Oracle Database 11*g*

New Features for DBAs and Developers

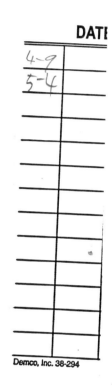

Sam R. Alapati and Charles Kim

Apress®

Oracle Database 11g: New Features for DBAs and Developers

Copyright © 2007 by Sam R. Alapati and Charles Kim

ISBN-13 (pbk): 978-1-59059-910-5

ISBN-10 (pbk): 1-59059-910-1

Printed and bound in the United States of America 9 8 7 6 5 4 3 2 1

Lead Editor: Jonathan Gennick
Technical Reviewer: Robert Blok
Editorial Board: Steve Anglin, Ewan Buckingham, Tony Campbell, Gary Cornell, Jonathan Gennick,
    Jason Gilmore, Kevin Goff, Jonathan Hassell, Matthew Moodie, Joseph Ottinger, Jeffrey Pepper,
    Ben Renow-Clarke, Dominic Shakeshaft, Matt Wade, Tom Welsh
Project Manager: Sofia Marchant
Copy Edit Manager: Nicole Flores
Copy Editor: Kim Wimpsett
Associate Production Director: Kari Brooks-Copony
Production Editor: Kelly Winquist
Compositor: Susan Glinert
Proofreader: April Eddy
Indexer: Broccoli Information Management
Cover Designer: Kurt Krames
Manufacturing Director: Tom Debolski

Distributed to the book trade worldwide by Springer-Verlag New York, Inc., 233 Spring Street, 6th Floor, New York, NY 10013. Phone 1-800-SPRINGER, fax 201-348-4505, e-mail orders-ny@springer-sbm.com, or visit http://www.springeronline.com.

For information on translations, please contact Apress directly at 2855 Telegraph Avenue, Suite 600, Berkeley, CA 94705. Phone 510-549-5930, fax 510-549-5939, e-mail info@apress.com, or visit http://www.apress.com.

To Jim Gray (Microsoft Technical Fellow), who is deeply missed by the database world, which remembers him with fondness and respect for both his professional brilliance and his warm personal qualities. Jim Gray is responsible for several fundamental database technologies, especially in online transaction processing. Jim Gray is still missing after embarking on a solo one-day boating trip from San Francisco on January 28, 2007, to immerse his mother's ashes at sea. In 1997 Jim Gray received the A.M. Turing Award (which is considered by some to be the Nobel Prize for computer science) for his "seminal contributions to database and transaction processing research and technical leadership in system implementation." Jim Gray is the author of Transaction Processing: Concepts and Techniques, which has been the classic reference in the field for the last several years. Much of what we do in online transaction processing today flows directly from Jim Gray's seminal contributions, and all of us who work with relational databases owe an immense debt to him.

—Sam R. Alapati

I dedicate the completed endeavor of this book to my parents, Wan Kyu and Chong Sik Kim, who made incredible sacrifices for my sisters and me. I thank you for my upbringing, education, work ethic, and any and all accomplishments. Thank you for exemplifying what it means to be a follower of Christ. As a parent myself now, I know that you are truly good and Godly parents.

—Charles Kim

Contents at a Glance

Contents

About the Authors

 **SAM ALAPATI** is an Oracle DBA for the Boy Scouts of America, working at their national office in Los Colinas, Texas. Prior to this, Sam worked at Sabre, Oracle Corporation, and NBC. Sam has previously published *Expert Oracle9i Database Administration*, *Expert Oracle Database 10g Administration*, and *Oracle Database 11g RMAN Recipes*, as well as two OCP certification books for Oracle Press. Sam has been working with relational databases since 1985, starting with the Ingres database. Sam holds the OCP certification for Oracle DBAs as well as the HP-UX System Administrator certification.

 **CHARLES KIM**, director of database technologies at Novara Solutions, is an Oracle Certified DBA, Red Hat Certified Technician, and Microsoft Certified Professional. He has more than 17 years of IT experience and has worked with Oracle since 1991. Prior to this, Charles served at Fidelity National Information Services as the chief Oracle database engineering counsel and also worked at GMAC Mortgage, i2 Technologies, and Oracle Corporation. Charles also serves as a technical editor for Oracle Press.

Charles has presented advanced topics for IOUG and Oracle OpenWorld on such topics as RAC/ASM and 7×24 high availability considerations using Oracle Advanced Replication, Hot Standby, and Quest Shareplex. Charles manages the DBAExpert.com web site and provides technical solutions to Oracle DBAs and developers.

Charles is the author of the Maximum Availability Architecture case study at Oracle's web site (http://www.oracle.com/technology/deploy/availability/htdocs/FNF_CaseStudy.html).

Acknowledgments

First and foremost, I'd like to acknowledge my gratitude for Charles Kim, my coauthor. It's a privilege to write a book with a consummate Oracle professional such as Charles. Charles has made writing this book a great pleasure, and he worked hard to meet our short deadlines, this being a "new features" book, whose contents always seem to be in a flux.

No Oracle-based book, let alone a "new features" book, can be conjured from thin air. I want to acknowledge the wonderful efforts of the Oracle Beta folks, who made the Oracle Database 11g Beta release available to me by extending an invitation to be part of their beta testing team. I benefited immensely by the high-quality e-studies and other technical studies made available by Oracle Corporation to the beta participants, as well as from the access to the beta software itself. I want to acknowledge in particular Lynn Snyder and Debbie Migliore, as well as Sheila Cepero, all from Oracle Corporation, for all their help over the last year while I was testing this exciting new offering from Oracle Corporation.

Jonathan Gennick, the editor, has as usual left his powerful mark on the book. I can't think of any part of this book that didn't benefit from Jonathan's conscientious and superb editing at both the technical as well the editorial level. Robert Blok, the technical editor, helped by pointing out several aspects that needed clarification. I owe thanks to the professional competence that the project manager, Sofia Marchant, brought to bear on the book. Sofia's kindness and cool efficiency over the past few months while managing a book under short deadlines is what helped Charles and I finish this book on time. Kim Wimpsett, the copy editor, did a superb job, going to great lengths to nail down numerous issues regarding style, terminology, consistency, and accuracy (although I think I've imposed a considerable burden on her by adding more new features in each iteration of the review process!). Kelly Winquist, the production editor, admirably managed the stupendously difficult task of getting this book out in time without compromising quality. April Eddy, the proofreader, did a brilliant job, without which my less than perfect typing skills would have been fully evident to the world. April has not only caught several insidious typos but also zoomed in on several tricky usage situations, always pointing out the correct approach. I'm grateful for the efforts of Sofia, Kim, Kelly, and April as well as the entire production group for going way beyond any call of duty and cheerfully moving the book along under the stress of looming deadlines. It's customary for the author to thank the editorial and production folks, I suppose, but I simply can't imagine this book being ready in time and in good shape without the supreme effort and dedication shown by the previously mentioned people.

My managers, Dave Campbell and David Jeffries, have been supportive of my endeavors, and I'm grateful for their encouragement over the years. My colleagues—Rob Page, Lance Parkes, Stan Galbraith, Dan Nelson, Dabir Haidar, Sabrina Kirkpatrick, and Carla Wallace—have also been helpful to me at work, and I appreciate their help and friendship. I also want to acknowledge my friends at work, Debra Kendrew, Myra Riggs, and especially Leticia Salazar; Leticia has been very helpful during the past few months in helping take care of a lot of my affairs at work.

Nothing I do in my personal and professional lives would be possible without the constant support and encouragement of my family. I'd like to express my gratitude for the love, affection, and sacrifice of my parents, Appa Rao and Swarna Kumari; my brothers, Hari Hara Prasad and Siva Sankara Prasad; and my sisters-in law, Aruna and Vanaja. At home, the love and support of my wife, Valerie, sustains me. Valerie's support and immense sacrifices have been crucial to the writing of this, as well as all my other books. Writing this book has meant time away from my children, Nina, Nicholas, and Shannon, and I can only promise that I'll make it up to them soon!

—Sam R. Alapati

Most important, I want to thank my dear wife, Melissa, and our three boys, Isaiah, Jeremiah, and Noah, for their unceasing support during the project and sacrificing precious family time. Without their prayers and encouragement, I could not have completed this project.

On a professional note, I would like to thank Leisa Pitner (`http://leisapitner.com`) for surrendering nights to rush edits and revisions of the chapters on last-minute notice. Leisa Pitner has served in several key roles in information technology ranging from business process engineer to director of internal applications for a 1 billon dollar software company. She has successfully facilitated the transformation of process and culture across multiple industries, leveraging her system's design and business process engineering background.

I would like to thank David Sweet, director of development practice at Novara Solutions, for contributing the PL/SQL and Java portions to Chapter 11. David has been working with Oracle since 1987 and, in my opinion, is one of the most elite developers in the industry.

I would like to extend an appreciation to Nitin Vengurlekar, member of the technical staff at Oracle and author of the *Automated Storage Administration* book. We shared a few battle scars of the book-authoring process. His review of Chapter 9 provided great insight and enhanced the overall quality of the chapter.

I can't forget the folks on Oracle's High Availability product development team, especially Joe Meeks and Larry Carpenter, for reviewing Chapter 10 and encouraging me to go forward. Thank you for the valuable input and recommendations.

My sincere gratitude goes to Debbie Migliore, director of Server Technologies Program Office, and her team for providing exceptional beta support and directing me to the right resources over the years. Debbie's team works implausible hours and plays a crucial role in delivering quality to each Oracle release.

I cannot say enough good things about the project management and editorial staff at Apress: Jonathan Gennick, Sofia Marchant, Kim Wimpsett, Kelly Winquist, and April Eddy. Thank you all for your "extra mile" efforts and at times holding my hand through some of the editing processes to provide a superior book.

Last but not least, thank you, Kirti Deshpande, for the last-minute review of Chapter 8. Kirti is well recognized in the Oracle industry for his books: *Performance Tuning 101* and *Oracle Wait Interface*.

—Charles Kim

Introduction

Oracle Database 11g contains several major innovations in the areas of change management, fault diagnosability, performance management, Data Guard administration, storage management, and data warehousing, among other areas. Besides the database administration changes, there are significant improvements in application development–related features, including natively compiled PL/SQL code, PL/SQL inlining, and enhanced triggers. In addition to the major standout changes, there are hundreds of smaller but significant changes as well, making the database more robust, better performing, easier to use, and more secure.

In this introduction, we summarize the key features of the new release, which are covered throughout the book.

Change Management

Change management is right at the very top of Oracle Database 11g's best new features. Considerable uncertainty surrounds database and server upgrades. Oracle Database 11g makes it easy for you to test an upgrade or other changes by testing and comparing the performance before and after the change. Oracle calls this the Real Application Testing feature, and it consists of two key new features that provide advanced change management capabilities:

- The Database Replay feature lets you capture database workloads from a production database and replay them on a test server, where you can realistically test changes using the captured production workload.

- The other change management tool is the SQL Performance Analyzer, which helps you identify the effect of system changes on the performance of SQL statements.

Enhanced Database Automation

Oracle Database 11g provides several useful automatic database management features. Chief among these are the following:

- The automatic memory management feature lets you automate both the system global area (SGA) and the program global area (PGA) components of Oracle's memory by setting a single initialization parameter named `memory_target`.

- The Automatic SQL Tuning feature involves the automatic running of the SQL Tuning Advisor during the nightly maintenance window and even the automatic implementation of the SQL profile recommendations made by the advisor.

- Automatic Database Diagnostic Monitor (ADDM) now covers Oracle Real Application Clusters, in addition to single database instances.

Performance Management

Besides the automatic running of the SQL Tuning Advisor every night, several innovations improve database performance. The key performance-related improvements include the following:

- Automatic Workload Repository baseline enhancements now let you create moving window baselines and baseline templates, in addition to fixed baselines.

- SQL Plan Management lets you automatically control SQL plan evolution.

- Multicolumn statistics provide more useful data to the optimizer in cases where columns are related.

- Private statistics let you test optimizer statistics before publishing them for usage by the query optimizer.

- The server-side result cache enables the caching of SQL and PL/SQL results, thus dramatically increasing performance. There is also a new client-side result cache.

- The SQL Test Case Builder lets you easily create test cases so you can reproduce a problematic SQL incident on another system.

Enhanced Fault Diagnosis Capability

Oracle Database 11g provides a consolidated fault diagnostic capability, including the following components, to make fault diagnosis and repair easier than ever:

- The automatic diagnostic repository lets you consolidate all diagnostic data in one central location outside the database.

- Automatic Health Monitor lets you perform both proactive and reactive database health checks.

- Support Workbench helps with several diagnostic tasks, including transmitting incident reports to Oracle Support.

- Incident Packaging Service is an efficient way of packaging all diagnostic data in an editable package to send to Oracle Support.

Data Guard Enhancements

Oracle packs significant new features in the Oracle Database 11g Data Guard technology stack. The latest and greatest Data Guard advancements are as follows:

- Real-time query standby database

- Snapshot standby database

- Logical standby database improvements

- Redo log compression

- Data Guard Broker enhancements

- Recovery Manager (RMAN) integration with Data Guard

- Rolling upgrades with the physical standby

- Fast-start failover improvements

Storage Management Improvements

With Oracle Database 11*g*, numerous improvements have been incorporated into automated storage management (ASM). Pertinent new ASM features include the following:

- Rolling upgrades

- ASM fast disk resynchronization

- ASM preferred read failure groups

- ASM diskgroup attributes for backward compatibility

- Separation of the DBA and SA roles via the sysasm role

- New manageability options for the check, mount, and drop commands

- A copy command to copy files between diskgroups, across ASM instances, and between ASM and the operating system

- ASM extensions such as diskgroup metadata backup and restore and block repair

Direct NFS provides simplicity and performance for database implementations on network-attached storage (NAS). Customers have opted for NFS solutions over block devices for simplicity and lower cost, and Direct NFS makes NFS implementations even simpler and faster.

General Database Management

Quite a few new database management features are useful, including the following:

- Invisible indexes let you test new indexes without affecting performance, since you can toggle an index's status between visible and invisible.

- There are new partitioning schemes—referential, internal, system, and virtual column partitioning.

- Virtual columns let you use dynamically computed table columns that use functions to produce new columns from existing columns.

- Invisible indexes let you test the usage of indexes by letting you make them available to the optimizer only when you want to do so.

- Read-only tables let you keep users from modifying the contents of key tables.

- The easy addition of columns with default values means you can add the columns online without taking a performance hit.

- SecureFiles are completely reengineered LOBs designed for performance and security, and they include capabilities such as encryption, deduplication, and compression.

- Data Pump incorporates data encryption, masking, and compression.

Enhanced Security

Security features in Oracle Database 11g will make security enforcement easier for the database administrators. Oracle has taken security more seriously than ever. Key security enhancements include the following:

- Tablespace encryption takes you beyond the transparent table-level encryption in the previous release and enhances database security.

- Case-sensitive passwords and stronger password verification comply with regulatory requirements.

- Data remapping masks data at rest.

- Fine-grained network access from the database protects the database ecosystem.

- The SHA-1 encryption algorithm with SALT replaces the password hashing algorithm.

- Security support is added to Enterprise Manager Database Console.

- TDE with hardware security module integration provides the highest level of TDE security.

- OCI security captures the level of information for bad packets, delays/drops database connections after n number of bad packets, configures the maximum number of server connection attempts, and enables banner pages for login and auditing.

Application Improvements

For the application developer, Oracle Database 11g provides several useful enhancements:

- Pivot operations provide cross-tabular reports for executive management reports by transforming rows into columns and aggregating data in the process.

- Unpivot operations rotate data from columns into rows.

- PL/SQL can now directly create native compiled PL/SQL code without a C compiler.

- The cross-session PL/SQL function result cache allows the developer to request that the result of a PL/SQL function call be cached in the SGA and returned from the cache if the same arguments are passed to the function in future calls.

- Inlining in PL/SQL is an optimization where the PL/SQL compiler replaces calls to subprograms (functions and procedures) with the code of the subprograms.

- The new SIMPLE_INTEGER datatype provides faster performance than PLS_INTEGER.

- Triggers can now control the order of triggers firing, can be created in ENABLED or DISABLED status, and compound triggers maintain a common state over the life of a DML operation.

- A new argument to REGEXP_INSTR() and REGEXP_SUBSTR() allows you to select the *n*th subexpression in the regular expression being evaluated.

- Binary XML introduces advantages to the XML world in the database. Binary XML format generally reduces the verbosity of XML documents, and thus the cost of parsing is reduced.

- The XML schema evolution capability enables certain kinds of changes to XML schemas with zero downtime.

- XQuery adds two new functions, XMLExists and XMLCast.

- The new XMLIndex is available for indexing the internal structure of the XML data and improving the performance of XML retrieval.

- New to XDK are the XMLDiff and XMLPatch SQL operators to compare and patch XML documents.

Partitioning New Features

New to Oracle Database 11*g* are numerous techniques for partitioning table data to increase the performance and organization of your corporate data. These partitioning techniques include the following:

- Reference partitioning allows tables with a parent-child relationship to be logically equi-partitioned by inheriting the partition key from the parent table without duplicating the key columns.

- Interval partitioning automatically creates maintenance partitions for range partitions.

- Extended composite partitioning allows data to be partitioned along two dimensions.

- Virtual column partitioning allows virtual columns to be defined as partition key columns.

High-Availability Enhancements

There are several highly useful innovations concerning backup and recovery, flashback technology, and SQL repair and data recovery. You can now create virtual private catalogs to control access to the central RMAN recovery catalog.

- A new feature called *network-aware duplication* lets you create a duplicate database without any prior backups of the source database by using the datafiles of the running database instead.

- The flashback transaction backout feature lets you undo an entire transaction, along with its dependent transactions, with a single click.

- The flashback archive feature lets you track data stored in any Oracle table, for any length of time you want, while providing automatic historical data management.

- SQL Repair Advisor provides alternative workarounds in the form of SQL patches to get around failed SQL statements without having to change the SQL statements themselves.

- Data Recovery Advisor lets you effortlessly recover from data failures by getting repair advice and recommendations that you can implement.

- Virtual private catalogs provide greater security by limiting users to only a subset of the base recovery catalog.

- There is improved block media recovery performance with the help of flashback logs.

- You can merge recovery catalogs.

- You can perform parallel backups of datafiles using the new `section size` parameter during backups.

- Online patching enhancements make it easy to apply patches with no downtime.

Advanced Compression

Oracle Database 11g provides new compression capabilities, as summarized here:

- The new release lets you compress OLTP data that's subject to normal data manipulation language (DML) activities.

- You can compress export data during a Data Pump operation, instead of just compressing the metadata.

As you can see, there's a quite bit of exciting new features in Oracle Database 11g. So, without much ado, let's dive into a discussion of the new features!

CHAPTER 1
■■■
Installing, Upgrading, and Managing Change

The best way to start reviewing the new features and changes offered by the Oracle Database 11g release is by first installing the software. As a DBA, you must also be wondering what it takes to upgrade from your current version of Oracle (8i, 9i, or 10g) to the Oracle Database 11g version. Well, this chapter discusses the changes in the Oracle installation procedures as well as the database upgrade process and the revolutionary new Oracle feature called Real Application Testing that helps you anticipate potential problems inherent in both software and application upgrades.

Oracle Database 11g introduces several new features related to installing the server software. These new features include several changes in the install options, new components you can install, an enhanced Optimal Flexible Architecture (OFA) to lay out your datafiles and the flash recovery area. Some of the older components such as iSQL*Plus are no longer included in the Oracle 11g release, while newer components have been added. We'll review the new installation options, as well as several new initialization parameters, in this chapter.

Once you install the new Oracle 11g binaries, your attention will naturally turn to upgrading your current Oracle databases running on older versions of the Oracle server software. There are several changes in both the manual upgrade method and the Database Upgrade Assistant (DBUA). The pre-upgrade information tool has been revised to provide more information.

Change management is one of the top priorities of the Oracle Database 11g release. Organizations typically face considerable problems when making changes in their production systems, be it an upgrade to a newer release of the database software or code changes in the applications. Simulated workloads often fail to accurately represent the true production database workloads. Oracle Database 11g provides two powerful solutions, Database Replay and SQL Performance Analyzer (as part of a broader feature called Real Application Testing). We devote considerable attention to the Database Replay and SQL Performance Analyzer features in this chapter. Finally, we discuss several interesting new features in database software patching.

This chapter covers the following main topics:

- New features in the server installation

- Oracle Database 11g installation

- New features in database creation

- Database upgrade new features

- Real Application Testing

- Database software patching

New Features in Server Installation

The installation process for the Oracle server software is essentially the same in the Oracle Database 11g and 10g versions. Invoking the Oracle Universal Installer (invoked by runInstaller on Unix/Linux and setup on Windows) remains the same, and the Oracle Universal Installer performs the same operating system checks as in the older versions. There are, however, a few important changes when installing Oracle Database 11g, which we summarize in the following sections.

Changes in the Optimal Flexible Architecture

The Oracle 11g installation process contains changes in the way you specify the Oracle base, the Oracle home, and the flash recovery area. In addition, there is a new infrastructure called the *automatic diagnostic repository*, which serves as a consolidated location for all database diagnostic information.

Choosing the Oracle Base Location

The Oracle base directory is the top-level directory for installing Oracle software, and the OFA-recommended path for this directory is /mount_point/app/<oracle software owner>. For example, a typical Oracle base directory path is /u01/app/oracle, where oracle is the Oracle software owner. The Oracle base is recommended as an environment variable, as in the earlier Oracle versions, but in future versions Oracle is likely to make this a mandatory variable. The Oracle Universal Installer now provides a list box for you to edit or select the Oracle base. The Oracle Universal Installer automatically derives the default Oracle home location from the Oracle base location you provide. The Oracle home directory is a subdirectory of the Oracle base directory, and that's where you install all your Oracle software. You can edit the location offered by the Oracle Universal Installer if you want to specify a different directory as the Oracle home location. Oracle recommends you specify the same Oracle base for multiple Oracle homes created by a user.

Choosing the Datafile and Flash Recovery Area Locations

In Oracle Database 11g, by default, all datafiles are located one level below the Oracle base. The flash recovery area is also one level below the Oracle base, and Oracle recommends you create this on a disk that is separate from the ones hosting the datafiles. In Oracle Database 10g, by contrast, both the flash recovery area and the datafiles are located in the Oracle home directory. The datafile location and the flash recovery area in an Oracle Database 11g release database then would look like the following, assuming you chose /u01/app/oracle as your Oracle base location:

```
/u01/app/oracle/oradata
/u01/app/oracle/flash_recovery_area
```

The Oracle Universal Installer will warn you if you don't put the datafiles and the flash recovery area in separate locations.

Automatic Diagnostic Repository

The automatic diagnostic repository (ADR) is a new Oracle Database 11g feature, meant for the consolidation of all diagnostic data, including various trace files. The goal of the ADR is to provide a single directory location for all error data you'll need for diagnosing and resolving problems, thus leading to faster error resolution and troubleshooting. The ADR is simply a directory location that you specify through the new initialization parameter `diagnostic_dest`. The ADR replaces the traditional use of the diagnostic directories such as `bdump`, `cdump`, and `udump`, where you had to go to manually seek out the necessary trace file and error files during troubleshooting. The ADR uses standard methods to store diagnostic data not only for the Oracle database but also for other Oracle products. The diagnostic data is then read by special automatic diagnostic tools to provide a quick turnaround time for troubleshooting problems related to various Oracle products.

Under the ADR, you have the different directories such as `cdump`, `alert`, and so on. The alert log that you're used to viewing in the vi editor on Unix is now an XML-based file. You can read this file using the new `adrci` command-line tool. We discuss the ADR in detail in Chapter 2.

If you choose to use the ADR, you must give the Oracle Universal Installer a directory location for the ADR base. To consolidate diagnostic data, Oracle recommends you choose the same ADR base for all Oracle products.

▪Note If `ORACLE_BASE` is not set, warnings will appear in the alert log. Although `ORACLE_BASE` is a recommended environment variable, this variable will become a requirement in future releases.

By default, the ADR's base directory for storing diagnostic data is set to the Oracle base location. However, you can set an alternate location for the ADR by setting a value for the new initialization parameter `diagnostic_dest`. The ADR directory has the name `$ORACLE_BASE/diag` and contains several subdirectories, the most important of which is the `rdbms` directory. In the `rdbms` directory, diagnostic files are organized by database name and instance name. For example, for a database with the database name `orcl` and an instance name of `orcl1`, the trace files, including the alert log in the traditional text format, are located in the following directory (the Oracle base is `/u01/app/oracle`):

```
/u01/app/oracle/diag/rdbms/orcl/orcl1/diag
```

As this directory structure indicates, you can store the diagnostic data for multiple databases (as well as other Oracle products) under the same ADR base. For more on ADR, please see Chapter 2, which discusses the new fault diagnosability infrastructure.

Changes in the Install Options

There are several important install option changes for Oracle Database 11g, as summarized here:

- The Oracle Configuration Manager, which gathers configuration information pertaining to the software stored in the Oracle home directories, is integrated with the Oracle Universal Installer as an optional component.

- The Oracle Data Mining option is selected by default with the Enterprise Edition installation and is installed automatically when you run the `catproc.sql` script after creating the database.

- The Oracle XML DB option has been removed, since it isn't an optional component any longer. The Database Configuration Assistant installs and configures it. When you manually run the `catproc.sql` script, the XML DB is created automatically.

- Oracle Database Vault is an optional component, and to install this option, you must choose the Custom installation option during installation.

As with any other release, the Oracle11g database version deprecates certain components available in older releases. The most important of the deprecated components are as follows:

- iSQL*Plus

- Oracle Workflow

- Oracle Enterprise Manager Java Console

- Oracle Data Mining Scoring Engine

- Raw storage support (installer only)

New Oracle Database 11g Components

In Oracle Database 11g, the following new components are available while installing the server software:

- *Oracle Application Express (APEX)*: Oracle's browser-based rapid application development tool, formerly known as Oracle HTML DB, is enhanced in Oracle Database 11g with prepackaged applications for blogs, storefronts, and discussion forums. There are also new reporting capabilities and support for drag-and-drop forms layout. APEX is now part of the base Oracle CD instead of the companion CD.

- *Oracle SQL Developer*: Oracle's free database development productivity tool is a graphical version of SQL*Plus and is enhanced with new tuning capabilities in Oracle Database 11g. These enhancements include database activity reporting and expanded support for version control and visual query building. SQL Developer is automatically installed when you choose to perform a template-based database installation by choosing an installation option such as General Purpose and Transaction Processing.

- *Oracle Real Application Testing*: This component, which is automatically installed with the Enterprise Edition installation, consists of two new features, Data Replay and the SQL Performance Analyzer, both of which we discuss later in this chapter.

- *Oracle Configuration Manager (OCM)*: This is offered as an optional component during the server installation. The OCM collects information about software configuration in the Oracle home directories and uploads it to the Oracle configuration repository.

- *Oracle Warehouse Builder*: This is an enterprise business intelligence design tool and is installed as part of the Oracle Database server software.

- *Oracle Database Vault*: This tool, which enables you to secure business data, is installed with the Oracle Database 11g as an optional component, instead of being a component of the companion CD as in previous releases. The Oracle Database Vault installation means you now have a baseline security policy for the database. Security-related initialization parameters are given default values following the installation of the Oracle Database Vault.

Role and Privilege Changes

If you are using automatic storage management (ASM), you can now optionally create an additional OS-level group while installing the software or even after the installation. In addition, there is a new optional system privilege in Oracle Database 11*g* exclusively for ASM administration. If you're migrating from a database release older than Oracle Database 10*g* (10.2), you must also be aware of the changes made to the connect role.

New Privileges Group and Database Role for ASM

In Oracle Database 11*g*, there is a clear-cut demarcation between database administration and ASM administration. Previously, you performed all ASM administration as a user with the sysdba privilege. There is a new system privilege called sysasm, which you should grant to the user who needs to perform ASM administrative tasks. Users will need the sysasm privileges to create an ASM instance or cluster using OS authentication. In prior versions of Oracle, you created the dba and oper operating system groups when installing Oracle software. In Oracle Database 11*g*, you can optionally create a third operating system group called the osasm group. Oracle recommends you grant ASM access only to members of the osasm group.

■**Note** There is a myriad of ASM enhancements for 11*g*, and thus we dedicate a chapter to reviewing the new features in managing ASM. Please refer to Chapter 9 for the new ASM features.

Both the new system privilege sysasm and the new operating system group osadm are optional in Oracle Database 11*g*. However, in future releases, Oracle may restrict access to ASM to members of the osadm operating system group in addition to requiring all ASM administrators to have the sysasm system privilege.

Deprecation of the connect Role

The connect role was deprecated in the Oracle Database 10.2 release. In fact, the role now has only the create session privilege, unlike in releases prior to Oracle Database 10.2, when it also had privileges other than create session. If you're upgrading to Oracle Database 11*g* from a release older than Oracle Database 10.2, any users with the connect role will cease to have all privileges other than the create session privilege.

After upgrading to Oracle Database 11*g* from release 9.2 or release 10.1, the connect role will have only the create session privilege; the other privileges granted to the connect role in earlier releases will be revoked during the upgrade. To identify which users and roles in your database are granted the connect role, use the following query:

```
SQL> select grantee from dba_role_privs
    where granted_role = 'CONNECT';
```

The upgrade script automatically takes care of adjusting the privileges of all Oracle-supplied users (such as sys, system, outln, and dbsnmp). For all other users with the connect role, you must explicitly grant all the privileges that were part of the old connect role after the upgrade is completed.

■**Note** In previous versions, it was sometimes a difficult process to switch a database manually from Database Control to Grid Control. In Oracle Database 11g, you can simply use the new EMCP API to switch a database from Database Control to Grid Control.

Installing Oracle Database 11g

The Oracle Universal Installer steps for installing the Oracle Database 11g release software are similar to the steps for the Oracle 10g release. There are a few changes, however, which we'll highlight when we show the installation steps in this section. You use the runInstaller executable to invoke the GUI-based Oracle Universal Installer. If you've downloaded the server software from the Oracle web site, you must first uncompress the downloaded file. This will create a directory named database, under which you'll find the runInstaller script. Start the installation process by moving to the database directory and typing the following:

```
$ ./runInstaller
```

If you're installing from a DVD, invoke the installer by supplying the full path for the database directory on the DVD:

```
$ /<directory_path>/runInstaller
```

If you pass the minimal operating system requirements, the Oracle Universal Installer will open. Once the Oracle Universal Installer GUI shows up, the following are the steps in the installation process:

1. On the Select Installation Method page, you can select either Basic Installation or Advanced Installation. Select Advanced Installation, and click Next.

■**Tip** Set the TMP and TMPDIR environment variables if /tmp is too small for the installation.

2. Select Installation Type. You're given three choices—Enterprise Edition, Standard Edition, and Custom. Choose Enterprise Edition, and click Next.

3. On the Install Location page, specify the path for the Oracle base and Oracle home locations, which is where the Oracle Universal Installer will install the database files. Click Next.

4. On the Product-Specific Prerequisite Checks page, the Oracle Universal Installer will verify that your environment meets the minimum requirements for installing the various products you want to install. These checks include the kernel parameters, swap space requirements, validation of the Oracle base location, and network configuration requirements. It's a good idea to go ahead and fix any warnings produced by the Oracle Universal Installer at this stage, say by updating the kernel on a Linux system, although you can get away with not doing so in most cases since the Oracle Universal Installer offers you the choice of continuing despite a warning. Once you pass the requirement checks, click Next.

5. Select Configuration Option. You can choose to create a database, configure ASM, or just install the Oracle 11g binaries. For the last option, choose Install Software Only, and click Next.

6. You'll see the Privileged Operating System Groups page next, as shown in Figure 1-1. This step is new in Oracle Database 11g. In addition to the sysdba and sysoper privileges you're familiar with, Oracle now recommends you create the new system privilege called sysasm for enabling the management of ASM. Oracle also recommends you create a new Unix/Linux group now, called osasm, for ASM administrators.

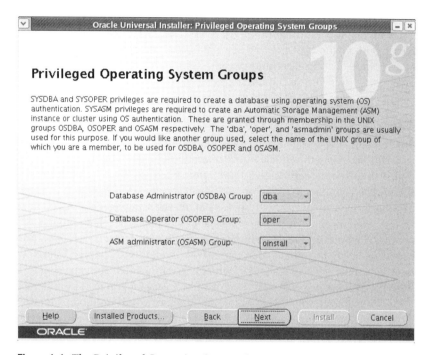

Figure 1-1. *The Privileged Operating System Groups page*

7. On the Summary page, the Oracle Universal Installer summarizes the installation, including the names of all the components it will install. Click Next after reviewing the summary.

8. On the Install page, you'll see the progress of the installation. Once the installation finishes successfully, exit the Oracle Universal Installer by first clicking Exit and then clicking Yes.

If you choose to create a new starter database (step 5), the Oracle Universal Installer invokes the Database Configuration Assistant (DBCA) to create the database. We discuss creating a new database with the DBCA in the following section. You'll see the new features we discuss there (such as specifying the automatic memory configuration details) if you choose to create a new database during installation itself by choosing the Create a Database option here. By default, Oracle includes the new Secure Configuration option, which configures the database with auditing options as well as password policy and expiration settings. If you want, you can disable the new enhanced security controls during the installation.

Also, if you choose to create the starter database during the installation, you'll get an option to configure the Oracle Configuration Manager. You'll need to configure the Oracle Configuration Manager in order to associate the database configuration information with Oracle MetaLink. You can then link your service requests to MetaLink with your configuration information. Chapter 2 explains more about the Oracle Configuration Manager in the context of the new Support Workbench feature.

New Features in Database Creation

You can create a new Oracle database either with manual commands at the SQL prompt or with the help of the Database Configuration Assistant (DBCA). Oracle Database 11g contains some changes in both methods of creating new databases. Some changes such as new initialization parameters are, of course, common to both techniques, so first we'll cover the new initialization parameters in Oracle Database 11g.

New Initialization Parameters

When you create a new Oracle Database 11g version database, you'll want to know about some important changes regarding the Oracle initialization parameters. There are both new initialization parameters and some deprecated parameters. A few significant new initialization parameters in Oracle 11g affect the implementation of certain key new Oracle 11g features. You don't necessarily have to set any of these new parameters when you're upgrading to Oracle Database 11g—or even when creating a new Oracle 11g database, for that matter.

You can now create a traditional text initialization parameter file or a server parameter file from the current values of the initialization parameters in memory. Chapter 3 shows you how to do this. Another new Oracle Database 11g feature is that the initialization parameter settings are recorded in the alert log in a way supposed to make it easy for you to copy and paste those settings if you want to create a new parameter file. When you start up the instance, Oracle writes all initialization parameter values to the alert log in valid syntax, so you can copy and paste this into a new initialization parameter file if you want.

Oracle's wonderful compatibility feature means that your 9i or 10g database will work under the Oracle 11g software with nary a change. The lowest possible setting you can use for the compatible initialization parameter is 10.0.0 before you upgrade to the Oracle Database 11g release. The default value is 11.1.0, and the maximum value is 11.1.0.n.n. When you set the compatible parameter to the minimum value of 10.0.0, the newly upgraded database can avail of only a small subset of the new features of Oracle Database 11g. However, some of these new initialization parameters control several of the most important innovations of Oracle 11g, topics that we discuss later this book. Scan through the following sections to see which initialization parameters you must use, if you want to adopt key new Oracle 11g features. All these parameters will be explained in more detail in the relevant chapters later in this book. The following sections are a quick summary of the most important initialization parameter changes in Oracle 11g.

Memory-Related Parameters

One of the biggest changes in Oracle Database 11g is the new *automatic memory management* feature under which both the major components of Oracle's memory allocation—the shared global area (SGA) and the program global area (PGA)—will be automatically expanded and shrunk, based on the needs of the instance. All you need to do is set the values for two memory-related parameters, `memory_target` and `memory_max_target`:

- The `memory_target` parameter sets the system-wide usable memory and lets Oracle tune both the SGA and PGA, changing the values of the SGA and the PGA automatically based on the demands of the running Oracle instance. You can dynamically change the value for this parameter using the `alter system` command.

- The `memory_max_target` parameter sets the maximum value of memory Oracle can use. That is, the value you set for the `memory_max_target` parameter is the maximum value up to which you can adjust the `memory_target` parameter's value.

You can enable automatic memory management by setting the value of the `memory_target` parameter and the `memory_max_target` parameter in the initialization parameter file when creating a new database. You can also add them later to the initialization parameter file after database creation, but you have to bounce the database for automatic memory management to take effect. Here's an example showing how to specify the new memory-related parameters, if you started your database with an initialization parameter file:

- `memory_max_target` = 500MB

- `memory_target` = 350MB

- `sga_target` = 0

- `pga_aggregate_target` = 0

This set of initialization parameters ensures that the server allocates 350MB of memory to Oracle right away. Oracle will allocate this memory among the SGA and the PGA. You can dynamically change the value of the `memory_target` parameter up to the maximum of 500MB set by the `memory_max_target` parameter. Note that you must set both the `sga_target` and `pga_aggregate_target` initialization parameters to 0 if you don't want to set any minimum values for the sizes of the SGA and the PGA. For testing purposes on both Linux and Windows servers, you can use as little as 120MB as the value for the `memory_target` parameter.

We discuss the automatic memory management feature in detail in Chapter 3.

PL/SQL Native Compilation Parameter

In Oracle Database 11*g*, it's easier than ever to enable PL/SQL native compilation, which offers greater performance benefits. In Oracle Database 10*g*, you had to use the initialization parameter `plsql_native_library_dir` to set a directory, as well as specify the `plsql_native_library_sbdir_count` parameter to enable native compilation of PL/SQL code. In addition, you also had to use the `spnc_commands` file in the `plsql` directory under the Oracle home. In Oracle Database 11*g* you use just one initialization parameter, `plsql_code_type`, to turn on native compilation. You don't need a C compiler, and you don't have to manage any file system DLLs either. You don't need to create any directories or use the `spnc_commands` file. You can also adopt native compilation for Java. We explain native compilation in more detail in Chapter 4.

■Note Real native compilation is rumored to be twice as fast as C native. The Whetstone benchmark runs 2.5 times faster under real native compilation.

The diagnostic_dest Parameter

The initialization parameter `diagnostic_dest` is new in Oracle 11*g*. This parameter points to the location of the new automatic diagnostic repository. The `diagnostic_dest` parameter replaces the `user_dump_dest`, `background_dump_dest`, and `core_dump_dest` initialization parameters in past releases. The database ignores any values you set for these parameters if you've also set the `diagnostic_dest` parameter.

If your Oracle base location is `/u01/app/oracle`, your database name is `orcl`, and the instance name is also `orcl`, then by default the ADR home directory will take the following form:

```
/u01/app/oracle/diag/rdbms/orcl/orcl
```

■Note You can set a different ADR for each instance of a Real Application Cluster (RAC). Oracle recommends that you do so, specifying the same value for the parameter for each instance.

In the `orcl` directory, you'll find various subdirectories such as `alert`, `incident`, and `trace`. The `trace` directory is where the `user_dump_dest` and `core_dump_dest` files used to go in earlier releases.

You can specify that the ADR be located in a nondefault location by setting the `diagnostic_dest` initialization parameter. The basic directory for the ADR, known as the ADR home, will have the following directory structure:

```
<diagnostic_dest>/diag/rdbms/<dbname>/<instname>
```

If you set the `diagnostic_dest` parameter to `/u05/app/oracle`, the database name is `orcl`, and the instance name is `orcl1`, then the following would be your ADR home directory:

```
/u05/app/oracle/diag/rdbms/orcl/orcl1
```

Chapter 2 discusses the ADR in detail.

New Result Cache–Related Parameters

You're familiar with the caching of queries in the shared pool component of the SGA. In Oracle Database 11*g*, Oracle has gone quite a bit further and caches the actual results of queries in memory. The caching is done in a new component of the SGA called the *result cache*. Result caching dramatically improves performance for frequently run queries when there are few changes in data.

For a table or view to be considered for result caching, you must alter the table using the `result_cache_mode` clause. You must set the new initialization parameter `result_cache_mode` to the appropriate value if you want the database to consider all queries or to only those queries that involve tables and views for which you have set the `result_cache` option. You can also cache PL/SQL function results in addition to SQL query results. In addition to the `result_cache_mode` option, there are several result cache–related initialization parameters, such as the `result_cache_max_result`, `result_cache_max_size`, and `result_cache_remote_expiration` parameters. You can also cache query results on the client side. When you use client-side query caching, you can specify the new parameters `client_result_cache_size` and `client_result_cache_lag`. We discuss all these new parameters as part of the result cache feature in Chapter 4.

■**Note** When you set the compatible parameter to 11.0.0 or greater, the server parameter file is written in a new format to comply with Oracle's HARD initiative, which helps prevent writing corrupted data to disk.

Parameter to Control DDL Lock Timeout

One of the important new features of the Oracle 11g database is the new DDL locking duration control feature. The `ddl_lock_timeout` parameter lets you specify the length of time a DDL statement will wait for a DML lock. This feature comes in handy when you want to perform online reorganization, where a DML lock by a user may prevent a DDL operation from succeeding. You can practically specify that a DDL statement wait forever by setting the parameter to the maximum allowed value, which is 1,000,000 seconds. We discuss the `ddl_lock_timeout` parameter in detail in Chapter 3.

SecureFiles-Related Parameter

The new Oracle SecureFiles feature is a major revamping of the implementation of Large Objects (LOBs). By using the new initialization parameter `db_securefile`, you can specify whether to treat a LOB file as a SecureFiles file. Please see Chapter 12 for a detailed discussion of SecureFiles.

■**Note** The `job_queue_processes` parameter has been moved to the basic initialization parameters list in Oracle Database 11g. Although this is not a big deal on the face of it, the point is that Oracle is saying you don't have to worry about setting a value for the `job_queue_processes` parameter in most cases, since it's classified as a basic initialization parameter. The `job_queue_processes` parameter can take a value from 0 to 1000. If you set it to 0, you can run DBMS_SCHEDULER jobs, but not the DBMS_JOB-based jobs. If you set the parameter to any value from 1 to 1000, both DBMS_JOB-based and DBMS_SCHEDULER-based jobs will run.

The db_ultra_safe Parameter

The new parameter `db_ultra_safe` sets default values for parameters, such as the `db_block_checking` parameter, that control protection levels. To be precise, you can control three corruption-checking parameters—`db_block_checking`, `db_block_checksum`, and `db_lost_write_protect`—by specifying values for the `db_ultra_safe` parameter.

The db_ultra_safe_parameter can take three values—off, data only, and data and index. By default, the db_ultra_safe parameter is set to off, meaning that any values you set for any of the three parameters won't be overridden. If you set the db_ultra_safe parameter value to data only, the following will be true:

- db_block_checking will be set to medium.

- db_lost_write_protect will be set to typical.

- db_block_checksum will be set to full.

If you set the db_ultra_safe parameter value to data and index, the following will be true:

- db_block_checking will be set to full.

- db_lost_write_protect will be set to typical.

- db_block_checksum will be set to full.

Security-Related Parameters

There are two important security-related initialization parameters that are new in Oracle Database 11g. The first parameter, sec_case_sensitive_logon, lets you enable and disable password case-sensitivity in the database. By default, password case-sensitivity is enabled in Oracle Database 11g.

The other new security-related initialization parameter is the parameter sec_max_failed_ login_attempts, which specifies the maximum number of times a client can make a connection attempt to a server. The default value of this parameter is 10.

Please see Chapter 5 for more details about the new case-sensitive password feature as well as the sec_max_failed_login_attempts parameter.

Optimizer-Related Parameters

There are several important new optimizer-related initialization parameters that are intended to support powerful new features such as SQL Plan Management, private statistics, and invisible indexes. We discuss all these features in subsequent chapters and merely introduce the relevant new initialization parameters in this section.

Oracle Database 11g replaces the old plan stability feature with the new SQL Plan Management feature. A change in the execution plan of an important SQL statement can potentially degrade performance. To avoid this performance degradation, the database selects optimal SQL plan baselines and prevents the optimizer from changing the execution plan of a statement until the new plan is found to be definitely superior to the existing SQL baseline plan (lower cost). You can enable automatic SQL plan capture so the database can capture and maintain SQL plan history using information from the optimizer.

By default, automatic plan capture is disabled, and you can enable it by setting the optimizer_capture_sql_plan_baselines parameter to true. Chapter 4 contains a detailed discussion of the SQL Plan Management feature.

Use the new initialization parameter `optimizer_use_sql_baselines` to enable the use of SQL plan baselines that are stored in what's called the SQL *management base*. If you enable SQL plan baselines, the cost optimizer will search in the SQL management base for a SQL plan baseline for the SQL statement being currently compiled. If there is a SQL plan outline available, the cost optimizer will select the baseline plan with the least cost.

A third new optimizer-related parameter, `optimizer_private_statistics`, allows you to specify the use of private statistics during the compilation of SQL statements. Please refer to Chapter 4 for details about the major optimizer-related new features.

Finally, the new parameter `optimizer_use_invisible_indexes` lets you enable and disable the use of invisible indexes, a significant new feature that we'll explain in Chapter 3.

DBCA Enhancements

The DBCA provides an alternative to the manual creation of a new Oracle database. In Oracle Database 11*g*, you should be aware of a couple of changes when you're creating a new database with the help of the DBCA. These changes pertain to security settings and the choice of memory allocation for the new database.

We summarize the changes in the DBCA by listing all the steps required to create a new database with the DBCA. Most of the steps are identical to the steps you followed in the Oracle Database 10*g* release, but there are two new steps and a couple of modified steps. Let's review the database creation steps when you use the DBCA to create a new Oracle 11*g* database:

1. On the DBCA Operations page, select the Create a Database option.

2. On the Database Templates page, select one of the following database types: Data Warehouse, General Purpose, or Transaction Processing.

3. On the Database Identification page, select the database name and the system identifier (SID).

4. On the Management Options page, select Database Control or Grid Control.

5. On the Database Credential page, specify passwords for accounts such as `sys` and `system`.

6. On the Security Settings page, choose the security settings for the new database (this is new in Oracle Database 11*g*). DBCA provides secure database configuration features by default. You can turn off security configuration in the new database if you want. Here are the important features related to secure database configuration:

   • Audit settings

   • Password profiles

   • Revoking grants to the `public` role

   You'll find more about secure database configuration in Chapter 6. Figure 1-2 shows the new Security Settings page.

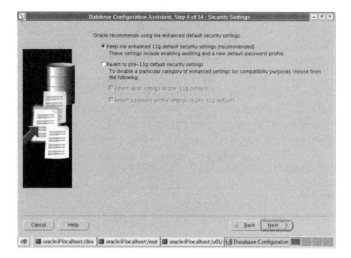

Figure 1-2. *DBCA's new Security Settings page*

7. On the Network Configuration page, select the listener(s) for which you plan to register the new database. (This is new in Oracle Database 11g.) Figure 1-3 shows the new Network Configuration page.

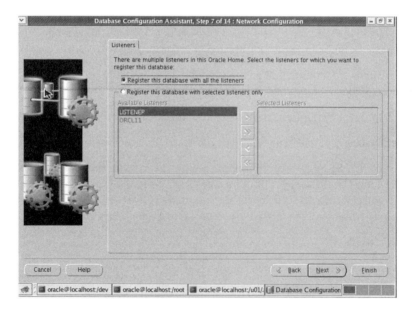

Figure 1-3. *DBCA's new Network Configuration page*

8. On the Storage options page, select the type of storage mechanism.

9. On the Database File Locations page, specify the Oracle software home and the directory for the database files, or select the Oracle-Managed Files (OMF) option for database files.

10. On the Recovery Configuration page, specify the archivelog/noarchivelog choice and the flash recovery area location.

11. On the Database Content page, specify the sample schemas and custom scripts to be run after database creation.

12. On the Initialization Parameters page, alter the default settings for various initialization parameters, such as memory, character sets, and so on. This screen lets you select among the three types of memory allocation—automatic memory management, automatic shared memory management, or manual shared memory management. (This option has been modified in Oracle Database 11*g*.) Figure 1-4 shows this page.

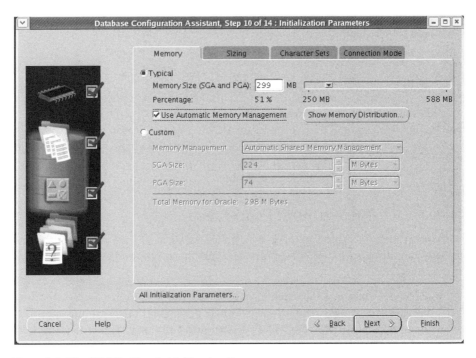

Figure 1-4. *The DBCA's New Initialization Parameters page*

13. On the Database Storage page, make changes in the storage structure of the database.

14. On the Database Creation Options page, choose from three options: Create Database, Save As a Database Template, or Generate Database Creation Scripts.

    In step 6, you can choose to use the new enhanced default security settings, or you can disable the security controls if you want. The default security controls are part of the new Secure Configuration option, which configures database auditing and password policy and expiration settings. Thus, the default configuration includes the Secure Configuration option, but you can check the Disable Security Settings box to disable the enhanced security controls. The new database is then installed with the default security options for Oracle Database 10*g* Release 2. You can configure the Secure Configuration option later by invoking the DBCA and altering the security settings of the database. Oracle strongly recommends you adopt the new Secure Configuration option. Note that if you install Oracle Database Vault, you can't change the Secure Configuration option using the DBCA.

In step 12, you get a chance to modify the default initialization parameter settings. The only real change in this section pertains to the allocation of Oracle memory. As in Oracle Database 10g, you can choose between Typical, which requires little or no configuration on your part, and Custom, which requires more configuration. If you choose the Typical method of memory allocation, Oracle automatically tunes memory for the instance using automatic memory management. The amount of memory Oracle allocates to the instance will be a percentage of the overall physical memory on the server. If you choose the Custom method, you must specify the memory you want to allocate to the Oracle instance, and you must also choose from one of the following three types of memory allocation:

- Automatic memory management (new in Oracle Database 11g)

- Automatic shared memory management

- Manual shared memory management

You select automatic management by first selecting the Typical option on the Initialization Parameters page and then selecting the Use Automatic Memory Management option. Automatic memory management, as explained earlier in this chapter, is new to Oracle Database 11g, and you can enable it through the new unitization parameters `memory_target` and `memory_max_target`. We explain automatic memory management in detail in Chapter 3.

New Oracle Background Processes

Some new Oracle background processes in Oracle Database 11g can help with some of the new features introduced as part of this release. Here are the important new background processes in Oracle Database 11g:

- *FBDA*: The flashback data archive process archives data from all tables that are enabled for flashback archive. The process stores all pre-change images of the table rows in the flashback archive following a DML operation such as an update or a deletion. Flashback archiving is an important Oracle Database 11g new feature that we discuss in Chapter 3.

- *SMCO*: The space management coordinator process is in charge of coordinating the work of space management–related tasks such as space reclamation, for example.

- *RCBG*: The result cache background process supports the new result cache feature.

You'll get a chance to review the key new background processes in more detail when we discuss the new features that use these background processes.

■**Note** On Windows servers, the Volume Shadow Copy Service infrastructure lets you make snapshots, called *shadow copies*. When you install Oracle Database 11g, the Oracle Shadow Copy Service Writer is automatically installed.

New Oracle-Supplied PL/SQL Packages

Several new Oracle-supplied PL/SQL packages provide support for various new features. We describe the most important packages briefly here; you'll find explanations regarding the use of each of these packages in later chapters:

- DBMS_CONNECTION_POOL: Supports the new database resident connection pooling feature (explained in Chapter 3)

- DBMS_SQLPA: Supports the new SQL Performance Analyzer feature, which we explain later in this chapter

- DBMS_ADDM: Facilitates the management of the Automatic Database Diagnostic Monitor

- DBMS_SPM: Supports the new SQL plan management feature (explained in Chapter 4)

- DBMS_AUTO_TASK_ADMIN: Supports the automated maintenance task (explained in Chapter 3)

- DBMS_COMPARISION: Lets you compare the database objects in two different databases (explained in Chapter 3)

- DBMS_SQLDIAG: Lets you manually invoke the new SQL Test Case Builder (explained in Chapter 2)

- DBMS_HM: Supports the new database health management feature. The package helps you run Health Monitor checks and retrieve the resulting reports. We discuss the Health Monitor in Chapter 2.

- DBMS_RESULT_CACHE: Supports the new result cache feature (explained in Chapter 4)

- DBMS_WORKLOAD_CAPTURE and DBMS_WORKLOAD_REPLAY: Support the new Database Replay feature, which we discuss later in this chapter

Of course, as with all new database releases, several of the older Oracle-supplied packages have been updated. Please refer to the *Oracle P/L SQL Packages* manual for full details on all Oracle packages that have been updated in Oracle Database 11*g*.

■**Note** In Oracle Database 10*g*, manual undo management using rollback segments was deprecated, but the default value for the undo_management initialization parameter was still manual. In Oracle Database 11*g*, by default the value of this parameter is set to auto. If you create a new database with the DBCA, Oracle automatically creates the undo tablespace for you. You can still operate a database in the manual undo management mode, but Oracle strongly recommends using automatic undo management owing to its benefits, and we concur.

Upgrading to Oracle Database 11*g*

Upgrading to the new Oracle Database 11*g* release is similar to the upgrade process in 10*g*, but it contains more sophisticated pre-upgrade checks as well as simplified error management. The changes in Oracle 11*g* simplify the database upgrade process while making it faster. Since both the DBUA and the manual upgrade processes utilize the same scripts, such as the `utlu111i.sql` and `utlu111s.sql` scripts, the improvements are common to both methods. The pre-upgrade and the post-upgrade scripts in Oracle 11*g* work the same way as they did in the Oracle 10*g* version.

Upgrading and the Compatibility Factor

The default compatibility value for Oracle Database 11*g* version 11.1 is 11.1. However, you can upgrade to Oracle Database 11*g* with a minimum compatibility value of 10.0.0. Before you perform the database upgrade, you must set the compatibility level for your new database by setting a value for the initialization parameter `compatible`. If you omit this parameter altogether from the new initialization parameter file, it defaults to 11.1.0. Oracle recommends you use the minimum value for the compatible parameter during the upgrade (10.0.0). This way, if your upgrade doesn't go well for some reason and you have to back out of the upgrade process, the upgraded database won't become incompatible with your previous (10*g.x*) release.

If you upgrade to 11.1 and keep the `compatible` parameter at 10.0.0.0, only a small portion of the new features, limited to those that don't make incompatible database structures on disk, will be allowed. The vast majority of the 11*g* features will make these permanent changes, however, so the lower compatibility level disables those new features. Once you confirm that the upgrade did finish successfully, you can change the value of the `compatible` parameter to 11.1 or greater, depending on the software release you installed. Just remember that once you do this and restart the database, you can't downgrade to the previous release.

Before you increase the setting of the `compatible` initialization parameter, back up the database, and either edit the initialization parameter (`compatible=11.1.0`, for example) or, if you're using the server parameter file, use the following statement to make the change:

```
SQL> alter system set compatible ='11.1.0' scope=spfile;
```

Once you change the value of the `compatible` parameter, shut down the database (`shutdown immediate`), and restart it with the `startup` command. To go back to the old compatibility level after this if something doesn't work right, you must return to the backup you made of the pre-upgrade database.

Upgrade Path to Oracle 11g

Whether you can directly upgrade your current Oracle database to Oracle 11*g* or have to perform an upgrade to an intermediate release first depends on your current Oracle database release. Oracle supports a direct upgrade to Oracle Database 11*g* Release 1, if you're migrating from a *9.2.04 or newer* release of the Oracle database software. If you want to upgrade to Oracle Clusterware 11*g* release 1 (11.1), then you must upgrade from an Oracle Clusterware release 10.2.0.3 or newer. Here's a summary of the upgrade path to Oracle 11*g* for Oracle database releases older than 9.2.04.

- 7.3.3 (or lower) ➤ 7.3.4 ➤ 9.2.0.8 ➤ 11.1

- 8.0.5 (or lower) ➤ 8.0.6 ➤ 9.2.0.8 ➤ 11.1

- 8.1.7 (or lower) ➤ 8.1.7.4 ➤ 9.2.0.8 ➤ 11.1

- 9.0.1.3 (or lower) ➤ 9.0.1.4 ➤ 9.2.0.8 ➤ 11.1

- 9.2.0.3 (or lower) ➤ 9.2.0.8 ➤ 11.1

> **Note** In general, Oracle's logic is that, for a direct upgrade, Oracle will support whatever version of the database software is supported at the time of general availability of the new product. This also includes compatibility information regarding database links and communications between the versions of Oracle.

As you can see, some of the older versions have to be migrated to multiple intermediate releases before you can upgrade to Oracle Database Release 1 (11.1). As in the Oracle Database 10*g* release, you can upgrade with the help of Oracle-provided scripts or use the DBUA to simplify matters. For certain databases, you can also consider using the Data Pump Export and Import utilities as well as the `create table as select` (CTAS) statement to copy all or part of a database into a new database created with the Oracle Database 11*g* server software.

You can upgrade an Oracle 8*i*, Oracle 9*i*, or Oracle Database 10*g* client to the Oracle 11.1 release. You can use the Oracle 11.1 client to access any Oracle 8*i*, Oracle 9*i*, Oracle Database 10*g*, and Oracle Database 11*g* (11.1) databases.

In the following sections, we'll review the changes in the manual upgrade first and then look at upgrading with the DBUA.

A Manual Upgrade Example

A manual upgrade of an Oracle database involves executing a set of Oracle-provided SQL scripts that are stored in the `$ORACLE_HOME/rdbms/admin` directory. The first script you run before starting the upgrade process is the `utlu111i.sql` script, also called the Pre-Upgrade Information Tool. In Oracle Database 11*g*, this utility provides more information than before to help you during the upgrade process.

If you're upgrading from Oracle Database 10*g* to Oracle Database 11*g*, you must copy three scripts (`utlu111.sql`, `utlu111s.sql`, and `utlu111x.sql`) from the 11*g* database's file system (`$ORACLE_HOME/rdbms/admin/`) to a staging directory on the 10*g* database's file system.

Before you can actually run the upgrade script provided by Oracle, you must gather information regarding the upgrade requirements by running the Pre-Upgrade Information Tool (invoked by the `utlu111i.sql` script). Once you make sure you've taken care of all the warnings and recommendations made by the Pre-Upgrade Information Tool, you can upgrade databases to the Oracle Database 11*g* release using the same type of scripts as in the previous releases. In this case, the database upgrade scripts are named in the following way:

- `utlu111i.sql`: This is the previously described pre-upgrade script.

- `catupgrd.sql`: This is the actual upgrade script and is similar to the script in previous releases. The major change now is that it has been restructured to support parallel upgrades of the database.

- `utlu111s.sql`: This is the upgrade status utility script, which you invoke after completing the database upgrade.

Here's a brief summary of the manual direct upgrade process from a 10.2 Oracle release database to the Oracle 11.1 release. Remember that Oracle supports a direct upgrade to the Oracle Database 11*g* release from a 9.2.0.4, 10.1, or 10.2 release database. You must log in as the owner of the Oracle 11.1 release Oracle home directory.

■**Note** Your database upgrade may take a long time since the database will collect optimizer statistics for any dictionary tables that are missing statistics or whose statistics were significantly changed during the upgrade. You can speed up the upgrade process by gathering statistics for these tables by using the DBMS_STATS.GATHER_DICTIONARY_STATS procedure before starting the upgrade.

1. Log in as the owner of the Oracle 11.1 release Oracle home directory, and copy the utlu111.i sql file from the $ORACLE_HOME/rdbms/admin directory to another directory such as /tmp.

2. Log in as the owner of the Oracle home directory of the database you want to upgrade, and run the utlu111.i sql script (from the /tmp directory, where you copied it to) to get the pre-upgrade information such as the necessary initialization parameter changes, tablespace space requirements, and so on. Spool the results of the script execution so you can review the output later. For example, the following is a run of the utlu111i.sql script on one of our own systems:

```
SQL> spool upgrade.log
SQL> @utlu111i.sql
Oracle Database 11.1 Upgrade Information Utility    03-23-2007 13:36:14
.
**********************************************************************
Database:
**********************************************************************
--> name:       ORCL
--> version:    10.2.0.1.0
--> compatible: 10.2.0.1.0
--> blocksize:  8192
.
**********************************************************************
Tablespaces: [make adjustments in the current environment]
**********************************************************************
--> SYSTEM tablespace is adequate for the upgrade.
.... minimum required size: 593 MB
.... AUTOEXTEND additional space required: 123 MB
--> UNDOTBS1 tablespace is adequate for the upgrade.
.... minimum required size: 454 MB
.... AUTOEXTEND additional space required: 429 MB
--> SYSAUX tablespace is adequate for the upgrade.
.... minimum required size: 306 MB
.... AUTOEXTEND additional space required: 66 MB
--> TEMP tablespace is adequate for the upgrade.
.... minimum required size: 61 MB
.... AUTOEXTEND additional space required: 41 MB
.
**********************************************************************
```

```
Update Parameters: [Update Oracle Database 11.1 init.ora or spfile]
***********************************************************************
WARNING: --> "streams_pool_size" needs to be increased to at least 50331648
WARNING: --> "session_max_open_files" needs to be increased to at least 20
.
***********************************************************************
Renamed Parameters: [Update Oracle Database 11.1 init.ora or spfile]
***********************************************************************
-- No renamed parameters found. No changes are required.
.
***********************************************************************
Obsolete/Deprecated Parameters: [Update Oracle Database 11.1 init.ora or spfile]
***********************************************************************
-- No obsolete parameters found. No changes are required
.
***********************************************************************
Components: [The following database components will be upgraded or installed]
***********************************************************************
--> Oracle Catalog Views                    [upgrade]      VALID
--> Oracle Packages and Types                [upgrade]      VALID
--> JServer JAVA Virtual Machine             [upgrade]      VALID
--> Oracle XDK for Java                      [upgrade]      VALID
--> Oracle Workspace Manager                 [upgrade]      VALID
--> OLAP Analytic Workspace                  [upgrade]      VALID
--> OLAP Catalog                             [upgrade]      VALID
--> EM Repository                            [upgrade]      VALID
--> Oracle Text                              [upgrade]      VALID
--> Oracle XML Database                      [upgrade]      VALID
--> Oracle Java Packages                     [upgrade]      VALID
--> Oracle OLAP API                          [upgrade]      VALID
--> Oracle interMedia                        [upgrade]      VALID
--> Spatial                                  [upgrade]      VALID
--> Expression Filter                        [upgrade]      VALID
--> Rule Manager                             [upgrade]      VALID
.
***********************************************************************
Miscellaneous Warnings
***********************************************************************
WARNING: --> Database contains stale optimizer statistics.
.... Refer to the 10g Upgrade Guide for instructions to update
.... statistics prior to upgrading the database.
.... Component Schemas with stale statistics:
....    SYS
.


PL/SQL procedure successfully completed.


SQL> spool off
```

Note that the `utlu111i.sql` script (also called the Pre-Upgrade Information Tool) will estimate the size requirements for the system and sysaux tablespaces. However, these tablespace size estimates may sometimes be unrealistically small. To avoid problems during the upgrade, Oracle recommends you set one datafile in each of these tablespaces to extend automatically during the upgrade (you can do this by using the `autoextend on maxsize unlimited` clause). The Pre-Upgrade Information Tool shows that in this particular case, there are no changes necessary before the upgrade to the Oracle 11*g* release. In general, the Pre-Upgrade Information Tool will recommend the following:

- Removing obsolete initialization parameters

- Adjusting initialization parameters

- Adding space to key tablespaces such as system and sysaux

3. Shut down the database cleanly (with the `shutdown immediate` command). If you're using a Windows system, stop the Oracle service first using the `net stop` command, and then delete the service using the `oradim` utility. Use the `oradim` utility from the Oracle Database 11*g* release to create a new Oracle Database 11*g* release instance.

4. Back up the database before starting the upgrade.

5. Make the necessary initialization parameter changes, remove any parameters shown as obsolete by the Pre-Upgrade Information Tool from the current `init.ora` file, and move that file to the new Oracle home under 11*g*. Ensure that the initialization parameter `compatible` is set to 11.1. If you are using a password file, you must move it to the new Oracle 11*g* Oracle home.

6. Change the environment variables `ORACLE_HOME`, `PATH`, and `LD_LIBRARY_PATH` so they point to the new Oracle Database 11*g* Release 1 (11.1) directories. Also, make sure you set the `ORACLE_SID` variable correctly to point to the database you're upgrading.

■**Note** If you take the sysaux tablespace offline after an upgrade, it could lead to potential performance issues, because the database upgrade script moves any SQL profiles you may have from the system tablespace to the sysaux tablespace when you upgrade from Oracle 10.1 to Oracle 11.1.

---

7. Log in to the server as the owner of the Oracle home directory for the new Oracle Database 11*g* release. Start SQL*Plus after first changing to the new 11*g* `$ORACLE_HOME/rdbms/admin` directory.

8. Start up the database in upgrade mode as shown here after logging in as a user with the `sysdba` privilege:

```
SQL> startup upgrade pfile=$ORACLE_HOME/dbs/initorcl.ora
```

We're assuming you're upgrading from a 10.*x* release to the Oracle Database 11*g* release. If you're upgrading from an Oracle Database 9*i* (Release 2) version, you must first create a sysaux tablespace.

9. Set up spooling so you have a log of the upgrade:

```
SQL> spool upgrade.log
```

10. Run the upgrade script, `catupgrd.sql`, located in the `$ORACLE_HOME/rdbms/admin` **directory**, to upgrade the database to the Oracle 11*g* release:

```
SQL> @catupgd.sql
```

The `catupgd.sql` script calls various upgrade scripts and shuts down the database after finishing the upgrade. It may upgrade or install several database components.

11. Once the upgrade script finishes successfully, restart the database in normal mode (not in upgrade mode) in order to initialize the system parameters:

```
SQL> startup
```

Starting up the database after the completion of the database upgrade clears the buffers and caches and ensures the integrity and consistency of the upgraded database.

12. Run the `utl111s.sql` script to view the results of the upgrade:

```
SQL> @utlu111s.sql
.
Oracle Database 11.1 Upgrade Status Utility        03-23-2007 15:03:58
.
Component                    Status     Version     HH:MM:SS
.
Oracle Server                VALID      11.1.0.1.0  00:14:01
JServer JAVA Virtual Machine  VALID      11.1.0.1.0  00:11:08
Oracle Workspace Manager     VALID      11.1.0.0.0  00:00:40
OLAP Analytic Workspace      VALID      11.1.0.1.0  00:00:25
OLAP Catalog .               VALID      11.1.0.1.0  00:00:50
Oracle OLAP API              VALID      11.1.0.1.0  00:00:31
Oracle Enterprise Manager    VALID      11.1.0.1.0  00:08:06
Oracle XDK                   VALID      11.1.0.1.0  00:00:58
Oracle Text                  VALID      11.1.0.1.0  00:00:45
Oracle XML Database          VALID      11.1.0.1.0  00:09:29
Oracle Database Java Packages VALID      11.1.0.1.0  00:01:00
Oracle interMedia            VALID      11.1.0.1.0  00:16:11
Spatial                      VALID      11.1.0.1.0  00:04:43
Oracle Expression Filter     VALID      11.1.0.1.0  00:00:13
Oracle Rules Manager         VALID      11.1.0.1.0  00:00:11
.
Total Upgrade Time: 01:13:55

PL/SQL procedure successfully completed.

SQL>
```

The utlu111s.sql script, also called the Post-Upgrade Status Tool, shows the status of various database components following the upgrade. In the example shown here, all database components have migrated successfully, with a VALID status. If you see any errors during the upgrade process, you can rerun the catupgrd.sql script as many times as necessary. Most of the time, any errors are because of problems such as an inadequate shared memory or lack of room in a tablespace. If you see a status of INVALID for any of the database components, running utlrp.sql as shown in the next step will most likely change the status to VALID.

13. Execute the utlrp.sql script to recompile the stored PL/SQL and Java code:

```
SQL> @utlrp.sql
```

You can run the following script to check there aren't any invalid objects left in the newly upgraded database:

```
SQL> select count(*) from dba_invalid_objects;
```

Once you ascertain that there aren't any invalid objects, you have finished upgrading your database to the Oracle Database 11g release. If the upgrade should fail for some reason, you must restore the pre-upgrade database from the backup you made before starting the upgrade.

If you have to rerun the upgrade, you can do so by shutting down the database and restarting the database in the upgrade mode (startup upgrade), as shown in step 7. You must run the catupgrd.sql script after this and check the status of the components in the end by running the utlu111s.sql script. If you want to cancel the upgrade altogether because of any reason, just restore the database from the backup made at the outset of the upgrade process.

At this point, you must reset any passwords you want (see the following note) and set thresholds for tablespace alerts, because the upgraded database disables all tablespace alerts (the alert threshold is set to null).

■**Note** In previous releases of the Oracle databases, passwords weren't case-sensitive. If you want to take advantage of the new Oracle Database 11g password case-sensitivity feature, you must reset the user passwords after the database upgrade is completed. Use the alter user statement for each user in the database to reset their passwords to a case-sensitive format. See Chapter 5 for a discussion of the new case-sensitive passwords.

Upgrading with the DBUA

You can use the DBUA to effortlessly upgrade a pre-Oracle Database 11g database to the 11g release. The DBUA now uses the new pre-upgrade script for estimating disk space, providing warnings, and so on. The DBUA works pretty similarly to the way it did in the Oracle Database 10g release. You just have an additional screen now that asks you to specify the diagnostic directory location. If you specify that you're performing a database upgrade after installing the Oracle Database 11g software, the DBUA starts up automatically after you install Oracle Database 11g. Otherwise, you can manually invoke DBUA when you want to upgrade a database to the Oracle Database 11g release.

For the past several major releases, Oracle has committed a huge amount of time and resources to the fine-tuning of the DBUA. The DBUA has become a reliable option and the "one-stop shop" for simplified upgrades, especially if you have lot of special database options installed in the database such as Oracle Text, Java, Advanced Replication, and Streams. The DBUA lets you upgrade both the database instance and the ASM instance simultaneously, whereas with a manual method, you must upgrade the ASM separately from the database.

Performance Testing the Upgrade

Whether you use the manual method or the DBUA to upgrade, you can use several new Oracle Database change management features to test the performance of the upgrade to the new release:

- *SQL Performance Analyzer (SPA)*: You can use the SQL Performance Analyzer to predict the impact of any change, such as an upgrade to a new release, on the SQL workload as captured by a SQL tuning set. We discuss the SPA later in this chapter.

- *Database Replay*: You can use the Database Replay feature to test the impact of the database upgrade on the production workload by capturing and replaying the production workload on a test system before you actually perform the upgrade on your production database. We discuss the Database Replay feature later in this chapter.

- *SQL Plan Management*: The SQL Plan Management feature relies on the use of SQL plan baselines, which represent efficient execution plans. When you adopt SQL Plan Management pursuant to a database upgrade, only those SQL plans are used that don't result in a performance regression. We discuss the SPA in detail in Chapter 3.

Of course, besides the new change management tools described here, you can also use traditional volume and load testing to predict the impact of the database upgrade under real-life conditions.

Downgrading After an Upgrade to 11*g*

You can downgrade to the major release from which you upgraded to 11*g*. For example, if you upgraded from 10.1 to 11.1, you can downgrade only to 10.1, but not to the 10.2 release. Once you upgrade to Oracle Database 11*g* Release 1(11.1), you can downgrade back to release 10.2 or 10.1, whichever you've upgraded from. If your original Oracle database release number is lower than 10.2.0.4, however, you must install the latest patch set for release 10.1.

Here are the steps for downgrading from the Oracle Database 11*g* Release 1(11.1) (you must be in the 11.1 environment before starting the downgrade process):

1. Start the instance in downgrade mode:

   ```
   SQL> startup downgrade pfile=spfileorcl11.ora
   ```

2. Spool the results of the downgrade process:

   ```
   SQL> spool downgrade.log
   ```

3. Execute the downgrade script, `catdwgrd.sql`, located in the `$ORACLE_HOME/rdbms/admin` directory.

   ```
   SQL> @catdwgrd.sql
   ```

Once all components are successfully downgraded, the database downgrade will be completed.

4. Turn off spooling once downgrading of the database is completed:

```
SQL> spool off
```

If you find any errors in the spool file downgrade log, you can rerun the downgrade script catdwgrd.sql as many times as necessary.

5. Shut down the instance:

```
SQL> shutdown immediate;
```

6. Restart the database after changing all environment variables to point to the correct directories for the release to which you're downgrading.

Rolling Upgrade Enhancements

A *rolling upgrade* lets you upgrade a database to a new server release or apply patches, all while the database is online. Obviously, a rolling upgrade lets you avoid downtime, because it means you can apply patches to a running, "live" database. In Oracle Database 10*g*, Oracle offered rolling upgrades to Oracle Data Guard (and logical standby databases) and Oracle Streams. In addition, you could also apply individual patches online for ORAC databases. In Oracle Database 11*g*, Oracle takes the rolling upgrade capability further by extending it to ASM-based databases. You can now perform a live upgrade of any ASM software from the Oracle Database 11.1 release to a newer release (11.2 and so on).

The rolling upgrade of ASM databases means you can continue to use all the features of a clustered ASM environment, even while you are performing a rolling upgrade of one of the nodes in the cluster. Please see Chapter 9 for more on rolling upgrades in Oracle Database 11*g*.

You can now also perform an Oracle Clusterware rolling upgrade, but you're limited to applying patch set upgrades. During the patch set upgrade, all instances of the Oracle RAC installation except the instance being upgraded continue to be available to users, thus reducing the total downtime during the upgrade to the new patch set release. We discuss the Oracle Clusterware upgrade in the next section.

■**Note** Oracle Database 11*g* uses parallelism and delays the compilation of PL/SQL objects during the database upgrade process, making the upgrade to the 11*g* release faster than earlier upgrades in earlier releases.

Oracle Clusterware Upgrade

Oracle Clusterware is the heartbeat of the RAC ecosystem. Oracle continues to make the upgrade procedures for Clusterware simpler with every release. The upgrade procedures for 10*g* to 11*g* is seamlessly straightforward. If you are familiar with the upgrade process from 10*g* Release 2 to 10*g* Release 2 patch set 3, you'll find they are identical to the upgrade procedures here.

The Clusterware upgrade is done in place. Unlike the ASM or database upgrade process where you install the binaries into a separate directory and run the DBUA utility, the Clusterware upgrade occurs in the source Clusterware's ORACLE_HOME. Since you are running RAC for high-availability considerations, you should perform rolling upgrades of the Clusterware stack. The following sections provide detailed instructions with screen shots of the Clusterware upgrade procedures from 10g Release 2 to 11g. Furthermore, the upgrade is performed in a rolling upgrade fashion.

Preparation for Upgrade

Before you can run the installation and upgrade your clusterware, you must first prepare your environment. First, the clusterware should be shut down completely. Next, you must run the supplied preupdate.sh script to reset the file permissions. This script attempts to shut down Clusterware also, but the recommendation is to perform a clean shutdown manually prior to this step.

You can comment out the last three lines of /etc/inittab so that the CRS daemons will not try to restart:

```
#h1:35:respawn:/etc/init.d/init.evmd run >/dev/null 2>&1 </dev/null
#h2:35:respawn:/etc/init.d/init.cssd fatal >/dev/null 2>&1 </dev/null
#h3:35:respawn:/etc/init.d/init.crsd run >/dev/null 2>&1 </dev/null
```

Next, you will tell the kernel to reread its inittab by issuing the init q command:

```
[root@rac1 upgrade]# init q
```

■**Note** Please exercise caution when you issue the init q command. The Q key is right below the 1 key, and if you are a fast and clumsy typist (like one of the authors), you can accidentally initiate an init 1, which tells the operating system to boot in single-user mode.

Now, you need to manually stop all the CRS background processes:

```
[root@rac1 upgrade]# /etc/init.d/init.crs stop
Shutting down Oracle Cluster Ready Services (CRS):
Stopping resources. This could take several minutes.
Error while stopping resources. Possible cause: CRSD is down.
Shutdown has begun. The daemons should exit soon.
```

Once you receive confirmation that the shutdown sequence has begun, you can validate that the processes are down using this script:

```
[root@rac1 upgrade]# ps -ef |grep -v grep| egrep -i "crs|css"
```

There should be nothing returned from this script.

Execute the Pre-update Script

In the upgrade directory from the CD software, run the preupdate.sh script as root. The upgrade directory is below the clusterware directory.

```
cd /home/oracle/software/11g/clusterware/upgrade
[root@rac1 upgrade]# ./preupdate.sh -crshome /apps/oracle/product/
CRS -crsuser oracle
Stopping resources. This could take several minutes.
Error while stopping resources. Possible cause: CRSD is down.
Oracle CRS stack is down now.
```

You will notice that the CRS shutdown attempt is made. Also, behind the scenes, it is changing the file and directory permissions to Oracle so that you can perform an upgrade. If this script is not executed prior to the upgrade, you will receive an error that resembles this:

```
Checking Cluster Synchronization Services (CSS) status ...
Actual Result: CSS Stack is running on the following nodes : rac1.
Check complete. The overall result of this check is: Failed <<<<
Problem: The cluster is not in a state suitable for upgrade.  One or more of the
following conditions have not been met: The Cluster Synchronization Service
(CSS) is running on one or more nodes in the cluster and/or appropriate
directories within the Oracle Home are not writable.
Recommendation: To upgrade Oracle 10g Release Clusterware, you must shutdown
CSS on all nodes, and ensure that specific directories within the
 Oracle 10g Release Clusterware Home are writable on all nodes.  In the upgrade/
 directory at the root of the Oracle Clusterware 11g Release 1 media
 there is a shell script 'preupdate.sh' that should be run as root on each node
 that you wish to upgrade prior to launching the installer.  This script will
 shutdown the Oracle 10g Release Clusterware stack on that node and prepare the
Oracle 10g Release Clusterware Home such that the upgrade can
take place.  The script can be invoked using the following command: 'preupdate.sh
-crshome <Oracle 10g Release Clusterware Home location> -crsuser
<Oracle 10g Release Clusterware user name>'.
```

Install and Upgrade Using runInstaller

Now let's proceed with the actual upgrade. The upgrade process starts by executing the runInstaller executable from the CD software:

```
$./runInstaller
```

This will take you to the Welcome screen, as depicted in Figure 1-5.

When you click Next, it will take you to the Specify Home Details page where you can confirm the source Clusterware home that needs to be upgraded to Oracle 11g Clusterware, as shown in Figure 1-6.

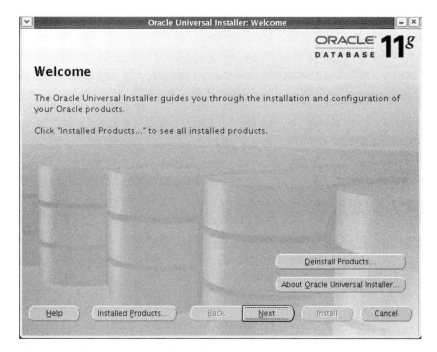

Figure 1-5. *Clusterware upgrade, Welcome screen*

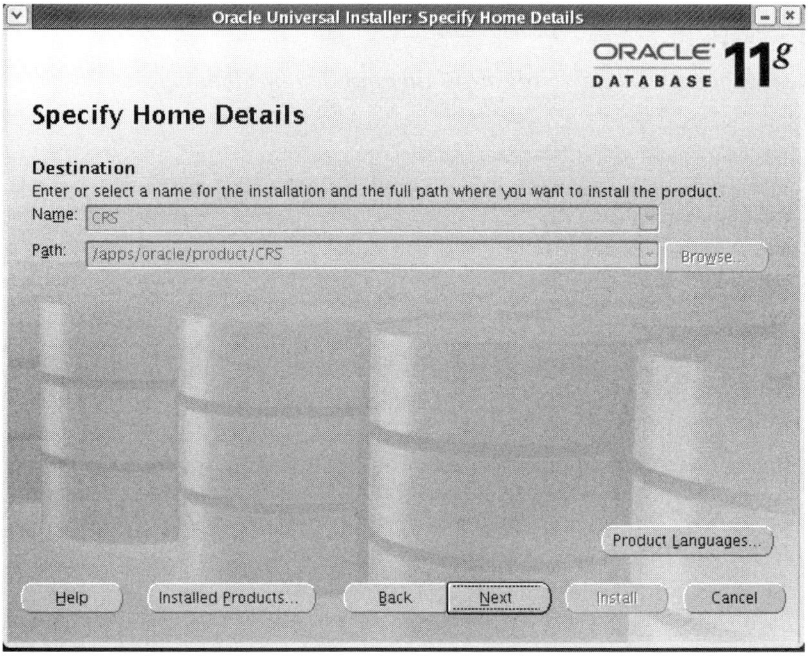

Figure 1-6. *Clusterware upgrade, Specify Home Details page*

When you click Next, you will be directed to the screen shown in Figure 1-7 to select the nodes you want to upgrade. For rolling upgrades, you should select only the node you are upgrading.

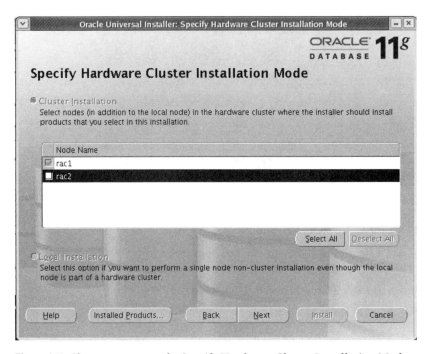

Figure 1-7. *Clusterware upgrade, Specify Hardware Cluster Installation Mode page*

■**Note** Optionally, prior to running the clusterware upgrade, you can single out the specific node by using the `updateNodeList` option: `./runInstaller -updateNodeList "CLUSTER_NODES=rac1" -local ORACLE_HOME=/apps/oracle/product/CRS`.

Once you pick the node(s), you can continue the upgrade with the system prerequisite checks, as shown in Figure 1-8. In this section, it is critical you make sure the overall status is Succeeded!

Once all the patches, swap space, memory, networks, CSS, OCR, voting disk, and so on are validated, you can continue. The upgrade process will take you to the Summary page, as shown in Figure 1-9.

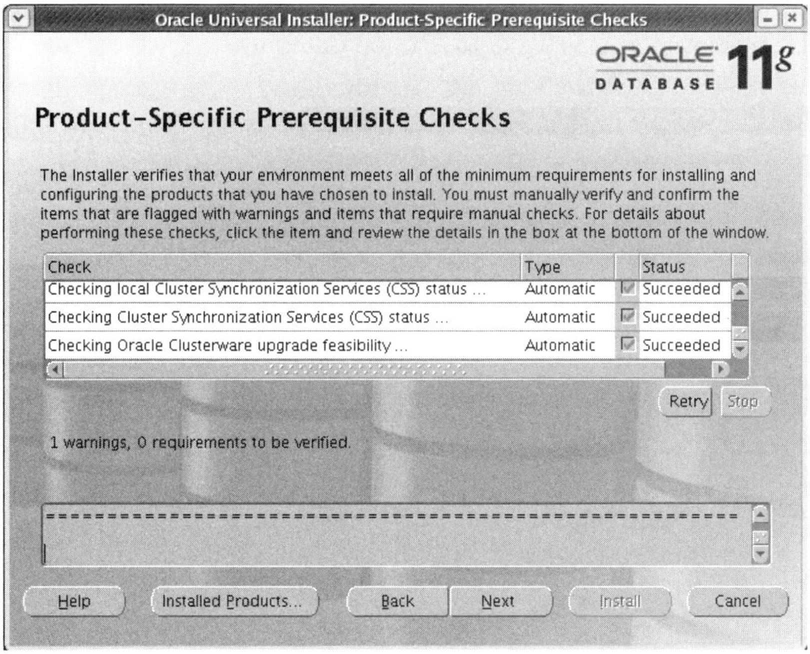

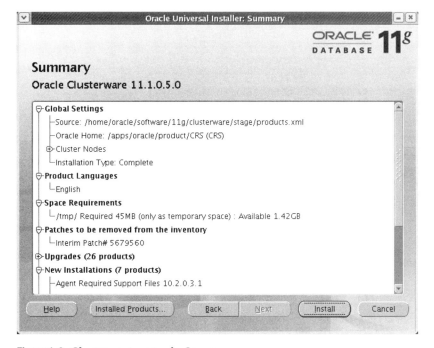

Figure 1-8. *Clusterware upgrade, Product-Specific Prerequisite Checks page*

Figure 1-9. *Clusterware upgrade, Summary page*

Once the installation is complete, you will be directed to the dialog box shown in Figure 1-10 to run the `rootupgrade` script from the `$ORA_CRS_HOME/install` directory.

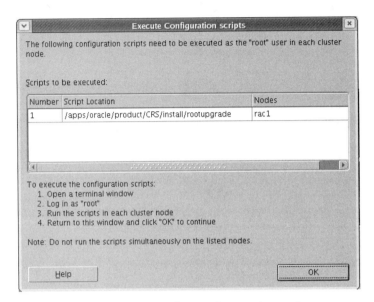

Figure 1-10. *Clusterware upgrade, running `-rootupgrade`*

As prompted, execute the `rootupgrade` script. The script will yield the following output:

```
[root@rac1 install]# ./rootupgrade
Checking to see if Oracle CRS stack is already up...

copying ONS config file to 11.1 CRS home
/bin/cp: `/apps/oracle/product/CRS/opmn/conf/ons.config' and `/apps/oracle/p
/apps/oracle/product/CRS/opmn/conf/ons.config was copied successfully to /ap
WARNING: directory '/apps/oracle/product' is not owned by root
WARNING: directory '/apps/oracle' is not owned by root
WARNING: directory '/apps' is not owned by root
Oracle Cluster Registry configuration upgraded successfully
Adding daemons to inittab
```

```
Attempting to start Oracle Clusterware stack
```

■**Note** You may have to reboot the box if the clusterware does not autostart after the upgrade.

Your clusterware may not autostart and may fail with the cluster verify utility (`cluvfy`). This is an optional requirement, and you can ignore the failure. You should confirm that there is nothing wrong if you get this error. Figure 1-11 shows the Configuration Assistants page, with the Failed status for the Oracle Cluster Verification Utility.

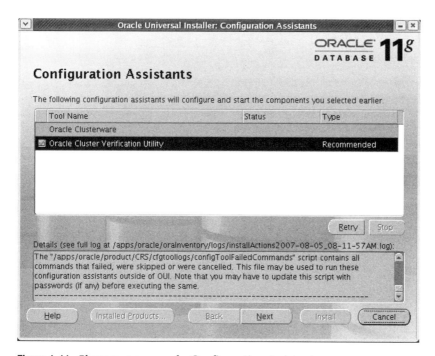

Figure 1-11. *Clusterware upgrade, Configuration Assistants page*

A simple bounce of the server can resolve this issue. The Next button will take you to the final screen of the upgrade, as shown in Figure 1-12.

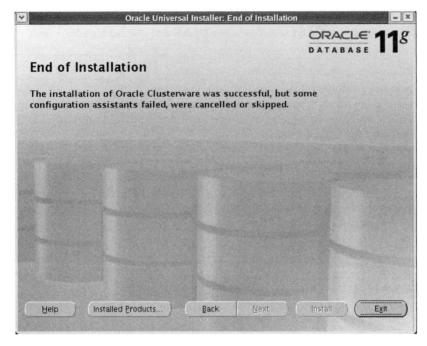

Figure 1-12. *Clusterware upgrade, End of Installation page*

Once the successful upgrade is complete and the CRS stack is back up and running, you can validate your rolling clusterware upgrade:

```
crs > crsctl query crs softwareversion
Oracle Clusterware version on node [rac1] is [11.1.0.5.0]
rac1.dbaexpert.com:/home/oracle
crs > crsctl query crs activeversion
Oracle Clusterware active version on the cluster is [10.2.0.3.0]
```

Upgrade Remaining Nodes of the RAC Environment

Repeat the same steps we showed here, starting from the "Prepare for Upgrade" section for every node in the cluster. Once the Clusterware upgrade is complete across all RAC nodes in the cluster, you can confirm that the Oracle Clusterware active version is the same as the software version:

```
crs > crsctl query crs activeversion
Oracle Clusterware active version on the cluster is [11.1.0.5.0]
rac1.dbaexpert.com:/apps/oracle/general/sh
crs > crsctl query crs softwareversion
Oracle Clusterware version on node [rac1] is [11.1.0.5.0]
```

The output shows the Oracle Clusterware version for each RAC node.

Real Application Testing

Adopting new technologies is too often a double-edged sword, making you more efficient and thus providing a competitive advantage while simultaneously introducing uncertainty and potential instability into key production systems. Change assurance, which involves making sure major changes such as new software releases and database upgrades don't negatively impact performance, has always been a prime concern for Oracle application developers and database administrators. Even if you can simulate real production workloads, the effort is just that—a simulation, not the real deal. In a world that is technologically advancing at a mind-numbing pace, you need to know which of the technologies have the potential to benefit you; therefore, you need to perform real testing with real data in real conditions.

Oracle Database 11*g* places considerable emphasis on the proactive testing of changes by making change assurance one of the cornerstones of the new release. It does this through the Real Application Testing feature; this feature encompasses two components, Database Replay and the SQL Performance Analyzer, that dramatically reduce the risks inherent in adopting changes by offering you a realistic method of testing changes using real-life workloads. The tools unearth problems and give you the opportunity to fix them before you actually introduce the changes into your production systems. Here's a brief summary of the two key components of Real Application Testing in Oracle Database 11*g*:

- *Database Replay*: You can use the Database Replay feature to test the impact of the database upgrade on the production workload by capturing and replaying the production workload on a test system before you actually perform the upgrade on your production database. Using the Database Replay reports from a test server, you can fix potential problems before they occur on the production database. We discuss the Database Replay feature later in this chapter.

- *SQL Performance Analyzer (SPA)*: You can use the SQL Performance Analyzer to predict the impact of any change, such as an upgrade to a new release, on the SQL workload as captured by a SQL tuning set. By knowing ahead of the actual upgrade about any adverse impact on performance and the root cause for it, you can prevent it from actually occurring in a production database after a database upgrade. We discuss the SPA later in this chapter.

In addition to the Database Replay and the SQL Performance Analyzer features, there's also a third new feature pertaining to change management, called SQL Plan Management, which replaces the stored outlines feature in earlier releases. The SQL Plan Management feature relies on the use of SQL plan baselines, which represent efficient execution plans. When you adopt SQL Plan Management pursuant to a database upgrade, only those SQL plans are used that don't result in a performance regression. We discuss the SPA in detail in Chapter 3. We discuss Database Replay and the SQL Performance Analyzer in detail in the following sections.

Database Replay

One of the major problems you face during an Oracle server software upgrade process or an application upgrade is the difficulty in simulating the actual production workload on the test databases. This is also true when you're moving to a totally new database configuration, say from a regular operating system file system to automatic storage management. Even if you use sophisticated testing suite software, it's not easy to accurately reproduce the true workload of a production database. Consequently, you are forced to test in an unrealistic setting and take your chances when you move to the new release of the server software or the application. It's not at all uncommon for DBAs and developers to bemoan the fact that the testing folks couldn't adequately "stress test" the changes before they were approved for the switch to production.

Note You can capture the workload for a single-instance Oracle database and replay it over a test system running in Oracle RAC configuration to get an idea about the performance improvement.

The Database Replay feature provides a solution to the vexing problem of reproducing production conditions in the testing and migration environments. By making it significantly easier to test potential database changes, Oracle Database 11*g* lowers the cost of database upgrades as well as other major changes such as operating system and storage system upgrades. Testing that usually would take months when done by scripts and traditional load simulation tools can be done at dazzlingly fast speeds now with the Database Replay feature. Database Replay lets you capture the actual workload on a production system and analyze it the same way by replaying it on a test system. The goal is to replicate the production environment *in toto* on a test system. Since the characteristics of the original workload such as concurrency and timing are maintained during the replay, you're essentially working with the same type of resource contention and other characteristics. This lets you easily identify any negatives that'll be potentially introduced by making the application, system, or software changes. The goal is to make sure the change you're making, such as a database upgrade, gets you only desirable results. Note that your test system must be running on the same or a newer version of the Oracle Database compared to the production system.

The key fact you must understand here is that Database Replay captures only the workload at the database level and ignores all client, application, and middle-tier interactions. The replay will capture the impact of any system changes that affect the database, such as an upgrade of the database itself, an upgrade of the operating system, or a switch to a new disk storage system. The production database is backed up and restored on a test system with identical configuration and environment. Your goal is to replicate the production system with the same application state as the original.

You can use Database Replay for testing the following types of changes:

- Database upgrades
- Operating system upgrades
- Storage system changes
- Configuration changes such as switching to an Oracle Real Application Cluster

Using Database Replay to replay a production workload consists of four steps:

1. Workload Capture records the production database workload.
2. Workload Preprocessing makes the captured workload replayable by converting it into replay files.

3. Workload Replay replays the production workload in the test database with actual timings, following the changes you want to test.

4. Analysis and Reporting deals with error reporting as well as reports on data divergence and performance divergence between the production and test environments. You can also enlist the ADDM for a deeper performance analysis.

Oracle provides an interface called the Workload Replay Client to let you interface with the Workload Replay feature using the command line. To access the Workload Replay Client, type wrc at the operating system command line, as shown here:

```
$ wrc
Workload Replay Client: Release 11.1.0.6.0 - Production on Sat Aug 25 21:45:01 2007
Copyright (c) 1982, 2007, Oracle.  All rights reserved.

FORMAT:
=======
 wrc [user/password[@server]] [MODE=mode-value] KEYWORD=value

Example:
========
   wrc  REPLAYDIR=.
   wrc  scott/tiger@myserver REPLAYDIR=.
   wrc  MODE=calibrate REPLAYDIR=./capture
 The default privileged user is: SYSTEM

Mode:
=====
wrc can work in different modes to provide additional functionalities.
The default MODE is REPLAY.

Mode       Description
-----------------------------------------------------------------
REPLAY     Default mode that replays the workload in REPLAYDIR
CALIBRATE  Estimate the number of replay clients and CPUs
           needed to replay the workload in REPLAYDIR.
LIST_HOSTS List all the hosts that participated in the capture
           or replay.

Options (listed by mode):
=========================

MODE=REPLAY (default)
---------------------

Keyword    Description
-----------------------------------------------------------------
USERID     username (Default: SYSTEM)
```

```
PASSWORD      password (Default: default password of SYSTEM)
SERVER        server connection identifier (Default: empty string)
REPLAYDIR     replay directory (Default:.)
WORKDIR       work directory (Default:.)
DEBUG         FILES, STDOUT, NONE  (Default: NONE)
              FILES  (write debug data to files at WORKDIR)
              STDOUT (print debug data to stdout)
              BOTH   (print to both files and stdout)
              NONE   (no debug data)
CONNECTION_OVERRIDE  TRUE, FALSE (Default: FALSE)
              TRUE   All replay threads connect using SERVER,
                     settings in DBA_WORKLOAD_CONNECTION_MAP will be ignored!
              FALSE  Use settings from DBA_WORKLOAD_CONNECTION_MAP
SERIALIZE_CONNECTS  TRUE, FALSE (Default: FALSE)
              TRUE   All the replay threads will connect to
                     the database in a serial fashion one after
                     another. This setting is recommended when
                     the replay clients use the bequeath protocol
                     to communicate to the database server.
              FALSE  Replay threads will connect to the database
                     in a concurrent fashion mimicking the original
                     capture behavior.


MODE=CALIBRATE
,,,

MODE=LIST_HOSTS
...
$
```

The first thing to note is that wrc can work in different modes to perform various tasks. The default mode is REPLAY, which we'll use to replay the workload that we capture. However, it may be necessary to run wrc in calibrate mode first to estimate the number of replay clients and servers (CPUs) needed to replay the captured workload. By default, the connection_override parameter is set to false, meaning that all replay threads connect using the server settings in the DBA_WORKLOAD_CONNECTION_MAP table.

Each thread of the multithreaded wrc (replay client) program submits a workload for a single session for replaying. You must first connect with the replay client to the test system before starting the workload replay, as we show later in this chapter. The Workload Replay Client will connect to the replay system and send database requests that are part of the captured database workload. You can manipulate several options of the wrc to control replay behavior, including scaling the login time and think time up and down. You can put these options to use for load and stress testing the production system on the test database.

Types of Data Captured in the Workload

The workload you capture from the production system consists of the following types of SQL calls:

- Data Manipulation Language (DML) statements

- Data Definition Language (DDL) statements

- Session control calls such as `alter session`

- System control calls such as `alter system`

Any background activities and scheduled jobs aren't part of the data capture. Client requests such as a direct path load of data from external files using SQL*Loader, database links, external tables, Oracle Streams, non-SQL-based object access, and distributed transactions are the types of data that *aren't* captured as part of the database workload.

Oracle recommends you use the Oracle Enterprise Manager (Database Control or Grid Control) to capture and replay the workload data. However, you can also use APIs available through the new Oracle packages `DBMS_WORKLOAD_CAPTURE` and `DBMS_WORKLOAD_REPLAY` to perform the workload capture and replay that are at the heart of the Database Replay feature. You use the procedures from the `DBMS_WORKLOAD_CAPTURE` package to capture the production workload and the procedures from the `DBMS_WORKLOAD_REPLAY` package to replay the captured production workload on the test system. You must have either the `dba` privilege or the `execute_catalog_role` privilege to use the two packages. In this chapter, we show you how to use the various procedures of these two key new Oracle packages to work with the Database Replay feature.

Before you can capture the workload, you must create a directory that'll hold the captured workload data. You must also back up the database before the capture process begins so you can replay the captured data on a system with an identical application state as that of the source database. You can use filters (with the `add_filter` procedure) to avoid capturing some user sessions such as the Oracle Enterprise Manager sessions or DBA actions, which aren't deemed part of the database workload for the purposes of change management.

■**Tip** Add the workload directory as part of your database OFA file system standards: `mkdir -p $ORACLE_BASE/admin/$ORACLE_SID/workload`.

We briefly describe how to perform each of the four key steps of Database Replay in the following sections.

Capturing the Workload

During the workload capture phase, Database Replay will capture all requests made by external clients to the Oracle database. These external client requests primarily include calls made by applications such as SQL*Plus and middle-tier components. Information pertaining to calls made by the external clients, such as SQL text and bind values, are collected and stored in what are known as *capture files* in a location chosen by you (in binary format).

Before you can start capturing the workload, you must do the following:

1. Back up the production database so you can restore it on the test system later for replaying the workload. The goal is to reproduce the application state of the production system by restoring the database before you replay the captured workload. You can use RMAN, a point-in-time recovery, Data Pump Export/Import, or a snapshot standby to back up the production database before starting the data capture.

2. Decide whether you want to restart the production database. You don't have to restart the production database before starting the workload capture, but note that any transactions that are underway when you begin the workload capture may not be captured.

3. If you decide to restart the production database, you must do so in restricted mode after logging in as the user sys. Once you start the capture process as shown here, you can open the database for all user sessions.

4. Create a directory with enough space to store the captured workload. Use the create directory SQL statement to create the directory object.

5. Determine whether some of the user sessions, such as DBA sessions, don't need to be captured as part of the workload. You can use *workload filters* to eliminate these sessions from the workload, as shown in the following example, which uses the add_filter procedure to filter parts of the workload from the data capture:

```
SQL> exec dbms_workload_capture.add_filter (fname => 'my_filter1',-
    > fattribute => 'user', fvalue => 'prod_dba');
```

You can remove any filters you create by executing the delete_filter procedure.

Use the start_capture procedure of the DBMS_WORKLOAD package to capture the database workload during a representative period of operation. Here's a simple example showing how to capture a database workload:

```
SQL> exec dbms_workload_capture.start_capture(name => -
    > ' aug20_peak', dir=> 'test_dir',duration=> 240);
```

The name parameter specifies the name of this workload capture process. The dir parameter refers to the directory object pointing to the directory you created for storing the captured workload data. Although you can stop the workload capture with the procedure stop_capture, here we use the duration parameter instead to limit the workload capture to 4 hours (240 minutes). If you choose to stop the workload capture before the end of the 4-hour duration, you can do so in the following way:

```
SQL> execute dbms_workload_capture.finish_capture ();
```

The execution of the finish_capture procedure ends the workload capture. It's a good idea at this point to generate a workload capture report to validate your data capture. Validation includes ascertaining that you did capture the correct workload and didn't miss any critical part of the production workload by accident. Of course, you must also make sure you can replay the captured data on the test server later. Execute the DBMS_WORKLOAD_CAPTURE.GET_CAPTURE_INFO procedure to generate a workload capture report, as shown here:

```
declare
   capture_id    number;
   capture_rpt   clob;
begin
   capture_id  :=  dbms_workload_capture.get_capture_info(dir => 'test_dir');
   capture_rpt  := dbms_workload_capture.report (capture_id => capture_id,
                     format => dbms_workload_capture.type_text);
end;
```

The procedure shown here produces a report in a text format. The report shows you a profile of both the workload that was captured and a profile of the workload that was excluded by using filters or that couldn't be captured because of version limitations. You also get statistics such as the number of logins and transactions the workload captured. Although the workload capture report is useful in many ways, it's the workload replay report that you'll see later that's really of more concern to you, because it tells you about the data and performance differences between the original system and the replay system.

Once you finish capturing the production system workload, it's time to prepare the workload for the replay on the test system, as shown in the next section.

Preprocessing the Data

Before you can replay the production data on a test server, you must first preprocess the data and initialize it. Preprocessing the workload entails converting the data into replay files, as well as creating the metadata necessary for replaying those files. Of course, you must preprocess the workload on a system that's running the same version of the Oracle Database as the one from which you captured the database workload.

Preprocessing essentially involves creating *replay files* from the processed data, which you can then replay on the test system. You process the workload in the test database where you're planning the replay. You can preprocess the data on the production system itself, but since preprocessing is a resource-intensive process, you're better off doing it on the test system. Processing the workload sets the stage for replaying the workload; it does this by transforming the workload into replay files.

To preprocess the workload data, you must first move the captured workload from the production system to a directory on the test system. So, create a directory object for this directory on the test system beforehand. Use the process_capture procedure to process the captured workload data:

```
SQL> exec dbms_workload_replay.process_capture (capture_dir => 'test_dir');
```

The process_capture procedure has only a single parameter, capture_dir, which points to the directory object holding the captured workload data. Once you preprocess the workload data, you can replay it on the same or a newer release of the Oracle database.

Performing the System Change

Now that you have moved the captured workload from the pre-change production system to the test system, make the system changes that it's your goal to test. For example, if you're planning to test a database upgrade, perform that upgrade now so you can replay the captured workload from the pre-change database to test the database upgrade.

Replaying the Workload

Before you start the workload replay, restore the test database so it reflects the same application state as the production database. You must also ensure that all external linkages and objects such as database links, external tables, directory objects, and URLs present in the production system are present in the test system as well. Oracle recommends you reset the system time on the test replay system to the time when you started the workload capture to avoid invalid data sets when dealing with workloads containing time-sensitive data, as well as to eliminate any potential job-scheduling issues.

You may want to start the database you restored in a restricted mode to avoid accidental changes to data during the workload replay. Replaying the workload requires several steps, which we summarize in the following sections.

Resolving External References

You must resolve all external references such as database links that are part of the captured workload. You must either disable or reconfigure all external references in the workload, if necessary, to make them accessible from the test system. These external references include database links, external tables, directory objects, and URLs.

Initializing the Replay Data

The next step is to *initialize* the replay data. Initializing the data, which you perform through the initialize_replay procedure, loads the metadata into tables, which will be used by the workload replay process:

```
SQL> exec dbms_workload_replay.initialize_replay(replay_name =>
    'test_replay',replay_dir => 'test_dir');
```

The replay_name parameter refers to the name of the replay. The replay_dir parameter points to the directory containing the captured workload that you want to replay on the test system.

Remapping External Connections

Once you initialize the workload data, you can query dba_workload_connection_map to view the connection mappings, if any external connections were made by the source (production) database users during the workload capture. You must now remap the connection strings that were utilized during the workload capture so the individual user sessions can connect to the external databases. You remap the external connection strings using the remap_connection procedure. The replay clients must connect to the replay system in order to replay the workload. On single-instance systems (not Real Application Clusters), the connection strings between the capture and the replay systems are mapped one-to-one.

Here's how you remap the external connections using the remap_connection procedure:

```
SQL> exec dbms_workload_replay.remap_connection (connection_id => 111,
    replay_connection => 'prod1:1521/mydb');
```

The connection_id parameter signifies a connection from the workload capture (generated during replay data initialization), and the replay_connection parameter (an optional parameter) specifies the new connection string to be used during the workload replay. If you leave the replay_connection parameter's value set to null (the default value), all replay sessions will connect to the default host, which is determined by the replay client's runtime environment.

■**Note** Although Database Replay is a new Oracle Database 11*g* feature, Oracle will be porting the change capture portion of this feature back to the Oracle Database 10*g* Release 2. You can replay any workload you capture on an Oracle Database 10.2.0.4 release or newer on an Oracle Database 11*g* based database. So if you are running the 10.2 version, you can use the Database Replay feature to check out the impact of an upgrade to the 11.*x* release of the database once the relevant code is ported to Oracle Database 10*g* Release 2.

Starting the Replay Clients

Before you can replay the workload, you must ensure that the replay clients connect to the test database. Each thread of the replay client (started by the executable wrc) submits a workload from a session. Once you process the workload data, you must start the replay client(s). The replay client connects to the database and drives the replay of the workload data. Before you can start the replay clients, make sure the replay directory contains the (preprocessed) workload files, the replay clients have access to that directory, and the replay user has the correct credentials to connect.

The wrc executable is run by default in replay mode. However, first run the wrc executable in calibrate mode to estimate the number of replay clients and hosts to replay your captured workload. Each replay client can handle multiple user sessions. If, for example, the captured workload was generated by 200 user sessions and a single host can handle only about 120 sessions, you'll need two hosts, with a replay client running on each of those hosts. This means you must install wrc on both the hosts. Here's how you run the wrc executable in calibrate mode:

```
$ wrc system/<system_password> mode=calibrate replay_dir=./test_dir
```

Once you figure out the number of hosts and replay clients you need to replay the actual workload, you then start the necessary replay clients by executing the wrc executable in the (default) replay mode, as shown here:

```
$ wrc system/<system_password> mode=replay replay_dir=./test_dir
```

By default, the connection_override parameter of the wrc executable is set to the value of false, meaning that all replay threads will simply use the connection mappings in the DBA_WORKLOAD_CONNECTION_MAP view to connect.

Preparing the Workload Replay

Before you start the actual workload replay, you must specify various workload replay options. The following are the three replay options you can configure to control the database replay:

- Mode: By default, a workload replay is performed in *synchronization* mode. If you think the workload is primarily composed of independent transactions, you must disable synchronization mode explicitly, because data divergence during the replay under these circumstances isn't something to worry about.

- Connection Time Scale: You can use the connect_time_scale parameter to calibrate the time between the workload capture and the session connect time during the replay. Use this parameter to adjust the number of concurrent users higher or lower during the workload replay.

- Replay Speed: To correct for longer time for completion of user calls during the workload replay, use the think_time_auto_correct parameter. The think_time_auto_correct parameter helps you adjust the concurrency level during the workload replay. To correct for elapsed time between user calls during the replay, use the think_time_scale parameter. If the replay is progressing slower than the data capture, by default the think time component of the replay will be automatically reduced (think_time_auto_correct is set to true by default).

Use the prepare_replay procedure to prepare the workload for the replay on the test system, including setting the replay options discussed earlier, as shown here:

```
SQL> dbms_workload_replay.prepare_replay (replay_name =>'replay1',
     replay_dir => 'test_dir', synchronization= FALSE);
```

Only the synchronization parameter needs explanation. By setting the synchronization parameter to the value of false (the default value is true), you're saying that the commit order in the workload capture may or may not be preserved during the replay. You can do this in a situation where there are numerous independent transactions that don't have to follow a certain commit order.

Once you've completed all the requirements for the workload replay, it's time to start the workload relay. Use the start_replay procedure to do this, as shown here. After making sure you have started at least one wrc replay client, issue the following command to replay the workload:

```
SQL> exec dbms_workload_replay.start_replay();
```

The start_replay procedure doesn't require any parameters. You can cancel the replay operation using the cancel_replay procedure, if you want, as shown here:

```
SQL> exec dbms_workload_replay.cancel_replay();.
```

The cancel_replay procedure directs all replay clients (wrc) to stop submitting workload from the captured sessions.

At the end of the workload replay, all AWR snapshots that correspond to the replay time period are automatically exported. If the export of the snapshots fails for some reason, you can manually export them by executing the export_awr procedure. You can then import these snapshots into the AWR schema owned by the user sys by executing the import_awr procedure.

Analyzing Workload Capture and Replay

Once you replay the workloads on the test system, you must analyze the data replay by generating a workload replay report. To measure the data and performance differences between the capture and the replay systems as well as a list of any errors during the workload replay, generate the workload replay report, as shown here:

```
declare
      cap_id    number;
      rep_id    number;
      rep_rpt   clob;
begin
   cap_id  :=  dbms_workload_replay.get_replay_info (dir => 'test_dir');
   select max(id)
    into rep_id
    from dba_workload_replays
    where capture_id = cap_id;
   rep_rpt  :=  dbms_workload_replay.report(replay_id  =>  rep_id,
                format => dbms_workload_replay.type_text);
end;
/
```

The get_ replay_info function returns the history of the workload capture and all the workload replays made based on the specified directory. You can associate the capture_id value returned by this function with the capture_id column of the DBA_WORKLOAD_REPLAYS table. The get_replay_info function also inserts a row into the DBA_WORKLOAD_REPLAY table for every replay you make from the specified replay directory. Note that we chose text as the value for the replay_type parameter. You can also specify HTML and XML as the values for this parameter.

Here is a sample report from the execution of the replay_report procedure:

```
Error Data

(% of total captured actions)
New errors:
7.3%
Not reproduced old errors:
1.0%
Mutated errors:
1.0%


Data Divergence

Percentage of row count diffs:
5.0%
Average magnitude of difference (% of captured):
2.5%
Percentage of diffs because of error (% of diffs):
25.5%


Result checksums were generated for 10% of all actions(% of checksums)
Percentage of failed checksums:
0.0%
```

```
Percentage of failed checksums on same row count:
0.0%

Replay Specific Performance Metrics

Total time deficit (-)/speed up (+):
12 min
Total time of synchronization:
24 min
Average elapsed time difference of calls:
0.2 sec
Total synchronization events:
3284218772
```

Careful examination of the report by looking for both data and performance divergence will give you a good idea about the potential issues subsequent to major changes such as a database upgrade to a new release. Database Replay's reporting tools let you get the following types of information:

- Data divergence, which is reflected in differences in the number of rows returned by queries.

- Errors during the workload replay.

- Performance comparison between the workload capture and workload replay. In this example, the total time deficit is shown to be 12 minutes after the change was implemented. Obviously, things are taking longer to process after the changes were made to the database, and you must, of course, investigate this further.

- Performance statistics as captured by AWR reports.

Note that a performance divergence could be both desirable as well as undesirable, since it's entirely possible that the replay system uses a more recent version of the database, thus providing improved performance. A data divergence is said to occur when the source and the replay systems return different number of rows in response to identical SQL queries or DML statements. Of course, any such data divergence merits serious investigation.

Oracle claims that Database Replay offers significant benefits when compared to third-party tools such as LoadRunner for testing large applications. Database Replay offers the great advantage that it tests virtually 100 percent of the actual production workload, compared to a third-party tool's artificially simulated workload that at best uses less than 10 percent of the actual workload. Database Replay is also much faster when compared to a third-party tool, completing a replay of a complex application in days compared to months. In one study (*Oracle Database 11g: Real Application testing and Manageability Overview*, available at http://technet.oracle.com), Oracle claims that it takes only half a month to test an entire e-business suite with Database Replay, compared to a total time of seven-and-a-half months with LoadRunner.

Oracle provides several DBA_WORKLOAD_* views to help monitor and manage the Workload Replay feature. For example, the DBA_WORKLOAD_REPLAYS view shows you all the workloads that have been replayed in a database. You can monitor the workload replay by using new views such as DBA_WORKLOAD_CAPTURES and DBA_WORKLOAD_FILTERS.

The SQL Performance Analyzer

One of the major problems you encounter during an Oracle database upgrade is the difficulty of predicting the impact of a database upgrade on the functionality as well as the performance of the database. In Oracle Database 11*g*, you can perform a what-if analysis of potential database changes and their impact on SQL performance using the powerful SQL Performance Analyzer. The SQL Performance Analyzer (SPA) performs fine-grained performance analysis of individual SQL statements and provides suggestions for solving the potential performance degradation of SQL statements consequent to a database upgrade, say, from the Oracle Database 11.1 release to the Oracle Database 11.2 release. The SPA provides these recommendations by comparing performance before the upgrade and following the upgrade. You thus have the opportunity to catch those SQL queries whose performance is likely to worsen following a database upgrade and tune them so you can avoid the performance degradation. Essentially, the SPA lets you compare and analyze two versions of workload performance in order to identify those SQL statements that are likely to be affected by the changes you are making.

■**Note** You can use a SQL workload that you captured into an STS on an Oracle Database 10.2.0.1 (and newer) release with the SQL Performance Analyzer feature in an Oracle Database 11*g* database.

Once the SPA identifies SQL execution plan modifications and performance regression brought about by changes such as a shift to a different optimizer level, for example, you can use the SQL Tuning Advisor to retain the original execution plans or tune the SQL statements that have regressed following a database change.

In addition to using the SQL Performance Analyzer for gauging the potential SQL performance changes after a database upgrade, you can also use it to analyze any changes in the database that can potentially impact SQL performance, such as the following:

- Database and application upgrades

- Hardware changes

- Operating system changes

- Initialization parameter changes

- SQL tuning actions such as the creation of SQL profiles

- Schema changes

You first need to decide whether you're going to run the SQL Performance Analyzer analysis on the production system or on an identically configured test system. If you decide to go with a test system, you can use RMAN's `duplicate` command to create your test version of the production database. Your test system, should you choose to go that route, must use the same database version and initialization parameters as the production database. If you use a test system for the replay, you can capture the SQL workload on the production system, import it into a test system, and run the SQL Performance Analyzer there to compare the pre-upgrade and post-upgrade SQL performance. We recommend you use a test system to avoid the extra load on the production system.

In this example, we'll show you how to use the SQL Performance Analyzer to help predict SQL performance changes following the upgrade of a database from the Oracle 10.2 release to the Oracle 11.1 release. We assume you're using a test database to run the analysis instead of running it on the production system. You must configure the test database as similarly as possible to the production system to get the most out of the SQL Performance Analyzer. Oracle recommends you use Oracle Enterprise Manager to run the SQL Performance Analyzer. However, we show you how to run the tool using the PL/SQL procedures in the new package DBMS_SQLPA, which provides the interface for the SQL Performance Analyzer. When you use this package to run the SQL Performance Analyzer, you create a SQL Performance Analyzer task to contain the results of the SQL replay trials you perform. You also use several new procedures in the DBMS_SQLTUNE package to conduct your performance analysis with the SQL Performance Analyzer.

■**Note** You can run the SQL Performance Analyzer on the production database from which you collect the SQL workload or on a similarly configured test database. Running the job on the production database entails some additional resource usage but gives you the most representative results. If performance is a big concern, then use a test database to run the analysis.

You can store the SQL workload that you capture in a SQL tuning set (STS). An STS is a database object that includes the SQL text of one or more SQL statements along with information pertaining to their execution environment, the execution plan, and the execution statistics. You can also specify that the STS include the execution plans and row source statistics for the SQL statements in the STS. Using an STS lets you collect and store the SQL information in a persistent database object, which you can modify and select from later on, just as you would data from a database table. An STS also makes it easy for you to export the SQL workload from the production system to the test system and provide the workload as input to the SQL Performance Analyzer.

You can use any of the following sources to load statements into an STS:

- The automatic workload repository (AWR)

- A cursor cache

- Another STS

Once you capture the SQL statements that comprise the SQL workload on the production system in a SQL tuning set, you follow these steps to perform a SQL Performance Analyzer task:

1. *Measure the pre-change SQL workload performance*: The SQL Performance Analyzer executes the SQL statements that are part of the STS that you create and generates the execution plan and execution statistics for those statements. The SPA stores the execution information in the STS.

2. *Make the system changes*: After the first run of the SQL Performance Analyzer, you make the changes that you want to test on the testing system. For example, you may want to test the migration to a different release of the database by installing the new release and changing the initialization parameter optimizer_features_enable to the new version.

3. *Measure the post-change SQL workload performance*: The SQL Performance Analyzer collects the SQL performance data again, after you make the database change you're testing.

4. *Compare the SQL performance*: The SQL Performance Analyzer will compare the SQL performance before and after the changes you made. The goal is to identify changes in the execution plans of the SQL statements that are part of the captured workload. Statistics such as the execution times, buffer gets, and disk reads are some of the metrics that serve as the basis for comparing SQL performance.

Capturing the Production System SQL Workload

Your first task in running the SQL Performance Analyzer is to capture a representative SQL workload from the production system so you can analyze its performance before and after the database upgrade. The SQL workload consists of not just the SQL statements but additional environmental information such as the SQL bind variable values and the execution frequency of the SQL statements. As mentioned earlier, you can use the AWR, a cursor cache, or an STS to load the production database SQL workload into an STS. The following sections cover the steps you must follow to capture the production system SQL workload into an STS.

Creating the SQL Tuning Set

The first thing you must do is create a new STS, which you can then execute on the production system, to capture the workload statistics:

```
SQL> exec dbms_sqltune.create_sqlset(sqlset_name => 'upgrade_set',
          description  => '11g upgrade workload';
```

The name of the new STS is upgrade_set, which we'll use to store the captured SQL workload on the production system. The parameter sqlset_owner in the create_sqlset procedure defaults to the name of the current schema owner. Note that the create_sqlset procedure creates just an empty STS, which you must load with the necessary SQL statements later.

Loading the SQL Tuning Set

Once you create your STS, you must load the SQL statements into it by using the load_sqlset procedure of the dbms_sqltune package, as shown here:

```
declare
  mycur dbms_sqltune.sqlset_cursor;
begin
  open  mycur for
    select value (P)
    from table (dbms_sqltune.load_sqlset(
      'parsing_schema_name <> ''SYS'' AND elapsed_time > 2500000',
      null,null,null,null,1,null,
      'ALL')) P;
```

```
    dbms_sqltune.load_sqlset(sqlset_name => 'upgrade_set',
                             populate_cursor => cur);

end;
/
PL/SQL procedure successfully completed.
SQL>
```

Now that you have captured a representative SQL workload from the production system, it's time to export this STS to the test system where you'll conduct the performance analysis.

Transporting the SQL Tuning Set

You must first create a staging table using the create_stgtab_sqlset procedure before you can export the STS you created in the previous step. This staging table is where you export the STS from the production database and subsequently import it from there to the test database. Here are the steps in transporting the STS you captured from the production system:

```
SQL> exec dbms_sqltune.create_stgtb_sqlset ( table_name => 'stagetab');
```

The previous code creates a new staging table named stagetab.

Once you create your staging table, it's time to export the STS into that table by using the pack_stgtab_sqlset procedure:

```
SQL> exec dbms_sqltune.pack_stgtab_sqlset(sqlset_name => 'upgrade_set',
        staging_table_name => 'stagetab');
```

After the export of the STS from the production system is complete, you're ready to import the STS into the test system.

Import the STS into the Test System

After you use the Data Pump Export utility to export the staging table stagetab (which contains the STS), use the Data Pump Import utility to load the staging table into your test system. After you import the staging table, you must run the unpack_stgtab_sqlset procedure in order to import the STS into the replay database:

```
SQL> exec dbms_sqltune.unpack_stgtab_sqlset (sqlset_name = '%',
        replace => true, staging_table_name => ('stagetab');
```

Once you successfully import the STS into the replay database, your next step is to create a SQL Performance Analyzer task, as explained in the next section.

Creating a SQL Performance Analyzer Task

To compare the execution of the captured production workload on the pre- and post-upgrade test environments, you must first create a SQL Performance Analyzer task, using the DBMS_SQLPA package. Use the create_analysis_task procedure to create a tuning task for the STS you created earlier:

```
SQL> exec dbms_sqlpa.create_analysis_task(sqlset_name => 'upgrade_set',
        task_name=> 'spa_task1');
```

Since you're specifying an STS as the source of the SQL workload, make sure you have already created and loaded the STS before creating the SPA task as shown here.

Analyzing the Pre-change SQL Workload

To get the best results from using the SQL Performance Analyzer, your test system must resemble the production system as closely as possible. After installing the Oracle Database 11 release software, you need to set the `optimizer_features_enable` parameter to match the production system version on which you captured the SQL STS, as shown here:

```
optimizer_features_enable=10.2.0
```

By setting the value of the `optimizer_features_enable` parameter to 10.2.0, you can generate SQL performance statistics for a 10.2 database you're about to upgrade to the 11*g* version. Now you are all set to capture the pre-upgrade SQL performance data. Use the `execute_analysis_task` procedure to analyze the SQL workload, as shown here:

```
SQL> exec dbms_sqlpa.execute_analysis_task (task_name => 'spa_task1',
          execution_type => 'test execute',
          execution_name= 'before_change');
```

The key parameter here is the `execution_type` parameter, which can take the values `explain plan`, which generates explain plans for the SQL statements in the SQL workload, and `test execute`, which actually executes all SQL statements in the workload. In our example, we specify `test execute` as the value for the `execution_type` parameter, because we want to execute all the SQL statements in our STS. Note that only DML queries are executed so as to prevent an adverse impact on the data.

Analyzing the Post-upgrade SQL Workload

To compare the effect of a system change, you must first make that change on the test system. In this example, we're trying to figure out the impact of a database upgrade from the 10.2 release to the 11.1 release. To test the impact of the database upgrade, you must first set the value of the initialization parameter `optimizer_features_enable` to the 11*g* version:

```
optimizer_features_enable=11.1
```

Once you do this, you can collect the SQL performance data post-upgrade by running the same `execute_analysis_task` procedure as you did before you made the change:

```
SQL> exec dbms_sqlpa.execute_analysis_task (task_name => 'spa_task1',
        execution_type => 'test execute', execution_name='after_change')
```

The final step is to compare the SQL performance between the two runs of the `execute_analysis_task` procedure.

Comparing the SQL Performance

You must execute the `execute_analysis_task` for a third and final time in order to compare the SQL performance before and after the database upgrade. You must understand how to set the values for the `execute_type` parameters for this third and final execution of the execute_tuning_task procedure. Since two executions of execute_analysis_task, both of the execution type test execute, already exist, you must now pass the value compare performance to the execution_type parameter so the procedure can analyze and compare the SQL performance data from the two workload analyses you conducted.

Here's how you invoke the execute_analysis_task procedure to compare SQL performance before and after the system change:

```
SQL> exec dbms_sqltune.execute_analysis_task (task_name =>

        'spa_task1',
        execution_type => 'compare performance',
        execution_params =>
        dbms_advisor.arglist('comparision_metric',
                        'disk_reads',);
```

In this example, we used disk_reads as the value for the comparision_metric parameter, which lets you specify a variety of statistics to measure the performance impact of the system changes you make. Other possible values for this parameter include elapsed_time, optimizer_cost, direct_write, parse_time, buffer_gets, and so on.

Generating the SQL Performance Analyzer Report

Once you finish running the comparison analysis, it's time to generate a report showing the results. You can generate the results of the SQL performance comparison in report form by executing report_analysis_task, as shown here:

```
var report clob;
exec :report := dbms_sqlpa.report_analysis_task('spa_task1', 'text',
            'typical','summary');
set long 100000 longchunksize 100000 linesize 120
print :report
```

In this example, we chose to generate a text report (HTML and XML are the other options) and summary as the value for the section parameter (all is the other option).

Analyzing the Performance Report

The SQL Performance Analyzer report in this example uses the disk_reads comparison metric to evaluate the database change you made (different optimizer level). The report contains three main sections: general information, result summary, and result details. The result summary section shows overall performance statistics pertaining to the entire SQL workload as a whole, indicating whether performance will improve or degrade after the database changes you're putting in place.

The report provides detailed execution statistics for each of the SQL statements in the STS you provide and summarizes the findings by saying whether the performance of a statement has regressed and whether its SQL execution plan has changed. Wherever the report indicates a performance regression, it also will contain a root cause analysis and recommendations to improve the execution plan of that SQL statement. You can then tune the regressed statements using the recommendations.

> **Note** Oracle Database 11*g* deprecates the use of stored outlines to preserve execution plans for SQL statements. The stored outlines feature is replaced by a newer and more powerful feature called SQL Plan Management that employs SQL plan baselines, which are sets of known good execution plans for SQL statements. Under this, the optimizer maintains a history of execution plans for SQL statements. When an execution plan changes, SQL Plan Management evaluates the new plan during the next maintenance window, and if it finds that the new plan is indeed better, it will replace the old plan with the new execution plan.

The SQL Performance Analyzer offers benefits such as a low overhead for data capture and integration with the cost optimizer when compared to third-party tools that perform similar tasks. In addition, the SQL Performance Analyzer offers the additional advantage that it's integrated with other Oracle tools such as the SQL Tuning Advisor and the SQL Plan Management feature. You can use both the SQL Tuning Advisor and the new SQL Plan Management feature to carry out the SQL Performance Analyzer recommendations made after the system change. You can place the new execution plans generated as a result of the system change you implemented in the SQL plan baseline repository. Thus, you can ensure that the optimizer will pick only previously validated execution plans. Following this, the database can automatically validate the plans seeded by you in the SQL plan baseline, or you can manually validate them yourself. Chapter 4 discusses the SQL plan baselines feature.

Database Software Patching

Once the Oracle Database 11*g* server software is installed, you might want to upgrade your databases to the new release. Before you go live on your 11*g* production database environment, check for any available patch set release. Patch sets don't provide additional functionality, but they provide bug fixes and don't need certification for installation on the system. Similarly, check for any critical path updates, which are the security updates made available by Oracle on a quarterly basis. Applying critical path updates secures your new database from any significant security vulnerabilities that were discovered by Oracle. Just as important, you should make sure to check the bug database and carefully consider critical bugs and pertinent bugs that may cause database outage situations.

New Features in Database Control for Patching

A software patch is a software update to fix defects in the software (bug fixes). A patch is thus supposed to fix bugs but doesn't involve any new functionality as such. Periodically Oracle releases maintenance releases, which are known as *patch sets*. Patch sets are a set of integrated product fixes. For example, if you're using Oracle Database 11*g* Release 11.1.0.1 software, a new patch set might be termed 11.1.0.3. In Oracle Database 10*g*, Database Control and Grid Control provided the crucial patch advisory. However, the Patch Prerequisite Check feature wasn't available in Database Control. In Oracle Database 11*g*, Database Control is enhanced by providing the Parch Prerequisite Check feature. In addition, Database Control now has the Software Library feature as well. You can stage a patch once in the Software Library and use it for multiple deployments.

Enterprise Manager now searches proactively for patches that are relevant to a specific customer's environment. Your installation and your database feature usage determine the search for patches. A daily patch job will run to correlate with the patch metadata on MetaLink. When the patch job finds relevant patches for your environment, it sends you an alert and enables you to apply that patch. As soon as a new one-off patch becomes available, you will be alerted by the proactive MetaLink patch advisory if the patch is relevant to your database environment. Thus, you can count on reliable deployment with this automation of patching.

The Provisioning Pack lets you automatically deploy software, patches, and applications. You can do the following things with the Provisioning Pack:

- Bare-metal provisioning of operating systems and software images

- Cloning installations and software images, for example, RAC or CRS

- Patching

- Using the Deployment Procedure Manager

OEM Database Control simplifies the staging and application of new patches and patch sets. Database Control can automatically stage a new patch set by proactively searching for it and downloading it from Oracle MetaLink to your server directories. Database Control supports all types of patches, including critical patch updates (CPUs), interim patches, and patch sets. Here are some of the key features concerning patching in Oracle Database 11*g*:

- Live update of MetaLink best practices

- Support for sudo

- Support for Pluggable Authentication Modules (PAM)–based authentication

In Oracle Database 10*g*, Database Control had a limited amount of patch management capabilities. In the Oracle Database 10*g* release, you could do only two patch-related activities through Database Control:

- Applying a patch

- Viewing a patch cache

In Oracle Database 11*g*, you still have the two links that are similar to the patching links in Oracle Database 11*g*. The Stage Patch link corresponds to the Apply Patch link. The View Patch Cache link is the same as in the previous release. However, the Database Software Patching page in Oracle Database 11*g* is much more detailed and offers more tools. On the Database Control home page, click Software and Support to reach the Database Software Patching page. You can go to the following pages from that page.

- *Patch Advisor page*: The Patch Advisor page shows you the currently applicable patches to your installation. The page contains patch advisories in two sections.

■**Note** You can't use feature-based patch application in Database Control 11*g*, since you won't get any feature usage–based patch advisories.

- *Critical security patches*: Critical security patches (also called *critical patch updates*) are periodic patch releases by Oracle to fix major security holes.

- *Patch recommendations by feature*: Lists all patch recommendations based on the database feature.

- *Patch Cache page*: Any patches you download from the Oracle MetaLink to the Enterprise Manager are saved in the Enterprise Manager repository. You can view the current patches in the repository by clicking the View Patch Cache link, which takes you to the Patch Cache page. This page shows, in a tabular format, all the patches you downloaded from MetaLink. The advantage of the using the patch cache is that you need to download a patch only once and stage it to multiple destinations. If you haven't downloaded a patch, that's OK too, since Enterprise Manager will automatically download the necessary path from MetaLink when the patch job runs.

- *Oracle Patch Prerequisite Checker page*: Click Path Prerequisites in the Database Software Patching section to get to the Oracle Patch Prerequisite Checker page. Here, you can select the software updates from MetaLink or the Software Library. You can stage the updates to a staging location and run prerequisite checks on those updates.

- *Stage Patch page*: This page lets you select patches from MetaLink, based on search criteria you provide.

- *Apply Patch page*: This page lets you select the patches to apply. You can select patches from MetaLink for the Software Library.

Emergency Hot Patching (Online Database Patching)

You can use the online database patching feature in Oracle Database 11*g* to apply emergency, one-off patches to the database server software, while the database is online. This means you can now patch Oracle executables with no downtime. This feature is especially useful for diagnostic patches. Some one-off patches can be done online now.

▓**Hint** Patches can now be installed with the `runInstaller` executable instead of `opatch`. This was one of the enhancements added to 10.2.0.3.

The new online patching capability is integrated with OPatch. Besides installing a new patch, you can uninstall a patch without bringing the database offline. Similarly, you can also enable and disable one-off patches online. You can use the online patching capability to patch many one-off patches online. There is also a subset of online upgradeable patches for Real Application Cluster environments. Oracle plans eventually to enable the online patching of its periodically released critical path updates.

Database Change Management Pack

The Change Management Pack offers you the capability to compare database object definitions before and after changes in the databases. The pack enables you to capture and compare
database object definitions from different points in time. Using the Change Management Pack,
you can easily associate application modules with the database schema objects. After an application upgrade, for example, you can assess the impact of the changes on the dependent database
objects so you can modify the application modules in accordance with the changes in the
database schema. In addition, you can track changes to initialization parameters as well as
authorization and storage settings.

You can use the following types of sources to compare the database objects:

• Two databases

• Two baselines

• A database and a baseline

Please refer to the Chapter 4 to learn more about dictionary baselines and dictionary
comparisons.

Software and Database Cloning

Oracle Database 11*g* offers gold-image cloning (*gold images* are tested and approved software
images) of software on the same server or cluster. Note the following points about software cloning:

• You can clone multiple Oracle homes in parallel.

• You can pre-patch images to a level you select.

• You have a choice of the Software Library or the host itself to get the source image.

You can optionally perform configuration tasks following the cloning job, such as creating
a database. In Oracle Database 10*g*, Database Control offered you only the following two sources
for cloning a database:

• A running database instance in archivelog or noarchivelog mode

• A saved working directory from a previous cloning operation

In Oracle Database 11*g*, Database Control provides you with vastly enhanced cloning
capabilities. You have the following four source types you can choose from now:

• Copy an online database files over Oracle Net, without any prior backups.

• Copy an online database's files via staging areas.

• Use RMAN whole-database backups.

• Use a special backup made by a previous database cloning operation.

You can get to the Clone Oracle Home page by clicking the Software and Support link
on the Database Control home page and then clicking the Clone Oracle Home link in the
Configuration section.

Database Diagnosability and Failure Repair

One of the major thrusts of Oracle Database 11*g* is in the area of fault management, which includes error diagnosing and repairing database failures. When you encounter a critical database error such as a corrupted datafile, for example, most of your attention is focused on *fixing* the problem after the fact. It's not easy to bring the same level of attention to the *prevention* of the problem. In Oracle Database 11*g*, Oracle provides a first-rate advanced diagnosability infrastructure to help you undertake proactive steps to prevent and proactively detect problems and quickly diagnose and resolve critical errors, such as those caused by code bugs and data corruption. The new infrastructure also helps ease interaction with Oracle Support.

In Oracle Database 11*g*, all critical errors in the database are tagged as *problems*, and each time one occurs, the database creates an *incident* with a unique ID. The Automatic Diagnostic Repository (ADR) holds all diagnostic data about critical errors. When the database encounters a critical error, it creates a new incident and automatically captures all relevant diagnostic data for that problem and stores it in the ADR. Oracle likens the new diagnostic framework to an airplane "black box," helping you analyze the causes of a database problem even if the database itself can't be accessed. A new tracing system that always lives in the database memory lets you collect diagnostic data for critical database errors. Since the collected data is stored separately from the database in the ADR, the data will survive a database crash and help you diagnose the problem. If necessary, the database might run a health check to gather more data about a problem. The DBA can also run manual proactive health checks.

Oracle Database 11*g* also introduces the Incident Packaging Service (IPS), which creates consolidated *incident packages* that are bundles of diagnostic information relating to critical errors. You can view, modify, add, or delete diagnostics data from these incident packages and then create a ZIP file of the package to transmit to Oracle Support.

Oracle Database 11*g* provides new tools to investigate and resolve database critical errors in your database. For simple problems, you can use the new GUI-based Support Workbench facility, accessible through Database Control. For more complex problems where you need to customize your incident reporting, you may want to use the new adrci command-line tool, which provides access to the diagnostic data stored in the ADR.

One of the most important new features of the Oracle Database 11*g* release is the Data Recovery Adviser (DRA), which helps you fix problems such as data corruption and missing datafiles. The Data Recovery Advisor is a tool that's based on RMAN's backup and recovery capabilities. You can access this advisor either by using Database Control or by executing various new RMAN commands that are designed for investigating and fixing problems. The Data Recovery Advisor shows problems, their level of seriousness, and their impact on the database. The advisor recommends repair options for problems such as corrupted or lost datafiles and can perform automatic repair of the problems it finds.

Here are main topics we'll review in this chapter:

- The fault diagnosability infrastructure

- Investigating and resolving problems

- Database health checks

- Data Recovery Advisor

- Support Workbench

- Repairing SQL failures with the SQL Repair Advisor

- Database health checks

- SQL Test Case Builder

- Improvements in handling data corruption

Although we discuss the new diagnosability and problem resolution features of Oracle Database 11g in several sections of this chapter, the underlying theme for all these new features is the concept of the new fault diagnosability infrastructure anchored by the ADR, which is the unified storehouse of all diagnostic data. So, we'll discuss the ADR first, before we cover the other new features related to diagnosing and fixing database problems and failures.

The Fault Diagnosability Infrastructure

Although we discuss several diagnostic and repair tools in this chapter, the real contribution of Oracle Database 11g is in providing a unified framework for diagnosing and resolving problems, the new automatic diagnostic repository. In previous releases, the diagnostic data was spread over different file systems and wasn't consolidated in any way. Thus, when you had to troubleshoot a critical error or upload various log files, trace files, and core dumps to the Oracle Support folks, you had to gather all this material from disparate sources and upload it via FTP. In Oracle Database 11g, there is a new infrastructure for database diagnosability, the heart of which is the Automatic Diagnostic Repository (ADR). The ADR is a dedicated repository on your file system, used for storing both traditional diagnostic data sources, such as the alert log, trace files, and dump files, and new types of diagnostic data, such as the Health Monitor reports.

All diagnostic and repair tools rely on the ADR to resolve problems. For example, when a critical problem occurs in the database, it causes Oracle to create an incident and to file away all diagnostic data for this incident in the ADR. Using the new incident packaging framework, you can then send this diagnostic data to Oracle Support and resolve the problem. Similarly, the Health Monitor, which is the new proactive diagnostic checking framework, stores the results of its checks in the ADR. The Data Recovery Advisor uses this data to repair the problem.

Currently, you use the initialization parameters background_dump_dest, core_dump_dest, and user_dump_dest to specify where the database should store all diagnostic data, including the all-important alert log file. Starting with the Oracle Database 11g release, all database diagnostic data will be stored in the new ADR. The great benefit of the ADR is that you can access the diagnostic data for a database even when the database is down or can't be opened for general access because of problems. The ADR stores the diagnostic data not only for all database instances but also for all other Oracle components and features as well, such as automatic storage management (ASM), Cluster Ready Services (CRS), and others. The ADR uses a consistent diagnostic data format across these various products.

The ADR provides the following benefits in serving as the repository for all the databases' diagnostic data:

- A unified directory structure

- Consistent diagnostic data formats for diagnostic data not only from multiple Oracle instances but also from multiple products

- The same set of tools to analyze diagnostic data across instances

The ADR consists of all the familiar Oracle database diagnostic files, such as the following:

- The alert log

- Trace files

- Core and dump files

In addition to the previously mentioned diagnostic files, the ADR contains new Oracle Database 11g release diagnostic data such as the following:

- Incident packages

- SQL test cases

- Data repair records

Note In Oracle Database 11g, you can no longer read the alert log that is located in the $ORACLE_BASE/diag/rdbms/$INSTANCE_NAME/$ORACLE_SID/alert directory directly, since it is now an XML file (named log.xml), not text file. In addition to all the standard information regarding database operation, the alert log will now also contain information regarding incidents. The alert log file you are used to seeing in previous versions of Oracle is located in the $ORACLE_BASE/diag/rdbms/$INSTANCE_NAME/$ORACLE_SID/trace directory.

We advise DBAs to quickly transition to the ADR. DBAs are accustomed to Oracle's Optimal Flexible Architecture and the standard set of directories in the $ORACLE_BASE/admin/$ORACLE_SID directories. The ADR's new directory structures and the newly implemented XML alert log file will take a little time for DBAs to get used to using. On a positive note, the ADR implements a standard layout for DBAs no matter who originally set up the server, and every server will have the same look and feel for directory structures as they move from one server to another.

Problems and Incidents

There are two new diagnostic-related concepts in Oracle Database 11*g* around which the entire fault diagnosability infrastructure revolves: *problems* and *incidents*. We'll take a minute to define these critical terms before we wade into the details of the fault diagnosability infrastructure:

- Any critical error in the database is defined as a *problem*. Typically these include familiar Oracle database errors denoted as ORA-600 errors and errors such as ORA-04031 (out of shared pool memory). All metadata concerning a database problem is stored in the ADR. Each problem is assigned a *problem key*, which helps identify and describe that problem. The problem key contains the Oracle error number and error argument values. Here's an example (part of the output from a show incident command in the adrci tool, which we explain later in this chapter):

```
INCIDENT_ID    PROBLEM_KEY         CREATE_TIME
------------   ------------------  ---------------------------
8801           ORA 600 [4899]      27-MAR-07 06.14.41.04-05:00
```

- An incident is a one-time occurrence of a particular problem. Thus, if the same problem occurs multiple times, you'll have one problem and many incidents to denote the multiple occurrence of that problem. A frequently occurring problem is denoted by a large number of incidents. Each incident has its own incident ID, as shown in the previous example.

The database does three things when a particular incident occurs:

- It creates an alert for that incident and assigns the appropriate level of severity for that alert.

- It makes an entry regarding the incident in the alert log.

- It gathers and stores the relevant diagnostic data for that incident in the appropriate subdirectory in the ADR.

You can't disable the automatic incident creation for critical errors. A problem is created automatically when the first incident occurs. Once the last incident is removed from the ADR, the problem metadata is deleted as well.

The ADR limits the dumping of diagnostic data to a certain number of incidents under any one problem. Two retention policies dictate how long the ADR retains the diagnostic data it accumulates for various incidents:

- The "incident metadata retention policy" determines how long the ADR retains metadata. The default retention period is for one year.

- The "incident files and dumps retention policy" determines how long the ADR retains dump files for the incidents. The default retention period is one month.

You can change either or both the retention polices using the Incident Package Configuration link on the Support Workbench page in Database Control. The background process MMON automatically purges expired ADR data.

Incident Packaging Service

In Oracle Database 11*g*, all diagnostic data relating to a particular error is tagged with that error's incident number. Thus, when you have to send diagnostic data to Oracle Support, you don't have to go rummaging through your trace file, dump files, and alert logs to see which files you must send to Oracle Support. You can now automatically gather and package all diagnostic data and files concerning a critical error for sending them to Oracle Support in the form of a ZIP file. This feature is called the Incident Packaging Service (IPS).

Besides automatically identifying the required files for problem resolution, IPS also lets you customize the package by adding other information as well as diagnostic data for related incidents. You'll see the IPS in action in the section "Packaging Incidents" later in this chapter.

Structure and Location of the ADR

One of the ways in which the ADR provides great diagnostic help is by always being available for problem diagnosis, since it is located outside the database. Thus, following a database crash, you can access the ADR without any hindrance. The database creates the ADR by default— the only thing you need to specify is the location for it. Use the new initialization parameter `diagnostic_dest` to specify the root directory for the ADR, as shown here:

```
diagnostic_dest = /u05/app/oracle
```

This root directory for the ADR is called the *ADR base*. Oracle will create an ADR even if you omit the `diagnostic_dest` initialization parameter. In such a case, the database will create the ADR in one of the following locations:

- If you set the `ORACLE_BASE` environmental variable, the `diagnostic_dest` default value is set to the same directory.

- If you haven't set the `ORACLE_BASE` variable, Oracle will set the `diagnostic_dest` parameter value to `$ORACLE_HOME/log` by default.

In an Oracle Real Application Cluster (RAC) environment, you can set a node's ADR base either on local storage or on shared storage.

■**Note** In Oracle Database 11*g*, you don't need to set the traditional *_dest initialization parameters such as the `user_dump_dest` parameter. Instead, just provide a value for the new initialization parameter `diagnostic_dest`. The `diagnostic_dest` parameter is a dynamically modifiable initialization parameter—you can modify it with the `alter system` command.

The ADR stores diagnostic data for all Oracle products. The ADR allocates a separate *home directory* for each instance of each Oracle product. Thus, a single ADR base can contain multiple *ADR homes*, each pointing to a different Oracle instance. Each ADR home is the root directory for all the diagnostic files for a database instance or any other Oracle product or component. The location of an ADR home is shown by the following directory path:

```
ADR_base/diag/product_type/product_id/instance_id/
```

For example, if you set the `diagnostic_dest` parameter to `/u05/app/oracle`, the ADR home for an Oracle database with an identical SID and database name of `prod1`, would be as follows:

`/u05/app/oracle/diag/rdbms/prod1/prod1/`

In the previous example, `product_type` is `rdbms` since you're dealing with a database. In each ADR home directory, you'll find subdirectories where Oracle stores diagnostic data for that instance. The following are the important subdirectories in the ADR home directory:

- `alert`: Contains the alert log for the instance (in XML format)

- `cdump`: Contains the core files

- `hm`: Contains Health Monitor reports

- `incident`: Contains subdirectories for each incident, containing all trace dumps for an incident

- `incpkg`: Contains the incident packages you create for uploading to Oracle Support

- `ir`: Contains the incident reports for the instance

- `trace`: Stores user session trace files

You can query the V$DIAG_INFO view to find out where all the ADR-related locations are:

```
SQL> select name, value from v$diag_info;
```

```
NAME                          VALUE
------------------            --------------------------
Diag Enabled                  TRUE
ADR Base                      /u01/app/oracle
ADR Home                      /01/app/oracle/diag/rdbms/prod/prod1
Diag Trace                    /u01/app/oracle/diag/rdbms/prod/prod1/trace
Diag Alert                    /u01/app/oracle/diag/rdbms/ prod/prod1/alert
Diag Incident                 /u01/app/oracle/diag/rdbms/prod/prod1/incident
Diag Cdump                    /u01/app/oracle/diag/rdbms/ prod/prod1/cdump
Health Monitor                /u01/app/oracle/diag/rdbms/ prod/prod1/hm
Default Trace File            /u01/app/oracle/diag/rdbms/ prod/prod1/
                              trace/eleven_ora_9417.trc
Active Problem Count          3
Active Incident Count         8

SQL>
```

As you can see, the V$DIAG_INFO view also shows the number of active problems and incidents in the database.

Now that you have learned about the basic structure of the new fault diagnosability infrastructure, you can turn your attention to investigating and resolving problems by using this diagnostic framework.

Investigating and Resolving Problems

Although you can access all the diagnostic data stored in the ADR through the Support Work-bench facility in Database Control, Oracle also provides a powerful new command-line tool called the adrci (ADR Control Interface) to manage ADR data. You can use the adrci tool along with two new Oracle-supplied packages, DBMS_HM and DBMS_SQLDIAG, to investigate and report problems, as well as to fix the problems where possible. The adrci tool is a command-line alternative to the Support Workbench and offers additional functionality such as the ability to list and query trace files. In the following two sections, we first discuss using the adrci tool and then examine problem resolution through the Support Workbench.

Using the Command-Line Tool adrci

Oracle provides a new command-line tool called adrci to help you mine the diagnostic data stored in the ADR. Besides letting you view the diagnostic data that the database stores in the ADR, adrci provides another and much more important function—it lets you package incident and problem information into ZIP files for sending to Oracle Support. This diagnostic data can include familiar data such as trace and dump files, alert log entries, and the new Oracle Database 11g Health Monitor reports.

You can use adrci in interactive mode or use adrci commands inside operating system scripts for batch execution. Next, we'll briefly review how to use adrci in both modes.

Using adrci in the Command-Line Mode

To log into the adrci and issue commands from there, just type adrci at the command line after logging in as the owner of the Oracle software installation:

```
$ adrci

ADRCI: Release 11.1.0.6.0 - Beta on Sun Aug 26 20:05:42 2007

Copyright (c) 1982, 2007, Oracle.  All rights reserved.

ADR base = "/u01/app/oracle"
adrci>
```

Once you see the adrci prompt, you can start entering adrci commands. Note that in the interactive mode, you can enter each command separately at the adrci command line, or you can execute scripts consisting of adrci commands. To view a list of all adrci commands, type help at the adrci prompt or just type adrci -help at the command line, as shown in the following example:

```
$ adrci -help
Syntax:
   adrci [-help] [script=script_filename]
         [exec = "one_command [;one_command;...]"]
```

```
Options      Description                        (Default)
----------------------------------------------------------
script       script file name                   (None)
help         help on the command options        (None)
exec         exec a set of commands             (None)
----------------------------------------------------------
$
```

Type exit or quit to exit the adrci command-line interface.

Using adrci in Scripts and in Batch Mode

In addition to using adrci interactively, you can also use adrci commands within scripts and operating system batch files. To incorporate a group of adrci commands into a script, simply create a file with all the adrci commands you want to execute, and then execute the script at the adrci prompt.

To use adrci commands in a shell script or a Windows batch file, you simply invoke adrci using the command-line parameter exec to which you pass the adrci commands you want to execute. That is, you must use the following syntax in your batch file when invoking adrci:

```
adrci exec="command[; command]..."
```

For example, if you want to use the two adrci commands show homes and show incident in a script, use the following syntax:

```
adrci exec="show homes; show incident"
```

Note that each of the commands must be separated by a semicolon (;). Here's an example showing how to use the ADR command-line interface to do the equivalent of the usual vi alert$ORACLE_SID.log command, which lets you read the alert log in a text editor:

```
adrci exec="set homepath diag/rdbms/orcl/orcl1; set editor vi; show alert -V"
```

Alternatively, you can pipe adrci commands to a shell script, as shown in the following script example, which lets you see all the alert log entries that contain the word ORA-, which indicates an Oracle-related error:

```
adrci << EOF
set homepath diag/rdbms/orcl/orcl1
show alert -p "message text like '%ORA-%'"
EOF
```

You can use the entire set of adrci commands in batch mode.

Setting the Homepath

All adrci commands you issue will run under your ADR root directory, which is the ADR base. Issue the show base command to see the location of the ADR base:

```
adrci> show base
ADR base is "/u01/app/oracle"
adrci>
```

When you issue any `adrci` command, it's in the ADR home defined in the "current" ADR *homepath* that Oracle searches for diagnostic data. If you don't set the ADR homepath explicitly, all ADR homes under the ADR base will be current. ADR commands always operate on the diagnostic data in the current ADR home. So if you issue a command such as `show tracefile`, for example, `adrci` will show you all the trace files in each of the ADR homes that are current. The `show homes` command shows all available ADR homes:

```
adrci> show homes
ADR Homes:
diag/rdbms/auxdb/auxdb
diag/rdbms/eleven/eleven
diag/rdbms/orcl11/orcl11
adrci>
```

Although the `show homes` command shows three different ADR homes for the three different Oracle instances, the ADR homepath itself isn't set, as shown by executing the `show homepath` command:

```
adrci> show homepath

adrci>
```

It's important to understand that if you don't set any ADR homepath, all instance homes under the ADR base are considered to be active or current homes. In our case, all three ADR homes under the ADR base are "current" by default. If you want `adrci` commands to apply to only a single ADR home, you can do so by using the `set homepath` command, which lets you change the current home path:

```
adrci> set homepath diag/rdbms/orcl1/orcl1
adrci> show homepath
diag/rdbms/orcl1/orcl1
adrci>
```

You can set the ADR homepath to multiple ADR homes if you want. When you do this, those `adrci` commands that can simultaneously work with multiple ADR homes (for example, `show incident` and `show alert`) will search the diagnostic data under all the ADR homes defined in the current ADR path. You can issue all other `adrci` commands only if a single ADR home is current. If you issue such a command when multiple ADR homes are current, `adrci` will issue an error. For example, an attempt to create a package with the `ips` command (the `ips` command creates an incident package, and we explain this later in this chapter) when you have multiple home paths set will lead to this error:

```
adrci> ips create package;
DIA-48448: This command does not support multiple ADR homes
adrci>
```

Obviously, you must set a single ADR homepath by using the `set homepath` command before you can create an incident package with the `ips` command.

Viewing the List of Commands

You can see what adrci commands are available by typing the command help at the adrci command line:

```
adrci> help
```

If you want to see what adrci command-line options are available, type adrci -help at the command line.

You can get additional information for a single command by typing the command name after the keyword help. The following command, for example, lets you find out the syntax and usage details for the show incident command:

```
adrci> help show incident
  Usage: SHOW INCIDENT [-p <predicate_string>]
                       [-mode BASIC|BRIEF|DETAIL]
                       [-last <num> | -all]
                       [-orderby (field1, field2, ...) [ASC|DSC]]

  Purpose: Show the incident information. By default, this command
will only show the last 50 incidents which are not flood controlled.

  Options:
    [-p <predicate_string>]: The predicate string must be double-quoted.

    [-mode BASIC|BRIEF|DETAIL]: The different modes of showing incidents.
    ...

    Examples:
    show incident
    show incident -mode detail
    show incident -mode detail -p "incident_id=123"

adrci>
```

In the following sections, we highlight some of the key tasks you can perform with the adrci tool.

Viewing the Alert Log

In Oracle Database 11g, the alert log is stored as both a text file and as an XML-formatted file. You can use adrci to view the XML-formattted alert log without the XML tags. Just type show alert at the adrci prompt to view the contents of the alert log:

```
adrci> show alert

Choose the alert log from the following homes to view:

1: diag/tnslsnr/localhost/listener
2: diag/rdbms/oracle11/oracle11
3: diag/rdbms/orcl11/orcl11
```

```
4: diag/rdbms/auxdb/auxdb
5: diag/rdbms/eleven/eleven
6: diag/rdbms/nina/nina
Q: to quit

Please select option: 3

Output the results to file: /tmp/alert_15987_3086_orcl11_1.ado
Starting ORACLE instance (normal)
2007-02-15 11:42:14.307000 -05:00
LICENSE_MAX_SESSION = 0
LICENSE_SESSIONS_WARNING = 0
Shared memory segment for instance monitoring created
Picked latch-free SCN scheme 2
Using LOG_ARCHIVE_DEST_10 parameter default value as USE_DB_RECOVERY_FILE_DEST
Autotune of undo retention is turned on.
. . .
adrci>
```

■**Note** There are two alert logs for each instance in Oracle Database 11*g*. There is an XML-based alert log in the `alert` directory under the ADR home directory, and there is a regular text-based alert log file in the `trace` directory under the ADR home directory.

In the example shown here, we've provided several options for the alert log file, because we haven't set a homepath before issuing the `show alert` command. Once you set the homepath for a specific database instance, the `show alert` command will act differently, as shown here:

```
adrci> set homepath diag/rdbms/orcl11/orcl11
adrci> show alert

ADR Home = /u01/app/oracle/diag/rdbms/orcl11/orcl11:
*************************************************************************
Output the results to file: /tmp/alert_18327_3086_orcl11_1.ado
_7_[?47h_[?1h_=_[1;24r_[m_[H_[2J_[24;1H"/tmp/alert_18327_3086_orcl11_1.ado" 71412L,
 5078426C_[1;1H2007-02-15 11:42:13.093000 -05:00
Starting ORACLE instance (normal)
2007-02-15 11:42:14.307000 -05:00
LICENSE_MAX_SESSION = 0
LICENSE_SESSIONS_WARNING = 0
...
adrci>
```

The command will show the complete alert log (stripped of the XML tags). In addition, adrci outputs the complete contents of the current alert log file to the /tmp directory, as shown in both examples of the show alert command. You can use the show alert command with the -tail option to see only the last 20 to 30 messages of the alert log, as shown here:

```
adrci> show alert -tail
```

If you want to see the last 100 messages in the alert log, you can issue the command show alert -tail 100. The alert -tail commands are similar to the tail commands you use in viewing Unix and Linux text files in that they let you actively monitor the additions to a file. You can see whether there are any ORA-600 errors in the alert log by issuing the following command:

```
adrci> show alert -P "MESSAGE TEXT LIKE '%ORA-600%'*
```

If you want to capture the contents of the alert log to a different file without the XML tags, you can do so by using the spool command before issuing the show alert command, as shown here:

```
adrci> spool /u01/app/oracle/strip_alert.log
adrci> show alert
adrci> spool  off
```

We don't want to bore you with the many ways to look at your beloved alert log in Oracle Database 11g, but we'll be remiss if we don't mention that you can still directly access a text-only alert log as in the old days by simply looking up the path for the Diag Trace entry in a query (select *) of the V$DIAG_INFO view. For example, in our case, the Diag Trace entry has the path /u01/app/oracle/diag/rdbms/orcl11/orcl11/trace. From here, you can open the alert log in a text editor and view it to your heart's content. This is the textual format alert log, similar to what you used in the older releases of the database. This means that Oracle now generates two alert logs for the instance, one in text format and the other in XML format.

Listing Trace Files

You can get a listing of all available trace files in the current ADR homepath by using the show tracefile command:

```
adrci> show tracefile
```

The show tracefile command lists all the available trace files.

Viewing Incidents

Use the show incident command to view all open incidents. The report will show you the incident ID, problem time, and creation time for each incident encountered by the database and logged in the ADR. If you have multiple current adrci homes in your adrci homepath, the show incident command will display open incidents from all the instances in the various ADR homes.

Here's an example showing the output of the show incident command with multiple current ADR homes:

```
adrci> show incident

ADR Home = C:\ORCL11\APP\ORACLE\DIAG\diag\rdbms\auxdb\auxdb:
*************************************************************************
0 incident info records fetched

ADR Home = C:\ORCL11\APP\ORACLE\DIAG\diag\rdbms\eleven\eleven:
*************************************************************************
INCIDENT_ID     PROBLEM_KEY                  CREATE_TIME
------------    --------------               --------------------------
8801            ORA 600 [4899]               17-MAR-07 06.14.41.04-05:00
16417           ORA 7445 [ACCESS_VIOLATION]  17-MAR-07 06.15.46.7905:00
2 incident info records fetched

ADR Home = C:\ORCL11\APP\ORACLE\DIAG\diag\rdbms\orcl11\orcl11:
*************************************************************************
INCIDENT_ID          PROBLEM_KEY               CREATE_TIME
-------------------  --------------------      --------------------------
113769               ORA 1578 [2] [66598]      27-MAR-07 10.00.10.91-05:00
113770               ORA 1578                  27-MAR-07 10.00.11.86-05:00
113771               ORA 1578                  27-MAR-07 10.00.12.10-05:00
3 incident info records fetched
adrci>
```

The show incident command reveals that for the first database (auxdb) there aren't any open incidents. For the second database (eleven) there are two open incidents, and for the third database (orcl11) there are three open incidents.

If you want to drill down to a particular incident, you can do so by using the show incident command with the -p option, as shown here (only the last part of the output is shown):

```
adrci> show incident -mode detail -p "incident_id=113769"
...
------------------------------------------------------------
INCIDENT FILES:
   INCIDENT_ID     113769
   OWNER_ID        1
   BFILE           C:\ORCL11\APP\ORACLE\DIAG\diag\rdbms\orcl11\orcl1
                   \incident\incdir_113769/orcl11_j003_4244_i113769.trc

Incident file number: 1


------------------------------------------------------------
1 incident info records fetched
adrci>
```

The show incident command has two options: *predicate string* (-p) and *mode* (-mode). You can use the predicate string to specify various field names, such as the field incident_id in this example. You must enclose the field names with a pair of double quotes. For a list of all the field names you can use in a predicate string, type `describe incident` at the `adrci` command line, as shown here:

```
adrci> describe incident
Name                         Type           NULL?
-----------------------      ----------     --------
INCIDENT_ID                  number
PROBLEM_ID                   number
CREATE_TIME                  timestamp
CLOSE_TIME                   timestamp
...
SUSPECT_COMPONENT            text(64)
SUSPECT_SUBCOMPONENT         text(64)
ECID                         text(64)
IMPACT                       number
adrci>
```

In addition to the predicate string (-p) option, we also used the -mode option (detail) in this example to specify that the output be shown in detail. The other settings for the -mode option are basic and brief, both of which provide shorter displays of the output.

Packaging Incidents

One of the most useful new features of Oracle Database 11g is the new framework for packaging incidents for easy transmission of diagnostic data to Oracle Support. An incident package represents at least one problem. When you create an incident package, you add one or more problems to the package, and the Support Workbench will then automatically add relevant trace files and dump files for those problems. By default, each incident package includes only the first and last three incidents per each problem. The incident package contains all diagnostic data pertaining to a particular incident, or it can range over a period of time, with data for all incidents during that time interval.

Once you create an incident package, you can add or remove files from the incident package. You can also edit the external files that are part of the package to delete sensitive data.

To create a self-contained incident package with all supporting diagnostic data for an incident (or a group of incidents or a time interval), you must follow these steps:

1. *Create a logical package*: You must first create a logical package, so named since it doesn't exist in the form of a separate file you can actually send somewhere—it merely exists as metadata in the ADR. You may create an empty logical package with no diagnostic data, or you can create an incident number or problem number or time interval–based logical package, which will automatically contain the diagnostic data for the relevant problems/incidents. You use the command `ips create package` to create a logical package. There are many variations on this command. You can choose to create a package based on a particular problem number, incident number, problem key, or time period.

2. *Add diagnostic data to the logical package.* This is an optional step, which applies only if you created an empty logical package in step 1. The problem and incident-based logical packages already contain the relevant diagnostic data.

3. *Generate the physical package (zipped file):* In the final step, you generate the actual zipped physical file, ready for sending to Oracle Support. You can always add extra information to the ZIP file by creating incremental ZIP files for the same logical package. Here's an example showing a complete (COM) ZIP file, with an associated incremental (INC) ZIP file for the same logical package:

```
ORA603_20060906165316_COM_1.zip
ORA603_20060906165316_INC_2.zip
```

Once you're ready to upload the package to Oracle Support, you use the Support Workbench or the `adrci` utility to collect all files that the incident package's metadata refers to and package them in a ZIP file before uploading it to Oracle Support. We'll first show how to create incident packages with the `adrci` utility.

You use special `adrci` commands called IPS commands to manage packages in `adrci`. Here are the steps to package an incident so you can send it for analysis to the folks at Oracle Support:

1. Use the `ips create package` command to create a new logical package. In this example, we show how to create an empty logical package, which means you don't have to specify an incident or a time interval:

```
adrci>ips create package
Created package 1 without any contents, correlation level typical
adrci>
```

Note that the usage of a semicolon to end the `adrci` commands is optional. The packages you create are serially numbered, starting with 1. In this example, the `ips create package` command results in the creation of package 1, since this is the first package ever created under this ADR base.

2. Since you created an empty logical package in step 1, you must add diagnostic information to that package. You can add incidents and files to the logical package. The following example shows how to add a particular incident to your logical package:

```
adrci>ips add incident 113769 package 1;
kaged: ADD INCIDENT
Cmd: --- incid 113769
Cmd: --- pkgid 1
adrci>
```

At this stage, your package still doesn't have any actual diagnostic data. All it has is the metadata for the incident that you want Oracle Support to diagnose. In the next step, you create the actual physical package that you'll send to Oracle Support.

3. Generate the physical package by issuing the `ips generate package` command. When you issue this command, `adrci` collects all the required diagnostic files and packages them into a ZIP file:

```
adrci>ips generate package 4 in /u01/app/oracle/adrci/support
Cmd: GENERATE PACKAGE
Cmd: package id is 4
Cmd: file C:\ORCL11\APP\ORACLE
Cmd: --- mode full
adrci>
```

The ips generate command shown here creates a ZIP file in the /u01/app/oracle/adrci directory, which you can then send to the Oracle Support for diagnostic support. The file you create this way is called a *complete* ZIP file. If you want to add or change any diagnostic data later, you can do so by generating an *incremental* ZIP file. Use the keyword incremental with the ips generate package command to generate an incremental ZIP file:

```
adrci> ips generate package 5 in /u01/app/oracle/adrci/support incremental
```

Here's an example showing how to name a complete and an incremental ZIP file, respectively:

```
ORA222_20070304124515_COM_1.zip
ORA222_20070304124515_INC_2.zip
```

In this example, the first file has the COM tag in its file name, indicating that it's a complete ZIP file. The second file uses the INC tag, meaning it's an incremental ZIP file. The files are processed in sequential order, with the complete file being processed first, followed by any incremental files, if any exist.

In this example, we showed how to use the ips create package command. Here are the variations of this command:

- ips create package creates an empty package.

- ips create package problem creates a package based on a problem ID.

- ips create package problem key creates a problem key–based package.

- ips create package incident creates a package based on an incident ID.

- ips create package time creates a package for a specified time range.

You can configure various aspects such as incident metadata retention period by using the adrci tool. Issue the ips show configuration command to review all the available configuration parameters. Here's an abbreviated output of the ips show configuration command:

```
adrci> ips show configuration
*********************************************************************
IPS CONFIGURATION PARAMETER
*********************************************************************
PARAMETER INFORMATION:
    PARAMETER_ID            1
    NAME                    CUTOFF_TIME
    DESCRIPTION             Maximum age for an incident to be
                            considered for inclusion
    UNIT                    Days
    VALUE                   90
```

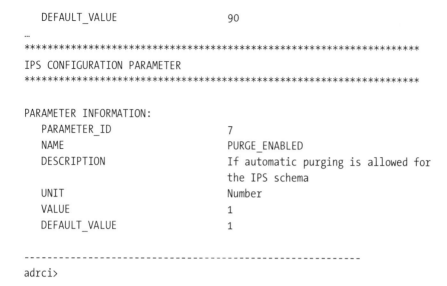

```
DEFAULT_VALUE                     90
...
**********************************************************************
IPS CONFIGURATION PARAMETER
**********************************************************************

PARAMETER INFORMATION:
    PARAMETER_ID                  7
    NAME                          PURGE_ENABLED
    DESCRIPTION                   If automatic purging is allowed for
                                  the IPS schema
    UNIT                          Number
    VALUE                         1
    DEFAULT_VALUE                 1


-----------------------------------------------------------
adrci>
```

Although you can employ the powerful and easy-to-use adrci tool to investigate problems and package and upload the incident packages to Oracle Support, the Support Workbench is the recommended tool to use, especially for simpler problems.

The Support Workbench

The Support Workbench is a new Enterprise Manager–based facility to help you investigate and report critical errors. The Support Workbench lets you gather diagnostic data and easily upload the data to Oracle Support. You can run health checks, invoke the IPS to package relevant diagnostic data for problems, and file and track service requests with Oracle Support. The Support Workbench also lets you repair several types of problems by providing access to various Oracle advisors, such as the new SQL Repair Advisor and the SQL Test Case Builder.

In the following sections, you'll learn how to resolve database problems through the Support Workbench. You'll then look at using the Support Workbench home page for viewing existing problems and creating "user-reported" problems.

Using the Support Workbench Home Page

You can view all current incidents and their descriptions by accessing the Support Workbench home page. Follow these steps to access the Support Workbench home page:

1. Click the Software and Support link on the Database home page.

2. In the Support section, click Support Workbench.

3. In the Support Workbench home page, you can see all problems found in the previous 24 hours.

4. Click All from the View list to see all problems.

You can also get all details for any incident as well as view the checker findings for that incident using the Support Workbench. In addition, you can employ the Support Workbench to collect additional diagnostics for any incident. Although critical errors are automatically added to the ADR and consequently tracked by the Support Workbench, you can add a problem to the Support Workbench yourself by clicking the *Create User-Reported Problem* link on the Support Workbench home page. User-created problems may be called for in situations where the database doesn't issue a critical incident alert but you know that there is a serious performance problem in the database. Creating a user-reported problem is similar to creating a pseudo-problem within the Support Workbench framework, allowing you to take advantage of the Workbench workflow for fixing the problem.

Whether it's a system-generated problem or a user-reported problem, you can use the Support Workbench to add diagnostic data for aiding problem diagnosis and upload the diagnostic data to Oracle Support by following the simple investigative and reporting procedure that we explain in the following section.

Using the Support Workbench to Resolve Problems

Although using the adrci tool to investigate problems and create packages in order to resolve those problems is indeed straightforward, Oracle recommends you use the Database Control–based Support Workbench to take care of your database problems. For simpler problems, the Support Workbench may turn out to be all you need to fix the problem. In cases where you need to capture additional diagnostic data or customize the diagnostic data in certain ways before sending it in to Oracle Support, you may fall back on the adrci tool.

■**Tip** You must install the Oracle Configuration Manager if you want to use the Support Workbench to upload incident packages to Oracle Support.

You can use the Support Workbench out of the box for all problem resolution actions, except for uploading the diagnostic information to Oracle Support. To be able to upload the zipped incident packages to Oracle Support directly from the Support Workbench, you must first install the Oracle Configuration Manager. The Oracle Configuration Manager enables you to link your system configuration information with your MetaLink account. Thus, when you lodge a request with Metalink, you can link your configuration details to that request. The easiest way to install the Oracle Configuration Manager is while installing the Oracle software, where you're offered a choice to install it along with the other binaries. Figure 2-1 shows the Oracle Configuration Manager installation screen during the Oracle server installation. You can also install the Oracle Configuration Manger after the installation. Please refer to the Oracle manual *Oracle Configuration Manager Installation Guide* for details. If you don't install the Oracle Configuration Manager, you must upload the incident package files yourself the old-fashioned way, through MetaLink.

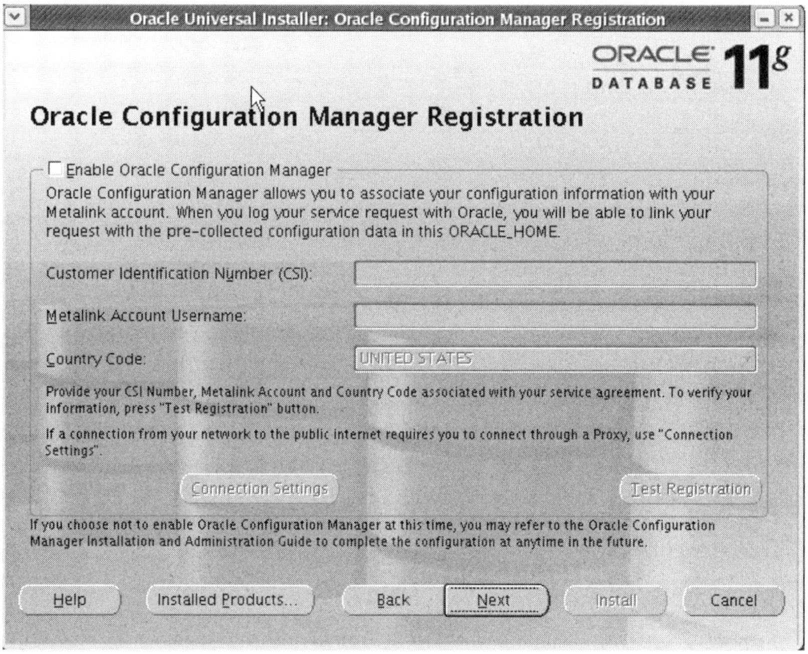

Figure 2-1. *Oracle Configuration Manager registration*

Here are the steps to follow to resolve a critical error using the Support Workbench:

1. Check for critical error alerts. You'll find all critical database error alerts on the Database home page of Database Control. On that page, examine the table of alerts in the Alerts section. Any alert with a severity level marked by a red *X* in the Severity column and the text *incident* in the Category column is a critical error alert. Figure 2-2 shows the alert table with a number of critical errors indicating possible Oracle data block corruption. A count of all active incidents is also shown in the Diagnostic Summary section on the home page.

2. Investigate the problem. Click the link provided in the Message column in the table of alerts in the Alerts section. This will take you to the Alert Details page, shown in Figure 2-3. The Alert Details page provides the problem information and details such as the severity and the time stamp of the problem that raised the alert. You can also display finds from the automatic health checks run by the database. You can also add comments in a text box provided for that purpose. At this point, you can choose to run additional health checks to get more findings on the problem. You can also invoke the SQL Test Case Builder to gather data for a problem SQL so Oracle Support can reproduce the problem.

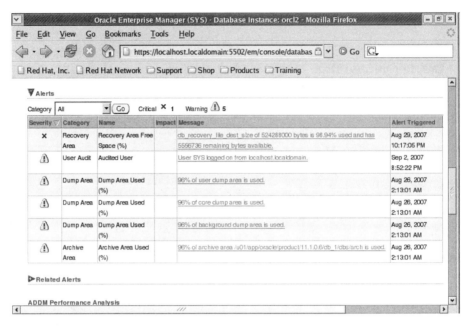

Figure 2-2. *The table of alerts on the Database home page*

Figure 2-3. *The Alert Details page*

3. Create a service request. Once you decide to ask Oracle Support for help in resolving the problem, you must first create a service request. On the Problem Detail page, click Go to Metalink. Enter your MetaLink credentials, and create a service request, just as you would normally.

■**Tip** For enterprise-class database support environments, we recommend creating a generic Metalink user ID with the DBA distribution list to log service requests. When Oracle Support analysts respond, all the DBAs are made aware that Oracle is working on their issues.

4. Create the incident package, and upload data to Oracle Support. Before the Support Workbench creates the physical file for an incident package, it calls the IPS to *finalize* the incident package. Finalizing involves adding any data such as trace files that are correlated by item or process ID or by similar criteria. Adding diagnostic data that's correlated to the main incident could be helpful in many cases. You have a choice of two types of packaging—Quick Packaging or Custom Packaging. Quick Packaging is simpler but won't let you add or edit the diagnostic information you're about to upload. Custom Packaging gives you greater control by letting you edit diagnostic data or add fields before uploading to Oracle Support. In this example, we'll use the Quick Packaging process, so click Quick Package in the Investigate and Resolve section of the Problem Details page. Enter your package name and a description. Click Next, and follow the instructions on the remaining pages of the Quick Packaging Wizard. Once you are ready to upload the package, click Submit on the Review page. Of course, this assumes your system is connected to the Internet.

   Once you create a custom incident package, you can choose among several packaging tasks available on the Package Details page, such as editing the packaged incident files or adding external files to the incident package.

5. Track the service request. Once you upload the diagnostic information to Oracle Support, you can revise the Problem Details page to perform additional activities such as adding an Oracle bug number to the problem information, adding comments to the problem activity log, and running Oracle advisors such as the Data Recovery Advisor to help repair critical errors.

6. Close the problem (incident). Once you resolve a problem, you can close the incident. On the Support Workbench home page, click View in the Problem Details page that appears, select the incident you want to close, and click Close. By default all incidents, both open and closed, are closed after 30 days. You can, if you want, disable this automatic closure of incidents on the Incident Details page.

By accessing the Incident Packaging Configuration page from the Related Links section of the Support Workbench, you can configure various rules for generating packages and incident data retention.

From the Support Workbench, you can run key Oracle advisors such as the Data Recovery Advisor and SQL Repair Advisor to implement repairs. You can access these advisors by clicking the Self-Service tab in the Investigate and Resolve section of the Problem Details page. You can also access the advisors by going to the Checkers Findings subpage of the Incident Details page. The SQL Repair Advisor helps you repair SQL statement failures by applying an Oracle-supplied patch as a workaround. The Data Recovery Advisor helps fix data failures such as block corruption and missing datafiles.

In the following section, we explain how to use one of the new advisors, the SQL Repair Advisor. We explain the Data Recovery Advisor later in this chapter.

Repairing SQL Failures with the SQL Repair Advisor

The Support Workbench doesn't serve just as a tool to upload diagnostic data to Oracle Support. You can also launch the new SQL Repair Advisor tool from the Support Workbench. In Oracle Database 11g, you can run the SQL Repair Advisor to fix a failed SQL statement. The advisor usually recommends applying a patch to fix the failed statement. If you accept the recommendation(s) and apply the SQL patch, the optimizer chooses an alternate execution path, and the SQL code will work successfully, without having to change the original SQL statement at all. If the SQL Repair Advisor fails to recommend a patch to make the SQL work, you can use the Support Workbench to package the incident files and relevant data and send them to Oracle Support. Here's a quick summary of the steps to invoke the SQL Repair Advisor from the Support Workbench home page:

1. Go to the Problem Details page, and click the specific problem message resulting from the failed SQL statement.

2. Click SQL Repair Advisor in the Investigate and Resolve section on the Self Service tab.

3. Enter the appropriate options to run the advisor immediately or at a scheduled time later.

4. Click Submit.

5. On the SQL Repair Results page that appears, click View to examine the Report Recommendations page.

6. Once you're sure you want to implement the recommendations, click Implement.

Once the SQL Repair Results page comes back with a confirmation message, you're done. When you migrate to a newer release of the Oracle database, you may want to remove any patches installed through the SQL Repair Advisor's recommendations. You can disable or remove a patch by going to the Database Control home page and navigating to Server ➤ SQL Plan Control ➤ SQL Patch ➤ Disable (or Drop).

You can also use various procedures from the new DBMS_SQLDIAG package to create and execute diagnostics tasks with the SQL Repair Advisor. The SQL Repair Advisor will, in most cases, produce a SQL patch as a workaround for the problem SQL query. Here are the steps to create a task and apply and test a SQL patch offered by the SQL Repair Advisor:

1. Once you identify a problem SQL statement, the first step is to create a diagnosis task using the create_diagnosis_task procedure:

```
SQL> declare
  2  report_out clob;
  3  task_id  varchar2(50);
  4  begin
  5  task_id := dbms_sqldiag.create_diagnosis_task(
  6  sql_text=>'delete from t1 where rowid != (select max(rowid)
  7                  from t1 group by empno)',
  8  task_name=>'test_task1',
```

```
  9  problem_type=> dbms_sqldiag.problem_type_compilation_error);
 10* end;
SQL> /

PL/SQL procedure successfully completed.
SQL>
```

The next step is to execute the diagnosis task.

2. Use the task name from the previous step (test_task1) to execute the diagnostic task, which generates the workaround for the problem SQL:

```
SQL> exec dbms_sqlldiag.execute_diagnosis_task('test_task1',

PL/SQL procedure successfully completed.

SQL>
```

When you execute the diagnostic task, Oracle usually provides a workaround to fix the problem, but sometimes there may not be any recommendations.

3. Access the analysis of the diagnosis task by executing the report_diagnsotic_task procedure, as shown here:

```
SQL> declare rep_out  clob;
  2 begin
  3  rep_out := dbms_sqldiag.report_diagnosis_task('test_task1',
  4             dbms_sqldiag.type_text);
  5  dbms_output.put_line ('Report  : '  ||  rep_out);
  6*end;
SQL> /

Report               : GENERAL INFORMATION
SECTION
-------------------------------------------------------------------
Tuning Task Name         : test_task1
Tuning Task Owner        : SYS
Tuning Task ID           : 3531
Workload Type            : Single SQL Statement
Execution Count          : 1
Current Execution        : EXEC_3531
Execution Type           : SQL DIAGNOSIS
Scope                    : COMPREHENSIVE
Time Limit(seconds)      : 1800
Completion Status        : COMPLETED
Started at               : 08/26/2007 20:03:51
Completed at             : 08/26/2007 20:03:54
Schema Name              : SYS
SQL ID                   : 25wx5x05jx02v
```

```
SQL Text                    : delete from t1 where rowid != (select
                              max(rowid) from t1 group by empno)

...
PL/SQL procedure successfully completed.

SQL>
```

In cases where the SQL Repair Advisor is able to find a fix for the problem SQL, it recommends a SQL patch. Although a SQL patch is similar to a SQL profile, it's used only as a workaround to compile a failing SQL statement.

4. If there is a patch recommendation in the previous step, run the `accept_sql_patch` procedure to accept the patch:

```
SQL> exec dbms_sqldiag.accept_sql_patch (task_name=>'test_task1',
     task_owner=> 'SYS')
```

Once you implement a SQL patch, rerun the problem SQL statement to verify that the critical error is gone. You should also see the use of the SQL patch in the explain plan for the SQL statement now. You can query the `DBA_SQL_PATCHES` view to find out the name of all the patches offered by the SQL Repair Advisor. You can drop a patch by executing the `drop_sql_patch` procedure.

Database Health Checks

Proactive checking of various database components can help you avoid potential problems. Release 11*g* of the Oracle Database provides a new monitoring framework called the Health Monitor, which runs diagnostic checks on database components such as the file system, memory, and transaction integrity. Each check generates a report containing findings as well as recommendations to fix the problem. The Health Monitor automatically examines the database to check the state of the various components of the database whenever there is a database error. The goal of these checks that are automatically made pursuant to errors in the database is to catch dangerous things such as file corruptions, physical and logical block corruptions, and data dictionary corruption before they can seriously damage the database. These checks result in a report of the database error and, in most cases, also recommendations to fix the problem. You, as the DBA, also have the option to proactively run database health checks using the same mechanism as the automatic checks made by the database.

Whenever there's a critical error in the database, the database automatically runs the Health Monitor to diagnose the problem. The Health Monitor logs all its findings in the ADR, from where the Data Recovery Advisor can access the results in order to generate reports or repair the problems. You can also run the Health Monitor manually, either following a database problem or as a regular part of your DBA activities, through Database Control or with the help of the new Oracle-supplied package, `DBMS_HM`.

Checks, Failures, and Repairs

Checks (also called *checkers* or *health checks*) are diagnostic operations or procedures that are registered with the new Health Monitor to help assess the health of your database or other Oracle components. If a database check results in the discovery of a database *failure*, Oracle maps that failure to a database *repair*.

In Oracle Database 11*g*, the database will perform automatic *reactive* checks for you. Each time there's an error of any kind, the database will automatically invoke a database checker to search for failures related to that error. This is called a *reactive check*, since it's made in response to an event in the database. However, Oracle recommends you schedule periodic *proactive* checks during periods of low database usage. You can perform a proactive database check through RMAN or the Database Control/Grid Control. If an automatic reactive check shows a problem in a particular database component, it's a good idea to further investigate the problem with a proactive check of the affected database component.

A failure represents a diagnosed problem and is defined as persistent data corruption that's detected by a database checker, such as the Redo Check checker, which checks the integrity of the redo logs, for example. If a checker diagnoses a database failure, it records that information in the ADR. You'll be able to employ the new Data Recovery Advisor (explained later in this chapter) to get advice on failures and repair them if those failures are recorded in the ADR.

Types of Health Monitor Checks

You can perform various types of Health Monitor checks, including checking datafiles for corruption, performing redo checks, and verifying the integrity of core database dictionary objects, such as tab$ and col$. The V$HM_CHECK view (the current definition of the view doesn't have the description column!) describes all the available types of Health Monitor checks, as shown here:

```
SQL> select name,description from v$hm_check;

NAME                            DESCRIPTION
------------------------------  ----------------------------------------
HM Test Check                   Check for HM Functionality
DB Structure Integrity Check    Checks integrity of all database files
Data Block Integrity Check      Checks integrity of a datafile block
Redo Integrity Check            Checks integrity of redo log content
Logical Block Check             Checks logical content of a block
Transaction Integrity Check     Checks a transaction for corruptions
Undo Segment Integrity Check    Checks integrity of an undo segment
All Control Files Check         Checks all control files
CF Member Check                 Checks a multiplexed control file
All Datafiles Check             Check for all datafiles in the database
Single Datafile Check           Checks a datafile
Log Group Check                 Checks all members of a log group
Log Group Member Check          Checks a particular member of a group
Archived Log Check              Checks an archived log
Redo Revalidation Check         Checks redo log content
IO Revalidation Check           Checks file accessability
```

```
Block IO Revalidation Check     Checks file accessability
Txn Revalidation Check          Revalidate corrupted txn
Failure Simulation Check        Creates dummy failures
Dictionary Integrity Check      Checks dictionary integrity

21 rows selected.

SQL>
```

You can view the input parameters that you can specify for the health checks by using the V$CHECK_PARAM view.

You can run the health checks in two modes—DB-online (database in the open or mount state) and DB-offline (database in the nomount mode, with just the instance up). You can perform most Health Monitor checks even when the database is offline. The column offline_ capable in the V$HM_CHECK view shows whether you can perform an offline check for a particular type of check

As mentioned earlier, although the database is capable of detecting failures by the automatic execution of checkers, that process is set off only when the database encounters a problem such as corrupted data. By running various checks manually, you can catch failures before they cause extensive damage. We'll discuss manual checks in the following section.

Manual Checks

Although the database automatically performs reactive checks, it's a good idea to proactively run the checkers on a regular basis to detect potential failures that haven't affected the database yet. Reactive checks are run only when a failure affects the database, say, when a user tries to retrieve data from a corrupted data block. However, a corrupted data block won't automatically cause a failure alert to be lodged in the database if users haven't accessed that block after it was corrupted. Manual checks help catch such hidden failures that may strike during the course of a busy day and potentially hinder the availability of the database.

You can perform manual database checks by using Database Control or by using the DBMS_HM PL/SQL package. In addition, you can also perform database corruption checks using the new RMAN validate command. We'll first look at how to run checks using the DBMS_HM package.

Manual Checking Using the DBMS_HM Package

As mentioned earlier, Oracle makes the Health Monitor functionality available through the DBMS_HM package. Use the run_check procedure of the DBMS_HM package to run a proactive health check. Here is the structure of the run_check procedure:

```
PROCEDURE RUN_CHECK
Argument Name           Type            In/Out      Default?
---------------------   ------------    ----------  ---------
 L_CHECKNAME            VARCHAR2        IN
 L_RUNNAME              VARCHAR2        IN          DEFAULT
 L_TIMEOUT              NUMBER          IN          DEFAULT
 L_PARAMS               VARCHAR2        IN          DEFAULT
```

Here's what the different arguments of the run_check procedure stand for:

- CHECKNAME: Name of the database check. This is a mandatory argument and must exactly match a check name from the V$HM_CHECK view.

- RUNNAME: This is an optional argument that lets you specify a name for the check run.

- TIMEOUT: Optionally, you can set a limit on the length of time a check can run.

- PARAMS: This is an input parameter that controls the execution of the check. You can view the various types of inputs by querying the V$HM_CHECK_PARM view.

In the following example, we show you how to perform a database crosscheck, which tests the integrity of all datafiles in the database. Just pass the type of check and a name for the test run to the run_check procedure, as shown here:

```
SQL> exec dbms_hm.run_check('DB Structure Integrity
    Check','testrun1');

PL/SQL procedure successfully completed.

SQL>
```

The Health Monitor saves the report of all its database checks in the ADR home of this database instance. The show hm_run command shows a summary of all checker executions that are registered in the ADR. These are the same checker runs that will be visible from the V$HM_RUN view. Here are sample results of the show hm_run command:

```
adrci> show hm_run
************************************************************************
HM RUN RECORD 19
    RUN_ID                      342
    RUN_NAME                    testrun1
    CHECK_NAME                  Data Block Integrity Check
    NAME_ID                     3
    MODE                        0
    START_TIME                  2007-07-22 17:50:17.845880 -04:00
    RESUME_TIME                 <NULL>
    END_TIME                    2007-07-22 17:50:17.886126 -04:00
    MODIFIED_TIME               2007-07-22 17:50:17.886126 -04:00
    TIMEOUT                     0
    FLAGS                       0
    STATUS                      6
    SRC_INCIDENT_ID             0
    NUM_INCIDENTS               0
    ERR_NUMBER                  48615
    REPORT_FILE                 <NULL>
...
19 rows fetched

adrci>
```

You can view a detailed report of a particular execution of a check by the Health Monitor by using the adrci command show report:

```
adrci> show report hm_run testrun1
<?xml version="1.0" encoding="US-ASCII"?>
<HM-REPORT REPORT_ID="HM_RUN_7">
    <TITLE>HM Report: HM_RUN_7</TITLE>
    <RUN_INFO>
        <CHECK_NAME>Data Block Check</CHECK_NAME>

        <FINDING_NAME>Multiple corrupted blocks</FINDING_NAME>
         <FINDING_MESSAGE>datafile 2 contains corrupt blocks</FINDING_MESSAGE>
        <FINDING_MESSAGE>tablespace SYSAUX is unavailable</FINDING_MESSAGE>
        <FINDING_MESSAGE>block 66578 in datafile 2 is corrupt</FINDING_MESSAGE>
    </HM-REPORT>
adrci>
```

The Health Monitor report shown in the previous example reveals block corruption in datafile 2, which happens to belong to the sysaux tablespace.

All Health Monitor reports are stored in the V$HM_RUN view. But you must generate the reports first, using either the adrci tool as shown in this example or using the DBMS_HM package, as shown in the following example:

```
SQL>
SQL> var v_output CLOB
SQL> begin
SQL> :v_output := dbms_hm.get_run_report ('test_run_1');
SQL> end;
SQ1L> /
```

To print the report, do the following:

```
set long 100000
set pages 0
print :v_output
<?xml version="1.0" encoding="US-ASCII"?>
<HM-REPORT REPORT_ID="test_run_1">
    <TITLE>HM Report: test_run_1</TITLE>
    <RUN_INFO>
        <CHECK_NAME>'DB Structure Integrity Check'</CHECK_NAME>
        <RUN_ID>161</RUN_ID>
        <RUN_NAME>test_run_1</RUN_NAME>
        <RUN_MODE>MANUAL</RUN_MODE>
        <RUN_STATUS>COMPLETED</RUN_STATUS>
```

```
            <RUN_ERROR_NUM>0</RUN_ERROR_NUM>
            <SOURCE_INCIDENT_ID>0</SOURCE_INCIDENT_ID>
            <NUM_INCIDENTS_CREATED>0</NUM_INCIDENTS_CREATED>
            <RUN_START_TIME>2007-04-04 17:02:14.555390 -05:00</RUN_START_TIME>
            <RUN_END_TIME>2007-04-04 17:02:14.613107 -05:00</RUN_END_TIME>
        </RUN_INFO>
        <RUN_PARAMETERS/>
        <RUN-FINDINGS/>
</HM-REPORT>
```

In addition to using `adrci` or the `DBMS_HM` package to get the report for a database check, you can directly query the V$HM_RUN view to get information about the checks. For example, you can issue the following query to see the results of a check, as shown here:

```
SQL> select name,check_name,run_mode,status from v$hm_run;

NAME        CHECK_NAME                    RUN_MODE    STATUS
---------   ----------------------------  --------    ---------
HM_RUN_1    DB Structure Integrity Check  REACTIVE    COMPLETED
testrun1    Data Block Integrity Check    MANUAL      COMPLETED
...
20 rows selected.

SQL>
```

The `run_mode` column tells you whether a particular health check was proactive (manual) or reactive. Proactive checks are checks made by you. You can also get details about the findings by querying the V$HM_FINDING view and can get recommendations for fixing the problems by querying the V$HM_RECOMMENDATION view. You can also access the Health Monitor reports through Database Control, as we explain later in this chapter.

Manual Checks Using Database Control

You can also run a Health Monitor check through Database Control by using the following steps:

1. Click Advisor Central on the Database home page.

2. Click Checkers to go to the Checkers subpage.

3. Click the checker you want to run.

4. Enter values for each parameter for the checker run.

5. Click Run. After confirming your choices, click Run again to start the check.

Figure 2-4 shows the various checkers provided by Database Control. Each of the checkers has a different number of parameters and arguments.

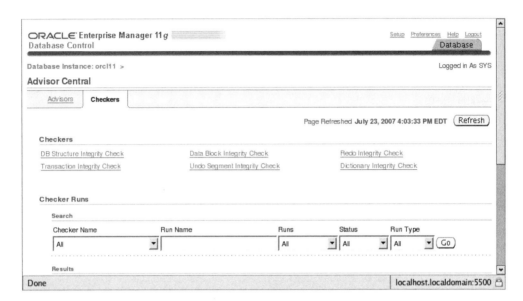

Figure 2-4. *The Checkers subpage in Database Control*

Manual Checks with the RMAN Validate Command

In previous releases of the Oracle Database, you could use the backup ... validate command
to validate your backups. Essentially, what this command helped you do was check for both
logical and physical intrablock corruption in the datafiles and also whether the datafiles could
be backed up by RMAN. The command doesn't actually perform the actual backup but only
validates the datafiles so you can ensure you'll have usable and valid backups when you use
RMAN to back up those datafiles.

■**Tip** Oracle recommends DBAs run proactive database checks, especially on those database components
that have received errors.

In Oracle Database 11*g*, there is a new command called validate that has semantically
similar options as the older backup ... validate command but can validate at a much finer
level of granularity. Whereas you could use the backup ... validate command at only the
database level, you can use the validate command to perform the same job at the backup set,
tablespace, datafile, or even at the data block level. You may even use it to check the integrity
of the flash recovery area or all recovery files.

If you think there are failures that haven't been trapped automatically by the database, run
the validate command to check for missing files and corrupt data blocks. The validate command
helps you invoke a database health check to assess the failure when it finds any type of data
failure. RMAN logs the failure information in the ADR. You can then use the Data Recovery
Advisor's list failure, advise failure and repair failure commands in RMAN to view the
failures and repair them. By default, the validate command looks for physical corruption of

data blocks. By including the check logical clause, you can make the validate command look for logical intrablock corruption as well.

■**Note** You can have intrablock (within the data block) and interblock (between data blocks) corruption. The latter is a particular type of logical corruption that isn't caught by the RMAN validate command.

Here's an example showing how to check for block corruption throughout the database using the new validate command:

```
RMAN> validate database;

Starting validate at 02-APR-07
using target database control file instead of recovery catalog
allocated channel: ORA_DISK_1
channel ORA_DISK_1: SID=155 device type=DISK
...
channel ORA_DISK_1: validation complete, elapsed time: 00:17:07
List of Datafiles
==================
File Status Marked Corrupt Empty Blocks Blocks Examined High SCN
---- ------ -------------- ------------ --------------- ----------
1    OK     0              12542        72960           4351550
   File Name: C:\ORCL11\APP\ORACLE\ORADATA\ORCL11\SYSTEM01.DBF
   Block Type Blocks Failing Blocks Processed
   ---------- -------------- ----------------
   Data       0              48959
   Index      0              9143
   Other      0              2316
...
including current control file for validation
including current SPFILE in backup set
channel ORA_DISK_1: validation complete, elapsed time: 00:00:02
List of Control File and SPFILE
===============================
File Type    Status Blocks Failing Blocks Examined
------------ ------ -------------- ---------------
SPFILE       OK     0              2
Control File OK     0              594
Finished validate at 02-APR-07

RMAN>
```

Unlike the RMAN backup ... validate command, the validate command lets you parallelize the validation by dividing each file into sections. You must use the option section size to parallelize the validation. Chapter 6, which covers backup and recovery new features, discusses both the validate command and the new backup parameter section_size in detail.

Data Recovery Advisor

The Data Recovery Advisor (DRA) tool is a new integrated solution that detects and analyzes database failures, determines the optimal repair strategies, optionally executes the repairs, and verifies their success. A database *failure* is broadly defined here as a corruption of data or the loss of data, including the loss of entire datafiles. Since the DRA can perform even proactive failure diagnosis and repair, it can potentially help limit the damage that could be caused by a data failure. You can access DRA through the RMAN client or Enterprise Manager.

The ultimate goal of the DRA is to reduce the mean time to recovery (MTTR) by the provision of an automated data repair tool that enhances the Oracle Database's reliability. The DRA performs an automatic diagnosis of database failures, presents you with the repair options, and carries out the repair upon your approval of its recommendations. The DRA consolidates multiple related failures so you can repair them efficiently. Since the DRA recommends optimal repair options, it's preferable to a manual determination of the correct repair options by the DBA, which is prone to judgmental errors.

The DRA is built on the new approach to problem diagnosis and repair involving the Oracle Database 11g concepts of problems, incidents, and failures, defined earlier in this chapter. You can use the DRA to diagnose and fix failures such as a lost or misnamed datafile, physical data block corruption, inconsistencies in the database (one datafile is older than the others, for example), I/O failures, and a down database. The main goals of the DRA are as follows:

- Detection of data failures before a database process discovers the error, thus limiting potential damage by extensive corruption of data

- Automatic detection, reporting and repair of database failures

- Cutting back on database downtime

- Minimizing disruptions for users

The Health Monitor performs an automatic check (data integrity check) whenever it encounters a database error. The data integrity check looks for any data failures that resulted from the database error that initiated the automatic check. If the check diagnoses a failure, it records pertinent information such as the errors, the symptoms, and its findings in the ADR. The failure assessments are executed and also stored in the ADR. The DRA groups related findings into a database failure, with each failure being assigned a severity level (critical or high, for example). The DRA maps the failures to both automatic and manual repair options. When the DBA requests advice on the repair of a particular failure, the Data Recovery Advisor presents the choices to you along with its advice. You can then perform the repair manually or have the DRA perform the repairs for you.

It's important to understand that all database errors logged in the alert log, such as an ORA-600 error, don't automatically qualify as a failure. A failure represents a problem such as persistent data corruption that is diagnosed by a diagnostic procedure (checker) registered with the Health Monitor. A serious database error will invoke a data integrity check, which looks for failures related to that error. Once the database detects a failure, it records it in the ADR. Only then can you call on the Data Recovery Advisor to generate repair advice. Of course, you can launch a proactive data integrity check anytime through the Health Monitor. Any failures that are detected by such proactive checks are treated exactly the same as if the check were issued by the database following an error. In addition, you can also employ the `validate` command (using RMAN) to check for block corruption, as shown earlier in this chapter and in Chapter 6 (backup and recovery). Both the `validate` and `backup` commands in RMAN invoke an automatic data integrity check.

You can use the DRA both through RMAN as well as through Enterprise Manager. In Enterprise Manager, the DRA is integrated with the Support Workbench as well as the Health Monitor, both of which we discussed earlier in this chapter. We'll show you how to use the DRA through both of these interfaces in the following sections.

Managing the Data Recovery Advisor Through RMAN

RMAN provides several new commands that help you perform various tasks related to the management and resolution of database failures through the help of the Data Recovery Advisor. We briefly discuss these commands in the following sections.

Viewing Failures

Use the `list failure` command to view a list of database failures, as shown here:

```
RMAN> list failure;
```

The results of the `list failure` command are captured in the V$IR_FAILURE view. The DRA consolidates related failures into a single failure. If ten data blocks are corrupted in the same datafile, the DRA will show you a single consolidated failure, although you can drill down to the subfailure level if you want. You can list a failure individually by issuing the `list failure ... detail` command.

You can restrict the `list failure` command's output by specifying options such as `critical`, `high`, `low`, or `closed`, which results in the output being limited to only those failures with a particular priority level or status. By default, the `list failure` command shows all failures with the `critical` and `high` priorities. You can also exclude specific failures from the output. Here are some examples showing how you can customize the output of the `list failure` command:

```
RMAN> list failure critical;
RMAN> list failure open;
RMAN> list failure closed;
```

The first command shows only those failures that have a priority level of `critical`, and the second command shows only currently `open` failures. The failure status remains `open` until you invoke a repair action; once you repair the failure, its status will be `closed`.

It's important to understand that the `list failure` command doesn't initiate any data integrity checks but merely lists the results of automatically executing prior checks that were initiated in response to errors in the database.

Dealing with Failures

If the database failure is critical, you of course have no choice but to fix it pronto. Once you fix a failure, the failure is closed automatically. However, some failure may really be trivial or irrelevant to your case. In such a situation, you can use RMAN's `change failure` command to explicitly close an open failure even if you haven't done anything to remedy the situation. You can also use this command to change the priority level of a failure. You can change the priority from high to low, or vice versa. You can't, however, change a priority level of critical, because this will result in an error.

Here's an example showing how to use the change failure command to change the priority level of a failure:

```
RMAN> change failure 3 priority low;
```

If you change the status of a failure to closed before the problem is actually solved, the Data Recovery Advisor will re-create the failure with a different ID when the checker that detected the failure the first time is run again.

Getting Repair Advice

The RMAN advise failure command advises on all failures that are recorded in the automatic diagnostic repository. By default, the command lists only those failures that have a critical or high level of priority. In addition to producing a summary of all input failures, the command also provides a single recommended repair option for each failure. Often, the advise repair command presents both manual as well as automated repair options.

At the end of the output of the advise failure command, RMAN generates a script listing the details of the recommended repair option. If you want to perform the repair yourself, you can use this script as is or make your own modifications to it.

A careful perusal of the RMAN-produced script can often help you avoid a time-consuming repair job. The script, also referred to as a *manual checklist*, is useful under circumstances where you can fix the failure yourself with a minor change, instead of RMAN fixing the same problem through a laborious restore and recover operation. For example, you can easily recover a deleted reference table from a test/acceptance environment rather than have RMAN restore and recover the whole production database.

After you run the advise failure command, you can view the manual advice by querying the V$IR_MANUAL_CHECKLIST view, as shown here:

```
SQL> select advise_id, rank, message from v$ir_manual_checklist;

ADVISE_ID   RANK     MESSAGE
------      ------   -------------------------------------------
21          0        if file /u01/app/oracle/nick/users01.dbf
                     was unintentionally renamed or moved,
                     restore it
21          0        if file /u01/app/oracle/nick/example01.dbf
                     was unintentionally renamed or moved,
                     restore it

SQL>
```

The MESSAGE column shows a summary of the repair advice offered by the DRA.

The `advise failure` command may offer just manual options or automatic repair options as well. You must, of course, perform manual actions yourself, but the DRA can perform all the automatic repair options that it suggests. Wherever possible, the DRA consolidates a set of repairs so it can fix multiple failures in a single repair job.

When the DRA recommends an automatic repair option to fix a failure, it always creates a repair script that shows the exact RMAN commands it'll use to repair the failure. For example, a script for an automatic fix of a missing datafile failure will look like the following:

```
# restore and recover datafile
restore check readonly datafile 1;
recover datafile 1;
```

If you prefer to control the repair activity yourself, you can execute the repair script manually yourself (even when you are offered an automatic repair option), without having the DRA automatically execute it.

Repairing the Failures

Once RMAN provides its repair recommendations for failures, you can choose to run the `repair failure` command to fix and close a specific failure. If the `advise failure` command recommends any manual repairs, first perform these repairs before asking the Data Recovery Advisor to automatically undo the failure. You must issue the `report failure` command only after using an `advise failure` command. Here's the basic `repair failure` command:

```
RMAN> repair failure;
```

If you try to use the `repair failure` command without issuing the `advise failure` command first, you'll get the following error:

```
RMAN> repair failure;
using target database control file instead of recovery catalog
RMAN-00571: ========================
RMAN-00569: =============== ERROR MESSAGE STACK FOLLOWS ===============
RMAN-00571: =====================================================================
RMAN-03002: failure of repair command at 03/29/2007 14:44:11
RMAN-06954: REPAIR command must be preceded by ADVISE command in same session
RMAN>
```

If you don't use any options, by default the `repair failure` command will use the single recommendation made by RMAN in the previously run `advise failure` command.

If you'd rather not have RMAN actually repair the failure but merely want to examine RMAN's repair actions and comments, use the `preview` option with the `repair failure` command, as shown here:

```
RMAN> repair failure preview;
```

The `repair preview` command merely previews the repair process but doesn't actually start the repair job itself. The results of the `repair failure` command are captured in the V$IR_REPAIR view. The following query shows how:

```
SQL> select repair_id,advise_id,summary,rank
     from v$ir_repair;

REPAIR_ID   ADVISE_ID    SUMMARY                    RANK
----------- ---------    --------------------       --------
   23          21        NO DATA LOSS OPTION           1
   69          67        NO DATA LOSS OPTION           1
   82          80        NO DATA LOSS OPTION           1

SQL>
```

The SUMMARY column indicates that the repair action for all three failures is NO DATA LOSS OPTION, meaning that the failure can be repaired with no data loss.

Repairing a Missing Datafile Problem

We'll walk you through a missing datafile problem so you can understand how the Database Repair Advisor performs its job. In the following example, the database can't be opened because of a missing datafile:

```
SQL> startup
ORACLE instance started.
Total System Global Area  615055360 bytes
Fixed Size                  1324864 bytes
Variable Size             239757504 bytes
Database Buffers          369098752 bytes
Redo Buffers                4874240 bytes
Database mounted.
ORA-01157: cannot identify/lock data file 4 - see DBWR trace file
ORA-01110: data file 4: 'C:\ORACLE\PRODUCT\10.2.0\ORADATA\NICK\USERS01.DBF'
SQL>
```

The following are the steps you must follow in order to repair the problem with the help of the Data Recovery Advisor:

1. Start the RMAN client and use the database repair commands you reviewed in the previous section to fix the missing datafile problem, starting with the list failure command:

   ```
   RMAN> list failure;

   List of Database Failures
   Failure ID Priority Status    Time Detected Summary
   ---------- -------- --------- ------------- ------------------------------
   4          HIGH     OPEN      29-MAR-07     multiple datafiles are missing

   RMAN>
   ```

   You can also execute a variation of the list failure command to get the individual subfailures that may have been consolidated under a single failure by the DRA by passing the unique identifier for a specific failure to the list failure command and specifying the keyword detail. Here's an example:

```
RMAN> list failure 4 detail
```

The list failure command shown here will list all the individual failures consolidated into the failure with the unique identifier 4.

2. Use the advise failure command to get recommendations regarding the failure:

```
RMAN> advise failure;

List of Database Failures
Failure ID Priority Status    Time Detected Summary
---------- -------- --------- ------------- ------------------------------
4          HIGH     OPEN      29-MAR-07     multiple datafiles are missing

analyzing automatic repair options; this may take some time
allocated channel: ORA_DISK_1
channel ORA_DISK_1: SID=152 device type=DISK
analyzing automatic repair options complete

Manual Checklist
================
if file C:\ORACLE\PRODUCT\10.2.0\ORADATA\NICK\USERS01.DBF was
unintentionally renamed or moved, restore it

if file C:\ORACLE\PRODUCT\10.2.0\ORADATA\NICK\EXAMPLE01.DBF was
unintentionally renamed or moved, restore it

Automated Repair Options
========================
Option Strategy     Repair Description
------ ------------ ------------------
       no data loss restore and recover datafile 4, restore and
       recover datafile
  Repair script: C:\ORCL11\APP\ORACLE\NICK\DIAG\diag\
  rdbms\nick\nick\hm\reco_1139896242.hm


RMAN>
```

3. Before repairing the problem, use the repair failure preview command to see how RMAN plans to repair the problem:

```
RMAN> repair failure preview;

Strategy     Repair script
------------ -------------
no data loss C:\ORCL11\APP\ORACLE\NICK\DIAG\diag\
rdbms\nick\nick\hm\reco_1139896242.hm
```

```
contents of repair script:
  # restore and recover datafile
  restore check readonly datafile 4, 5;
  recover datafile 4, 5;
```

```
RMAN>
```

4. Finally, direct RMAN to repair the problems it found earlier:

```
RMAN> repair failure;

Strategy      Repair script
------------  -------------
no data loss C:\ORCL11\APP\ORACLE\NICK\DIAG\diag\rdbms\nick\nick\hm\reco_1139896
242.hm

contents of repair script:
  # restore and recover datafile
  restore check readonly datafile 4, 5;
  recover datafile 4, 5;

Do you really want to execute the above repair (enter YES or NO)? yes
executing repair script

Starting restore at 29-MAR-07
using channel ORA_DISK_1

channel ORA_DISK_1: starting datafile backup set restore
channel ORA_DISK_1: specifying datafile(s) to restore from backup set
Finished restore at 29-MAR-07

Starting recover at 29-MAR-07
using channel ORA_DISK_1

starting media recovery
RMAN-08187: WARNING: media recovery until SCN 1741717 complete

Finished recover at 29-MAR-07
repair failure complete
Do you want to open the database (enter YES or NO)? yes

RMAN>
```

When you choose to let the Data Recovery Advisor open the database, as shown in this example, the database is opened automatically, since the recovery has already been completed in the previous step.

Managing the DRA with Database Control

Oracle recommends using Database Control to manage the Data Recovery Advisor. Once you log in to Database Control, choose Availability ➤ Manage ➤ Perform Recovery ➤ Perform Automated Repair to get to the Perform Recovery page, shown in Figure 2-5. You can also get a list of all database failures (in decreasing order of priority) and a description of each failure from the Database Recovery Advisor page, by going to Advisor Central and clicking on the Data Recovery Advisor link.

The Perform Recovery page of Database Control has two main sections: Oracle Advised Recovery and User Directed Recovery. You can always access the Customized Repair section to perform data restore and recovery at the datafile, tablespace, or database level. Here, you're interested in the new Oracle Advised Recovery section of the Perform Recovery page, which is how you access the new Data Recovery Advisor.

The Oracle Advised Recovery section of the Perform Recovery page has a button called Advise and Recover, which is gray if the Data Recovery Advisor hasn't detected any failures in the database. Click the Advise and Recover button, which will be highlighted when the DRA discovers any data errors such as corrupt data blocks, for example.

You can also access the DRA from the Support Workbench when the problem you are dealing with involves data corruption or some other type of data failure. In fact, the DRA is automatically recommended when dealing with these types of problems. There are two ways you can access the DRA from the Support Workbench:

- From the Checker findings subpage on the Support Workbench home page

- From the Problem Details page

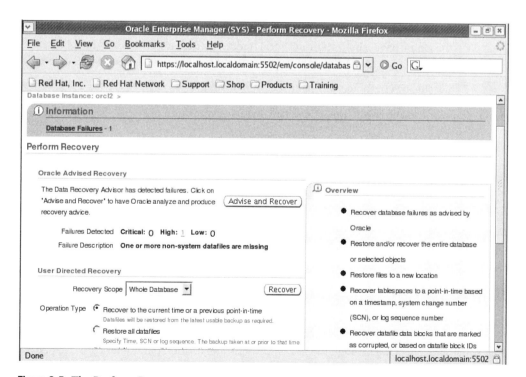

Figure 2-5. *The Perform Recovery page*

SQL Test Case Builder

When you're reporting a problem to the Oracle Support folks, it's often difficult to gather and reproduce the exact scenario under which the problem occurred. The new SQL Test Case Builder lets you easily capture information regarding a SQL problem and upload it to Oracle Support, so Oracle Support can reproduce the problem and test it. The SQL Test Case Builder gathers data such as the SQL query particulars, object definitions, stored code such as packages, initialization parameters, and optimizer statistics. The SQL Test Case Builder doesn't collect the actual data used by the query.

You can use either Database Control or the new DBMS_SQLDIAG package to access the SQL Test Case Builder. Here are the key procedures in the DBMS_SQLIDIAG package that deal with the SQL Test Case Builder functionality:

- The explain_sql_testcase function explains a SQL test case.

- The get_sql function imports a SQL test case.

- The export_sql_testcase procedure exports a SQL test case to a directory.

- The export_sql_testcase_dir_by_inc function generates SQL test cases that correspond to an incident ID.

- The export_sql_testcase_dir_by_txt function generates SQL test cases that correspond to a SQL statement.

It's a snap to build a SQL test case from Database Control. Note that you can use the SQL Test Case Builder from Database Control only when a SQL-related incident occurs. Here are the steps to access the SQL Test Case Builder from Database Control:

1. On the Home page, click Advisor Central under Related Links to access the Advisor Central page. Click SQL Advisors and then the link Click Here to Go to Support Workbench.

2. To investigate a particular problem, click an incident ID.

3. Click Oracle Support in the Investigate and Resolve section.

4. Click Generate Additional Dumps and Test Cases

5. To run the SQL Test Case Builder for a specific incident, click the icon in the Go To Task column.

You must provide a name for the output as well as a directory to save it. The output consists of commands that'll let you re-create the environment and the objects to test the problem SQL query or queries.

Improvements in Handling Data Corruption

Oracle Database 11g provides several new innovations that help catch incidents of data corruption before they mushroom into major problems. These include the new integrated mechanism for data corruption checking through the use of the new initialization parameter db_ultra_safe and *lost-write detection* through the use of a standby database. We discuss these and other data corruption–related new features in the following sections.

Protecting the Database from Data Corruption

In previous releases of the Oracle database, you had to employ initialization parameters such as db_block_checking and db_block_checksum to check for various types of data corruption. However, these parameters operated independently of each other, and there was no overall mechanism to control database corruption. Oracle Database 11g provides the new initialization parameter db_ultra_safe to offer better protection against data corruption. This parameter lets you proactively detect data corruption, thus enhancing the high-availability capabilities of the Oracle database.

In Oracle Database 11g, it takes less time to discover block corruptions, because several database components and utilities are capable of detecting and recording corrupt data blocks in the V$DATABASE_BLOCK_CORRUPTION view. The database maintains an accurate tally of the block corruptions in the database by updating this view as appropriate when data block corruption is detected and when the corrupt blocks are repaired.

You still use the db_block_checking and db_block_checksum initialization parameters in the Oracle Database 11g release, but now you can use the db_ultra_safe initialization parameter to control the setting of these two parameters in order to provide a consistent data protection mechanism. In addition to these two parameters, the db_ultra_safe parameter also controls the setting of the new db_lost_write_protect initialization parameter. Furthermore, the db_ultra_safe parameter controls other types of data protection behavior in the database, such as requiring automatic storage management (ASM) to perform sequential mirror writes.

The db_ultra_safe initialization parameter offers flexibility by allowing you to set various levels of protection from data corruption. Chapter 1 summarizes the various levels to which you can set the db_ultra_safe parameter.

Lost-Write Detection Using a Physical Standby Database

Occasionally, your database may signal the completion of a block write before the write is actually stored on disk, because of the malfunctioning of the storage hardware or software. This is known commonly as the *lost-write* form of data corruption. Oracle Database 11g provides a new initialization parameter called db_lost_write_protect, which lets you use a physical standby database to detect data corruption due to a lost-write form of data corruption. If you're already using a physical standby database for any reason, you can now leverage your efforts in maintaining that standby database by letting it perform a comprehensive lost-write data corruption detection.

If you set the value of the db_lost_write_protect parameter to typical (the default value), the instance will log all buffer cache block reads in the redo log files for all read/write tablespaces. However, to enable the recording of all reads including read-only tablespaces, you need to set the value of the db_lost_write_protect parameter to full instead of the default value of typical.

The lost-write protection feature works best in a Data Guard environment, where you set the db_lost_write_protect parameter in both the primary database and the standby database. During the application of redo while performing a managed recovery, the standby database detects lost writes on the primary database when the block SCNs on the primary database are found to be lower than the SCNs on the standby database. If, on the other hand, the SCN on the primary database is higher than that on the standby database, there is a lost write on the standby database. Repairing the standby database lost writes entails the re-creation of the entire standby database or just the affected files.

You can encounter a lost write during the normal database operation or during a media recovery. To generate the lost-write error that occurs during normal operation, you must recover the database (or the tablespace) to the SCN when the stale block read corruption occurred. If you encounter a lost-write error during a media recovery, you must open the database with the `resetlogs` option, thus losing all data after the `resetlogs` SCN.

CHAPTER 3

■■■

Database Administration

Oracle Database 11g provides several significant enhancements in the areas of database manageability that alleviate the burden of the day-to-day activities of DBAs. You already saw some of the key new administration-related features in Chapter 2, where we discussed administration features such as the fault diagnosability infrastructure, the Health Monitor, and the Data Repair Advisor. In this chapter, we focus on several important Oracle Database 11g features that affect the performance of day-to-day administrative tasks. We discuss the new features pertaining to performance tuning in Chapter 4 and new security features in Chapter 6.

This chapter discusses new Oracle database features that fall into the following categories:

- Database automation

- New flashback-related features

- Database administration enhancements

- SQL*Plus enhancements

- Online application maintenance

- The advanced table compression feature

- Enterprise Manager new features

- Oracle Scheduler new features

We'll begin with the most useful Oracle Database 11g database administration features related to database automation.

Database Automation

Automating routine DBA tasks not only enhances your productivity but also diminishes the chances of making on-the-job errors. Higher database availability, proactive database management, and improved performance are all benefits of automating database management processes. Oracle has continually automated the DBA tasks, making vast strides in memory and storage management in recent releases of the database. In Oracle Database 11g, you'll find that the following areas have been further automated:

- *Memory management:* Oracle Database 11*g* introduces a much simplified, unified tuning method for both the SGA and the PGA.

- *Database maintenance tasks feature:* This now includes a new task, the Automatic SQL Tuning Advisor task. We discuss automatic SQL tuning in Chapter 4.

- *Partition management:* The new Partition Advisor, a part of the SQL Access Advisor, provides advice on partitioning methods for tables, indexes, and materialized views. We discuss the Partition Advisor in Chapter 12.

- *Streams management:* The Streams Performance Advisor helps you identify replication bottlenecks. We discuss this advisor in Chapter 9.

- *Data Repair:* The Data Repair Advisor identifies and fixes problems such as SQL exceptions, missing files, bad data blocks, and bad undo records. We discuss the Data Repair Advisor in Chapter 2.

In the following sections, we discuss the new automatic memory management feature and the additions to the automated database maintenance tasks feature.

Automatic Memory Management

Over the past couple of releases (starting with Oracle Database 9*i* primarily), Oracle has been steadily moving toward completely automating the allocation of memory for Oracle instances. The process of automation really started with Oracle Database 9*i* (sga_target), continued in Oracle Database 10*g* (automatic PGA management with the pga_target parameter), and now culminates in Oracle Database 11*g* with the introduction of a new capability called *automatic memory management*, which provides a completely hands-off way to manage memory. With this method, a single parameter called memory_target lets you automate memory allocation for both the SGA and PGA components of Oracle's memory.

Once you set the memory_target parameter, Oracle automatically allocates the SGA and the PGA memory and automatically redistributes memory between these two components as dictated by the database workload. Oracle recommends you use automatic memory management to simplify the allocation of memory to Oracle instances.

Oracle still supports the manual management of memory as well as the partially automatic memory management introduced in Oracle Database 9*i* and Oracle Database 10*g*. To avoid confusion, here are the different ways you can manage Oracle memory allocation in Oracle Database 11*g*:

- *Automatic memory management:* This is new to Oracle Database 11*g* and involves the use of the memory_target (and memory_max_target) initialization parameter.

- *Automatic shared memory management and automatic program global area management:* These use the sga_target and pga_target parameters to set values for the SGA and aggregate PGA. The database then tunes the SGA and PGA components.

- *Manual shared memory management:* This means you manually set values for each component of the SGA, such as the buffer cache and the shared pool, with parameters such as db_cache_size and shared_pool_size.

- *Manual PGA memory management:* This involves setting various *_AREA_SIZE parameters (for example, HASH_AREA_SIZE) to control the size of the SQL work areas.

You can still use manual shared memory and PGA management as well as automatic SGA and automatic PGA management in Oracle Database 11g. However, Oracle strongly recommends switching to the simple and efficient automatic memory management, which we discuss in detail here. Automatic memory management unifies the management of the SGA and the PGA. The memory allocation mechanism adjusts automatically to changes in database workload and practically eliminates any out-of-memory errors. Oracle uses an indirect memory transfer mechanism to move memory back and forth between the PGA and the SGA. The memory transfer utilizes the operating system, which frees the shared memory and releases it to the operating system, from where other components can request additional memory.

You can still set specific minimum values for the various caches using familiar parameters such as `shared_pool_size` and `db_cache_size`. If you do set values for any of these parameters, the database won't autotune them any longer, instead taking the values that you manually set as the minimum values for those caches.

New Automatic Memory Initialization Parameters

There are two key new memory-related initialization parameters in Oracle Database 11g that let you set up automatic memory management for a database instance. You set the target memory size initialization parameter, named `memory_target`, to specify the memory you want to allo-cate for an Oracle instance. The optional second parameter is the maximum memory size initialization parameter (or `memory_max_size`), and it sets the maximum memory you can allocate to the instance.

The `memory_max_size` parameter's value sets the ceiling on the value of the `memory_target` parameters. The `memory_max_size` parameter is static, while the `memory_target` parameter is dynamic. Thus, you can calibrate the value of the `memory_target` parameter up and down, as long as you don't exceed the maximum possible value for memory allocation, which is the value set for the `memory_max_size` parameter.

Adopting Automatic Memory Management

You can choose automatic memory management for Oracle's memory management either when you're creating a new database or later. We'll discuss both cases.

At Database Creation Time

If you want to specify automatic memory management during database creation, set a value for the `memory_target` and `memory_max_target` parameters in the initialization parameter file before you execute the `create database` SQL statement, as shown here:

```
memory_target = 1000m
memory_max_target = 1500m
```

If you're using the DBCA to create the new database and choose Advanced Installation, you can select the automatic memory management option during database creation. If you choose the Basic Installation option instead, automatic memory management is the default.

You can arrive at a tentative size for the `memory_target` parameter by adding the memory allocations you currently make using the `sga_target` and `pga_target` parameters. You can set the value of the `memory_max_target` parameter based on the physical memory you have avail-able for the instance. Note that even with the automatic memory management method, you can still set minimum values for both the SGA and the PGA.

■ **Note** `memory_target` is a dynamic parameter, but `memory_max_target` is a static parameter.

After Database Creation

If you want to convert to automatic memory management, you can do so by using the two automatic memory-related parameters, `memory _target` and `memory_max_target`. Even though `memory_target` is a dynamic parameter, you can't switch to automatic memory management while the database is running. Once you add the new memory parameters, you must restart the database for the parameters to take effect and automatic memory management to come into force. Here are the steps:

1. If you're using an `init.ora` file for your initialization parameters, just add the two automatic memory parameters, `memory_target` and `memory_max_target`, as shown in the previous section, and then restart the database. If you're using a server parameter file instead, use the following command to record the new memory parameters in your spfile first:

   ```
   SQL> alter system set memory_target = 1000m scope = spfile;
   SQL> alter system set memory_max_target = 2500m scope = spfile;
   ```

   If you omit setting the `memory_max_target` parameter, the value of the parameter defaults to the value you set for the `memory_target` parameter.

2. Shut down and restart the instance for automatic memory management to come into force. Once you do this, you can adjust the value of the `memory_target` parameter dynamically, without an instance restart. The `memory_max_target` parameter isn't dynamic, so the value you set for it in the previous step will come into force only after the instance restart.

If you adopt automatic memory management by setting the `memory_target` parameter to a value greater than 0, then the following will be true:

- If you don't set the `sga_target` and `pga_target` parameters (or set both of these parameters to zero), Oracle will completely automate memory management and will not use any minimum values for either `sga_target` or `pga_target`. When the instance starts, it gives 60 percent of the memory target to the SGA and 40 percent to the PGA.

- Any values you set for the `sga_target` and `pga_target` parameters are treated as the minimum values for those parameters. The size of the `memory_target` parameter will be equal to the sum of the `pga_target` and `sga_target` parameter values.

- If you set either the `sga_target` or `pga_target` parameter, Oracle will autotune both the parameters and will set the value of the parameter you didn't specify to the difference between `memory_target` and the value of the parameter you did set.

- If you omit the `memory_max_target` parameter, it defaults to the value you set for the `memory_target` parameter. If, on the other hand, you set the `memory_max_target` parameter but omit the `memory_target` parameter, the `memory_target` parameter will default to zero. However, after starting the instance, you can dynamically change the `memory_target` parameter to any value up to the value you set for the `memory_max_target` parameter.

You can simply use Database Control to turn the automatic memory management feature on by following these steps:

1. On the database home page, click the Server tab.

2. Click the Memory Advisors link in the Database Configuration section.

3. On the Memory Advisors page, click the Enable button to enable automatic memory management.

You can check current memory allocation under automatic memory management by using the show parameter memory command:

```
SQL> show parameter memory

NAME                          TYPE         VALUE
------------------------      -----------  -----
hi_shared_memory_address      integer          0
memory_max_target             big integer   252M
memory_target                 big integer   240M
shared_memory_address         integer          0
SQL>
```

The query shows that the memory_target parameter is set at 240M and the memory_max_target parameter is at 252M.

▪Note In Oracle Database 11*g*, there is a new SGA component known as the *result cache*. You can't tune this component by setting the initialization parameter memory_target. You must use the new initialization parameter result_cache_size to specify the amount of SGA that can be used by the result cache. The parameter can take a range of values from 0 to an operating system–dependent maximum. The default value is 128KB. You disable the result cache feature by setting the result_cache_size parameter to a value of 0. Chapter 4 discusses the result cache feature.

Monitoring Memory Allocation

For guidance on the appropriate value for the memory_target parameter, use the V$MEMORY_TARGET_ADVICE view, which provides advice on memory sizing based on the current values for the memory_target parameter and the potential decrease or increase in the db_time parameter, which indicates the time spent by the instance on database calls, based on increasing or decreasing the value of the memory_target parameter.

```
SQL> select * from v$memory_target_advice;

MEMORY          SIZE_FACTOR   ESTD_DB_TIME    TIME_FACTOR   VERSION
_SIZE
------------    ------------  -------------   ------------  --------
356                  1            206              1           0
445                1.25           204             .9919         0
712                  2            204             .9919         0
623                1.75           204             .9919         0
534                1.5            204             .9919         0
```

In this example, the memory_target parameter is set at 356MB. As you can see from the estd_db_time column, there is no significant reduction in db_time, even if you double the value of the memory_target parameter. However, if you see a substantial reduction in db_time that correlates to higher memory_target parameter values, you must consider raising the value of the memory_target parameter.

The sga_target parameter is dynamic, so you can always use an alter system statement to calibrate the size of the parameter. Since the database needs some of the components to be at a certain minimum size, it prevents you from setting the value too low for the parameter.

The V$MEMORY_DYNAMIC_COMPONENTS view shows the current status of all memory components:

```
SQL> select component,current_size,min_size,max_size
     from v$memory_dynamic_components;

COMPONENT               CURRENT_SIZE   MIN_SIZE      MAX_SIZE
--------------------    ------------   -----------   ----------
shared pool               62914560      25165824      62914560
large pool                 4194304             0       4194304
java pool                  4194304       4194304       4194304
streams pool                     0             0             0
SGA Target                 8880384      88080384      88080384
DEFAULT buffer cache       8388608       8388608      20971520
PGA Target                58720256      58720256      58720256

16 rows selected.
SQL>
```

Note that although you don't have to set them anymore, the database will internally set and manage the sizes of both the sga_target and pga_target parameters.

You may on occasion get the following error (the following was on a Linux system) when you use automatic memory management to allocate memory to the Oracle instance:

```
SQL> startup
ORA-00845: MEMORY_TARGET not supported on this system
```

Contrary to what the error seems to indicate, the previous error more likely means that the kernel parameter /dev/shm wasn't correctly sized on your system. Make sure the /dev/shm allocation is at least equal to the sga_max_size parameter's value.

Automated Database Maintenance Tasks

In the Oracle Database 10*g* release, Oracle for the first time provided the automated mainte-nance tasks feature with which you could schedule predefined database maintenance tasks during various maintenance windows. The primary focus of these maintenance tasks is to collect information about things such as optimizer statistics and segment free space.

Oracle Database 11*g* enhances the automated maintenance tasks feature by adding a new automated maintenance task—the SQL Tuning Advisor task. In addition, there are improve-ments in the management of maintenance windows and resource allocation. You can now have a separate maintenance window for *each day of the week.* In Oracle Database 10*g*, to control the allocation of CPU resources to the automatic system tasks, you had to create a resource plan and then assign that plan to a maintenance window. Oracle Database 11*g* comes with a default resource manager plan enabled. This default plan contains a subplan that controls the resources consumed by the automated maintenance tasks.

Oracle Database 11*g* provides a new PL/SQL package, `DBMS_AUTOTASK_ADMIN`, to manage the automated management tasks. In addition, you can employ Database Control to manage autotasks. We'll cover the improvements in the three areas of automatic maintenance task management where there are enhancements in the Oracle Database 11*g* release—default automated maintenance tasks, maintenance windows, and the resource manager plan for automated tasks—in the following sections.

Automated Maintenance Tasks

Oracle Database 11*g* comes with three predefined automatic maintenance tasks, two of which you're familiar with from Oracle Database 10*g*:

- The Automatic Optimizer Statistics Collection task collects statistics for all objects with no or stale statistics.

- The Automatic Segment Advisor task provides advice on which database segments have free space that you can reclaim.

Oracle Database 11*g* adds a new automatic maintenance task, called *Automatic SQL Tuning Advisor* task, which examines SQL statement performance and makes SQL profile recommen-dations to improve the statements. If you want, you can also configure the Automatic SQL Tuning Advisor task so it automatically implements its SQL Profile recommendations. We discuss the Automatic SQL Tuning Advisor task in detail in Chapter 4, along with the other new performance-tuning features.

■**Note** All three predefined automated maintenance tasks run in all maintenance windows.

You can query the new view DBA_AUTOTASK_TASK to find out the names and status of the automatic tasks in your database, as shown in the following example:

```
SQL> select task_name,operation_name,status
     from dba_autotask_task;


TASK_NAME                     OPERATION                  STATUS
--------------------------    -----------------------    --------
gather_stats_prog             auto optimizer stats job   ENABLED
auto_space_advisor_prog       auto space advisor job     ENABLED
AUTO_SQL_TUNING_PROG          automatic sql tuning task  ENABLED
SQL>
```

The output of the query shows that all three of the predefined automated maintenance tasks are enabled by default.

New Maintenance Windows

All automated maintenance tasks are scheduled to run during the Oracle Scheduler maintenance window, which is part of the window group named `maintenance_window_group`. A maintenance window is simply a time span during which a job could be run by the Oracle Scheduler. The window usually is run according to a repeating interval such as every Sunday between 12 a.m. and 6 a.m., for example. The Oracle Scheduler creates a job when the window "opens" for each maintenance task that's scheduled to run during the maintenance window. When the automated task job completes, the Oracle Scheduler automatically drops that job. Unlike the other two automated maintenance tasks, the Automatic SQL Tuning Advisor runs only once during each maintenance window. If you have a long maintenance window, the database runs the other two maintenance tasks every four hours.

Upon installing Oracle Database 10g, two schedule windows were predefined: a `WEEKNIGHT_WINDOW` and a `WEEKEND_WINDOW`. In Oracle Database 11g, there are seven predefined maintenance windows, five for each of the weekdays and two windows for the two days in the weekend, Friday and Saturday. Each of the seven predefined windows is named after the day of the week, as in `MONDAY_WINDOW` and `SUNDAY_WINDOW`, for example. Each of the weekday windows starts at 10 p.m. and ends at 2 a.m., providing a time span of four hours to execute scheduled maintenance tasks. The two weekend windows provide a much longer time span of 20 hours each. You can view all the predefined maintenance windows by querying the DBA_AUTOTASK_SCHEDULE view, as shown here:

```
SQL> select * from dba_autotask_schedule;


WINDOW_NAME           START_TIME                        DURATION
-----------------     ---------------------------------- ---------
MONDAY_WINDOW         09-APR-07 10.00.00.000000 PM -05:00   04:00:00
MONDAY_WINDOW         16-APR-07 10.00.00.000000 PM -05:00   04:00:00

...
FRIDAY_WINDOW         04-MAY-07 10.00.00.000000 PM -05:00   04:00:00

...
SATURDAY_WINDOW       14-APR-07 06.00.00.000000 AM -05:00   20:00:00

...
SUNDAY_WINDOW         06-MAY-07 06.00.00.000000 AM -05:00   20:00:00
32 rows selected.
SQL>
```

Note that there's a separate window for each day of the month, named for the day of the week. When a maintenance task runs past the operational window, it continues to completion, based on the priority you allocate to that task.

Default Resource Manager Plan

All maintenance windows use the resource plan DEFAULT_MAINTENANCE_PLAN by default, with the automated tasks running under the subplan ORA$AUTOTASK_SUB_PLAN. You can query the DBA_RSRC_PLAN_DIRECTIVES view to find out the resource allocations for this subplan. You can change the resource allocation for any of the automated maintenance tasks by changing the resource allocation for the subplan ORA$AUTOTASK_SUB_PLAN. Of course, this will also involve adjusting resource allocation for other subplans or groups in the DEFAULT_ MAINTENANCE_PLAN resource plan to keep the total resource allocation at 100 percent. Please refer to the Oracle manual titled *Database Administrator's Guide* for more details on resource allocation.

Each of the automated maintenance tasks belongs to a special resource consumer group. The following query on the DBA_RSRC_CONSUMER_GROUPS view shows the various resource consumer groups.

```
SQL> select consumer_group, mandatory from dba_rsrc_consumer_groups;

CONSUMER_GROUP                  MAN
------------------------------- ---
ORA$AUTOTASK_URGENT_GROUP       YES
BATCH_GROUP                     NO
ORA$DIAGNOSTICS                 YES
ORA$AUTOTASK_HEALTH_GROUP       YES
ORA$AUTOTASK_SQL_GROUP          YES
ORA$AUTOTASK_SPACE_GROUP        YES
ORA$AUTOTASK_STATS_GROUP        YES
ORA$AUTOTASK_MEDIUM_GROUP       YES
INTERACTIVE_GROUP               NO
OTHER_GROUPS                    YES
DEFAULT_CONSUMER_GROUP          YES
SYS_GROUP                       YES
LOW_GROUP                       NO
AUTO_TASK_CONSUMER_GROUP        NO

14 rows selected.
SQL>


SQL>
```

Note that there is a separate High Priority consumer group for each of the three automatic maintenance tasks (space_group, sql_group, stats_group). In addition, there is also a consumer group named health_group for supporting the Health Monitor (explained in Chapter 2), which performs automatic database health checks. All three maintenance tasks run in all predefined maintenance windows, but you can disable any of the tasks by using the disable procedure of the DBMS_AUTO_TASK_ADMIN package. Similarly, you can modify a maintenance window or create a new maintenance window to suit your needs.

The main automated database management functions include modifying the automated tasks, managing the maintenance windows, and allocating resources for the various windows. We briefly cover each of these functions in the following sections.

Modifying the Automatic Tasks

DBAs and developers can now use the new DBMS_AUTO_TASK_ADMIN package to modify maintenance task execution. You can use this package to enable and disable automatic maintenance tasks in some or all maintenance windows. You can disable *all* automatic maintenance tasks, for example, by executing the disable procedure without any arguments, as shown here:

```
SQL> execute dbms_auto_task_admin.disable;
```

You can reenable all the automated tasks with the enable procedure, as shown in the following example:

```
SQL> execute dbms_auto_task_admin.enable;
```

The client_name column in the DBA_AUTOTASK_OPERATION view identifies the client (for example, the SQL Tuning Advisor), and the operation_name column identifies the actual automatic maintenance task (for example, automatic sql tuning task), as shown by this query:

```
SQL> select client_name,operation_name,status from dba_autotask_operation;

CLIENT_NAME                      OPERATION_NAME            STATUS
-------------------------------  ------------------------  --------
auto optimizer stats collection  auto optimizer stats job  ENABLED
auto space advisor               auto space advisor job    ENABLED
sql tuning advisor               automatic sql tuning task ENABLED
```

If you would rather disable only a specific task, specify the client_name parameter when executing the disable procedure, instead of executing it without any parameters. You can disable a maintenance task for a specific window by using the window_name argument, as shown in this example:

```
begin
    dbms_auto_task_admin.disable(
    client_name    => 'sql tuning advisor',
    operation      => NULL,
    window_name    => 'FRIDAY_WINDOW');
end;
```

The preceding PL/SQL code will disable the maintenance task temporarily until you reenable it.

Modifying the Maintenance Windows

You can customize the predefined maintenance windows or create more convenient windows by using the DBMS_SCHEDULER package. You can remove a maintenance window by using the remove_window_group_member procedure, as shown here:

```
begin
    dbms_scheduler.remove_window_group_member(
    group_name    => 'MAINTENANCE_WINDOW_GROUP',
    window_list   => 'EARLY_MORNING_WINDOW');
END;
```

Use the create_window procedure of the DBMS_SCHEDULER package to create a new window. To create a maintenance window, you must add this new window to the window group maintenance_window_group. Call the add_window_group_member procedure to add your new window to the group named maintenance_window_group. Here's an example:

```
begin
    dbms_scheduler.create_window(
    window_name      => 'LATE_NIGHT_WINDOW',
    duration         => numtodsinterval(2, 'hour'),
    resource_plan    => 'DEFAULT_MAINTENANCE_PLAN',
    repeat_interval  => 'FREQ=DAILY;BYHOUR=22;
                        BYMINUTE=0;BYSECOND=0');
end;
```

Once you create the new window named late_night_window, you must add it to the window group maintenance_window_group by using the add_window_group_member procedure, as shown here:

```
begin
    dbms_scheduler.add_window_group_member(
    group_name      => 'MAINTENANCE_WINDOW_GROUP',
    window_list     => 'LATE_NIGHT_WINDOW');
end;
```

The create_window procedure creates the new window called LATE_NIGHT_WINDOW and adds it to the window group named maintenance_window_group. The duration attribute of the create_window procedure sets the window duration at two hours, and the repeat_interval attribute specifies that this window be open daily starting from 10 p.m.

Use the set_attribute procedure of the DBMS_SCHEDULER package to modify any attributes of a maintenance window, such as the duration of the maintenance window, for example. Use the DBMS_SCHEDULER package's enable and disable procedures to disable a maintenance window before changing its attributes and then to reenable the window once you change its attributes. You can remove a maintenance window by using the remove_window_group_member procedure.

Tracking Job Runs

You can track the various maintenance job runs by issuing a query such as the following on the DBA_AUTOTASK_HISTORY view:

```
SQL> select client_name,job_name,job_start_time
     from dba_autotask_job_history;

CLIENT_NAME          JOB_NAME                JOB_START_TIME
-----------------    --------------------    ---------------------------
auto optimizer       ORA$AT_OS_OPT_SY_1      15-MAR-07   10.00 PM -05:00
stats collection
auto space advisor   ORA$AT_SA_SPC_SY_22     19-MAR-07   10.00 PM -05:00
sql tuning advisor   ORA$AT_SQ_SQL_SW_103    28-MAR-07   10.00 PM -05:00
SQL>
```

Notice that all three database maintenance jobs run daily at 10 p.m. by default.

You can use the following procedures from the DBMS_AUTO_TASK_ADMIN package to perform various management tasks relating to the automatic maintenance tasks:

- get_p1_resources: This procedure returns the percentage of resources allocated to each of the four high-priority resource groups relating to the maintenance tasks.

- set_pi_resources: Use this procedure to modify the resource allocation to each of the resource groups used by the automatic maintenance task (AUTOTASK) clients.

- set_attribute: This procedure lets you set attributes for a task, a client, or an operation.

- override_priority: You can use this procedure to override task priorities at the client, operation, and task level. For example, you can set the priority of a task to urgent, thereby making it jump to the top of the maintenance window the next time the database executes that task.

■**Note**   There are some important additions to Oracle Scheduler's capabilities, which we will discuss towards the end of this chapter.

Flashback-Related New Features

Oracle9*i* Database and Oracle Database 10*g* introduced and developed several flashback-related features that enhanced the ability of DBAs and developers to perform the logical repair of data, besides providing means to produce "as-if" reports using historical data. In Oracle Database 11*g*, Oracle takes the flashback concept further by giving you two very useful features. The *flashback data archive*, which is the underlying technology behind the new Oracle Total Recall option, lets you track, store, and manage historical changes in data (that is, all versions of a table's rows over time) and lets you easily query the historical data. The *flashback transaction backout* feature lets you back out unwanted transactions effortlessly with a one-step transaction backout operation. We'll review the flashback data archive feature in the following section, followed by a discussion of the flashback transaction backout feature.

Total Recall and the Flashback Data Archive

Oracle Database 10g release introduced several flashback-related features that helped you perform various logical data correction and recovery tasks, such as recovering an accidentally dropped table or rewinding the database or transaction to a previous point in time. To perform their magic, all flashback features (except for flashback database, which depends on flashback logs) rely on the undo data stored in the undo tablespace. During every transaction that involves a change in a table's data, the Oracle server copies "old" pre-change data to the undo segments in the undo tablespace. This undo data is useful in recovering databases, in providing data consistency, and, more important for this discussion, in helping roll back unwanted transactions before you commit the changes.

Although the undo data is stored in a tablespace and thus is of a persistent nature, there's a limit on how far back you can go in terms of retrieving older data—the undo tablespace can't serve as a historical archive of all the changes that were made to a table's data. Although the undo tablespace in an Oracle database performs several functions, the most important of which is the maintenance of transaction consistency, the undo management's main function isn't to serve as an archival record of all changes made to data over time.

In addition to the problem of a space-restricted amount of stored undo data, another limitation of undo data is that you can't collect undo data for a limited set of tables or transactions. Let's say you are interested in tracking changes in only two tables over time. Oracle's undo management feature doesn't let you specify that only the undo of these two important tables be saved—it's an all-or-nothing deal when it comes to storing undo data.

Oracle Database 11g takes flashback technology further by introducing a major new flashback-related feature, called the *flashback data archive*. Oracle actually calls the new feature Total Recall, with flashback data archive as the underlying technology. The flashback data archive feature provides a new time dimension to your data, enabling you to automatically track and record all changes made to a table row securely and effortlessly.

In some types of applications, such as applications dealing with compliance reporting and audit reports, sometimes you'd need to examine the entire history of a piece of data. That is, you'd need to have access to the entire history of a table row, from its inception to the present time, showing all the changes that row went through. If you aren't using the flashback data archive feature, you can use a flashback query when you want to see some historical information, but the SCN or the timestamp you specify in the flashback query must be less than the duration of your undo retention setting for the database. Flashback data archiving removes this limitation on data retention inherent in undo management as currently implemented by Oracle—you can retain historical data for as long as you want, without regard for the length of undo retention or the amount of flashback logs.

■**Note** The flashback data archive feature tracks and stores transactional changes to rows in only the table or tables you explicitly specify. In other words, the archiving isn't done en masse for all tables in the database.

Regulatory oversight and compliance requirements due to regulations such as HIPAA and Sarbanes-Oxley have led to a serious need for retaining data over long periods of time. Long retention periods that span several years of time mean you need an efficient and secure long-term history management system to assure compliance with the new regulations. Current methods include implementing a historical data management system at the application level or using triggers to archive data. Using business logic to implement historical data management leads to greater application complexity, making it hard to deal with changes in retention requirements and database upgrades, besides lacking a tamper-proof method of securing the data. Triggers involve a performance overhead and lack a central management interface.

The flashback data archive feature overcomes these limitations of current techniques to maintain historical data. Using this feature, you can have the database automatically track all changes to a specified table or a set of tables and store and maintain an archive of historical data. You can implement archiving both for new and existing tables. Since all the historical data pertaining to any given row is stored in the flashback data archive, you can easily use "as-if" historical flashback SQL queries on the data, either to track the changes in a record or to perform decision support tasks. By storing changes to tracked tables over long periods of time, you can always perform a query to check the data as of a time that's way in the past, without worrying about the dreaded "snapshot too old" error. In addition, you can employ the flashback data archive feature to enforce digital shredding policies—all unwanted data will simply disappear after the specified retention period is up!

You can profitably employ the flashback data archive feature for the following purposes:

- Change tracking

- Integrated lifecycle management (ILM)

- Auditing

- Generating reports

- Compliance and reporting

The database server automatically stores changes made to any selected table in the flashback data archive. You can retain data long term, for many years, or forever, if you want. Once you save the data, you can't modify it in any way since the flashback data archive allows only a read-only access to the historical data it stores. You can, however, purge some or all of the data in the flashback data archive according to your guidelines.

■**Note** A flashback data archive doesn't necessarily save all transaction changes "forever." The length of the retention period you choose for the flashback data archive determines how long the changes for a table will be retained.

What Is the Flashback Data Archive?

A flashback data archive is a new database object that holds historical data for one or several tables, along with the storage retention and purging polices for that data. The archive is simply one or more tablespaces that you dedicate for saving all transactional changes for one or more tables in the database. The database writes all original data in the buffer cache to the undo tablespace as undo data. A new background process named Flashback Data Archiver Process (FBDA) will collect and write the original data to a flashback data archive, thus creating a history of all table data. To enable flashback archiving, you must either create a table with the `flashback data archive` clause or use the `alter table` statement to enable archiving for existing tables.

Note the following key facts about the flashback data archives:

- There's a one-to-many relationship between a flashback data archive and tables.

- You can have multiple flashback data archives in your database, say, one for very long-term durations such as five years and the others for shorter time retention periods such as six months or a year.

- You can denote a particular tablespace as the default flashback data archive.

- The new Oracle background process (FBDA) collects the original data from the buffer cache and records it in the tablespace designated for a flashback data archive.

- Oracle will automatically purge the flashback data archive the day after the *retention period* expires.

Here's a summary of the architecture of the flashback data archive: once you enable a table for archiving, the FDAP creates an internal history table for that table. The history table will have all the columns of the original table plus some time stamp columns to track the transaction changes.

When you update or delete a row in the tracked table, the FDAP process marks the transactions and the corresponding undo records for archival. The history table will have the before image of the row before you committed the `delete` or `update` transaction. An `insert` transaction won't cause any records to be added to the history table, since that new row doesn't have a prior history.

The FDAP process wakes up at system-determined intervals (the default is five minutes) and copies the undo data for the marked transactions to the history table. So when you make a change to a table, that change won't immediately show up in the history table. It'll take a few minutes for you to see the changes in the history table. If the database is generating a high amount of undo data, it adjusts the sleep time of the FDAP background process so it can read undo data from the buffer cache faster.

Until the FDAP process completes recording the pre-transaction (undo) data in the history table, the database won't reuse the undo records that are marked for archival. Once the FDAP process completes the history generation, these undo records become candidates for recycling again.

Here's an example that shows how the history table archives data following transactions that update or delete data from a table that's being currently tracked in the FDAP. The first transaction inserts a new row into the `departments` table:

```
SQL> insert into hr.departments
     values (300,'New Department',200,1700);

1 row created.
SQL> commit;

Commit complete.

SQL>
```

The preceding transaction, since it involves an insertion of a new row, will be not add any history records to the history table hr.SYS_FBA_HIST_70308. The following update statement will add a record, however:

```
SQL> update departments
     set department_name='Last Department'
     where department_id=300;

1 row updated.

SQL> commit;
```

The next transaction deletes the updated row. Again, a new row is written to the history table:

```
SQL> delete from hr.departments where department_id=300;

1 row deleted.

SQL> commit;

Commit complete.
SQL>
```

If you query the history table hr.SYS_FBA_HIST_70308 now, you'll find all the pre-change table data that the FBDA background process has captured from the undo records:

```
SQL> select  department_id, department_name, manager_id, location_id
     from hr.SYS_FBA_HIST_70308;
DEPT_ID   DEPT_NAME           MANAGER_ID     LOCATION_ID
-------   ----------------    -----------    ------------
300       New Department      200            1700
300       Last Department     200            1700

SQL>
```

As you can see, only the update and delete statements led to the addition of a history record to the history table—the insert statement didn't.

Benefits of Using a Flashback Data Archive

The flashback data archive feature offers the following key benefits:

- You can use a centralized management interface that lets you easily implement administrative tasks such as setting common retention policies for related groups of tables and automatic purging of aged-out data from the archive.

- You can view the archived data from any past point in time easily using the as of clause of the flashback query feature.

- You can capture historical data without any changes in the underlying application at all.

- It's easy to implement without any application changes and has a low performance overhead because of an efficient strategy for archiving data, as we explain later.

- You incur low storage requirements for storing the historical data because the data is stored in compressed format. The database also automatically partitions the internal history tables using a range-partitioned scheme, without any work on your part whatsoever.

- You can store critical data extremely securely because users, including DBAs, can't directly update the historical data.

Managing the flashback data archive includes performing tasks such as creating a new flashback data archive, altering the characteristics of a flashback data archive, and turning flashback logging on and off. We explain how to manage flashback data archives in the following sections.

Creating a Flashback Data Archive

To create a flashback data archive, you must either have the DBA role or have the system privilege `flashback archive administer`. Here's a query that shows how to query the DBA_SYS_PRIVS view to check who has been granted this privilege:

```
SQL> select * from dba_sys_privs where privilege like '%FLASH%';

GRANTEE                 PRIVILEGE                       ADM
----------------        ----------------------------    --------
SYS                     FLASHBACK ANY TABLE             NO
DBA                     FLASHBACK ANY TABLE             YES
DBA                     FLASHBACK  ARCHIVE ADMINISTER   YES
```

Grant the `flashback archive administer` privilege to the user `hr` so that user can manage a flashback data archive. Here's the example:

```
SQL> grant flashback archive administer to hr;

Grant succeeded.

SQL>
```

You create a flashback data archive by using the `create flashback` statement. You must first create the tablespace that'll host the flashback data archive. You can specify the following things while creating a new flashback data archive:

- A name for the flashback data archive

- Whether the flashback data archive is the default archive for the database

- The name of a tablespace you've created earlier

- A quota for this flashback data archive in the tablespace you choose as the host for the archive

- A retention period for the flashback data archive

The two key parameters are `quota`, which determines the amount of space in a tablespace that the flashback data archive can use, and `retention`, which determines how long the historical data is retained in the archive before the database automatically purges it (you can also manually purge the historical data). Here's an example that shows how to create a flashback data archive in the tablespace flash_tbs1:

```
SQL> create flashback data archive flash1
     tablespace flash_tbs1
     retention 4 year;

Flashback Data Archive created.

SQL>
```

The `retention 4 year` clause means the flashback data archive `flash1` will retain data up for a period of four years. Note that there is no `quota` clause in the `create flashback data archive` statement, meaning the archive can take up all the space available in the tablespace flash_tbs1. You can limit the amount of space the flashback data archive takes up in a tablespace by specifying a value for the `quota` clause, as shown in the following example:

```
SQL> create flashback data archive flash1
     tablespace flash_tbs1
     quota 2000m
     retention 4 year;

Flashback Data Archive created.

SQL>
```

The amount of space you must allocate for a flashback data archive will depend on the amount of transactions in the tables you're archiving and the duration of the archiving retention period. Before the flashback data archive uses up its allotted quota or, in the absence of a `quota` clause, before the archive uses up the entire tablespace, Oracle issues an out-of-space alert for the flashback data archive. This gives you time to purge older data in the archive or increase the tablespace quota or add more datafiles to the tablespace housing the flashback data archive, depending on the case.

■**Note** To enable flashback historical tracking for a table, the user must have the `flashback archive` `object` privilege on the flashback data archive that you want to use for that table.

You can drop a flashback data archive by using the `drop flashback archive` command:

```
SQL> drop flashback archive flash1;
```

Of course, once you drop a flashback data archive, the data you archived disappears, although the tablespace that housed the flashback data archive will remain intact, since it may contain other data besides the flashback data archive. You can't drop or even modify the contents of the tracking table that stores the actual data changes, since that defeats the purpose of creating tamper-proof historical data archives for auditing and security purposes.

Altering a Flashback Data Archive

Use the `alter flashback` command to change things such as the length of the retention time, making a flashback data archive the default flashback data archive for the database, adding space to the flashback data archive, or purging data from it. The following are examples of the several ways you can use the `alter flashback` command to manage the flashback data archive:

```
SQL> alter flashback archive flash1
     set default                   # makes flash1 the default archive

SQL> alter flashback archive flash1
     add tablespace flash_tbs1   # adds space to the flashback archive

SQL> alter flashback archive flash1
     modify tablespace
     flash_tbs1 quota 10G;       # changes the quota for the archive

SQL> alter flashback archive flash1
     modify retention 2 year;    # changes the archive retention time
```

The following two commands show how to add a tablespace to a flashback data archive and remove the tablespace when you want it:

```
SQL> alter flashback tablespace flash1
     add tablespace flash_tbs2;

SQL> alter flashback tablespace flash1
     remove tablespace flash_tbs2;
```

■ **Tip** All tables in a particular flashback data archive are subject to the same retention time.

Although the data in a flashback data archive is automatically purged upon the expiry of the retention time period, you can always remove unwanted data from a flashback data archive. If you want to empty the flashback data archive, you can do so by specifying the `purge all` clause. You can alternatively use the `before timestamp` or `before scn` clause to selectively purge data from the flashback data archive. Here are some examples showing how to purge data from a flashback data archive:

```
SQL> alter flashback archive flash1
     purge all;                          # purges all archived data

SQL> alter flashback archive flash1
     purge before
     timestamp (systimestamp - interval '2' day);

                                         # purges data older than 2 days

SQL> alter flashback archive flash1
     purge before scn 123456;            # purges all data before the
                                           specified scn
```

It's important to remember that the database will automatically purge the archived data a day after the retention period expires.

Enabling and Disabling Flashback Data Archiving

Once you create a flashback area, you must *enable* flashback logging for those tables whose transactional changes you want to archive. You can't turn flashback archiving on at the database or tablespace level. You must explicitly turn flashback archiving on for each table whose changes you want to track. To enable flashback data archive logging, you must have the flashback archive object privilege on the flashback archive you want to use as well as the create tablespace system privilege. Of course, the DBA role automatically contains these privileges.

By default, flashback logging is turned off for every table in the database. After you create one or more flashback data archives in your database, any table you create with the flashback data archive clause or any table you alter with the flashback data archive clause will have flashback logging enabled automatically.

To enable flashback logging for a table from its inception, modify your create table statement to include the flashback archive clause, as shown here:

```
SQL> create table test11 (
  2 name varchar2(30),
  3 address varchar2(50))
  4*flashback archive fla4;


Table created.
SQL>
```

If you've designated a certain flashback data archive as the default flashback data archive for the database, you can omit the name of the flashback data archive (fla4 in this example) and instead simply use the clause flashback archive. If you don't specify a flashback data archive by name, the database will use the default flashback data archive for all create table and alter table statements that specify a flashback archive clause.

One of the wonderful features of the flashback data archive capability is that you can enable archiving for already existing tables. This saves you the bother of having to re-create existing tables in order to take advantage of the flashback data archive feature. Use the flashback archive clause to enable flashback archiving for an existing table, as shown here:

```
SQL> alter table employees
     flashback archive;
```

Since we didn't specify a specific flashback data archive, the database will archive the data from the employees table to the default flashback data archive. The following query shows this:

```
SQL> select * from dba_flashback_archive_tables;
```

TABLE_NAME	OWNER	FLASHBACK_ARCH_NAME	ARCH_TABLE_NAM
EMPLOYEES	HR	FLASH1	SYS_FBA_HIST_70313

In this example, employees is the name of the table whose changes you want the database to track. The history table for recording the changes is given a system-generated name, SYS_FBA_HIST_70313 in this case, and its owner is the user HR, who is also the owner of the original table that's being tracked. You can't directly update the history table, but you can use the as of SQL construct to query the historical data.

You must set your default flashback data archive (using the set default clause, as shown earlier) before you can use a flashback data archive. The following query shows you've set a default flashback data archive:

```
SQL> select flashback_archive_name,status from
     dba_flashback_archive;
```

FLASHBACK_ARCHIVE_NAME	STATUS
FLASH1	DEFAULT

If you want to explicitly specify storing the table changes in a specific flashback data archive, you can do so in the following manner:

```
SQL> alter table employees
     flashback archive flash1;
```

You can turn off the flashback logging to the flashback data archive for a specific table anytime by executing the following command:

```
SQL> alter table employees
     no flashback archive;
```

If you've enabled flashback logging for any other tables, the changes made to those tables will continue to be stored in the flashback data archive.

Flashback Data Archive Limitations

There are certain limitations on using the flashback archive. For any flashback-enabled table, you can't use the drop column DDL command (you can, however, use the add column command). The only way to drop a column belonging to a table that's flashback data archive enabled is to turn flashback archiving off first. Unfortunately, this has the severe side effect of erasing all flashback archive data from the flashback data archive!

Monitoring Flashback Data Archives

There are some new views associated with the flashback data archive feature, which we summarize here:

- DBA_FLASHBACK_ARCHIVE_TABLES lets you view which tables have flashback data archiving enabled. Here's an example:

```
SQL> select * from dba_flashback_archive_tables;

TABLE_NAME   OWNER   FLASHBACK_ARCHIVE    ARCHIVE_TABLE_NAME
---------    -------  ------------------   --------------------
EMPLOYEES    HR      FLASH1               SYS_FBA_HIST_70313
```

- DBA_FLASHBACK_ARCHIVE lets you see all the flashback data archives in the database:

```
SQL>  select flashback_archive_name,retention_in_days
      from dba_flashback_archive;

         FLASHBACK_ARCHIVE_NAME     RETENTION_IN_DAYS
         ----------------------     -----------------
             FLASH1                        365
```

- DBA_FLASHBACK_ARCHIVE_TS provides information about the tablespaces used for flashback data archives:

```
SQL> select flashback_archive_name, tablespace_name, quota_in_mb
     from dba_flashback_archive_ts;

FLASHBACK_ARCHIVE _NAME      TABLESPACE_NAME   QUOTA_IN_MB
----------------------       ---------------   -----------
FLASH1                       FLASH1            80
```

Using Flashback Data Archives: Examples

You can use flashback data archives for a wide range of tasks, including accessing historical data, auditing, and recovering data. In the following sections, we provide brief examples that demonstrate the versatility of the flashback data archive feature. Make sure you create one or more flashback data archives first. You must also use the alter table command to enable the flashback data archive feature for a table, if you didn't specify archiving when you created the table.

Accessing Older Data

You can retrieve data from a specified point in time by specifying the as of clause, as shown by the following query:

```
SQL> select patient_number, doctor_name, count
     from patient_info as of
     timestamp to_timestamp ('2007-01-01 00:00:00',
     'YYYY-MM-DD HH23:MI:SS');
```

The as_of formulation is especially useful for pinpointing the state of the pertinent data at a specific point in time in the past. Look at the following example, which helps you correct erroneously entered table data when you aren't sure about the exact point in time. First check the current salary information for an employee from the hr.employees table:

```
SQL> select salary from hr.employees where
     last_name='Zlotkey';

     SALARY
------------
     10500
SQL>
```

Now, user *hr* wrongly updates the salary column for employee Zlotkey, giving the employee a raise of 50,000 instead of 5,000, and then commits the update:

```
SQL> update hr.employees set salary=salary+50000
     where last_name='Zlotkey';

1 row updated.

SQL> commit;

Commit complete.

SQL>
```

To set matters right, you must update employee Zlotkey's salary to its value before the erroneous update made by user *hr*. Just make sure you specify a time that falls before the erroneous update. If you know that the update was made about an hour ago (but not quite an hour), you can revert the salary column's value to what it was an hour ago by running the following SQL:

```
SQL> update hr.employees set salary =
     (select salary from hr.employees
     as of timestamp (systimestamp - interval '60' minute);
     where last_name='Zlotkey')
     where last_name='Zlotkey';

1 row updated.

SQL> commit;
Commit complete.

SQL>
```

The previous update statement uses the flashback data archive to update the salary information for Zlotkey. In this example, we use the expression systimestamp - interval '60' minute to specify that the database needs to retrieve the necessary values that prevailed an hour ago. You can also use values such as the following:

```
systimestamp - interval '60' second
systimestamp - interval '7' day
systimestamp - interval '12' month
```

Generating Reports

You can use the historical data in a flashback data archive to create reports that range over a long period of time. Here's an example that uses the versions_between clause to retrieve data between two time periods:

```
SQL> select * from patient_info
     versions between timestamp
     to_timestamp ('2007-01-01 00:00:00', 'YYYY-MM-DD HH23:MI:SS')
     and maxvalue
     where name ='ALAPATI';
```

The preceding query generates a report of all changes made to the patient_info table for the name ALAPATI from January 1, 2007, until the present time.

Information Lifecycle Management

Information lifecycle management (ILM) applications often require that you be able to retrieve a specific version of a row in a table. In the absence of a flashback data archive, you have the onerous burden of managing and storing multiple versions for each row in a table. Flashback data archiving works as a boon for ILM applications. Simply use the versions between clause to retrieve all available versions of a table row that fall between two specified time periods. The following example shows how to do this:

```
SQL> select * from patient_info
     versions between timestamp
     to_timestamp ('2007-01-01 00:00:00', 'YYYY-MM-DD HH24:MI:SS')
     and
     to_timestamp ('2007-06-01 00:00:00', 'YYYY-MM-DD HH24:MI:SS')
     where name='ALAPATI';
```

The preceding SQL statement will fetch all versions of the requested row that fall in the six-month time period specified by the version between clause.

Flashback Transaction Backout

In Oracle Database 10g, Oracle introduced the twin flashback features flashback version query and flashback transaction query to allow you to undo erroneous changes to data following logical corruptions in the database. Following a suspected data error, you'd first employ the flashback version query to identify the versions of the rows in a table that pertain to the erroneous transaction. Once you identify the culprit transaction(s), you'd then use the flashback transaction query to audit all the changes made by that transaction. Using the SQL code provided by the UNDO_SQL column of the flashback transaction query, you'd then undo the changes made by the erroneous transaction. Thus, the flashback transaction query offered a powerful means to undo logical corruption in your database.

In Oracle Database 11g, you can use the new flashback transaction backout feature to perform the tasks you had to perform by using both the flashback version query and the flashback transaction query together. Often, a data failure could cause other dependent transactions to be executed, using the corrupted data. *Flashback* transaction backout is a new *logical recovery feature* that lets you return a target transaction as well its dependent transactions to their original state. The flashback transaction backout feature identifies and fixes the initial transaction as well as the dependent transactions, thus completely undoing the effects of a logical data corruption. Undoing an entire set of inserts, updates, and deletes in one fell swoop ensures that the transaction atomicity and consistency principles are maintained. You can thus perform a logical recovery of the database while the database is online by executing a single backout command (a single execution of the `transaction_backout` procedure). If you're using Database Control, you can back out a transaction with a single click. A dependent transaction can have the one of the following types of relationships to the target transaction:

- A write-after-write (WAW) relationship where a dependent transaction modifies the same data that was modified by the target transaction

- A primary key constraint relationship, where a dependent transaction inserts the same primary key that was deleted by the target transaction

The database undoes the transaction changes by executing what are called *compensating transactions*, which revert the data affected by the unwanted transactions to their original states. Flashback transaction relies on undo data (and the redo generated for the undo blocks) to create the compensating transactions. Thus, you must have both the necessary undo data and the archived redo logs to undo a set of unwanted transactions.

Prerequisites for Flashback Transaction Backout

You must first enable *supplemental logging* in the database and then grant certain special privileges to users who want to use the flashback transaction backout feature. To enable supplemental logging in your database, use the following commands:

```
SQL> alter database add supplemental log data;
SQL> alter database add supplemental log data (primary key) columns;
```

In addition to turning supplemental logging on, grant the following privileges to the users who need to use the flashback transaction backout feature:

```
SQL> grant execute on dbms_flashback to hr;
SQL> grant select any transaction to hr;;
```

A user must have the `flashback` privilege, which you can grant by granting the `execute` privilege on the `DBMS_FLASHBACK` table. In addition, the user needs the `select any transaction` privilege.

If users want to back out transactions in their own schema, no additional privileges are necessary. If a user wants to back out transactions in another schema, however, you must also grant DML privileges to that user on all tables that'll be affected by the transaction backout operation.

Using the TRANSACTION_BACKOUT Procedure

The idea of a *compensating transaction* is crucial to the transaction backout feature. A compensating transaction backs out one or more transactions by using undo data. Use the DBMS_FLASHBACK package's transaction_backout procedure to back out unwanted transactions easily. Here's the structure of the transaction_backout procedure:

```
PROCEDURE TRANSACTION_BACKOUT
   Argument Name            Type              In/Out    Default?
   -------------------      ----------------  -------   ---------
   NUMTXNS                  NUMBER            IN
   NAMES                    TXNAME_ARRAY      IN
   OPTIONS                  BINARY_INTEGER    IN        DEFAULT
   TIMEHINT                 TIMESTAMP         IN
```

There are four parameters in the transaction_backout procedure:

- Numtxns: This is the number of transactions to be backed out.

- Names: This is the list of transactions to be backed out (by name).

- Timehint: If you identify transactions by name, you can provide a time hint, such as a time that's before the start of any transactions.

- Options: This specifies the order in which specified transactions and their dependent transactions are backed out.

The transaction_backout procedure merely analyzes the dependencies among the transactions, performs the DML operations, and provides a report. The procedure doesn't automatically commit these DML operations, however. All the procedure does is keep other transactional dependencies from affecting the backout operation by holding necessary locks on the affected table rows as well as on the tables themselves. You must explicitly issue a commit statement for the backout to become permanent.

The database will automatically provide a transaction name for the backout operation, but explicit naming of the operation by you facilitates auditing later. If your execution of the transaction_backout procedure completes successfully, it means the single transaction has been backed out and there are no dependent transactions. How long a backout operation takes will depend on the amount of redo generated by the transaction that's being backed out—the larger the amount of redo logs, the longer it takes to complete the transaction backout operation.

You can run the transaction_backout procedure with four options, as explained here:

- cascade: Backs out all transactions, including the dependent transactions, which are backed out first, before backing out their parent (target) transactions.

- nocascade: Expects the specified transaction not to have any dependents. This is the *default* value.

- nocascade_force: Backs out only the target transaction, ignoring dependent transactions.

- nonconflict_only: Backs out only those rows in the target transaction that don't conflict.

Note that the default value of nocascade expects that the transaction pending a backout has no dependent transactions.

TRANSACTION_BACKOUT Reports

You can examine the DBA_FLASHBACK_TRANSACTION_STATE and DBA_FLASHBACK_TRANSACTION_REPORT views for details about the transaction backout operation. The transaction_backout procedure populates both of these views. If a transaction appears in the DBA_FLASHBACK_TRANSACTION_STATE view, it means the transaction has been successfully backed out of the database. For each backed-out transaction, the DBA_FLASHBACK_TRANSACTION_REPORT view provides a detailed report.

You can also use Database Control to perform a transaction backout operation if you don't want to use the DBMS_FLASHBACK package directly.

Database Administration New Features

Oracle Database 11g adds several important weapons to the toolkit of DBAs to facilitate the day-to-day management of the database as well as providing additional object management capabilities. In the following sections, we discuss the most important of these enhancements.

Virtual Columns

Sometimes you might want to store data in a column based on the evaluation of an expression. Oracle Database 11g provides a new type of column you can include in a table, called a *virtual column*. Virtual columns are similar to normal table columns, with two major differences:

- You can't write to a virtual column.

- A virtual column is populated by the evaluation of an expression.

You can derive the virtual column from evaluating an expression on columns from the same table, from constants, or as the result of evaluating a SQL or PL/SQL function. You'll see the values under a virtual column only when you query that column, but the values aren't permanently stored on disk, as is the case for normal columns. The values in a virtual column are calculated only when it's queried by dynamically computing a function or a column expression.

You can do the following things with a virtual column:

- Use them in both DDL and DML statements.

- Collect statistics on them.

- Define indexes on them. The indexes you define are similar to function-based indexes you create on normal columns. Behind the scenes, Oracle creates a function-based index on the virtual column when you create an index on that column.

Creating a Table with a Virtual Column

To create a virtual column, you must use the clause generated always as after the virtual column name when you create a table. Here's an example showing how to incorporate a virtual column in a table:

```
SQL>  create table emp (
  2    empno      NUMBER(5) PRIMARY KEY,
  3    ename      VARCHAR2(15) NOT NULL,
  4    ssn        NUMBER(9),
  5    sal        NUMBER(7,2),
  6*   hrly_rate  NUMBER(7,2) generated always as (sal/2080));

Table created.
SQL>
```

Line 6 in the previous example creates the virtual column hrly_rate. If you want, you can also use the keyword virtual after this line to make it syntactically complete, but the keyword is purely optional. The following example shows how to use the optional keyword virtual as part of a table creation statement that also creates a check constraint on the virtual column:

```
SQL>  create table emp3
  2    (sal number (7,2),
  3    hrly_rate number (7,2) generated always as (sal/2080)
  4    virtual
  5*   constraint HourlyRate CHECK (hrly_rate > 8.00));

Table created.
SQL>
```

The column hrly_rate is a virtual column since the column values are generated by evaluating the expression sal/2080 for each row in the table emp. The generated always as clause means the values of the virtual column are created on the fly in response to a query on the virtual column. The values for the hrly_rate column for each employee are derived by dividing the employee's annual salary by the total number of hours the employee worked during that year. The column expression can refer to a user-created function. A virtual column can use any scalar datatype or the XML type.

You can modify a table containing a virtual column just as you would a table with only normal columns by using the alter table statement.

Adding a Virtual Column to a Table

You can add a virtual column to an existing table just as you would a normal column. In the following example, we show how to add a new virtual column named income, which is derived by computing the product of the salary and commission_pct columns for each row:

```
SQL> alter table employees add (income as (salary*commission_pct));
Table altered.
SQL>
```

Note that in this `alter table` statement we haven't specified a datatype for the new virtual column named income. Oracle will automatically assign a datatype for the column, based on the data type of the two columns, `salary` and `commission_pct`, that are part of the column expression that defines the virtual column.

When you create a new virtual column, the values for that column are automatically computed based on the column expression. If you query the `employees` table now, you'll see values in the new virtual column `income`, as shown in the following example:

```
SQL> select salary, commission_pct, income
     from employees1;

     SALARY    COMMISSION_PCT   INCOME
----------    --------------   -------
       7000              .15      8050
      10000              .35     13500
       9500              .35     12825
       7200              .10      7920
       6800              .10      7480
SQL>
```

Although you can see the virtual column values when you query the table, the data isn't stored on disk but is calculated from the virtual column expression each time you query it.

Virtual Columns Limitations

The following are restrictions on virtual columns:

- You can create virtual columns only on ordinary (heap-organized) tables. You can't create virtual columns on an index-organized table, an external table, a temporary table, an object, or a cluster.

- You can't create a virtual column as a user-defined type, LOB, or RAW.

- All columns in the column expression must belong to the same table.

- The column expression must result in a scalar value.

- The column expression in the `generated always as` clause can't refer to another virtual column.

- You can't update a virtual column by using it in the `set` clause of an `update` statement.

- You can't perform a `delete` or an `insert` operation on a virtual column.

■**Note** You can now encrypt an entire tablespace. Chapter 5, which deals with new security-related features, discusses the new transparent tablespace feature.

New Data Partitioning Schemes

In Oracle Database 11g, there are several new partitioning techniques to facilitate storing large amounts of data as well as increasing the performance of queries based on the partitioned tables. We list the four new partitioning schemes here. You'll find a more detailed discussion of the new partitioning schemes in Chapter 12, which discusses new data warehousing features in Oracle Database 11g.

- *Reference partitioning* enables you to logically equipartition tables with parent-child relationships by inheriting the partitioning key from the parent table.

- *Interval partitioning* lets you automate the creation of range partitions by creating partitions on demand.

- *System partitioning* enables application controlled partitioning.

- *New composite partitioning schemes* let you perform logical range partitioning along two dimensions.

- *Virtual column partitioning* lets you use partitioning key columns defined on a table's virtual columns (discussed earlier in this chapter), thus overcoming limitations where the partitioning needs aren't being served by the currently defined table columns.

Allowing DDL Locks to Wait for DML Locks

In previous releases, by default, any DDL locks wouldn't wait for a DML lock but would fail right away if they couldn't obtain the DDL lock. In Oracle Database 11g, you can use the new initialization parameter `ddl_lock_timeout` to specify the duration for which a DDL statement will wait for a DML lock.

The default value of the `ddl_lock_timeout` parameter is zero, meaning that DDL statements won't wait for a DML lock. The maximum value of 1,000,000 seconds means you can potentially set the wait duration for as long as 11.5 days. You can use the `alter session` statement to specify the duration of wait for a DML lock, as shown here:

```
SQL> alter session set ddl_lock_timeout = 30;

Session altered.

SQL>
```

Explicit Locking of Tables

If you want to add a column to a table, Oracle requires that an exclusive lock be requested when you issue the DDL command to add the column. If Oracle fails to obtain an immediate DDL lock on the table in question, the DDL command will fail right away. Oracle Database 11g lets you allow a DDL command to wait for a specified length of time before it fails because of its inability to acquire the necessary DML lock on the table.

Oracle now allows new syntax with the `lock table` command that lets you specify the maximum time a statement should wait to obtain a DML lock on a table. This feature is handy for operations such as adding a column to a table that users are frequently updating. The new syntax of the `lock table` command is as follows:

```
LOCK TABLE ... IN lockmode MODE [NOWAIT | WAIT integer]
```

Here's what the mode parameters nowait and wait mean:

- If you want the database to return control to you immediately upon finding that a necessary table is already locked by other users, specify the nowait option.

- You can use the wait parameter to specify the number of seconds the lock table statement can wait in order to acquire a DML lock. You can set the value of this parameter to any integer value you want—there's no limit.

- If you don't specify either wait or nowait, the database will wait until the locked table is available and then lock it before returning control to you.

Invisible Indexes

Suppose you have a situation where you have to create a huge index for some special queries but don't want the optimizer to change its query plans based on this index. Furthermore, the situation may call for dropping and re-creating the index often, which leads to problems because the index building takes considerable time. In Oracle Database 11g, you can create an index as an *invisible index,* which really means the index won't be visible to the cost optimizer when it's figuring out the execution plans.

You can use the invisible index only by specifying the index hint in your SQL statements. In sum, this means you can make selective use of an index, choosing to employ the index only when you want it, not when the optimizer thinks it's necessary. As far as the optimizer is concerned, the index simply doesn't exist, unless *you* reveal its existence!

The following situations make the invisible index a handy feature:

- You want to test the usefulness of a new index but don't want to change the optimizer's execution plans before you are sure about the usefulness of the new index. You can now make the index invisible and have the optimizer generate execution plans without that index. If the performance is the same or better, you may decide to drop that index for good. If, on the other hand, the performance is better with the index, you want to make that index visible, that is, change it back to a normal index or change its status to visible, as we show later.

- You want to use an index for a temporary purpose, such as during an application upgrade, but don't want the index to be considered by the optimizer subsequently.

Although an invisible index is unknown to the cost optimizer unless you cause the index to be considered by using the index hint, the index continues to be maintained just as any other normal index. This means when you add new data to the table or modify existing data, the invisible index will be updated accordingly by the database.

Creating an Invisible Index

By default, all indexes are visible to the optimizer. The new visible|invisible clause of the create index statement lets you designate the visibility of an index. If you don't use this clause, Oracle creates the index as a normal index. You can create an invisible index by simply appending the keyword invisible at the end of the normal create index statement, as shown here:

```
SQL> create index name_idx1 on test_tbl1(name) invisible;
Index created.
SQL>
```

You can also specify a tablespace while creating the invisible index, as the following example shows:

```
SQL> create index name_idx2 on test_tbl2(name) invisible
    tablespace example;
Index created.
SQL>
```

The index name_idx2 is stored in the tablespace example, just as any other normal visible index. The database will update this index as necessary following all DML operations.

Making an Existing Index Invisible

Besides the ability to create a new index as invisible from its inception, you can also change the status of an existing index from a normal index into an invisible index. This gives you the ability to toggle the status of an index, sometimes making it available to the optimizer and at times invisible to the optimizer. Here's the command to make an existing index invisible:

```
SQL> alter index name_idx1 invisible;
Index altered.
SQL>
```

Once you make an existing index invisible as shown here, the optimizer won't be able to "see" the index any longer when it's figuring out the most efficient or optimal execution plan. You can use the alter index ... visible statement to make the invisible index visible to the optimizer, as shown here:

```
SQL> alter index name_idx1 visible;
Index altered.
SQL>
```

Thus, once you create an invisible index, you can toggle its status between visible and invisible as you want.

As in the case of the normal indexes, you can't create two indexes on the same column, even if one of them is an invisible index. If you try to create an invisible index on an already indexed column, you'll get this error:

```
SQL> create index name_idx2 on test1(name) invisible;
                              *
ERROR at line 1:
ORA-01408: such column list already indexed
SQL>
```

As the preceding example hints, the care and feeding of an invisible index isn't really different from that of regular indexes.

How the Optimizer Treats the Invisible Index

When you execute a SQL query that involves an invisible index, the cost optimizer will disregard the index. You can make an invisible index visible to the cost optimizer in two ways. If you want the optimizer to take into account all invisible indexes in the databases, you can do so by setting the new initialization parameter `optimizer_use_invisible_indexes` to `true`. When you do this, the optimizer will treat all invisible indexes as normal indexes. The default value of this parameter is set to `false`, meaning that the use of invisible indexes is disabled by default. The database maintains the invisible indexes as any other normal index, but the optimizer will ignore them by default. You can enable the use of invisible indexes at the session or the system level, as shown here:

```
SQL> alter session set optimizer_use_invisible_indexes=true;
SQL> alter system set optimizer_use_invisible_indexes=true;
```

Setting the initialization parameter `optimizer_use_invisible_indexes` to `true` (the default is `false`, meaning the invisible indexes are indeed invisible) makes all invisible indexes visible to the optimizer. If you want the optimizer to take only a specific invisible index into account rather than all the invisible indexes in the database, you can do that as well by using the *index hint* in a query. When the optimizer "sees" the index hint embedded in the `select` statement, it takes that index into account when figuring out an optimal execution plan for a query. If you remove the index hint from the query, the index remains invisible to the optimizer.

Let's first look at the explain plan output for the following `select` statement without the index hint:

```
SQL> set autotrace on

SQL> select edba_document_id
     from edba_documents where edba_document_id=1280;
```

Here's the explain plan output without the index hint:

```
  SQL> select edba_document_id
       from edba_documents
       where edba_document_id=1280;
Elapsed: 00:00:00.00

Execution Plan
----------------------------------------------------------------------------
Plan hash value: 2995896303


----------------------------------------------------------------------------
| Id  | Operation          | Name          | Rows  | Bytes | Cost (%CPU)| Time     |
----------------------------------------------------------------------------
|   0 | SELECT STATEMENT   |               |     1 |     3 |     7   (0)| 00:00:01 |
|*  1 |   TABLE ACCESS FULL| EDBA_DOCUMENTS |     1 |     3 |     7   (0)| 00:00:01 |
----------------------------------------------------------------------------
```

```
Predicate Information (identified by operation id):
--------------------------------------------------

    1 - filter("EDBA_DOCUMENT_ID"=1280)
```

You can clearly see that the optimizer does not pick up the index hint and opts to perform a full table scan. If you want the optimizer to take the invisible index into account, you must use the index hint, as shown in the following example:

```
  1  select /*+ index (edba_documents EDBA_DOCUMENTS_I10) */
  2  edba_document_id
  3  from edba_documents
  4* where edba_document_id=1280
19:07:35 SQL> /
Elapsed: 00:00:00.00

Execution Plan
---------------------------------------------------------------------------------
--
Plan hash value: 2328900544


---------------------------------------------------------------------------------
--
| Id  | Operation        | Name              | Rows  | Bytes | Cost (%CPU)| Time
|
|   0 | SELECT STATEMENT |                   |     1 |     3 |     1   (0)|
00:00:01 |
|*  1 |   INDEX RANGE SCAN| EDBA_DOCUMENTS_I10 |     1 |     3 |     1   (0)|
00:00:01 |
---------------------------------------------------------------------------------
--
Predicate Information (identified by operation id):
---------------------------------------------------------------------------------
--

    1 - access("EDBA_DOCUMENT_ID"=1280)
```

The explain plan for the select statement with the index hint reveals that the optimizer performs an index range scan instead of a full table scan, owing to it taking the invisible index into account.

Checking the Visibility Status of an Index

Oracle Database 11g has added a new column named visibility to the DBA_INDEXES table to enable the checking of an index's visibility status. Use the following command to check the visibility status of an index:

```
SQL> select index_name, visibility from dba_indexes
    where index_name like '%NAME_IDX%';

INDEX_NAME        VISIBILITY
------------      -----------
NAME_IDX2         INVISIBLE
NAME_IDX1         INVISIBLE
SQL>
```

By default, all indexes are visible, unless you explicitly create them as invisible indexes.

Read-Only Tables

In earlier releases of the Oracle database, you could have read-only tablespaces but not read-only tables. One of the more useful but simple to implement new features in Oracle Database 11*g* is the *read-only* table feature. Simply specify the clause read only in the alter table statement as shown in the following example, where we first create a normal read-write table and then convert that into a read-only table:

```
SQL> create table  test1 (name varchar2(30));
Table created.

SQL> alter table test1 read only;

Table altered.
SQL>
```

The new column READ_ONLY in the DBA_TABLES view shows whether a column has read-only status. You can return a read-only table to a read-write status by using the read write clause in the alter table statement, as shown in the following example:

```
SQL> alter table test1 read write;

Table altered.
SQL>
```

Once you put a table in a read-only mode, you can't issue any DML statements such as update, insert, or delete. You also can't issue a select for update statement involving a read-only table. You can issue DDL statements such as drop table and alter table on a read-only table, however. You can use the read-only feature to prevent changes to a table's data during maintenance operations. You can perform maintenance operations on any of the indexes that you have defined on the read-only table, prior to changing their status to read-only. You can, of course, use this feature for security reasons, where you want to grant users the ability to read but not modify table data.

Temporary Tablespace Management

There are several improvements in the management of temporary tablespaces in Oracle Database 11*g*. Chief among these are the new capabilities to shrink temporary tablespaces and tempfiles and to specify a temporary tablespace during the creation of temporary tables. We'll cover both of the temporary tablespace innovations in more detail in the following sections.

Shrinking Temporary Tablespaces and Tempfiles

Often you'll find you need to reduce the space that you had allocated to the temporary tablespace. It's not uncommon to see huge tempfiles floating around on disk, even after a massive sort job has finished. You have increased the allocation temporarily for a large job and want to reclaim the space after the job is completed. In previous releases of the Oracle database, you just couldn't do this, because there was no way to reduce the size of the temporary tablespace. You could drop the large temporary tablespace and re-create it with a smaller size, but you have to ensure that the users aren't using the temporary tablespace for sorting operations during that time.

In Oracle Database 11*g*, you can *shrink* the temporary tablespace by specifying the new clause shrink space in an alter tablespace statement. You can also shrink tempfiles using the new command alter tablespace shrink tempfile, thus making the temporary tablespace smaller. Here are a couple of examples, the first one showing how to shrink a temporary tablespace and the second showing how to shrink a tempfile:

```
SQL> alter tablespace temp shrink space;
SQL> alter tablespace temp shrink
    tempfile '/u01/app/oracle/oradata/or11/temp01.dbf';
```

If you have multiple datafiles in the temporary tablespace, the shrink space clause will shrink all the tempfiles to a database-determined minimum size, which is about 1m. The minimum size the tablespaces are shrunk to take into account the tablespace storage requirements. If you want the temporary tablespace/tempfile to be at least a certain size, you can use the keep clause to specify a lower bound for the tablespace/tempfile, as shown in the example here, which shrinks the temporary tablespace named temp.

```
SQL> alter tablespace temp shrink space
    keep 100m;
```

In the keep clause in this example, 100m is the value for the size subclause. Let's look at the logic Oracle uses to shrink the temp tablespace. In the following example, there are two 1GB tempfiles. The command to shrink the temp tablespace to 1GB was issued immediately afterward.

```
SQL> alter database tempfile '+DATA/o11g/tempfile/temp.263.617809819'
    resize 1000m;
Database altered.

SQL> alter database tempfile '+DATA/o11g/tempfile/temp.290.618408247'
    resize 1000m;
Database altered.

SQL> alter tablespace temp shrink space keep 1000m;

Tablespace altered.
```

Now, query the V$TEMPFILE view to see the amount of space remaining in the temporary tablespace:

```
SQL> select file#, name, bytes/1024/1024 MB from v$tempfile;

FILE#   NAME                                     MB
------  -----------------------------------   --------
1       +DATA/o11g/tempfile/temp.263.617809819   999.9375
2       +DATA/o11g/tempfile/temp.290.618408247     1.0625
```

Instead of equally evenly shrinking the two tempfiles to 500MB each, Oracle shrinks one tempfile all the way down to 1MB and the other down by just 1MB, with the size of the tempfile going down to 999MB.

If you want to specify a particular tempfile when specifying a minimum space for it after shrinking, you can do so as well, as shown in the following example:

```
SQL> alter tablespace temp shrink space
     tempfile '/u01/app/oracle/oradata/prod1/temp02.dbf'
     keep 100m;
Tablespace altered.
SQL>
```

The previous statement will not shrink the entire temp tablespace—it shrinks the specified tempfile, but only down to the 100MB level you specified with the keep clause. All other temp-files that are part of the temp tablespace will remain unaffected.

The new view DBA_TEMP_FREE_SPACE shows you temporary space usage information, as shown here:

```
SQL> select * from dba_temp_free_space;

TABLESPACE_NAME   TABLESPACE_SIZE   ALLOCATED_SPACE   FREE_SPACE
---------------   ---------------   ---------------   ------------
   TEMP               41943040          41943040        40894464

SQL>
```

The information in the DBA_TEMP_FREE_SPACE view is derived from existing views.

Specifying Temporary Tablespace for Global Temporary Tables

Prior to Oracle Database 11g, when you created a global temporary table, you couldn't specify the tablespace for that table. The global temporary table would be created in your default temporary tablespace as a result. This meant the global temporary table would be forced to use the extent size of the default temporary tablespace, no matter what its sort usage size is.

In Oracle Database 11g, you can specify a temporary tablespace clause when you create a global temporary table. Here's the new command:

```
SQL> create global temporary table global_temp1 (c varchar2(20))
     on commit delete rows tablespace temp;
```

You can thus ensure that the database allocates the appropriate extent sizes to match your sort usage. This is especially handy when your database performs several types of temporary space usage with different sort resize requirements.

Creating an Initialization Parameter File from Memory

In previous Oracle releases, you used the `create pfile from spfile` statement to create a text initialization parameter (`init.ora`) file from the server parameter file. In Oracle Database 11*g*, you can create the text initialization parameter file using the current system-wide parameter settings by specifying the new option `memory` when creating the pfile. When you specify `memory` instead of `spfile`, the instance generates the initialization parameter values that are currently in force. You simply issue the following statement to create the `init.ora` file from the current system-wide parameter settings in use by the instance:

```
SQL> create pfile from memory;
File created.
SQL>
```

You can also use the `memory` clause to create an spfile, as shown here:

```
SQL> create spfile from memory;
File created.
SQL>
```

The ability to create the pfile or spfile entirely from memory is wonderful, since that provides a fallback option when you lose your initialization file or the server parameter file, or both, provided the instance is up. In the following example, an attempt to create a new `init.ora` file from the server parameter file fails, because the server parameter file is lost:

```
SQL> create pfile from spfile;
create pfile from spfile
*
ERROR at line 1:
ORA-01565: error in identifying file
'/u01/app/oracle/product/11.1/db_1/dbs/spfileauxdb.ora'
ORA-27037: unable to obtain file status
Linux Error: 2: No such file or directory
Additional information: 3
SQL>
```

In cases such as this, you simply use the `create pfile from memory` statement to re-create your `init.ora` file entirely from the instance memory. An interesting thing about the initialization parameter file you re-create this way is that the file will contain about 150 initialization parameters altogether, including many parameters you haven't explicitly set. Oracle will simply take both the default values of parameters you didn't set values for and the values for the explicitly set parameters and put them in the new initialization file. Here's an example:

```
# Oracle init.ora parameter file generated by instance orcl11 on 04/14/2007 14:11:30
_always_anti_join='CHOOSE'
...
skip_unusable_indexes=TRUE
user_dump_dest='/u01/app/oracle/diag/rdbms/auxdb/auxdb/trace'
```

You'll see all the parameters currently in force for the instance when you use the memory option to generate your parameter file.

Restore Point Enhancements

Oracle Database 10g introduced *restore points*, which are associated with the system change number (SCN) of the database when you create a restore point. Restore points serve as user-defined bookmarks to specific points in time when the database was in a good or normal state. Restore points are highly useful when you're flashing back a database, because they eliminate the need for determining the SCN or the timestamp for the point in time to which you want to flash back the database. You simply specify the restore point instead.

Oracle Database 11g introduces significant enhancements in the restore point syntax, allowing you to create restore points specific to a particular SCN or point in time, as well as the capability to preserve the restore points. In addition, you use them to implement archival backups.

Creating Restore Points "as of" an SCN or a Timestamp

In earlier releases, when you issued the create restore point command, the database created a restore point associated with the SCN at the time of the restore point creation. You can now create a restore point for a specific SCN in the past or a past point in time. You use the as of construct to create a restore point corresponding to a previous SCN or timestamp. Of course, the SCN you specify must be a valid SCN from a past time period.

Let's see how you can use the as of clause to create a restore point with an older SCN or timestamp. First, check the current SCN of the database:

```
SQL> select current_scn from v$database;

CURRENT_SCN
-----------
    2409686

SQL>
```

Next, create a restore point, restore1, as of the SCN 2400000, which is older than the current SCN of 2409686:

```
SQL> create restore point restore2 as of scn 2400000;

Restore point created.
SQL>
```

Instead of an SCN, you can use a timestamp with the `as of` clause to specify a past period of time, as shown here:

```
SQL> create  restore point restore3 as of timestamp
    to_date('08-01-2007');

Restore point created.

SQL>
```

Of course, the database must be able to go back to the time point you select with the `timestamp` clause.

Preserving Restore Points

Often you may create restore points to use with the flashback features. In such a case, you want to make sure the restore points aren't automatically deleted by the database, say because it has reached the maximum number of restore points, in which case it drops the oldest restore point in the database. In Oracle Database 11g, you can specify the `preserve` clause to indicate that the database can't automatically drop the restore point. Here's an example:

```
SQL> create restore point restore4 preserve;

Restore point created.

SQL>
```

You can check whether a restore point is preserved by querying the V$RESTORE_POINT view in the following way:

```
SQL> select name, preserved from V$RESTORE_POINT;

NAME              PRESERVED
---------         ---------
RESTORE4          YES
RESTORE1          NO
RESTORE2          NO
RESTORE3          NO

SQL>
```

Note that a *guaranteed restore point* is always preserved, unlike normal restore points. A preserved restore point isn't the same as a guaranteed restore point, which enables you to flash back a database to a restore point regardless of the setting for the `db_flashback retention_ target` parameter. A preserved restore point is simply a normal restore point that requires that you explicitly delete it.

Using Restore Points for Creating Archival Backups

In Oracle Database 11*g*, you can use restore points during the implementation of archival backups. We explain archival backups in Chapter 6.

Database Resident Connection Pooling

Traditionally, Oracle offered you two different types of server processes, which handle the requests of use processes. These are the dedicated server process, which handles one user process at a time, and the shared server process, which serves multiple user processes simultaneously through dispatchers. By default, an Oracle database always allows a dedicated server process, but the shared server process needs special configuration. Shared server processes offer an efficient way to scale up when faced with large numbers of user connections by eliminating the need to start a dedicated server for each user connection.

It's common for web-based client applications that have similar database credentials and that use identical schema to share or reuse sessions. Huge numbers of client connections also mean memory requirements become a problem if connections and scalability of the middle tier and database tiers are an issue. Web-based applications aren't always "active" throughout a session. Rather, they show bursts of activity, and they don't maintain state through the time they are connected to the database. You can use database connection pooling so a small number of database sessions can service a large number of end users, increasing both performance and scalability. However, technologies such as PHP can't take advantage of connection pooling via the application server, since they require a separate database connection for each web server process. Even if an application can use application-server-level connection pooling, it will still be stymied by a high number of database connections when dealing with large numbers of application servers.

In Oracle Database 11*g*, you can configure scarce resources even better in a large-user environment by using the new *database resident connection pooling* (DRCP) feature. DRCP employs a pool of dedicated servers for servicing larger numbers of connections and is capable of handling tens of thousands of simultaneous connections to the database while using very little memory when compared to both a dedicated server and a shared server approach. Applications that currently can't avail of application server connection pooling, as well as applications that run on large application server farms, can take advantage of this feature to increase scalability. DRCP is especially designed to help architectures that use multiprocess, single-threaded application servers (PHP with Apache, for example) that are incapable of middle-tier connection pooling. Using DRCP, these applications can now effortlessly scale to tens of thousands of simultaneous connections.

DRCP is similar to the traditional dedicated server connection model, which is the default method of connection to an Oracle database but doesn't need an exclusive dedicated server for each user connection throughout the lifetime of the connection. The server in DRCP works just like the dedicated server while the user connection is actually working with it, but is referred to as a *pooled server*. The pooled servers combine an Oracle server process and user session, just as a dedicated server does. The server is a pooled server rather than a dedicated server, because each connection acquires a server for a temporary period from a pool of servers. When the user connection is done using the database, it relinquishes the server connection back to the server pool. In a dedicated server connection method, on the other hand, the server connection is terminated only after the client connection is terminated. So, even if a client isn't actively using the dedicated server, the connection is maintained for the lifetime of the connection, wasting crucial memory resources in the bargain.

By enabling resource sharing among middle-tier client applications, you can now scale up to a large number of user connections with a much smaller resource usage.

How DRCP Works

When you use a dedicated server, the instance creates a new server process in response to a new client connection request, along with a new client session. Under DRCP, a connection broker assigns the new client connection to a pooled server, if one is already available. The client connection will release the pooled server back to the connection pool once its request is serviced by the database. In both the dedicated server and shared server methods, the client connection releases the memory and other resources back to the instance only after the termination of the session.

If the connection broker can't find an available free pooled server to assign to the new client connection, it will create a new pooled server. However, if the number of pooled servers is at the maximum level, the connection broker won't be able to create a new pooled server. The client connection will have to go into a wait queue until an existing pooled server is released back to the connection pool by the client connections that are using the available pooled servers. Both the dedicated server method and the DRCP method allocate memory from the program global area (PGA). However, the big advantage of using the DRCP method lies in the fact that the memory requirement is proportional to the number of active pooled servers in the connection pool, and not to the number of client connections, as is the case under the dedicated server approach. Here's an example that shows the tremendous gains you can achieve in memory usage by switching to DRCP from traditional dedicated server connections.

Let's say there are 10,000 client connections, with each client session requiring 200KB of memory and each server process requiring 5MB. Let's assume that the maximum number of pooled servers is 200. Here are the total requirements for a dedicated server approach and the new DRCP method:

```
Dedicated server
Total memory required = 10000 X (200KB + 5MB) = 520GB

Database Resident Connection Pooling
Total Memory Required = 200 X (200KB + 5MB) =  1.04 GB

Shared Server
1000 X 200KB + 200 X 5MB =  21GB
```

You can see that DRCP requires only a little more than 1GB of memory for the 10,000 users, whereas the dedicated server approach will require a mammoth 520GB of memory!

■**Note** You can't shut down the database after connecting through a pooled server. You also can't use encryption and certificates or connect to a connection pool on a different instance through a database link.

Enabling and Disabling DRCP

You don't have to create a database-resident connection pool, since the database already comes with the resident pool configured. The default connection pool has the name `SYS_DEFAULT_CONNECTION_POOL`. All you have to do to enable DRCP in a database is to simply *start* the database-resident connection pool. Use the new Oracle package `DBMS_CONNECTION_POOL` to do so, as shown here:

```
SQL> connect sys/sammyy1 as sysdba
SQL> exec dbms_connection_pool.start_pool();

PL/SQL procedure successfully completed.
SQL>
```

You can specify a single parameter with the `start_pool` procedure, `pool_name`, but currently only the default pool name, `SYS_DEFAULT_CONNECTION_POOL`, is supported. Check the status of the connection pool with the following query:

```
SQL> select connection_pool, status, maxsize from dba_cpool_info;

CONNECTION_POOL                STATUS      MAXSIZE
--------------------------     ---------   ---------
SYS_DEFAULT_CONNECTION_POOL    ACTIVE      40
SQL>
```

You use the `start_pool()` procedure only once to start the connection pool. The connection pool you start with the `start_pool()` function survives instance shutdowns. When you restart an instance, the connection pool will be automatically restarted as well, provided you have enabled the DRCP before the database shutdown. You can stop the connection pool and thus disable DRCP by using the `stop_pool` procedure, as shown here:

```
SQL> exec dbms_connection_pool.stop_pool();

PL/SQL procedure successfully completed.
SQL>
```

The `stop_pool()` procedure stops the connection pool and takes it offline. Note that when you restart the instance, the connection pool starts automatically. You don't have to use the `start_pool` procedure each time your restart the instance.

When you enable DRCP, clients connect to the new background process named connection monitor (CMON), which manages the server-side connection pool, instead of connecting to a dedicated server. A client that uses a common username will use a previously allocated session. When the applications disconnects from the database, it returns the dedicated server process to CMON, which puts the process back in the connection pool to serve other client requests.

Applications can invoke the DRCP connection method in two ways. They can specify `:POOLED` in the EZ Connect string, or if they are using tnsnames.ora, they can specify `SERVER=POOLED` in the TNS connect string. Here is an example showing how to leverage DRCP in a TNS connect string:

```
mydb = (DESCRIPTION=(ADDRESS=(PROTOCOL=tcp) (HOST=myhost.company.com)
      (SERVER=POOLED)))
```

If you're using an EZ Connect string instead, specify DRCP in the following way:

```
myhost.comany.com:1521/mydb.company.com:POOLED
```

■**Note** OCI applications linked with Oracle Database 11*g* client libraries would also work unaltered with older releases of the database server. If you deploy the applications with the DRCP connect string, they will work with an 11*g* server only if DRCP is enabled on that server.

Oracle has extended the OCISessionPool APIs so they work with DRCP. To maximize the gains from DRCP, Oracle recommends that these applications using the OCISessionPool APIs specify the *connection class* attribute (to set the logical name for the application) when obtaining a session using OCISessionGet(). In addition, they must set the *session purity* attribute to SELF. By doing this, the application is set up to reuse a pooled session. When you specify the connection class and session purity as suggested here, the session will be obtained from and released back to the DRCP. In addition, the connections to the connection broker are cached, thus improving performance.

Configuring DRCP

You can configure the connection pool based on your database's usage requirements. Here are the main DRCP configuration parameters:

- inactivity timeout: The maximum idle time allowable to a pooled server before it is terminated

- max_lifetime_per_session: Sets the time to live (TTL) duration for a pooled session

- max_uses_per_session: The maximum number of times a pooled server can be released to the connection pool

- max_size and min_size: The maximum and minimum number of pooled servers in the connection pool

- max_think_time: The maximum time a client can remain inactive after obtaining a pooled server from the connection pool

If you want to adjust the values of several or all the configuration parameters of the connection pool, you can do so by executing the configure_pool procedure of the DBMS_CONNECTION_POOL package. If you want to adjust the value of a single connection pool configuration parameter, you can execute the alter_param procedure of the DBMS_CONNECTION_POOL package, as shown here:

```
SQL> exec dbms_connection_pool.alter_param(' ','INACTIVITY_TIMEOUT','3600')
```

In the example here, the alter_param procedure specifies a value of 3600 seconds (1 hour) as the value for the inactivity_timeout parameter, meaning that a pooled server is allowed a maximum idle time of one hour before the server is terminated.

After making any configuration changes, you can always return to the original settings for the connection pool by executing the restore_defaults procedure, as shown here:

```
SQL> exec dbms_connection_pool.restore_defaults()
```

The `restore_defaults` procedure restores the default values for all connection pool configuration parameters.

Monitoring DRCP

You can use the following data dictionary views to monitor database resident connection pooling:

- `DB_CPOOL_INFO`: Shows the name of the connection pool, its status, the maximum and minimum number of connections, and the timeout for idle sessions

- `V$CPOOL_STAT`: Shows pools statistics such as the number of session requests and wait times for a session request

- `V$CPOOL_CC_STATS`: Shows details about the connection class-level statistics

Use DRCP to improve the scalability of your databases and applications and to share resources among multiple middle-tier client applications. If you want to support a large number of client connections with small memory requirements or if you have client applications that can share or reuse sessions, DRCP will be very useful for you. If you want to reduce memory usage, DRCP is the way to go. Also consider using DRCP if client applications use the database only intermittently and session affinity isn't a requirement across client requests.

Comparing and Converging Database Objects

It's typical for replication environments to share database objects such as tables and indexes. These objects are known as *shared database objects*, since multiple databases share them. Shared database objects are commonly used by materialized views and Oracle Streams components, which maintain copies of the same tables and other objects in multiple databases. Replication environments such as these strive to keep the common database objects synchronized at the multiple sites. However, it's not uncommon for shared database objects to become unsynchronized, with the result that a table will have a different number of rows and/or different data in the rows when compared to the same table in another database. These data divergences, caused by network problems, user errors, configuration changes, materialized view refresh problems, and so on, may result in a failure to capture data changes on a database or to successfully transfer them to all databases in the configuration.

Oracle Database 11g provides the new `DBMS_COMPARISON` package, which lets you compare database objects in different databases. If the comparison process shows there are important differences in data between two databases, you can use the same package to converge the data in both databases so the two databases are consistent datawise. You can compare and converge the following types of data:

- Tables

- Views on single tables

- Materialized views

- Synonyms for the previous three types of objects

In an example a little later, we compare two tables on different databases that have the same name and the same columns. However, you can compare two tables that have different names, as well as tables that have different columns, as long as the columns share the same data type. You can also compare (and converge) a subset of columns and rows instead of an entire table or a materialized view.

Comparing Data

In the following example, we compare a simple shared database object, which is a table in the user HR's schema. To ensure that we can show how to converge data, we first change the data in three rows of the shared database object (table departments) in the remote database. We then use the DBMS_COMPARE package to perform a comparison of the two tables on the two databases and then use the same package to merge the differences so the two tables are in sync once again.

The only requirement for using the DBMS_COMPARE package is that the two tables we're comparing have at least one column that the package can identify as an index column. This index column must uniquely identify each row that's part of the comparison, meaning the index has to be either a primary key constraint or a unique constraint on a non-null column. Otherwise, the package can't compare the two objects. The table rmp has a primary key column in both databases, so we're OK here.

1. Create a database link from the primary database (or11) to the secondary database (tenner). In the example, we use the user system as the owner of the database link to ensure that the user has the necessary privileges to execute the procedures in the DBMS_COMPARISON package and the privileges to access and modify tables in both databases. The remote database is named tenner and so is our database link to that database from the primary database or11.

```
SQL> create database link tenner
     connect to system identified by sammyy1
     using tenner.world;
Database link created.
SQL>
```

The next step is to create a divergence between the data in an identical table on the two databases.

2. On the secondary database, make some changes in the scott.emp table so the data diverges from the hr.emp table on the primary database:

```
SQL> delete from emp where ename='MILLER';
1 row deleted.
SQL> update emp set sal=10000 where ename='FORD';
1 row updated.
SQL> insert into emp values (9999,'ALAPATI','DBA',7792,'20-JUN-
     00',50000,10000,30);
1 row created.
SQL> commit;
Commit complete.
SQL>
```

Now that we made sure the emp table in the two databases diverges, it's time to run the create_comparison procedure to trap the data divergence between the two tables.

3. Create a comparison for the hr.emp table on the two databases by running the create_comparison procedure, as shown here:

```
SQL> begin
  2  dbms_comparison.create_comparison(
  3  comparison_name => 'compare1',
  4  schema_name     => 'scott',
  5  object_name     => 'emp',
  6  dblink_name     => 'tenner');
  7* end;
SQL> /

PL/SQL procedure successfully completed.
SQL>
```

4. Execute the compare function to see whether the create_comparison procedure has found any differences between the two tables.

```
SQL> declare
  2  consistent boolean;
  3  scan_info dbms_comparison.comparison_type;
  4  begin
  5  consistent := dbms_comparison.compare(
  6  comparison_name => 'comp1',
  7  scan_info => scan_info,
  8  perform_row_dif => TRUE);
  9  DBMS_OUTPUT.PUT_LINE('Scan ID: '||scan_info.scan_id);
 10  IF consistent=TRUE THEN
 11  DBMS_OUTPUT.PUT_LINE('No differences were found.');
 12  ELSE
 13  DBMS_OUTPUT.PUT_LINE('Differences were found.');
 14  end if;
 15* end;
SQL> /
Scan ID: 4
Differences were found.

PL/SQL procedure successfully completed.

SQL>
```

5. The compare function uses the scan ID 4 and prints the statement "Differences were found."

6. Since there are differences, you can run the following query, which uses the views DBA_COMPARISON and DBA_COMPARISON_SCAN_SUMMARY to tell us how many differences were found during the table comparison:

```
SQL>select c.owner,
  2 c.comparison_name,
  3 c.schema_name,
  4 c.object_name,
  5 s.current_diff_count
  6 from dba_comparison , dba_comparison_scan_summary s
  7 where c.comparison_name = s.comparison_name and
  8 c.owner = s.owner and
  9 s.scan_id  = 1;


OWNER     COMP_NAME    SCHEMA_NAME   OBJECT_NAME   CURRENT_DIF_COUNT
-------   ----------   -----------   -----------   -----------------
SYSTEM    COMP1        SCOTT         EMP           3



SQL>
```

The current_diff_count column from the DBA_COMPARISON_SCAN_SUMMARY view shows that there are three rows that are different between the emp table in the or11 database and the emp table in the tenner database. The differences could be because a row is present in one but not the other database, or the row is present in both databases but with different data in the row.

Converging Data

Since we've discovered a data divergence between the local and the remote databases, we may want to synchronize the emp table in the two databases so they have identical data. You do this by using the converge procedure of the DBMS_COMPARISON package, as shown here:

1. Connect to the remote database from the local database as the system owner, who happens to be the owner of the database link that we created earlier between the two databases:

```
$ sqlplus sytem/sammyy1@or11
SQL>
```

2. Execute the converge procedure of the DBMS_COMPARISON package to synchronize the data between the two databases:

```
SQL> declare
  2    scan_info     DBMS_COMPARISON.COMPARISON_TYPE;
  3  begin
  4    DBMS_COMPARISON.CONVERGE(
  5      comparison_name  => 'comp1',
  6      scan_id          => 4,
  7      scan_info        => scan_info,
  8      converge_options => DBMS_COMPARISON.CMP_CONVERGE_LOCAL_WINS);
  9    DBMS_OUTPUT.PUT_LINE('Local Rows Merged:
                            '||scan_info.loc_rows_merged);
```

```
10    DBMS_OUTPUT.PUT_LINE('Remote Rows Merged:
                       '||scan_info.rmt_rows_merged);
11    DBMS_OUTPUT.PUT_LINE('Local Rows Deleted:
                       '||scan_info.loc_rows_deleted);
12    DBMS_OUTPUT.PUT_LINE('Remote Rows Deleted:
                       '||scan_info.rmt_rows_deleted);
13* end;
SQL> /
Local Rows Merged: 0
Remote Rows Merged: 2
Local Rows Deleted: 0
Remote Rows Deleted: 1

PL/SQL procedure successfully completed.

SQL>
```

In this example, we chose to replace the data in the emp table at the remote database with the data from the emp table on the local database. To do this, we use cmp_converge_local_wins as the converge option, meaning that the data from the local database trumps that in the remote database. However, we could also have chosen to do the reverse by specifying cmp_converge_remote_wins instead, which would have required that the remote database table's data replace the local database table's data.

The converge procedure may modify or delete data from one of the databases to synchronize the data in both databases. The output that is printed after the converge procedure finished its execution shows that two rows in the remote database were merged, because they were different from the rows in the local database. Merging here means the local table's rows replace the rows in the remote table. One row shows up in the Remote Rows Deleted column. This was a row that was found in the remote database, but not in the local database. Since we chose to make the remote database data conform to the local database data, the converge procedure deletes that row from the remote database. Assuming there were no further changes made during the data synchronization process, the two tables in the local and remote databases are now completely synchronized.

Note that you can also compare and converge different types of database objects at two databases. For example, you can compare and converge a table on one database and a materialized view on the other.

SQL*Plus New Features

The SQL*Plus interface has several interesting 11g release innovations, including the new error logging feature and the incorporation of default SQL*Plus settings in the SQL*Plus executable itself instead of in the traditional glogin.sql file.

SQL*Plus Error Logging

When you're troubleshooting code errors, it's common to use the show errors command in SQL*Plus to identify the errors in a PL/SQL statement. Other than this, there was no way to check code errors, and the errors were not stored for later examination. In Oracle Database 11g, there's a new SQL*Plus command called set errorlogging, which stores all errors resulting from the execution of any SQL, PL/SQL, and even SQL*Plus commands in a special error logging table.

By default, the set errorlogging command causes any query errors to be written to the default table SPERRORLOG. You can specify your own table name for the error logging table, instead of using this default table name. For each error, the error logging feature logs the following bits of information:

- The username

- The time when the error occurred

- The name of the script that contains the query, if a script was used

- A user-defined identifier

- The ORA, PLS, or SP2 error message

- The query statement that caused the error

By default, error logging is turned off, as you can see from the following query:

```
SQL> show errorlogging
errorlogging is OFF
SQL>
```

You can turn error logging on with the set errorlogging command, as shown here:

```
SQL> set errorlogging on;
```

If you issue the show errorlogging command again to ensure that error logging has been successfully turned on, you'll see something interesting:

```
SQL> connect hr/hr
SQL> show errorlogging
errorlogging is ON TABLE HR.SPERRORLOG
SQL>
```

Not only does the database turn error logging on, but it also creates a new table called hr.sperrorlog to hold the error messages. The prefix to the error table is the same as the name of the schema owner who sets error logging on. In this case, we logged in as the user hr, so the error log is created in the hr schema.

The following example shows how to query the error logging table, sperrorlog, to retrieve the error messages and the SQL statements or PL/SQL code that generated those error messages:

```
SQL> select username,statement,message
     from sperrorlog;

USERNAME        STATEMENT                  MESSAGE
---------  --------------------------   ---------------------------
HR         create table  employees as   ORA-00955: name is already
           select * from employees      used by an existing object
```

```
HR         select names from employees       ORA-00904: "NAMES":
                                             invalid identifier
```

```
SQL>
```

The first message indicates that the table creation statement failed because there is already a table with an identical name. The second message shows that the error was because of the presence of an invalid column name in a `select` statement.

Default Settings in the SQL*Plus Executable

In previous versions of the Oracle database, a site profile script for SQL*Plus, called `glogin.sql`, was automatically created while installing the server. DBAs used this script to configure environmental variables for all users who logged into SQL*Plus. The `glogin.sql` script would run first whenever any user attempted a connection to SQL*Plus, followed by the user profile script, `login.sql`.

In Oracle Database 11g, the `glogin.sql` site profile file is still installed as usual and called by SQL*Plus, but it's blank now, as shown by the following output:

```
--
-- Copyright (c) 1988, 2005, Oracle.  All Rights Reserved.
--
-- NAME
--   glogin.sql
--
-- DESCRIPTION
--   SQL*Plus global login "site profile" file
--
--   Add any SQL*Plus commands here that are to be executed when a
--   user starts SQL*Plus, or uses the SQL*Plus CONNECT command.
--
-- USAGE
--   This script is automatically run
--
```

For the SQL*Plus Instant Client, you no longer need a `glogin.sql` file.

New SQL*Plus Connection Syntax

In Oracle Database 11g, the SQL*Plus `connect` command is enhanced, as shown here:

```
CONN[ECT] [{ logon | / } [AS {SYSOPER | SYSDBA | SYSASM}]]
```

Notice that the `as` clause now permits privileged connections to SQL*Plus from users who are given the new `sysasm` privilege. As Chapter 9 explains, in Oracle Database 11g, Oracle has consciously separated automatic storage management (ASM) administration from regular database administration.

Enhanced SQL*Plus BLOB Support

In Oracle Database 11g, you can query and print tables and objects that contain the BLOB and BFILE datatypes.

Online Application Maintenance

Often DBAs are often forced to perform object reorganization, also called *online application maintenance*, while the database is in use. Oracle's online table reorganization feature lets you modify a table's structure while users continue to use it online. Oracle lets you perform both in-place object reorganization where you modify database objects without making an intermediate copy of the objects and copy-based reorganization where you first make changes to intermediate objects. Online table and index reorganizations use the copy-based approach.

Oracle Database 11g offers better online redefinition capabilities that go a long way to reducing the headaches we all had to endure during most redefinition projects. The following sections summarize the new online redefinition capabilities.

Support for New Objects

Oracle Database 11g provides support for redefining more types of objects online.

- You can redefine tables with materialized views and view logs.

- You can also redefine tables consisting of triggers with the `follows` or `preceding` clause (see Chapter 11 for an explanation of these triggers). These two new trigger clauses establish an ordering dependency between multiple triggers on a table.

Enhanced Online Index Creation and Rebuild

It is usually much faster to rebuild an index online rather than to drop and re-create it. Even though Oracle has provided an online index creation and rebuilding feature for quite a while, the results of trying to rebuild an index online were unpredictable in a real-life production environment. Although Oracle claimed that the online create/rebuild process applied exclusive locks on the underlying table only during the beginning and ending of the index creation/rebuild process for "brief" periods of time, it was common to experience a considerable slowdown in the execution of DML statements by the rest of the users in the database.

In Oracle Database 11g, Oracle finally provides a real online index creation and rebuild feature by making it unnecessary to apply an exclusive lock (X) on the underlying tables. Instead, the database will use shared exclusive locks (SX) on the objects, thus enabling DML to continue uninterrupted while the DDL is executing. The changing of the locking strategy applies to the following types of statements, among others:

- `create index online`

- `rebuild index online`

- `create materialized view log`

None of the commands listed here requires exclusive locks in Oracle Database 11g.

Enhanced Default Column Value Functionality

When you add a new column to a table, that column initially has `null` values. You can add a column with a `not null` constraint only if the table has new rows or if you supply values for the new column by specifying the `default` clause. If you specify the `default` clause while adding the column, however, Oracle immediately issues an update for each row with the default value for the new column. During this row update, the database applies an exclusive lock on the table, thus limiting access to other users.

In Oracle Database 11*g*, when you add a column with a default value, Oracle doesn't immediately update the rows of the table. Let's use a simple example to drive home the value of this important new feature.

First, let's add a new column called BONUS to the `employees` table:

```
SQL>  alter table employees add
  2* (bonus number(7,2) not null);

alter table employees add
            *
ERROR at line 1:
ORA-01758: table must be empty to add mandatory (NOT NULL) column

SQL>
```

This first attempt failed since you can't add a column with a `not null` constraint to an already populated table—obviously, table `employees` isn't an empty table. You can, however, do this:

```
SQL> alter table employees add
     (bonus number(7,2) default 500 not null);

Table altered.

SQL>
```

Before the Oracle Database 11*g* release, the database would let you add the column without a problem, but there was a price to pay. Since the table isn't empty, Oracle applies an exclusive lock on the table to update all rows in the table with the default value for the new column you just added. If the table had a large number of rows, this meant that the database generated a huge amount of undo and redo logs, and in general, the performance of the database was affected. In Oracle Database 11*g*, any default values you specify for a column you specify as `not null` are stored in the *data dictionary* instead of the table. This, of course, means the addition of a new column is almost instantaneous, thus eliminating a major hurdle for DBAs in adding new columns to tables. All the addition of the new column involves is updating the data dictionary once, with a single value denoting the default value of the new column. This is true regardless of the size of the table. In addition, you have the big advantage of not using any space for adding the default values for the new column!

Online Reorganization of Materialized Views

Until now, if a table contained materialized views, that table was ineligible for an online table reorganization, unless you were prepared to drop and re-create dependent materialized views and materialized view logs for those tables. In Oracle Database 11g, you can perform an online reorganization of tables with materialized views and materialized view logs. You simply clone the materialized view logs on the interim table, with the procedure DBMS_REDEFINITION.COPY_TABLE_DEPENDENTS, just as you would other objects dependent on the table being reorganized, such as triggers and indexes.

After redefining a table with a materialized view log, you must make sure you completely refresh the materialized views at the end of the table reorganization, since the ROWID logs are invalidated during the table reorganization.

Minimal Invalidation of Dependent Objects

In previous versions of the Oracle database, during an online redefinition, the database automatically invalidated all dependent views and PL/SQL packages. In Oracle Database 11g, all dependent objects aren't automatically invalidated any longer. The database marks as invalid only those dependent views, synonyms, and other objects that are logically affected. If an object that's referenced has identical column names and types following the online redefinition, its status continues to remain valid. Previously, for example, if you dropped a column from a table that you were redefining online, all procedures and views that depended on the table were invalidated, even when it was not logically required. Under the new concept of a *fine-grained dependency management*, object dependencies are tracked only at the level of an element within each unit. Now, Oracle invalidates only the subset of procedures and views that actually use the dropped column. Note that the new object-invalidating behavior doesn't affect triggers, because all triggers on a table that's being redefined online are invalidated as before.

Oracle Database 11g uses more precise dependency metadata than in previous releases, called *fine-grained dependencies*. In earlier releases, object dependency metadata was recorded with the precision of the entire object; for example, view V depends on table T. If the view V depended on just the first three columns of the table T and you added a new column to table T, the view would be invalidated, even though the new column didn't logically affect it. In Oracle Database 11g, the view V will not be invalidated when a change in an object doesn't directly affect the view. For example, a column addition such as the one explained here won't result in the invalidation of the view.

Oracle also uses similar fine-grained dependency management for PL/SQL objects such as procedures and functions. In current releases, if you add a new element or change an element in a PL/SQL package, you invalidate all the procedures in that package. In Oracle Database 11g, a new program element invalidates other procedures or functions only if that object has a specific dependency on the changed or new element.

Fine-grained dependency management leads to an overall reduction in the invalidation of objects following changes to objects, and you don't need to configure anything to avail of this new feature. You'll have enhanced application availability especially when you're upgrading applications.

Oracle Advanced Table Compression Option

With some data volumes doubling roughly every two to three years, mounting storage costs as well as application scalability and performance issues make data compression an attractive technique for organizations. Oracle Database 11*g* takes data compression to new heights with its Oracle Advanced Compression option, which, unlike the older table compression technology, you'll have to separately license from Oracle. The Oracle Advanced Compression option includes new OLTP compression capabilities, but it goes way beyond mere table compression. The Oracle Advanced Compression option includes the following types of compression:

- Compression of OLTP table data

- Compression of unstructured data with SecureFiles

- Compression of backup data produced by RMAN through the new fast RMAN compression technique

- Compression of the table data during a Data Pump export (in Oracle Database 10*g*, you could compress only the metadata from an export job, not the table data itself)

- Compression of redo data during its transmission to a standby database during redo gap resolution after a network or standby server outage

Beginning with the Oracle 9*i* release, you could use table compression in an Oracle database. The table compression feature allowed you to specify that the database compress data while loading it through bulk load operations. These operations include the `create table as select` (CTAS) and direct path load techniques. However, the data compression capability was aimed at data warehousing environments only. In Oracle Database 10*g*, you could compress a heap-organized table, but Oracle recommended compressing just read-only tables, which are mostly used in data warehouse settings, since the compression algorithm wasn't optimized for normal Data Manipulation Language (DML) activity. Although you can issue DML commands against a compressed table, for performance reasons Oracle recommended avoiding DML operations on the compressed tables.

■**Note** You must set the database compatibility level to at least 11.1 for compression in an OLTP environment.

The overhead of compression in OLTP environment made the pre-Oracle Database 11*g* compression techniques unsuitable for fast-paced OLTP-based databases. In Oracle Database 11*g*, the table compression feature has been enhanced to support OLTP environments. Oracle uses new algorithms to provide a powerful new online transaction processing (OLTP) compression capability that allows the database to compress data during all types of DML activities, such as insert, delete, and update. The performance improvement during compression of data, which makes it appealing for OLTP uses results from a deduction in the overhead of the writing of data during compression. Thus, compression is now a viable option for both OLTP and data warehouse environments.

How the New Compression Feature Works

During a block compression, Oracle eliminates all duplicate values within a block by storing only a single copy of the column value that has duplicates in a special table that holds compression metadata, called the *symbol table*. Instead of multiple duplicate values in a block, you then have several short references to those values stored in the symbol table. Oracle stores the symbol table that contains the metadata used to compress data within the data block itself. This local database symbol table usage is what offers you superior performance during OLTP data compression by severely reducing the I/O when the database accesses any of the compressed data.

Storage and Performance Gains

Oracle claims you'll save your storage requirements by about two to three times (Oracle claims a compression ratio of 3.5:1) when you use the new table compression feature. Since Oracle can read the compressed data without having to uncompress the compressed data blocks, not only will there *not* be a performance hit, which is what you expect during table compression, but there will be an improvement in performance. This reduction in I/O results from the reduced need for I/O, since Oracle needs to access fewer blocks of data when dealing with duplicated data. For the same reason, your buffer cache requirements would go down as well, since you can save more compressed data in the cache.

Although the new table compression feature doesn't pose any additional burden on performance during reading the compressed data and can actually make for speedier query execution, writing compressed data is an altogether different proposition, because compressing data for writing to disk requires the database to perform additional work. Oracle has come up with a batch mode compression strategy, whereby the database doesn't incur the overhead of compressing data each time it needs to write that data to disk. Rather, the database waits until the uncompressed data in a data block reaches a critical threshold to compress the entire components of the block. Oracle then allows more new data to be written to the block in which it is compressing the data, until the block can't gain any more from further compression of the data in it.

Implementing OLTP Table Compression

You can specify table-level compression when you create a table, as shown here:

```
SQL> create table comp_tbl
    ...
    compress for all operations;
```

The compress for all operations clause specifies that the database compress all DML operations on the table comp_tbl, which happens to be a table used for DML operations. In addition, the compression applies to all bulk load (direct-path insert) operations, which are more common in a data warehouse environment. The compress for all operations clause is new in Oracle Database 11*g* and is designed for compression during DML operations in an OLTP environment. If, on the other hand, you were to specify table compression only for bulk load operations, as in Oracle Database 10*g*, specify the compress for direct_load operations option or simply the compress option. Thus, both the following statements will result in the compression of data during a direct-path load only:

```
SQL> create table test_tbl1
     ...
     compress for direct_load operation;

SQL> create table test_tbl2
     ...
     compress;
```

You can also specify compression for an already existing table. However, the database will compress only the new data that is entered in the table. All the previously existing data will remain uncompressed.

Compressing Unstructured Data

The new Oracle SecureFiles feature offers an alternative to traditional Large Objects (LOBs) for storing unstructured data such as documents, XML files, and spreadsheets. The Advanced Compression option lets you reduce the storage needs for SecureFiles data by the process of deduplication, which eliminates redundant copies of SecureFiles data. When you have multiple copies of the same document floating around your organization, the database uses SecureFiles deduplication to store only a single image of the SecureFiles data. The numerous copies of that document are replaced by pointers to the single image. If the company chairman sends a 10MB vision document to all 100,000 employees of the company, you'd normally need 1000GB of disk storage to store all 100,000 copies of the vision document. With SecureFiles deduplication, all you'll need is merely 10MB, which is the size of a single document. The SecureFiles feature offers you reduced storage requirements and better performance.

Please refer to Chapter 8 for more about SecureFiles.

Compressing Backup Data

RMAN provided backup compression in Oracle Database 10g. Although RMAN doesn't need to uncompress the compressed data during a recovery, because of the extensive compression ratio, backup times are longer since the compression of data before backing it up imposes an overhead.

The Oracle Advanced Compression option increases the performance of compressed RMAN backups while reducing the storage needs. The new ZLIB compression algorithm offered by RMAN in Oracle Database 11g reduces the compression ratio by 20 percent, and the compressed backups are up to 40 percent faster than those in the previous release of the database.

Please see Chapter 6 for more details about the new RMAN compression technique.

Compressing Data Pump Export Data

Oracle Database 10g Release 2 offered you the ability to compress a Data Pump export job's metadata, but not the table data itself. In Oracle Database 11g, you can choose to compress the export data while performing the export. Although you can compress a normal export dump file with operating system utilities such as gzip, you'd uncompress it again before importing the data. With the new Data Pump data compression, you don't have to uncompress the compressed dump file before importing data, since Data Pump import automatically uncompresses the compressed dump file during the import job.

Please see Chapter 7 for more details on the new Data Pump compression feature.

Compressing Network Data

Network or standby server failures can prevent redo log data from being transported to a standby server when you're using Data Guard. Oracle will automatically synchronize the redo data between the primary and secondary servers after the resolution of the failure. This synchronization process, also called a *redo gap resolution*, can prove to be time-consuming if the database has to transmit a large amount of redo data over the network. Oracle Advanced Compression compresses the redo data that needs to be transmitted over the network, thus increasing the throughput of the redo gap resolution process. Oracle estimates that compression enhances high availability by helping synchronize the standby database up to two times faster with compressed redo data.

For more on the compression of redo data during a redo gap resolution, please refer to Chapter 6.

Enterprise Manager New Features

There are several changes in Oracle Database 11g Enterprise Manager Database Control regarding database administration tasks. We'll show you the main new features in Enterprise Manager in this section. We discuss the new performance-related Enterprise Manager features in Chapter 4.

In Oracle Enterprise Manager 10g, you had only three main tabs on the database home page: Performance, Administration, and Maintenance. In Oracle Enterprise Manager 11g, you have the following tabs:

- *Performance*: The customizable Performance tab lets you view session performance details as well as memory, disk, and CPU utilization. Chapter 4 discusses the new performance pages in detail.

- *Availability*: This tab helps you manage backup and recovery, including Oracle Secure Backup.

- *Server*: This tab helps you manage storage, configuration, security, the query optimizer, the Oracle Scheduler, and the Resource Manager.

- *Schema*: This tab lets you manage database objects and perform change management.

- *Data Movement*: This tab covers Data Pump export and import, Streams, and advanced replication.

- *Software and Support*: This tab helps you manage software configuration and patching, the Deployment Procedure Manager, and Real Application Testing. We explained how to use most of these features in Chapter 1.

In the following sections, we outline some of the key new features in Oracle Enterprise Manager 11g.

The Availability Tab

You can perform back and recovery tasks, including using Oracle Secure Backup, from the Availability tab. The Availability tab has two major sections, Backup/Recovery and Oracle Secure Backup. The Backup/Recovery section has two sections, Setup and Manage. Click the View and Manage Transactions link in the Manage section to access the LogMiner tool. The LogMiner tool lets you browse transactions by time or an SCN range. You can query results by record or transaction basis.

The LogMiner tool is integrated with the Oracle Database 11*g* flashback transaction feature. LogMiner shows all dependent transactions, and it can undo an entire transaction, including its dependent transactions.

The Server Tab

The Server tab includes sections such as Storage, Database Configuration (initialization parameters), Security, Oracle Scheduler, Statistics Management, and Resource Manager. You'll find the Oracle Scheduler on the Server tab. A new addition to the Oracle Scheduler links is the Automated Maintenance Tasks tab, which lets you enable, disable, and configure the three automated maintenance tasks in Oracle Database 11*g*: Optimizer Statistics Gathering, Segment Advisor, and Automatic SQL Tuning. Figure 3-1 shows the Automated Maintenance Tasks page.

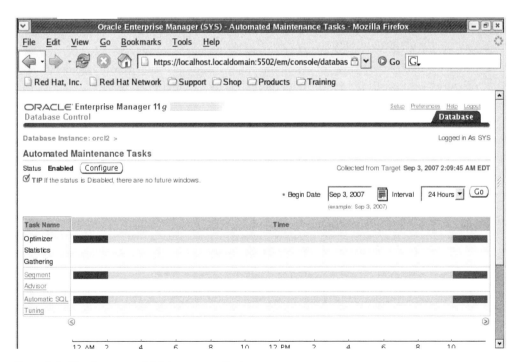

Figure 3-1. *The Automated Maintenance Tasks page*

Notice that there are three automatic maintenance tasks that are scheduled through the Oracle Scheduler, instead of two tasks in Oracle Database 10*g*. The automatic maintenance task framework manages important maintenance tasks such as Automatic SQL Tuning, Segment

Advisor, and Optimizer Statistics Gathering. The Optimizer Statistics Gathering job, of course, collects optimizer statistics on various database objects during the daily maintenance window. The Segment Advisor, as in the older release, shows the amount of unused space you can reclaim from various segments. By having key maintenance tasks as part of a framework, you can exert control over their scheduling and resource usage.

The new automatic maintenance task introduced in this release is the Automatic SQL Tuning Advisor task, which identifies ways to improve the execution plans for high-load SQL statements.

New Related Links

In Oracle Enterprise Manager 11*g*, you have a set of new links in the Related Links section on the home page. Here's a summary of the important new links.

Policy Groups Link

The Policy Groups link lets you manage all policy groups defined in your database. You'll have predefined policy groups such as Secure Configuration for Oracle Database and Secure Configuration for Oracle Listener. The Secure Configuration for Oracle policy group ensures that your database is following best-practice security configuration settings in order to make the database secure. The Policy Groups page has three tabs leading to the following pages:

- *Policy Group Evaluation Results page*: Summarizes how the targets are adhering to the standards of the policy group.

- *Policy Group Library page*: Shows all the policy groups available in your organization. Figure 3-2 shows the Secure Configuration for Oracle Database page.

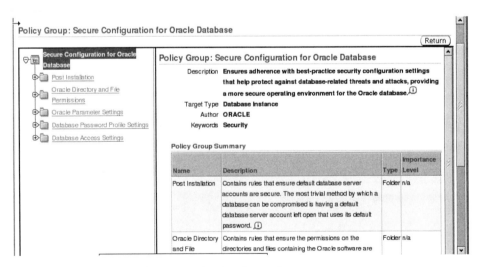

Figure 3-2. *The Secure Configuration for Oracle Database page*

- *Policy Group Evaluation Errors page*: Shows any errors that occurred during the evaluation of the targets.

Scheduler Central

The Scheduler Central page lets you monitor and manage three types of jobs:

- Jobs that you scheduled through the Oracle Scheduler

- Jobs being managed by the Enterprise Manager

- The three automated maintenance tasks (Optimizer Statistics Gathering, Segment Advisor, and Automatic SQL Tuning task) that run automatically for database maintenance

Baseline Metric Thresholds

The Baseline Metric Thresholds page has two tabs: Metric Analysis and Threshold Configuration. The Metric Analysis tab lets you identify the metrics that have a bearing on recent problems in the database. Once you find out which metrics are strongly correlated with recent database problems, you can then set thresholds for those metrics using the Threshold Configuration tab. The Threshold Configuration tab lets you view the current configuration of baseline metric thresholds and also edit those threshold settings. You can also invoke the Advanced Metric Analysis tab from here in order to test the threshold levels for various metrics.

SQL Worksheet

The iSQL*Plus interface has been removed in Oracle Database 11g. Instead, you have the new SQL Worksheet to execute SQL statements.

Advisor Central

You can access all database advisors, including the new SQL Performance Analyzer and the Data Recovery Advisor, by clicking the Advisor Central link. You can run an advisor, change the default parameters for the advisor, and review the results of the advisor from the Advisor Central page.

Metric and Policy Settings

The Metric and Policy Settings page has two tabs: Metric Thresholds and Policies. Use the Metric Thresholds page to specify metric settings for a monitored target. The Polices tab takes you to a table that allows you to add and customize polices for a specific target. For example, you can select a policy rule that checks whether the default temporary tablespace has been set to the system tablespace.

LogMiner Support

LogMiner is a familiar Oracle tool, which can directly access the redo logs to help you locate the changes made and roll back user errors or a logical corruption of data, in addition to helping you perform audit functions. You can use LogMiner through the SQL*Plus command-line interface. In prior versions, the only GUI to LogMiner was through the installation of a stand-alone Java console especially for the LogMiner tool. In Oracle Database 11g, you don't have to perform this installation, since you can now access LogMiner directly through Enterprise Manager Database Control. We'll briefly review how you can use the new Database Control interface to the LogMiner tool.

Earlier in this chapter, you learned about the new flashback transaction feature. The LogMiner tool is integrated fully with the flashback transaction feature and lets you view a transaction along with all of its dependent transactions.

To use the LogMiner tool, you must first enable supplemental logging in the database, as shown here:

```
SQL> alter database enable supplemental log data (primary key, unique
     index) columns;

Database altered.
SQL>
```

Once you have enabled supplemental logging in the database, you're ready to use the LogMiner tool to search the redo logs for transactions. To access LogMiner through the Database Control interface, use the following steps.

1. From the Database home page, click the Availability tab.

2. In the Manage section on the Availability tab, click the View and Manage Transactions link.

Figure 3-3 shows the LogMiner page in Database Control.

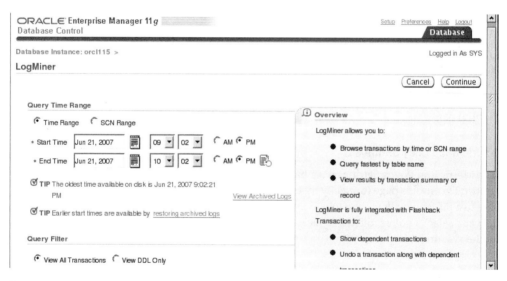

Figure 3-3. *The LogMiner page in Database Control*

Database Diagnostic Pack and Tuning Pack

As in Oracle Database 10*g*, you require separate Oracle licensing to use the premium functionality embedded in the OEM Database Control (and Grid Control). You can use the Management Pack Access page to control access to the premium packs, as shown in Figure 3-4.

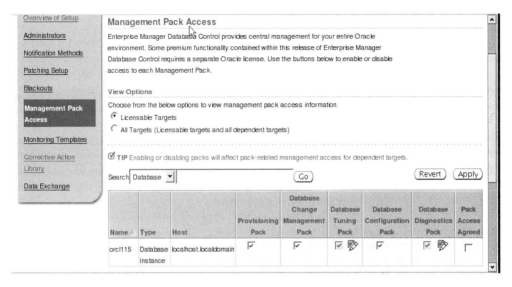

Figure 3-4. *The Management Pack Access page in Database Control*

Figure 3-4 shows the Management Pack Access page in Database Control. You can use this page to enable or disable access to each of the premium packs that require additional Oracle licenses in the Oracle Database 11*g* release.

The Database Diagnostic Pack and the Database Tuning Pack are essentially identical to their counterparts in Oracle Database 10*g*. The diagnostic pack provides the diagnostic tools ADDM, AWR, and so on. The Tuning Pack provides access to tuning advisors such as the SQL Tuning Advisor and the SQL Access Advisor. To enable or disable the Database Diagnostic Pack and the Database Tuning Pack, set the new initialization parameter `control_management_pack_access`. This parameter can take the following three values:

- `none`

- `diagnostic`

- `diagnostic+tuning`

For example, to enable access to both the diagnostic pack and the tuning pack, you must use the following setting for the `control_management_pack_access` parameter:

```
control_management_pack_access = diagnostic+tuning
```

By default, you have access to both the diagnostic and tuning packs. The `control_management_pack_access` parameter is dynamic.

Oracle Scheduler New Features

Oracle Scheduler functionality has been enhanced in the new release. Among the important new features of Oracle Scheduler are the concepts of a lightweight job, remote external jobs, and support for Data Guard. We'll explore these features in the following sections.

Lightweight Jobs

A Scheduler job is a task you schedule to run one or more times. Jobs contain two things: the action to be taken and its schedule. You can create a job by explicitly specifying the action to be performed by the job and its schedule in the job definition itself, and you can also create a job by using an existing program object and schedule object to specify the action and the frequency of execution.

In Oracle Database 10*g*, there was simply only one type of job you could create. Oracle Database 11*g* lets you create two types of jobs: regular jobs and lightweight jobs. *Regular jobs* are the jobs supported by the Scheduler in Oracle Database 11*g*. Regular jobs entail quite a bit of overhead, because they have to be created and dropped after each execution by the Scheduler. Regular jobs offer advantages such as the ability to use other users' programs, and they offer fine-grained control over the privileges to run the job.

A *lightweight job* inherits the privileges, and in some cases the job metadata itself, from a *job template*. Lightweight jobs aren't self-contained jobs like regular Scheduler jobs, since they inherit the job characteristics from the job template. If the Scheduler needs to create and drop a large number of jobs every day, lightweight jobs are preferable to regular jobs. Use regular jobs for tasks that you need to execute infrequently. Lightweight jobs, since they aren't database objects, don't cause overhead by having to create and drop them. In addition, they are faster to create and need less space for storing their metadata.

You create a lightweight job by using the create_job procedure of the DBMS_SCHEDULER package. In addition to the usual arguments that you must supply to create a regular job, you also specify the value LIGHTWEIGHT for the new attribute job_style. You don't have to specify the job_style attribute when creating a regular job. The following example shows how to create a lightweight job by specifying a program as a job template.

The following statement creates a lightweight job that uses the program test_prog as a job template:

```
begin
dbms_scheduler.create_job (
    job_name          => 'lightweight_job1',
    template          => 'test_prog',
    repeat_interval   => 'freq=daily;by_hour=9',
    end_time          => '30-DEC-07 12.00.00 AM
                          Australia/Sydney',
    job_style         => 'LIGHTWEIGHT',
    comments          => 'New lightweight job');
end;
/
```

In the example, the template attribute refers to the program (or stored procedure) that contains the job action. Note that you must use a job template when creating a lightweight job. That is, you can't create a lightweight job that contains all the information in the job creation statement itself. You also can't assign privileges directly in a lightweight job because the job will acquire or inherit the privileges from the job template.

Remote External Jobs

A Scheduler job that runs outside the Oracle database, such as an operating system shell script, is known as an *external job*. You specify the value `executable` for the `job_type` attribute when dealing with an external job. These external jobs, which you are familiar with from the Oracle Database 10*g* release, are called *local external jobs* now, since they run locally on the same host where the scheduling database is running.

Oracle Database 11*g* introduces a new type of operating system external job, called a *remote external job*, which runs, not on the host that's running the Oracle database but on a remote host. The database uses a *Scheduler agent* (formally known as Oracle External Scheduler Agent) on a remote host to start remote external jobs and return their results to the scheduling database. The remote host needs only the Scheduler agent and not an Oracle database. The Scheduler agent must register separately with each of the Oracle databases that you want to grant permission to in order to run a remote external job on the server hosting the Scheduler agent.

Installing, Registering, and Managing the Scheduler Agent

Before you can create and schedule a remote external job, you must first install and configure the Scheduler agent. You can do this by installing Oracle Database Gateway. For our Linux server, we downloaded and installed Oracle Database Gateway 11*g* Release 1 (11.1.0.6.0) for Linux x86 from the Oracle web site (you can also install it from the database CD pack). Here are the installation configuration and registration steps for the Scheduler agent:

1. Run the Oracle Universal Installer from the directory where you saved the Oracle Database Gateway software files, as shown here:

   ```
   $ /11g/gateways/runInstaller
   ```

   Of course, you must first unzip the downloaded installation file (`linux_11gR1_gateways.zip` in our case) before you can invoke the Oracle Universal Installer.

2. On the Select a Product to Install page, which appears after the Welcome page, select Oracle Scheduler Agent 11.1.0.6.0.

   On the Oracle Scheduler Agent page, specify the Scheduler agent host name and port number.

3. Once the installation of the agent is complete, you must run the `root.sh` configuration script as the root user. A successful installation is reported with a message on the End of Installation page. Click Exit to leave the Oracle Universal Installer.

   Once you install the Scheduler agent, it's time to register the agent with the database that you'll be using to run external jobs on the host housing the agent. Before you can register the agent with a particular database, you must first "set up" that database by issuing the following command as the user `sys`:

   ```
   $ @ORACLE_HOME/rdbms/admin/prvtrsch.plb
   ```

4. Once you run the `prvtrsch.plb` script, you must set a registration password for the Scheduler agent using the `set_agent_registration_pass` procedure, as shown in the example here:

```
SQL> exec dbms_scheduler.set_agent_registration_pass('sammyy1')

PL/SQL procedure successfully completed.

SQL>
```

In this example, `sammyy1` is the Scheduler agent registration password for the database host. Now you're ready to register the Scheduler agent with a database. Here's the command to register a Scheduler agent with a database:

```
$ schagent -registerdatabase database_host database_xmldb_http_port
```

You can find out the value for the `database_xmldb_http_port` (the port on which the database listens for HTTP connections) by issuing the following query:

```
SQL> select dbms_xdb.gethttpport() from dual;
```

Once you register the agent with the database that will run remote external jobs on the agent's host server, start the Scheduler agent with the following command (on a Unix/Linux server):

```
$ schagent -start
Scheduler agent started
$
```

You can stop the Scheduler agent with the following command:

```
$ schagent -stop
Scheduler agent stopped
$
```

You can disable remote external jobs by dropping the database user `remote_scheduler_agent`. This will disable the registration of all new Scheduler agents as well as all remote external jobs. You can create the user again by executing the `prvtrsch.plb` script again.

Now that you've learned how to create and manage the Scheduler agent, let's look at how you actually create a remote external job.

Creating a Remote External Job

Creating a remote external job is a bit more intricate than creating a local external job. In addition to the usual job attributes, you must supply the following additional information when creating a remote external job:

1. You must specify a credential for the remote external job. Oracle recommends specifying the credential even for local external jobs, but it isn't mandatory to do so. Before you can specify a credential for a remote external job, you must first create that credential using the `create_credential` procedure, as shown here:

```
SQL> exec dbms_scheduler.create_credential('testcredential',
        'salapati','sammyy1');
```

In the example, the database creates a credential named testcredential, with the username salapati and password sammyy1. You can grant any user in the database the privilege to use a credential by using the grant statement, as shown here:

```
SQL> grant execute on testcredential to newuser;
```

Once you create a credential, you can specify the credential for any external job by using the set_attribute procedure, as we'll show in our example in this section. You can view all the credentials in a database by querying the DBA_SCHEDULER_CREDENTIALS view.

2. You must use the destination attribute when creating a remote external job to specify the destination host and port. You can find the port number, which is the port on which the Scheduler agent listens, by viewing the file schagent.conf, located in the Scheduler agent home directory (on the remote host).

The following example shows how to create a remote external job:

```
begin
dbms_scheduler.create_job(
    job_name            => 'deletelogs',
    job_type            => 'executable',
    job_action          => '/u01/app/oracle/deletelogs',
    repeat_interval     => 'freq=daily; byhour=23',
    enabled             =>  false);
dbms_scheduler.set_attribute(' deletelogs', 'credential_name',
        'testcredential');
dbms_scheduler.set_attribute ('deletelogs', 'destination', 'app123:12345');
dbms_scheduler.enable(' deletelogs');
end;
```

The create_job procedure shown here creates a remote external job named *deletelogs*. The set_attribute procedure sets the credential name and the destination (host and port number) for the external job. Note that you must enable the new remote external job *deletejobs* using the enable procedure after setting the credential and destination attributes.

Scheduler Support for Data Guard

If you're using a physical standby database, then all Scheduler-related changes made on the primary database are applied to the physical standby database, like any other database change. For primary database and logical standby databases, you can now specify that a job can run only if the database is in the primary database role or only when the database is in the logical standby database role.

Use the set_attribute procedure of the DBMS_SCHEDULER package to set the job attribute database_role to either primary or logical standby. Upon a swtichover or a failover, the Scheduler will automatically run the job specific to the role. In the case of a failover, the job event log will show all successful DML changes on the primary database until the time of the failover.

The following example shows how to run a job in the two database roles: the primary database role and the logical standby database role. We create two copies of a job and assign different values for the database_role attribute (primary and logical standby) to each of the copies.

If you want to run a job in both roles, you can do so by copying the job and then changing the database_role attribute value to the required value (primary or logical standby) after enabling the copied job.

In the following example, we create a job named *test_primary* on the primary database. We then make a copy of this job and change the database_role attribute value to logical standby. When the primary database becomes a logical standby database, the copied job will run as per the schedule.

```
begin
dbms_scheduelr.create_job(
job_name        => 'test_primary',
program_name    => 'test_prog',
schedule_name   => 'test_sched');
dbms_scheduler.copy_job('test_primary','test_standby');
dbms_scheduler.enable(name=>'test_standby');
dbms_scheduler.set_attribute('test_standby','database_role','logical_standby');
end;
/
```

You can query the DBA_SCHEDULER_JOB_ROLES view to ensure that the job roles are switched, as shown here:

```
SQL> select job_name,database_role
     from dba_scheduler_job_roles;

JOB_NAME             DATABASE_ROLE
-------------        ----------------
TEST_PRIMARY         PRIMARY
TEST_STANDBY         LOGICAL STANDBY
```

The query reveals that our primary and standby jobs are assigned the correct job roles.

CHAPTER 4

■ ■ ■

Performance Management

Oracle Database 11g adds several weapons to the arsenal of the DBA looking to improve performance and scalability. Automatic native compilation of PL/SQL code means you'll now get much faster PL/SQL performance automatically when you upgrade applications to the new release. The new server cache feature dramatically increases performance for SQL queries as well as for PL/SQL functions by retrieving results straight from the cache instead of reexecuting code. There is also a new client-side result caching feature for OCI applications.

The new SQL Plan Management (SPM) feature helps you stabilize SQL execution plans to prevent a performance regression due to unexpected changes in the execution plans of SQL statements. By default, in Oracle Database 11g, the database automatically tunes SQL statements by running a new daily task called the Automatic SQL Tuning Advisor task as part of the automated task management feature.

There are major innovations in the use of the Automatic Database Diagnostic Monitor (ADDM), including the ability to run the ADDM in dual modes at the database level and at the cluster level to help diagnose performance problems in an Oracle Real Application Cluster (RAC) environment. There are significant improvements in the automatic workload repository (AWR) baselines, including the new concept of moving window baselines and baseline templates. You can now configure adaptive thresholds for various database alerts based on AWR's new system_ moving_window baseline. The database advisor framework, introduced in Oracle Database 10g, is extended in this release.

Here are the main topics we discuss in this chapter:

- SQL and PL/SQL performance improvements

- New result caching functionality

- Automatic SQL Tuning Advisor task

- SQL Access Advisor enhancements

- ADDM enhancements

- Adaptive cursor sharing

- Performance-related changes in Database Control

- Optimizer and statistics collection enhancements

- SQL Plan Management

We'll now review the major new performance-related features in the Oracle Database 11*g* release, starting with SQL and PL/SQL performance improvements.

SQL and PL/SQL Performance Enhancements

Oracle Database 11*g* introduces several enhancements in PL/SQL programming and execution. Some of these improvements are transparent, such as the PL/SQL result cache, which caches execution results so that frequently executed identical PL/SQL statements can use those results instead of executing the same statement repeatedly.

In addition to performance-improving enhancements, several language features improve the functionality and usability of PL/SQL programming. You'll learn about these programming enhancements in Chapter 11. Let's turn to a review of the important PL/SQL performance-enhancing new features.

Automatic "Native" PL/SQL Compilation

In previous releases of the database, Oracle transformed all PL/SQL code to C code, which in turn was compiled by a third-party C compiler. This posed a problem in organizations that didn't want to or couldn't install a C compiler on their servers. In Oracle Database 11*g*, Oracle directly translates the PL/SQL source code to the DLL for the server. In addition, Oracle bypasses the file system directories by doing the linking and loading itself.

Except setting one new initialization parameter, you don't need to configure anything to take advantage of the PL/SQL native compilation. This parameter is plsql_code type, which you can use to turn automatic native PL/SQL compilation on and off. Tests performed by Oracle showed a performance improvement of up to 20 times with native PL/SQL compilation.

Using Real Native Compilation

By default, the database interprets PL/SQL code instead of directly compiling it. You can use PL/SQL native compilation now without any third-party software such as a C compiler or a dynamic link library (DLL) loader. The new initialization parameter plsql_code_type specifies the compilation mode for PL/SQL library units and can take one of two values: interpreted or compiled.

- If you set the parameter to interpreted, the database will compile all PL/SQL code to PL/SQL bytecode format, and the PL/SQL interpreter engine will execute them.

- If you set the parameter to native, most PL/SQL code will be compiled to machine code and executed natively without the involvement of an interpreter, thus making execution faster.

The default value of the plsql_code_type parameter is set to interpreted. To turn on native PL/SQL compilation, set the plsql_code_type initialization parameter as follows:

```
plsql_code_type=native
```

You can change the value of the plsql_code_type parameter dynamically, with either an alter system or alter session statement. However, the switch in compilation mode won't affect the PL/SQL units that have already been compiled. Once the database compiles a PL/SQL unit, all recompilations will continue to use the original mode in which that unit was compiled, be it native or interpreted.

Oracle Database 11g generates DLLs from the PL/SQL source code and stores the code in the database catalog from where it loads the code directly without having to stage it on a file system first.

Oracle claims the following regarding real native PL/SQL compilation:

- Compilation is twice as fast as C native compilation.

- The Whetstone Benchmark shows that real native compilation is two-and-a-half times faster than C native compilation.

Setting Up a PL/SQL Program Unit for Native Compilation

In this section, we'll show how to set up the PL/SQL native compilation for a single procedure. To enable native compilation of our test procedure, first change the value of the plsql_code_type parameter from its default value of interpreted to native, either by placing this in the parameter file or by using the alter system or alter session command. Once you do this, the database will natively compile any PL/SQL program unit you create.

```
SQL> select name, value from v$parameter where
     name like '%plsql%';
NAME                          VALUE
--------------------          ----------------------
plsql_code_type               INTERPRETED
plsql_optimize_level          2
...
9 rows selected.

SQL>
```

The other way is to take an already created PL/SQL program unit, which is going to be interpreted by default, and use the alter <PLSQL unit type> statement to enable PL/SQL native compilation. In the example here, you first create a test procedure with the plsql_code_type parameter still set to the default value of interpreted.

```
SQL>  create or replace procedure test_native as
  2     begin
  3     dbms_output.put_line('Test Procedure.');
  4*    end test_native;
SQL> /
Procedure created.
SQL>

SQL> select plsql_code_type
  2  from all_plsql_object_settings
  3  where name='TEST_NATIVE';
```

```
PLSQL_CODE_TYPE
--------------------------
INTERPRETED
SQL>
```

Once you create the test procedure (test_native), you issue the alter procedure statement in the following way to change the code type to native:

```
SQL> alter procedure  test_native compile plsql_code_type=native;

Procedure altered.

SQL>
```

You can confirm that the test procedure is now compiled for native execution by executing the following query on the DBA_PLSQL_OBJECT_SETTINGS view:

```
SQL> select plsql_code_type
  2  from all_plsql_object_settings
  3* where name='TEST_NATIVE';

PLSQL_CODE_TYPE
--------------------------
NATIVE

SQL>
```

The plsql_code_type column has the value native for the test procedure named test_native, indicating that the alter procedure statement has succeeded.

Recompiling a Database for PL/SQL Native Compilation

If you want to recompile all existing PL/SQL modules in your database to native, you must start your database in upgrade mode and execute the dbmsupgnv.sql script provided by Oracle. Here are the steps:

1. Shut down the database in normal or immediate mode:

   ```
   SQL> shutdown immediate;
   ```

2. Edit the parameter file for the instance, and set the plsql_code_type parameter to native, as shown here:

   ```
   plsql_code_type=native
   ```

3. Also make sure the value of the plsql_optimize_level parameter is at least 2 (which is the default):

   ```
   plsql_optimize_level=3
   ```

4. Start the database in upgrade mode:

```
SQL> connect sys/sammyy1 as sysdba
Connected to an idle instance.
SQL> startup upgrade
ORACLE instance started.
...
Database opened.
```

5. Once the instance comes up, execute the $ORACLE_HOME/rdbms/admin/dbmsupgnv.sql
script as the user sys:

```
SQL> @$ORACLE_HOP ME/rdbms/admin/dbsupgnv.sql
OC>############################################################
DOC>############################################################
DOC>    dbmsupgnv.sql completed successfully. All PL/SQL procedures,
DOC>    functions, type bodies, triggers, and type bodies objects in
DOC>    the database have been invalidated and their settings set to
DOC>    native.
DOC>
DOC>    Shut down and restart the database in normal mode and
DOC>    run utlrp.sql to recompile invalid objects.
SQL>
```

The dbmsupgnv.sql script updates the execution mode of all PL/SQL modules to native.

6. Shut down and restart the database after the updating of the PL/SQL units is complete.
Since the update invalidates all the PL/SQL units, run the utlrp.sql script located in
the $ORACLE_HOME/rdbms/admin directory to recompile all the invalidated PL/SQL units:

```
SQL> shutdown immediate;
SQL> startup
ORACLE instance started.
...
Database opened.
SQL> @$ORACLE_HOME/rdbms/admin/utlrp.sql
...
SQL> Rem END utlrp.sql
SQL> exit
```

Once you update your database to compile PL/SQL in native mode, you don't have to use
any alter <PL/SQL unit> commands any longer. By default, the database will now execute all
PL/SQL units in native mode.

The effect of the recompilation process isn't permanent. If you decide to take the database
back to the default mode of interpreted execution, follow the same process as shown here, with
one exception—just replace the dbmsupgnv.sql script with the dbmsupgin.sql script.

Faster DML Triggers

This is one of the new features of Oracle Database 11g that doesn't require you to do anything to reap the benefits! All DML triggers run much faster in Oracle Database 11g. According to one of Oracle's internal tests, there was a 25 percent improvement in the performance speed of a row-level update trigger fired during DML. Please see Chapter 11 for several new trigger-related features.

Adaptive Cursor Sharing

Using bind variables reduces the amount of shared memory the database needs to allocate to parse SQL statements, because bind variables reuse a single cursor for multiple executions of the same (or similar) SQL statement. Bind variables, because they reduce parse time and memory usage, enhance the performance and scalability of the database, especially when you have a large number of concurrent users. The initialization parameter cursor_sharing determines which SQL statements can share the same cursor. Setting the cursor_sharing parameter to exact stipulates that only identical statements can share a cursor. Setting the parameter to force means statements that differ in some literals can share a cursor. Setting the parameter to the value similar leads to the same behavior as setting it to force unless the different values of the literals affect the degree of optimization of the execution plan.

However, cursor sharing inherently conflicts with SQL optimization, because specifying literal values instead of bind values provides richer information to the optimizer, leading to the evolution of better plans. For this reason, forced cursor sharing especially could lead to suboptimal execution plans. In some cases, some users of a SQL statement may get highly optimal executions, while others may get quite inferior executions because of the specific values of the actual bindings.

Columns with heavily skewed data distribution need different execution plans based on the actual values of the bind variables in a SQL query, and when you bind variables, you may end up with suboptimal execution plans as a result. Oracle uses the concept of *bind peeking*, under which the optimizer examines the bind values the first time you execute a statement in order to evolve an optimal execution plan for subsequent executions of that statement. The optimizer will look at the bind variable values during the first hard parse and base its plan strategy on those values. Bind variable peeking helps you only when the optimizer first generates the execution plan for a new SQL statement. However, if the data is heavily skewed, bind peeking has little value, because different data for the bind variables requires different execution plans, making the use of literals a better strategy. For example, if the values the optimizer sees during its "peeking" warrant using an index, it'll continue to use the index even for other values of the bind variable when a full scan may be a better strategy!

Oracle Database 11g takes a major step to resolve the inherent conflict between cursor sharing and query optimization by introducing the concept of *adaptive cursor sharing*. Under adaptive cursor sharing, the SQL statements automatically share a cursor. Oracle generates multiple execution plans for a statement that uses bind variables, when it detects that the cost of doing so for a particular SQL statement outweighs the benefit of a lower parse time and memory usage flowing from using the same cursor. Oracle still attempts to keep the number of generated child cursors to a minimum to take advantage of cursor sharing. In a nutshell, what Oracle is attempting to do is avoid the "blind sharing" of cursors while minimizing the number of child cursors.

■**Note** Adaptive cursor sharing is an automatic feature of Oracle Database 11*g*, and you can't turn it off.

How Adaptive Cursor Sharing Works

The key to adaptive cursor sharing is the bind sensitivity of a cursor and the concept of a bind-aware cursor. A query is considered *bind-sensitive* if the optimizer performs bind peeking when figuring out the selectivity of the predicates and a change in bind variable values potentially leads to different execution plans. If a cursor in the cursor cache has been marked for bind-aware cursor sharing, the cursor is called *bind-aware*.

■**Note** Adaptive cursor sharing works independently from the setting of the `cursor_sharing` parameter. It doesn't matter whether the user supplies the bindings or whether the literals are replaced by system-generated bind variables, which is the case if you set the `cursor_sharing` parameter to `force`.

Adaptive cursor sharing uses bind-aware cursor matching. Unlike in previous releases, the cursors can be bind-sensitive now. We'll now show a simple example that illustrates how adaptive cursor sharing works in practice.

Let's say you have the following SQL query that the database executes multiple times:

```
SQL> select * from hr.employees where salary = :1
     and department_id = :2;
```

The previous SQL statement uses two bind variables, one for the `salary` column and the other for the `department_id` column.

The first time the database executes the SQL statement, there is a hard parse. If the optimizer peeks at the bind values and uses histograms to compute the selectivity of the predicate with the two bind variables, the cursor is marked as a bind-sensitive cursor. The predicate selectivity information is stored in a cube, let's say (0.15, 0.0025). Once the database executes the query, it stores the execution statistics of the cursor in the cursor. Under adaptive cursor sharing, the database monitors the query execution of a new SQL statement for a while and gathers information to help decide whether it should switch to bind-aware cursor sharing for the query.

When the database executes a SQL statement the next time with a different pair of bind values, the database performs a soft parse as usual and compares the execution statistics to those stored in the cursor. Based on all the previous execution statistics for this cursor, the database makes a decision whether to mark this cursor as bind-aware.

If the cursor is marked bind-aware, the database uses *bind-aware cursor matching* during the next soft parse of the query. Each time the database executes the query, it performs a cursor sharing check using the predicate's bind variable selectivity estimates, which are stored in the selectivity cubes. Each plan has a selectivity range or cube associated with it. If the new bind values fall within this range, they will use the same plan. That is, if the selectivity of the predicate with the new pair of bind values is within the existing cube or range of values, the database uses the same execution plan as that of the existing child cursor.

If the selectivity of the predicate doesn't fall inside the existing cube, then the database can't find a matching child cursor. As a result, the database performs a hard parse, generating a new child cursor with a different execution plan. If two hard parses generate an identical execution plan, the child cursors are merged.

Briefly, bind-aware cursor sharing means that the database will share an execution plan when the bind values are roughly equivalent. The optimizer will delineate a selectivity range for an execution plan, and it'll use the same plan if the new bind values fall within this selectivity range. If the binds are not equivalent according to the selectivity range, the optimizer will generate a new execution plan with a different selectivity range.

Monitoring Adaptive Cursor Sharing

The V$SQL view has several new database views as well as new columns that help you monitor adaptive cursor sharing in the database. Since adaptive cursor sharing is automatic, you don't have to actually do anything. Here's a brief description of the new views:

- *V$SQL_CS_HISTOGRAM*: Shows the distribution of the execution count across the execution history histogram

- *V$SQL_CS_SELECTIVITY*: Shows the selectivity cubes or ranges stored in cursors for predicates with bind variables

- *V$SQL_CS_STATISTICS*: Contains the execution information gathered by the database to decide on whether it should use bind-aware cursor sharing and includes buffer gets and CPU time, among the statistics

In addition to these new views, the V$SQL view has two important new columns to support adaptive cursor sharing. The IS_BIND_SENSITIVE column shows whether a cursor is bind-sensitive. The IS_BIND_AWARE column shows whether a cursor in the cursor cache has been marked to use bind-aware cursor sharing. Here's a simple query showing the two new columns:

```
SQL> select sql_id, executions, is_bind_sensitive, is_bind_aware
     from v$sql;

SQL_ID                    EXECUTIONS             I       I
--------------------      -------------------    ---     ---
57pfs5p8xc07w             21                     Y       N
1gfaj4z5hn1kf             4                      Y       N
1gfaj4z5hn1kf             4                      N       N
...
294 rows selected.

SQL>
```

If the IS_BIND_SENSITIVE column shows Y, it means the optimizer is planning to use multiple execution plans, depending on the value of the bind variable. If the IS_BIND_AWARE column shows Y, it means the optimizer knows that the bind variable values result in different data patterns. In this case, the optimizer may hard-parse the statement.

New Result Caching Functionality

Oracle Database 11*g* introduces several new caching features that let you utilize memory more efficiently, which results in faster query processing. There are actually two types of caching features: the *server result cache* that caches SQL query results as well as PL//SQL function results in the SGA and the *OCI consistent client cache (client cache)* that lets you cache query results on the client. The client cache is especially useful when you're using large-scale stateless web applications driven by frameworks such as PHP. We'll review the two types of caching features in the following sections, starting with the server result cache.

Using the Server Result Cache to Enhance Performance

The server result cache is a new concept of Oracle Database 11*g* that enables the database to cache SQL query and PL/SQL function results in memory. The database serves the results for frequently executed SQL queries and PL/SQL functions straight from the cache instead of reexecuting the actual query or function all over again. You can imagine the dramatic savings in resource usage (for example, IO) as well as the improved response times when you use cached results. Both logical as well as physical IO waits are virtually eliminated since the database fetches the necessary results from memory. The actual server result cache contains a *SQL query result cache* and a *PL/SQL function result cache*, both of which share an identical infrastructure.

All database sessions can share the cached results of a query, as long as they share execution plans even partially. Oracle's internal tests show that the server result cache leads to gains as high as a 200 percent improvement in performance for workloads that are read-intensive.

In Oracle Database 11*g*, there is a new SGA component called *result cache*, which is actually part of the shared pool in the SGA. By default, the server result cache uses a small part of the shared pool, even when you don't explicitly allocate memory for the cache. The default maximum size depends on the size of the SGA as well as the memory management method you're using. However, to set the size for the result cache memory size, you use the `result_cache_max_size` initialization parameter. If you're manually managing the shared pool, make sure you increase the shared pool size when you increase the result cache size, since the result cache draws its memory from the shared pool. Once you set the result cache memory size, the automatic shared memory management infrastructure will automatically manage the memory you allocate for the server-side result cache.

The new PL/SQL package `DBMS_RESULT_CACHE` provides various procedures to administer the result cache feature, including monitoring and managing the cache. The V$RESULT_CACHE_* views let you determine the success of a cached SQL query or a PL/SQL function by determining the cache-hit success of the query or function.

In the following sections, you'll learn how the two components of the server result cache—the SQL query result cache and the PL/SQL result cache—work. You'll also learn how to manage the two types of caches, which together make up the server result cache.

SQL Query Result Cache

You can now cache the results of frequently executed SQL query results in the SQL query result cache. It doesn't take a rocket scientist to figure out that extracting results from the cache takes far less time than actually running the SQL query. You'll see significant database-wide performance improvements when you use the SQL query result cache.

Query result caching is ideal in the following circumstances:

- The query processes a large number of rows to yield just a handful of rows or even a single row.

- The database executes the query frequently, with little or no changes in the data itself.

Thus, although technically speaking you can apply the SQL query result cache to any kind of workload, data warehousing applications are the most common beneficiaries of the cache.

■**Note** In an Oracle RAC environment, each of the nodes has its own result cache that can't be used by the other instances in the RAC.

The database automatically invalidates the cached results of a SQL query when there is a change in the data that's part of the query or a change in any of the objects that are part of the query.

Administering SQL Query Result Caching

Three new initialization parameters—result_cache_mode, result_cache_max_size, and result_cache_max_result—are crucial in managing the server-side result cache. The initialization parameter result_cache_mode determines whether and under what circumstance query result caching will apply. The result_cache_max_size initialization parameter determines the size of the result cache memory allocation. We'll talk about the three result cache–related initialization parameters in the following discussion.

You can control when the database uses the SQL query result cache by setting the result_cache_mode initialization parameter. If you turn caching on, a ResultCache operator is added to the execution plan of the cached SQL query. The setting of the result_cache_mode parameter determines when the optimizer will add the ResultCache operator to a query's execution plan. Here are the three possible values for the parameter:

- The default value of this parameter is manual, which means the result cache operator will be added (results cached) only if you use the new result_cache hint in the SQL query.

- If you set the value to auto, the cost optimizer will determine when it should cache the query results, based on factors such as the frequency of execution, the cost of execution, and how frequently the database objects that are part of the query are changing.

- If you set the value to force, the database caches the results of all SQL statements, as long as it's valid to cache the result. That is, the database will cache the results of all SQL statements where it's possible to do so.

Here's how you use the alter system statement to enable result caching in a database:

```
SQL> alter system set result_cache_mode = force
```

Note that the `force` option means the database will cache the results of all SQL statements. By setting the result caching mode to manual, as shown here, you disable automatic query caching by the database:

```
SQL> alter system set result_cache_mode = manual;
```

Once automatic query caching is disabled, you must use the `result_cache` hint in your queries to enforce query result caching.

■Note You can add the `result_cache` hint to SQL queries, subqueries, and inline views.

The `result_cache_mode` parameter helps you enable the query result cache at the *database level*. You can enable just *session-level caching* by setting the parameter using the `alter session` statement. You can override the setting of the `result_cache_mode` initialization parameter by specifying the new optimizer hints `result_cache` and `no_result_cache` in order to turn SQL query caching on and off. The hints will override both the `auto` and `force` settings of the `result_cache_mode` parameter.

If you set the `result_cache_mode` parameter to manual, you must then specify the `result_cache` hint in a query so the database can cache the query results. The `result_cache` hint tells the database to cache the current query's results and to use those results for future executions of the query or query fragment. If you set the `result_cache_mode` parameter to `auto` or `force`, on the other hand, the database will try to cache the results of all the queries. If you don't want to cache the results of any query under these circumstances, you must specify the `no_result_cache` hint in the query. The `no_result_cache` hint, like the `result_cache` hint, overrides the value set for the `result_cache_mode` parameter.

Here's how you'd use the `result_cache` hint in a query to turn query caching on for that query:

```
SQL> select /*+ result_cache */
       avg(income), region
       from employees
       group by region;
```

Although the `result_cache_mode` initialization parameter determines whether the database caches the query results, the `result_cache_max_size` parameter determines the maximum amount of the SGA that the database can allocate to the result cache. Note that the result cache size you set by using this parameter applies to both components of the server-side result cache—the SQL query result cache as well as the PL/SQL result cache.

Even if you don't set a specific size for the result cache, the `result_cache_max_size` parameter always has a positive default size, derived mainly from the `memory_target` parameter (or the `sga_target` or `shared_pool_size` parameter, if you configure one of them). By default, the cache takes 0.25 percent of the `memory_target` parameter's value, 0.5 percent of the `sga_target` value, and 1 percent of `shared_pool_size`, if you set it. However, the maximum allocation can't exceed 75 percent of the size of the shared pool. In the following example, we haven't used the `result_cache_max_size` parameter in the parameter file. However, the database internally allocated a default amount of 393,216 bytes for the parameter (`Maximum Cache Size` in the output). In the example, we generate a server result cache *usage report* employing the `DBMS_RESULT_CACHE` package:

```
SQL> set serveroutput on
SQL> exec dbms_result_cache.memory_report

Result   Cache   Memory   Report
[Parameters]
Block Size      = 1024 bytes
Maximum Cache Size  = 393216 bytes (384 blocks)
Maximum Result Size = 19456 bytes (19 blocks)
[Memory]
Total Memory = 13412 bytes [0.017% of the Shared Pool]
... Fixed Memory = 10560 bytes [0.013% of the Shared Pool]
... State Object Pool = 2852 bytes [0.004% of the Shared Pool]
... Cache Memory = 0 bytes (0 blocks) [0.000% of the Shared Pool]

PL/SQL procedure successfully completed.

SQL>
```

Since we haven't cached any SQL query results in the cache, the *cache memory* is 0 bytes, as shown in the output. The maximum value for this parameter is dependent on the operating system you're using. You can completely disable result caching of any kind by explicitly setting the result_cache_max_size parameter to zero. After setting the parameter to zero, the memory report will show the following:

```
SQL> exec dbms_result_cache.memory_report;

Result   Cache   Memory   Report
Cache is disabled.

PL/SQL procedure successfully completed.

SQL>
```

The memory_report procedure displays the memory usage reports for the result cache. The result_cache_max_size parameter is static, so you can't modify it without restarting the database.

You may be wondering, what if a single large SQL query result takes up the entire result cache? By default, any single query result is limited to a maximum of 5 percent of the result cache (the size of which is set with the result_cache_max_size parameter). However, you can modify this default value by using the result_cache_max_result parameter, which specifies the maximum proportion of the result cache any single query result can take up, in percentage terms. You can set any percentage value between 0 and 100 for the result_cache_max_result parameter.

There is a third result cache–related initialization parameter called result_cache_remote_expiration. You can use this dynamic initialization parameter to specify the time (in minutes) for which query results involving tables in remote databases stay valid. The default value of this parameter is 0, meaning the database won't cache any results involving remote objects. Exercise care when you set this parameter to a positive value, since you may get incorrect results if the remote tables in the query have been modified in the meanwhile.

Viewing the Result Cache with EXPLAIN PLAN

You will notice that the explain plan for any query with a result_cache hint will contain the ResultCache operator, as shown in the following example:

```
SQL> explain plan for select /*+ result_cache +*/
    department_id,avg(salary);

Explained.

SQL> select plan_table_output from table (DBMS_XPLAN.DISPLAY());

PLAN_TABLE_OUTPUT
--------------------------------------
Plan hash value: 1192169904

| Id | Operation           | Name| Rows  | Bytes | Cost(%CPU)| Time     |
-------------------------------------------------------------------------------
|  0 | SELECT ST           | | 11        | 77    |4  (25)    |00:00:01 |

|  1 |   RESULT CACHE      | 4t7p9c4m3xty05wpjas75taw9j|   |   |

|  2 |     HASH GROUP BY   | | 11        | 77    | 4  (25)| 00:00:01 |

|  3 |       TABLE ACCESS FULL| EMPLOYEES  |  107   |  74  | 3 (0) | 00:00:01 |


Result Cache Information (identified by operation id):
-------------------------------------------------------

   1 - column-count=2; dependencies=(HR.EMPLOYEES);
 name="select /*+ result_cache +*/ department_id,avg(salary)
from hr.employees

PLAN_TABLE_OUTPUT
----------------------
group by department_id"


15 rows selected.

SQL>
```

You can use the cache_id value provided in the explain plan to find details about the cached query results using the V$RESULT_CACHE_OBJECTS view, as shown here:

```
SQL> select status,name,namespace
     from v$result_cache_objects where
     cache_id='4t7p9c4m3xty05wpjas75taw9j';
```

STATUS	NAME	NAMESPACE
Published	select /*+ result_cache +*/ department_id,avg(salary)	SQL

```
SQL>
```

The STATUS column's value (Published) in the V$RESULT_CACHE_OBJECTS view reveals that the result for this query is available for use. The other possible values for the STATUS column are new (result under construction), bypass, expired, and invalid. The NAMESPACE column shows that this is a SQL statement. The other value for the NAMESPACE column is PLSQL.

Examples of Query Result Caching

We'll use a simple example to show how the SQL query result cache feature works. First specify result caching for your query using the result_cache hint. Before you create the newly cached SQL query, flush the server result cache as well as the shared pool so you start fresh with the new query whose results you want to store in the server result cache.

```
SQL> exec dbms_result_cache.flush

PL/SQL procedure successfully completed.

SQL> alter system flush shared_pool;

System altered.

SQL>
```

The DBMS_RESULT.CACHE_FLUSH procedure purges the server result cache. In this example, we used a simple invocation of the flush procedure, but you can also specify that the database retain the free memory in the cache as well as the existing cache statistics. Alternately, instead of flushing the entire contents of the server result cache, you can execute the invalidate procedure instead to specify only those results that depend on a specified database object or are owned by a specific user. You most likely are familiar with the alter system flush shared_pool statement, which flushes the shared pool, so you have no prior executions of the test SQL queries in the shared pool already.

Here's the test SQL query, with the result_cache hint:

```
SQL> select /*+ result_cache q_name(Query1) */
     last_name,salary
     from emp
     order by salary;
```

Note that we provided the optional `q_name` parameter within the `result_cache` hint to specify a name (Query1) for our new SQL query whose results the database will store in the server result cache. If you check the execution plan for the new SQL query, you'll see that the query uses the `result_cache` optimizer hint:

```
SQL> explain plan for
     select /*+ result_cache q_name(Query1) */
     last_name,salary
     from hr.employees
     order by salary;

Explained.

SQL> @$ORACLE_HOME/rdbms/admin/utlxpls

PLAN_TABLE_OUTPUT
-------------------------------------------------------------------------------
Plan hash value: 3447538987


-------------------------------------------------------------------------------
| Id | Operation      | Name | Rows  | Bytes | Cost
(%CPU)| Time |

PLAN_TABLE_OUTPUT
---------------------------------------------------------------------
|  0 | SELECT STATEMENT   | |   107 | 1284 |    4  (25)| 00:00:01 |

|  1 |  RESULT CACHE     | 6xt7gzhawg9jg8m503j2njzdxm | | |
        | |

|  2 |   SORT ORDER BY   | |   107 | 1284 |    4  (25)| 00:00:01 |

|  3 |   TABLE ACCESS FULL| EMPLOYEES  |  107 | 1284 |   3  (0)| 00:00:01 |

PLAN_TABLE_OUTPUT
-------------------------------------------------------------------------------


Result Cache Information (identified by operation id):
-----------------------------------------------------

   1 - column-count=2; dependencies=(HR.EMPLOYEES);
name="select /*+ result_cache q_name(Q1) */
last_name,salary
```

```
PLAN_TABLE_OUTPUT
-----------------------------------
from hr.employees
order by salary"

15 rows selected.

SQL>
```

Now that you know that the execution plan includes the result cache, execute the actual query, as shown here:

```
SQL> select /*+ result_cache q_name(Query1) */
     last_name,salary
     from hr.employees
     order by salary;
```

When you first execute the query with the result_cache hint, the result_cache operator checks the server result cache to see whether it already contains the results for this query. If the results are present there, of course, no execution is necessary and the query returns the results from the server result cache. In this example, since there are no prior results in the server result cache (we actually purged the result cache before we issued our query), the first execution of the test query will execute the SQL statement and store the results in the server result cache. Execute the same statement again so it can use the cached results now. Query the V$RESULT_CACHE_STATISTICS view to examine the usage statistics for the new query:

```
SQL> select name, value from v$result_cache_statistics;
```

NAME	VALUE
Block Size (Bytes)	1024
Block Count Maximum	384
Block Count Current	32
Result Size Maximum (Blocks)	19
Create Count Success	1
Create Count Failure	0
Find Count	1
Invalidation Count	0
Delete Count Invalid	0
Delete Count Valid	0

```
10 rows selected.

SQL>
```

The create count success column shows a value of 1, meaning the database successfully created one query whose results will be cached in the server result cache. The Find Count column also has a value of 1, meaning the cache results were found successfully by the second execution of the query.

The example here used a simple SQL query, but you can just as easily cache the results of an inline view as well by specifying a result_cache hint. Here's an example:

```
SQL> select prod_subcategory, revenue
  2  from (select /*+ result_cache */ p.prod_category,
  3  p.prod_subcategory,
  4  sum(s.amount_sold) revenue
  5  from products p, sales s
  6  where s.prod_id = p.prod_id and
  7  s.time_id between to_date ('01-JAN-2007','dd-mon-yyyy')
  8  and
  9  to_date('31-Dec-2007','dd-MON-yyyy')
 10  group by rollup(p.prod_category,p.prod_subcategory))
 11* where prod_category = 'Women';
```

In the inline view shown here, some of the optimizations such as view merging and column projection aren't employed. Thus, the view takes a longer time to execute the first time, but the cached results mean that later executions will finish very fast. Note that in addition to caching results of the queries with identical predicate values, the caching feature ensures that queries using a different predicate value for the column inside the where clause (prod_category) will also get back their results quickly.

Here's a simple example showing the dramatic improvement in query performance when you use the result cache.

1. First, check to ensure that the database isn't currently caching query results:

   ```
   SQL> show parameter result_cache
   ```

NAME	TYPE	VALUE
client_result_cache_lag	big integer	3000
client_result_cache_size	big integer	0
result_cache_max_result	integer	5
result_cache_max_size	big integer	672K
result_cache_mode	string	MANUAL
result_cache_remote_expiration	integer	0

   ```
   SQL>
   ```

   Note that result_cache_mode has the value MANUAL, meaning result caching is turned off at the database level. You can override this by using the result_cache hint in your queries. Of course, you can set the value of the result_cache_mode parameter to either auto or force, as explained earlier, to turn caching on at the database level.

2. Execute the following query first, and check the time it takes to get the results back:

```
SQL> select * from
  2  (select * from (select manager_id,department_id,  max(e.salary) maxsalary
  3  from emp1 e
  4  group by e.manager_id, department_id)
  5  order by maxsalary desc)
  6* where rownum =3;
```

MANAGER_ID	DEPARTMENT_ID	MAXSALARY
100	90	7000
100	80	14000
100	20	13000

```
Elapsed: 00:00:19.80
SQL>
```

The elapsed time is almost 20 seconds for this query.

3. From a different session, turn on system-wide server query result caching using the following command:

```
SQL> alter system set result_cache_mode=force;

System altered.

SQL>
```

4. Return to the first session to run your test query again, and note the execution time:

```
SQL> /

...
Elapsed: 00:00:18.14
SQL>
```

5. Issue the query again, now that the query results are cached by the database, and check the timing:

```
SQL> /
...
Elapsed: 00:00:00.01
SQL>
```

6. Note the dramatic improvement in query timing because of the use of the query result cache, since all the database had to do was merely get the cached result set for the server result cache!

Managing the Query Result Cache

You manage the SQL query result cache through the DBMS_RESULT_CACHE package (we've used this package earlier in this section), which provides you statistics that help manage the memory allocation for the query result cache. Here are the key procedures of the DBMS_RESULT_CACHE package:

- exec dbms_result_cache.flush: Removes all results and clears the cache memory

---

> **Note** If the number of cached results keeps growing, the result cache could be eventually filled up. The result cache will grow, but only until it reaches the maximum size set by the result_cache_max_size parameter. You must manually purge results from the cache to prevent the cache from filling up. First disable the cache before you purge it, because you can't purge while the cache is in active use.

- exec dbms_result_cache.invalidate (ABC', 'TESTTAB'): Invalidates cache results for a specified object
- select dbms_result_cache.status from dual: Shows status of the result cache
- exec dbms_result_cache.memory_report: Shows result cache memory usage

You can also use the following views to find out details about the query result cache:

- V$RESULT_CACHE_STATISTICS: Shows cache settings and memory usage statistics
- V$RESULT_CACHE_OBJECTS: Lists all cached objects and their attributes
- V$RESULT_CACHE_DEPENDENCY: Shows the dependency information between the cached results and dependencies
- V$RESULT_CACHE_MEMORY: Shows all memory blocks and their statistics

The V$RESULT_CACHE_OBJECTS view shows both cached results and all dependencies. The STATUS column can take the following values:

- new: The cached result is still being built.
- published: The cached result is available for use by other queries.
- bypass: Other queries will bypass the cached result.
- expired: The cached result has crossed the expiration time limit.
- invalid: The cached result is unavailable for use by other queries.

Here's a query that shows the type, status, and name of objects in the result cache:

```
SQL> select type,status,name from v$result_cache_objects;
```

```
TYPE                STATUS          NAME
----------------    ------------    -------------------------------
Dependency          Published       HR.COUNT_EMP
Dependency          Published       HR.EMPLOYEES
Result              Published       "HR"."COUNT_EMP"::8."COUNT
                                        EMP"#fac892c7867b54c6 #1
Result              Published       select /*+ result_cache q_name(Q1) */
                                        last_name,salary from hr.employees
                                        order by salary
```

```
SQL>
```

The output of the previous query shows that there are two cached results in the result cache, and that both are available for use.

The following limitations apply with regard to the operation of the query result cache:

- When dealing with bind variables, a query can reuse a cached result only for identical variable values. Different values for the bind variables or different bind variable names lead to a cache miss.

- Oracle won't cache results if the query uses a noncurrent version of the data because of the enforcement of the read consistency principle.

- Oracle won't cache results if there are pending transactions on the tables that are part of the query.

- Oracle won't cache flashback queries.

- All queries containing the following are ineligible for query result caching:

  - Nondeterministic PL/SQL functions

  - Currval and nextval

  - SQL functions such as sysdata and current_date

  - Temporary tables

  - Dictionary tables

PL/SQL Function Result Cache

PL/SQL functions sometimes return results of computations performed by queries that involve PL/SQL functions. When you're dealing with frequently executed PL/SQL functions whose queries access infrequently changing data, the PL/SQL function result cache feature lets you specify that the function's results be cached. Once you do this, when the database invokes a function with similar arguments as the cached function, instead of reexecuting that function, the database returns the cached results of the earlier execution of that function instead. Of course, performance would be dramatically improved. If any of the tables that are part of the functions' queries undergo a DML change, the database purges the PL/SQL result cache.

You can cache the results of PL/SQL functions executed by a session in the SGA and make them available to all other sessions in the database. You don't have to design a cache management policy to take advantage of this new feature—it is completely automatic. Frequently invoked complex PL/SQL functions that operate on relatively fixed data are ideal candidates for caching.

Enabling PL/SQL Result Caching

As we mentioned earlier, both server-side result caches—the SQL query result cache and the PL/SQL result cache—share the same infrastructure. The database uses the same result cache buffer for both SQL query result caching as well as PL/SQL function result caching. Thus, PL/SQL result caching is automatically enabled in the database, with a default amount of cache size memory (based on the SGA size) as long as you don't explicitly turn caching off by setting the result_cache_max_size parameter to zero.

An Example

You can activate the PL/SQL function result cache by using the result_cache clause in a PL/SQL function, as shown in the following example:

```
SQL> create or replace function count_emp (dept_no number)
  2  return number
  3  result_cache relies on(emp)
  4  is
  5  emp_ct number;
  6  begin
  7  select count(*) into emp_ct from emp
  8  where department_id=dept_no;
  9  return emp_ct;
 10  end;
 11  /

Function created.

SQL>
```

The previous code enables result caching on the function count_emp. The relies_on clause is optional, and you use it to indicate that the function relies or depends on the table (*emp* in this example) for its results. You can use the relies_on clause to specify tables or views on which the function depends. You can also specify a set of tables or views with the relies_on clause. The clause ensures that the database purges (invalidates) the server result cache when the dependent table undergoes a DML operation. This automatic purging of the results maintains cache consistency.

Once you create a function that populates the result cache using the result_cache option, it's time to test the function. To do this, you must call the PL/SQL function from inside a SQL query, as shown here:

```
SQL> select dept_name, count_emp(dept_id) "employee count"
     from depts
     where dept_name='Accounting';

DEPARTMENT_NAME            EMPLOYEE_COUNT
-----------------          -------------------------
Accounting                 2

SQL>
```

When you issue the previous SQL query for the first time, it invokes the PL/SQL function and stores the results it retrieves in the result cache. When you subsequently execute the same query, it'll simply retrieve the results directly from the result cache. You can examine the V$RESULT_CACHE_STATISTICS view, as in the case of the SQL query cache, to view the usage statistics for the PL/SQL result cache. All columns such as create count success and find count hold the same meaning for the PL/SQL result cache, as they did for the SQL query result cache.

If you apply a code patch to a PL/SQL unit such as a procedure, then the results in the PL/SQL result cache won't reflect the correct results for that PL/SQL unit, unless you bounce the instance. In cases such as these, you can bypass the result cache, as shown here:

1. Place the result cache in bypass mode:

   ```
   SQL> exec dbms_result_cache.bypass(true)

   PL/SQL procedure successfully completed.
   ```

2. Flush the existing cached results:

   ```
   SQL> exec dbms_result_cache.flush

   PL/SQL procedure successfully completed.
   ```

3. Apply the PL/SQL code patch.

4. Turn off the PL/SQL result cache bypass mode:

   ```
   SQL> exec dbms_result_cache.bypass(false)

   PL/SQL procedure successfully completed.
   ```

When you turn result cache bypassing on, the database doesn't use any cached results, and no results are stored there until you turn bypass mode off. Please refer to Chapter 11 for a more programmatic discussion of the PL/SQL cross-section result cache, as well as a listing of the limitations of the cache.

OCI Consistent Client Cache

The OCI consistent client cache, also called simply the *client cache*, extends server-side query caching by letting the client machines leverage their memory to cache query results. The client cache resides in the OCI client process memory and can store tables or entire data sets, usually on the application server. Instead of having the server repeatedly execute frequently used

SQL queries, the client simply gets the results from the client cache directly, saving unnecessary round-trips between the client and the server. Increased scalability results from the lower CPU usage. Oracle's benchmark studies show that for simple queries such as the ones that use lookup tables, involving usually a read but not a write, performance gains could be dramatic, as high as a 500 percent reduction in elapsed time and a 200 percent drop in CPU time.

■**Note** You must use Oracle Database 11*g* client libraries and connect to an Oracle Database Release 1 (11.1) or newer server to take advantage of the client-side query cache feature.

Queries from different client sessions that have a match in things such as their SQL text and bind values share the cached query result sets. This leads to a significant reduction in response time for frequently executed SQL queries as well as an increase in scalability.

The best aspect of the client cache feature is that you don't have to make any changes to your application code to take advantage of it. Any application that uses an Oracle Database 11*g* OCI client can avail of the client cache. The OCI clients include ODBC, ODB.NET, PHP, JDBC-OCI (Thick) Driver, and various Oracle precompilers.

The OCI client cache is particularly suitable for queries involving lookup tables that produce repeatable result sets or small static result sets. This type of caching is also ideal for frequently executed queries. Once you enable client result caching, the result can be cached on the client or on the server. When you think the results aren't consistent any longer or simply incorrect, you can disable the client caching feature.

The Mechanics of Query Result Set Caching

You use the following two new initialization parameters to configure the client result cache:

- `client_result_cache_size`: You can turn on client result caching by setting this parameter to a value greater than zero. The parameter sets the maximum size of the client per-process result cache size in bytes. By default, the parameter has a value of zero, meaning the client cache is disabled by default (in contrast, the server cache is enabled by default). The value of this parameter (in bytes) sets the limit on the result set cache for each client process. The database assigns all OCI client processes a result cache that is equal to the value of this parameter. The `client_result_cache_size` parameter ranges from a minimum value of 0 to a maximum value that's dependent on the operating system. You must restart the database after setting the initial value for this parameter or after making an adjustment, since it's a static initialization parameter. You can override the `client_result_cache_size` parameter with the client configuration parameter `oci_result_cache_max_size`.

- `client_result_cache_lag`: This parameter sets the maximum time since the latest round-trip to the server after which the OCI client query makes a fresh round-trip to get new data for the cached queries on the client.

You can also use an optional client configuration file (or make the settings part of the `sqlnet.ora` file on the client) to enable and disable OCI client caching for OCI client processes that use the file. The settings in the client configuration file override the client cache settings made through the server parameter file on the server. Any OCI client process that uses the configuration file will have OCI client caching enabled for it. You can set the following optional parameters for clients in the client configuration file.

- `oci_result_cache_max_size`: Sets the maximum size of the query cache for a process (in bytes). This parameter overrides the value set for the `client_result_cache_size` initialization parameter on the server.

- `oci_result_cache_max_rset_size`: Sets the maximum size (in bytes) of a single query result in the query cache for a process.

- `oci_result_cache_max_rset_rows`: Sets the maximum size of a query result set (in rows) for a process.

Enabling and Disabling Client Caching

OCI applications enable and disable client result caching by using `OCIStmtExecute()` mode with the mode values `OCI_RESULT_CACHE` and `OCI_NO_RESULT_CACHE` to override the SQL hints `no_result_cache` and `result_cache`.

Intra Unit Inlining

Intra unit inlining, also called *procedure inlining* when applied to PL/SQL procedures, is another Oracle Database 11*g* new feature that promises tremendous gains in PL/SQL performance. Oracle claims that by using this new feature appropriately, you could achieve performance gains by a factor of two to ten times. Intra unit inlining is a process that replaces a call to a procedure, function, subroutine, or method with a copy of the body of that object, which always runs much faster than the actual procedure, function, or subroutine. The database automatically finds candidates for inlining, but you can influence the process with the initialization parameter `plsql_optimization_level` and the `pragma inline` directive. Oracle suggests you inline only small, frequently run procedures. The PL/SQL performance tool `plstimer` can help you identify procedures that may benefit from inlining.

By setting the initialization parameter `plsql_optimize_level` to a value of 3, you can make the PL/SQL complier search for PL/SQL calls that are candidates for inlining and inline the most promising of those calls. You can also specify the `plsql_optimization_level` parameter dynamically inside a procedure, as shown here:

```
SQL> alter procedure test compile
     plsql_optimize_level = 3
     reuse settings;
```

You can also use the `pragma inline` directive inside a subroutine to direct the database to inline the subroutine. Please see Chapter 11 for more details on the intra unit inlining feature.

Automatic SQL Tuning

Although a DBA could manually tune poorly performing SQL statements, the large number of distinct SQL statements in any real-life production database and the expertise it requires to write good SQL code, design fast data access, and work with explain plans and trace output makes manual tuning quite a daunting task, besides being extremely time consuming.

Oracle Database 10*g* gave you two excellent performance tuning tools, the SQL Tuning Advisor and the Automatic Database Diagnostic Monitor (ADDM), to facilitate tuning SQL queries. As candidates for tuning, ADDM picks high-load SQL statements that provide the biggest bang for the buck in the form of improved performance. You must look at the ADDM reports and then run the SQL Tuning Advisor to receive recommendations for improving performance. The SQL Tuning Advisor makes recommendations to improve problem SQL queries, due either to a poorly designed query or to a query that wasn't making use of optimal statistics. The SQL Tuning Advisor's recommendations might include gathering statistics, adding indexes, creating a SQL profile, or modifying the SQL statements.

Even when you got recommendations from the SQL Tuning Advisor that saved you the rigors of performing a manual SQL tuning, in Oracle Database 10*g* you were still in charge of evaluating and then actually implementing the recommendations made by the SQL Tuning Advisor. In Oracle Database 11*g*, Oracle goes much further in automating the entire SQL tuning process, as we explain in the next section.

Automation of SQL Tuning in Oracle Database 11*g*

In Oracle Database 11*g*, the new Automatic SQL Tuning Advisor task runs nightly by default. As is the case with the other two automated management tasks—the Optimizer Statistics Gathering and Automatic Segment Advisor tasks—the Automatic SQL Tuning Advisor task is enabled by default when you create a database or migrate an Oracle 10*g* database to the 11*g* release. The new automatic task, named the Automatic SQL Tuning Advisor task (`sys_auto_sql_tuning_task`), runs automatically every night, as part of the automatic maintenance task framework, looking for ways to speed up the performance of high-load SQL statements by improving their execution plans.

■**Note** As with all automated tasks in the database, you must set the initialization parameter to `typical` (not `basic`) to enable automatic SQL tuning. The ADDM gets its data from the AWR—if you turn off the AWR snapshots or if you lower the retention period for AWR data to less than the default period of eight days, the database disables automatic SQL tuning.

The Automatic SQL Tuning Advisor task does the following things:

- Identifies inefficient SQL statements

- Runs the SQL Tuning Advisor to get recommendations for improving the problem statements

- Tunes problem statements by *implementing* the SQL profile recommendations made by the SQL Tuning Advisor

In the following sections, we'll cover how the new automatic SQL tuning feature works in Oracle Database 11*g*.

Identifying Candidates for SQL Tuning

The Automatic SQL Tuning Advisor job runs every night during the maintenance window of the automated maintenance tasks feature. You don't need to provide any SQL tuning sets for the job, because the tuning task selects the workload based on its analysis of database performance. The Automatic SQL Tuning Advisor task depends on the AWR for the selection of candidates for further analysis. Automatic SQL tuning pulls SQL from the AWR that was at the top of the list of SQL queries that performed poorly during four different time periods, which it calls *buckets*. These four buckets are based on weekly, daily, hourly, or top SQL in a single SQL execution based on response time. Automatic SQL tuning combines the top queries from the four buckets into one by assigning weights.

The database considers the following types of queries ineligible for automatic SQL tuning, although you can still tune them (except ad hoc SQL queries) manually using the SQL Tuning Advisor:

- Parallel queries

- Ad hoc SQL

- Any SQL statement that wasn't executed more than once during the past week

- DDL statements

- Queries that are still at the top of the poorly performing query list, even after profiling

- Recursive SQL statements

Running the Automatic SQL Tuning Advisor

The first step in automatic SQL tuning is to find the bad SQL statements to tune. Once the Automatic SQL Tuning Advisor task generates a list of candidate SQL statements, the advisor orders the candidate SQL list in the order of importance. The SQL Tuning Advisor then tunes each of the candidate SQL statements in the order of importance and recommends SQL profiles to improve the performance of the SQL statements.

Implementing the Recommendations

If the SQL Tuning Advisor finds an existing SQL profile, it checks the optimizer statistics to ensure they do exist and that they are up-to-date. If not, it lets the gather_stats_task job know about it so it can collect the necessary statistics.

The automatic SQL tuning process may make other recommendations besides the adoption of a SQL profile, such as creating new indexes, refreshing statistics, or even restructuring the SQL statements. However, you must review and manually implement these other recommendations yourself, as in Oracle Database 10g. The database implements only the SQL profiles automatically.

An interesting aspect here is that the database doesn't automatically implement all SQL profiles that the SQL Tuning Advisor generates during the tuning process. It implements only those SQL profile recommendations that will improve performance by at least threefold. To be more precise, here are the requirements a SQL profile must satisfy before the database automatically implements it:

- There should be a threefold improvement in the sum of the CPU time and IO time.

- Neither CPU time nor IO time must deteriorate because of the new SQL profile.

The reason for the previous set of requirements is to ensure that any contention caused by the new SQL profile doesn't make performance actually worse than running the query without the SQL profile. The automatic SQL tuning process tests SQL statements with and without the SQL profile before making the recommendation to accept the new profile.

The automatic SQL tuning process doesn't modify the offending SQL statement in any way, and you can reverse its actions any time by removing the new profiles that it implemented.

Managing Automatic SQL Tuning

Managing the automatic SQL tuning feature involves configuring the automatic SQL tuning feature on and off, and second, managing the scheduling of the task during the maintenance window. You also need to configure the parameters of the Automatic SQL Tuning Advisor task. These task parameters include actions such as setting time limits on the tuning tasks, turning SQL profile implementation on and off, and even disabling the testing of new SQL profiles, if the time to implement the changes is a major concern.

Like most components of the advisor framework, you can tune automatic SQL tuning through Enterprise Manager Database Control (or Grid Control) or through Oracle-supplied PL/SQL packages. Next we'll cover how you can manage automatic SQL tuning through Enterprise Manager Database Control.

Using Database Control

The easiest way to manage most components of the automatic SQL management framework is by using Database Control. Follow these steps to manage automatic SQL tasks through Database Control:

1. Click the Server tab on the home page of Database Control.

2. On the Server page, click the Automated Maintenance Tasks link in the Oracle Scheduler section.

3. On the Automated Maintenance Tasks page, click the Automatic SQL Tuning link.

4. You'll now be on the Automatic SQL Tuning Result Summary page. To turn automatic SQL tuning on and off, go to the Configure Automatic SQL Tuning page by clicking the Configure button in the Task Status section of this page. If you want, you can enable the feature only for some days of the week.

5. Click the View Report link in the Task Activity Summary section to view the Automatic SQL Tuning Result Details page, shown in Figure 4-1. Here, you can view all recommendations made by the SQL Tuning Advisor, and you can choose to implement some or all of the recommendations from this page. At the bottom of the same page, you can view a histogram showing the pre-change response time and another showing the tuning benefit.

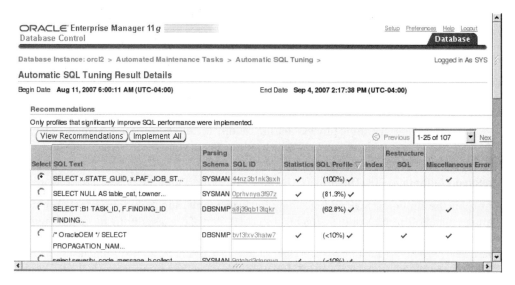

Figure 4-1. *The Automatic SQL Tuning Result Details page*

Using the DBMS_AUTO_TASK_ADMIN Package

Use the DBMS_AUTO_TASK_ADMIN package to enable and disable the Automatic SQL Tuning Advisor task and to control various aspects of executing the SQL Tuning Advisor task. Here's a summary of the main procedures you can use to control the execution of the Automatic SQL Tuning Advisor task:

- enable: Lets you enable a previously disabled operation, client, target type or target to be enabled again

- disable: Lets you prevent executing requests from a specific client or operation

- get_client_attributes: Returns select client attribute values

- get_p1_resoruces: Returns the percentage of resources allocated to each automatic maintenance task's High Priority Consumer group

- set_p1_resources: Sets the resource allocation for each High Priority Consumer group used by the automatic maintenance task clients

- override_priority: Lets you override task priorities

SQL Access Advisor Enhancements

Oracle introduced the SQL Access Advisor in the Oracle Database 10*g* release to help you determine efficient access structures such as indexes, materialized views, and materialized view logs. The SQL Access Advisor either takes the actual database workload (SQL cache) or derives a hypothetical workload or a SQL tuning set as the basis for making recommendations for better execution of SQL statements. You can run the advisor in limited mode or in comprehensive mode, as was the case with this advisor in Oracle Database 10*g*.

In Oracle Database 10g, the SQL Access Advisor provided recommendations regarding indexes, materialized views, and materialized view logs. New in Oracle Database 11g, the advisor will also recommend *partitions* for tables, indexes, and materialized views. The partition enhancements are part of the Partition Advisor, which is integrated into the SQL Access Advisor.

The SQL Access Advisor now shows you the expected gains of implementing its recommendations. In addition, the advisor also reports intermediate results by breaking up the workload into parts. These intermediate results are called *publish points*.

Partitioning Recommendations

In addition to the normal recommendations to create or drop indexes, materialized views, and materialized view logs, you'll now also get recommendations to *partition* existing tables and indexes. The advisor may also recommend adding a partitioned index on a table or a materialized view or adding a new partitioned materialized view. In some case, the advisor may recommend replacing the current table partitioning with a more efficient partitioning scheme.

The SQL Access Advisor may recommend range, interval, list, hash, range-hash, and range-list partitioning schemes for base tables and indexes. It may recommend local, range, and hash partitioning schemas for partitioning indexes.

To implement its partition recommendations, the SQL Access Advisor generates an implementation script, which may invoke an external package such as the DBMS_REDEFINITION package, and partitions the base table online. If the table that the advisor is going to partition has any bitmap indexes defined on it, the DBMS_REDEFINITION package may fail. In this case, you must drop the bitmap indexes before the advisor implements its partitioning recommendations and create the indexes after the table partitioning is completed.

Here are some key things to note about the partition recommendations:

- If the partitioning recommendation is one of several other recommendations such as creating indexes beside the partitioning recommendation, you can't implement the other recommendations only and decide not to partition the table or index. This is because the other recommendations are contingent upon the implementation of the partitioning recommendations.

- The SQL Access Advisor recommends only single-column interval and hash partitioning, with interval being the default. Hash partitioning is designed to take advantage of partition-wise joins.

- The advisor recommends partitions only for tables that have at least 10,000 rows.

- The partitioning recommendations may take a considerable amount of time to complete, if the table is large.

- Partitioning recommendations are limited to workloads that contain predicates or join table columns of type NUMBER or DATE only.

- You'll need additional storage if the DBMS_REDEFINITION package is invoked, since that package creates a temporary copy of the table during the online reorganization of a table.

Accessing Intermediate Results

As you are probably aware, the SQL Access Advisor takes a considerable amount of time to execute, especially when you run it in comprehensive mode. In Oracle Database 11*g*, you can access the *intermediate results* while the advisor is still executing. This gives you the opportunity to cut short an advisor run if the intermediate results aren't appealing to you. Similarly, if the intermediate results show evidence that the recommendations will lead to a significant benefit, you can cut short the advisor run by interrupting it midstream.

The SQL Access Advisor bases its partitioning recommendations on its analysis of a significant proportion of the workload. Thus, if you interrupt an advisor task early in the game, the advisor may not include any base table partitioning recommendations in the intermediate results. If you decide to interrupt, wait for a substantial portion of the workload to complete so you can get the partitioning recommendations as well.

To accept the intermediate results, you must formally interrupt the advisor task. The advisor will then stop executing the task and mark it as interrupted. Following this, you can either ask the advisor to complete the recommendation process or choose to accept the recommendations and generate scripts for implementing them.

New DBMS_ADVISOR Procedures

Two new procedures in the DBMS_ADVISOR package have a bearing on the SQL Access Advisor. These are the add_sts_ref and copy_sqlwkld_to_sts procedures.

ADD_STS_REF Procedure

You can use the add_sts_ref procedure to link a SQL Access Advisor task to the SQL tuning set. The advisor task can use this link to access the SQL tuning set for analysis purposes. Here's the structure of the add_sts_ref procedure:

Argument Name	Type	In/Out	Default?
TASK_NAME	VARCHAR2	IN	
STS_OWNER	VARCHAR2	IN	
WORKLOAD_NAME	VARCHAR2	IN	

Here's an example showing how to use the add_sts_ref procedure to link a task (task1) to a SQL tuning set (sts_1):

```
SQL> exec dbms_advisor.add_sts_ref ("task1', 'hr', 'sts_1');
```

Once you create a link between the advisor task and the SQL Tuning Advisor task, the STS can't be altered or deleted, thus providing a stable view of the workload for the advisor.

COPY_SQLWKLD_TO_STS Procedure

The copy_sqlwkld_to_sts procedure transfers the contents of a SQL workload object to an STS. The copy_sqlwkld_to_sts procedure has the following attributes:

Argument Name	Type	In/Out	Default?
WORKLOAD_NAME	VARCHAR2	IN	
STS_NAME	VARCHAR2	IN	
IMPORT_MODE	VARCHAR2	IN	DEFAULT

The workload_name attribute refers to the source SQL workload, and the sts_name attribute points to the target STS into which you'll be importing the SQL Workload object. The import_mode attribute can take the value append, new, or replace and determines the handling of the data in the target STS upon the import of the SQL Workload object. Here's an example showing how to use the copy_sqlwkload_to_sts procedure:

```
SQL> exec dbms_advisor.copy_sqlwkld_to_sts ('workload_1',
     'sts_1', 'new');
```

Oracle will create a new STS if the STS you specify doesn't exist.

Optimizer and Statistics Collection Enhancements

Oracle Database 11g provides several enhancements in the optimizer statistics collection area. One of the important new features is the *extended statistics* feature, which lets the optimizer collect statistics on correlated columns in a table, thus providing better selectivity estimates. You can also collect *expression statistics* on expression functions. The statistics that you can collect for column groups and expressions are called *extended statistics*. The other important enhancement is the new concept of private and public statistics, with private statistics being statistics that you've collected but not yet published for use by the cost optimizer. We'll cover the interesting new features in the following sections.

Multicolumn Statistics

One of the key things the cost optimizer considers during its execution plan evaluation is the *selectivity* (or *cardinality*) of the column in the where clause of a query. The number of different values in a column determines the column's selectivity. When a column in a table has many different values, that column has good selectivity, and a column with many values that are the same has poor selectivity. If you build an index on a column with good selectivity, the optimizer is able to access the necessary row faster than it will access a row with lower selectivity.

If a column has poor selectivity—for example, a certain value that's the same in more than 95 percent of the table's rows—it's likely that the cost optimizer will opt for a full table scan, regardless of the existence of an index on that column. If, on the other hand, there are several distinct column values such that no column value is in more than 1 or 2 percent of the table's rows, the optimizer is likely to choose the index for accessing the rows when you issue a query that contains a where clause containing this column.

Several queries, however, contain multiple columns from a table, each with a different degree of selectivity. Some of these columns are related, but the optimizer doesn't know about the nature of these relationships. For example, in a table containing products and their prices, some products have higher prices than others. However, the cost optimizer, which bases its calculations on the statistics it gathers on individual columns, doesn't know of this relationship. The optimizer can't estimate the combined selectivity of multiple columns when there is skewed data—that is, data where the different values in a column aren't evenly distributed among all rows but rather are bunched together. For the optimizer to estimate the true cardinality of the data, it must know whether the addition of another column to a given column would reduce the result set. Correlated statistics on multiple columns could provide significantly better cardinality estimates than single column statistics or histograms. Adding an additional predicate could reduce the result set when the two columns are strongly correlated.

Oracle Database 11*g* introduces extended statistics (also called *multicolumn statistics*) wherein you can collect statistics on a set of columns together, thus enabling the optimizer to compute the selectivity of multiple single-column predicates accurately. Since closely related columns can affect the combined selectivity for the columns taken as a group, gathering statistics on the related columns as a group (column group) means the optimizer will have a more correct estimate of the selectivity for the group of columns as a whole, which is your real focus in queries involving predicates using the related columns. This innovation could mean that a query that used a full table scan in prior releases may now use an index scan, making the query run much faster.

The following example makes the concept of multicolumn statistics clearer. Let's take the customers table in the sh schema, which has two related columns, cust_state_province and country_id. You get the following results when you query the customers table:

```
SQL> select count(*)
     from customers
     where cust_state_province = 'CA';

COUNT(*)
-------------
    3341

SQL>
```

If you add the country_id column to the query, the results are still the same:

```
SQL> select count(*)
     from customers
     where cust_state_province = 'CA'
     and country_id = 52790;

COUNT(*)
-------------
    3341

SQL>
```

The COUNTRY_ID 52790 is for the United States. If the COUNTRY_ID column has a different value, such as 52775, the results are quite different:

```
SQL> select count(*)
     from customers
     where cust_state_province = 'CA';

COUNT(*)
-------------
    0

SQL>
```

The optimizer doesn't have any idea about the relationship between the CUST_TATE_PROVINCE and COUNTRY_ID columns. However, if you gather statistics on the two columns as a group, the optimizer has a far better estimate of the selectivity for the group, instead of relying on generating the selectivity estimate for the two columns separately from the statistics on the individual columns.

Creating Multicolumn Statistics

Although the database creates column groups by default by analyzing the workload in the database, you can create your own column groups by using the DBMS_STATS package. Here's the syntax of the create_extended_stats function, which lets you create a column group:

```
FUNCTION CREATE_EXTENDED_STATS RETURNS VARCHAR2
 Argument Name        Type               In/Out     Default?
 --------------       ---------------    ---------  -----------
 OWNNAME              VARCHAR2           IN
 TABNAME              VARCHAR2           IN
 EXTENSION            VARCHAR2           IN
```

The ownname argument stands for the schema owner's name, and if you're using the current schema, you can specify null as the value for this attribute. The tabname attribute is for the table name, and the extension attribute is where you list the related columns that are going to be part of your new column group.

The following example shows how to create a column group named group1 consisting of two related columns—CUST_STATE_PROVINCE and COUNTRY_ID—from the table orders:

```
SQL> declare
     group1 varchar2(30);
     begin
        group1:=dbms_stats.create_extended_stats(null,'customers','
        (cust_state_province,country_id)');
     end;
SQL> /

PL/SQL procedure successfully completed.

SQL>
```

Executing this PL/SQL procedure creates a new column group `group1` consisting of the `STATE_PROVINCE` and `COUNTRY_ID` columns and adds that group to the `customers` table. You can check what extensions providing multicolumn statistics exist in the database by issuing the following query:

```
SQL> select extension_name, extension
    from dba_stat_extensions
    where table_name='CUSTOMERS';

EXTENSION_NAME                   EXTENSION
-------------------              --------------------------------------------
SYS_STU#S#WF25Z#QAHIHE#MOFFMM    ("CUST_STATE_PROVINCE","COUNTRY_ID")

SQL>
```

The `show_extended_stats` function returns the name of the column group you created as a *virtual column*, with a database generated column name. Here's the query:

```
SQL> select
    sys.dbms_stats.show_extendedstats_name('sh','customers',
    '(cust_state_province,country id)') col_group_name from dual);

COL_GROUP_NAME
------------------------------------------------------
SYS_STU#S#WF25Z#QAHIHE#MOFFMM
SQL>
```

Utilizing the virtual column `SYS_STU#S#WF25Z#QAHIHE#MOFFMM`, which represents the true nature of the correlation between the `CUST_STATE_PROVINCE` and the `COUNTRY_ID` columns, the cost optimizer now has the correct estimate of the true selectivity of the two correlated columns. A virtual column, as its name suggests, isn't physically part of the table, but the optimizer is aware of it when it's evaluating different execution plans.

Gathering Statistics for Column Groups

When you know that some columns of a table are correlated in a skewed manner, you can let the optimizer know that the data is skewed so it can compute better selectivity estimates. The way to do this is by gathering histograms on the skewed column group, as shown in the following example:

```
SQL> exec sys.dbms_stats.gather_table_stats(null,'customers',-
    method_opt => 'for all columns size skewonly')
```

Earlier, you learned how to create a new column group using the `create_extended_stats` procedure. You can automatically create a new column group as part of statistics gathering as well, as shown here:

```
SQL> exec sys.dbms_stats.gather_table_stats(null,'customers',
    method_opt => 'for all columns size skewonly
                            for columns  (cust_state_province,country_id)
                            skewonly')
```

You specify the new column group you want to create by using the `for columns` clause. The procedure will both create the new column group as well as gather statistics on that group in a single step.

Deleting Extended Statistics

You can remove any extended statistics you created by executing the `drop_extended_statistics` procedure, as shown in the following example:

```
SQL> exec dbms_stats.drop_extended_stats(null,'customers',-
    '(country, state)');

PL/SQL procedure successfully completed.
SQL>
```

You can use the `drop_extended_statistics` procedure for removing any extended statistics that you created for a function on a column.

Expression Statistics for Functions and Expressions

Another area where the cost optimizer has trouble making true selectivity estimates is for columns to which you apply a function or an expression. For example, it's common to use the `upper` and `lower` functions when using columns such as `LAST_NAME` and `FIRST_NAME` in a query expression, as shown in this example.

```
SQL> select count(*)
    from employees
    where lower(state) ='tx';
```

Because of the application of a function to the `state` column, the optimizer can't get accurate estimates of the selectivity of that column. In Oracle Database 11*g*, you let the optimizer get better selectivity estimates by gathering expression statistics on the expression function.

Suppose that the users input a value for the last name of the customers in uppercase. You can then create extended statistics on the expression `UPPER (last_name)` so the optimizer can get the correct count of the number of rows:

```
SQL> exec dbms_stats.create_extended_stats -
    (null,' customers','(lower(cust_state_province))')
```

As with the column groups, you can both create new extension statistics and gather statistics at the same time by using the `DBMS_STATS` package, as shown in this example:

```
SQL> exec dbms_stats.gather_table_stats (null,'customers_obe',-
    >  method_opt => 'for all columns size skewonly for -
    >  columns (upper(last_name))  -
    >  skewonly');
```

You can monitor expression statistics with the DBA_STAT_EXTENSION view, and you can drop the extension statistics from a table with the drop_extended_statistics function of the DBMS_STATS package.

Changing Statistics Preferences

In Oracle Database 10g, you used the DBMS_STATS package's GET_PARAM function to return the default values of parameters for several procedures that belong to the DBMS_STATS package. The GET_PARAM procedure is obsolete in Oracle Database 11g. Instead, there is a more powerful new function called GET_PREFS, which will get you the default values of various preferences. The GET_PREFS function has parameters such as cascade, degree, estimate_percent, granularity, publish, and stale_percent, each of which is called a *preference*. Here's an example of how you can use the get_prefs function to get the preferences for a certain parameter, in this case the stale_percent parameter:

```
SQL> select dbms_stats.get_prefs('stale_percent',
     'sh','product_descriptions')
     stale_percent from dual;


STALE_PERCENT
-----------------------
    20
```

If you provide the schema, the table name, and a preference, the previous function will return the values specified for that table. If you don't specify any values for that table, the function will return the global preference, if you specified one. If you don't specify either a global preference or a table specific preference, the function will return the default values for that preference.

Setting Preferences

The set_param procedure that enabled you to set default parameter values for various DBMS_STAT procedures in the previous version of the Oracle database is now obsolete. Instead, there is a new procedure, set_global_prefs, that lets you set global statistics preferences for the various parameters. You need the sysdba privilege to set global preferences using the set_global_prefs procedure.

The following example shows how to use the set_global_prefs procedure:

```
SQL>exec dbms_stats.set_global_prefs('estimate_percent','70');

PL/SQL procedure successfully completed.

SQL>
```

Confirm the change in the estimate_percent parameter's value in the table product_descriptions by using the following query:

```
SQL> select dbms_stats.get_prefs ('estimate_percent', 'oe',
     'product_descriptions') estimate_percent from dual;

ESTIMATE_PERCENT
------------------------------
70

SQL>
```

The set_global_prefs procedure will set global preferences for all parameters you can set for the various procedures of the DBMS_STATS package. You can also set the preferences at the database level (set_database_prefs), schema level (set_schema_prefs), and individual table level (set_table_prefs).

Removing Statistics Preferences

You can use new procedures of the DBMS_STATS package to delete current statistics preferences. Here are the different statistics preferences deletion procedures:

- delete_table_prefs: Deletes statistics preferences for a specific table

- delete_schema_prefs: Deletes statistics preferences for a specific schema

- delete_database_prefs: Deletes statistics preferences for all tables in the database, other than those owned by Oracle

Exporting and Importing Statistics Preferences

You can also *export* statistics preferences at the database (export_database_prefs), schema (export_schema_prefs), or table (export_table_prefs) level. The following example exports statistics preferences at the database level:

```
SQL> exec dbms_stats.export_database_prefs('hrtab',statown=>'hr');
```

The previous procedure will export the statistics preferences of all tables (except those owned by SYS) to the table hrtab. Similarly, you can *import* statistics preferences from a specified statistics table where you first exported them at the database level (import_database_prefs), schema level (import_schema_prefs), or table level (import_table_prefs).

Keeping Statistics Pending vs. Publishing Statistics Immediately

In prior database versions, once the DBMS_STATS procedure (or the analyze command) collected statistics, the statistics were immediately offered for use by the cost optimizer. In other words, the *publishing* of the statistics was automatic. This is still the default behavior in Oracle Database 11*g*, with the important distinction that you can now opt *not to publish* the statistics automatically, thus giving you an opportunity to test the new statistics to see whether they actually improve query performance. You can view the default behavior regarding the publishing of statistics by using the get_prefs function as shown here:

```
SQL> select dbms_stats.get_prefs('publish') from dual;

DBMS_STATS.GET_PREFS('PUBLISH')
--------------------------------------------------
TRUE

SQL>
```

In Oracle Database 11g, there is a distinction between *public* and *private* statistics, the former being statistics that have been published for use by the cost-based optimizer in its query optimization process and the latter being statistics that have been gathered but aren't yet published, that is, not made available to the cost-based optimizer. You can choose to collect private statistics at the database level or at the table level, thus offering you great flexibility in how you use this powerful new feature. By default, statistics that the database collects are stored in the data dictionary. The database will store private statistics that you collect in a private area pending their publishing, thus making them unavailable to the cost-based optimizer, which can use only those statistics stored in the data dictionary.

Pending Statistics

How do you test the usage of private statistics by the cost-optimizer? The statistics you categorize as private have a pending status at first, before they're published. This is the reason why the private statistics are also called *pending* statistics. After verifying the query performance, you can opt to publish the pending statistics by running the publish_pending_stats procedure in the DBMS_STATS package. If the query performance isn't acceptable, you can delete the pending statistics by running the delete_pending_stats procedure instead.

Making Pending Statistics Available to the Optimizer

Once you test the impact of the new statistics, you can decide whether to publish them. You can make the private statistics available to the cost-based optimizer by setting the initialization parameter optimizer_use_private_statistics to true. The default value of this parameter is false, meaning the cost optimizer ignores pending statistics by default. Once you change the parameter setting to true, the optimizer will take into account the pending statistics in preference to the published statistics it has for a table or schema.

In the following example, we use the set_table_prefs procedure we explained earlier in this chapter in order to specify that a certain table's statistics not be published automatically. In other words, we are directing the database to collect private instead of public statistics for this table, and these statistics will be in pending mode until you decide on their acceptance. In the example, we turn off automatic publishing of statistics for the table product_descriptions, owned by the user oe. Here's the example:

```
SQL> exec dbms_stats.set_table_prefs ('oe','
    product_descriptions','publish','false');

PL/SQL procedure successfully completed.

SQL>
```

You can also change the publish settings at the schema level instead of the table level. The set_table_prefs procedure we execute here doesn't set off an immediate statistics collection, private or public, for the specified table. It stipulates only that when the database collects statistics the next time for the product_descriptions table, it shouldn't immediately publish the statistics. Instead of publishing the statistics that it gathered for the table product_descriptions, the database will store them in the DBA_TAB_PENDING_STATS table.

You can confirm that the product_descriptions statistics will be private (pending) by issuing the following select statement again:

```
SQL> select
     dbms_stats.get_prefs('publish','oe','product_descriptions')
     from dual;

DBMS_STATS.GET_PREFS('PUBLISH','OE','PRODUCT_DESCRIPTIONS')
-----------------------------------------------------------
FALSE

SQL>
```

The value of false in the previous query means that the statistics for the OE table won't be automatically published but kept private (pending).

Collecting Private Statistics

First, execute the delete_table_statistics procedure to delete any existing statistics for the table product_descriptions. Here's the code:

```
SQL> exec dbms_stats.delete_tables_stats
     ('oe','product_descriptions');

PL/SQL procedure successfully completed.

SQL>
```

Once you get rid of all the statistics on the table product_descriptions, collect fresh statistics for the table by issuing the following command:

```
SQL> exec dbms_stats.gather_table_stats('oe','product_descriptions');

PL/SQL procedure successfully completed.

SQL>
```

The database won't publish the statistics you collected by executing the previous gather_ table_stats procedure, since you earlier set the publish preference to false. You can verify first that these statistics aren't public by querying the USER_TABLES view in the following manner:

```
SQL> select table_name, last_analyzed, num_rows from
     user_tables
     where table_name='PRODUCT_DESCRIPTIONS';
```

```
TABLE_NAME              LAST_ANALYZED           NUM_ROWS
-------------           ----------------        ------------------
```

```
SQL>
```

The query on the USER_TABLES view shows public statistics only, and thus there is nothing showing that the database actually collected any statistics for the product_descriptions table. However, if you query the USER_TAB_PENDING_STATS view, which holds information about private statistics, you'll see something else:

```
SQL> select table_name, last_analyzed, num_rows from
     user_tab_pending_stats
     where table_name='PRODUCT_DESCRIPTIONS';
```

```
TABLE_NAME              LAST_ANALYZED       NUM_ROWS
-------------------     --------------      -----------------
PRODUCT_DESCRIPTIONS    29-MAY-07           8634
```

```
SQL>
```

The USER_TAB_PENDING_STATS view shows pending statistics for tables, partitions, and subpartitions owned by the user issuing the command.

Testing, Publishing, and Deleting Pending Statistics

You can use the export_table_statistics procedure to export the pending statistics to a different database and test them there. If the query results aren't encouraging with the pending statistics, you can delete pending statistics by executing the delete_pending_stats procedure, as shown here:

```
SQL> exec dbms_stats.delete_pending_stats('HR','EMPLOYEES');
```

You can choose to make pending statistics permanent, that is, publish them, by using the publish_pending_statistics procedure, as shown in this example:

```
SQL> exec dbms_stats.publish_pending_stats('HR','EMPLOYEES');
```

If you want to publish all statistics collected for a particular schema, you can do so by executing this procedure:

```
SQL> exec dbms_stats.publish_pending_stats('HR',null);
```

You can publish all pending statistics in the database by executing the following procedure:

```
SQL> exec dbms_stats.publish_pending_stats(null, null);
```

By default, private statistics are turned off, as shown by the default setting of false for the new Oracle Database 11g initialization parameter optmizer_use_private_statistics.

SQL Plan Management (SPM)

It's not uncommon at all for DBAs to confront situations where a well-functioning system encounters performance problems because of a regression in the execution plans of SQL statements. Execution plans for SQL statements could change for a number of reasons, including the upgrade of the Oracle database or the operating system software, changes in optimizer versions, optimizer statistics or optimizer parameters, data changes, schema definition and metadata changes, deployment of new application modules, adding and dropping indexes, and so on. In earlier versions, Oracle provided features such as stored outlines and SQL profiles to enable the stability of execution plans over time. However, all these required you, the DBA, to decide to use and implement the plan stability features.

Oracle Database 11*g* introduces a new plan stabilization feature called SQL Plan Management that lets the database control the evolution of SQL execution plans through *SQL plan baselines*. The goal of SPM is to preserve the performance of your SQL code in the face of changes such as database upgrades, system and data changes, and application upgrades and bug fixes. You can currently use SQL profiles through Oracle's automatic SQL tuning feature to produce well-tuned execution plans, but that is a purely *reactive mechanism*, which doesn't help you when there are drastic changes in your system. Oracle has designed SPM as a *preventative mechanism* that aims to preserve the performance of SQL statements in the face of numerous types of changes that we listed earlier. Whereas a SQL profile contains statistics that will improve the execution plan for a SQL statement, a SQL plan baseline contains hints for the optimizer to generate a better execution plan for a SQL statement.

Once you enable this new plan stabilization feature, new execution plans generated by changes in factors such as optimizer statistics, for example, are accepted only if they don't lead to a deterioration in performance. The cost-based optimizer manages the SQL plan baselines and uses only known and verified plans. After verification, the optimizer uses only comparable plans or plans that yield better performance than the current execution plans. SPM builds SQL plan baselines of known good execution plans. SQL Plan Management aims to replace the plan stability feature in earlier releases of the Oracle database. The older stored outlines feature is deprecated in this release, and Oracle recommends that you migrate your stored outlines to SQL plan baselines.

The database stores an execution plan as a SQL baseline, thus maintaining the plan for a set of SQL statements. Provided the database has the necessary optimizer statistics, the optimizer first evolves a best-cost plan and then tries to match it with a plan in the SQL plan baseline. If the optimizer finds a match, it uses this plan. Otherwise, the optimizer will evaluate all the accepted plans in the SQL baseline and choose the lowest cost plan for executing the statement.

■**Note** The database tracks SQL plan history only for statements that execute multiple times. Ad hoc queries aren't, by definition, eligible for tracking.

SPM involves three distinct steps or stages—capturing, selecting, and evolving SQL plan baselines. The following sections summarize the three phases.

Capturing SQL Plan Baselines

The first phase involves capturing the SQL plan baselines. To support SPM and the performance verification of newly evolved execution plans, the optimizer maintains a plan history for each repeatable SQL statement containing the different execution plans generated for that statement. The optimizer considers a SQL statement repeatable if the database parses or executes that statement multiple times after the optimizer logs the statement in the SQL statement log that it maintains.

You can load the SQL plan outlines automatically or use manual bulk-loading procedures. First we'll discuss the automatic approach to creating and maintaining plan history for SQL statements, using the optimizer-provided data. Then we'll show how to do this manually.

Automatic SQL Plan Capture

You can enable automatic loading of SQL plan baselines by setting the initialization parameter `optimizer_capture_plan_baselines` to true, as shown here:

```
SQL> alter system set optimizer_capture_sql_plan_baselines=true;
System altered.
```

The default value of the `optimizer_capture_sql_plan_baselines` parameter is `false`, meaning automatic plan capture is turned off by default. By setting the parameter's value to `true` in the parameter file, or with the `alter system` or `alter session` statement, you let the database automatically start recognizing repeatable SQL statements and create a plan history for them.

The database uses the optimizer details about each SQL statement to reproduce the execution plan for it. The first plan for each SQL statement is marked for use by the optimizer. At this point, both plan history and the SQL plan baseline are identical, since there's only a single SQL statement to consider. All new plans that the optimizer generates subsequently for a SQL statement become part of the plan history. During the final *SQL plan baseline evolution* phase, the database will add to the SQL plan baseline any plan that's verified not to lead to a performance regression.

■**Note** If you manually load plans directly from the cursor cache, those plans are automatically marked as SQL baseline plans by default.

Manual SQL Plan Loading

In addition to this automatic tracking of repeatable SQL statements, you can also manually seed plans for a set of SQL statements (SQL tuning set). You can supply the SQL plans as an alternative or in addition to the automatic capture of SQL by the database. An important distinction between automatically capturing SQL plans and manually loading SQL plans is that the database adds *all manually loaded plans* to a SQL plan baseline as accepted plans, without subjecting them to verification for performance.

You can use the new `DBMS_SPS` package to load SQL plans directly into a SQL plan baseline. You can use a cursor cache as the source of the SQL plans or load the plans from SQL tuning sets and AWR snapshots. In the following example, we show how to load SQL plans manually from an STS. Make sure you create and load the STS first, before executing the load_plans_ from_sqlset function, as shown here:

```
SQL> declare
  2   result number;
  3   begin
  4   result :=dbms_spm.load_plans_from_sqlset (sqlset_name =>
         'sqlset1');
  5   end;
  6  /

PL/SQL procedure successfully completed.

SQL>
```

The previous function loads all SQL plans from an STS into SQL plan baselines. The plans aren't verified, as we mentioned earlier, and are added as accepted plans to an existing or new SQL baseline. If you want to load plans from the AWR, first load the SQL plans from the AWR into the STS before executing the load_plans_from_sqlset procedure. You can alternatively load any SQL plans you want from the cursor cache using the load_plans_from_cursor_cache function, as shown here:

```
SQL> declare
  2   result number;
  3   begin
  4    result := dbms_spm.load_plans_from_cursor_cache (sql_id =>
         '7ztv2z24kwOsO');
  5   end;
  6  /

PL/SQL procedure successfully completed.

SQL>
```

In this example, we load a plan from the cursor cache by providing its SQL ID. Instead of the SQL ID, you can also use the SQL statement text or the SQL handle to load a SQL statement into a SQL plan baseline.

SQL Plan Baseline Selection

During the selection phase, the database automatically selects SQL plans for every SQL statement that avoids a performance regression. The cost optimizer adopts a conservative plan selection strategy that works in this way: each time the database compiles a SQL statement, the optimizer will build a best-cost plan and try to match it with a plan in the SQL baseline and then use that plan if there is a match. If the optimizer doesn't find a match in the SQL baseline, it selects the cheapest plan from the SQL baseline for execution. In this case, the optimizer's best-cost plan (which doesn't match any of the plans in the plan history) is added as a new plan to the baseline. The database doesn't use this new plan automatically since it is as yet a nonaccepted plan. The database can use this plan only after it verifies that it doesn't lead to performance regression or if it's the only available plan.

Evolving SQL Plan Baselines

A SQL plan baseline can't remain static over time; it has to evolve with the changes in your system by analyzing the good and the not so good plans over a period of time. The database doesn't automatically implement all SQL plans generated by the cost-based optimizer. A SQL plan is deemed an *acceptable plan* only after verification of its performance as compared to the SQL plan baseline performance, and the SQL plan baseline consists of all the acceptable plans for a specific SQL statement. Evolving a SQL plan means changing a nonaccepted plan into an accepted plan.

■**Tip** All plans generated by the optimizer become part of the plan history but aren't automatically integrated into the plan baseline. SPM integrates into the SQL plan baseline only "acceptable" plans that don't lead to a performance regression.

The *original plan baseline* will always consists of at least one plan, which, of course, will be the first execution plan generated by the optimizer for a given SQL statement. The database continuously evaluates new nonaccepted plan performance by comparing the plan performance with a plan selected from the SQL plan baseline. All the plans that don't lead to a performance regression are changed into accepted plans and integrated into the SQL plan baseline.

There are three ways to evolve a SQL plan baseline—manually by running the SQL Tuning Advisor task, by using the DBMS_SPM package, and by using the SQL Tuning Advisor. We'll review the three methods briefly in the following sections.

Manually Loading Plans into the Baselines

As described earlier, when you manually load SQL baselines by using SQL tuning sets or the cursor cache as the source for the statements, the plans you load are considered accepted plans, which makes them equivalent to a verified plan.

Using the DBMS_SPM Package to Evolve Plans

The function DBMS_SPM.EVOLVE_SQL_PLAN_BASELINE evolves baselines associated with one or more SQL statements. The function compares the execution performance of a nonaccepted plan, and if it finds the performance better than the SQL plan baseline performance, it changes the nonaccepted plan into an accepted plan. Here's an example:

```
SQL>  declare
   2      report clob;
   3    begin
   4      report := dbms_spm.evolve_sql_plan_baseline(
   5                    sql_handle => 'aq8yqxyyb4Onn');
   6    end;
   7  /
```

You must grant a user the `administer_sql_management object` privilege so they can execute the `evolve_sql_plan baseline` procedure.

Evolving Plans with the SQL Tuning Advisor

When you run the SQL Tuning Advisor, it may sometimes recommend the acceptance of a SQL profile when the advisor runs across a plan whose performance is better than any plan in the SQL plan baseline. If you implement the recommendation by accepting the SQL profile, the SQL Tuning Advisor automatically adds that plan to the SQL plan baseline. In Oracle Database 11g, as we explained in the SQL Tuning Advisor discussion, the Automatic SQL Tuning Advisor task that runs nightly during the maintenance window automatically implements the SQL profile recommendations made by the SQL Tuning Advisor. Thus, any tuned high-load SQL statements automatically become part of the SQL plan baselines for those statements.

■**Note** If you want to set the number of possible plans to a single plan, you can do so by using fixed SQL plan baselines. You can also use fixed-plan baselines when migrating a stored outline by making the stored outline a fixed SQL plan baseline. The optimizer will then pick the fixed plan even if it finds other plans with lower costs. The optimizer won't automatically add new plans to a fixed plan baseline. You can evolve a fixed SQL plan baseline manually, however, by manually loading new plans from an STS or a cursor cache.

Displaying SQL Plan Baselines

You can examine the SQL plan baselines for any SQL statement using the `DISPLAY_SQL_PLAN_BASELINE` function of the `DBMS_XPLAN` package, as shown here:

```
SQL> select * from table(
  2  dbms_xplan.display_sql_plan_baseline(
  3  sql_handle=>'SYS_SQL_2d02582d7a04c30b',
  4  format =>'basic';));

PLAN_TABLE_OUTPUT
------------------------------------------------------------------------
SQL handle: SYS_SQL_2d02582d7a04c30b
SQL text: select * from hr.employees order by last_name
------------------------------------------------------------------------


------------------------------------------------------------------------
Plan name: SYS_SQL_PLAN_7a04c30b6d8b6a03
Enabled: YES    Fixed: NO    Accepted: YES    Origin: MANUAL-LOAD
------------------------------------------------------------------------
PLAN_TABLE_OUTPUT
------------------------------------------------------------------------
Plan hash value: 3447538987
```

```
-----------------------------------------
| Id  | Operation          | Name        |
-----------------------------------------
|   0 | SELECT STATEMENT   |             |
|   1 | SORT ORDER BY      |             |
|   2 | TABLE ACCESS FULL  | EMPLOYEES   |
-----------------------------------------

20 rows selected.

SQL>
```

As shown here, the function DISPLAY_SQL_PLAN_BASELINE displays and provides information about the baseline plans.

Managing the SQL Management Base

The optimizer is in charge of automatically managing the SQL management base (SMB), which is part of the data dictionary and stores the statement log maintained by the optimizer. The SMB also stores the SQL plan histories and the SQL plan baselines. Unlike the data dictionary, which is stored in the system tablespace, the database stores the SMB in the sysaux tablespace. You can configure the SMB to occupy anywhere between 1 and 50 percent of the size of the sysaux tablespace; the default allocation is 10 percent. A background process that runs once a week will issue an alert if the SMB exceeds its space allocation. You can increase the space allocation percentage, increase the size of the sysaux tablespace, or purge SQL plan baselines and SQL profiles from the SMB to make more room for new data.

Use the new view DBA_SQL_MANAGEMENT_CONFIG to see the configuration parameters of the SQL management base. There are two configuration parameters you can modify, space_budget_percent and plan_retention_weeks. The space_budget_percent parameter shows the current SMB space limit in the sysaux tablespace, and the plan_retention_weeks parameter shows how long the database will retain the data in the SMB before automatically purging it. You can view the current values for both of these parameters by issuing the following statement:

```
SQL> select parameter, parameter_value from dba_sql_management_config;

PARAMETER                              PARAM_VALUE
------------------------------------   -------------------
SPACE_BUDGET_PERCENT                   10
PLAN_RETENTION_WEEKS                   53

SQL>
```

This query shows the default values for the two configuration parameters related to the SQL management base. The database will retain unused plans for 53 weeks before purging them. You can also purge individual plans with the help of the purge_sql_plan_baseline function. You can change either of the two configuration parameters by using the configure procedure of the new DBMS_SPM package. The following example shows how to change the setting for the space_budget_percent parameter:

```
SQL> execute dbms_spm.configure ('space_budget_percent', 30);
```

A scheduled purging job that runs as an automated task in the maintenance window takes care of purging unused plans. The purging job automatically removes any execution plan that the optimizer hasn't used in more than a year. You can, however, change this default purging behavior and specify that a used plan not be purged for a period as long as 10 years, as shown in the following example (520 weeks is 10 years):

```
SQL> execute dbms_spm.configure ('plan_retention_weeks', 520);
```

The execution of the `configure` procedure in the example ensures that all execution plans in the SQL management base are retained for 10 years.

Managing SQL Plan Baselines

You can use the DBA_SQL_PLAN_BASELINES view to see the current SQL plan baselines for SQL statements. Besides various SQL plan and SQL identifiers, execution statistics, and timestamps, the view contains the following key columns:

- `origin`: Tells you how the SQL plans were created. There are four possible values for this column:

  - `manual-load`

  - `manual-sqltune`

  - `auto-capture`

  - `auto-sqltune`

- `enabled`: Shows whether the plan baseline is enabled.

- `accepted`: Shows whether the plan baseline is accepted.

- `fixed`: Shows whether the plan baseline is fixed.

Here's an example showing how you can get details about plan baselines from the DBA_SQL_PLAN _BASELINES view:

```
SQL> select sql_handle, origin,enabled,accepted from
  2  dba_sql_plan_baselines;
```

SQL_HANDLE	ORIGIN	ENABLED	ACCEPTED
SYS_SQL_2d02582d7a04c30b	MANUAL-LOAD	YES	YES
SYS_SQL_6a74b7e2315d3858	AUTO-CAPTURE	YES	YES
SYS_SQL_827bc97a47b3e31d	AUTO-CAPTURE	YES	YES
SYS_SQL_9ce6569c74a9b77f	MANUAL-LOAD	YES	YES
SYS_SQL_df1c094103fb0616	AUTO-CAPTURE	YES	YES

```
SQL>
```

The query shows whether the plan was captured automatically or manually, as well as whether it is accepted and enabled.

You can alter any of the attributes of a SQL plan baseline by using the DBMS_SPM.ALTER_SQL_PLAN_BASELINE function. You can also import and export SQL plan baselines using Oracle Data Pump and procedures from the DBMS_SPM package.

ADDM Enhancements

In Oracle Database 10g, Oracle introduced the Automatic Database Diagnostic Monitor, which uses the automatic workload repository snapshots to provide diagnosis regarding SQL statements, IO, and CPU usage in the database. The ADDM is based on the single-minded goal to reduce "DB time." ADDM provides you with quick results that help pinpoint the root cause of a performance problem, besides telling you what the nonproblem areas are, so you don't waste your time chasing down unproductive avenues.

Instance ADDM and Database ADDM

You can run the ADDM in two distinct modes in Oracle Database 11g. In the first mode, called the *instance ADDM*, the monitor provides traditional instance-level performance evaluation. The instance ADDM is what you have in Oracle Database 10g. Oracle calls the new ADDM mode introduced in the new release *database ADDM*, and its goal is to analyze and report on Oracle RAC installations. In this mode, the ADDM report will contain an analysis of the cluster as a unit besides an analysis of each of the instances that are part of the the cluster. Oracle's target for the database ADDM is database administrators rather than application developers, for whom the instance ADDM is more relevant.

The instance ADDM runs automatically after the database takes each AWR snapshot, and it produces the same reports that it did in the Oracle Database 10g database. Depending on whether you run the ADDM in global or instance mode, you'll have global findings or local findings.

The global ADDM is appropriate only for an ORAC setup, where the tool can analyze the performance of the entire cluster together as one unit. For example, the DB time is computed as the sum of the database times for all instances in the ORAC cluster. Global ADDM also reports facts such as CPU consumption and server performance at the aggregate cluster level, thus giving you an overall view of how the ORAC installation is performing. You can also perform a partial analysis of just a subset of the instances in a cluster. This is known as the *partial analysis ADDM*. If you are concerned about the performance of only some but not all instances in a cluster, partial analysis ADDM will provide results faster than an exhaustive database ADDM analysis.

Running ADDM Over a Specific Time Period

You can now run an ADDM task for any specific range of time you want, instead of being able to run it only over a pair of snapshots. This is a great help, especially when there is a hung database or a sharp spike in activity in the database that hasn't been captured yet by an AWR snapshot.

Specifying the Type of ADDM Task

You can use the DBMS_ADVISOR package's set_default_task_parameter procedure to specify the type of ADDM analysis you want to run. You set the values for the instance and the instance's parameters to select among a database ADDM, instance ADDM, or partial analysis ADDM.

Advisor Findings

The various advisors that are part of the management advisory framework issue findings. Oracle Database 11g names and classifies the advisor findings, making it easier for you to keep track of the frequency with which various findings occur. There is a new view named DBA_ADVISOR_FINDINGS that lets you look up all finding names. Here's a query that lets you view all findings in the database:

```
SQL> select finding_name from dba_advisor_finding_names;

FINDING_NAME
-----------------------------------
normal, successful completion
"Administrative" Wait Class
...
Buffer Busy
...
Undersized instance memory

80 rows selected.

SQL>
```

There is also a new FINDING_NAME column added to the DBA_ADVISOR_FINDINGS view, which lets you make queries such as the following:

```
SQL> select finding_name,impact from dba_advisor_findings;

FINDING_NAME                              IMPACT
-----------------------------------       -------------
normal, successful completion             0
normal, successful 0
I/O Throughput                            34077700
Undersized instance memory                140000000
Hard Parse                                256895416
...

78 rows selected.
SQL>
```

Classification of findings applies to all types of advisors, not just the ADDM, and helps you find the frequency with which different findings are issued.

Using the New DBMS_ADDM Package

The DBMS_ADDM package is a new package in the Oracle Database 11g Release 1, designed to make it easier to manage ADDM. Here's a brief summary of the main procedures and functions of this package:

```
analyze_db: creates a Database ADDM (global) task.
SQL> exec dbms_addm.analyze_db('Database ADDM Task 1', 1,2);

analyze_inst: creates an Instance ADDM (local) task.
SQL> exec dbms_addm.analyze_inst('Instance_ADDM_Task 1'1,2);

analyze_partial: creates a task for analyzing some of the instances only.
SQL> exec dbms_addm.analyze_partial(('Instance_ADDM_Task 1'1,2);

get_report: produces a text report of the ADDM task results
SQL> select dbms_addm.get_report('partial_analysis_report') from dual;

Delete: deletes an ADDM task of any type
SQL> exec dbms_addm.delete('Instance_ADDM_Task 1');
```

Note that you must pass the beginning and ending snapshot IDs when creating any type of an ADDM task. Here's an example of an instance ADDM execution with a pair of snapshots.

```
SQL> var task_name varchar2(100);
SQL> begin
SQL> :task_name := 'Instance ADDM Task 1';
SQL> dbms_addm.analyze_inst (:task_name, 10, 15);
SQL> end;
```

To get a text report of the previous task, run the get_report procedure, as shown here:

```
 set long 100000
 set pagesize 50000
SQL> select dbms_addm.get_report(:tname) from dual;
```

The DBMS_ADDM package lets you add various *directives* when you create a new ADDM task to help you control the work of the ADDM. Here's a description of the various procedures you can use to create directives to limit the work of the ADDM:

- insert_finding_directive: Creates a directive that limits the reporting of a specific finding type

- insert_sql_directive: Creates a directive to limit the reporting on a specific SQL

- insert_segment_directive: Creates a directive to prevent the Automatic Segment Advisor from running on certain segments

- insert_parameter_directive: Creates a directive to prevent the modification of values for a specified system parameter

Here's an example that shows how to create an ADDM directive to filter out findings relating to undersized instance memory:

```
SQL> var task_name varchar2(100);
SQL> begin
        dbms_addm.insert_finding_direcive (null,
        'Undersized   Instance Memory Directive',
         'Undersize instance memory',
         5,
         10);
         :task_name := 'ADDM Task 1';
         dbms_addm_analyze_inst(:task_name,1,2);
      end;
SQL> /
```

The example shown here creates an instance ADDM task with a finding directive that limits the display of the "Undersized instance memory" finding only if that finding is related to at least five active sessions during the time of the ADDM analysis. In addition, the finding must be responsible for at least 10 percent of the database time during the analysis period. You can delete any directive you create with the DELETE_* procedures. For example, the delete_finding_directive procedure will delete a finding directive.

AWR Baselines

The AWR generates automatic snapshots of performance data on an hourly basis. You can also manually generate snapshots with the DBMS_WORKLOAD_REPOSITORY package. The ADDM then uses the data thus collected in the AWR.

In Oracle Database 10g, you learned how to use AWR baselines, which provide a frame of reference for comparing performance and advisor reports between two periods. An AWR baseline is simply database performance data from a set of AWR snapshots, representing database performance at an optimum level. When a performance problem occurs, the database compares performance data from a previous "good" period with the performance of a similar workload. You create a baseline with the create_baseline procedure of the DBMS_WORKLOAD_REPOSITORY package and drop it by executing the drop_baseline procedure.

■**Note** In Oracle Database 11g, the default retention for the snapshot data is eight days to ensure that the AWR always has a full week's worth of performance data.

You could create and delete only simple fixed baselines in Oracle Database 10g. A fixed baseline uses a fixed period that you specify. Oracle Database 11g adds more sophistication to the management of AWR baselines by providing the capability to create more complex and productive baselines. Oracle Database 11g contains the following enhancements relating to AWR baselines:

- Moving window baselines

- Baseline templates

- Ability to rename baselines

- Ability to set expiration dates for baselines

You can still use the AUTOMATIC_WORKLOAD_REPOSITORY package's procedures create_snapshot, drop_snapshot, modify_snapshot settings, create_baseline, and drop_baseline to manage snapshots and baselines. In Oracle Database 11g, you have access to new procedures that let you manage the added functionality of the AWR baselines.

We'll briefly describe the AWR baseline enhancements in the following sections.

Moving Window Baselines

A moving window baseline doesn't require you to specify a pair of snapshots. The range of the baseline keeps "moving" or changing continuously. By default, Oracle automatically creates a system-defined moving window named system_moving_window, whose time span corresponds to the entire AWR retention period, which is eight days by default now (instead of seven days). The default moving window baseline will always use AWR data from the previous eight days. Here's how you can view the moving window baseline information:

```
SQL> select baseline_name,baseline_type,start_snap_time,end_snap_time
     from dba_hist_baseline;
```

BASELINE	BASELINE_TYP	START_SNAP	END_SNAP
SYSTEM_ MOVING WINDOW	MOVING_WINDOW	05-JUN-07	13-JUN-07

```
SQL>
```

Note that the eight-day span for system_moving_window is a default value, which you can modify. However, the time range for this window must be always the same as the AWR retention period. Therefore, if you want to specify a 30-day time span for the system_moving_window, you must first raise the AWR retention period to 30 days, up from its default of eight days. (In Oracle Database 10g, the default was seven days.) Use the new modify_baseline_window_size procedure of the DBMS_WORKLOAD_REPOSITORY package to modify the size of the default moving window:

1. You must change the retention period of the AWR, since your default moving window size has to correspond to the AWR retention period, whose default value is eight days. Here's how you change the retention period to 15 days (21600 minutes):

```
SQL> execute dbms_workload_repository.modify_snapshot_settings
     (retention =>  21600);

PL/SQL procedure successfully completed.

SQL>
```

You can set the size of the retention period to anywhere from one day to ten years.

2. Once you set the new AWR retention period, you can modify the default moving window size as shown here:

```
SQL> execute dbms_workload_repository.modify_baseline_window_size (window_
    size = 15, dbid => 3863017760);

PL/SQL procedure successfully completed.

SQL>
```

The window_size parameter sets a new window size for the default moving window baseline. In this case, we set the new window size to 15 days, which is greater than the default AWR retention period of eight days. You can set only a window size that is equal to or less than the AWR retention setting. In cases such as this, where you want to specify a window size greater than the default AWR retention setting, you must first execute the modify_snapshot_settings procedure to change the AWR retention setting.

Baseline Templates

Oracle Database 11*g* provides the ability to create *baseline templates*, which enable you to create AWR baselines automatically for a specific period, whether that period is in the past or in the future. The big advantage to using a baseline template to create baselines is that you don't need to supply the starting and ending snapshot identifiers for the create_baseline procedure. Oracle Database 11*g* provides you with two types of AWR baselines: single and repeating. A single baseline is static in nature. A repeating baseline is dynamic and changing since it captures performance over changing periods. Oracle also provides you with baseline templates to create both types of AWR baselines:

- You can use a single baseline template to create a baseline for a single period that must be contiguous, such as one that covers the testing of a new application or an upgrade.

- You use a repeating baseline template to create a baseline on a repeating schedule, such as when you want to capture the performance during the execution of a key batch job over a period. You can specify that the database automatically remove older baselines after a certain time.

Generating a Template for a One-Time Baseline

The following syntax enables you to specify a template for the creation of a single AER baseline in some future period:

```
dbms_workload_repository.create_baseline_template(
    start_time                in date,
    end_time                  in date,
    baseline_name             in varchar2,
    template_name             in varchar2,
    expiration                in number,
    dbid                      in number default null);
```

Note that you can use the expiration attribute to set the time (in days) for which Oracle must maintain a baseline. The default value is null, meaning the database will never drop a baseline.

Generating a Template for a Repeating Baseline

You can specify a template for creating a repeating baseline using the following procedure:

```
dbms_workload_repository.create_baseline_template(
    day_of_week               IN         VARCHAR2,
    hour_in_day               IN         NUMBER,
    duration                  IN         NUMBER,
    start_time                IN         DATE,
    end_time                  IN         DATE,
    baseline_name_prefix      IN         VARCHAR2,
    template_name             IN         VARCHAR2,
    expiration                IN         NUMBER,
    dbid                      IN         NUMBER DEFAULT NULL);
```

You can use the drop_baseline_template procedure to drop either a one-time or a repeating baseline template.

Ability to Rename Baselines

You can use the new rename_baseline procedure to rename an AWR baseline, as shown in the following example:

```
SQL> execute dbms_workload_repository.rename_baseline -
    (old_baseline_name =>'old_baseline', -
    new_baseline_name => 'new_baseline', dbid=3863017760);
```

The dbid parameter, as in the earlier example, is optional, and the database identifier for the local database will be used as the default value for dbid if you don't provide one.

Ability to Set Expiration Dates for Baselines

When you use the create_baseline procedure to create a new AWR baseline, you can specify the expiration time for that baseline by setting a value for the new expiration attribute of the procedure. The default value of null for the expiration attribute means that a baseline will never expire, which was the only behavior possible in Oracle Database 10g.

Baselines and Template Dictionary Views

There are several new DBA views to help you manage AWR baselines and templates. The three views that will help you the most are as follows:

- DBA_HIST_BASELINE (modified)

- DBA_HIST_BASELINE_TEMPLATE (new)

- DBA_HIST_BASELINE_DETAILS (new)

Adaptive Baseline Metric Thresholds

The Oracle database uses performance alerts to warn you about any violations of thresholds for various activities in the database. However, specifying when the database should issue an alert is a complex task. The setting of alert thresholds is a difficult task because the expected metric values can vary based on the instance load and workload type.

In the Oracle Database 11g release, the database uses the AWR baseline metric statistics to determine alert thresholds. Once the database computes baseline statistics for a specified baseline, you can align the metric thresholds with these AWR baselines. These thresholds are termed *AWR baseline metric thresholds*. Using AWR baselines as the source for the metric statistics lets you specify adaptive thresholds for database performance. The new metric thresholds are called *adaptive* since they're based on the `system_moving_window` baseline, which is, by definition, constantly changing.

You can define AWR baseline alert thresholds either through the PL/SQL interface or through Database Control. The following steps show you how to use Database Control to configure adaptive thresholds:

1. Click the Server tab on the Database home page.

2. Click the AWR Baselines link in the Statistics Management section.

3. You'll be on the AWR Baselines page. Click the Baseline Metric Thresholds link.

4. Select the metric type you want, and click Edit Thresholds.

5. On the Edit Thresholds page, specify critical and warning thresholds for the metric in the Thresholds Settings section.

6. Click Apply Thresholds to apply the threshold settings.

You must specify three threshold settings for each metric for which you choose to configure adaptive thresholds:

- *Threshold Type*: Choose from Significance Level, which indicates whether a metric is at or above a specified value (for example 1 in 100); Percentage of Maximum; and Fixed Values.

- *Warning*: Warning threshold.

- *Critical*: Critical threshold.

Enterprise Manager provides a starter set of thresholds based on online transaction processing (OLTP) or data warehouse workload profiles. Once you select the profile, the database automatically configures adaptive thresholds for the appropriate group of metrics for the workload you choose by using metrics data from the `system_moving_window` baseline.

Performance-Related Changes in Database Control

There are numerous changes in Database Control pertaining to database performance. Since Oracle Database 11g has introduced several new performance features, Database Control will, of course, support those new features. Our focus is on the main changes to the Performance page in Database Control.

Customized Performance Page

You can now set up a customized Database Performance page in Database Control to suit your purposes. Database Control stores the customized settings in its repository and retrieves them for your session's use when you log in again. You can customize things such as which charts appear on the Performance page in the Active Sessions section. You can also configure whether baseline values should appear in the Throughput and Services charts.

Click the Settings link to go to the Performance Page Settings page. The Performance Page Settings page has two sections. The Detailed Chart Settings section lets you choose defaults for displaying the instance activity charts. The Baseline Display Settings section lets you select if and how the AWR baseline values are displayed in the Performance page charts.

The Detailed Chart Settings section on the Performance Page Settings page lets you make the following display choices for the Performance page:

- *Default View*: You can select from Throughput, I/O, Parallel Execution, and Services.

- *Throughput Chart Settings*: You can choose Per Second or Per Transaction.

- *I/O Chart Settings*: You can choose from I/O Function, I/O Type, and Consumer Group.

Here are the steps to follow to change the display of the instance activity charts:

1. Click Settings on the Performance page.

2. Choose the default view you want to appear in the Average Active Session section by making a choice in the default view. You can choose among Throughput, I/O, Parallel Execution, and Services.

3. In Throughput Chart Settings, select Per Second or Per Transaction.

4. Under I/O Chart Settings, select from I/O Function, I/O Type, or Consumer Group as the default I/O breakdown on the I/O tab.

5. Click OK.

The Performance Page Settings page that appears now will reflect the new display choices you made, as shown in Figure 4-2.

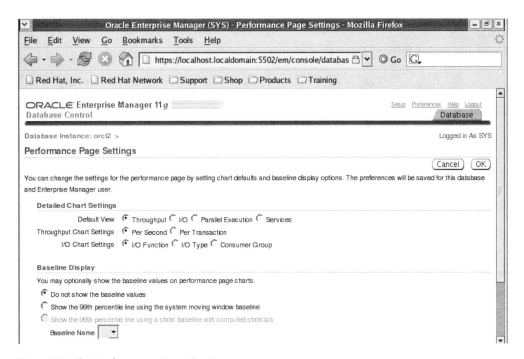

Figure 4-2. *The Performance Page Settings page*

If you want, you can also show the baseline values on the performance page charts.

Average Active Sessions

The average active sessions section on the Performance page offers a window into the performance of the database by showing, in graphical form, what proportion of time users are waiting and the time they spend actually doing something, such as IO. Monitoring user activity and probing further when there are spikes in CPU usage, for example, helps you identify the causes of poor performance.

ADDM Performance Analysis

On the Database Control Database home page, you can now see an ADDM performance analysis summary table, which provides you a quick overview of current ADDM findings. This is the same table as the one you'd get if you clicked ADDM Findings in the Diagnostic Summary section on the Database home page. Figure 4-3 shows the ADDM Performance Analysis table.

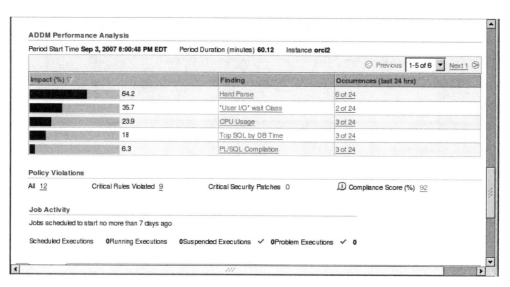

Figure 4-3. *The ADDM Performance Analysis table*

CHAPTER 5

■■■

Database Security

Oracle has made numerous enhancements to Oracle Database 11g security. In fact, Oracle has taken security more seriously than ever. Starting with Oracle Database 11g, passwords are now case-sensitive, and the password algorithm has changed to Secure Hash Algorithm (SHA-1) instead of the Data Encryption Standard (DES)–based hash algorithm. There is a significant amount of out-of-the-box security improvements geared to providing a higher sense of security for corporate environments. Oracle Database 11g introduces the concept of tablespace-level encryption to attack the data-at-rest concerns while addressing performance and feasibility concerns. Oracle Database 11g can govern fine-grained network access from the database. Enterprise Manager Database Console fully supports transparent data encryption and the majority of the security features introduced in Oracle Database 11g. Large Objects (LOBs) are completely reengineered for performance and security, including the ability to be encrypted.

These new features are just the beginning. Security features in Oracle Database 11g will make security enforcement easier for the database administrators.

Enterprise Database Security Concerns

One of the major concerns in the security industry is that DBAs typically have complete access to all the data. In high turnaround development environments, even developers can have full reign in the production databases. More and more developers are requesting DBA-level access in production and pre-production database environments. Inflexible delivery dates lead to compromise in database and system security.

Even though the database industry has a clear delineation of the roles and responsibilities between a production and development DBA, lots of DBAs perform both jobs because of budgetary constraints or the relative size of the company. This is especially true in small to medium-sized businesses. What companies fail to realize is that this makes data theft even easier if the person responsible for backups, audits, and operations also happens to know where the personally identifiable information resides.

With more and more security breaches and internal company employees selling sensitive data to competitors, database security is becoming a sensitive topic for a lot of companies. Regulators and auditors pressure database and system administration for compliance to Sarbanes-Oxley (SOX) and the Payment Card Industry (PCI) guidelines. Compliance to SOX and PCI are tedious and consume resources to enable auditing and lockdown processes. If there is sensitive data such as credit card numbers, Social Security numbers, or bank account information, encryption is also involved to protect both data at rest and data in motion. Even with the additional consumption of resources, companies are choosing to be compliant to mitigate internal threat.

Stronger Password Hash Algorithm

Starting in Oracle Database 11*g*, the SHA cryptographic hash function SHA-1 became the new algorithm for password hashing. SHA-1 is a 160-bit hash employed in several widely used security applications and protocols, including TLS and SSL, PGP, SSH, S/MIME, and IPsec. MD5, an earlier 128-bit widely used hash function, is considered its successor. From a performance perspective, SHA-1 is slightly slower than MD5 but produces a larger message digest, thus making SHA-1 more secure against brute-force attacks.

Hash functions generate the same output for a specified input and produce the same text for password values. SALT is a random value added to the data before it is encrypted. SALT in hashing algorithms strengthens the security of encrypted data by making it more difficult for hackers to crack using standard pattern-matching techniques. SALT is employed by the Oracle Database 11*g* user password hashing algorithm.

SHA-1 encryption commonly used in the industry provides much better security without forcing a network upgrade. Known in the industry as the *strong hash algorithm*, SHA-1 encryption algorithm enables Oracle Database 11*g* to meet stringent compliance regulations and strong password requirements.

Security Out of the Box

Oracle Database 11*g* heightens database security to another level. Oracle wants to make its customers aware that database security is critical. In recent years, internal employees contribute more and more to information security breaches. Now, when you create a database using the Database Configuration Assistant (DBCA), Oracle by default will create the database with the new level of security settings. These security settings include database audits of relevant SQL statements and privileges and modifications to the default profile. Moreover, DBCA will automatically set the AUDIT_TRAIL initialization parameter to DB.

■**Note** You can also modify the AUDIT_TRAIL parameter to EXTENDED_DB for enhanced auditing if your application requires SQL statement–level or bind variable information.

The new security settings checkbox will be set to default when creating a database using DBCA or when installing the Oracle Database 11*g* software. If you do not want to turn on Oracle Database 11*g*–enhanced auditing, Oracle provides another radio button to revert to the Oracle Database 10*g* and earlier security settings, which includes reverting the auditing and password profile options. Figure 5-1 shows the new Oracle Database 11*g* Security Settings page for database creation.

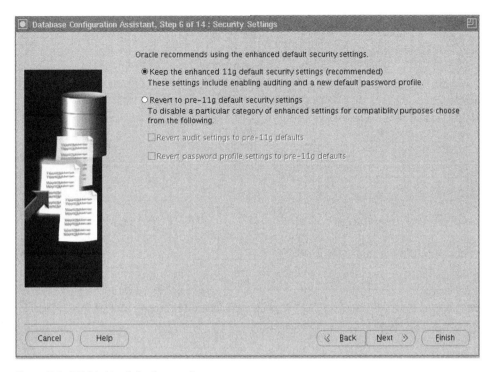

Figure 5-1. *DBCA 11g default security*

You have the flexibility to turn on auditing and disable the password profile option. Likewise, you can enable strong passwords but disable database auditing. The privileges that are audited by default are as follows:

```
SQL> select privilege, success, failure
from dba_priv_audit_opts
order by privilege;
```

PRIVILEGE	SUCCESS	FAILURE
ALTER ANY PROCEDURE	BY ACCESS	BY ACCESS
ALTER ANY TABLE	BY ACCESS	BY ACCESS
ALTER DATABASE	BY ACCESS	BY ACCESS
ALTER PROFILE	BY ACCESS	BY ACCESS
ALTER SYSTEM	BY ACCESS	BY ACCESS
ALTER USER	BY ACCESS	BY ACCESS
AUDIT SYSTEM	BY ACCESS	BY ACCESS
CREATE ANY JOB	BY ACCESS	BY ACCESS
CREATE ANY LIBRARY	BY ACCESS	BY ACCESS
CREATE ANY PROCEDURE	BY ACCESS	BY ACCESS
CREATE ANY TABLE	BY ACCESS	BY ACCESS
CREATE EXTERNAL JOB	BY ACCESS	BY ACCESS
CREATE PUBLIC DATABASE LINK	BY ACCESS	BY ACCESS

```
CREATE SESSION                          BY ACCESS        BY ACCESS
CREATE USER                             BY ACCESS        BY ACCESS
DROP ANY PROCEDURE                      BY ACCESS        BY ACCESS
DROP ANY TABLE                          BY ACCESS        BY ACCESS
DROP PROFILE                            BY ACCESS        BY ACCESS
DROP USER                               BY ACCESS        BY ACCESS
EXEMPT ACCESS POLICY                    BY ACCESS        BY ACCESS
GRANT ANY OBJECT PRIVILEGE              BY ACCESS        BY ACCESS
GRANT ANY PRIVILEGE                     BY ACCESS        BY ACCESS
GRANT ANY ROLE                          BY ACCESS        BY ACCESS

23 rows selected.
```

These privileges plus the AUDIT ROLE BY ACCESS and AUDIT SYSTEM BY ACCESS privileges make up the new Oracle Database 11g auditing-enabled features. Oracle Database 11g audits all privileges and statements using BY ACCESS.

■**Note** Oracle recommends you enable the default Oracle Database 11g security settings. Auditing enablement is the only way to become SOX or PCI compliant.

Some customers fret about the performance implications of turning on database auditing. The default database auditing options are negligible to performance since these audits are not at the transaction level. The default database auditing option also identifies who is logging into the system and logging off the system.

The DBCA utility enables you to turn off the auditing provided by Oracle Database 11g. Please note that setting and/or unsetting the Oracle Database 11g default security feature does impact the AUDIT_TRAIL initialization parameter, and the DBCA will ask permission to bounce the database. If you use the DBCA and unset the new auditing feature, you will revert to the default security features of Oracle Database10g Release 2.

■**Note** As with any other kind of auditing, please make sure to purge the AUD$ table. We recommend that the AUD$ table, which resides in the system tablespace, be moved to another tablespace to eliminate potential fragmentation and IO bottlenecks to the system tablespace. A shell script is available for download from the DBAExpert.com web site that moves the SYS.AUD$ table out of the system tablespace and re-creates the indexes associated with the table. This script also creates a user-friendly view on top of the SYS.AUD$ table that is significantly easier to read. The link to the site is http://www.dbaexpert.com/blog/?p=30.

When you have auditing enabled, it is imperative that you enable auditing of select, update, and delete on the SYS.AUD$ table by access. You do not want privileged accounts to be able to delete entries in the AUD$ table. Furthermore, you may want to know who is peeking into the auditing details.

In addition to the auditing settings, the default profile is also modified in the Oracle Database 11*g* automatic secure configuration. The new default profile is set with these settings:

- `PASSWORD_LOCK_TIME=1`

- `PASSWORD_GRACE_TIME=7`

- `PASSWORD_LIFE_TIME=180`

- `FAILED_LOGIN_ATTEMPTS=10`

- `PASSWORD_REUSE_MAX=UNLIMITED`

- `PASSWORD_REUSE_TIME=UNLIMITED`

The three profile settings, `PASSWORD_LOCK_TIME`, `PASSWORD_GRACE_TIME`, and `PASSWORD_LIFE_TIME`, are more restrictive in Oracle Database 11*g*.

Delayed Failed Logins

If a user tries to connect to the database multiple times using an erroneous password, the database will delay the response to the client after the third attempt. This is effective in Oracle Database 11*g* by default. The delays of response back to the client are repeated even if the connections are initiated from different IP addresses or hosts. Oracle preserves the performance of the database by increasing the delay for the user to try another password for up to ten seconds.

You can see in the following example that the first invalid password attempt produced an error output within a subsecond. Using the `time` or `timex` command, you can determine the amount of real time spent on waiting for the Unix prompt to return, as shown here:

```
$ time echo "select sysdate from dual;" |sqlplus -s ckim/xx
ERROR:
ORA-01017: invalid username/password; logon denied
...
    0.35s real     0.01s user    0.09s system
```

Continuing with this example, after the eighth iteration of the same invalid password login attempt, Oracle does not relinquish control back to the Unix session until after seven seconds. The delay is evident in the following example:

```
$ time echo "select sysdate from dual;" |sqlplus -s ckim/xx
ERROR:
ORA-01017: invalid username/password; logon denied
...

    7.26s real     0.02s user    0.05s system
```

Case-Sensitive Passwords

For added security, Oracle introduces case-sensitive passwords for databases created with the default Oracle Database 11g enhanced security. For databases not created with the default security, you can enable case sensitivity with the SEC_CASE_SENSITIVE_LOGON initialization parameter. The SEC_CASE_SENTITIVE_LOGON parameter must be set to TRUE to enable case-sensitive database passwords. You can set the case sensitivity using the ALTER SYSTEM command:

```
SQL> alter system set sec_case_sensitive_logon = TRUE;
```

Let's look at the password case sensitivity in action. First, the password for the rodba user will be changed:

```
  1* alter user rodba identified by RockAndRoll567
SQL> /
```

```
User altered.
```

The password of RockAndRoll567 is now case-sensitive since the SEC_CASE_SENSITIVE_LOGON parameter is set to TRUE. If you attempt to log in to the database as rodba with an all-lowercase password, you will receive an invalid password error, as shown here:

```
DBAPROD > sqlplus rodba/rockandroll567
```

```
SQL*Plus: Release 11.1.0.6.0 - Production on Thu Sep 13 04:56:25 2007
```

```
Copyright (c) 1982, 2007, Oracle.  All rights reserved.
```

```
ERROR:
ORA-01017: invalid username/password; logon denied
```

All users created or passwords modified in Oracle Database 11g will automatically adopt case-sensitive passwords. There is an exception to the case-insensitivity governance. We'll discuss this further in the upcoming section.

Basic Compliance with Industry Security Recommendations

The Center for Internet Security (CIS) is a nonprofit organization with the purpose of reducing the risk of business and e-commerce disruptions resulting from inadequate technical security controls. Many large corporations adopt CIS guidelines. Oracle Database 11g starts to provide some compliance to recommendations established by the CIS. Oracle Database 11g security enhancements such as strong passwords, auditing, and case-sensitive passwords are the initial building blocks to compliance with the security guidelines established by the CIS. CIS recommendations are significantly more secure than the default Oracle Database 10g or 11g database settings. You can download the latest CIS-recommended security assessment from the web site at http://www.cisecurity.org. The security documentation provides security lockdown procedures to mitigate a lot of potential security risks.

Another great web site to obtain the database-hardening recommendations is the SANS Institute at http://www.sans.org. SANS provides a comprehensive Excel spreadsheet of database security risks and suggestions to harden the database. Please be advised that you should carefully examine each recommendation from SANS and the CIS and make the appropriate implementation decisions based on your corporate security requirements. Some of the recommendations look great on paper, but without thorough testing in your application, they may cripple your application. Oracle Database 11*g* starts to provide additional security compliance, but the responsibility of hardening the database is the burden of the DBAs.

■**Tip** With heightened security, we strongly recommend that DBAs try to keep up with the quarterly security updates from Oracle. You can go to Oracle's web site at `http://www.oracle.com/technology/deploy/security/alerts.htm` to review current and previous security alerts posted by Oracle.

Upgrade Implications

When performing a database export and import of users from Oracle Database 9*i* or 10*g*, users' passwords will remain case-insensitive until you manually reset them. If you upgrade the database from a supported release using the DBUA or `catupgrade.sql` (please refer to Chapter 1 for all the approved versions) and want to leverage the new case-sensitive passwords, you must reset the passwords of existing users during the database upgrade procedure. The new strong password authentication will not be enabled for upgraded databases until each user password is manually reset using the `ALTER USER` statement.

If the database user had the `sysdba` or `sysoper` role, their passwords will also be imported to the `$ORACLE_HOME/dbs/orapw$ORACLE_SID` password file.

Password Versions

You can query the DBA_USERS view's `PASSWORD_VERSIONS` column to review the user password release level:

```
SQL>  select username,password_versions
  2  from dba_users
  3* order by username
SQL> /


USERNAME                         PASSWORD
-----------------------------    -------------------
ANONYMOUS
APEX_PUBLIC_USER                 10G 11G
BI                               10G 11G
CKIM                             10G 11G
CTXSYS                           10G 11G
DBSNMP                           10G 11G
DIP                              10G 11G
DSONG                            10G 11G
DSWEET                           10G 11G
EXFSYS                           10G 11G
FLOWS_030000                     10G 11G
```

```
FLOWS_FILES                  10G 11G
HR                           10G 11G
IX                           10G 11G
JJONES                       10G 11G
...
...
```

If the `PASSWORD_VERSIONS` column reflects a value of 10g, this implies the database account was upgraded to Oracle Database 11g but the password has not yet been modified. In this particular case, the `PASSWORD_VERSIONS` column remains case-insensitive. The password will remain case-insensitive until you change the password in Oracle Database 11g.

Case-Sensitive Password Files

You can incorporate password sensitivity into the `orapw` password file for `sysdba` and `sysoper` users. When creating the `orapw` password file, you can set the `ignorecase` option to `n` to designate that the password file record password entries in case-sensitive format. Let's see how you can set the case-sensitive password file with the `ignorecase` option:

```
orapwd file=$ORACLE_HOME/dbs/orapw$ORACLE_SID password=ORAcle123 \
entries=25 ignorecase=n
```

Not specifying the `ignorecase` parameter while creating the `orapw` file will cause Oracle Database11g to default to case-insensitive passwords.

Change Default User Passwords

A new view called DBA_USERS_WITH_DEFPWD is provided to flag database accounts with default passwords. This view includes both locked and unlocked accounts. As a best security practice, all users who show up as entries in this view should have their passwords changed. Safe password management will protect your database environment and make you less vulnerable to attacks by intruders. Let's see all the database accounts that have default passwords:

```
SQL> select username
     from dba_users_with_defpwd
     order by username
SQL> /

USERNAME
------------------------------
CTXSYS
DIP
EXFSYS
MDDATA
MDSYS
OLAPSYS
ORDPLUGINS
ORDSYS
OUTLN
```

```
SCOTT
SI_INFORMTN_SCHEMA
WK_TEST
WMSYS
XDB

14 rows selected.
```

A better query would be to cross-reference the DBA_USERS_WITH_DEFPWD view with the DBA_USERS view. This will identify database accounts with default passwords and active status. You can use the following query to find such culprits:

```
SQL> select username
     from dba_users_with_defpwd
     where username in
     (select username
     from dba_users
     where account_status='OPEN')
SQL> /

USERNAME
----------
SH
```

For this particular example, the sales history (SH) database account was intentionally enabled to provide this output. You can easily change the passwords for any accounts that the DBA_USERS_WITH_DEFPWD view lists as offenders. Let's change the password for the SH account to a strong password:

```
SQL> alter user sh identified by Oracl3D3v3lop3r123;

User altered.
```

This DBA_USERS_WITH_DEFPWD view reports only those accounts with default passwords for Oracle-supplied database accounts. It does not protect the database from other accounts that have weak passwords.

Database Links and Case Sensitivity

Since Oracle Database 9*i* and 10*g* are not case-sensitive, connecting to Oracle Database 11*g* can pose some complications. Oracle provides a set of rules to govern password management, and connection negotiation is between Oracle Database 11*g* and other versions of the database. Obviously, if you are connecting from Oracle Database 11*g* to another Oracle Database 11*g* using a database link, the password sensitivity remains case-sensitive.

First, look at what has to happen to make connections from a previous release of Oracle to a case-sensitive Oracle Database 11*g*. You must alter the password on Oracle Database 11*g* to the uppercase equivalent of the password designated in the database link's CONNECT TO USERNAME IDENTIFIED BY clause section. Oracle stores the password for the database links in uppercase.

Because database link passwords are stored in uppercase, the password in Oracle Database 11*g* should be set with uppercase.

Now let's see what kind of implications there are to initiate the database link from Oracle Database 11*g* to an older version of Oracle. Since Oracle Database 11*g* Release 1 is the first release to use password sensitivity, you do not have to worry about case sensitivity when creating database links to a prior release of Oracle.

Password Management

In previous releases, if a hacker has select access to the DBA_USERS view, the hacker can easily crack another user's password if the passwords are weak. Hackers can create a copy of the DBA_USERS view to a local database and perform an *offline attack*. Hackers can create a database account for username entries in the DBA_USERS view and can compare the hash value of the password column in the local DBA_USERS view with the production copy of the DBA_USERS view. There are various ways to determine passwords. One common practice is to compare passwords with millions of words in the dictionary to exploit weak passwords. Another common practice is to generate random alphanumeric passwords such as Oracle's RANDOM function and compare hash values.

Luckily, Oracle provides another level of security to the underlying data dictionary. The DBA_USERS view in Oracle Database 11*g* has the password column blanked out. The following query confirms that the password column no longer provides the hashed value of the password:

```
SQL> select username, password from dba_users order by username;
```

```
USERNAME                       PASSWORD
----------------------         ------------------------------
ANONYMOUS
APEX_PUBLIC_USER
BI
CKIM
CTXSYS
DBSNMP
DIP
DSONG
DSWEET
...
...
```

To obtain the hashed value of the encrypted password, you will need to have the select privilege on the USER$ table instead. Database users do not receive select privileges against the USER$ table via the SELECT_CATALOG_ROLE role. One of the ways to grant access to the USER$ table is by granting the SELECT ANY DICTIONARY role to the database account.

Here is the simple query of the USER$ table to view the hashed password values:

```
SQL> select name, password from user$;
```

■**Note** We strongly discourage giving direct select access of the `SYS.USER$` table to non-DBAs. This same logic applies for the `SELECT ANY DICTIONARY` role. DBAs will inherit select access against this table through the DBA role.

Create Password Verification Function

Oracle Database 11*g* addresses some of the weak password concerns by providing a stronger password verification function. The password verification function is in the `$ORACLE_HOME/rdbms/admin/utlpwdmg.sql` file. This file comes with two password verification functions. When you execute the `utlpwdmg.sql` script, it will create two password verification functions, an updated Oracle Database 11*g* version with higher security configurations and the Oracle Database 10g predecessor password function. The previous database version of the default profile is commented out, and the default profile is set to utilize the new `verify_function_11G` function as the built-in password verification standard.

The password verification function is not enabled by default. To create and enable the strong password verification function, you must execute the `utlpwdmg.sql` script. When you execute the `utlpwdmg.sql` script, the output will look something like this:

```
SQL> @?/rdbms/admin/utlpwdmg.sql

Function created. <-- This is the verify_function_11g


Profile altered.  <-- This enables the default profile with the new
                      password function.


Function created. <-- This is the legacy verify_function
```

The first function created is the new Oracle Database 11*g* strong password verification function. It also creates the Oracle Database 10*g* password verification function for legacy support. Oracle Database 10*g*'s `verify_function` contains some of the password verification checks that are available in Oracle Database 11*g*, but the differences are significant. For example, the minimum expected password length is four characters in Oracle Database 10*g*, and the minimum expected password length in Oracle Database 11*g* is eight characters.

Oracle password verification checks for valid passwords when users are created and passwords are modified. The new verification function provides enhanced security to mitigate weak passwords or passwords easily guessed. By leveraging Oracle Database 11*g*'s revised password verification utility, security administrators can be rest assured that another facet of password management is in compliance. These are the out-of-the-box password rules from Oracle Database 11*g*:

- Must be a minimum of eight characters. In Oracle Database 10g, the minimum length is four characters.

- Must be at least one letter and one digit. To our surprise, in Oracle Database 10g, the verify function expects one letter, one digit, and one punctuation mark.

- Cannot be simple or common (that is, `welcome1`, `abcdefg1`, or `change_on_install`).

- Cannot be `oracle` or `oracle` with the digits 1–100 appended.

- Cannot be the same as the username, the username spelled in reverse, or the username with 1–100 digits appended.

- Cannot be the same as the server name or the server name with the digits 1–100 appended.

- Must differ from the previous password by at least three characters. This is same in Oracle Database 10g.

■**Note** We strongly recommend DBAs implement strong and long passwords to avoid brute-force or dictionary attacks.

As mentioned earlier, executing the `utlpwdmg.sql` script as `sys` enables the default profile with the new Oracle Database11g password verification algorithm. At the end of the script, the `ALTER PROFILE` command sets the default profile with the Oracle 11g password verification function, as shown here:

```
alter profile default limit
        password_life_time                      180
        password_grace_time                     7
        password_reuse_time                     unlimited
        password_reuse_max                      unlimited
        failed_login_attempts                   10
        password_lock_time                      1
        password_verify_function                verify_function_11g;
```

If the Oracle-supplied password verification function does not suit your security requirements, you can always customize Oracle's function to tailor to your corporate security standards or even create your own personalized version. For example, if the minimum eight-character restriction is not adequate for your company, you can easily customize a component in the `utlpwdmg.sql` script to fit your security needs. The Oracle-supplied password length validation portion of the PL/SQL code reads as follows:

```
IF length(password) < 8 THEN
    raise_application_error(-20001, 'Password length less than 8');
END IF;
```

The password length portion of the logic can be changed to 12 characters, as shown here:

```
IF length(password) < 12 THEN
    raise_application_error(-20001, 'Password length less than 12');
END IF;
```

For some unforeseen reason, if you run into any problems after modifying the password verification function, you can disable the password verification function by setting the default `password_verify_function` profile to `null`, as shown here:

```
SQL> alter profile default
    limit password_verify_function null
SQL> /

Profile altered.
```

Change Database Account Passwords

Now we will look at the password verification utility at work. First we will attempt to change the password that differs from the last password by three characters using the password command from SQL*Plus.

■**Note** Oracle passwords can be changed using the traditional `alter user USERNAME identified by PASSWORD;` syntax, or they can be changed using the `password` command from SQL*Plus.

```
SQL> password
Changing password for RODBA
Old password:
New password:
Retype new password:
ERROR:
ORA-28003: password verification for the specified password failed
ORA-20011: Password should differ from the
old password by at least 3 characters

Password unchanged
```

Next, we attempt to change the password to something less than eight characters:

```
SQL> alter user rodba identified by rodba;
alter user rodba identified by rodba
*
ERROR at line 1:
ORA-28003: password verification for the specified password failed
ORA-20001: Password length less than 8
```

You will receive an error message stating that the password length is too short. Another rule is that passwords must have a numeric character in them. If you attempt to change the password to something that is eight characters or more but does not have a numeric character, you will receive another error message:

```
SQL> alter user rodba identified by ohmygodwhatishappening;
alter user rodba identified by ohmygodwhatishappening
*
ERROR at line 1:
ORA-28003: password verification for the specified password failed
ORA-20008: Password must contain at least one digit, one character
```

Likewise, if you add a number but the password is simple, then Oracle kindly lets you know:

```
SQL> alter user rodba identified by welcome1;
alter user rodba identified by welcome1
*
ERROR at line 1:
ORA-28003: password verification for the specified password failed
ORA-20006: Password too simple
```

You have seen examples of simple password verification checks. The simple password verification code of the stored function also checks to see whether the password equals any of the words in the following list:

- welcome1

- database1

- account1

- user1234

- password1

- oracle123

- computer1

- abcdefg1

- change_on_install

If any of the attempted passwords matches this list, the password verification function will let you know that you have a simple password. Another password security to consider is to disallow passwords that are in the dictionary. You can easily purchase text-based dictionaries and load their content into the database. The password verify function can easily be altered to check for an existence of a word in the dictionary. Of course, the dictionary word must be indexed for optimal data retrieval. The check can be complete in subseconds and would offer another level of security with stronger passwords.

Another password breach that Oracle will check for is if you have the same username and password. The password-length check of eight characters precedes the check for the same username and password check. In the next example, we have to create a username with a length greater than eight characters. Let's try to create a username charleskim with the same password:

```
SQL> create user charleskim identified by charleskim
  2   default tablespace tools
  3   temporary tablespace temp;
create user charleskim identified by charleskim
*
ERROR at line 1:
ORA-28003: password verification for the specified password failed
ORA-20002: Password same as or similar to user
```

The password verification function immediately output the ORA-20002 error message indicating that we could not create a database account with the same password. The password verification function also checks to see whether the password is the same as the username with the digits 1–100 appended to it. You can see in the following example that Charles99 violates this security requirement:

```
SQL> create user charles identified by charles99;
create user charles identified by charles99
*
ERROR at line 1:
ORA-28003: password verification for the specified password failed
ORA-20005: Password same as or similar to user name
```

The password verification function also checks to see whether the password is the same as the username spelled backward. For example, if you attempt to create a username called dbaexpert, the password verification function will make sure that the password cannot be trepxeabd:

```
SQL> create user dbaexpert identified by trepxeabd;
create user dbaexpert identified by trepxeabd
*
ERROR at line 1:
ORA-28003: password verification for the specified password failed
ORA-20003: Password same as username reversed
```

Oracle's password verification utility has great potential and can be enhanced to fit your security requirements. The utlpwdmg.sql script has great examples to build upon and is configurable to fit any company.

Tablespace Encryption

In Oracle Database 10g Release 2, Oracle introduced the new transparent data encryption (TDE) feature, which lets you easily encrypt a column's data in a table. The encryption is "transparent" because the Oracle database takes care of all the encryption and decryption details, with no need for you to manage any tables or triggers to decrypt data. Now, in Oracle Database 11g, you can encrypt an entire tablespace by simply using a pair of special clauses during tablespace creation.

Oracle has been gradually improving its encryption capabilities over the years. In Oracle 8i, Oracle introduced the DBMS_OBFUSCATION_TOOLKIT package and in the Oracle 10.1 release introduced the DBMS_CRYPTO package to facilitate encryption. Both the toolkit and the DBMS_CRYPTO package required the application to manage the encryption keys and call the API to perform the necessary encryption/decryption operations.

Prior to Oracle Database 11g, encryption was limited to a column or multiple columns of a table. When entering data in an encrypted column, Oracle transparent data encryption automatically encrypts the data. When the data is selected out of the table, it is automatically decrypted. Oracle Database 11g adds the functionality to encrypt a complete tablespace. This breaks the boundary of encryption at the column. Tablespace encryption also relies on encryption keys in a wallet outside the database.

When you encrypt a column, you have to be concerned about performance implications. The higher the level of encryption, the more CPU intensive the encryption and decryption function. Oracle supports up to AES 256-bit encryption.

Tablespace encryption eliminates the need for granular analysis of applications to determine which columns are candidates for encryption. You can use tablespace encryption to encrypt entire tables and associated indexes by moving the objects into an encrypted tablespace. The data from the encrypted tablespace is transparently decrypted at runtime.

Tablespace encryption will also encrypt objects that are stored as LOBs including BLOBs and CLOBs. However, if you create a table with a BFILE, it will encrypt all other columns except for the BFILE since BFILEs are stored outside the database. Similar to BFILEs, external tables are not encrypted.

Certain situations in column-level encryption prohibit its use. For example, you cannot encrypt a column that participates in an index scan. When you encrypt a column(s) for a table, there are limitations on certain queries. For example, in Oracle Database 10g, you cannot encrypt a column if it is part of a foreign key or used in another database. Encrypting the entire tablespace removes some of these restrictions. The following are additional considerations to using tablespace-level encryption:

- Function-based indexes

- Index range scans

- Datatype restrictions

- Partitioned/subpartitioned tables

Creating the Oracle Wallet

An Oracle Wallet is a container to store authentication and signing credentials. The tablespace encryption feature relies on the Oracle Wallet to store and protect the master key used in the encryption. There are two kinds of Oracle Wallets—encryption wallets and auto-open wallets. You must manually open an encryption wallet after database start-up, whereas the auto-open wallet automatically opens upon database start-up. The encryption wallet is commonly recommended for tablespace encryption. However, if you are dealing with unattended Data Guard environments, the automatic opening of the wallet comes in handy.

The Oracle Wallet, named `ewallet.p12` under both Windows and Unix/Linux-based systems, is a file in your directory system. The location where Oracle stores this file is operating system specific. However, you can specify a nondefault location by using the parameter `encryption_wallet_location` in the `sqlnet.ora` file, as shown here:

```
ENCRYPTION_WALLET_LOCATION =
 (SOURCE=
   (METHOD=file)
   (METHOD_DATA=
   (DIRECTORY=/apps/oracle/general/wallet)     )  )
```

To use TDE, you must have the `ALTER SYSTEM` privilege as well as a password for an Oracle Wallet. If you do not have an Oracle Wallet, you must create one and then add a master key to it. You can create the Oracle Wallet in several ways:

- By invoking the Oracle Wallet Manager through a GUI

- By invoking the Oracle Wallet Manager by issuing the command owm at the command line

- By using the mkstore command from the operating system command line

---

Tip Use the following syntax to create a wallet from the OS:

```
mkstore -wrl $ORACLE_BASE/admin/$ORACLE_SID/wallet –create
Enter password:
Enter
```

Wallet Requirements

TDE requires an Oracle Wallet encryption key be established and opened. Because the wallet is the essence of TDE, we will take you on a little tour to create a key and open it for use for the database. The easiest way to create a wallet is by using the ALTER SYSTEM command, which is the method we use here:

```
SQL> alter system set encryption key identified by "clidba123";

System altered.
```

The alter system statement shown here both creates the wallet if it does not already exist and adds a master key to it. You must replace the password with your own password for the wallet. The ALTER SYSTEM statement you issued in the previous example works in the following way:

- If you already have an Oracle Wallet, it opens that wallet and creates (or re-creates) the master encryption key.

- If you do not have an Oracle Wallet already, it creates a new wallet, opens the wallet, and creates a new master encryption key.

Since we created an encryption wallet, we must re-open the wallet after database start-up. To open the wallet (ewallet.p12) after database start-up, you can issue the following command:

```
alter system set wallet open identified by "clidba123";
```

Please remember that since the wallet was created with the double quotes around it, it needs to be opened with double quotes. Otherwise, you will receive the ORA- 28353 ("failed to open wallet") error. To verify that a wallet is open, you can query the V$ENCRYPTION_WALLET view:

```
SQL> select wrl_parameter, status from v$encryption_wallet
SQL> /

WRL_PARAMETER                       STATUS
----------------------------------  -----------
/apps/oracle/general/wallet         OPEN
```

> **■Note** As mentioned earlier, you can also create a wallet using the Wallet Manager. Using the owm command invokes the Wallet Manager. The owm utility is a Java application, so the DISPLAY parameter must point to a legitimate X-Windows client.

Encrypted Tablespace Caveats

There are several caveats to encrypted tablespaces. You cannot encrypt an existing tablespace. You can encrypt a new tablespace only at creation time. If you want to encrypt an existing tablespace, you must move the objects into a newly created encrypted tablespace using the various options such as CTAS, ALTER TABLE MOVE, exp/imp, online data redefinition, or expdp/impdp. Tablespace-level encryption makes it transparent to even developers. Developers do not have to be concerned about how to encrypt a column or what is required to maintain a high-performance data encryption environment.

If you are upgrading from Oracle Database 10g Release 2 to Oracle Database 11g and have set the compatibility mode to 11.1.0, you need to reissue the ALTER SYSTEM SET ENCRYPTION KEY command to create a master encryption key for tablespace encryption. This command will re-create the standard TDE master key and overwrite the existing one if one already exists. It also creates a new tablespace master encryption key. If the tablespace key already exists in the wallet folder, the ALTER SYSTEM SET ENCRYPTION KEY command will not rekey it.

> **■Caution** You cannot re-create the tablespace encryption key.

Additional restrictions apply to encrypted tablespaces:

- The NO SALT option cannot be used (for clarification on SALT, please refer to the beginning of this chapter).
- BFILES and external tables are not encrypted.
- Temporary and undo tablespaces cannot be encrypted.
- Transportable tablespaces must be in the same endian format.

Encrypting a Tablespace

Once you create the Oracle Wallet, creating an encrypted tablespace is a breeze. The tablespace creation statement for an encrypted tablespace has the following syntax:

```
create tablespace <tbsp_name>
encryption
default storage(encrypt)
```

The encryption clause in the second line does not actually encrypt the tablespace. You merely provide the encryption properties by setting values for the keyword encryption.

You may use the using clause to specify the name of the encryption algorithm you want to use. The supported encryption algorithms are as follows:

- *AES192*: Advanced Encryption Standard 192-bit encryption

- *3DES168*: Triple Data Encryption Standard 168-bit encryption

- *AES128*: Advanced Encryption Standard 128-bit encryption

- *AES256*: Advanced Encryption Standard 256-bit encryption

You can use the default algorithm of AES128, in which case you can omit the using clause altogether. The encrypt keyword is passed to the storage clause in the third line that performs the actual encryption of the tablespace. In the following sections, we review how to encrypt a tablespace.

The following is an example showing how to create a simple encrypted tablespace that uses the default AES 128-bit encryption. Since you do not have to specify the default encryption level, you do not specify the using clause for the encryption clause in the third line.

```
SQL> create tablespace docs_encrypted_default
  2  datafile '+DATA'
  3  encryption
  4  default storage (encrypt);

Tablespace created.
```

Next, we will create an encrypted tablespace with the AES 192-bit encryption. Notice the keywords encryption using 'AES192' default storage (encrypt) in the following example:

```
SQL> create tablespace docs_d_e
  2  datafile '+FRA' size 10m
  3  extent management local uniform size 128k
  4  segment space management auto
  5  encryption using 'AES192'
  6* default storage (encrypt)
/

Tablespace created.
```

Now all objects created in the docs_d_e tablespace will be encrypted. The beauty behind encrypted tablespaces is that the encryption consideration just becomes an object placement consideration. By designing an encrypted tablespace, the DBAs can place objects into the encrypted tablespace and be confident that the data is encrypted. Furthermore, both DBAs and data architects can collaborate and place objects into the encrypted tablespaces during the design phase.

Upon creating the encrypted tablespace, you can query the DBA_TABLESPACES view to review the encryption state. Oracle provides a new column called ENCRYPTED in the DBA_TABLESPACES view to reveal whether a tablespace is encrypted. In the following query, we are identifying the encryption attributes for tablespaces that start with the name DOC:

```
  1   select tablespace_name, encrypted
  2   from dba_tablespaces
  3*  where tablespace_name like 'DOC%'
SQL> /


TABLESPACE_NAME                         ENC
-------------------------------         ---
DOCS_D                                  NO
DOCS_D_E                                YES
DOCS_ENCRYPTED_DEFAULT                  YES
DOC_I                                   NO
```

Another provided view called V$ENCRYPTED_TABLESPACES reveals the encryption attributes of encrypted tablespaces:

```
SQL> desc V$ENCRYPTED_TABLESPACES
 Name                                Null?     Type
 -------------------------------     --------  -----------------------
 TS#                                           NUMBER
 ENCRYPTIONALG                                 VARCHAR2(7)
 ENCRYPTEDTS                                   VARCHAR2(3)
```

You can join this view with the V$TABLESPACE view based on the ts# column to determine which tablespace is encrypted and which encryption algorithm is being used. The following query produces output of all encrypted tablespaces including the encryption algorithm information:

```
SQL> select vt.name, vet.encryptionalg, vet.encryptedts
  2   from   v$encrypted_tablespaces vet,
  3          v$tablespace vt
  4*  where vet.ts#=vt.ts#
SQL> /


NAME                                  ENCRYPT       ENC
------------------------------------  -----------   -------
DOCS_ENCRYPTED_DEFAULT                AES128        YES
DOCS_D_E                              AES192        YES
```

Enterprise Manager Integration

Oracle from release to release continues to strengthen its graphical user interfaces (GUIs) for database management and configuration. This continues to be the case with Oracle Database 11*g* relative to security setup, management, and configuration.

Transparent Data Encryption with Enterprise Manager Database Console

You can create encryption keys and control security using the Oracle Enterprise Manager Database Console. One of the enhancements made in Oracle Database 11*g* is the integration of the wallet creation with Enterprise Manager Database Console. To enable TDE, the navigation path is Server ➤ Security (Transparent Data Encryption).

The new TDE setup screen looks like the screen displayed in Figure 5-2.

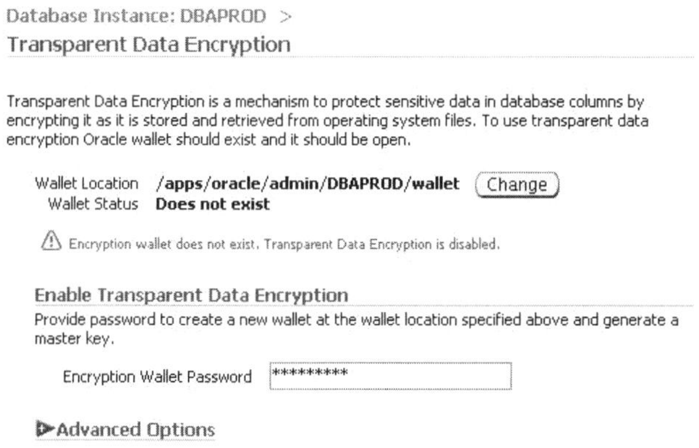

Figure 5-2. *TDE setup*

All you have to do is determine what you want your password to be. Once you create the wallet, you can proceed to other security-related options such as creating an encrypted tablespace. If you click the Advanced Option button, you will have the option to rekey the master key. You might want to do this is if you think your master key has been compromised.

You can revisit the screen in Figure 5-2 after each database bounce to open the wallet. By providing the master key password for the database, you are able to open the wallet.

Tablespace Encryption with Database Console

Earlier in this chapter, we demonstrated how to set up tablespace encryption using the conventional SQL syntax. All of the tablespace encryption features are also configurable using Database Console. You can navigate to the tablespace setup screen within Database Console by selecting Server ➤ Storage (Tablespaces) ➤ Create.

You will see the new encryption options provided, as shown in Figure 5-3.

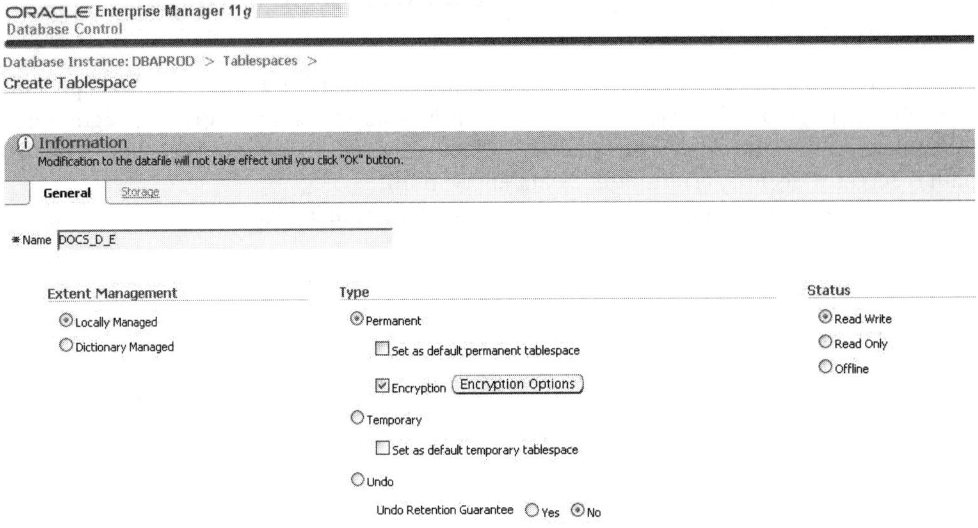

Figure 5-3. *Tablespace setup*

After you provide the tablespace name and add the specifics for the datafile(s), you can click Encryption Options and see the encryption algorithms provided by Oracle. Figure 5-4 shows all the encryption options you can set for the tablespace with Database Console.

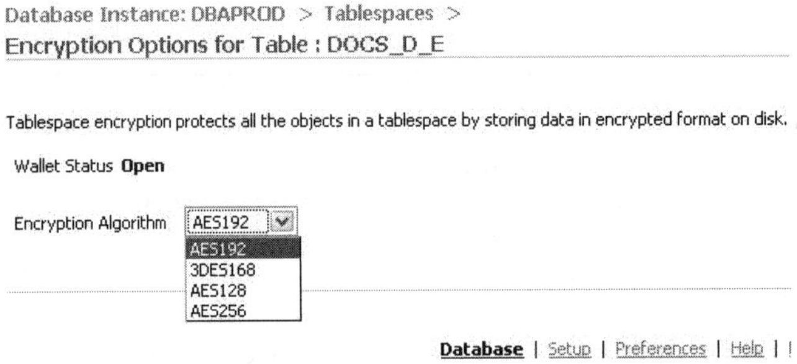

Figure 5-4. *Encryption algorithms*

A nice feature that Database Console added is the automatic detection of Oracle Wallet. Although you are attempting to create an encrypted tablespace using Database Console, if Oracle detects that a wallet is not open, Oracle will ask you whether you want to enable TDE, as depicted in Figure 5-5.

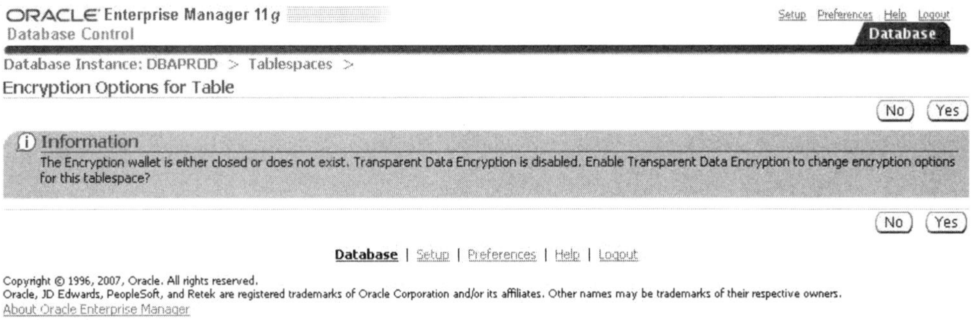

Figure 5-5. *Oracle Wallet detection*

Finally, before you finalize on the creation of your new tablespace, you can review the SQL syntax and confirm that it is as expected. The SQL syntax for the docs_d_e tablespace looks like Figure 5-6.

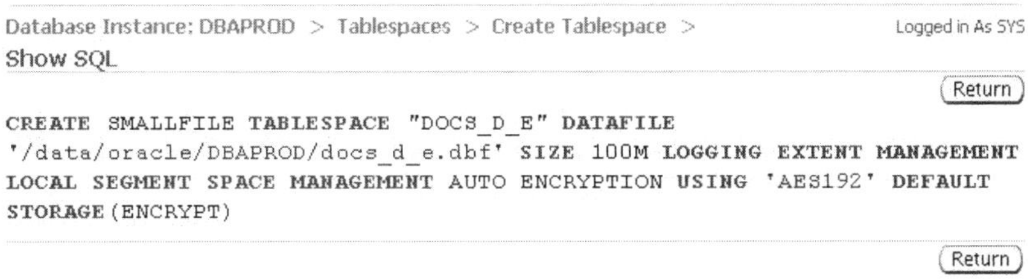

Figure 5-6. *Reviewing the SQL syntax*

Oracle's direction is to provide more and more SQL validation screens in their Database Console and Grid Control products. This allows seasoned veterans to review SQL syntax and provides great learning opportunities for new DBAs.

Policy Trend Overview

Enterprise Manager Database Console provides a new screen to display security compliance of your database. Your database is scored against a set of best-practice guidelines established by Oracle. You can navigate to the Policy Trend Overview screen from the main Enterprise Manager Database Console page. Look out for the link next to the Compliance Score (%) in the Policy Violations section. The Policy Trend Overview screen looks like Figure 5-7.

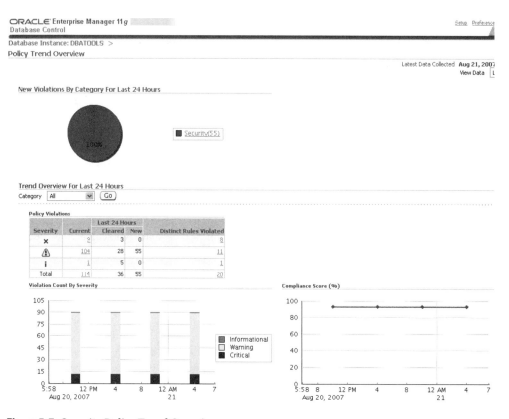

Figure 5-7. *Security Policy Trend Overview screen*

Additional Security Management Integration in Database Console

Oracle Enterprise Manager Database Console replaces the Policy Manager Java console. Although the Policy Manager tool remains available, you can administer the Oracle label security, application contexts, and virtual private database using the Enterprise Manager Database Console. The URLs to maintain Virtual Private Databases, Oracle Label Security, and application contexts are available by navigating to Database Console and selecting Server ➤ Security.

Enterprise Manager Database Console also replaces the Enterprise User Security management. You must modify the ldap.ora file before modifying the menu options for Enterprise User Security become available. The Enterprise Manager Security tool is still available.

UTL_ Package Network Access Management

Even with all the security lockdown improvements in Oracle Database 11g, Oracle still has quite a few packages that have execute permissions granted to PUBLIC. Based on the following query results, four particular packages pose network security concerns: UTL_SMTP, UTL_TCP, UTL_FILE, and UTL_HTTP.

```
  1  select  table_name, privilege
  2  from dba_tab_privs
  3  where (grantee = 'PUBLIC'
  4  and table_name like 'UTL%')
  5  and privilege = 'EXECUTE'
  6* order by table_name
SQL> /


TABLE_NAME                                PRIVILEGE
-------------------------------------     ----------
UTL_BINARYINPUTSTREAM                     EXECUTE
..
UTL_FILE                                  EXECUTE              <--
UTL_GDK                                   EXECUTE
UTL_HTTP                                  EXECUTE              <--
..
UTL_SMTP                                  EXECUTE              <--
UTL_TCP                                   EXECUTE              <--
UTL_URL                                   EXECUTE

24 rows selected.
```

As a rule, DBAs should revoke unnecessary privileges and roles from PUBLIC since all database accounts have privileges granted to PUBLIC. Specifically, you should revoke the four packages listed in Table 5-1 in a standard database build.

Table 5-1. *Revoke UTL Packages from* PUBLIC

Package Name	Description
UTL_SMTP	Allows e-mail messages to be sent from one arbitrary user to another arbitrary user
UTL_TCP	Allows outgoing network connections to be established by the database to any receiving (or waiting) network service
UTL_HTTP	Allows the database to request and retrieve data using HTTP
UTL_FILE	Allows PL/SQL interface to files on the operating system

Grant access to these four packages only on an as-needed basis with adequate business justification. When and if there are no options, grant access to the packages to specific database users.

Fine-Grained Access Control for UTL_* Network Packages

Packages such as UTL_TCP, UTL_SMTP, UTL_MAIL, UTL_HTTP, and UTL_INADDR provide access to network services to and from the database. If business requirements dictate that these packages become an essential element of the application, Oracle Database 11g provides a mechanism to refine the level of access. You can use the DBMS_NETWORK_ACL_ADMIN package to facilitate management of the UTL_* network access packages. Granting access involves several steps. First, you have to create an access control list (ACL) and configure the privilege definitions associated with the ACL. This is also known as defining the access control entries (ACEs). Next, you have to assign the ACL to one or more network hosts.

Create an Access Control List

All ACL definitions are stored in XML DB in the form of XML documents. The ACL XML files reside in the /sys/acls directory of the XML DB repository. ACLs can be defined using the APIs within the XML DB, but Oracle also provides DBAs with a simple command-line interface in the DBMS_NETWORK_ACL_ADMIN package. Look to using the CREATE_ACL procedure to create an XML file called dba.xml:

```
 1  BEGIN
 2    DBMS_NETWORK_ACL_ADMIN.CREATE_ACL (
 3    acl => 'dba.xml',
 4    description => 'Network Access Control for the DBAs',
 5    principal => 'RODBA',
 6    is_grant => TRUE,
 7    privilege => 'connect',
 8    start_date => null,
 9    end_date => null);
10* END;
SQL> /
PL/SQL procedure successfully completed.
```

Within the CREATE_ACL procedure, the ACL parameter defines the file name of the ACL. When you first create the ACL, the ACL must have at least one privilege setting.

Please note that this file name is case-sensitive. The description parameter is a short description of the file's purpose. The principal parameter defines the user or role for which you want to create the ACL. The principal must be a valid entry from the DBA_USERS view or from the DBA_ROLES view. Because it is a database-authenticated account or a role, the entry must be in uppercase. In this particular example, the rodba account is in uppercase as RODBA. The is_grant parameter specifies whether you want to grant the grant connect privilege or deny the grant. This parameter is a Boolean flag.

The privilege parameter has two valid value options: connect or resolve. The package required by the application determines this value. If the user needs access to an external network computer using the UTL_TCP, UTL_HTTP, UTL_SMTP, and UTL_MAIL packages, then the connect privilege is required. The resolve privilege is necessary if the requirement is to use the UTL_INADDR package to identify the host name based on the supplied IP address. The privilege is also case-sensitive.

The start_date is an optional parameter but must be in the TIMESTAMP WITH TIME ZONE format (YYYY-MM-DD HH:MI:SS.FF TZR). The start_date defines when this ACE will become valid. The start_date will be valid starting on the start_date entry and going forward. The default value is null. An example of the start date looks like this:

```
start_date => '2007-07-11 10:30:00.00 US/Pacific',
```

The last parameter, end_date, defines the end date for the ACE. This parameter has the same format as the start_date parameter:

(YYYY-MM-DD HH:MI:SS.FF TZR).

Since the dba.xml file is created, let's look inside the XML repository to confirm. We can query RESOURCE_VIEW to find the dba.xml ACL in the /sys/acls directory:

```
SQL> SELECT any_path
  2  FROM resource_view
  3* WHERE any_path like '/sys/acls/dba%'
SQL> /


ANY_PATH
--------------------------------------------------------
/sys/acls/dba.xml
```

You need to be cautious with too many entries in the ACL. ACLs are checked for each access to Oracle XML DB repository. The ACL check operation is a critical component of the XML DB performance. The number of entries in the ACL affects the performance of the XML DB. Oracle recommends that you share ACLs as much as possible between resources. In addition, ACL check operations perform best when the number of ACEs in the ACL is at 16 entries or less.

Add Access Control Entries

Once you create the initial ACL with the CREATE_ACL procedure, you can continue to add more privileges to the XML file. Use the ADD_PRIVILEGE procedure to add or revoke principals in the ACL. This example will add CKIM to the dba.xml file and grant him network access:

```
1  BEGIN
2  DBMS_NETWORK_ACL_ADMIN.ADD_PRIVILEGE (
3    acl => 'dba.xml',
4    principal => 'CKIM',
5    is_grant => TRUE,
6    privilege => 'connect',
7    start_date => null,
8    end_date => null);
9* END;
SQL> /


PL/SQL procedure successfully completed.
```

Again, the ACL file name and the principal are case-sensitive. What differentiates the ADD_ PRIVILEGE procedure from the CREATE_ACL procedure is that the ADD_PRIVILEGE does not have the description API for the ACL file name. At this point, you have built the foundation by defining the ACL and adding principals and privileges to the ACL. Now, let's assign network hosts and see this fine-grained access control for network services at work.

Assign Hosts

The ASSIGN_ACL procedure is used to authorize access to one or more network hosts. The network host can be internal or external to the company. In this particular example, you are allowing the database to be able to make HTTP calls to the dbaexpert.com web site. The dbaexpert.com site is a four-CPU server running Debian Linux version 2.4.

```
1  BEGIN
2    DBMS_NETWORK_ACL_ADMIN.ASSIGN_ACL (
3    acl => 'dba.xml',
4    host => 'dbaexpert.com',
5    lower_port => 80,
6    upper_port => 443);
7* END;
8  /
```

```
PL/SQL procedure successfully completed.
```

The lower port and upper port parameters are null by default. You should preface the lower and upper port ranges for tighter security. The lower port defines the lower boundaries of the allowable port ranges. The upper port defines the upper boundaries for the allowable port ranges. These port ranges should be defined only for connect privileges; they should not be set for resolve privileges. There is another caveat to the port ranges. If you omit one of the parameters but define the other, then both parameters take the value of the one you provided. For example, if you set lower_port to 80 and do not define the port value for upper_port, the upper_port parameter automatically inherits the value of 80.

■**Tip** You can use the XML DB HTTP protocol to view the contents of the dba.xml file. You can view the dba.xml ACL for this particular server using this URL: http://rac104.dbaexpert.com:8080/sys/acls/dba.xml.

Since you created the ACL, assigned privileges/principals, and authorized network entities, you can validate that the ACL permissions worked accordingly. Take a look at the UTL_HTTP.REQUEST API to retrieve a web page from the dbaexpert.com web site to confirm that the network access rights work as planned:

```
SQL> select utl_http.request('http://www.dbaexpert.com') from dual;

UTL_HTTP.REQUEST('HTTP://WWW.DBAEXPERT.COM')
--------------------------------------------------------------------------------
<!DOCTYPE html PUBLIC "-//W3C//DTD XHTML 1.0 Transitional//EN"
"http://www.w3.org/TR/xhtml1/DTD/xhtml1-transitional.dtd">
<html xmlns="http://www.w3.org/1999/xhtml">
<head>
<meta http-equiv="Content-Type" content="text/html; charset=iso-8859-1" />
```

```
<title>Database Experts</title>
<link rel="SHORTCUT ICON" href="favicon.ico"></link>
<link href="css/dbaStyle.css" rel="stylesheet" type="text/css" />
<!--Tree Menu-->
<script language="JavaScript" src="tree.js"></script>
<script language="JavaScript" src="tree_items.js"></script>
<script language="JavaScript" src="tree_items_top.js"></script>
<script language="JavaScript" src="tree_tpl.js"></script>
</head>
...
...
...
```

Since this example returns a valid HTML page, you can conclude that the ACL host assignment worked as planned. If the sufficient ACL privileges or ACL assignments are not provided, you will receive the dreaded ORA-24247 error:

```
SQL> select utl_http.request('http://dbaexpert.com') from dual;
       *
ERROR at line 1:
ORA-29273: HTTP request failed
ORA-06512: at "SYS.UTL_HTTP", line 1577
ORA-24247: network access denied by access control list (ACL)
ORA-06512: at line 1
```

■**Note** If you are testing the setup using the DBMS_NETWORK_ACL_ADMIN package, make sure you commit. All changes to the ACL are transactional. Records must be committed like any other database records.

Maintain Access Control Lists

Two more procedures to maintain the fine-grained access of UTL APIs are DROP_ACL and DELETE_PRIVILEGE. Use the DROP_ACL procedure to remove the XML file from the /sys/acls directory. Use DELETE_PRIVILEGE to remove an access control entry from the XML file. For example, if you want to remove CKIM's ACE from the dba.xml control list, you would simply execute the following:

```
  1  begin
  2    dbms_network_acl_admin.DELETE_PRIVILEGE
  3    (ACL =>'dba.xml',
  4      PRINCIPAL => 'CKIM');
  5* end;
SQL> /

PL/SQL procedure successfully completed.
```

■Note So far, all of the examples have been using a database user. You can assign the principal to a database role. In this particular example, we will assign `connect` privileges to the DBA role:

```
 1  BEGIN
 2    DBMS_NETWORK_ACL_ADMIN.ADD_PRIVILEGE (
 3      acl => 'dba.xml',
 4      principal => 'DBA',
 5      is_grant => TRUE,
 6      privilege => 'connect',
 7      start_date => null,
 8      end_date => null);
 9* END;
SQL> /
```

In the same manner, if you want to delete the ACL, Oracle provides the DROP_ACL procedure. In the following example, Oracle will delete the /sys/acls/dba.xml file from the XML DB repository:

```
 1  begin
 2    dbms_network_acl_admin.drop_acl
 3    (ACL=>'dba.xml');
 4* end;
SQL> /
```

```
PL/SQL procedure successfully completed.
```

Query Your Access Control List

There are two new data dictionary views to query the access rights for users and authorized hosts: DBA_ACL_NETWORKS and DBA_NETWORK_ACL_PRIVILEGE. You can query the DBA_NETWORK_ACL_PRIVILEGE view to query network privileges granted or denied for the access control list. Since start_date and end_dates are permissible for network privileges, you can query this view to see when certain users have access.

First, look at the assigned network privileges listed for the dba.xml file:

```
SQL>  select host, lower_port, upper_port, acl
  2   from dba_network_acls
  3* where acl='/sys/acls/dba.xml'
SQL> /
```

```
HOST                      LOWER_PORT        UPPER_PORT    ACL
--------------------      -----------       -----------   --------------------
dbaexpert.com                      80               443    /sys/acls/dba.xml
```

You can see the lower and upper bounds for the open ports and that access to the dbaexpert.com has been punched for security access. The next step would be to find out who the principals are for the `dba.xml` ACL. Let's see how DBAs can query the DBA_NETWORK_ ACL_PRIVILEGES view privileges granted to principals:

```
SQL> select acl, principal, privilege, is_grant
    from dba_network_acl_privileges
SQL> /
```

ACL	PRINCIPAL	PRIVILEGE	IS_GRANT
/sys/acls/dba.xml	JWARD	connect	false
/sys/acls/dba.xml	APP_SUPPORT	connect	true
/sys/acls/dba.xml	RODBA	connect	true
/sys/acls/dba.xml	CKIM	connect	true
/sys/acls/dba.xml	DBA	connect	true
/sys/acls/dba.xml	SALAPATI	connect	true
/sys/acls/dba.xml	APPLICATION_ SERVER_ACCOUNTS	connect	true
/sys/acls/dba.xml	DSWEET	connect	false
/sys/acls/dba.xml	RODBA	connect	false

```
9 rows selected.
```

You can use the following query to determine user permissions for network host connections:

```
SQL> select host, lower_port, upper_port, acl,
 2          decode(
 3          dbms_network_acl_admin.check_privilege_aclid
            (aclid, 'CKIM', 'connect'),
 4           1, 'GRANTED', 0, 'DENIED', null) privilege
 5  from dba_network_acls
 6  where HOST in
 7   (select * from
 8    table(dbms_network_acl_utility.domains('dbaexpert.com')))
 9 order by dbms_network_acl_utility.domain_level(host) desc,
10          lower_port, upper_port
SQL> /
```

HOST	LOWER	UPPER	ACL	PRIVILEGE
dbaexpert.com	80	443	/sys/acls/dba.xml	GRANTED

■**Note** Only DBAs should have access to the DBA_ACL_NETWORKS and DBA_NETWORK_ACL_PRIVILEGE views. These views are available through SELECT_CATALOG_ROLE.

Users can check their access rights to the network and domain by querying the USER_ NETWORK_ACL_PRIVILEGES view. This view is granted to the public, so all database users have select access to it. By logging in with your session, you can query the view to see that your access entry exists in the dba.xml file and that you have been granted rights to the dbaexpert.com web site. For example:

```
SQL> select host, lower_port, upper_port, status privilege
  2  from user_network_acl_privileges
  3  where host in
  4  (select * from
  5  table(dbms_network_acl_utility.domains('dbaexpert.com'))) and
  6  privilege = 'connect'
  7* order by dbms_network_acl_utility.domain_level(host) desc, lower_port
SQL> /


HOST              LOWER_PORT   UPPER_PORT    PRIVILEGE
---------------   ----------   -----------   ---------
dbaexpert.com             80          443    GRANTED
```

Order Your Access Control List

The order of the access control entries in the ACL play an important role in security. Oracle reads the access entries from the top down. If the first entry is a role that allows access to the network but the second entry restricts you from the network, you will still be able to access the network because you are part of the first role that allows you access to the network. If you were denied from the network in the first entry but granted access to the network through a role in the second entry, you would be denied access because of the order precedence.

You can use the position parameter of the ADD_PRIVILEGE procedure to specify the order in the ACL. In this example, the principal JWARD is placed at the beginning of the ACL with the deny flag and with a position value of 1. Next, the APP_SUPPORT database role is granted network access with a position value of 2. Even though the JWARD user account has the APP_SUPPORT database role assigned to him, he will not have access because the JWARD principal is denied the network access privilege prior to the APP_SUPPORT role in the ACL:

```
BEGIN
 DBMS_NETWORK_ACL_ADMIN.ADD_PRIVILEGE (
    position => 1,
    acl => 'dba.xml',
    principal => 'JWARD',
    is_grant => FALSE,
    privilege => 'connect',
    start_date => null,
    end_date => null);
END;
/
```

```
BEGIN
 DBMS_NETWORK_ACL_ADMIN.ADD_PRIVILEGE (
    position => 2,
    acl => 'dba.xml',
    principal => 'APP_SUPPORT',
    is_grant => TRUE,
    privilege => 'connect',
    start_date => null,
    end_date => null);
END;
/
```

In the dba.xml file, you will see the order of the privilege assignment or denial. A <grant> XML tag with a false value indicates that the network access is denied. This is evidenced in the output of the dba.xml file for JWARD:

```
 - <a:acl description="Network Access Control for the DBAs"
xmlns:a="http://xmlns.oracle.com/xdb/acl.xsd"
xmlns:plsql="http://xmlns.oracle.com/plsql"
xmlns:xsi="http://www.w3.org/2001/XMLSchema-instance"
xsi:schemaLocation="http://xmlns.oracle.com/xdb/acl.xsd
http://xmlns.oracle.com/xdb/acl.xsd" shared="true">
  <a:security-class>plsql:network</a:security-class>
- <a:ace xmlns:a="http://xmlns.oracle.com/xdb/acl.xsd">
  <a:grant>false</a:grant>
  <a:principal>JWARD</a:principal>
- <a:privilege>
  <plsql:connect xmlns:plsql="http://xmlns.oracle.com/plsql" />
  </a:privilege>
  </a:ace>
- <a:ace xmlns:a="http://xmlns.oracle.com/xdb/acl.xsd">
  <a:grant>true</a:grant>
  <a:principal>APP_SUPPORT</a:principal>
- <a:privilege>
  <plsql:connect xmlns:plsql="http://xmlns.oracle.com/plsql" />
  </a:privilege>
  </a:ace>
- <a:ace>
  <a:grant>true</a:grant>
  <a:principal>RODBA</a:principal>
+ <a:privilege>
  <plsql:connect xmlns:plsql="http://xmlns.oracle.com/plsql" />
  </a:privilege>
  </a:ace>
 ...
 ...
```

sysasm Privilege for Automatic Storage Management

The sysasm system privilege is added to Oracle Database 11g to provide enhanced security for ASM. This privilege delineates the roles and responsibility of the ASM administrator. Now, either the system administrator or the SAN administrator can manage the ASM instance. Starting from Oracle Database 11g, Oracle recommends that customers use the sysasm role instead of the sysdba role to administer ASM instances. For more information, please refer to Chapter 9.

LOB Encryption Enhancements

SecureFiles is a completely reengineered LOB storage that promises performance, security, compression, and encryption. The introduction of the SecureFiles encrypts the new LOBs in the latest encryption algorithms. SecureFiles provide encryption capabilities while providing additional capabilities such as compression and deduplication. For all the new developments in Oracle LOB encryption, please refer to Chapter 12.

Data Pump Encryption

Oracle Database 11g introduces the encryption of Data Pump dump files. In the previous release, only the metadata could be encrypted at AES-128, AES-192, and AES-256 modes. In addition, Data Pump provides APIs to remap data during the export and import operations. The combination of both encryption and data remapping capabilities provide a significant level of protection in this new release. For details of all the new enhancements related to Data Pump, please refer to Chapter 7.

RMAN Virtual Private Catalog

In Oracle Database 11g, you can restrict access to the recovery catalog by granting access to only a subset of the metadata in the recovery catalog. You can create a subset virtual catalog for groups and database users. The subset that a user has read/write access to is termed a *virtual private catalog*, or just *virtual catalog*. The central or source recovery catalog is now also called the *base recovery catalog*. For complete details on RMAN virtual private catalogs, please refer to Chapter 6.

RMAN Backup Shredding

Backup shredding is a key management feature available in Oracle Database 11g. DBAs can destroy encryption keys of TDE backups without having physical access to backup media. By destroying the encryption keys, this allows DBAs to render backups inaccessible. For complete details on backup shredding, please refer to Chapter 6.

TDE with LogMiner Support

Oracle Database 11g's enhances LogMiner to support TDE. Oracle Logical Standby relies on LogMiner to examine the redo logs to generate SQL statements for the SQL Apply process. The wallet must be open to decrypt encrypted columns. To open the wallet, the database must be in a mounted state to populate the V$LOGMNR_CONTENTS view.

TDE with Data Guard SQL Apply

LogMiner TDE support allows logical standby to support TDE. Oracle's logical standby database has several datatype limitations. Prior to Oracle Database 11g, if the primary database supported any kind of encryption using TDE, the logical standby database option for data protection had to be dismissed. Starting with Oracle Database 11g, the logical standby database fully supports TDE. This support enables a logical standby database to be acceptable by more customers and a wider variety of applications, especially in companies with advanced security requirements. For complete details relative to TDE and Data Guard Logical Standby, please refer to Chapter 10.

Oracle Audit Vault

In a nutshell, Oracle's Audit Vault is a secure database to store and analyze audit information collected from other databases and OS audit trails. Oracle Database 11g enhances Streams support for the Audit Vault. Oracle Streams achieves support for Audit Vault by allowing the Audit Vault to control the Streams configuration. When you integrate Streams with the Audit Vault, you will be prohibited at the source database from making changes.

Furthermore, Oracle Streams introduces the functionality to capture changes introduced by the sys and system database accounts. This allows for Oracle Streams to forward information to the Audit Vault database audit trail.

TDE with Hardware Security Module Integration

The majority of Oracle's security enhancements engage the TDE. TDE works in conjunction with the master key in proprietary encrypted software called Oracle Wallet, a PKCS#12 (public key cryptography standards devised and published by RSA Security) file encrypted using a password. PKCS#12 is a personal information exchange syntax standard.

Oracle Wallet has to be open to allow the key to encrypt the database columns and tablespaces. For the majority of the companies, Oracle Wallet implementation is adequate. For companies that necessitate more stringent security requirements, hardware solutions can provide the supplemental protection.

In a TDE implementation, Oracle's master key must reside in memory to perform cryptographic operations. Hackers can attack Oracle by dumping the physical system memory to retrieve the key. To mitigate this security risk, Oracle broadens TDE functionality, allowing hardware security modules (HSMs) to be used for enhanced physical and logical protection of the master keys. Because encryption and decryption functions using the master key occur inside the HSM, it prevents exposure of the master key to a server's memory. HSMs provide secure computational space (memory) to perform encryption and decryption algorithms. HSM implementation is a secure alternative to Oracle Wallet.

Oracle Database 11g TDE integrates with hardware solutions such as Ingrian (http:// www.ingrian.com) to provide the highest level of security for TDE. Ingrian is a hardware-based security appliance that provides centralized encryption capabilities for application and database data. Additionally, Ingrian stores all the encryption keys in its hardware appliances and offloads the encryption overhead off the application and database servers. Security administrators consider key management an integral component to corporate security. It is a security risk to have encryption keys stored in the database, file systems, applications, or web servers.

This is so because so many people have access to all these layers. With HSM, the keys are not stored in an operating system but at the physical device.

You can configure HSMs such as Ingrian to be tamper-resistant. Ingrian is certified to FIPS 140-2 Level 3, the widely accepted standard of government-specified best practices for network security. Private keys are generated and stored in encrypted form within the HSM. Keys stored in the HSM are protected from physical attacks and cannot be compromised even by stealing the Ingrian appliance. Attempts made to tamper with or probe the card will result in the immediate destruction of all private key data, making it virtually impossible for either external or internal hackers to access this vital information.[1]

The HSM product will be configured by the security administrator. Once the HSM product is configured successfully, you can proceed to modify your `sqlnet.ora` file and change the `METHOD` value. Earlier in the chapter, you learned how to create a wallet and the method of the wallet in the operating system designated as a file. When you set up an HSM product, you must assign the `METHOD` option the value of HSM, as shown here:

```
ENCRYPTION_WALLET_LOCATION=
  (SOURCE=(METHOD=HSM)(METHOD_DATA=
  (DIRECTORY=/apps/oracle/admin/DBATOOLS/wallet)))
```

The `DIRECTORY` value in this example is not required by the HSM but may be by other Oracle products such as RMAN. The `DIRECTORY` option is also mandatory when migrating from a software-based wallet. The `DIRECTORY` path is used to locate the old wallet file.

Your vendor will provide the appropriate PKCS#11 (an API defining a generic interface to cryptographic tokens) library file. TDE integration with HSM must utilize this library file provided by the vendor to interface with the HSM. You will need to copy the library file to a location in your operating system accessible to the database server. A new database user is also required for the database to communicate with the HSM. Once done, you will have to generate the master encryption key for the HSM and open the new wallet with the designated user ID and password using the following syntax:

```
alter system set encryption key identified by user_Id:password;
```

You can optionally use the `MIGRATE USING wallet password` clause if you are migrating from an existing software-based wallet. The `MIGRATE` clause will decrypt the existing column encryption keys and then encrypt them with the newly created, HSM-based master encryption key.

There will be additional setup requirements provided by the HSM vendor to integrate Oracle TDE with HSM. Once the HSM and TDE integration is complete, HSM can be used just like any other software wallet.

Oracle Advanced Security Features

In addition to the security features available for mainstream DBAs, Oracle Database 11*g* strengthens its premier advanced security options. The Oracle Kerberos client adds support for encryption algorithms such as 3DES and AES, thus making Kerberos more secure. Additionally, the enhanced Kerberos operates seamlessly with Microsoft and MIT Key Distribution

---

1. Best practices for employing encryption to achieve maximum security from Ingrian Networks

Centers. Other Kerberos improvements are evident in the cross realm and in sysdba strong authentication support.

Kerberos Cross-Realm Support

Oracle Database 11g enhances the Oracle Kerberos implementation to support cross-realm authentication. Effective in Oracle Database 11g, a principal in one realm can authenticate to a principal in another Kerberos realm. By sharing an encryption key between two realms, Kerberos implements cross-realm authentication. The benefit of this feature is that it makes Kerberos an acceptable solution for customers with strong security authentication requirements. This eliminates the need to manage certificates and PKI.

Here is an example of creating an externally authenticated Oracle user that corresponds to a Kerberos user. For two realms, US.DBAEXPERT.COM and KR.DBAEXPERT.COM, these principals could be krb_ckim@US.DBAEXPERT.COM and krb_ckim@KR.DBAEXPERT.COM:

```
SQL> connect / as sysdba;
SQL> create user "KRB_CKIM@KR.DBAEXPERT.COM" identified externally;
SQL> grant create session to "KRB_CKIM@KR.DBAEXPERT.COM";
```

Oracle Database 11g advanced security lifts the 30-character limitation for Kerberos principal accounts.

sysdba Strong Authentication

Oracle has had support for strong authentication since Oracle Database 8i for PKI, Kerberos, and Radius implementations. However, sysdba and sysoper connections were never supported. In Oracle Database 11g, sysdba and sysoper accounts can connect using strong authentication. This release solidifies strong authentications to the database including those made as sysdba and sysoper.

Oracle Call Interface Enhancements

Starting with Oracle Database 11g, numerous initialization parameters allow DBAs to have a more granular level of security for OCI applications. These parameters are sec_* initialization parameters:

```
SQL> show parameter sec_

NAME                                 TYPE         VALUE
------------------------------------ -----------  -------------
sec_case_sensitive_logon             boolean      TRUE
-- sec_max_failed_login_attempts     integer      10
-- sec_protocol_error_further_action string       CONTINUE
-- sec_protocol_error_trace_action   string       TRACE
-- sec_return_server_release_banner  boolean      FALSE
...
```

The initialization parameters in the previous listing that start with dash dash sec (-- sec) are the initialization parameters specific for OCI. In addition, Oracle enables the DBAs to set banner and audit pages through sqlnet.ora parameters. These features enable the DBAs to secure databases for all applications that leverage OCI. The OCI security enhancements are enabled for databases starting in Oracle Release 1(11.1) and for any version of the client. Oracle Database 11*g* OCI security allows you to harden the database further by enabling you to do the following:

- Set the level of information captured for perceived bad packets on the server.

- Drop or delay database connections because of bad packet overflow.

- Configure the maximum number of connection attempts.

- Control the display of database release information.

- Set up the banner for unauthorized access.

Set the Level of Information Captured for Bad Packets

First we'll show what you can do in Oracle Database 11*g* relative to bad packets received on the database tier. Bad packets can be received because of network protocol errors or malicious attacks by hackers to send a large amount of bad packets. Either way, bad packets can create havoc to the database environment by causing disk space outages or denial of service.

Now, you can leverage the SEC_PROTOCOL_ERROR_TRACE_ACTION database initialization parameter to determine the level of information you want to capture for bad packets. This parameter accepts the values for NONE, TRACE, LOG, and ALERT. The default setting for this parameter is TRACE. When SEC_PROTOCOL_ERROR_TRACE_ACTION is set to TRACE, trace files generate on the database server. You can leave this setting for debugging purposes. The LOG value produces an entry in the alert log file but does not generate a trace file. This is the preferable option for a lot of DBAs. You can set this parameter to LOG, and if problems persist, you can change the parameter to ALERT. By setting the parameter to ALERT, Oracle will produce an entry in the alert log file and yet generate a trace file. Lastly, SEC_PROTOCOL_ERROR_TRACE_ACTION can be set to NONE to specify that you do not want to generate a trace file or produce alert log entries for bad packets. You can set this parameter to LOG using the alter system command, as shown here:

```
SQL> alter system set sec_protocol_error_trace_action = LOG;

System altered.
```

Delay or Drop Database Connections

Not only can Oracle Database 11*g* protect you from a flood of bad packets to the database server, but it can also protect you by disconnecting or deferring the connections made to the server. The initialization parameter SEC_PROTOCOL_ERROR_FURTHER_ACTION controls this behavior. By default, this parameter value is set to CONTINUE and does not stop connections from being dropped or deferred. You can modify the behavior of server continuity by using the following syntax:

```
  1* alter system set sec_protocol_error_further_action = "(DROP,30)"
SQL> /

System altered.
```

The DROP option will drop the database connection after n number of bad packets. In this particular example, the client will disconnect from the database after 30 bad packet transfers to the database. The database will go into self-preservation mode. The worst-case scenario for the client is that it may have to reestablish the connection to the database. If you consider database disconnectivity too harsh, you can use the DELAY value to delay the client by n seconds before the database will accept another packet from the client for the same session. Let's look at setting the DELAY option:

```
SQL> alter system set sec_protocol_error_further_action = "(DELAY,15)";

System altered.
```

In this particular example, the client connection will forcibly delay sending packets by 15 seconds. This allows the database to protect itself from denial-of-service attacks. The risk to the client is that the application may suffer from degraded performance.

Configure Maximum Number of Server Connection Attempts

The maximum number of OCI authentication attempts is set to 10 by default. For security reasons, you may want to change this setting to a number acceptable to your security administrators. You can change this behavior by setting the SEC_MAX_FAILED_LOGIN_ATTEMPTS initialization parameter. Unfortunately, modification to the SEC_MAX_FAILED_LOGIN_ATTEMPTS parameter requires a database bounce. You can change the SEC_MAX_FAILED_LOGIN_ATTEMPTS parameter using the following ALTER SYSTEM command:

```
SQL> alter system set sec_max_failed_login_attempts = 5 scope=spfile;

System altered
```

In this particular example, the OCI connection allows only five authentication attempts before it is disconnected.

Control the Display of Database Release Information

Just like you can see the database version in SQL*Plus, you can display the database version banner for OCI connections. SEC_RETURN_SERVER_RELEASE_BANNER controls this behavior. The default value for SEC_RETURN_SERVER_RELEASE_BANNER is FALSE, which means Oracle displays the version number to the client. Therefore, by default, Oracle will display only the high-level version information to the client, as shown here:

```
Oracle Database 11g Enterprise Edition Release 11.1.0.0.0 - Production
```

If you set SEC_RETURN_SERVER_RELEASE_BANNER to YES, then Oracle will disclose the full version of the database including the release number. You can do this by using this syntax:

```
SQL> alter system set sec_return_server_release_banner = TRUE
    scope=spfile;

System altered.
```

This parameter also requires a database restart. Once this parameter is set to TRUE, OCI clients will see the full version of the database, as shown here:

```
Oracle Database 11g Enterprise Edition Release 11.1.0.6 - Production
```

Set Up the Banner and Auditing for Unauthorized Access

Oracle enables the capability to set up a banner page for unauthorized access. Many security administrators consider the banner page for initial login to be crucial to warn the hackers that unauthorized access will not be tolerated. You can enable banners for unauthorized access by setting the SEC_USER_UNAUTHORIZED_ACCESS_BANNER parameter in the sqlnet.ora file. This parameter needs to point to the location of a text file that has the unauthorized banner page. For example, you can specify this banner page in your sqlnet.ora file:

```
SEC_USER_UNAUTHORIZED_ACCESS_BANNER = /apps/oracle/general/banner/access.txt
```

An example of an enterprise corporate-authorized banner page looks something like this:

```
--   SECURITY ALERT:
--   Access to this system is for authorized
--   Database Technology Innovations (DTI) employees only.
--   By accessing this system you agree to be bound by DTI Computer
--   Users and Information Security policies. Your activity on this system
--   may be monitored, and by logging on, you signify your consent to such
--   monitoring. Unauthorized use detected may be subject to investigation
--   and disciplinary action and/or reporting to law enforcement and/or
--   civil action. If you do not agree to these terms you must disconnect
--   immediately.
```

Oracle Database 11g does not just stop at providing a banner page for unauthorized access but also allows the setup of an audit page to warn clients that their connections are being audited. Respectively, you can set up an auditing banner to warn clients by adding an entry in the sqlnet.ora file similar to what you see here:

```
SEC_USER_AUDIT_ACTION_BANNER = /apps/oracle/general/banner/audit.txt
```

By default, these parameters are not set. In addition, you must modify the client to make proper OCI calls to take advantage of these security settings. The OCI_ATTR_ACCESS_BANNER call will retrieve the access banner information from the database server. Likewise, you can invoke the OCI_ATTR_AUDIT_BANNER call to retrieve audit banner text from the server.

CHAPTER 6

■■■

Backup and Recovery

Oracle Database 11g provides several useful and powerful features relating to the management of backup and recovery and provides several enhancements to RMAN, which is the main Oracle backup and recovery tool. The following are the key new features and enhancements in the backup and recovery area:

- Data Recovery Advisor

- Enhanced block media recovery

- Tighter integration of RMAN and Data Guard

- Enhanced archived redo log management

- Virtual private recovery catalogs

- Network-enabled database duplication without the use of prior backups

- Long-term backups

- Multisection backups

- New validate command

In addition to these features, there are also new configuration options for backup compression, a new archived redo log failover feature, use of substitution variables in RMAN command files and stored scripts, and several other interesting new backup and recovery–related features in this release, which all contribute to making RMAN even more robust and powerful for backing up and recovering Oracle databases.

The Data Recovery Advisor is indeed one of Oracle Database 11g's stellar achievements, and it ranks right up there in the list of RMAN new features. We discussed this exciting new feature in Chapter 2, as part of the database diagnosability new feature, and we discuss the rest of the new backup and recovery–related features in this chapter.

Enhanced Block Media Recovery

Block media recovery, which enables you to recover corrupt blocks in a datafile, was available in prior versions of the Oracle database. Random IO errors, as well as memory corruptions that are written to disk, are usually responsible for data block corruption. Block media recovery, by letting you restore and recover only the corrupted blocks in a datafile, enhances database availability. The affected datafiles can remain online while you're fixing the corrupt blocks. Block media recovery is an ideal solution for repairing physical corruption in a limited number of known data blocks and lets you avoid the costly alternative of a complete restore and recovery of the affected datafile.

During a block media recovery, RMAN searches the database backups for a good version of the corrupted data blocks. It first restores the good data blocks and then performs a recovery by using archived redo logs, just as it does in the case of a complete datafile recovery. Of course, the restore and recovery are way faster in a block media recovery operation, since you are recovering only a limited number of data blocks, instead of recovering the entire datafile.

Before the Oracle Database 11g release, you used the `blockrecover` command to perform block media recovery. Using this command, you could specify a datafile (or a tablespace) and the data block numbers you wanted to recover. In Oracle Database 11g, there is a new command to perform block media recovery, named the `recover ... block` command. The `recover ... block` command replaces the `blockrecover` command, which isn't available in Oracle Database 11g.

The new `recover ... block` command is more powerful and efficient than the old `blockrecover` command, since it searches the flashback logs first before searching backups for the necessary good data blocks during data block corruption fixes. Searching the flashback logs is a whole lot quicker than searching the database backups for those same data blocks. Of course, RMAN will search the flashback logs for older uncorrupted versions of the corrupt blocks only if you happen to be using the flashback database feature and have enabled flashback logging. This is one more reason for you to implement the flashback database feature.

While the block media recovery is going on, any attempt by users to access data in the corrupt blocks will result in an error message, telling the user that the data block is corrupt.

Preconditions for Using the recover ... block Command

To use the `recover ... block` command, you must meet the following prerequisites:

- The database must be mounted or open.

- You must enable flashback logs if you want RMAN to first search the flashback logs for good versions of the corrupt blocks.

- The database must be in archivelog mode, since RMAN needs the archived redo logs to perform the block recovery.

- You can use only full or level 0 backups of the relevant datafiles, not proxy copies.

During a block media recovery, RMAN searches the flashback logs for good versions of the corrupted data blocks. Once it finds them, it'll first restore the blocks and then perform a media recovery on those blocks, using archived redo logs for the recovery. Thus, archived redo logs are essential for the block media recovery process to work. If some redo records are missing, it's possible that RMAN may still be able to recover the necessary block information from the archived redo logs. However, if you have lost or can't access an entire redo log file, block media recovery will fail.

Identifying the Corrupt Blocks

There are basically two types of data corruption: physical or media corruption, where the database fails to recognize the corrupted data block, and logical corruption, where the database recognizes the data block but the block's contents are logically inconsistent. Block media recovery can repair only the first kind of block corruption, in other words, physical corruption.

The V$DATABASE_BLOCK_CORRUPTION view always records information about the corrupt blocks when the database encounters one. The following commands will reveal corrupt data blocks and record that information in the V$DATABASE_BLOCK_CORRUPTION view:

- `analyze table` and `analyze index`

- `list failure`

- `validate`

- `backup ... validate`

■**Tip** Another trick DBAs often use in order to handle database corruption is to perform a full database export to `/dev/null`:

```
exp file=/dev/null log=/tmp/full.log full=y userid="'/ as sysdba'"
```

The export command shown here will scan all data blocks and report on the corrupted data blocks.

In addition, the `dbverify` utility will also reveal block corruption. The alert log as well as the user trace files will record the corruption messages. A typical block corruption message would look like this:

```
ORA-01578: ORACLE data block corrupted (file # 2, block # 4)
ORA-01110: data file 2: '/u01/app/oracle/oradata/prod1/data01.dbf'
ORA-01578: ORACLE data block corrupted (file # 3, block # 95)
ORA-01110: data file 3: '/u01/app/oracle/oradata/prod1/data01.dbf'
```

Once you see error messages such as this, it's time to go work with the `recover ... block` command to recover the corrupted data blocks, as we explain in the next section.

Using the recover ... block Command

Once you identify corrupt data blocks, start RMAN, and issue the `recover ... block` command to fix the corrupted blocks. RMAN will automatically look in the flashback logs first before looking in the backups for a good version of the corrupted blocks. You can choose to fix only selected corrupt blocks or all corrupted blocks in one step. We show both methods in the following sections.

Recovering Specific Data Blocks

You can use the `recover ... block` command to recover one or a set of corrupt data blocks. You must specify the datafile number and the affected data blocks, as shown here:

```
RMAN> recover datafile 2 block 24
   2> datafile 4 block 10;
```

You can specify various options such as the from backupset option, which specifies a certain backup set, or the from tag option, which specifies that RMAN must recover the corrupt data blocks from a backup with a specific tag. Here's an example of how you can specify the from tag option:

```
RMAN> recover datafile 2 block 24
   2> datafile 4 block 10
   3> from tag=sundaynight;
```

You can, if you want, recover all corrupt blocks at once, as explained in the following section.

Recovering All Corrupt Data Blocks

Use the recover corruption list command to recover all corrupted data blocks that are listed in the V$DATABASE_BLOCK_CORRUPTION view. First, execute the validate database command to populate the V$DATABASE_BLOCK_CORRUPTION view with information about all physically corrupted data blocks in the database. Then run the recover corruption list command to recover all the corrupted blocks.

Let's use a simple example to show how to recover all corrupt data blocks with the recover corruption list command. First issue the validate database command to see whether there are any corrupt data blocks in the database:

```
RMAN> validate database;

Starting validate at 20-MAY-07
allocated channel: ORA_DISK_1
channel ORA_DISK_1: SID=174 device type=DISK
channel ORA_DISK_1: starting compressed full datafile backup set
channel ORA_DISK_1: specifying datafile(s) for validation
input datafile file number=00002 name=C:\ORCL11\APP\ORACLE\ORADATA\ORCL1101.DBF
input datafile file number=00001 name=C:\ORCL11\APP\ORACLE\ORADATA\ORCL1101.DBF
input datafile file number=00003 name=C:\ORCL11\APP\ORACLE\ORADATA\ORCL11S01.DBF
input datafile file number=00005 name=C:\ORCL11\APP\ORACLE\ORADATA\ORCL11E01.DBF
input datafile file number=00004 name=C:\ORCL11\APP\ORACLE\ORADATA\ORCL111.DBF
channel ORA_DISK_1: validation complete, elapsed time: 00:12:05
List of Datafiles
=================
File Status Marked Corrupt Empty Blocks Blocks Examined High SCN
---- ------ -------------- ------------ ---------------- --------
1    OK     0              12499        72960            12591563
   File Name: C:\ORCL11\APP\ORACLE\ORADATA\ORCL11\SYSTEM01.DBF
   Block Type Blocks Failing Blocks Processed
   ---------- -------------- ----------------
   Data       0              48999
   Index      0              9146
   Other      0              2316
```

```
File Status Marked Corrupt Empty Blocks Blocks Examined High SCN
---- ------ -------------- ------------ ---------------
2    OK     37              20609         91976           12673599
   File Name: C:\ORCL11\APP\ORACLE\ORADATA\ORCL11\SYSAUX01.DBF
   Block Type    Blocks Failing          Blocks Processed
   ----------    --------------          ---------------
   Data              0                       26850
   Index             0                       22864
   Other             0                       21653


...
channel ORA_DISK_1: specifying datafile(s) for validation
including current control file for validation
channel ORA_DISK_1: validation complete, elapsed time: 00:00:02
List of Control File and SPFILE
===============================
File Type    Status Blocks Failing Blocks Examined
------------ ------ -------------- ---------------
Control File OK     0              594
Finished validate at 20-MAY-07

RMAN>
```

The output of the `validate database` command reveals that there are corrupt data blocks in some datafiles. You can also query the V$DATABASE_BLOCK_CORRUPTION view at this point to see whether corrupt data blocks exist. You can do this because the V$DATABASE_BLOCK_CORRUPTION view stores all the blocks marked corrupt by the `validate database` command. Issue `recover corruption list` to recover all the blocks marked corrupt in the V$DATABASE_BLOCK_CORRUPTION view.

```
RMAN> recover corruption list;

Starting recover at 20-MAY-07
using channel ORA_DISK_1

channel ORA_DISK_1: restoring block(s)
channel ORA_DISK_1: specifying block(s) to restore from backup set
restoring blocks of datafile 00002
channel ORA_DISK_1: reading from backup piece C:\ORCL11\APP\ORACLE\PRODUC0\
DB_1\5SIFHTAF_1_1
channel ORA_DISK_1: restored block(s) from backup piece 1
channel ORA_DISK_1: block restore complete, elapsed time: 00:00:12
channel ORA_DISK_1: restoring block(s)
channel ORA_DISK_1: specifying block(s) to restore from backup set
restoring blocks of datafile 00002
channel ORA_DISK_1: reading from backup piece …
```

```
starting media recovery
starting media recovery
media recovery complete, elapsed time: 00:00:01

Finished recover at 20-MAY-07

RMAN>
```

Once the database recovers all the physically corrupted data blocks, it removes the information about the previously corrupted data blocks from the V$DATABASE_BLOCK_CORRUPTION view.

RMAN Management Enhancements

Oracle Database 11g implements several general enhancements in the RMAN management area. These improvements include new RMAN persistent configuration parameters, the introduction of substitution variables in RMAN scripting, multisection backups wherein RMAN backs up a large datafile in sections, improved archived redo log management, archived redo log failover, the new backup shredding feature, and the optimized backup of undo data. There is also a new archival backup feature and a new `validate` command in this release. We'll cover these new backup and recovery management–related features in detail in the following sections.

Scripting with RMAN Substitution Variables

You can now use substitution variables in RMAN command files, which you can then incorporate in shell scripts. Using substitution variables lets you create dynamic command files that you can use for multiple backup jobs. All you have to do is pass different values for the substitution variables for different RMAN jobs.

Include the new clause `using` to specify the substitution variables you're using in the RMAN command file. Use the familiar *integer* syntax (&1, &2, and so on) to indicate the substitution variables to which you'd like to assign values. Here's a simple example that shows how to create a dynamic backup shell script:

1. Create an RMAN script named `backup.cmd` that uses two substitution variables:

   ```
   # backup.cmd
   connect sys/<sys_password>@prod1
   run {
   backup database
   tag &1
   format '/u01/app/oracle/backup/&2%U.bkp'
   keep forever;
   }
   exit;
   ```

   The script shown here will back up the database using two substitution variables (&1 and &2), one for the backup tag and the other for the string value in the `format` specification.

2. Create the shell script to run the backup script you created in step 1:

```
#!/bin/tcsh
# script name: yearly_backup.sh
set tag=$1
set format =$2
rman  @backup.cmd using  $tag $format
```

Note that you have to specify the `using` clause when employing a dynamic command file. The `using` clause will specify which substitution variables will be used. In this example, the two substitution variables are `tag` and `format`.

3. Specify the arguments for the `tag` and `format` variables when you invoke the backup shell script, as shown in the following example:

```
$ yearly_backup.sh longterm_backup back0420
```

The example shows how to execute the shell script `yearly_backup` with two dynamic parameters, `longterm_backup` (tag) and `back0420` (format string).

The previous example showed you how to create a dynamic command file. You can also employ substitution variables in a `create script` command to create a *dynamic stored script*. To do this, simply specify the substitution variables for all values that you want to be dynamically updated. Before you can create a dynamic stored script, you must specify the `using` clause when you start RMAN at the command line and also pass the initial values for the substitution variables you want to use in the stored script. Once you invoke RMAN in this fashion, you must create the dynamic stored script. Here's how to create a dynamic stored script that uses substitution variables:

1. Create a command file with the `create script` statement using substitution variables for those values that you want to pass dynamically at script execution time. Here's the command file with the `create script` statement:

```
create script quarterly{
backup
tag &1
format '/u01/app/oracle/bck/&2%U.bck'
keep forever
restore point &3
database;
}
```

The `create script` statement includes three substitution variables, &1, &2, and &3, which stand for tag, part of the `format` string, and restore point, respectively. We'll name this command file `testcmd1` and use it to create the stored script.

2. Connect RMAN to both the target database and the recovery catalog (since we're using the `keep forever` clause). Also, specify the initial values for all three of the substitution variables:

```
$ rman target sys/sammyy1 catalog rman/rman using test_backup  bck0707 FY07Q3

Recovery Manager: Release 11.1.0.6.0 - Production on Thu Aug 23 13:46:15 2007

Copyright (c) 1982, 2007, Oracle.  All rights reserved.

connected to target database: ORCL2 (DBID=611115374)
connected to recovery catalog database

RMAN>
```

3. Once you log in to RMAN after specifying the initial values for the substitution variables, you must create the stored script using our command file (testcmd1) from step 1. Create the stored script by running the command file you created earlier:

```
RMAN> @testcomd1

RMAN> create script quarterly {
    2> backup
    3> tag bck0707
    4> format '/u01/app/oracle/bck/test_backup%Ubck'
    5> keep forever
    6> restore point FY07Q3
    7> database;
    8> }
starting full resync of recovery catalog
full resync complete
created script quarterly

RMAN> **end-of-file**
```

Notice how RMAN replaced the three substitution variables with the actual values you supplied at the command line when you invoked RMAN in step 2.

4. In future executions of the stored script, you can specify values for the three substitution valuables as part of a run block, as shown here:

```
run
{
  execute script quarterly
  using
  prod_backup
  prodbck0707
  FY0704;
}
```

You can see that the introduction of substitution variables make creating dynamic RMAN stored scripts quite easy, just as in the case of creating dynamic RMAN command files.

New RMAN Configuration Parameters

There are a couple of important new persistent configuration parameters for RMAN. Issue the
show all command at the RMAN prompt to see all the configuration parameters in Oracle
Database 11g. The compression algorithm and the archivelog deletion policy parameters are
new in the Oracle Database 11g release:

```
RMAN> show all;

using target database control file instead of recovery catalog
RMAN configuration parameters for database with db_unique_name ORCL2 are:
CONFIGURE RETENTION POLICY TO REDUNDANCY 1; # default
CONFIGURE BACKUP OPTIMIZATION OFF; # default
CONFIGURE DEFAULT DEVICE TYPE TO DISK; # default
CONFIGURE CONTROLFILE AUTOBACKUP OFF; # default
CONFIGURE CONTROLFILE AUTOBACKUP FORMAT FOR DEVICE TYPE DISK TO '%F'; # default
CONFIGURE DEVICE TYPE DISK PARALLELISM 1 BACKUP TYPE TO BACKUPSET; # default
CONFIGURE DATAFILE BACKUP COPIES FOR DEVICE TYPE DISK TO 1; # default
CONFIGURE ARCHIVELOG BACKUP COPIES FOR DEVICE TYPE DISK TO 1; # default
CONFIGURE MAXSETSIZE TO UNLIMITED; # default
CONFIGURE ENCRYPTION FOR DATABASE OFF; # default
CONFIGURE ENCRYPTION ALGORITHM 'AES128'; # default
CONFIGURE COMPRESSION ALGORITHM 'BZIP2'; # default
CONFIGURE ARCHIVELOG DELETION POLICY TO NONE; # default
CONFIGURE SNAPSHOT CONTROLFILE NAME TO '/u01/app/oracle/product/
11.1.0.6/db_1/dbs/snapcf_orcl2.f'; # default

RMAN>
```

You can now choose the compression algorithm RMAN uses for compressing a backup. You
have a choice of two different compression algorithms. Query the V$RMAN_COMPRESSION_
ALGORITHM view to find out what compression algorithms you can choose from, as shown in
the following example:

```
SQL> select algorithm_name, algorithm_description,
     is_default from
     v$rman_compression_algorithm;

ALGORITHM_NAME      ALGORITHM_DESCRIPTION                IS
------------------  ---------------------------------    --------
ZLIB                optimized for speed                  NO
BZIP2               optimized for maximum compression    YES

SQL>
```

The default compression algorithm, BZIP2, provides a better compression ratio but performs
the compression more slowly than the ZLIB algorithm. The alternate compression algorithm,
ZLIB, is faster but doesn't offer the best compression ratio. Use the following command to
switch to the ZLIB compression algorithm from the default BZIP2 algorithm:

```
RMAN> configure compression algorithm 'zlib';

new RMAN configuration parameters:
CONFIGURE COMPRESSION ALGORITHM 'zlib';
new RMAN configuration parameters are successfully stored

RMAN>
```

This command will switch the RMAN compression algorithm from the default compression algorithm BZIP2 to the alternate compression algorithm ZLIB. You must set the initialization parameter compatibility to at least 11.0.0 to use the ZLIB compression algorithm.

The other important new configuration parameter is the specification of an archived redo log deletion policy. By default, there is no archived redo log policy, as shown by the output of the show all command for the archivelog deletion policy parameter (CONFIGURE ARCHIVELOG DELETION POLICY TO NONE). We discuss the configuration of an archived redo log deletion policy later in this chapter.

Backing Up Large Files in Sections

In Oracle Database 10*g*, the unit of an RMAN backup and restore was the file level. That is, you had to back up or restore an entire datafile but couldn't break up the backup/recovery into a subfile chunk. Since you can now have an Oracle file theoretically as large as 2 terabytes, there comes a point when it becomes impractical to back up and restore at the file level. Oracle Database 11*g* offers a way out of this predicament by letting you back up and restore a large file in *sections*. The backups you perform at the section level are known as *multisection backups*. Each backup piece of a backup set that belongs to a multisection backup will contain blocks from a single file section, which is a contiguous set of blocks in a file.

■**Tip** The multisection backups feature can be one of the options you can adopt to handle larger datafile size standards. Lot of DBAs today have maximum file size limitations. The file size limitation, which was originally 4GB or 10GB, can be increased to an arbitrary number such as 32GB. If you are on an ASM file system, the single file size of 32GB will not be an issue since the data is scattered across all the disks in the disk group. You can alleviate the fear of slow backups and have a single point of contingency by using multisection backups.

In a multisection backup, each RMAN channel backs up a different section of a datafile. Thus, you can enhance backup performance by specifying a multisection backup and use multiple channels to back up a large datafile. Multisection backups thus offer tremendous performance benefits, since you can back up a single datafile in parallel in multiple sections. You also don't have to back up a large file all over again if the backup fails midway—you need to back up only those sections that weren't backed up prior to the backup failure.

You can have up to 256 sections per datafile. RMAN makes uniform-sized sections, except the very last one, which may or may not be the same size as all the other sections. You can specify different `section size` values for different files, within the same backup job.

Performing Multisection Backups

Use the new `backup` command clause `section size` to perform multisection backups. Each backup piece then will be limited to the value you set for the `section size` parameter. If you don't specify a value for the sections with the `section size` parameter, RMAN computes an internal default section size for that backup job. Each section of the backup corresponds to a separate backup piece in a backup set.

The following is an example showing how using the `section size` parameter breaks up the backup of a datafile into multiple sections of the same size. Here are the steps you must follow in order to make a multisection backup:

1. Connect to the target database:

   ```
   $ rman target sys/<sys_password>@target_db
   ```

2. Configure channel parallelism. In this example, we use a parallel setting of 3 for the SBT device, so we configure three SBT channels, as shown here:

   ```
   {allocate channel c1 device type sbt
    parms 'env=(ob device 1=testtape1)';
   allocate channel c2 device type sbt
    parms 'env=(ob device 1=testtape2)';
   allocate channel c3 device type sbt
    parms 'env=(ob device 1=testtape3)';
   ```

3. Execute the `backup` command, specifying the `section size` parameter:

   ```
   RMAN> backup
       2> section size 500m
       3> tablespace example;
   ```

Let's say that our tablespace example has one datafile, sized 1500m. The `section size` parameter breaks up the datafile backup into three chunks of 500m apiece. Each of the three channels you specified backs up a contiguous set of blocks, known as a *section*, with each section going to a different backup piece.

▓**Note** You can't specify the `section size` parameter along with the `maxpiecesize` parameter.

You must set the initialization parameter `compatibility` to at least 11.0 when performing multisection backups, since it's not possible to restore multisection backups with a release earlier than 11.0.

You can also use the `section size` clause with the `validate datafile` command. We'll show an example of this later in this chapter, when we discuss the new version of the `validate` command.

Managing Multisection Backups

The `SECTION_SIZE` column in both the V$BACKUP_DATAFILE and RC_BACKUP_DATAFILE views shows the number of blocks in each section of a multisection backup. Of course, a whole file backup will show a value of zero in this column. If you haven't performed any multisection backups, the `SECTION_SIZE` column will have a zero value. The V$BACKUP_SET and RC_BACKUP_SET views tell you which backups are multisection backups. The following example shows a query on the V$BACKUP_DATAFILE view:

```
SQL> select piece, multi_section from v$backup_datafile;

PIECES          MUL
-------         --------
1               NO
2               YES
7               YES
4               NO

SQL>
```

The query shows that backup pieces 2 and 7 are multisection backups since they each have a value of YES for the column `MULTI_SECTION`.

Creating Archival (Long-Term) Backups

You can use the `backup ... keep` command in Oracle Database 11g to retain backups for longer periods than specified by your retention policy for RMAN backups. Using this command, you can make *archival backups* that you can retain for years, if you want, for purposes such as meeting regulatory requirements. You can also use archival backups for periodically restoring a database for testing purposes. These archival backups contain all the files necessary to restore and recover a database.

In Oracle Database 10g, you used the keep option to override any configured retention policy for a backup. The keep option made the backup exempt from a retention policy for a specified period of time. The `keep forever` option (requires a recovery catalog) specified that a backup or copy never expired. In Oracle Database 11g, you use the keep and `keep forever` options to essentially do the same thing as before. However, some of the options from the previous release aren't used now, and there is a new option called `restore point`. Since the `backup ... keep` command is at the heart of the archival backups feature, we'll cover this command in more detail in the following sections.

The backup ... keep Command in Oracle Database 10g

Before Oracle Database 11g, the `backup ... keep` command had the following options:

- `keep` to mark as exempt and `unkeep` to mark the undoing of a backup's exemption from the configured backup retention policy

- `logs` to specify that RMAN must retain the archived redo logs necessary for a recovery as long as the relevant backup is available, and the `nologs` option to specify that the archived redo logs to recover the backup not be kept

- `forever` and `until time` to specify the length of time for which to exempt a backup from the configured backup retention policy

---

■**Note** You must use a recovery catalog if you specify the `keep forever` clause.

Changes in the backup ... keep Command

In the new version of the `backup ... keep` command, the `keep`, `nokeep`, `forever`, and `until time` options are retained. However, the `logs` and `nologs` options aren't there any longer. Instead, you have a new option, `restore point`. The `restore point` option lets RMAN automatically create a restore point corresponding to the SCN that RMAN must recover the target database backup to in order to make the database consistent. In other words, the `restore point` clause specifies the time to which RMAN can recover the archival backup. You must, of course, specify a restore point name when you use the `restore point` clause, as you'll see in the section "Creating an Archival Backup" later in this chapter.

Archival Backups

The primary purpose of the `backup ... keep` command in Oracle Database 11*g* is to specify a backup as a self-contained archival backup exempt from any backup retention policy you might have configured. In addition to being exempt from the backup retention policy, the archival backup is an *all-inclusive backup*, in the sense that all the files needed to restore and recover the database are part of the archival backup. Note that this all-inclusive archival backup is backed up to a single disk or tape. The archival backups can be put to historical usage, or they can be used to restore the production databases on another system for testing.

Previously, if you retained an online backup for a lengthy period, RMAN automatically retained all the archived redo logs for that period, assuming you might want to perform a point-in-time recovery in the time spanned by that period. Archival backups are somewhat different, since your goal isn't a point-in-time recovery but rather a need to keep a backup for a specified length of time, along with all the archived redo logs necessary to recover that backup. Thus, when you specify the `keep` option (`keep forever` or `keep until`), RMAN saves only the backups for the datafiles and just those archived redo logs necessary to recover the online backup and necessary autobackup files. Thus, the archival backup as a whole occupies far less space than saving a regular RMAN backup for a long period.

■**Note** Since RMAN doesn't apply its configured retention policies for archival backups, you'll end up filling up your flash recovery area if you store your archival backups in that location. You can avoid this by storing archival backups in a location other than the flash recovery area.

Creating an Archival Backup

You can create an archival backup in two ways. You can make a backup exempt from a retention policy by using the backup ... keep command, as explained earlier. The other way you can make an archival backup is by altering the status of an existing backup using the change command. Let's create an archival backup using both of these methods.

First, we'll create an archival backup using the backup ... keep command. We'll create an archival backup that's retained for one year without being considered obsolete, regardless of the configuration of your backup retention policy. Here's the command:

```
RMAN> backup database
    2> format 'c:\archives\db_%U.bkp'
    3> tag quarterly
    4> keep until time 'sysdate + 365'
    5> restore point firstquart07;


Starting backup at 21-MAY-07
using channel ORA_DISK_1
backup will be obsolete on date 20-MAY-08
archived logs required to recover from this backup will be backed up
channel ORA_DISK_1: starting full datafile backup set
channel ORA_DISK_1: specifying datafile(s) in backup set
input datafile file number=00001
...
channel ORA_DISK_1: backup set complete, elapsed time: 00:00:08
Finished backup at 21-MAY-07

RMAN>
```

In this example, we used the keep until time clause, which makes RMAN mark this backup obsolete as soon as the time you specify (sysdate+365) has passed. Of course, if you specify the keep forever clause instead, the backup never becomes obsolete. That is, the backup will never be eligible for deletion by the backup retention policy. Here's how you specify the keep forever clause in your backup command:

```
RMAN> backup database
    2> format 'c:\archives\db_%U.bkp'
    3> tag quarterly
    4> keep forever'
    5> restore point finyear2007;
```

RMAN never deletes the archival backup you create with the previous backup command since the backup never becomes obsolete (you can use the change command to alter the status of this as well as any other backup, as we'll show later in this chapter). You can also make a *temporary archival backup* that you plan on deleting soon after you create it, instead of keeping it for a long period of time. This kind of backup would be ideal when you want to restore a backup to a different host and then delete it soon after that. If, for example, you want the backup to be obsolete after only one day, overriding the configured retention policy, you can do so by specifying the clause keep until sysdate+1, as shown in the following example:

```
RMAN> backup database
    2> format '/u01/app/oracle/tmp_bck/%U'
    3> tag proddb
    4> keep until 'sysdate+1'
    5> restore point prod07;
```

The backup database command shown here creates a temporary archival backup with the tag proddb, which becomes obsolete after just one day. Here's what happens when you issue the backup ... keep until time (or a backup ... keep forever) command:

- The database performs a redo log switch so the redo information in the current online redo log is archived. This is to make the database consistent upon a recovery.

- RMAN makes a backup of all datafiles, archived redo logs, the controlfile, and the server parameter file.

- The archived redo log consists of only the redo logs necessary to recover the database to a consistent state.

- The command supports an optional restore point clause, which you can specify to create a normal restore point. This restore point captures the SCN right after the backup is completed.

- The controlfile autobackup will store the restore point created by RMAN, so it can be used when you restore the controlfile.

Note You can create archival backups (with the keep or keep forever clause) only if you're using a recovery catalog. You can't use the keep or keep forever clause for backup files in the flash recovery area.

When you specify the keep clause in a backup command (keep until time, keep forever), RMAN creates multiple backup sets. For this reason, you must ensure that the format clause can create multiple backup pieces in the various backup sets. The easiest way to do this is to specify the %U parameter, as shown in the example earlier in this section.

The second method of creating an archival backup is to simply use the keep option of the change command to alter the status of a regular backup to that of an archival backup. Here's a simple example:

```
RMAN> change backup
    2>  tag 'weekly_bkp'
    3>  keep forever;
```

The change command converts a routine weekly backup in this case to an archival backup that never becomes obsolete (keep forever). The change command thus changes the exemption status of a backup or copy vis-à-vis the configured retention policy. If you want to make a long-term backup that's ineligible for deletion into one that's eligible for deletion (that is, eligible for the obsolete status), you can do so by issuing the change ... nokeep command, as shown here:

```
RMAN> change copy of database controlfile nokeep;
```

■**Note** You can't use the change ... keep command for backup files stored in the flash recovery area.

The nokeep option brings the long-term image copies for both datafiles and controlfiles back under the purview of the configured retention policy, thus guaranteeing that eventually they become eligible for the obsolete status again.

Restoring an Archival Backup

The easiest way to restore an archival backup is by using the duplicate command after creating a temporary instance. Here's a quick summary of the procedure:

1. Prepare the auxiliary instance, which includes the duplicate command's usual preparatory steps for creating an auxiliary instance, such as creating the password file and the initialization parameter file. You must also establish Oracle Net connectivity to the auxiliary instance and start the auxiliary instance.

2. Connect to the recovery catalog, the target, and the auxiliary instances, as shown here:

```
RMAN> connect target sys/<sys_password>@prod1
RMAN> connect catalog rman/rman@catdb
RMAN> connect auxiliary /
```

3. Issue the list restore point all command to see the available restore points in the database:

```
RMAN> list restore point all;

SCN      RSP Time  Type   Time     Name
-------  --------  -----  -------  --------------
3074299                   21-MAY-07 FIRSTQUART07

RMAN>
```

4. Issue the duplicate database command, making sure you specify the restore point to which you'd like to restore the database, using the archival backup:

```
RMAN> duplicate database
    2> to newdb
    3> until restore point firstquart07
    4> db_file_name_convert='/u01/prod1/dbfiles/',
    5>'/u01/newdb/dbfiles'
    6> pfile = '/u01/newdb/admin/init.ora';
```

The duplicate command shown here creates a new controlfile instead of restoring the controlfile of the target database. The restore point you created earlier with the keep command and the SCN corresponding to it are recorded in both the recovery catalog if you're using one and the target database controlfile. Since you need the SCN for duplicating the database until the restore point that you specified (firstquart07), you must either use a recovery catalog or use the target database controlfile, as long as the restore point is still there and hasn't been overwritten.

The New Validate Command

In Oracle Database 10g, you had access to two backup validation commands. The validate backupset command lets you validate a specific backup set when one or more backup pieces were suspected to be damaged or even missing. RMAN would check all the backup pieces in the backup set and see whether their checksums were correct to verify that the backup set was OK and good for use in a recovery situation. You can still use this command when you suspect corruption in a backup set.

In addition to the validate backupset command, the previous release of the Oracle database provided the backup validate command to perform checks on specified files to confirm that they could be backed up correctly. The backup validate command checks for both physical and logical corruption in the datafiles. In addition, the command also verifies that all database files are indeed where they are supposed to be. For example, you can issue the backup validate command to check all database files as well as the archived redo logs of a database by issuing the following command:

RMAN> backup validate database archivelog all.

RMAN would go through all the motions of an actual backup, except it doesn't produce any backup sets—it merely reads each datafile and archived redo log to confirm that they aren't corrupted and that they can be backed up successfully. Any corruptions found would be recorded in the V$DATABASE_BLOCK_CORRUPTION view.

In Oracle Database 11g, you can use the new validate command to check for corruption at a finer level of granularity than the old backup validate command. You can use this command to validate datafiles, backup sets, and even individual data blocks. Note that the new validate command is semantically equivalent to the backup validate command in the previous release.

You use the validate command to check for things such as missing datafiles or corrupt data blocks. You also run the command to assure yourself that a backup set is restorable. If RMAN finds that the validate command has trapped any errors, it automatically triggers a failure assessment. If any failures are found, RMAN will log it into the automatic diagnostic repository. You can use the Data Recovery Advisor command list failure to view all the failures logged in the ADR. Chapter 2 explains the ADR in detail.

Validating with the validate Command

We'll present some examples that show how to validate various database objects in order to illustrate the range of the new validate command. Here's an example showing how to validate a backup set by using the validate command:

```
RMAN> validate backupset 7;

Starting validate at 21-MAY-07
using target database control file instead of recovery catalog
allocated channel: ORA_DISK_1
channel ORA_DISK_1: SID=193 device type=DISK
channel ORA_DISK_1: starting validation of datafile backup set
channel ORA_DISK_1: reading from backup piece C:\ORCL11\APP\ORACLE\PRODUCT\11.1.
0\DB_1\DATABASE\5TIFHU1H_1_1
channel ORA_DISK_1: piece handle=C:\ORCL11\APP\ORACLE\PRODUCT\11.1.0\DB_1\DATABA
SE\5TIFHU1H_1_1 tag=TAG20070419T081823
channel ORA_DISK_1: restored backup piece 1
channel ORA_DISK_1: validation complete, elapsed time: 00:00:01
Finished validate at 21-MAY-07

RMAN>
```

You can validate an individual block in a datafile by specifying the datafile and block numbers, as shown in the following example:

```
RMAN> validate datafile 2 block 24;
```

The block-level validation shown here is the lowest level of granularity that you can go to with the validate command. On the other extreme, you can use the validate command to check the entire database at once, as shown in the following example:

```
RMAN> validate database;

Starting validate at 21-MAY-07
using channel ORA_DISK_1
channel ORA_DISK_1: starting compressed full datafile backup set
channel ORA_DISK_1: specifying datafile(s) for validation
input datafile file number=00002 name=C:\ORCL11\APP\ORACLE\ORADATA\1\SY01.DBF
...
channel ORA_DISK_1: validation complete, elapsed time: 00:11:24
List of Datafiles
=================
File Status Marked Corrupt Empty Blocks Blocks Examined High SCN
---- ------ -------------- ------------ --------------- ----------
1    OK     0              12542        72960           7236557
  File Name: C:\ORCL11\APP\ORACLE\ORADATA\ORCL11\SYSTEM01.DBF
  Block Type Blocks Failing Blocks Processed
```

```
---------- -------------- ----------------
  Data        0               48959
  Index       0               9143
  Other       0               2316
...
channel ORA_DISK_1: specifying datafile(s) for validation
including current control file for validation
channel ORA_DISK_1: validation complete, elapsed time: 00:00:02
List of Control File and SPFILE
===============================
File Type    Status Blocks Failing Blocks Examined
------------ ------ -------------- ---------------
Control File OK     0                594
Finished validate at 21-MAY-07
```

RMAN>

The `validate` command begins with the message "Starting validate" and not "Starting backup," as is the case when you issue the `backup ... validate` command. The semantics, however, of the new `validate` command are similar to those of the old `backup ... validate` command, and both commands work in a similar fashion. The big advantage to using the new `validate` command is that it can check at a more granular level than the old `backup ...` `validate` command, including at the data block level. You can also apply the new `validate` command to a much larger number of objects, including such objects as the recovery area.

■**Note** The `validate` command checks only for intrablock corruption both physical and logical in nature. It doesn't check for interblock corruption.

Speeding Up Validation with the Section Size Clause

If you want to validate a very large datafile fast, use the `section size` clause with the `validate` command. The `section size` clause works similarly to the `section size` clause during a multi-section backup, which we discussed earlier in this chapter. Make sure you first configure multiple backup channels in order to parallelize the datafile validation when you run the `validate` command. The following example shows how to parallelize the validation of a large datafile by using the `section size` clause to break up the job into two parallel streams:

```
RMAN> run
2> {
3> allocate channel ch1 device type disk;
4> allocate channel ch2 device type disk;
5> validate datafile 2 section size = 500m;
6> }
```

```
allocated channel: ch1
channel ch1: SID=193 device type=DISK
allocated channel: ch2
channel c2: SID=191 device type=DISK

Starting validate at 21-MAY-07
...
validating blocks 1 through 32768
...
validating blocks 32769 through 65536
including current control file for validation
channel ch1: validation complete, elapsed time: 00:00:17
========================================================
File Status Marked Corrupt Empty Blocks Blocks Examined High SCN
---- ------ -------------- ------------ -----------------
1    OK     0              12542        72960             7373884
  File Name: C:\ORCL11\APP\ORACLE\ORADATA\SYSTEM01.DBF
...
Finished validate at 21-MAY-07
released channel: ch1
released channel: ch2
```

RMAN>

The validate command skips all unused blocks in the datafiles it's validating. Set the section size clause's value higher, and increase the number of backup channels to make the validation job significantly faster. You must configure multiple channels when specifying the section size clause. Remember that the section size clause applies only to the validation of datafiles.

Validate Command Options

Besides the options we illustrated in the previous section, you can also specify the following options with the validate command:

- validate recovery area

- validate recovery files

- validate spfile

- validate tablespace <tablespace_name>

- validate controlfilecopy

- validate backupset <primary_key>

Configuring an Archived Redo Log Deletion Policy

Oracle Database 11g provides several key enhancements in the management of archived redo logs. Oracle Database 11g lets you configure a persistent policy regarding when archived redo logs are eligible for deletion. The archived redo log deletion policy applies to logs stored on disk and applies to all archived redo log destinations, including the flash recovery area.

Deleting Archived Redo Logs

You can delete unwanted archived redo logs either manually or let RMAN delete them automatically. You can use either the `delete ... archivelog` or `backup ... delete input` commands to delete archived redo logs yourself. RMAN automatically deletes only those archived redo logs that are in the flash recovery area. There's no default RMAN archived redo log deletion policy. RMAN decides whether an archived redo log is eligible for deletion based on criteria such as whether a certain number of backups have been made and whether all archived redo logs have been successfully transferred to the necessary destinations. To be precise, when you don't configure an archived redo log deletion policy, RMAN will deem an archived redo log eligible for deletion if that log satisfies *both* of the following conditions.

■**Note** The archived redo log deletion policy you configure doesn't apply to the archived redo logs that are part of a backup set.

- If you have specified the `log_archived_dest_n` parameter, the archived redo log must have been successfully transferred to all the remote destinations you specified. This applies to archived redo logs in the flash recovery area as well as those that are stored in a non-flash-recovery-area location.

- You must have already backed up that archived redo log at least once (either to disk or tape), *or* the archived redo log must be obsolete. Whether an archived redo log is deemed obsolete depends on the backup retention policy in force. Any archived redo log necessary to support a guaranteed restore point or the flashback database feature isn't considered obsolete by the backup retention policy.

Remember that when you configure an archived redo log deletion policy, the following will be true:

- Both the `backup ... delete` and `delete ... archivelog` commands take the configured policy into account.

- The flash recovery area takes the configured policy into consideration as well.

Configuring an Archived Redo Log Deletion Policy

As mentioned in the previous section, by default there isn't an archived redo log deletion policy (it is set to `none`). To configure your own archived redo log deletion policy, use the `configure` command, with the `archived redo log deletion policy` clause. The following example shows how to configure a typical archived redo log deletion policy for archived redo logs made to a tape device:

```
RMAN> configure archivelog deletion policy
   2> to backed up 2 times to sbt;

new RMAN configuration parameters:
CONFIGURE ARCHIVELOG DELETION POLICY TO BACKED UP 2 TIMES TO 'SBT_TAPE';
new RMAN configuration parameters are successfully stored

RMAN>
```

The policy that was configured here specifies that all archived redo logs are eligible for deletion only after they have been backed up two or more times to tape. In this example, we specified sbt (tape) as the device type. However, you can also specify disk as the device type instead of sbt. RMAN will make sure that the number of archived redo log backups that you require RMAN to keep exist on the particular device type you specify in the command.

Let's say you configured an archived redo log deletion policy as shown earlier, stipulating that an archived redo log be backed up twice before being eligible for deletion. When you subsequently issue a backup ... archivelog command, RMAN will back up an archived redo log only if there are less than two copies of that log and will skip the backup of the log otherwise. Sound familiar? Well, this behavior is similar to what you'd get if you had specified the not backed up 2 times clause in a backup archivelog command. You can, however, override the archived redo log deletion policy you configured by specifying the force clause in the backup archivelog command.

Once you configure an archived redo log deletion policy, it's enabled automatically and comes into force immediately. If you ever want to disable the policy, you can do so by issuing the following command:

```
RMAN> configure archivelog deletion policy to none;
```

When you issue the command shown here, the database will revert to the out-of-the-box setting for deletion of the archived redo logs, which was explained earlier.

Archived Redo Log Deletion in a Data Guard Setup

You can configure an archived redo log deletion for any standby destination or just for mandatory standby destinations. You can also specify whether the archived redo logs should be merely transferred or applied to the standby database before being considered for deletion. The following discussion explains how to use the configure archivelog deletion policy command, depending upon what your requirements are regarding the two criteria—the number of databases and the status of the archived redo log application.

■**Note** Foreign archived redo logs, which are logs received by a logical standby database for a LogMiner session, are outside the purview of any archived redo log deletion policy you create.

- Specify the `to applied on standby` clause if you want RMAN to delete the archived redo logs after the logs have been *applied* to all the mandatory standby destinations. To be eligible for deletion, the archived redo logs must in addition also satisfy any `backed up ... times to device type` policy that's in force. If you want the archived redo logs to be considered for deletion only after they are applied on all remote standby destinations, use the `to applied on all standby` clause. Here are our two examples of our command for specifying deletion of the archived redo logs after they are applied to remote destinations:

```
RMAN> configure archivelog deletion policy to applied on standby;
RMAN> configure archivelog deletion policy to applied on all standby;
```

  The first command is applicable only to required standby destinations, and the second applies to all standby destinations.

- Specify the `to shipped on standby` clause if you want RMAN to delete the archived redo logs after the logs have been merely *transferred* to all the mandatory standby destinations. To be eligible for deletion, the archived redo logs must in addition also satisfy any `backed up ... times to device type` policy that's in force. If you want the archived redo logs to be considered for deletion only after they are applied on all remote standby destinations, use the `to shipped on all standby` clause. Here are our two examples of the command for specifying deletion of the archived redo logs after they are applied to remote destinations:

```
RMAN> configure archivelog deletion policy to shipped on standby;
RMAN> configure archivelog deletion policy to shipped on all standby;
```

The first command is applicable only to required standby destinations, and the second applies to all standby destinations.

Archived Redo Log Failover

If RMAN finds that the archived redo log in one or more archived redo log locations is corrupt or is missing during an archived redo log backup, it can now complete the backup successfully by using logs from an alternative location. This is called the *archived redo log failover* feature. If, for example, you're backing up the redo logs to the flash recovery area and RMAN finds that one or more redo logs in the flash recovery area are corrupted, it will search for a good archived redo log from outside the flash recovery area. This failover to non-flash-recovery areas during a backup is automatic and guarantees that even if a disk hosting the flash recovery area is damaged, the backup of the flash recovery area won't fail.

We'll show a simple example to illustrate how the archived redo log failover feature works. Let's say you have two archived redo log locations, `/u01/app/oracle/arch1` and `/u01/app/oracle/arch2`. You issue the following command to back up the archived redo logs:

```
RMAN> backup archivelog
  2> from sequence 90
  3> until sequence 100;
```

Now, assume that log 100 is missing in the `/u01/app/oracle/arch1` directory. When you're archiving redo logs to multiple locations, RMAN selects only one copy of each archived redo log when it's backing up the archived redo logs. RMAN will back up redo logs 90–99 from the

/u01/aapp/oracle/arch1 directory and the redo log 100 from the second archived redo log location, /u01/app/oracle/arch2.

Backup Shredding

Oracle Database 11*g* lets you render encrypted backups inaccessible by destroying the encryption key of the backup. You don't need to physically access the backup media to perform this task, also called *backup shredding*. Backup shredding is disabled by default. Here's how you configure backup shredding:

```
RMAN> configure encryption external key storage on;
```

Alternatively, you can use the set encryption command as shown here to configure backup shredding:

```
RMAN> set encryption external key storage on;
```

To actually use the backup shredding feature, you must use the delete force command, as shown here:

```
RMAN> delete force backup;

using target database control file instead of recovery catalog
allocated channel: ORA_DISK_1
channel ORA_DISK_1: SID=153 device type=DISK

RMAN>
```

Note that you can't shred RMAN backups protected with a password.

Optimized Backing Up of Undo Data

Up until this release, during a backup, all undo data in the undo tablespace was backed up. The undo data might include both committed as well as uncommitted data. The committed data that's recorded in the undo tablespace doesn't serve any useful purpose, since that data is also recorded in the data blocks upon committing the relevant transactions. In Oracle Database 11*g*, during a backup, the committed data isn't backed up, thus leading to a saving of storage space as well as faster backups for large OLTP-type databases.

Since the new optimized undo backup is automatically enabled, you don't have to configure anything special to take advantage of this feature.

Active (Network-Based) Database Duplication

Prior to Oracle Database 11*g*, database duplication through RMAN always meant *backup-based duplication*, since the duplicate database relied on the source database's datafile and archived redo log backups. In Oracle Database 11*g*, you can directly duplicate a database over the network without having to back up and provide the source database files. This direct database duplication is called *active database duplication* or *network-aware database duplication*. This is definitely one of Oracle Database 11*g*'s more useful innovations, since you can create duplicate databases and standby databases directly from a live production database, with only an overhead in terms of additional CPU and network utilization for the duplication process. RMAN simply copies the target database files to the destination server (it can be the same server) over a network connection.

Until the Oracle Database 11*g* release, duplicating a destination database with RMAN meant you had to have all of the following:

- A source database

- A copy of the source database on the source database (or on disk)

- A copy of the source database on the destination server

When you use the network-enabled active database duplication, the process of duplicating is considerably simpler. You don't need any previously made backup of the source database, and you are able to duplicate a live production database to a duplicate instance or create a physical standby database over the network without actually restoring a previously existing backup. You can perform this network-aware, backup-less database duplication either with Database Control or through RMAN. You still use the RMAN `duplicate database` command, but with a new clause named `from active database`, to let RMAN know you aren't using backups as the source but are instead using the network for the database duplication. The database files are directly copied over the network connection from the source database to the new destination database.

Unlike in the case of a normal backup-based database duplication, you don't have to use the `until` clause when performing an active database duplication. RMAN automatically selects the time based on when the copying of the online datafiles to the destination database is completed, so it can recover the datafiles to a consistent point in time. Because RMAN doesn't copy the online redo log files and apply them to the duplicate database, it must always perform an incomplete recovery. RMAN can recover the duplicate database to the point in time of the latest archived redo log on the source database.

Prerequisites

Here are the requirements you must satisfy before starting active database duplication over the network:

- Both the target and destination databases must be on an identical operating system platform.

- Oracle Net must be aware of both the target and duplicate instances.

- Both the target and destination databases must have the same `sysdba` password, enforced through the use of password files.

- The source database can be either in the open or in the mount state.

- If the target database is open, it must be in archivelog mode.

- If the target database is in the mount state, you must have shut it down cleanly before bringing it up in the mount state.

- You must provide a network service name when connecting to the auxiliary instance, even if you're performing the duplication on the same server, since you're performing a network-based database duplication.

- By default, RMAN will not copy the password file from the target to the duplicate destination. You must specify the `password file` clause inside the `duplicate database` command to copy the password file.

- In a Data Guard environment, the contents of the password file must be the same.

■**Note** With the ever-increasing security concerns, most companies are adopting secure shell (SSH) as the corporate standard for Unix shell access. Using SSH, you can remotely synchronize the password file (and even automate this process using `cron`). The following `tar` command piped to SSH can be used to perform such synchronization:

```
cd $ORACLE_HOME/dbs; tar cvf - orapw$ORACLE_SID
|ssh $REMOTE_HOST "cd $ORACLE_HOME/dbs; tar xvf -"
```

The source database remains fully accessible to users while you're performing the database duplication, which is yet another great feature of the active database duplication technique. Of course, be prepared to take a slight hit on CPU usage and network bandwidth consumption during the datafile duplication.

■**Note** In previous releases, RMAN couldn't duplicate a tablespace that wasn't made read/write after transporting the tablespace. If you set the database compatibility to 11.0.0 or greater, RMAN will automatically duplicate a transportable tablespace whose status you didn't change to read/write after the tablespace transport.

Necessary Spfile Modifications

In Oracle Database 10g, you didn't copy the spfile as part of a database duplication process. You had to first copy the spfile to the destination server and modify it to suit the duplicate database's requirements. In Oracle Database 11g, you can specify the `spfile` clause in the `database duplication` command for both the new active database duplication (network-enabled duplication) as well as traditional backup-based database duplication. By specifying the new `spfile` clause, you direct RMAN to copy the source database's spfile to the destination server. For this to happen, you must have started the source database with a server parameter file. Before RMAN processes the `duplicate database` command, it first copies over this spfile, modifies it based on the settings in the `spfile` clause, and starts up the auxiliary instance with this modified server parameter file. If you use the spfile command in your `duplicate database` command, you must start the auxiliary instance with a traditional text-based (`init.ora`) initialization parameter file (`init.ora`).

When you duplicate a database, RMAN has to generate names for the duplicate database's datafiles, controlfiles, online redo log files, and tempfiles. If you're using the same directory structure on a different host, you can use identical database file names as the source database. You must specify the `nofilenamecheck` clause in the `duplicate database` command when you do this to avoid errors. If the duplicate host uses a different directory structure or you want to rename the database files for some reason, you must adopt a strategy to generate the new datafile names during the database duplication process.

The simplest way to generate file names is to specify the `spfile` clause in the `duplicate` command, as shown here:

```
duplicate database
...
spfile
...
```

The `spfile` clause lets you set all the file name–related parameters (except the `db_file_name_convert` parameter). If you're using the backup-based duplication method, RMAN restores the server parameter file from a backup of the source database server parameter file. If you are using the active database duplication method, on the other hand, RMAN will copy the server parameter file currently being used by the source database. RMAN copies or restores this spfile to the default location for the auxiliary instance on the host where it's running. If you don't specify the `spfile` clause, you must copy the server parameter file yourself. You can also specify a normal text-based initialization parameter (pfile) by specifying the `pfile` parameter instead of the `spfile` parameter as part of the `duplicate` command.

■**Tip** Oracle recommends specifying the `spfile` clause in the `duplicate` command for both backup-based duplication as well as the new active database duplication technique to set all the necessary parameters involving file names and even other initialization parameters such as `memory_target`, `sga_target`, and so on.

You can provide values for the `parameter_value_convert` clause when you use the spfile to specify all path names except the `db_file_name_convert` and `log_file_name_convert` parameters. The real purpose of the `parameter_value_convert` clause is to set the values of a bunch of initialization parameters when creating the duplicate database. RMAN will update the initialization parameter values in the spfile it copied (or the backed-up spfile if you are using the backup-method of duplication) based on the values you provide for the `parameter_value_convert` and `set` parameters. RMAN will then start the new duplicate (auxiliary) instance with the updated server parameter values.

If you specify the `spfile` clause with the `duplicate` command, you must have started the auxiliary instance already with a text-based initialization parameter file (with one required parameter, `db_name`). If you haven't specified the `from active database` clause in the `duplicate` command, RMAN will copy the binary server parameter file and restart the auxiliary instance based on the modified settings gathered from the `spfile` clause. If you specify the `from active database` clause in the `duplicate` command, then the source instance must be using a server parameter file.

If you don't want to use the `spfile` clause technique for naming the duplicate files, you can use alternative file-naming techniques. You can also choose to use the `spfile` clause to name the files and supplement that technique with one or more of the alternative techniques.

Use the Oracle-recommended `spfile` clause in the duplicate command to set all necessary parameters involving file names for the duplicate database. This is by far more straightforward and easier than using the alternative technique of `db_file_name_convert` and other file name–converting parameters. The following are the various options you can use to rename files when you're duplicating a database:

- `spfile ... parameter_value_convert 'string_pattern'` specifies conversion strings for all initialization parameters specifying path names, except two: `db_file_name_convert` and `log_file_name_convert`. In addition to specifying path names, the `parameter_value_convert` clause also lets you update any string values.

- Use `spfile ... set 'string_pattern'` to set the `log_file_name_convert` parameter for the online redo log files. The `set` clause lets you specify initialization parameters to the values you want. For example, you can use the `set` clause to specify initialization parameters such as `sga_target` or turn off replication options. In essence, the `set` functionality amounts to temporarily stopping the database duplication process in midstream after restoring the server parameter file and issuing the `alter system set` statement to change the initialization parameter values. The `parameter_value_convert` clause is processed before the `set` clauses, and values you set for an initialization parameter using the `set` clause will override any identical initialization parameter settings that you specify through the `parameter_value_convert` clause.

- Use the `db_file_name_convert 'string_pattern'` to specify file-naming rules for creating the duplicate database's datafiles and tempfiles.

Here's a simple example that shows how to use the `spfile` clause within the duplicate command to name datafiles and log files of the duplicate database during the duplication process:

```
RMAN> duplicate database to dupdb
    2> from active database
    3> db_file_name_convert '/u01/app/oracle','/u05/app/oracle'
    4> spfile
    5> parameter_value_convert '/u01/app/oracle','/u05/app/oracle'
    6> set log_file_name_convert '/u01/app/oracle','/u05/app/oracle'
    7> set sga_max_size '3000m'
    8> set sga_target '2000m';
```

The `db_file_name_convert` clause substitutes the string /u05/app/oracle in the names of the duplicate database's datafiles (and tempfiles). The `parameter_value_convert` clause in our example specifies the string /u05/app/oracle to be used in all initialization parameters that specify file names for the duplicate database, except the `db_file_name_convert` and `log_file_name_convert` parameters. Note the use of the multiple `set` clauses to specify various initialization parameters, including the `log_file_name_convert` parameter, which specifies the substitution of /u05/app/oracle in the file names of the duplicate database's online redo log files.

Performing Active Duplication

You use the familiar RMAN command, `duplicate database`, to perform active database duplication, with one important modification—you add the new clause `from active database` to indicate that the source database files must be copied directly from the target database rather than from the target database backups, as is the case in normal database duplication.

You can create a duplicate database on a different server using an identical directory structure as the target database by using the following basic active database duplication command:

```
RMAN> connect target sys/oracle@prod1
RMAN> connect auxiliary sys/oracle@dupdb
RMAN> duplicate target database to dupdb
    2> from active database
    3> spfile
    4> nofilenamecheck;
```

The spfile clause means that RMAN will copy the target database's spfile over to the destination database. If the destination database is on a different server, the spfile is copied to the new server. Of course, since we aren't specifying any additional subclauses under the spfile clause to either set or modify any initialization parameters, the source database's spfile is copied intact to the destination instance. The nofilenamecheck clause is mandatory because you're specifying that the duplicate database's file names be identical to those of the source database (and the two databases are on different hosts).

In the following sections, we'll explore the specific steps you must take to perform active database duplication.

Setting Initialization Parameter Values

If you don't have any further clauses after the spfile clause, all the settings in the source database are copied over to the destination database's spfile. If you want to override the source database settings for any initialization parameters of the destination database, you can do so by using one or more set clauses. The set clause specifies the value of a specified initialization parameter. Here is an example showing how to set values for various parameters:

- set db_file_name_convert '/disk1','/disk10'

- set log_file_name_convert '/disk1','/disk10'

- set sga_max_size 500m

- set sga_target 250m

In the example shown in the previous section, since the files on the destination server and the target server are identical, you didn't have to specify any additional clauses in your database duplication command to dictate the naming convention for the datafiles or log files.

An Active Database Duplication Example

Let's duplicate a database to learn how powerful the active database duplication feature is. For simplicity, we'll perform the database duplication on the same server as the target database. You don't need any backups to start the database duplication process. In the example, the source and the duplicate databases are on the *same host*, so we make sure we use different datafile names. No matter that the two databases are on the same host, the backup still works through a transfer of files over the network through the Oracle Net connection. That's why the first step for active database duplication is to establish Oracle Net connectivity.

1. To make sure the source database can connect to the auxiliary instance by means of a net service name, you must make the net service name available on the source database instance. Add the auxiliary instance, which we named test1, to the listener.ora file on the server hosting the source database, as shown here (you must also restart or reload the listener after this):

```
SID_LIST_LISTENER =
(SID_DESC =
(GLOBAL_DBNAME = prod1)
(ORACLE_HOME = /u01/app/oracle/product/10g/)
(SID_NAME =prod1)
    )
(SID_DESC =
(GLOBAL_DBNAME = test1)
(ORACLE_HOME = /u01/app/oracle/product/10g/)
(SID_NAME =test1)
)
)
```

Also add the following information to the tnsnames.ora file, located in the $ORACLE_HOME/network/admin directory.

```
test1 =
(DESCRIPTION =
(ADDRESS_LIST =
(ADDRESS = (PROTOCOL = TCP)(HOST = prod1)(PORT = 1521))
)
(CONNECT_DATA =
(SERVER = DEDICATED)
(SERVICE_NAME = test1)
)
)
```

The tnsnames.ora entry shown here maps the net service name test1 to the connect descriptor for a database named test1.

2. The next step is to create an initialization parameter file for the auxiliary instance. Since we're using the more straightforward spfile technique for naming the duplicate files, we can get by with a minimum of just a single parameter (db_name) in the spfile to denote the name of the duplicate database. We'll set the values for the initialization parameters db_file_name_convert and log_file_name_convert directly in the duplicate database command itself, rather than in the spfile. The simple spfile for our auxiliary instance would then look like this:

```
db_name=test1
```

If you didn't use the spfile technique for naming the duplicate database files, you'd have had to set parameters such as db_file_name_convert and log_file_name_convert in your initialization parameter file.

3. When you perform active database duplication, you must use a password file for the auxiliary instance. You'll need the password file so the target instance can connect directly to the auxiliary database instance during the duplication process. Use the same sysdba password in this password file as that of the source database. You can create a password file with the orapwd utility, as shown here:

```
$ orapwd file=orapwtest1 password=<sys_pwd> entries=20  ignorecase=n
```

■**Note** If you have several passwords in the source database password file, you can have RMAN copy the source database's password file to the duplicate database by specifying the password file clause with the duplicate database command. If you're creating a physical standby database instead of duplicating a database, RMAN will automatically copy the source database's password file to the target database, without any need for the password file clause.

---

4. Using the SQL*Plus command line, start the new auxiliary database in nomount mode:

```
$ export ORACLE_SID=test1
$ sqlplus /nolog
SQL> connect /sys/sammyy1 as sysdba
Connected to an idle instance
SQL> startup nomount
Oracle Instance started.
Total System Global Area        113246208 bytes
Fixed Size                        1218004 bytes
Variable Size                    58722860 bytes
Database Buffers                 50331648 bytes
Redo Buffers                      2973696 bytes
SQL> exit
```

The startup command will use the spfile you created in step 2 to start the auxiliary instance in the nomount state, since you don't have a controlfile yet for the new instance. Since you specified the spfile clause in the duplicate database command, RMAN will copy the source database parameter file to the destination host.

5. Set the ORACLE_SID environment variable to that of the source database, prod1, and start RMAN. You can leave the source database open or in the mount state. If the source database is open, it must be running in archivelog mode. You must connect to the source database, which you are duplicating to the auxiliary instance. Here's how you start up RMAN and connect to the source (target) database.

■**Note** If you're performing active database duplication, you must use a password file for both the target and the auxiliary instances, with an identical sysdba password.

```
$rman target sys/sammyy1@eleven
Recovery Manager: Release 11.1.0.3.0 - Beta on Sun May 20 08:07:53 2007
Copyright (c) 1982, 2006, Oracle.  All rights reserved.
connected to target database: ELEVEN (DBID=3481681133)
```

Note that as long you have established connectivity, you can start the RMAN client on any server.

6. Next, establish a connection to the auxiliary instance by specifying the keyword auxiliary, as shown here:

```
RMAN> connect auxiliary sys/sammyy1@test1
connected to auxiliary database: TEST1 (not mounted)
RMAN>
```

We're not using a recovery catalog in this example. If you're using the recovery catalog, you must of course also connect to the recovery catalog at this point.

7. Issue the duplicate target database command to create the duplicate database:

```
RMAN> duplicate target database
    2> to test1
    3> from active database
    4> spfile
    5> parameter_value_convert
        '/u01/app/oracle/eleven/eleven','/u10/app/oracle/test1'
    6> set log_file_name_convert
          '/u05/app/oracle/eleven', '/u10/app/oracle/test1'
    7> db_file_name_convert '/u10/app/oracle/eleven',
              '/u10/app/oracle/test1';

Starting Duplicate Db at 20-MAY-07
using target database control file instead of recovery catalog

contents of Memory Script:
{
   sql "declare worked boolean;
        begin worked := dbms_backup_restore.networkFileTransfer(
                ''auxdb'', null, null,
...
executing Memory Script

...
Starting backup at 20-MAY-07
...
Finished backup at 20-MAY-07

...
```

```
contents of Memory Script:
{
   set until scn  901715;
   recover
   clone database
   delete archivelog
   ;
}
...
starting media recovery
...
media recovery complete, elapsed time: 00:00:01
Finished recover at 20-MAY-07
...
database opened
Finished Duplicate Db at 20-MAY-07

RMAN>
```

RMAN automatically updates the spfile on the server hosting the duplicate database based on the values you provided through the parameter_value_convert and set clauses of the duplicate database command. RMAN then starts the auxiliary instance with the updated spfile and proceeds to copying the source database files over the network. Once this is done, it recovers the duplicate database and opens it with the resetlogs option, thus creating a new set of online redo logs.

In our simple example here, we duplicated an entire database to the same server. You can also use the active duplication technique to duplicate a database to a different server. You can also perform duplication to a past point in time, as well as file system–to–ASM and ASM-to-ASM duplications over the network, just as in the case of traditional backup-based database duplication.

How Network-Enabled Duplication Works

The from active database clause of the RMAN duplicate command starts the database duplication process. RMAN utilizes the network connection to copy the source database files to the auxiliary instance. After copying the datafiles, RMAN performs a database recovery by using a *memory script* (so named because it exists only in memory) before opening the duplicate database.

The following duplicate database command shows how much simpler the duplication command is when you perform the database duplication on a different host with an identical directory structure as well as datafile names:

```
RMAN> duplicate database
   2> to newdb
   3> from active database
   4> spfile
   5> nofilenamecheck;
```

You must specify the nofilenamecheck clause in this case, since you're using the same directory structures for both the source and destination databases. If you want RMAN to copy the entire password file from the source database to the duplicate database, specify the optional `password file` clause in the `duplicate database` command. In this example, the password file was created manually instead of specifying the `password file` clause.

When you perform active database duplication over the network, the various files that are part of the database duplication are copied or re-created, as shown in the following list:

- Datafiles are copied from the source database.

- Controlfiles are re-created but will be copied from the source database if you specify the `for standby` clause.

- Tempfiles are re-created in the location set by the `db_create_file_dest` parameter.

- Online redo log files are re-created.

- Archived redo logs are copied from the source database, but only if needed for duplication.

- The server parameter file is copied from the source database, but only if you use the `spfile` clause.

- The password file is copied for standby databases always, but for a duplicate database, it's copied only if you specify the `password file` option in the `duplicate database` command.

- Flash recovery area files aren't copied during the duplication. Similarly, the duplication doesn't re-create the flashback log files, the password file, or the block change tracking file.

To create a standby database instead of a duplicate database, just replace the `to auxdb` part of the `duplicate database` command with the `for standby` clause, as shown in the following example:

```
RMAN> duplicate target database
   2> for standby
   3> from active database
   4> spfile
```

Please refer to Chapter 10 for complete details on duplicating databases for physical standby databases using the active database duplication method.

It's easy to duplicate a non-ASM file-based database to an ASM file system. To do this, first create an ASM disk group, before running the `duplicate database` command. Here's an example:

```
RMAN> duplicate target database
   2> to newdb
   3> from active database
   4> spfile
   5> parameter_value_convert
       '/u01/app/oracle/oradata/prod1/', '+DISK2'
   6> set db_create_file_dest = +DISK2;
```

The `duplicate database` command shown here creates a database with all of its datafiles, controlfiles, and online redo logs in the ASM disk group +DISK2.

If you want faster duplication of a database, you must increase the number of disk channels on the source database, which leads to a parallel copying of the source database files.

Recovery Catalog Management

There are two significant changes in Oracle Database 11*g* in the way you manage the RMAN recovery catalog:

- You can now merge two or more recovery catalogs using the new `import catalog` command. You can use a variation of the `import catalog` command to move a recovery catalog to a new database.

- You can limit the RMAN metadata that a specific user can access by creating virtual private catalogs.

The following sections show how to merge recovery catalogs as well as introduce the new virtual private catalog feature.

Merging Recovery Catalogs

It's common for DBAs to create multiple recovery catalogs, each for a different Oracle version, in order to store RMAN data for multiple Oracle databases. In some companies, DBAs even separate development/QA and production recovery catalogs. The management of the multiple recovery catalogs often gets to be a problem. Oracle Database 11*g* lets you designate a single catalog schema for all your Oracle databases by using the new `import catalog` command to import a recovery catalog schema into another recovery catalog schema. You can merge an entire recovery catalog, or just the metadata pertaining to a specific database or databases, into another recovery catalog

Before Oracle Database 11*g*, there was no way to combine contents from one recovery catalog to another without having to actually use the export and import utilities to perform a data migration between two recovery catalogs.

To illustrate the recovery catalog merging feature, we'll use multiple recovery catalogs, one of which will serve as the destination target, meaning the recovery catalog into which you want to merge one or more other recovery catalogs.

In Oracle Database 11*g*, you can merge recovery catalogs with the new `import catalog` command. In the following example, the destination recovery catalog schema is located in the recovery catalog database rman11. The `list incarnation` command shows that there are currently two databases (`ELEVEN` and `ORCL11`) registered in this recovery catalog:

```
RMAN> list incarnation;

List of Database Incarnations
DB Key  Inc  DB Name  DB ID       STATUS  Reset SCN  Reset Time
------  ----  ------  ----------  ------  ---------  -----------
192     207  ELEVEN   3481526915  PARENT         1   22-NOV-06
192     193  ELEVEN   3481526915  CURRENT   909437   13-MAR-07
1        15  ORCL11   3863017760  PARENT         1   22-NOV-06
1         2  ORCL11   3863017760  CURRENT   909437   03-MAR-07
RMAN>
```

There is also a Release 10.2 recovery catalog schema called rman10, owned by another user, with one database (TENNER) registered in it, as shown by the following list incarnation command:

```
RMAN> list incarnation;

List of Database Incarnations
DB Key  Inc DB Name DB ID       STATUS Reset SCN  Reset Time
------- -- -------- ----------- ------- -------- ----------
1       8   TENNER   1166569509  PARENT      1   30-AUG-05
1       2   TENNER   1166569509  CURRENT 534907 13-MAR-07

RMAN>
```

Our goal is to merge the Release 10.2 recovery catalog into the Release 11.1 recovery catalog, creating a consolidated recovery catalog schema with all three databases registered in it. Here are the steps to do this:

1. First connect to the destination recovery catalog, as shown here:

   ```
   $ rman
   RMAN> connect catalog rman/rman@rman11
   ```

2. Issue the import catalog command, and specify the connection string for the source catalog whose metadata you want to import into the destination catalog to which you're currently connected. The following example shows how to execute the import catalog command:

   ```
   RMAN> import catalog rman1/rman1@rman10;

   Starting import catalog at 08-APR-07
   connected to source recovery catalog database
   import validation complete
   database unregistered from the source recovery catalog
   Finished import catalog at 08-APR-07
   RMAN>
   ```

3. Issue the list incarnation command to verify that all three databases from both recovery catalogs are now part of the rman11 recovery catalog:

   ```
   RMAN> list incarnation;

   List of Database Incarnations
   DB Key Inc DB Name DB ID     STATUS   Reset SCN  Reset Time
   ------ ----------- --------           ---------------- --- ---------- -
   1411  1418 TENNER   66569509 PARENT   1          30-AUG-05
   1411  1412 TENNER 1166569509 CURRENT  534907     13-MAR-07
   192    207 ELEVEN 3481526915 PARENT   1          22-NOV-06
   ```

```
192      193 ELEVEN 3481526915 CURRENT   909437   13-MAR-07
1         15 ORCL11 3863017760 PARENT    1        22-NOV-06
1          2 ORCL11 3863017760 CURRENT   909437   03-MAR-07

RMAN>
```

If you now run the list incarnation command on the source recovery catalog (rman10), you'll find that the single database that was part of that catalog is no longer registered in it, the metadata about the database having been imported to the rman11 recovery catalog. Here are the results of running the list incarnation command on the source recovery catalog:

```
RMAN> list incarnation;

RMAN>
```

The reason you don't see any databases registered in the source database now is because RMAN automatically unregisters all databases from the source recovery catalog once it imports the databases from that catalog into the destination recovery catalog. If you want to retain the databases in the source catalog and don't want RMAN to automatically unregister the databases after importing the metadata for those databases, use the no unregister clause with the import catalog command, as shown here:

```
RMAN> import catalog rman1/rman1@rman10 no unregister;
```

The previous command uses the no unregister clause to direct RMAN to retain the imported database IDs in the source recovery catalog. By default, the imported database IDs are automatically removed upon their import into the destination recovery catalog.

Importing a catalog into another and merging it with the destination catalog takes place without you having to connect to a target database. You simply need to connect to the source and destination recovery catalogs from the RMAN client.

The import catalog command will import the metadata for all the databases that are currently registered in the source catalog schema into the destination catalog schema. If you'd rather import a specific database or a set of databases from the source recovery catalog, you may do so by using a slightly different form of the import catalog command, specifying either the DBID or database name of the database(s) you want to import:

```
RMAN> import catalog rman10/rman10@tenner dbid = 123456, 123457;
RMAN> import catalog rman10/rman10@tenner db_name = testdb, mydb;
```

If a database is registered in both the source and destination target recovery catalogs, first unregister that database from one of the catalogs before proceeding. You can't perform an import when a database is simultaneously registered in both the source and destination catalogs.

You can issue the import catalog command only if the source database's version is identical to the version of the RMAN client you're using. If the source recovery catalog schema is from a lower version than that of the RMAN client, you must first upgrade the lower version recovery catalog schema using the upgrade catalog command. If the source recovery catalog schema belongs to a higher version, you must perform the import with an RMAN executable of a higher version as well.

Here are some additional points to remember about using the `import catalog` command:

- RMAN lets you register a target database in multiple recovery catalogs. However, you shouldn't register a database in both the source and destination recovery catalog schemas before you perform a recovery catalog import.

- A catalog import operation is an all-or-nothing affair. If your import operation fails in the middle, all changes are rolled back.

- If you have identically named global stored scripts in multiple recovery catalogs, RMAN automatically renames the scripts from the source recovery catalog (the format for the renamed files is `copy of script_name`).

Moving a Recovery Catalog to Another Database

You can use the `import catalog` command to move the recovery catalog from one database to another. Here are the steps to move a recovery catalog to a different database:

1. Create a new recovery catalog in the destination database that will store the moved recovery catalog. The new recovery catalog won't have any databases registered in it.

2. Issue the `import catalog` command to import the source recovery catalog into the new recovery catalog you just created on the destination database, after first connecting to the new recovery catalog. The following example shows this:

```
$ rman
RMAN> connect catalog rman/rman@target_db
RMAN> import catalog rman10/rman10@source_db;
```

The `import catalog` command imports the source recovery catalog contents into the new recovery catalog.

Virtual Private Catalogs

It's common to encounter situations where certain users may require access to the recovery catalog so they can view some metadata, but you are compelled to give them access to the entire recovery catalog. That is, there was no way to give just partial access to the recovery catalog. In Oracle Database 11g, you can restrict access to the recovery catalog by granting access to only a subset of the metadata in the recovery catalog. The subset that a user has read/write access to is termed a *virtual private catalog*, or just *virtual catalog*. The virtual private catalog feature lets you separate responsibilities between individuals in an organization, thus ensuring compliance with a basic security requirement. You can create a virtual private catalog for a specific group of users or for groups of databases.

Before this release, any user you granted access to a recovery catalog automatically had access to the entire metadata stored in there. That is, the user could view data from all the databases registered in the recovery catalog. The owner of the centralized base recovery catalog can now create restricted users, limiting the metadata they can access from the base catalog.

▇**Tip** Oracle recommends you create a central recovery catalog as the repository for all your Oracle databases. The new Oracle Database 11g recovery catalog merging feature helps you achieve this goal with ease.

The central or source recovery catalog is now also called the *base recovery catalog*. There is no set limit on the number of virtual private catalogs you can create on a base recovery catalog. A virtual private catalog is nothing but a set of synonyms and views on the base recovery catalog. The main recovery catalog owner grants privileges to the owner of each virtual catalog, which enables the virtual catalog owner to either connect to a target database or register it themselves (if they are granted the `register database` privilege). After this point, there is virtually no difference between how you use a virtual private catalog and the centralized base catalog. The sole difference is that a virtual private catalog owner can access only those databases for which they have been given access, while the base catalog owner can access all the registered databases in the base recovery catalog.

Creating a Virtual Private Catalog

Creating a virtual private catalog involves two steps. First you must create a user who will own the new virtual catalog. Next you must create the virtual private catalog. You then grant the new user restricted access to the base recovery catalog by giving the user read/write access to the user's own RMAN metadata, which is what a virtual private catalog is. The following example shows you how to create a virtual private catalog:

1. Create a new database user (if the database user who will own the virtual private catalog doesn't already exist) who will own the virtual recovery catalog:

```
SQL> connect sys/<sys_password> as sysdba
SQL> create user virtual1 identified by virtual1
     temporary tablespace temp
     default tablespace vp_users
     quota unlimited on vp_users;

User created.
SQL>
```

Once you create the new user, your next step is to grant this user the necessary privileges to use a virtual private catalog.

2. Using SQL*Plus, grant the new user who will own the virtual private catalog the `recovery_catalog_owner` role in order for the user to use the virtual private catalog you are going to create:

```
SQL> grant recovery_catalog_owner to virtual1;

Grant succeeded.

SQL>
```

Exit from SQL*Plus after this, and start RMAN.

3. Connect to the base recovery catalog as the base recovery catalog owner, and grant necessary privileges to the new virtual private catalog owner to access metadata for specified databases. You do this by using the new RMAN command grant. In this example, we grant the user access to two database, test1 and test2:

```
$ rman

Recovery Manager: Release 11.1.0.1.0 - Beta on Sun Apr 8 13:19:30 2

Copyright (c) 1982, 2005, Oracle.  All rights reserved.

RMAN> connect catalog rman/rman@nick

connected to recovery catalog database

RMAN> grant catalog for database test1, test2 to virtual1;

Grant succeeded.
RMAN>
```

The grant catalog for database command grants recovery catalog access for the databases test1 and test2 to the user virtual1, who is the new virtual catalog owner you created. Note that instead of the database names, you can use the DBID for a database as well.

■**Note** A virtual private catalog owner can create a local stored script, but has only read-only access to global scripts.

---

4. Since the virtual private catalog owner has the catalog for database privilege, that user can log in to the base recovery catalog and create the virtual private catalog:

```
RMAN> connect catalog virtual1/virtual1@catdb

connected to recovery catalog database

RMAN> create virtual catalog;

found eligible base catalog owned by RMAN
created virtual catalog against base catalog owned by RMAN

RMAN>
```

The new user virt_user1 owns the virtual catalog created by the previous command. Since the base recovery catalog owner has granted rights (with the grant catalog command) for the

two databases, test1 and test2, the user virt_user1 will see only those two databases registered in the new virtual catalog the user has just created. You can confirm that the user virt_
user1 can access only the test1 and test2 databases and not all the registered databases in the
base recovery catalog by issuing the list incarnation command, as shown next.

> **Note** If the virtual catalog owner doesn't have the sysdba or sysoper privilege on the target database,
then that owner can't perform most RMAN operations.

```
RMAN> list incarnation;

List of Database Incarnations
DB Key Inc DB Name DB ID       STATUS  Reset SCN Reset Time
------- ------- -------- ---------------- --- -----------
192   207 TEST1   3481526915   PARENT  1         22-NOV-06
192   193 TEST1   3481526915   CURRENT 909437    13-MAR-07
1      15 TEST2   3863017760   PARENT  1         22-NOV-06
1       2 TEST2   3863017760   CURRENT 909437    03-MAR-07

RMAN>
```

However, the base recovery catalog owner can see all databases in the main catalog by
issuing the list incarnation command, as shown here:

```
RMAN> list incarnation;

List of Database Incarnations
DB Key Inc DB Name  DB ID     STATUS  Reset SCN  Reset Time
------ ------- ----------- -------- ------ --- -----------
192    207 TEST1 481526915    PARENT  1          22-NOV-06
192    93  TEST1 3481526915 CURRENT  909437     13-MAR-07
1      15  TEST2 3863017760 PARENT   1          22-NOV-06
1       2  TEST2 3863017760 CURRENT  909437     03-MAR-07
12     150 TEST3 3533598612 PARENT   1          10-MAR-07
12     150 TEST3 3533598612 CURRENT 909437      15-APR-07

RMAN>
```

The user virt_user1 can create local RMAN stored scripts within this virtual catalog. However,
the user will have only read privileges on any global scripts in the base recovery catalog.

The virtual catalog owner virtual1 can use the virtual private catalog to store the metadata for all backups of a database. Here's an example that shows how to do this:

```
RMAN> connect target sys/sammyy1@prod1;
RMAN> connect catalog virtual1/virtual1@catdb;
RMAN> backup database plus archivelog;
```

In the previous example, you connect to the target database first and then connect to the base recovery catalog but specify the virtual1 schema in the connect catalog command. This means the backup metadata is stored in the recovery catalog owner virtual1's schema, that is, in the virtual private catalog.

Managing Virtual Private Catalogs

The grant command lets you grant two important virtual recovery catalog–related privileges—catalog for database and register database. The catalog for database privilege, which you've seen earlier, lets you grant recovery catalog access to a specific database that you can denote by either the database name or its DBID. Note that one of the catalog operations granted is the ability to register and unregister the database from the recovery catalog. The base recovery catalog owner can optionally grant a virtual recovery catalog owner the right to register new target databases in the recovery catalog by specifying the register database clause with the grant command. Here's an example:

```
RMAN> grant register database to virt_user1;
```

The register database clause implicitly grants the catalog for database privilege as well. The virtual private catalog owner can register new databases by issuing the register database command. The databases that the virtual private catalog owner thus registers are also registered in the base recovery catalog.

The base recovery catalog owner can always unregister a database that has been registered by a virtual catalog user from the base recovery catalog and thus from the virtual recovery catalog, which is nothing but a subset of the base recovery catalog.

Just as the grant command lets the base catalog owner grant various privileges to the recovery catalog users, the revoke command makes it possible to take those rights away. The base recovery catalog owner can revoke a virtual catalog user's access to a specific database by using the revoke catalog command and specifying the database name after first connecting to the base recovery catalog. You specify the catalog for database clause within the revoke command to remove recovery catalog access to a database from a user, as shown in the following example:

```
RMAN> connect catalog rman/<password>@catdb;
RMAN> revoke catalog for database test1 from virt_user1;
```

Note the following about the revoke command:

- You can use the register database clause to revoke the ability of a recovery catalog user to register new databases.

- Use the all privileges from clause to revoke both the catalog and register privileges from a user, as shown in the following example:

  ```
  RMAN> revoke all privileges from virt_user1;
  ```

Of course, the previous command revokes all privileges on the virtual private catalog, meaning both the catalog and register privileges that have been granted to the virtual recovery catalog user. The base recovery catalog owner can revoke just the ability to register new databases from a virtual private catalog owner by using the revoke command in the following manner:

```
RMAN> revoke register database from virtual_user1;
```

When you issue the previous command, the virtual catalog owner can't register new databases in the recovery catalog. However, the virtual catalog owner will continue to have the `catalog` privilege for all registered databases. The `catalog` privileges include the privilege to register and unregister those databases for which the `catalog for database` privilege was granted.

Dropping a Virtual Private Catalog

Virtual private catalog owners can drop the private recovery catalog they own by issuing the `drop catalog` command. Here's an example showing how to drop a virtual private catalog:

1. Log in as the virtual catalog owner to the base recovery catalog:

   ```
   RMAN> connect catalog virt_user1/<password>@catadb;
   ```

2. Issue the `drop catalog` command:

   ```
   RMAN> drop catalog;
   ```

All the metadata pertaining to the virtual catalog owner is deleted from the base recovery catalog when you issue the `drop catalog` command.

Virtual Private Catalogs in Earlier Oracle Database Releases

The `drop catalog` command shown in the previous section works only if you're using an Oracle Database 11*g* or higher RMAN executable. If you're using an Oracle Database 10*g* or earlier RMAN executable, you must execute the following command as the virtual recovery catalog owner to drop the virtual catalog:

```
SQL> rman.dbms_rcvcat.drop_virtual_catalog;
```

In the previous command, `rman` is the owner of the base recovery catalog.

Similarly, if you're using an Oracle Release 10.2 or earlier of RMAN, you first connect to the *base* recovery catalog as the virtual catalog owner and execute the `create_virtual_catalog` procedure shown here:

```
SQL> execute
    base_catalog_owner.dbms_rcvcat.create_virtual_catalog;
```

If all your target databases are from Release 11.1 or newer, you don't need to perform the procedure shown here. Contrary to what the name of the procedure indicates, the procedure doesn't create a virtual private catalog. You'll need to execute the procedure before you can work with a target database that belongs to an older release.

Enhanced RMAN Integration with Data Guard

Oracle Database 11*g* provides better integration between RMAN and Data Guard. The following are the main enhancements in the Data Guard/RMAN area.

Configuring RMAN Without a Database Connection

You can now connect to any database in a Data Guard setup and make persistent RMAN configuration changes for any other standby site in the Data Guard configuration. That is, you don't have to connect to the particular database you're making RMAN configuration changes to, unlike in the previous releases. The new for db_unique_name clause, which you can use with the configure, show, list, and report schema commands, makes it possible for you to view and make changes to the persistent RMAN configuration for a database without connecting to that database using the keyword target. Most of the RC_* views, such as the RC_DATAFILE and RC_RMAN_OUTPUT views, now contain a new column named DB_UNIQUE_NAME that relates a specific row to a standby site.

Viewing Configuration Information

You can view configuration information configuration by using the db_unique_name option of the show command. You must be connected to a recovery catalog and any target database that is mounted or open in order to use the for db_unique_name clause. You can also use this option after executing the set dbid command. Here's an example showing how to use the for db_unique_name option:

```
RMAN> show for db_unique_name <site_name>;
```

The previous command will show the persistent RMAN configuration settings for the site you specify with the site_name clause. You can similarly use the for db_unique_name option as part of the list, report, and show schema commands, as shown here:

```
RMAN> list for db_unique_name <site_name>;
RMAN> report for db_unique_name <site_name>;
RMAN> report schema for db_unique_name <site_name>;
```

The for db_unique_name clause isn't applicable to just a single site. You can use any of the commands listed in this section—show, list, report, and report schema with the for db_unique_name option and the all clause—to view the configuration or other information for all sites. That is, you just replace the site_name clause with the all clause to make the command apply to all sites. For example, to view the current persistent configuration settings set for all sites in your Data Guard configuration, issue the following command:

```
RMAN> show for db_unique_name all;
```

You can use the list, report, and report schema commands in the same way.

Making Configuration Changes for a Site

Use the for db_unique_name clause of RMAN's configure command to make persistent configuration changes to a specific standby site, without actually connecting to it. The for db_unique_name clause leads RMAN to automatically connect to the specified standby site and update its controlfile with the new configuration changes.

If you use the for db_unique_name clause with the all option instead of the site_name option, RMAN will connect to all databases registered in the recovery catalog and will update their controlfiles with the new settings.

Renaming a Standby Site

You can rename a standby site in the recovery catalog by using the `change db_unique_name` command, as shown here:

```
RMAN> change db_unique_name
   2>  from <old db_unique_name> to <new db_unique_name>;
```

The previous command will associate the RMAN metadata for the old `db_unique_name` to the new `db_unique_name` you provided.

Removing a Standby Site

You can remove information about a specific standby site from the recovery catalog with the help of an enhanced `unregister` command, wherein you can use the `db_unique_name` clause to specify a particular standby site name. You must be connected, of course, to the recovery catalog and any mounted target database when you issue the command, which has the following syntax:

```
RMAN> unregister db_unique_name site_name;
```

If you want to get rid of the actual backups for a standby site, add the `including backups` clause to the previous command. This command is applicable to both primary and standby databases.

Restoring a Backup Controlfile to a Standby Controlfile

In Oracle Database 11g, you don't need to back up a standby controlfile on the primary database when creating a standby database. You also don't need to create a backup controlfile on all your standby sites. RMAN performs an automatic reverse synchronization of the necessary data to all the (physical) standby databases.

Use the new `restore controlfile` command to restore a backup controlfile to a standby controlfile and to restore the controlfile for the primary database from the standby controlfile backups as well. There are three variations of the `restore controlfile` command, as shown here:

```
# following command restores the standby database or the primary database control
# file according to the database role which is defined in the recovery catalog.

RMAN> restore controlfile;

# following command restores the primary database control file
# using both the current control file and standby control file backups.
RMAN> restore primary controlfile;

# following command restores the standby control file using
# both the current control file and standby control file backups.

RMAN> restore standby controlfile;
```

During the restore of the controlfile, RMAN performs the actions so the controlfile is converted to a standby controlfile the first time that controlfile is mounted.

Resynchronizing the Recovery Catalog

You can resynchronize the RMAN recovery catalog from a remote database using an enhanced `reysnc catalog` command, which does the resynchronization when you add the new `db_unique_name` option.

Before you use the `resync catalog` command to perform the recovery catalog resynchronization, however, you must first define the connect identifiers for the standby databases in your Data Guard configuration by using the `configure` command with the new clause `connect identifier`.

Here's how you define a connect identifier for a specific standby site in your Data Guard configuration:

```
RMAN> configure db_unique_name <site_name>
    2> connect identifier <connect_identifier_name>;
```

You must enclose the connect identifier name you supply in quotes. The database you are connected to through RMAN will connect automatically to the remote standby site using the connect identifier you create, as the privileged user `sys`.

Although RMAN can use the connect identifier to process information back and forth with the remote standby site, in this chapter, our interest is in using the connect identifier as part of the `resync catalog` command. You can use the `resync catalog` command to resynchronize the catalog with a specific standby site's information (by using the `site_name` clause), or if you have configured connect identifiers for all databases in your Data Guard configuration, use the `all` clause in the `resync catalog` command. Here's an example:

```
RMAN> resync catalog
    2> from db_unique_name all;
```

Oracle recommends you define the connect identifier for all databases in your Data Guard configuration.

Backup File Accessibility Groups

In Oracle Database 11g, all `backup`, `restore`, and `recover` commands automatically figure out the correct file names for each of the standby sites in the Data Guard configuration. This transparency is extremely useful when you're dealing with databases that contain a large number of datafiles or use an automatic storage management (ASM) file system or an Oracle Managed Files (OMF) file system, where the file names tend to be unwieldy.

You can create a group of sites that can share backups for a device type by using the new `configure group` command to create a group of standby sites, formally known as a *backup file accessibility group*. A standby site can belong to multiple groups. Here's how you create a new group of standby sites:

```
RMAN> configure group <group_name>
    2> for device type disk
    3> site_nameA, site_nameB, site_nameC;
```

Make sure you connect to the recovery catalog before executing the command shown here. The target database you're connected to can be mounted or open. The previous command creates a backup file accessibility group with three standby sites, whose backups are accessible by each of the three sites. Besides providing the ability to share backups among the group members, RMAN also lets the `restore` and `recover` commands use the backup file accessibility groups during file restoration from backups.

Block Change Tracking Support in Standby Databases

RMAN has provided a block change tracking feature in earlier releases of the Oracle database. The block change tracking feature improves backup performance considerably by backing up only the changed data blocks during incremental backups. Block change tracking is recommended because it avoids having to scan entire datafiles for changed data when the database may be undergoing modifications in only a small percentage of the data blocks in the database.

In Oracle Database 11g, for the first time, you can set up block change tracking in a standby database. Please see Chapter 10 for an explanation of the block change tracking in a Data Guard environment.

CHAPTER 7

■■■

Data Pump

DBAs and developers have been using the Export and Import utilities since the early releases of Oracle (versions 6/7) to make logical data backups for development, quality assurance, and even production environments. Oracle Database 10g introduced a new tool called Data Pump that will eventually replace the Export and Import utilities. The objective of the Data Pump utility is to take advantage of modern database features and provide scalability to ever-growing database workloads and sizes. Since Oracle 9i Database, Oracle has no longer made improvements to the exp or imp utilities.

Data Pump provides significant performance improvements over the conventional Export and Import utilities, especially in the world of large objects and VLDB databases. Data Pump claims to be up to two times faster than conventional exports. Oracle Database 11g makes significant enhancements to the Data Pump tool, adding new features such as data encryption, compression, data remapping capabilities, and file reusability. Data Pump allows faster data extraction and now even provides security compliance for data at rest.

■**Note** Oracle's direction is to eventually deprecate the traditional Export utility. Obviously, the deprecation timeline for the Import utility will be significantly prolonged, because a lot of customers will have in-house export dump files from previous releases of Oracle.

API Enhancements

Data Pump uses the following two Oracle PL/SQL packages:

- DBMS_DATAPUMP (also referred to as the Data Pump API)

- DBMS_DATAPUMP (also referred to as the Metadata API)

The Data Pump utilities (expdp and impdp) simply make calls to the DBMS_DATAPUMP API to perform data extractions or imports. Oracle Database 11g provides a new API that will provide additional security for companies that need to remap sensitive data for data at rest or transform data during import operations. The data_remap procedure has been introduced in the DBMS_DATAPUMP package to allow data transformation of pertinent data for Data Pump jobs of data in user tables. The datatype, structure, and format are still preserved during this operation. This feature to transform data during the export is particularly useful while refreshing the production database to the QA or development environment, and we'll discuss it further in the data_remap section later in this chapter. This is the definition of the data_remap procedure:

```
PROCEDURE data_remap (
            handle        IN  NUMBER,
            name          IN  VARCHAR2,
            table_name    IN  VARCHAR2,
            column        IN  VARCHAR2,
            function      IN  VARCHAR2,
            schema        IN  VARCHAR2 DEFAULT NULL
    );
```

Several enhancements to existing APIs have been introduced in Oracle Database 11g. Here are some of the key new features:

- In the add_device procedure, Oracle added the reuse_file API to indicate whether an existing dump file should be reused (overwritten) prior to an export operation.

- The set_debug procedure is enhanced to enable debug/trace features for trace parameters or events

- The Data Pump APIs have been improved to restart worker processes after failures without terminating the Data Pump job. This feature can be particularly useful in parallel options of Data Pump.

- Data Pump now supports editable XML. You can now extract the metadata for a particular object, modify it as needed, and convert the metadata as DDL and create the revised object to the same or a different database.

- The Metadata API allows for transformation of local indexes on a single partition to an index on a nonpartitioned table.

- The table_export object type is enhanced to support advanced queue tables, and all dependent objects for the table are exported.

Compression Enhancements

By far, the compression capability is one of the greatest new features of the Data Pump utility in Oracle Database 11g. Oracle Data Pump takes the database exports to another level of usability by natively providing the compression option. In Oracle Database 10g, you were able to compress only the metadata relative to your Data Pump extracts. In Oracle Database 11g, Oracle provides the mechanism to compress both data and metadata during the extract operation. To make full use of all these compression options, the compatible initialization parameter must be set to at least 11.1.

In the previous release of Oracle, DBAs created a Unix pipe and performed the export or Data Pump extract using the pipe as the target file. Behind the scenes, another Unix process compressed the output of the Unix pipe. The following script demonstrates how DBAs performed export compression prior to Oracle Database 11g using the old exp utility:

```
if test -p $TARGET/exp/$ORACLE_SID.export.pipe
then
  rm -f $TARGET/exp/$ORACLE_SID.export.pipe
  mknod $TARGET/exp/$ORACLE_SID.export.pipe p
else
  mknod $TARGET/exp/$ORACLE_SID.export.pipe p
fi

$NOHUP gzip \
 <$TARGET/exp/$ORACLE_SID.export.pipe \
 >$TARGET/exp/$ORACLE_SID.$TODAY.exp.gz &

echo "**************************************************"
echo "${ORACLE_SID}'s Full database export started -- \c"
date

exp "'/ AS SYSDBA'" buffer=31457280 \
    full=y \
    compress=n \
    consistent=n \
    direct=n \
    rows=$YNFlag \
    statistics=none \
    file=$TARGET/exp/$ORACLE_SID.export.pipe \
    log=$LOGFILE 1> /dev/null 2>&1
```

Without the use of Unix pipes, DBAs often do not have enough space on disk to perform the export. Although it does not take a rocket scientist to implement Unix pipes, it still involves a DBA with some in-depth Unix expertise.

As mentioned before, the metadata_only compression option was available in Oracle Database 10g. Oracle Database 11g adds the all and data_only options to the compression option. The available options for the COMPRESSION parameter are as follows:

```
compression={all | data_only | metadata_only | none}
```

The all option enables compression for the entire export operation, and the data_only option results in just the data being written to the dump file in compressed format.

Let's see how much space the COMPRESSION parameter can save us. In the first example, we will perform a full database Data Pump export using the compression option and compare the size of the dump file with a noncompressed Data Pump dump file. Here we perform a full database export using Data Pump with the compression=all option to a file named full.compress.dmp:

```
$ expdp full=yes userid="'/ as sysdba'" \
        dumpfile=dbadir:full.compress.dmp compression=all

Export: Release 11.1.0.6.0 - Production on Sunday, 23 September, 2007 9:13:50

Copyright (c) 2003, 2007, Oracle.  All rights reserved.
```

```
Connected to: Oracle Database 11g Enterprise Edition Release 11.1.0.6.0 - Production
With the Partitioning, OLAP, Data Mining and Real Application Testing options
Starting "SYS"."SYS_EXPORT_FULL_01":  full=yes userid='/******** AS SYSDBA'
    dumpfile=dbadir:full.compress.dmp compression=all
Estimate in progress using BLOCKS method...
Processing object type DATABASE_EXPORT/SCHEMA/TABLE/TABLE_DATA
Total estimation using BLOCKS method: 238.5 MB
...
...
```

Even though the estimated size from Data Pump is 238.5MB, the actual size of the dump file is a little less than 84MB, as you see here:

```
-rw-r----- 1 oracle oinstall  87973888 Sep 23 09:31 full.compress.dmp
```

Performing the same export without the compression option produces a file that is substantially larger. The following Data Pump export produces a file called full.dmp approximately 248.6MB in size:

```
DBA11g > expdp full=yes userid="'/ as sysdba'" dumpfile=dbadir:full.dmp
```

```
-rw-r----- 1 oracle oinstall 260665344 Sep 23 08:48 full.dmp
```

Comparing the file sizes, the noncompressed dump file is 248.6MB in size, while the compressed dump file is approximately 83.9MB in size. You clearly see that the compression option for Data Pump can save you a significant amount of space. DBAs may wonder how Data Pump compression compares to compression utilities like gzip. Using the gzip utility, we compress the full.dmp file. The size of the full.dmp.gz compresses down to 72.99MB:

```
-rw-r----- 1 oracle oinstall 76539609 Sep 23 08:48 full.dmp.gz
```

You can see that the gzip compression performs slightly better than the Data Pump compression using the compression=all option. The compression difference is negligible as you consider the ease of use factor. In conclusion, you should replace Unix pipes with Data Pump compression.

■**Note** By specifying the user ID of "'/ as sysdba'", export and import dumps can be automated without having to supply a password in the automation script. Please note that it is a single tick surrounded by a double quote on each side.

Let's continue our example and perform a Data Pump export against a single table. In this example, the CUST table is created as an image of the CUSTOMER table in the SH schema. In addition, the primary key is dropped, and data is quadrupled to examine the level of compression that Oracle is capable of producing for a table with 222,000 rows. Here we will perform a table-level export of the SH.CUST table:

```
DBA11g1 > expdp tables=sh.cust userid=sh/sh123456 dumpfile=oratmp:cust.dmp

Export: Release 11.1.0.6.0 - Production on Sunday, 23 September, 2007 15:08:08

Copyright (c) 2003, 2007, Oracle.  All rights reserved.

Connected to: Oracle Database 11g Enterprise Edition Release 11.1.0.6.0 - Production
With the Partitioning, OLAP, Data Mining and Real Application Testing options
Starting "SH"."SYS_EXPORT_TABLE_01":  tables=sh.cust userid=sh/********
  dumpfile=oratmp:cust.dmp
Estimate in progress using BLOCKS method...
Processing object type TABLE_EXPORT/TABLE/TABLE_DATA
Total estimation using BLOCKS method: 47 MB
Processing object type TABLE_EXPORT/TABLE/TABLE
Processing object type TABLE_EXPORT/TABLE/STATISTICS/TABLE_STATISTICS
. . exported "SH"."CUST"                            39.37 MB  222000 rows
Master table "SH"."SYS_EXPORT_TABLE_01" successfully loaded/unloaded
******************************************************************************
Dump file set for SH.SYS_EXPORT_TABLE_01 is:
  /tmp/cust.dmp
Job "SH"."SYS_EXPORT_TABLE_01" successfully completed at 15:09:33

rac1.dbaexpert.com:/home/oracle
DBA11g1 > ls -l /tmp/cust.dmp
-rw-r-----  1 oracle oinstall 41377792 Sep 23 15:09 /tmp/cust.dmp
```

The size of the noncompressed dump file is approximately 39.46MB. Now using the compression=all option, we produce a compressed dump file named cust.compress.dmp, as shown here:

```
$ expdp tables=sh.cust userid=sh/sh123456 \
        dumpfile=oratmp:cust.compress.dmp compression=all
Export: Release 11.1.0.6.0 - Production on Sunday, 23 September, 2007 15:11:11

Copyright (c) 2003, 2007, Oracle.  All rights reserved.

Connected to: Oracle Database 11g Enterprise Edition Release 11.1.0.6.0 - Production
With the Partitioning, OLAP, Data Mining and Real Application Testing options
Starting "SH"."SYS_EXPORT_TABLE_01":  tables=sh.cust userid=sh/********
dumpfile=oratmp:cust.compress.dmp compression=all
Estimate in progress using BLOCKS method...
Processing object type TABLE_EXPORT/TABLE/TABLE_DATA
Total estimation using BLOCKS method: 47 MB
Processing object type TABLE_EXPORT/TABLE/TABLE
Processing object type TABLE_EXPORT/TABLE/STATISTICS/TABLE_STATISTICS
. . exported "SH"."CUST"                            9.101 MB  222000 rows
Master table "SH"."SYS_EXPORT_TABLE_01" successfully loaded/unloaded
```

```
*****************************************************************************
Dump file set for SH.SYS_EXPORT_TABLE_01 is:
  /tmp/cust.compress.dmp
Job "SH"."SYS_EXPORT_TABLE_01" successfully completed at 15:12:23
```

The dump file size is significantly reduced relative to the noncompressed Data Pump export at approximately 9.13MB:

```
-rw-r----- 1 oracle oinstall 9576448 Sep 23 15:12 /tmp/cust.compress.dmp
```

Comparing the two files, the noncompressed dump file is 39.46MB in size, and the compressed dump file is 9.13MB in size. The gzipped version of the cust.dmp file produces a file that is 8.96MB in size:

```
-rw-r----- 1 oracle oinstall  9392929 Sep 23 15:09 cust.dmp.gz
```

Again, the compression difference between Data Pump compression and gzip is negligible. Let's perform a Data Pump export using the compression=data_only option. Using our same table as before, we will create a dump file called cust.compress.data.dmp:

```
$ expdp tables=sh.cust userid=sh/sh123456 \
    dumpfile=oratmp:cust.compress.data.dmp compression=data_only

Export: Release 11.1.0.6.0 - Production on Sunday, 23 September, 2007 15:29:17

Copyright (c) 2003, 2007, Oracle.  All rights reserved.

Connected to: Oracle Database 11g Enterprise Edition Release 11.1.0.6.0 - Production
With the Partitioning, OLAP, Data Mining and Real Application Testing options
Starting "SH"."SYS_EXPORT_TABLE_01":  tables=sh.cust userid=sh/********
dumpfile=oratmp:cust.compress.data.dmp compression=data_only
Estimate in progress using BLOCKS method...
Processing object type TABLE_EXPORT/TABLE/TABLE_DATA
Total estimation using BLOCKS method: 47 MB
Processing object type TABLE_EXPORT/TABLE/TABLE
Processing object type TABLE_EXPORT/TABLE/STATISTICS/TABLE_STATISTICS
. . exported "SH"."CUST"                              9.101 MB  222000 rows
Master table "SH"."SYS_EXPORT_TABLE_01" successfully loaded/unloaded
*****************************************************************************
Dump file set for SH.SYS_EXPORT_TABLE_01 is:
  /tmp/cust.compress.data.dmp
Job "SH"."SYS_EXPORT_TABLE_01" successfully completed at 15:30:26
```

You can see that the data_only option produces a file that is about 9.14MB in size, as shown here:

```
-rw-r----- 1 oracle oinstall  9588736 Sep 23 15:30 cust.compress.data.dmp
```

Encryption

In addition to the COMPRESSION parameter, the encryption option tremendously enhances the Data Pump tool, particularly in the face of today's ever-changing compliance regulations. Because of an ever-increasing theft of sensitive data, more companies are required to encrypt data in motion and data at rest. Oracle Database 11*g* Data Pump complies with regulatory requirements by providing the ENCRYPTION parameter to specify varying levels of encryption algorithms to satisfy data-at-rest requirements. In addition to the ENCRYPTION parameter, ENCRYPTION_PASSWORD and ENCRYPTION_ALGORITHM parameters are available to further secure your data. In the coming section, we will demonstrate how these parameters can be effectively implemented to further secure your export dump files.

Specifying Encryption

The ENCRYPTION parameter has the following options:

```
encryption = {all | data_only | encrypted_columns_only |
              metadata_only | none}
```

The default value for the ENCRYPTION parameter depends upon the combination of encryption-related parameters that are used. To enable encryption, you must specify either the ENCRYPTION or ENCRYPTION_PASSWORD parameter, or both.

The only option that may need explanation is the ENCRYPTED_COLUMNS_ONLY value, which specifies that only encrypted columns are written to the dump file set in encrypted format. The ENCRYPTION parameter needs to be coupled with the ENCRYPTION_ALGORITHM parameter. The default value for the ENCRYPTION ALGORITHM parameter is AES128-bit encryption. The ENCRYPTION_ALGORITHM parameter specifies which cryptographic algorithm should be used to perform the encryption. Oracle supports three algorithms:

- AES128

- AES192

- AES256

■Note The Advanced Encryption Standard (AES) was adopted as an encryption standard by the U.S. government. It has been analyzed extensively and is now used worldwide; it is commonly used in place of its predecessor, the Data Encryption Standard (DES). AES became effective as a standard May 26, 2002. As of 2006, AES is one of the most popular algorithms used in symmetric key cryptography.

The ENCRYPTION_ALGORITHM parameter must be used in conjunction with either the ENCRYPTION or ENCRYPTION_PASSWORD parameter.

Choosing an Encryption Mode

The encryption mode specifies the type of security to apply when encryption and decryption operations are performed. There are three ENCRYPTION_MODE options:

- dual

- password

- transparent

Using the transparent encryption mode is equivalent to performing a TDE-enabled export. If Oracle Wallet is open, no intervention is required by the DBAs to perform a transparent encrypted export.

If the ENCRYPTION_PASSWORD parameter is specified and Oracle Wallet is open, Oracle uses the dual mode for encryption. If Oracle Wallet is not available on the target database, you can use the ENCRYPTION_PASSWORD parameter that was specified at the time of export to decrypt the data during import.

The following example shows how to perform a TDE-enabled Data Pump export:

```
expdp dumpfile=oratmp:tde.dmp tables=rodba.docs \
    parallel=2 encryption_mode=transparent    \
    encryption=all userid="'/ as sysdba'"
```

Let's look at the password encryption mode. This option indicates that the password has to be provided to perform an import. To be able to import a password-encrypted export dump, the password must be provided during the import operation. The following Data Pump export uses the password ENCRYPTION_MODE with the default encryption algorithm of AES128-bit encryption:

```
expdp dumpfile=dbadir:encrypted.dmp schemas=rodba      \
    userid=rodba/oracle123  encryption_mode=password \
    encryption_password=oracle123
```

Using password mode is by far the easiest way to start performing encrypted Data Pump exports. Let's add a higher level of cryptography to the equation:

```
expdp dumpfile=dbadir:encrypted.dmp.compressed tables=rodba.docs \
    userid=rodba/oracle123  encryption_mode=password        \
    encryption_password=oracle123 ENCRYPTION_ALGORITHM=aes256
```

By specifying the encryption algorithm of AES256, the highest level of encryption is set for the export dump file.

The dual encryption mode can be used when you need to restore to an alternate server on which the Oracle Wallet file is not accessible. The dual mode provides flexibility of using either TDE or the password option during the export/import operation. To perform dual Data Pump exports, you can invoke the expdp utility with the following parameters:

```
expdp dumpfile=oratmp:tde.dualdmp tables=rodba.docs \
    parallel=2 encryption_mode=dual              \
    encryption=all userid="'/ as sysdba'" encryption_password=11g
```

Please be aware that you are required to specify a password when *exporting* in either `dual` or `password` mode.

You can specify a password to encrypt column data, metadata, or table data in the export dump file if an encryption password was supplied exporting the data. The `ENCRYPTION_PASSWORD` parameter has several restrictions. First, the `ENCRYPTION_PASSWORD` parameter is not valid for export dump files created with the `transparent` encryption mode. In addition, the `ENCRYPTION_PASSWORD` parameter works only with Oracle Database 11g Enterprise Edition. Data Pump exports over the network of user-defined external tables with encrypted columns are not supported if the `ENCRYPTION_PASSWORD` parameter is supplied with the `ENCRYPTED_COLUMNS_ONLY` parameter. Lastly, the encryption attributes for all columns must match between the exported table and the target table.

Let's see how we can enforce a password to be supplied during an import operation. Here we take an export of the `DOCUMENTS` table using the `ENCRYPTION_PASSWORD` parameter:

```
expdp expdp dumpfile=dbadir:documents.dmp tables=documents        \
      userid=sh/sh123456 encryption_password=oracle123            \
      reuse_dumpfiles=y encryption_mode=password


Export: Release 11.1.0.6.0 - Production on Sunday, 23 September, 2007 18:17:50

Copyright (c) 2003, 2007, Oracle.  All rights reserved.

Connected to: Oracle Database 11g Enterprise Edition Release 11.1.0.6.0 - Production
With the Partitioning, OLAP, Data Mining and Real Application Testing options
Starting "SH"."SYS_EXPORT_TABLE_01":  dumpfile=dbadir:documents.dmp tables=documents
 userid=sh/******** encryption_password=******** reuse_dumpfiles=y
 encryption_mode=password
Estimate in progress using BLOCKS method...
Processing object type TABLE_EXPORT/TABLE/TABLE_DATA
Total estimation using BLOCKS method: 128 KB
Processing object type TABLE_EXPORT/TABLE/TABLE
Processing object type TABLE_EXPORT/TABLE/STATISTICS/TABLE_STATISTICS
. . exported "SH"."DOCUMENTS"                         5.929 KB       3 rows
Master table "SH"."SYS_EXPORT_TABLE_01" successfully loaded/unloaded
******************************************************************************
Dump file set for SH.SYS_EXPORT_TABLE_01 is:
  /home/oracle/documents.dmp
Job "SH"."SYS_EXPORT_TABLE_01" successfully completed at 18:19:03
```

After a successful export with the `ENCRYPTION_PASSWORD` parameter of `oracle123`, we confirm that an import cannot occur without specifying a password. The following example produces an ORA-39174 error since the password is not provided during the import operation:

```
impdp dumpfile=dbadir:documents.dmp tables=documents \
      userid=sh/sh123456


Import: Release 11.1.0.6.0 - Production on Monday, 03 September, 2007 7:12:35
```

```
Copyright (c) 2003, 2007, Oracle.  All rights reserved.

Connected to: Oracle Database 11g Enterprise Edition Release 11.1.0.6.0 - Production
With the Partitioning, OLAP, Data Mining and Real Application Testing options
ORA-39002: invalid operation
ORA-39174: Encryption password must be supplied.
```

As you can see next, if the correct password is supplied (the original password used to create the export dump), we are able to successfully import the documents table:

```
impdp dumpfile=dbadir:documents.dmp tables=documents \
      userid=sh/sh123456 encryption_password=oracle123

Import: Release 11.1.0.6.0 - Production on Sunday, 23 September, 2007 18:20:09

Copyright (c) 2003, 2007, Oracle.  All rights reserved.

Connected to: Oracle Database 11g Enterprise Edition Release 11.1.0.6.0 - Production
With the Partitioning, OLAP, Data Mining and Real Application Testing options
Master table "SH"."SYS_IMPORT_TABLE_01" successfully loaded/unloaded
Starting "SH"."SYS_IMPORT_TABLE_01":  dumpfile=dbadir:documents.dmp tables=documents
            userid=sh/******** encryption_password=********
Processing object type TABLE_EXPORT/TABLE/TABLE
Processing object type TABLE_EXPORT/TABLE/TABLE_DATA
. . imported "SH"."DOCUMENTS"                          5.929 KB       3 rows
Processing object type TABLE_EXPORT/TABLE/STATISTICS/TABLE_STATISTICS
Job "SH"."SYS_IMPORT_TABLE_01" successfully completed at 18:20:21
```

Reusing a Dump File

One simple new feature added to Oracle Database 11g is the ability to reuse an existing Data Pump dump file in an Oracle directory. Even though the feature seems trivial, it is yet another granular feature that can provide easier manageability to both DBAs and developers. This particular feature is a great enhancement in the world of ASM since Data Pump directories can reside inside ASM. Unless you have access to the asmcmd utility, you will have to use SQL to delete the files in ASM. The asmcmd utility is not available to developers.

The REUSE_DUMPFILE option takes a parameter of [Y/N]. The following example reuses the dump file named encrypted.dmp:

```
expdp dumpfile=oratmp:encrypted.dmp tables=rodba.docs            \
      userid="'/ as sysdba'" encryption_mode=password            \
      encryption_password=oracle123 ENCRYPTION_ALGORITHM=aes256 \
      reuse_dumpfiles=Y
```

If the dump file exists, it is overwritten with this new export. If the dump file does not exist, then Data Pump creates a new file having the name specified.

Remapping Data

Oracle Database 11*g* provides the REMAP_DATA parameter, which allows you to transform data during the export or import operation. To perform a data remap operation, you must create a stored package function and supply the package.function name to the REMAP_DATA parameter as a command-line option.

In the following example, the SALARY column data will be transformed to illustrate the data remapping feature. The salary of every employee can be remapped to $35,000 before storing the data on disk. A simple package with a single function is provided to remap the salary column. The edba_remap function must be passed into the REMAP_DATA parameter of Data Pump.

```
create or replace package edba_remap
is
function remap_sal (p_sal number) return number;
end;
/

create or replace package body edba_remap
is
function remap_sal
(p_sal number) return number
as
v_sal number := 35000;
begin
  return v_sal;
end;

end;
/

SQL>
Package created.
SQL>
Package body created.
```

We now have a package function to remap our SALARY column to the value $35,000. Let's export the EMP table and remap the salary information. The REMAP_DATA parameter accepts the schema name.table_name.column_name value followed by a colon followed by a package. function_name value. In the following example, the SALARY column of the EMP table for the RODBA schema is being remapped to $35,000 during the export:

```
expdp dumpfile=oratmp:emp.dmp tables=rodba.emp \
    userid=rodba/oracle123 reuse_dumpfiles=y \
    remap_data=rodba.emp.sal:edba_remap.remap_sal
```

Once the export is complete and the salary information is remapped, let's import the data into another schema and confirm that the salary information did actually get changed:

```
impdp tables=rodba.emp remap_schema=rodba:ckim \
    userid=rodba/oracle123 dumpfile=oratmp:emp.dmp
```

Here's what the employee information looks like after the import is complete:

```
  1* select ename, sal from emp
SQL> /


ENAME             SAL
---------- ----------
WARD            35000
JONES           35000
MARTIN          35000
BLAKE           35000
CLARK           35000
SCOTT           35000
KING            35000
TURNER          35000
ADAMS           35000
JAMES           35000
FORD            35000
Sam             35000
Charles         35000

13 rows selected.
```

The REMAP_DATA option worked as expected, and all the employee salaries are updated to $35,000. Other great use cases for the REMAP_DATA parameter of Data Pump include tasks such as changing Social Security information, banking information, credit card information, and so on. By generating random numbers using the DBMS_RANDOM package, you can dynamically change sensitive data at either export time or import time. For example, the remap_ssn function in the following edba_remap_ssn package replaces Social Security numbers with random, numerical values:

```
create or replace package edba_remap_ssn
is
function remap_ssn return number;
end;
/

create or replace package body edba_remap_ssn
is
function remap_ssn return number
IS

v_ssn NUMBER;
begin
```

```
SELECT dbms_random.value(100000000,999999999) into v_ssn FROM dual;

return v_ssn;
end;

end;
/
```

You can customize functions similar to the `remap_ssn` function to custom-tailor sensitive tables for your corporate databases.

■Tip Perform data remapping during the export operation so that the data at rest on the file system does not include any sensitive information. It is much easier to steal a dump file than it is to get privileges to access the database.

Remapping a Table

Oracle Database 11*g* provides the ability to import a table into another table using the `REMAP_TABLE` option. The `REMAP_TABLE` option can be used to change the name of a specific table (partitioned and nonpartitioned) during import.

Some restrictions that you may need to consider are as follows:

- If partitioned tables were exported in transportable mode, then each partition and subpartition must be promoted to its own table. The transportable mode is a new Oracle Database 11*g* feature that specifies whether a table/partition/subpartition is transportable.

- Tables will not be remapped if they already exist even if the `TABLE_EXISTS_ACTION` is set to truncate or append.

- The export has to be performed in a nontransportable mode.

The following are two examples of specifying the `REMAP_TABLE` parameter, one without partitions and the other with partitions where exports occur in the transportable mode:

```
impdp dumpfile=oratmp:docs.dmp \
      remap_table=rodba.docs.docs2 userid=rodba/oracle123

impdp dumpfile=oratmp:docs.dmp \
      remap_table=rodba.docs:part1.docs3 userid=rodba/oracle123
```

Notice that the `REMAP_TABLE` option is designated as [schema.]old_tablename[.partition]:new_tablename.

Export and Import of Partitions

Oracle Database 11g adds the ability to allow partitions to be exported and imported with Data Pump using the TRANSPORTABLE=ALWAYS option. In previous releases, the transportable tablespace mechanism of Data Pump could be specified only at the tablespace level.

Now, Oracle Database 11g provides the mechanism to export/import partitions/subpartitions without having to move an entire table or exchange partitions by introducing the PARTITION_ OPTIONS parameter. The default behavior is to departition a partitioned table export to a new table at import time. If the TRANSPORTABLE option is not set during export or the partition name is not specified as a filter, the expected behavior would be none.

Allowable values for PARTITION_OPTIONS are as follows:

- none: Creates the table as it was on the source database. This option cannot be used if the transportable option was set with the partition/subpartition filter during the export.

- departition: Creates each partition/subpartition as a new table. The new table name will be a derived name from the table and partition name. If the export was performed with the TRANSPORTABLE option and partition/subpartition was specified, the import must be done using the departition option.

- merge: Combines all partitions/subpartitions into a single table. This option cannot be used if the TRANSPORTABLE option was set with the partition/subpartition filter during the export.

Let's take a look at an example of how to use the departition option to import a single partition of a table. Here we have a list-partitioned table called KB:

```
SQL>  create table kb
  2  (doc_id number,
  3    category varchar2(55),
  4    note varchar2(4000))
  5    partition by list (category)
  6  (
  7  partition p_dg values ('DG') tablespace kb1,
  8  partition p_plsql values ('PLSQL') tablespace kb2,
  9  partition p_default values (default) tablespace kb3
 10* )
 /
Table created.
```

By querying the DBA_TAB_PARTITIONS view, you can confirm that the P_PLSQL partition resides on the KB2 tablespace. We will perform a single row insert into the P_PLSQL partition with the DOC_ID of 1001:

```
SQL> insert into kb
  2  values
  3  (1001, 'PLSQL', 'PL/SQL in Oracle Database 11g is faster and better!')
  4  /

1 row created.
```

Document identifier 1001 will be established as the baseline data for this demonstration. Behind the scenes, the KB2 tablespace is converted into a read-only tablespace. Next, we unload the P_PLSQL partition of the KB table using Data Pump export with the TRANSPORTABLE=ALWAYS option, as shown here:

```
DBA11g > expdp tables=sh.kb:p_plsql userid=sh/sh \
          directory=dbadir dumpfile=p_plsql.dmp \
          logfile=logdir_p_plsql.log            \
          reuse_dumpfiles=Y                      \
          transportable=always


Export: Release 11.1.0.6.0 - Production on Saturday, 01 September, 2007 23:46:03

Copyright (c) 2003, 2007, Oracle.  All rights reserved.

Connected to: Oracle Database 11g Enterprise Edition Release 11.1.0.6.0 - Production
With the Partitioning, OLAP, Data Mining and Real Application Testing options
Starting "SH"."SYS_EXPORT_TABLE_01":  tables=sh.kb:p_plsql userid=sh/********
directory=dbadir dumpfile=p_plsql.dmp logfile=logdir_p_plsql.log
 transportable=always
Processing object type TABLE_EXPORT/TABLE/PLUGTS_BLK
Processing object type TABLE_EXPORT/TABLE/TABLE
Processing object type TABLE_EXPORT/TABLE/END_PLUGTS_BLK
Master table "SH"."SYS_EXPORT_TABLE_01" successfully loaded/unloaded
******************************************************************************
Dumpfile set for SH.SYS_EXPORT_TABLE_01 is:
  /home/oracle/p_plsql.dmp
******************************************************************************
Datafiles required for transportable tablespace KB2:
  +DATA/dba11g/datafile/kb2.294.632183817
Job "SH"."SYS_EXPORT_TABLE_01" successfully completed at 23:46:14
```

The Data Pump export log indicates that the KB2 tablespace datafile resides in the DATA diskgroup in the ASM instance. The datafile, +DATA/dba11g/datafile/kb2.294.632183817, is required to transport the KB2 tablespace.

We will now take the Data Pump export file p_plsql.dmp and the +DATA/dba11g/datafile/kb2.294.632183817 datafile and perform a copy of the datafile followed by an import into another database. The easiest way to take a datafile out of ASM is to copy the datafile out of ASM to the file system using the cp command (another Oracle Database 11g new feature, discussed in detail in Chapter 9). Here the +DATA/dba11g/datafile/kb2.294.632183817 file is copied to the /tmp directory on the operating system:

```
ASMCMD [+] > cp -irf +DATA/dba11g/datafile/kb2.294.632183817 /tmp/kb2.dbf
source +DATA/dba11g/datafile/kb2.294.632183817
target /tmp/kb2.dbf
copying file(s)...
file, /tmp/kb2.dbf, copy committed.
```

Next, we will copy the kb2.dbf file into the ASM instance on another server. Using any kind of secure copy or file transfer utility, transfer the /tmp/kb2.dbf and p_plsql.dmp files to the target database server. Once the files are successfully copied to the target server, using the same ASM copy command (cp) syntax used earlier in the asmcmd utility, copy the kb2.dbf file into the ASM diskgroup, as shown here:

```
ASMCMD [+DATA/DBA11G1/DATAFILE] > cp /home/oracle/kb2.dbf .
source /home/oracle/kb2.dbf
target +DATA/DBA11G1/DATAFILE/kb2.dbf
copying file(s)...
file, +DATA/dba11g1/datafile/kb2.dbf, copy committed
```

Now, we can import the P_PLSQL partition of the KB table using the PARTITION_OPTIONS=DEPARTITION option in conjunction with the TRANSPORT_DATAFILES option of the Data Pump import utility, as shown here:

```
DBA11g1 > impdp userid="'/ as sysdba'"      \
          partition_options=departition \
          dumpfile=dbadir:p_plsql.dmp    \
          logfile=logdir:p_plsql.log     \
          transport_datafiles='+FRA/dba11g1/kb2.dbf'

Import: Release 11.1.0.6.0 - Production on Sunday, 02 September, 2007 1:46:32

Copyright (c) 2003, 2007, Oracle.  All rights reserved.

Connected to: Oracle Database 11g Enterprise Edition Release 11.1.0.6.0 - Production
With the Partitioning, OLAP, Data Mining and Real Application Testing options
Master table "SYS"."SYS_IMPORT_TRANSPORTABLE_01" successfully loaded/unloaded
Starting "SYS"."SYS_IMPORT_TRANSPORTABLE_01":  userid='/******** AS SYSDBA'
partition_options=departition dumpfile=dbadir:p_plsql.dmp logfile=logdir:p_plsql.log
 transport_datafiles=+FRA/dba11g1/kb2.dbf
Processing object type TABLE_EXPORT/TABLE/PLUGTS_BLK
Processing object type TABLE_EXPORT/TABLE/TABLE
Processing object type TABLE_EXPORT/TABLE/END_PLUGTS_BLK
Job "SYS"."SYS_IMPORT_TRANSPORTABLE_01" successfully completed at 01:46:37
```

Logging in as the SH user, you can verify the partition KB:P_PLSQL is created as [table_name]_[partition_name]. In the following example, you notice a table called KB_P_PLSQL created from the earlier example and that the row we inserted exists in the departitioned table:

```
SQL> desc kb_p_plsql
 Name                     Null?         Type
 ----------------         --------      ------------
 DOC_ID                                 NUMBER
 CATEGORY                               VARCHAR2(55)
 NOTE                                   VARCHAR2(4000)
```

```
SQL> select doc_id, category, note
    from kb_p_plsql
    where doc_id=1001
SQL> /

   DOC_ID   CATEGORY      NOTE
---------- ------------  ------------------------------
     1001   PLSQL         PL/SQL in Oracle Database 11g
                          is faster and better!
```

Ignoring Errors

Oracle Database 11g introduces the DATA_OPTIONS parameter to ignore errors encountered during imports when nondeferred constraint violations are encountered while load operations are being performed to tables, partitions, or subpartitions. For import operations, the only valid option to the DATA_OPTIONS parameter is skip_constraint_errors. The skip_constraint_errors value specifies that the import operation will continue as nondeferred constraints are violated. Errors will be logged to the logfile, and the import will continue.

Here's an example using the skip_constraint_errors option:

```
impdp rodba/oracle123 tables=docs content=data_only \
dumpfile=oradmp:docs.dmp data_options=skip_constraint_errors
```

External Tables Based on Data Pump

The concept of an external table was introduced in Oracle 9i Database. Oracle 9i Database introduced external tables using the ORACLE_LOADER driver. External tables were introduced strictly as read-only data; they were used only to load data into the database, and not to write it back out again. In Oracle Database 10g, Oracle introduced the ORACLE_DATAPUMP driver, enabling you to create external tables that used Data Pump to move data into and out of the database.

In Oracle Database 11g, Oracle enhances the Data Pump API and the ORACLE_DATAPUMP access driver. One such improvement ensures that a row error will not cause a table load to abort. In Oracle Database 10g, without the reject limit clause, a single row error in an external table caused the entire table load to fail. DBAs had to investigate the error, resolve the error causing the failure, and reload the table. In Oracle Database 10g, you can create a Data Pump export dump file using the create table syntax similar to what is shown here:

```
 1  create table docs_10g
 2  organization external
 3  (
 4  type oracle_datapump
 5  default directory dbadir
 6  access parameters
 7  (logfile dbadir:docs)
 8  location ('docs.dmp')
 9  )
```

```
 10* as select * from docs
SQL> /
```

Table created.

In Oracle Database 11g, you can modify this script to take advantage of the new COMPRESSION and ENCRYPTION options. You do this by supplying additional options to the ACCESS PARAMETERS clause. See the following example of creating a compressed external table. Please pay particular attention to the ACCESS PARAMETERS clause:

```
 1   create table docs
 2   organization external
 3   (
 4   type oracle_datapump
 5   default directory dbadir
 6   access parameters
 7   (logfile logdir:docs compression enabled)
 8   location ('docs.dmp')
 9   )
10* as select * from documents
SQL> /
```

Table created.

In addition to specifying the COMPRESSION option, you can also specify both COMPRESSION and ENCRYPTION options, as shown in the following example:

```
SQL> create table docs
 2   organization external
 3   (
 4   type oracle_datapump
 5   default directory dbadir
 6   access parameters
 7   (logfile logdir:docs compression enabled encryption enabled)
 8   location ('docs.dmp')
 9   )
10   as select * from documents
11   /
```

Table created.

To use the encryption option, TDE must be set up first; otherwise, you will receive an ORA-28365 alert indicating that the wallet is not open. For information about how to enable TDE, please refer to Chapter 5.

Now, let's read the external table based on the encrypted and compressed dump file. The following query confirms that the data content is accurate and accounted for:

```
SQL> select doc_id, name
  2  from docs;

  DOC_ID    NAME
  -------   --------------------------------------
    1002    Redhat Linux System Administration.doc
    1003    RMAN for DBAs.doc
    1004    Java for Oracle Developers.doc
...
...
```

One great benefit of using the external table feature to write out Data Pump export dumps is that you can perform complex joins and data transformations while extracting data into export dump files. External tables can be created with the PARALLEL option. You can also select from views or even join views to derive the underlying Data Pump extract. This mechanism of writing dump files significantly simplifies porting data from one database to another. On top of this, you can perform comparisons of the data before committing to the production database.

Stored Procedure to Generate External Table Using a Data Pump

Here's a simple stored procedure to generate DDL for external tables using Data Pump dump files. This stored procedure generates the syntax to create an external table using Data Pump. The stored procedure is called gen_dp and accepts multiple parameters. All but one parameter is required. The only required parameter is the table name. All other parameters have default values and can be overridden by assigning the appropriate parameter with values.

The intent of this script is to provide an automated mechanism to generate an external table using a Data Pump dump file for a specific table. This script can increase Data Pump usability, acceptance, and productivity in your organization. Here are the basic assumptions that the gen_dp stored procedure makes:

- The default directory name is called oratmp and is mapped to a file system directory.

- The name of the target table (the table that will be created) will be the source table name appended with a _dp.

- The logfile will be named the same as the source table.

- The dump file will be named as the source table name appended by .dmp.

- The external table dump file will not be encrypted.

- The external table dump file will not be compressed.

You can customize these default settings to fit your database environment. The following script uses the ORACLE_DATAPUMP type and the appropriate entries to ACCESS PARAMETERS to generate the syntax to create an external table:

```
set serveroutput on
CREATE OR REPLACE PROCEDURE gen_dp
(
p_table_name IN VARCHAR2,
p_table_name_extension IN VARCHAR2 := '_dp',
p_directory IN VARCHAR2 := 'oratmp',
p_dumpfile IN VARCHAR2 := 'sat',   -- sat = same as table
p_logfile IN VARCHAR2 := 'sat',    -- sat = same as table
p_compression IN VARCHAR2 := 'disabled',
p_encryption IN VARCHAR2 := 'disabled'
)
AS
v_dumpfile VARCHAR2(100) := p_dumpfile;
v_logfile VARCHAR2(100) := p_logfile;
v_compression VARCHAR2(30) := p_compression;
v_encryption VARCHAR2(30) := p_encryption;

BEGIN

IF v_dumpfile = 'sat' THEN
  v_dumpfile := p_table_name||'.dmp';
END IF;
IF v_logfile = 'sat' THEN
  v_logfile := p_table_name;
END IF;

IF lower(v_compression) = 'enabled' THEN
  v_compression := 'compression enabled';
elsif lower(v_compression) = 'disabled' THEN
  v_compression := '';
END IF;

IF lower(v_encryption) = 'enabled' THEN
  v_encryption := 'encryption enabled';
ELSIF lower(v_encryption) = 'disabled' THEN
  v_encryption := '';
END IF;

DBMS_OUTPUT.PUT_LINE ('create table '||p_table_name||p_table_name_extension);

DBMS_OUTPUT.PUT_LINE (' organization external');
DBMS_OUTPUT.PUT_LINE ('(');

DBMS_OUTPUT.PUT_LINE (' type oracle_datapump ');

DBMS_OUTPUT.PUT_LINE (' default directory '||p_directory);
```

```
DBMS_OUTPUT.PUT_LINE (' access parameters ');

DBMS_OUTPUT.PUT_LINE (' ( logfile '||v_logfile||' '||v_compression||'
 '||v_encryption||')' );
DBMS_OUTPUT.PUT_LINE (' location ('||chr(39)||v_dumpfile||chr(39)||')' );
DBMS_OUTPUT.PUT_LINE (')');
DBMS_OUTPUT.PUT_LINE (' as');
DBMS_OUTPUT.PUT_LINE (' select * from '||p_table_name);

END;
/
```

■ **Note** By default, the gen_dp procedure generates SQL syntax that is Oracle Database 10*g* and 11*g* compliant. To take advantage of the Oracle Database 11*g* features, use the p_compression=>'enabled' and p_encryption=>'enabled' parameters.

Let's execute the gen_dp script. Accepting all the default values, let's generate the syntax to create an external table called DOCS_DP deriving the data from the DOCS table:

```
SQL> exec gen_dp('docs');

create table docs_dp
organization external
(
type oracle_datapump
default directory oratmp
access parameters
( logfile docs   )
location ('docs.dmp')
)
as
select * from docs
PL/SQL procedure successfully completed.
```

■ **Note** Since the gen_dp procedure executes DBMS_OUTPUT to display output, you must have serveroutput on.

If you have TDE enabled for the database, you will want the script to generate the syntax to take advantage of encryption. The p_encryption parameter can be passed a string value of enabled to enable encryption, as shown here:

```
begin
  gen_dp(p_table_name => 'docs',
         p_encryption => 'enabled');
end;
/
```

Execution of the gen_dp procedure with the p_encryption parameter generates the following SQL syntax with the encryption enabled option to the ACCESS PARAMETERS parameter:

```
create table docs_dp
organization external
(
type oracle_datapump
default directory oratmp
access parameters
( logfile docs  encryption enabled)
location ('docs.dmp')
)
as
select * from docs
```

To take advantage of the COMPRESSION option, you can enable the p_compression parameter to the gen_dp procedure, as shown here:

```
begin
gen_dp(p_table_name => 'docs',
       p_compression => 'enabled',
       p_encryption => 'enabled');
end;
/
```

Executing the gen_dp procedure with both encryption and compression enabled yields the following output:

```
create table docs_dp
organization external
(
type oracle_datapump
default directory oratmp
ACCESS PARAMETERS
( logfile docs compression enabled encryption enabled)
location ('docs.dmp')
)
as
select * from docs
```

If you are storing Data Pump dump files inside ASM, you should be aware that Data Pump log files cannot reside inside ASM. To effectively utilize ASM, the dump files can reside in ASM, but the log files must reside on the file system. Attempting to store a log file inside of ASM will yield an error that resembles the following Oracle error message:

```
ERROR at line 1:
ORA-29913: error in executing ODCIEXTTABLEOPEN callout
ORA-29400: data cartridge error
error opening file +data/DBA11g/DUMPSET/docs2.log
```

CHAPTER 8

■■■

Oracle Streams

With the technological advances in computers and the spread of the Internet, the need has grown to share information within the corporation throughout the disparate regions of the globe. The internationalization of products and the demand for readily available information create the increasing requirements for data replication. Of all the replication technologies available, Oracle Streams can provide a single enterprise solution for data sharing for Oracle databases. One key benefit that Oracle Streams provides is the ability to replicate data between different versions of Oracle. Unlike Oracle Logical Standby, Oracle Streams also allows you to replicate a database between different operating systems. In addition, architects can selectively pick and choose what table they want to replicate. Application architects can even filter the data subset within a table using what is called Streams *rules*. These rules are similar to `where` clauses in a SQL statement.

With the advancements within the Enterprise Manager Database Console, the Streams setup process can be completed easily using the Streams Setup Wizard. By utilizing the Streams Setup Wizard, DBAs can set up and replicate the whole database, specific schemas, or specific tables between two or more database links. Alternatively, Oracle Streams can also be set up from command-line APIs.

Note Streams configuration is not covered in this chapter. For detailed Oracle Streams configuration steps, please visit the `http://www.dbaexpert.com/blog/?p=31` web page.

Oracle Database 11g focuses on the new database innovations to the Streams product. This chapter will concentrate on the key new features introduced with Oracle Streams:

- Synchronous capture

- Combined capture and apply

- Performance Advisor

- Compare and repair

- Topology

- Split and merge of destinations

Later, the chapter will focus on usability improvements of Streams that allow for easy management of the Streams environment.

Synchronous Capture

Oracle Database 11*g* pioneers another mechanism to perform data capture at the source database called *synchronous capture*. Synchronous capture utilizes an internal mechanism to capture deltas to tables immediately as transaction executes. Synchronous capture collects data modifications as they occur without mining through redo logs or archivelogs. In the implementation of synchronous capture, redo logs are not involved. Row LCRs are visible in the persistent queue, which consists of stored messages on disk, not in memory, as soon as the commits are issued. Synchronous capture identifies each modified row, converts it into a row LCR, and enqueues it directly to disk. Once LCRs are written to disk, the standard Streams processing controls the remaining process. It is important to note that the synchronous queue LCRs contain all the columns of the table even when not all of them are modified.

With synchronous capture, DML changes made to the underlying tables are captured as soon as commits occur. DML changes that are supported are `insert`, `update`, `delete`, and `merge` commands. Behind the scenes, the `merge` statement is converted into an `insert` or an `update`.

■**Note** Synchronous capture can be associated only with an `ANYDATA` queue, not with a typed queue. You use the `set_up_queue` procedure from the `DBMS_STREAMS_ADM` package to create the commit-time queues for synchronous capture.

There are situations where you want to utilize the synchronous capture process. First, Streams is available only with an Oracle Enterprise Edition license. If you want to use Streams with the Standard Edition, you must use the synchronous option.

The synchronous option should be used cautiously. You should not turn on synchronous capture for all the tables for high-volume OLTP transaction databases. You should consider setting up synchronous capture for a few tables that do not have high transaction volumes. Another great candidate is for databases that are not in archivelog mode or can enable the traditional Streams log-based capture.

Restrictions on Synchronous Capture

Please bear in mind the restrictions associated with synchronous capture. First, it is applicable only for DML. DDL changes cannot participate in synchronous capture. Second, synchronous capture will not capture changes on IOTs if the IOT has any of these datatypes: LONG, LONG RAW, CLOB, NCLOB, BLOB, BFILE, ROWID, and XMLType. Synchronous capture cannot capture changes made to temporary tables or object tables. Synchronous capture can enqueue messages only from a commit-time queue. In addition, changes to sequence values are not captured. SQL*Loader in direct load mode is not supported. Similar to the conventional Oracle Streams, the users `sys`, `system`, and `ctxsys` cannot participate in synchronous capture.

Synchronous capture rules must be a positive rule set. Negative rules are prohibited. The only rules that are valid for synchronous captures are rules specified at the table level or for subset of rows. Rules must be added using the `add_table_rules` or `add_subset_rules` procedure from the `DBMS_STREAMS_ADM` package.

The following commands are ignored in a synchronous capture:

- `plan`

- `call`

- `explain`

- `lock`

- `alter system`

- `alter session`

- `set role`

- `dbms_redefinition`

- Rules created by the `DBMS_RULE_ADM` package

- Calls to the PL/SQL (but the underlying changes to database objects are captured)

Configuring Synchronous Capture

The capture user must be set up to capture DML changes applicable for the rule set. This can be accomplished by invoking the `DBMS_CAPTURE_ADM.ALTER_SYNC_CAPTURE` procedure.

As stated before, the synchronous capture must use the `ANYDATA` queue. To create the `ANYDATA` queue, you can use the `DBMS_STREAMS_ADM.SET_UP_QUEUE` procedure. For example:

```
begin
dbms_streams_adm.set_up_queue
  (queue_table => ' STREAMS_ADMIN.STREAMS_QUEUE_TABLE ',
  queue_name => ' STREAMS_ADMIN.STREAMS_QUEUE ',
  queue_user => ' RODBA ');
end;
/
```

■**Note** The default value for `QUEUE_TABLE` is `streams_queue_table`, and the default value for `QUEUE_NAME` is `streams_queue`.

To start the synchronous capture process, you have several procedures from which to choose:

- `DBMS_STREAMS_ADM.ADD_TABLE_RULES`

- `DBMS_STREAMS_ADM.ADD_SUBSET_RULES`

- `DBMS_CAPTURE_ADM.CREATE_SYNC_CAPTURE`

A synchronous capture can capture changes only at the table level. Schema-level or data-base-level configurations cannot be set up for synchronous capture. You can invoke the add_table_rules or add_subset_rules procedure to configure synchronous capture.

Using the new create_sync_capture procedure, you can set up a synchronous capture at the source database. The create_sync_capture procedure takes these arguments:

- queue_name: Name of the queue as defined in the call to the set_up_queue procedure

- capture_name: Name of the sync capture process

- rule_set_name: Name of the positive rule set

- capture_user: Capture user

Here's an example of the create_sync_capture invocation with all the arguments relative to this example:

```
begin
dbms_capture_adm.create_sync_capture
 (queue_name => ' STREAMS_ADMIN.STREAMS_QUEUE ',
  capture_name => ' SYNC_DOCS_CAPTURE ',
  rule_set_name => ' STREAMS_ADMIN.SYNC_DOCS_RULE_SET ',
  capture_user => ' RODBA ');
end;
/
```

■**Note** The rule_set_name of sync_docs_rule_set must be defined already. You can use the create_rule_set procedure to create the rule set.

The procedure will create a synchronous capture called sync_docs_capture. You will also notice that the QUEUE_NAME of the streams queue coincides with the QUEUE_NAME from our set_up_queue procedure. Once the synchronous capture is defined, you can use the add_tables_rules or add_subset_rules procedure to add a table. Using subsets is required only when repli-cating partial/selected data; otherwise, there is no need to use subsets. In this example, we will use the add_subset_rules procedure to add the DOCS table where the DOC_ID >1000000:

```
begin
dbms_streams_adm.add_subset_rules
 (table_name => 'RODBA.DOCS',
  dml_condition => ' DOC_ID >1000000',
  streams_type => 'SYNC_CAPTURE',
  streams_name => 'SYNC_DOCS_CAPTURE',
  queue_name => 'STREAMS_QUEUE',
  include_tagged_lcr => FALSE);
END;
/
```

You can see that the `STREAM_NAME` argument takes the capture name from the previous `create_sync_capture` procedure. Also, there is an optional `DML_CONDITION` parameter to specify a where clause to the table. The synchronous capture will use the `SYNC_DOCS_RULE_SET` rule set name as specified from the `create_sync_capture` procedure.

Dropping Synchronous Capture

You can use the `DBMS_CAPTURE_ADM.DROP_CAPTURE` procedure to drop an existing synchronous capture. This procedure has two parameters, `CAPTURE_NAME` and `DROP_UNUSED_RULE_SETS`. By default, the `DROP_UNUSED_RULE_SETS` parameter is set to `FALSE`. If the `DROP_UNUSED_RULE_SETS` parameter is set to `TRUE`, the `drop_capture` procedure will also drop any rule sets specified by the `CAPTURE_NAME` parameter. However, if the rule set is used by another Streams client, it will not be dropped. In the following code example, we drop the `sync_docs_capture` synchronous capture:

```
begin
dbms_capture_adm.drop_capture
 (capture_name => 'SYNC_DOCS_CAPTURE',
  drop_unused_rule_sets => TRUE);
end;
/
```

DBA Views for Synchronous Capture

The view DBA_SYNC_CAPTURE_TABLES provides a listing of all the tables that are participating in synchronous capture for the database. For example:

```
SQL> select table_owner, table_name, enabled from dba_sync_capture_tables;

TABLE_OWNER    TABLE_NAME    ENA
------------   -----------   ---
RODBA          DOCS          YES
```

You can join this view with `DBA_STREAMS_TABLE_RULES` to correlate the stream name, rules, and subset operation information for each synchronous capture. Here's an example showing how that's done:

```
select r.streams_name, r.rule_name,
       r.subsetting_operation,t.table_owner,
       t.table_name, t.enabled
  from dba_streams_rules r,dba_sync_capture_tables t
 where r.streams_type = 'SYNCHRONOUS CAPTURE'
   and r.object_name = t.table_name;
```

You can also query the DBA_SYN_CAPTURE view to display the queue and rule set of each synchronous capture:

```
SQL> select capture_name, queue_name, rule_set_name, capture_user
  2*   from dba_sync_capture
SQL> /

CAPTURE_NAME         QUEUE_NAME        RULE_SET_NAME        CAPTURE_US
----------------     --------------    ------------------   ----------
SYNC_DOCS_CAPTURE    STREAMS_QUEUE     SYNC_DOCS_RULE_SET   RODBA
```

Combined Capture and Apply

Oracle Database 11g Streams launches a new feature called the *combined capture and apply*, which provides the capability for a capture process to send logical change records (LCRs) directly to an apply process without using a propagation. This feature cannot be used with synchronous capture. This feature can be used when the capture and apply processes are on the same database or on different databases. When combined capture and apply is in place, the LCRs are transferred using database links without staging the LCR in a queue.

When the database is started, the capture process automatically detects that the requirements for combined capture and apply are satisfied. The capture process will initiate a connection with the apply process and send the LCRs directly to the apply process. The capture process does not stage the LCR in the queue; likewise, the propagation and queues are not used to send and store LCRs.

Requirements for Combined Capture and Apply

Let's review the restrictions imposed when the capture and apply processes reside on the same database. First, capture and apply must use the same queue, and the compatible initialization parameter must be set to 11.1. This combined queue must have a single publisher and single consumer for the capture and apply processes. This queue must also have a single consumer for the buffered queue for the apply process.

There are different rules of governance when the capture and apply processes are on different databases. Obviously, both databases must have compatible set to 11.1.0 or higher. Also, the following rules apply:

- The propagation must be set up between the capture process queue and the apply process queue without an intermediate queue.

- The capture process queue must have a single consumer: the propagation between the capture process and the apply process queue.

- The apply process queue must have a single publisher: the propagation between the capture process and the apply process queue.

In the world of RAC, combined capture and apply can be architected to reside on the same instance, on different instances in the RAC cluster, or on different databases. Similar restrictions apply when the capture process and apply process are on different instances of the RAC database or on different databases.

If the requirements for combined capture and apply are met, Oracle Streams automatically detects and implements the optimized configuration, bypassing the propagation and queues to send and store LCRs.

Combined Capture and Apply Validation

You can view V$STREAMS_CAPTURE and V$STREAMS_APPLY_READER to obtain connect details and statistics relative to combined capture and apply. The V$STREAMS_APPLY_READER view has additional columns:

```
SQL> desc V$STREAMS_APPLY_READER
 Name                            Null?     Type
 ----------------------------    ------    -----
 SID                                       NUMBER
 SERIAL#                                   NUMBER
 APPLY#                                    NUMBER
 APPLY_NAME                                VARCHAR2(30)
 ..
 ..
 PROXY_SID                                 NUMBER
 PROXY_SERIAL                              NUMBER
 PROXY_SPID                                VARCHAR2(12)
 CAPTURE_BYTES_RECEIVED                    NUMBER
```

The PROXY_SID and PROXY_SERIAL columns are populated when communication for direct combined capture and apply is established. The PROXY_SID and PROXY_SERIAL columns are the SID and SERIAL of the apply process network receiver. The PROXY_SPID column provides the OS PID of the apply network receiver. The CAPTURE_BYTES_RECEIVED column provides the number of bytes received from the capture process. There are also three new columns introduced to the V$STREAMS_CAPTURE view:

```
SQL> desc V$STREAMS_CAPTURE
 Name                            Null?     Type
 -----------------------------   ------    -----------------------------
 SID                                       NUMBER
 SERIAL#                                   NUMBER
 CAPTURE#                                  NUMBER
 CAPTURE_NAME                              VARCHAR2(30)
 LOGMINER_ID                               NUMBER
 STARTUP_TIME                              DATE
 STATE                                     VARCHAR2(551)
 ..
 ..
 APPLY_NAME                                VARCHAR2(30)
 APPLY_DBLINK                              VARCHAR2(128)
 APPLY_MESSAGES_SENT                       NUMBER
 APPLY_BYTES_SENT                          NUMBER
```

The STATE column can have several different values depending on the condition of the capture process such as WAITING FOR APPLY TO START, WAITING FOR PROPAGATION TO START, or CONNECTING TO APPLY DATABASE. The APPLY_NAME and APPLY_DBLINK columns are populated when combined capture and apply processes are established. If the combined capture and apply conditions are satisfied, APPLY_DBLINK is populated with the remote database name. The APPLY_MESSAGE_SENT and APPLY_BYTES_SENT columns show the number of messages and bytes sent to the apply process.

Performance Advisor

Oracle Database 11g introduces another advisor to troubleshoot configuration issues and performance bottlenecks associated with your Streams environment. The Streams Performance Advisor uses database links to perform discovery of the Streams configuration. The overall objective of the Streams Performance Advisor is to recommend areas that can be modified for better performance such as identifying latency and throughput for each separate Streams component. Additional information collected includes calculating bottleneck components, top wait events, message rates, and transaction rates. When the Performance Advisor collects statistics about the Streams environment, it works backward. It starts from the apply process and works backward to the capture process. Along the way, the Streams Performance Advisor assigns a component ID to each component and a path ID to each path.

Streams Advisor Admin Package

The DBMS_STREAMS_ADVISOR_ADM package comes with a procedure named analyze_current_performance to gather and diagnose Streams performance statistics. This package in conjunction with a set of views—referred to as the Streams *topology views*—make up the Streams Performance Advisor. By default, this procedure does not require any parameters.

```
PROCEDURE ANALYZE_CURRENT_PERFORMANCE
 Argument Name          Type         In/Out   Default?
 ---------------        ---------    ------   ---------
 COMPONENT_NAME         VARCHAR2     IN       DEFAULT
 COMPONENT_DB           VARCHAR2     IN       DEFAULT
 COMPONENT_TYPE         NUMBER       IN       DEFAULT
```

First you must execute the analyze_current_performance procedure as the Streams administrator account:

```
execute dbms_streams_advisor_adm.analyze_current_performance;
```

This will allow the dynamic Streams views to be populated with the following information pertaining to the Streams environment:

- Capture process

- Propagation senders and receivers

- Apply process

- Queue

When you execute the `analyze_current_performance` procedure, you should run it more than once in the same session, especially if you are looking for rate, bandwidth, and event and flow control statistics. If you are looking for just the number of current messages in a queue, a single execution will provide you with this information.

Also, your goal is to keep the Streams topology statistics current. You should reexecute this procedure when any components are added to any database in the Streams environment.

■**Note** Synchronous capture and messaging client information is not gathered by the `DBMS_STREAMS_ADVISOR_ADM` package.

Streams Topology

What makes up the Streams topology? It is composed of databases in the Streams configuration, the Streams components for each database, and the flow of messages between the components. In the Streams topology, messages flow from one component to another component. This is referred to as a *stream path*. A path can be something as simple as a capture or synchronous capture process or an application enqueueing messages into a queue. Another path can be when the apply process dequeues the messages. A message will go through several paths queues and propagations before it reaches the apply process. The stream path ends when messages are dequeued by the apply process.

■**Note** As of Oracle Database 11*g* Release 1, Oracle Streams does not track paths when messages are dequeued by a messaging client by an application.

The Streams path begins from the capture process and ends with the apply process. Along the way, there can be multiple source/destinations before reaching the final apply process destination. The Streams topology assigns a number to each path. This allows for easy monitoring of the paths and location of messages along the path. The Streams topology also designates a number to a link between two components in a path, the beginning component and an end component. The positions of the link in the overall Streams path can resemble what is listed here:

1. The beginning component is the capture process, and the end component is the queue.

2. The beginning component is the queue, and the end component is the propagation sender.

3. The beginning component is the propagation sender, and the end component is the propagation receiver.

4. The beginning component is the propagation receiver, and the end component is the queue.

5. The beginning component is the queue, and the end component is the apply.

Streams Topology Views

Various Streams views provide detailed information and statistics about the Streams topology. Topology view information is gathered by executing the analyze_current_performance procedure as stated earlier. Table 8-1 shows various Streams topology views.

Table 8-1. *Streams Topology Views*

DBA Streams View	Description
DBA_STREAMS_TP_COMPONENT	Provides information about each Streams component at each database
DBA_STREAMS_TP_COMPONENT_LINK	Provides information about how messages flow between Streams components
DBA_STREAMS_TP_COMPONENT_STAT	Provides temporary information about performance statistics/session statistics of each Streams component
DBA_STREAMS_TP_DATABASE	Provides information about each database containing Streams components
DBA_STREAMS_TP_PATH_BOTTLENECK	Provides temporary information about Streams components, potentially delaying the flow of messages of a stream path
DBA_STREAMS_TP_PATH_STAT	Provides information about temporary statistics of each stream path

Some of the view information is temporary in nature and survives only the duration of the session. Views returning such temporary information include DBA_STREAMS_TP_COMPONENT_STAT, DBA_STREAMS_TP_PATH_BOTTLENECK, and DBA_STREAMS_TP_PATH_STAT. When the user disconnects the session, the temporary information is purged.

With each of the components, you must determine the component ID. This ID is assigned to each component and used throughout the topology mapping to track information about the component and what information flows in and out of the component. The component ID can be determined by querying the DBA_STREAMS_TP_COMPONENT view. You can query the DBA_STREAMS_TP_COMPONENT view on both the source and target databases to get a clear understanding of all the Streams components. The following query is issued from a source database:

```
select component_id, component_name, component_type, component_db
from dba_streams_tp_component
order by component_id
/
  ID Name                                          Type                  Database
---- --------------------------------------------- --------------------- ---------
   1 DBA11G2=>"STREAMS_ADMIN"."STREAMS_APPLY_Q"    PROPAGATION RECEIVER  DBA11G
   2 "STREAMS_ADMIN"."STREAMS_CAPTURE_Q"           QUEUE                 DBA11G2
   3 "STREAMS_ADMIN"."STREAMS_CAPTURE_Q"=>DBA11G   PROPAGATION SENDER    DBA11G2
   4 STREAMS_CAPTURE                               CAPTURE               DBA11G2
```

On the target database system, you will get another result to indicate that it is the destination:

```
ID Name                                   Type      Database
---- -------------------------------- -------- ----------
   1 "STREAMS_ADMIN"."STREAMS_APPLY_Q"   QUEUE     DBA11G
   2 STREAMS_APPLY                        APPLY     DBA11G
```

You can view the path to determine where a message is queued. To view the path information, you can use the following query:

```
select path_id, source_component_id, destination_component_id, position, active
from dba_streams_tp_component_link
order by path_id, position
SQL> /


   PATH_ID  SOURCE_COMPONENT_ID  DESTINATION_COMPONENT_ID  POSITION  ACT
---------- ------------------- ------------------------ -------- ---
         1                   1                        2        1 YES
```

The Streams topology provides information about where a message resides and what component of the path it is at. Another view called STREAMS_TP_PATH_BOTTLENECK identifies Streams performance problems:

```
select component_id, component_name, component_type, component_db
from dba_streams_tp_path_bottleneck
where bottleneck_identified ='YES'
 order by component_id
SQL> /


no rows selected
```

If you get the "no rows selected" output, then the Streams Performance Advisor could not identify any bottleneck components in your environment. If you get result sets returned from the query, this indicates you may have legitimate performance problems. You should check the status of these components. Next, you will have to put on your troubleshooting hat to diagnose the performance bottlenecks.

To display statistics for the components in the Streams topology, run the following query:

```
select component_id, component_name, component_type,
statistic_name, statistic_value, statistic_unit
from dba_streams_tp_component_stat
 order by component_id, component_name, component_type, statistic_name
SQL> /
```

■**Note** Oracle recommends that each apply process dequeues messages from only a single source. Oracle also recommends that each propagation sends changes to a separate queue.

DBMS_COMPARISON for "Compare and Repair"

Oracle Database 11g Streams introduces advancements in the DBMS_COMPARISON package. Oracle Streams now provides functionality that has been in Quest Shareplex since Oracle 8 i. Shareplex is one of Quest's enterprise products that performs redo and archivelog mining and provides a similar level of functionality to Oracle Streams. Lots of Oracle customers have preferred to utilize Quest Shareplex over Oracle Streams and Oracle Advanced Replication in the past for data replication because of its ease of use and maintenance. Oracle Streams now makes another big stride and fills this gap with the new data comparison and convergence APIs.

Even though the DBMS_COMPARISON package is introduced as a Streams feature, it can be used independently of Streams. You can use the DBMS_COMPARISON package to detect divergences and rectify discrepancies in a non-Streams environment.

Quest always had the capability to perform what they call a *compare and repair* operation. A compare and repair operation provides you with the ability to compare row for row of a source table against a remote target table. As of Oracle Database 11g, Oracle provides similar functionality that enables the comparison of the rows in an object, such as a table, against another object in the same or a different database. If there are deltas in the database objects, then the DBMS_COMPARISON package can be used to converge the database objects so that they are consistent.

The compare procedure does not support comparison of LONG, LONG RAW, ROWID, CLOB, NCLOB, BLOB, BFILE, user-defined types, or Oracle-supplied types such as XMLTypes.

DBMS_COMPARISON Requirements

The DBMS_COMPARISON package has database release requirements. The local database must be at least at Oracle version 11.1, and the remote database must be at least at Oracle version 10.1.0. DBMS_COMPARISON also requires that at least one index be available on the objects being compared, preferably a NUMBER column. In addition, the database character set of the source and target comparison database must be the same.

Supported Database Object Types

The DBMS_COMPARISION package can compare databases between live sources for the following types of database objects:

- Tables

- Single-table views

- Materialized views

- Synonyms for tables, single-table views, and materialized views

Data does not have to be compared against the same object type. You can compare a table with a view. You can also compare a table in one database against a materialized view on another database. Database objects can be of different types. Furthermore, the columns names can also be different as long as they are of the same datatype.

Comparison

Behind the scenes, Oracle does not perform row-for-row comparisons as you would expect. Oracle's comparison algorithm uses the ora_hash function to compute a hash value for a specified number of rows called a *bucket*. Buckets improve the performance of table scans by splitting the table into ranges of rows. Each range of rows is processed independently. The number of buckets determined for a compared object will be the number of rows in a specified table divided by the MAX_NUM_BUCKETS parameter in the DBMS_COMPARISION.CREATE_COMPARISON procedure. The MAX_NUM_BUCKETS parameter determines the number of rows performed per scan. If there are no differences found in the specified bucket of rows between the source and target tables, the bucket is split, and another scan is performed. If the split bucket from the previous process returns different results in the hash value, the buckets are split again, and another hash value comparison is performed. This process is repeated until the differing rows are identified or until the MIN_ROWS_IN_BUCKET threshold is reached. When the MIN_ROWS_IN_BUCKET is reached, the result is posted to the DBA_COMPARISON_SCAN_SUMMARY view.

By default, the number of MAX_NUM_BUCKETS and MIN_ROWS_IN_BUCKET parameters are set to 1000 and 10000, respectively, as shown in a snippet of code from the $ORACLE_HOME/rdbms/admin/dbmscmp.sql file:

```
-- Other Default values
CMP_MAX_NUM_BUCKETS    CONSTANT PLS_INTEGER  := 1000;
CMP_MIN_ROWS_IN_BUCKET CONSTANT PLS_INTEGER  := 10000;
```

Begin a comparison by first defining comparison boundaries including a table and column level of granularity using the create_comparison procedure:

```
begin
 dbms_comparison.create_comparison
 (comparison_name => 'COMPARE_DOCS',
  schema_name => 'RODBA',
  object_name => 'DOCS',
  dblink_name => 'DBA11g',
  column_list => ' DOCUMENT_ID,NAME ');
end;
/
```

Two additional parameters to the create_comparison procedure, SCAN_PERCENT and SCAN_MODE, allow you to specify the level of comparison and percentage of the table to scan. The following are valid values for SCAN_MODE:

- CMP_SCAN_MODE_FULL: The default mode where the complete table is scanned.

- CMP_SCAN_MODE_RANDOM: You can compare random portions of the table.

- CMP_SCAN_MODE_CYCLIC: You can cycle through a percentage threshold at a time. Subsequent scans continue where the last comparison ended.

- CMP_SCAN_MODE_CUSTOM: You can specify the amount of data that is compared at one time based on an index you specify.

Please note that data comparisons can affect the performance of the involved databases. You should consider the cyclic level of comparison since you can allocate, for example, 10 percent of the rowsets at a time and continue until the comparison completes. By using this approach, you can mitigate possible performance bottlenecks to the production database environment.

The SCAN_PERCENT parameter is applicable when the SCAN_MODE parameter is set to either CMP_SCAN_MODE_RANDOM or CMP_SCAN_MODE_CYCLIC.

Once the comparison is defined, we can run the comparison difference algorithm and collect the deltas between the source and the target. For each execution of the compare function, a scan ID is produced:

```
declare

v_comp boolean;
v_scan_info dbms_comparison.comparison_type;

begin
v_comp := dbms_comparison.compare
        (comparison_name => 'COMPARE_DOCS',
          scan_info => v_scan_info,
          perform_row_dif => TRUE);
dbms_output.put_line ('Scan ID: '||v_scan_info.scan_id);

if v_comp = TRUE then
  dbms_output.put_line ('No deltas were found.');
else
  dbms_output.put_line ('Deltas were found.');
end if;

end;
/
```

In this example, PERFORM_ROW_DIF is set to TRUE. With this parameter set, the individual row deviation's information will be collected. By setting this parameter to FALSE, deviation information will be collected only at the table level. Your output should look similar to the following:

```
Scan ID: 99
Deltas were found.
PL/SQL procedure successfully completed.
```

For optimal performance for object-level comparisons, you can adjust the MAX_NUM_BUCKETS and MIN_ROWS_IN_BUCKET parameters in the create_comparison procedure.

Comparison Maintenance

After much iteration of data comparisons, you may need to purge previous comparison collections. The nls_timestamp_format can be specified at the database level in the initialization parameter:

```
nls_timestamp_format='RRRR-MM-DD HH24:MI:SS'
```

To purge all previous comparisons, you can use the following procedure, specifying nulls for SCAN_ID and PURGE_TIME:

```
begin
  dbms_comparison.purge_comparison
 (comparison_name => 'COMPARE_DOCS',
  scan_id => NULL,
  purge_time => NULL);
end;
/
```

On the other hand, you can also purge an individual scan of a comparison. The requirement to perform this task are the comparison name and the scan ID. You can determine the SCAN_ID for a specified comparison name by querying the DBA_COMPARISON_SCAN_SUMMARY view:

```
select distinct root_scan_id
  from dba_comparison_scan_summary
 where comparison_name = 'COMPARE_DOCS';
```

Once the SCAN_ID is identified, you can perform the actual purge:

```
begin
 dbms_comparison.purge_comparison
 (comparison_name => 'COMPARE_DOCS',
  scan_id => 99,
  purge_time => NULL);
end;
/
```

You can also purge a plan for a specified period. All scans prior to that time period will be deleted. To purge all comparisons since April 15, 2007, as of noon, you can use the following:

```
begin
dbms_comparison.purge_comparison
 (comparison_name => 'COMPARE_DOCS',
  purge_time => '2007-04-15 12:00:00');
end;
/
```

You can also drop the comparison and all associated scans using the drop_comparison procedure:

```
exec dbms_comparison.drop_comparison('COMPARE_DOCS');
```

Rechecking a Prior Comparison

You can recheck the previous comparison scans using the DBMS_COMPARISION.RECHECK function. This function is capable of capturing in-flight data. It can also be used to provide a quick check of rows that are different. The recheck function checks the current data in the database objects for differences that were recorded in the specific comparison scan. The recheck function takes a parameter of the comparison name, scan ID, and row difference. Let's perform a recheck for a comparison on the DOCS table, which generated a SCAN_ID of 99:

```
set serveroutput on
declare
v_comp boolean;
begin

v_comp := dbms_comparison.recheck
        (comparison_name => 'COMPARE_DOCS',
         scan_id => 99);

if v_comp = TRUE then
  dbms_output.put_line('No deltas were found.');
else
  dbms_output.put_line('Deltas were found.');
end if;
end;
/
```

Your output is similar to the following:

```
Deltas were found.
PL/SQL procedure successfully completed.
```

Converging Shared Database Objects (Repair)

The primary purpose of the converge procedure is to resynchronize the differences from the source compared to the target database. Once you identify what is considered to be the "truth" database, albeit the target or the source, you can manually sync the row differences across the database link. The best option is to let Oracle synchronize the row differences identified in a comparison scan.

You can converge and specify whether the source or target is the master and should win on the conflict resolution. The following example specifies that the local database is the conflict winner:

```
set serveroutput on
declare
v_scan_info dbms_comparison.comparison_type;
begin

dbms_comparison.converge
                (comparison_name => 'COMPARE_DOCS',
                 scan_id => 99,
                 scan_info => v_scan_info,
                 converge_options => dbms_comparison.cmp_converge_local_wins);
```

```
  dbms_output.put_line ('Local Rows Merged: '||v_scan_info.loc_rows_merged);
  dbms_output.put_line ('Remote Rows Merged: '||v_scan_info.rmt_rows_merged);
  dbms_output.put_line ('Local Rows Deleted: '||v_scan_info.loc_rows_deleted);
  dbms_output.put_line ('Remote Rows Deleted: '||v_scan_info.rmt_rows_deleted);
end;
/
```

Your output is similar to the following:

```
Local Rows Merged: 0
Remote Rows Merged: 1
Local Rows Deleted: 0
Remote Rows Deleted: 1
PL/SQL procedure successfully completed.
```

By modifying this:

```
converge_options => dbms_comparison.cmp_converge_local_wins);
```

to this:

```
converge_options => dbms_comparison.cmp_converge_remote_wins);
```

you can specify the remote database server to be the master source. There are several DBA_COMPARISON_* views that provide detailed information about the comparisons, scans, and additional information captured by the DBMS_COMPARISON package. You can join the DBA_COMPARISON and DBA_COMPARISON_SCAN_SUMMARY views to produce a high-level report indicating the number of records that are out of sync using the following query:

```
select c.comparison_name, c.schema_name,
       c.object_name, cs.current_dif_count diff
  from dba_comparison c,
       dba_comparison_scan_summary cs
 where c.comparison_name = cs.comparison_name
   and c.owner = cs.owner
   and cs.scan_id = 99;


COMPARISON_NAME    SCHEMA_NAME    OBJECT_NAME    DIFF
---------------    -----------    ----------    ----
COMPARE_DOCS       RODBA          DOCS             1
```

Other pertinent views relevant to comparisons are as follows:

- DBA_COMPARISON_COLUMNS
- DBA_COMPARISON_SCAN
- DBA_COMPARISON_SCAN_VALUES
- DBA_COMPARISON_ROW_DIF

Splitting and Merging of a Destination

As with any kind of day-to-day operational support, rare but unfortunate situations will arise where the target server or database incurs an outage. In a hub-and-spoke configuration, if a destination in a Streams replication environment becomes unavailable, it can cause file system issues or possible performance degradations on the source system.

Splitting a Stream

For such situations, DBAs can split (temporarily offline) the unavailable destination from a Stream configuration using the DBMS_STREAMS_ADM.SPLIT_STREAMS procedure. The split_streams procedure creates cloned capture queue and processes on the source. In addition, a propagation is created with a disabled status. The split_streams procedure has these parameters:

```
PROCEDURE split_streams (
    propagation_name        IN      VARCHAR2,
    cloned_propagation_name IN      VARCHAR2 DEFAULT NULL,
    cloned_queue_name       IN      VARCHAR2 DEFAULT NULL,
    cloned_capture_name     IN      VARCHAR2 DEFAULT NULL,
    perform_actions         IN      BOOLEAN  DEFAULT TRUE,
    script_name             IN      VARCHAR2 DEFAULT NULL,
    script_directory_object IN      VARCHAR2 DEFAULT NULL,
    auto_merge_threshold    IN      NUMBER   DEFAULT NULL,
    schedule_name           IN OUT VARCHAR2,
    merge_job_name          IN OUT VARCHAR2);
```

The AUTO_MERGE_THRESHOLD is by default set to NULL or 0, which means the split stream is not automatically merged back with the original stream. If the result of CAPTURE_MESSAGE_CREATE_TIME in the V$STREAMS_CAPTURE view is within seconds of the AUTO_MERGE_THRESHOLD of the split_streams procedure with the original capture process, the two streams are automatically merged.

Merging the Streams

Once the issue on the target is resolved, you can merge the split stream back with the original stream using the merge_streams procedure in the same package:

```
PROCEDURE merge_streams (
  cloned_propagation_name IN VARCHAR2,
  propagation_name        IN VARCHAR2 DEFAULT NULL,
  queue_name              IN VARCHAR2 DEFAULT NULL,
  perform_actions         IN BOOLEAN  DEFAULT TRUE,
  script_name             IN VARCHAR2 DEFAULT NULL,
  script_directory_object IN  VARCHAR2 DEFAULT NULL);
```

As mentioned, this merge can be automated by setting the auto_merge_threshold parameter of the split_streams procedure to a nonzero value.

Once a fault is detected at a target destination, you can query the V$BUFFERED_QUEUES view to identify how many messages are in a buffered queue and how many of these messages have spilled to disk.

Merge Streams Job

You can use the merge_streams_job procedure when you need to determine whether the original capture and cloned capture processes are in the range of the specified merge threshold. If the threshold is within the range, then the merge_streams procedure is executed to merge the two streams.

```
PROCEDURE merge_streams_job (
  capture_name            IN VARCHAR2,
  cloned_capture_name     IN VARCHAR2,
  merge_threshold         IN NUMBER,
  schedule_name           IN VARCHAR2 DEFAULT NULL,
  merge_job_name          IN VARCHAR2 DEFAULT NULL);
```

Usability Improvements

Oracle Database 11g improves Oracle Streams to make the product easier to use, manage, and implement. Improvements include features such as the following:

- Message tracking

- Automated alerts

- Identifying newly supported tables

- Identifying minimum required checkpoint SCN

- Background process name changes

- Support for XMLTypes stored as CLOBs

- Support for TDE

- Support for Oracle Scheduler

Message Tracking

You can now monitor messages across all the databases. The V$STREAMS_MESSAGE_TRACKING view will capture all the areas of a message from capture to propagation to apply. This view provides information including timestamp, action, object name, and command type. Another benefit that this view provides is the ability to see the path of the message.

Streams message tracking is turned on by executing the set_message_tracking procedure:

```
begin
 dbms_streams_adm.set_message_tracking (tracking_label => 'DOC_TRACK');
end;
/
```

You can use the set_message_tracking procedure to assign a custom label. By default, the default label is called Streams_tracking. You can query the V$STREAMS_MESSAGE_TRACKING view to track the LCRs and the process flow through each of the clients. When you detect that LCRs are not being applied, this view can be helpful to diagnose the problems. This view will provide the necessary information to determine where in the process the LCRs are bottlenecked.

You can confirm that your tracking label is set for your session:

```
SQL> select dbms_streams_adm.get_message_tracking () from dual;


DBMS_STREAMS_ADM.GET_MESSAGE_TRACKING()
------------------------------------------
DOC_TRACK
```

To stop message tracking for the session, you can call the same procedure that you used to set message tracking on, except now, you will set the tracking label to NULL:

```
begin
dbms_streams_adm.set_message_tracking(tracking_label => NULL);
end;
/
```

Automated Alerts for Clients and Thresholds

Oracle Enterprise Manager Database Console detects when the Streams client is disabled or exceeds the specified threshold and triggers an alert. Oracle categorizes two kinds of alerts: stateful and stateless. A stateful alert is generally associated with a numeric value and has threshold-level settings for warning and critical levels. In Oracle Database 11g, Oracle provides alerts for Streams pool memory usage. Enterprise Manager Database Console would trigger a warning alert when the Streams pool memory hits 85 percent utilization. You can modify this threshold using Enterprise Manager Database Console or using the dbms_server_alert.set_threshold procedure.

A stateless alert is an alert that generates a single event and is not tied to a state. Here are all the valid conditions that would generate a stateless alert:

- A capture process aborts

- A propagation aborts after 16 consecutive errors

- An apply process aborts

- An apply process with an empty error queue encounters an apply error

Streams alerts can be viewed using the Enterprise Manager or via the database dictionary views. You can view DBA_OUTSTANDING_ALERTS for current stateful alerts and refer to DBA_ALERT_HISTORY for alerts that have been cleared from the DBA_OUTSTANDING_ALERTS view. The DBA_ALERT_HISTORY view also has information about the stateless alerts that have been cleared. Both of these views have two common columns: REASON and SUGGESTED_ACTION. Here's an example query from the DBA_OUTSTANDING_ALERTS view:

```
select reason, suggested_action
  from dba_alert_history
 where module_id like '%STREAMS%';
```

You can use the same query as earlier and change the view name to DBA_OUTSTANDING_ALERTS to get a list of the current stateful alerts.

Identifying Newly Supported Tables View

The DBA_STREAMS_NEWLY_SUPPORTED view displays information about tables that are newly supported by Oracle Stream. Even though this view is not new to Oracle Database 11g, you can query this view to determine what tables are supported with each version of the database. You can see that Oracle extends support for XMLTypes in release 11.1:

```
  1  select owner||'.'||table_name table_name, reason, compatible
  2  from dba_streams_newly_supported
  3* order by compatible desc
SQL> /


TABLE_NAME                      REASON                      COMP
----------------------          ------------------------    ----
OE.EDBA_PO                      table with XMLType column   11.1
OE.WAREHOUSES                   table with XMLType column   11.1
WKSYS.WK$_HTTPAUTH              IOT with row overflow       10.2
WKSYS.WK$_SYSINFO              IOT with row overflow       10.2
```

Identifying Minimum Required Checkpoint SCN

Oracle Database 11g adds a new column in the V$DATABASE view called MIN_REQUIRED_CAPTURE_CHANGE#. The purpose of this column is to indicate the minimum required checkpoint SCN for all local capture processes. You can join this to the V$ARCHIVED_LOG view to determine the required archivelogs.

Background Process Name Changes

Oracle renames their process names in Oracle Database 11g. Here are the naming convention changes:

- Capture process names have changed to cp00 to cpnn.

- Apply process names have changed to ap00 to apnn.

- Apply reader and apply servers have changed to as00 to asnn.

- LogMiner processes are now v000 to vnnn.

The values for nn can be 0–9 or a–z. You can see from the following output the new process names:

```
r11b > ps -fu oracle |grep -i ora_ |egrep -i "cp|ap|v0|as"
oracle   3810      1  0 04:35 ?        00:00:07 ora_cp01_r11b
r11a > ps -fu oracle |grep -i ora_ |egrep -i "cp|ap|v0|as"
oracle   20141     1  0 06:08 ?        00:00:00 ora_ap01_r11a
oracle   20143     1  0 06:08 ?        00:00:00 ora_as01_r11a
oracle   20145     1  0 06:08 ?        00:00:00 ora_as00_r11a
```

Support for XMLType Values Stored As CLOBs

Effective as of Oracle Database 11g, Oracle Streams extends support for XMLTypes stored as CLOBs. There is one little caveat worth mentioning, though. Old values for the XMLTypes stored as CLOBs are not logged. For conflict detection and resolution, you will need a TIMESTAMP column to be added to your table.

Support for Transparent Data Encryption

Oracle Database 11g Streams starts support for data encrypted with transparent data encryption. Oracle supports both column- and tablespace-level encryption. (Tablespace encryption is another Oracle Database 11g new feature that eliminates some of the complications of encrypted data relative to performance and referential integrity and is discussed more in Chapter 5.) Whether the data is encrypted via the column level or tablespace level, Streams components handle the column data in the same way.

By default, Oracle Streams handles the capture and apply processes similarly. If the source column or tablespace was encrypted with TDE, the Streams apply process will keep intact the level of encryption set at the target. The PRESERVE_ENCRYPTION apply parameter can change a column from TDE to non-TDE as it applies the messages on the target database. For example, the source database can enforce encryption with TDE, but if the target system does not have licensing for the Advanced Security Option, the column data can be decrypted before it is written to disk. By specifying PRESERVE_ENCRYPTION to N on the target apply process, data will be decrypted; on the other hand, if the target column is not TDE enabled and PRESERVE_ENCRYPTION is set to Y, you will receive an error. The row LCRs will also be moved to the error queue. You can set the preserve encryption using the set_parameter procedure:

```
SQL>  begin
  2       dbms_apply_adm.set_parameter (
  3       apply_name => 'APPLY_STREAM',
  4       parameter => 'preserve_encryption',
  5       value => 'n');
  6* end;
SQL> /

PL/SQL procedure successfully completed.
```

Intrinsically, Streams also supports TDE capture for downstream capture processes if the wallet is shared with the source database. The wallet file can be shared via the Network File System (NFS) mount or can be copied manually using the traditional secure file transfer protocols such as sftp or scp.

Support for Oracle Scheduler

In previous releases, Oracle Streams was configured to use job queue processes with the DBMS_JOB package for such tasks as propagation and event notification. DBMS_JOB has a dependency on the job_queue_processes initialization parameter being set. Oracle DBAs had to monitor for failed jobs, or worse, broken jobs. Oracle Database 11g Streams propagation uses Oracle Scheduler instead of DBA_JOBS. This allows for the following:

- Optimized propagated scheduling with a dedicated job for lowest propagation latency

- Shared job processing where propagation can be run in batch mode

- Event-driven processes where propagation is started where there are data to be propagated

Oracle Scheduler can be used to adjust the schedules of a Streams timetable. Propagation jobs use slave processes when needed to execute jobs.

CHAPTER 9

■■■

Storage Management

With Oracle Database 11g, numerous improvements have been incorporated into automated storage management (ASM) to provide higher availability, easier manageability, and better performance to the database community. This chapter will address the pertinent new ASM features introduced in Oracle Database 11g:

- Rolling upgrades

- ASM fast disk resynchronization

- ASM preferred read failure groups

- ASM diskgroup attributes for backward compatibility

- Separation of the DBA and SA roles via the sysasm role

- New manageability options for the check, mount, and drop commands

- A copy command to copy files between diskgroups, across ASM instances, and between ASM and the operating system

- ASM extensions such as diskgroup metadata backup and restore and block repair

Later in the chapter, the topic will change to another highly anticipated Oracle Database 11g feature called Direct NFS. RAC and non-RAC customers who leverage NFS today on filers can take advantage of Oracle's new Direct NFS. Direct NFS provides simplicity and performance for database implementations on network-attached storage (NAS). Customers have opted for NFS solutions over block devices for simplicity and lower cost, and Direct NFS makes NFS implementations even simpler and faster.

Automated Storage Management

Oracle Database 10g introduced ASM as an alternative to the file system for storing database files. ASM challenges file system management as we know it today by providing an integrated file system and volume manager in the database kernel. Many DBAs ask the same question: What does ASM buy me? There are many reasons why DBAs, SAs, and SAN administrators should consider ASM. Here are the most important reasons:

- Raw device performance

- Logical volume management

- Consolidation of storage management

- Mirroring/triple mirroring equivalence

- Striping

- Mirroring across heterogeneous storage arrays

- Mirroring across different storage vendors

- Real application cluster support

Misconceptions of ASM

Many DBAs have numerous misconceptions about ASM. By revealing "the truth" about ASM, DBAs, SAs, and SAN administrators can make cognitive decisions about implementing ASM. First, ASM does not automatically rebalance the IO. The rebalance activity of an ASM diskgroup happens only when adding or dropping disks from the diskgroup. Second, ASMLIB is available only for Linux and Windows. ASMLIB is a support library for ASM that simplifies the management and discovery of ASM disks. ASMLIB is not a requirement to implement ASM but is highly recommended. Third, you can implement ASM without RAC. Although ASM tends to be implemented with RAC, it performs well in stand-alone non-RAC environments too. With ASM, Oracle installs and configures a lightweight cluster agent called Cluster Synchronization Services (CSS). More and more companies are adopting ASM in a single instance for ease of manageability and performance.

On the same note, DBAs, SAs, and SAN administrators may be unaware of some hidden ASM features. You can leverage ASM mirroring technologies to simulate protection equivalence to mirroring and triple-mirroring technologies using normal and failure redundancy.

RMAN and ASM

Knowing RMAN is a must when considering ASM. DBAs who are not intimate with RMAN do not have a choice but to learn and become experts with RMAN. There are numerous ways to transfer files from and to ASM, but believe it or not, nothing compares in performance and ease of maintenance than RMAN. ASM has the option to utilize technologies such as WebDav or FTP in conjunction with XML DB, but this option complicates the environment and supportability.

■**Note** Although the `dbms_file_transfer` PL/SQL package provides the ability to copy, get, and put database-related files to/from ASM using the `copy_file`, `get_file`, and `put_file` procedures, RMAN performance is astronomically faster than `dbms_file_transfer`. In addition, the level of complexity of `dbms_file_transfer` compared to RMAN doesn't make it a preferable solution. `dbms_file_transfer` does have an advantage in that it does not require a backup.

Now with Oracle Database 11*g*, you can also use the new `asmcmd` copy command.

---

sysasm Privilege and osasm Group

Oracle Database 11*g* defines a new privilege called sysasm for the ASM instance. The primary purpose of the sysasm privilege is to manage the gray area of roles and responsibility introduced by ASM. The sysasm privilege separates the roles between the storage administrator, system administrator, and database administrator.

Eventually the sysdba privilege will be deprecated from the ASM instance. There will be a clear delineation between the RDBMS and ASM credentials. In Oracle Database 11*g*, the security credentials of sysdba will behave as they did with Oracle Database 10*g*. In future releases of Oracle, sysdba will be restricted from ASM. Separating the sysasm privilege from the sysdba privilege improves the security model since you are separating the role of the ASM administration from the role of database administration.

■**Note** Starting from Oracle Database 11*g*, Oracle's best practices recommend using the sysasm role instead of the sysdba role for ASM administration.

The following message is generated in the alert log file if the sysdba role is used to perform ASM maintenance:

```
WARNING: Deprecated privilege SYSDBA for command 'ALTER DISKGROUP CHECK'
```

The following code example illustrates the process necessary to grant the sysasm privilege and configure a new user for the sysasm privilege. Let's first create a user named ckim and grant that user the sysasm privilege:

```
SQL>  create user ckim identified by oracle123
default tablespace tools
temporary tablespace temp;

User altered.

SQL>  grant sysasm, sysoper to ckim;

Grant succeeded.
```

You can clearly see that the ckim user has the sysasm privilege granted in the V$PWFILE_USERS view:

```
SQL> select * from v$pwfile_users;
```

USERNAME	SYSDB	SYSOP	SYSAS
SYS	TRUE	TRUE	FALSE
CKIM	FALSE	TRUE	TRUE

Now, let's connect as the ckim user created in the earlier example. The user ckim now has privileges to perform sysasm-related tasks. In the following code, user ckim will unmount and remount all the diskgroups in the ASM instance:

```
[oracle@rac11]$  sqlplus ckim/oracle123 as sysasm

SQL*Plus: Release 11.1.0.6.0 - Production on Tue Sep 11 11:22:05 2007

Copyright (c) 1982, 2007, Oracle.  All rights reserved.


Connected to:
Oracle Database 11g Enterprise Edition Release 11.1.0.6.0 - Production
With the Partitioning, OLAP, Data Mining and Real Application Testing options

SQL> alter diskgroup data dismount;
Diskgroup altered.

SQL> alter diskgroup fra dismount;
Diskgroup altered.

SQL> alter diskgroup data mount;
Diskgroup altered.

SQL> SQL> alter diskgroup fra mount;
Diskgroup altered.
```

In Oracle Database 10g ASM, the sysoper privilege has similar privileges as the sysdba role; however, in Oracle Database 11g ASM, the sysoper privilege has similar restrictions and privileges enforced on the database side. The following are commands granted to the sysoper privilege:

- startup and shutdown
- alter diskgroup mount and alter diskgroup dismount
- alter diskgroup online disk and alter diskgroup offline disk
- alter diskgroup rebalance
- alter diskgroup check

sysoper is restricted from all the privileges required to create or drop diskgroups or disks such as create diskgroup, add/drop/resize disk, and so on. These privileges still require the sysdba or sysasm privilege. sysoper is restricted from privileges that create or destroy objects in the ASM instance.

Oracle Database 11g Enterprise Manager Database Console provides full support for user management of the ASM instance on the Users tab. This screen lists all the users who have administrative privileges against the ASM instance, as depicted in Figure 9-1.

In the upper-right corner of the screen, you will notice a button to create users. You will be prompted to enter the username, password, and list of roles to assign, as shown in Figure 9-2.

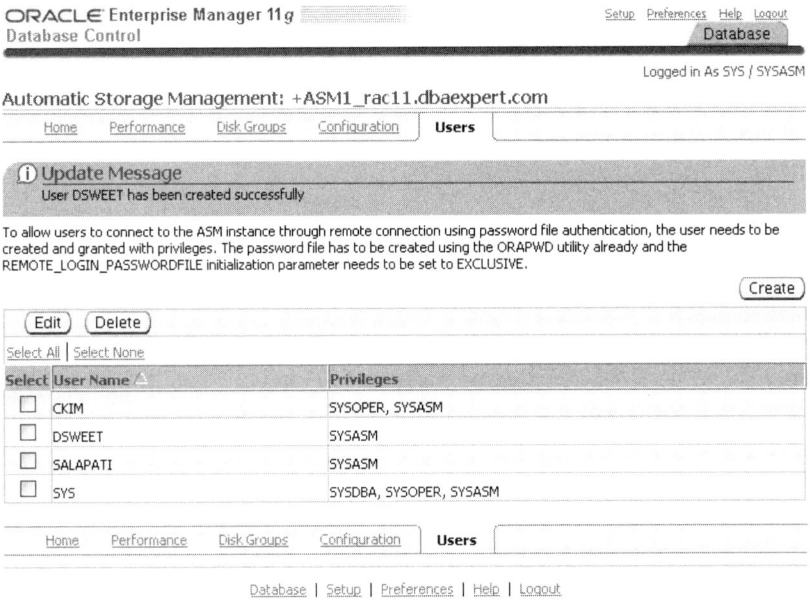
ORACLE Enterprise Manager 11g
Database Control
Setup Preferences Help Logout
Database
Logged in As SYS / SYSASM
Automatic Storage Management: +ASM1_rac11.dbaexpert.com
Home Performance Disk Groups Configuration Users
Update Message
User DSWEET has been created successfully
To allow users to connect to the ASM instance through remote connection using password file authentication, the user needs to be created and granted with privileges. The password file has to be created using the ORAPWD utility already and the REMOTE_LOGIN_PASSWORDFILE initialization parameter needs to be set to EXCLUSIVE.
Create
Edit Delete
Select All | Select None
Select User Name Privileges
CKIM SYSOPER, SYSASM
DSWEET SYSASM
SALAPATI SYSASM
SYS SYSDBA, SYSOPER, SYSASM
Home Performance Disk Groups Configuration Users
Database | Setup | Preferences | Help | Logout

Figure 9-1. *ASM user maintenance*

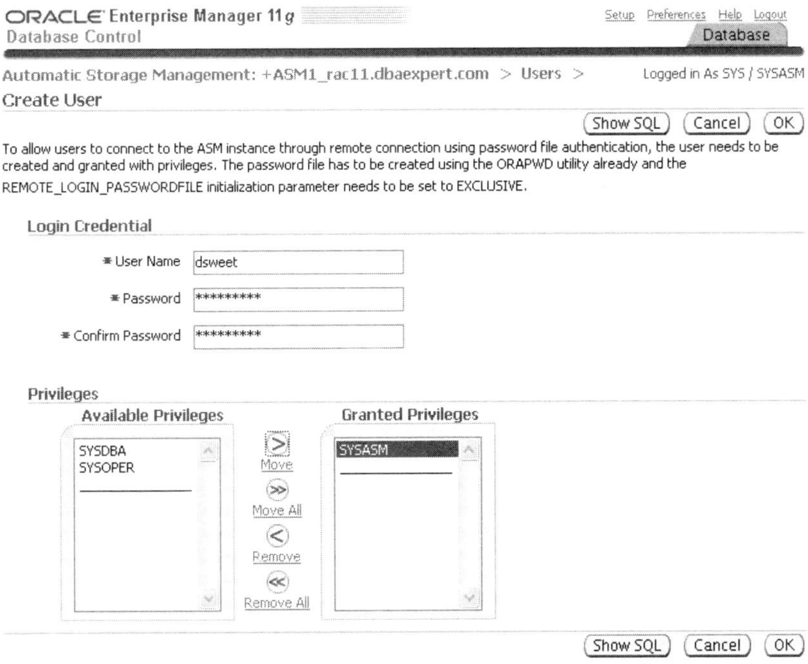
ORACLE Enterprise Manager 11g
Database Control
Setup Preferences Help Logout
Database
Automatic Storage Management: +ASM1_rac11.dbaexpert.com > Users >
Logged in As SYS / SYSASM
Create User
Show SQL Cancel OK
To allow users to connect to the ASM instance through remote connection using password file authentication, the user needs to be created and granted with privileges. The password file has to be created using the ORAPWD utility already and the REMOTE_LOGIN_PASSWORDFILE initialization parameter needs to be set to EXCLUSIVE.
Login Credential
* User Name dsweet
* Password *********
* Confirm Password *********
Privileges
Available Privileges
Granted Privileges
SYSDBA
SYSOPER
SYSASM
Move
Move All
Remove
Remove All
Show SQL Cancel OK

Figure 9-2. *ASM Create User screen*

The osasm Unix group is a new privileged operating system group available in Oracle Database 11*g* that complements the osdba and osoper groups. Prior to the installation process, the osasm group can be added to the /etc/group file. Unix accounts that are members of the osasm group can log in as sysasm using OS authentication.

Fast Rebalance

When you add new storage or remove disks from an existing diskgroup, you have to perform a rebalance operation. In a RAC configuration, all the ASM instances must communicate with each other during the rebalance activities to send lock and unlock extent map messages. This communication between the ASM instances degrades the performance of the rebalance activity.

Effective in Oracle Database 11*g*, what is known as *fast rebalance* can be performed to eliminate ASM messaging with other ASM instances. Fast rebalance improves the throughput of the rebalance activity. This feature is enabled by using the startup restrict or alter diskgroup ... mount restrict command. When the diskgroup is in restricted mode, databases are not allowed to access the datafiles.

In the previous release, one way that DBAs disabled this inter-ASM instance messaging was to shut down the remaining ASM instances during the rebalance activity.

ASM Upgrade

Before you start the upgrade process, you should install the Oracle Database 11*g* software to another ORACLE_HOME directory. Similar to the database upgrade method, there are two approaches to upgrading ASM to Oracle Database 11*g* ASM:

- Upgrading manually

- Using the Database Upgrade Assistant (DBUA)

Upgrading Manually

The manual upgrade process for ASM involves installing the ASM binary software to another directory and switching the ORACLE_HOME to the new location. You must perform some prerequisite steps prior to switching to the new ORACLE_HOME. Although you need to modify the diskgroup compatibility parameter, you can do this later.

Let's look at the steps required to perform a manual upgrade. First, the /etc/oratab or /var/opt/oracle/oratab file needs to be updated with the new ASM ORACLE_HOME location. Next, the ASM init.ora or spfile file needs to be copied from the old ORACLE_HOME to the new ORACLE_HOME. Appropriate changes, such as the directory locations for the diag and dump directories, need to be modified. If you have a password file, you need to copy the password file from the old ORACLE_HOME to the new ORACLE_HOME.

■**Note** For RAC environments, you can modify the new ASM home within the OCR using the srvctl utility:

```
srvctl modify asm -n racnode1 -i +ASM1
                -o /apps/oracle/product/11.1.0/asm -p init+ASM1.ora
```

You need to perform this command on all ASM instances participating in the RAC cluster.

If you are upgrading a non-RAC ASM instance, you will be required to reconfigure the Oracle CSS using the new ORACLE_HOME. You can do this by executing the localconfig command from the Oracle Database 11g ASM ORACLE_HOME before upgrading ASM:

```
cd $ORACLE_HOME/bin
[root@rac103 bin]# ./localconfig reset
Successfully accumulated necessary OCR keys.
Creating OCR keys for user 'root', privgrp 'root'..
Operation successful.
Configuration for local CSS has been initialized
Stale CSS daemon is running... killing it now
Cleaning up Network socket directories
Setting up Network socket directories
Adding to inittab
Startup will be queued to init within 30 seconds.
Checking the status of new Oracle init process...
Expecting the CRS daemons to be up within 600 seconds.
Cluster Synchronization Services is active on these nodes.
        rac103
Cluster Synchronization Services is active on all the nodes.
Oracle CSS service is installed and running under init(1M)
```

Once the CSS configuration is complete, you need to change your ORACLE_HOME to the new Oracle version 11.1 ORACLE_HOME and start the ASM instance. When everything is up and running, grant the new sysasm role to the administrative account user (sys), as shown here:

```
SQL> grant sysasm to sys;
```

If you have obsolete initialization parameters, you can address them now. To get a listing of all the obsolete initialization parameters, please refer to the ASM alert log file.

Upgrading Using DBUA

You can also perform the ASM upgrade to Oracle Database 11g using DBUA. Since Oracle Database 10g, Oracle development invested an enormous amount of hours on the upgrade utilities to deliver ease-of-upgrade processes. Similar to providing a simplified upgrade process in Oracle Database 10g, DBUA can be used to upgrade the ASM instance from Oracle Database 10g to Oracle Database 11g. The DBUA utility performs numerous activities during the upgrade process. First, the password file is copied from the Oracle 10.x ORACLE_HOME to the Oracle 11.1 ORACLE_HOME. Second, the oratab file is updated, and when the upgrade is complete, sys is granted the sysasm role. During the upgrade process, it will convert the init$ORACLE_SID.ora file to an spfile. In addition, the spfile will be relocated to the ASM instance if it was not there before the upgrade process. To initiate the upgrade process, change the directory to the new $ORACLE_HOME/bin directory, and launch DBUA:

```
[oracle@rac11.dbaexpert.com~]$ cd $ORACLE_HOME/bin
[oracle@rac11.dbaexpert.com~]$ ./dbua
```

The initial screen of the DBUA utility takes you to the ASM upgrade Welcome page, as shown in Figure 9-3.

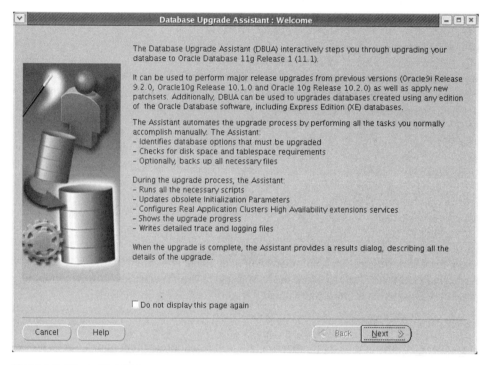

Figure 9-3. *The initial Welcome page*

Click the Next button, and the DBUA utility will redirect you to the Upgrades Operations page. At this point, click the Upgrade Automatic Storage Management Instance radio button, and click the Next button, as illustrated on Figure 9-4.

Just like the database, ASM upgrades can be achieved from different versions of Oracle. Please refer to Chapter 1 for the complete list of all supported versions. Clicking the Next button will take you to the Summary page, as shown in Figure 9-5, once all the information is collected about the source ASM ORACLE_HOME and target ORACLE_HOME.

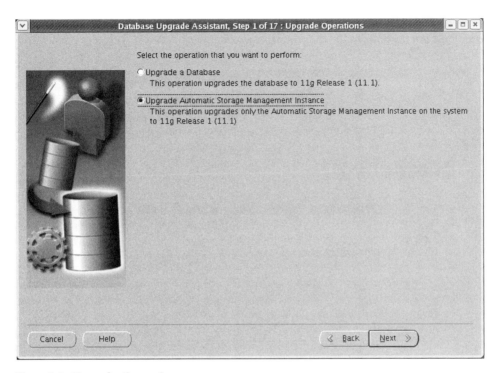

Figure 9-4. *Upgrades Operations page*

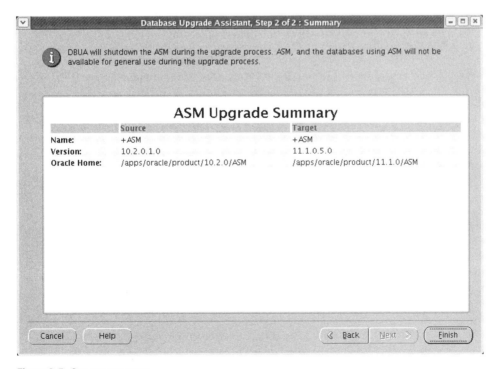

Figure 9-5. *Summary page*

You must click the Finish button. Once the ASM upgrade is complete, the Progress page will result in a 100 percent completion status, as shown in Figure 9-6.

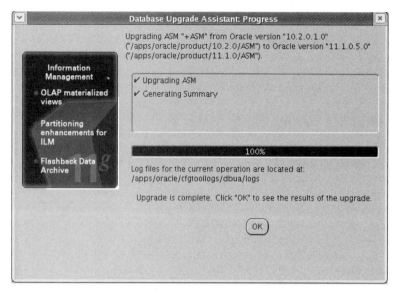

Figure 9-6. *ASM upgrade completion page*

You will receive a prompt to click the OK button to view the Upgrade Results page, as shown in Figure 9-7.

After a successful upgrade, you will see the following message in the Unix window that initiated the DBUA utility:

```
Database upgrade has been completed successfully, and the database is ready to use.
```

In Oracle Database 11*g*, a greater emphasis is on the ORACLE_BASE environment variable. In fact, oracle_base becomes one of the new underscore initialization parameters. The log files associated with the ASM upgrade using the DBUA utility are placed in the $ORACLE_BASE/cfgtoollogs/dbua/logs directory. You can go to this directory and view the ASMUpgrade.log file for additional details.

Figure 9-7. *Upgrade Results page*

Rolling Upgrades

Oracle Database 11*g* introduces the ability to perform rolling upgrades. Since this is introduced as a feature in Oracle Database 11*g* Release 1, customers will not be able to utilize it until Oracle Database 11*g* Release 2 or future patchsets. If you are upgrading from Oracle Database 10*g* ASM, you will not be able to utilize the rolling-upgrade feature. Prior to Oracle Database 11*g*, only the Oracle Clusterware component supported the rolling-upgrade concept. Prior to Oracle Database 11*g*, Data Guard also supported the concept of rolling upgrades with special setup considerations. Separating the ASM_HOME directory is considered a best-practice implementation. With the support of rolling upgrades in Oracle Database 11*g* ASM, splitting ASM home from the RDBMS home looks ever more appealing.

Typically, when applying a patch to an Oracle environment, the RAC clusterware is patched first in a rolling-upgrade fashion. Once the successful upgrade of the clusterware is confirmed, the ASM home software binary is upgraded. To upgrade the ASM binaries in Oracle Database 10*g* and 11*g* Release 1, all of the ASM instances in the RAC must be shut down. Once the ASM instance upgrade is validated, the RDBMS software stack and database environment is upgraded. Typically, the last environment to upgrade or patch is the RDBMS software stack, unless a known bug or issues in the clusterware or ASM prevents it otherwise.

■**Note** For Oracle Database 11 *g* early adopters, Oracle Clusterware and ASM software and instance can be upgraded independently of the RDBMS. Since optimizer changes between versions cause concerns for large database implementations, you can safely upgrade Clusterware and ASM relatively soon after the general availability of Oracle Database 11 *g*. You can leverage this same methodology for future releases of Oracle.

Enabling ASM Rolling Upgrades

The rolling upgrade of ASM will provide a higher level of availability for RAC implementations. Similar to the clusterware rolling-upgrade feature introduced in Oracle Database 10*g*, the Oracle ASM rolling-upgrade feature will provide higher uptime for RAC environments. To perform a rolling upgrade, you must place the ASM instance in rolling-upgrade mode. In addition, you should make sure all the ASM instances are at the same Oracle version. To enable the ASM instance for rolling migration mode, you can use this alter system syntax to start rolling migration to [database_version_number]:

```
SQL> alter system start rolling migration to 11.2.0.2;
```

This command does not actually perform the rolling migration but communicates with all the ASM instances in the RAC. This command informs the other ASM instance(s) of RAC that it is preparing to perform an upgrade and the states will be temporarily different. Once the rolling migration is enabled, you can query each ASM instance to view the current state of the ASM:

```
select sys_context ('sys_cluster_properties', 'cluster_state')
from dual
SQL> /
SYS_CONTEXT('SYS_CLUSTER_PROPERTIES','CLUSTER_STATE')
-----------------------------------------------------
Normal
```

If the ASM instance were participating in a rolling migration, the output of this query would indicate a "Rolling Migration" status. Once you confirm the state of the ASM instance is in rolling migration, you can now safely shut down the ASM instance and apply the software upgrade to the ASM home. Once you confirm the successful upgrade of the ASM software stack, you can now start the ASM instance, which will mount all the diskgroups.

Once upgraded, the ASM participates in the RAC in a different version from the other ASM instances. Only in the rolling migration state are different versions of the ASM instance(s) permissible. It is required that each ASM instance will be put into a rolling migration mode and shut down to prepare for the software upgrade.

A Step-by-Step Approach to Rolling Upgrades

Here is the step-by-step process to perform a rolling ASM upgrade:

1. Put the ASM instance in rolling migration mode, and communicate the status to the rest of the ASM instances. If new ASM instances join the RAC cluster, it is informed that the ASM instances are in rolling-upgrade mode:

   ```
   SQL> alter system start rolling migration to 11.2.0.2;
   ```

2. Shut down the ASM instance.

3. Apply the software upgrade to the ASM home.

4. Restart the ASM instance.

5. Repeat steps 3 and 4 for the remaining ASM instances in the cluster.

■**Note** Prior to performing any upgrade to ASM, rolling or nonrolling upgrade, you should make sure there are no rebalance activities taking place. You can query the V$ASM_OPERATION view to confirm this prior to any upgrade process.

During the ASM upgrade mode, ASM functionality is reduced. Only certain operations are permissible during this mode:

- Mount diskgroup

- Unmount diskgroup

- Database file operations, such as file open, close, resize, delete

- ASM and database instance shutdown, startup, and recovery

- Limited access to fixed views and packages

These are the disallowed operations:

- Rebalance

- Add/drop/online/offline disk

When the last ASM instance is upgraded, you need to disable rolling migration to enable full functionality to the ASM instances and to signal to all the ASM instances the new version state:

```
SQL> alter system stop rolling migration;
```

This command validates that all the RAC ASM instances are in the same version. If any members of the RAC ASM instances are on a different version, an error message will generate, and it will stay in rolling-upgrade mode. If there is no error message, the RAC ASM cluster will successfully update to the new upgraded version and begin to function with all the new features.

ASM Preferred Reads

In normal or high redundancy, ASM creates and maintains two or more copies of the ASM extent: a primary mirrored extent and secondary/tertiary mirrored extent. In Oracle Database 10g, the ASM instance always reads the primary copy of the mirrored extent unless the primary cannot be accessed, and then the secondary will be read.

Oracle Database 11g introduces the ASM preferred mirror read, which provides the database with the ability to read from the secondary mirrored extent first before reading the primary mirrored extent. This feature provides the greatest benefit for extended stretched RAC cluster implementations. With stretched RAC clusters, diskgroups are configured with the local primary copy in the local data center and the failure diskgroups at the remote data center. The remote RAC instance is now able to read a local copy of the ASM extent, thus significantly reducing the amount of network latency to read from the remote data center and effectively increasing performance of the applications. If that localized read fails, then ASM will make an effort to read from the secondary mirrored extent from the remote failure group.

In Oracle Database 10g, the ASM instance always reads the primary copy of the mirrored extent, even if this means accessing the extent across the interconnect, in other words, remote extent access. If the interconnect latency is high, then any remote node access will impact database performance.

Preferred Read Setup

Oracle enables ASM preferred reads through the initialization parameter `asm_preferred_read_failure_groups`. This parameter specifies the preferred read mirror names and allows each ASM instance to read from the localized mirror copy. This parameter accepts values in pairs of `diskgroup_name.failure group name` delimited by a period. This parameter will guarantee localized reads for the ASM instance. You can provide multiple values to this parameter by putting commas between the values.

This parameter is dynamically adjustable and can be modified with the `alter system` command. Even though this parameter is dynamically adjustable, this parameter does not take effect until the diskgroup is remounted. The `alter system` command updates the SGA structure of a disk in RDBMS to reflect whether it is a preferred read disk.

For normal and high redundancy diskgroups, there should be one failure group on each site of the extended cluster. For normal redundancy diskgroups, there should be two sites. Likewise, for high redundancy diskgroups, the extended cluster configurations should be three sites. If there are more diskgroups in one site over another (in other words, four failure groups and three extended RAC clusters), extents will end up mirrored to the same site, thus eliminating the high-availability benefit of setting up high redundancy.

Here's the syntax to create a normal redundancy so you can see how it is applicable to the preferred mirror reads:

```
create diskgroup DATA normal redundancy
failgroup fg1 disk 'ORCL:CTCVOL1',
                   'ORCL:CTCVOL2',
                   'ORCL:CTCVOL3'
failgroup fg2 disk 'ORCL:LTCVOL1',
                   'ORCL:LTCVOL2',
                   'ORCL:LTCVOL3'
SQL> /
```

The fg1 failgroup is recognized as a localized read from RAC node #1 in SiteA, while it is recognized as a remote mirror read from RAC node #2 in SiteB. Likewise, fg2 failgroup is recognized as a localized mirror read from node #2 in SiteB and as a remote mirror read from RAC node #1 in SiteA. For the SiteA servers, the ASM instances should read from the SAN storage devices that are from the SiteA data center:

```
asm_preferred_read_failure_groups = data.fg1
```

Set the parameter for the database servers in SiteB to the following:

```
asm_preferred_read_failure_groups = data.fg2
```

You can also configure the preferred read failure groups using Enterprise Manager Database Console. This option is the Preferred Read Failure Groups field on the Configuration tab of the ASM home page, as shown in Figure 9-8. You can specify a list of failure groups delimited by commas whose member disks will serve as the preferred read disks for this node.

Logged in As SYS / SYSASM

Automatic Storage Management: +ASM1_rac11.dbaexpert.com

| Home | Performance | Disk Groups | **Configuration** | Users |

Configuration Parameters

Disk Discovery Path `ORCL:DATA*, ORCL:FRA*`   (Revert) (Apply)
This path limits the set of disks considered for discovery. It should match the path or the directory containing the disk. e.g. /dev/raw/* for Linux based operating systems.

Auto Mount Disk Groups `FRA, DATA`
The list of the Disk Group names to be mounted by the ASM at startup or when ALTER DISKGROUP ALL MOUNT command is used.

Rebalance Power `1`
Higher values allows the operation to complete more quickly but takes more I/O bandwidth away from the database. Lower values causes rebalance to take longer but leave more I/O bandwidth for the database.

Preferred Read Failure Groups
Specify a comma-separated list of failure groups whose member disks will be preferred read disks for this node. If there is more than one mirror copy to read from, ASM will read from the preferred disk.

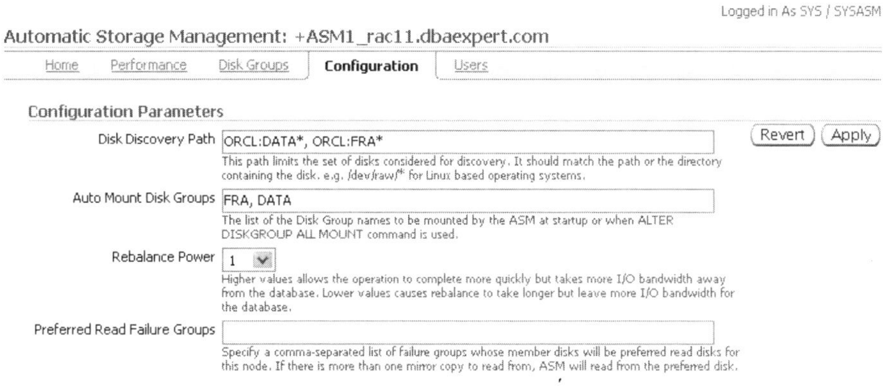

Figure 9-8. *ASM diskgroup preferred read*

Monitoring Preferred Reads

Oracle Database 11g adds the new column PREFERRED_READ to the V$ASM_DISK dynamic view. This column holds a Y or an N value to designate that the read is a localized and preferred read failure group. You can also view the performance characteristics of the ASM preferred read failure group by querying V$ASM_DISK_IOSTAT. The result of this view is to provide information at the ASM instance level:

```
SQL>  select instname, failgroup,
  2         read_time, write_time, bytes_read, bytes_written
  3* from v$asm_disk_iostat
SQL> /
```

INST NAME	FAIL GROUP	READ_ TIME	WRITE_ TIME	BYTES_ READ	BYTES_ WRITTEN
DBA11g1	DATA1	161904000	2641000	58054144	752128
DBA11g1	FRA1	1249000	2575000	1730560	3363840
DBA11g1	DATA2	188251000	3564000	61817344	3549696

ASM Restricted Mode

Oracle Database 11g ASM implements the restricted start-up option for maintenance mode. While in restricted mode, only the starting ASM instance has exclusive access to the diskgroups. When in restricted mode, databases will not be permitted to access the ASM instance. You can see that startup restrict; will mount all the diskgroups in restricted mode:

```
SQL> startup restrict;
ASM instance started

Total System Global Area   138158080 bytes
Fixed Size                 1296012 bytes
Variable Size              111696244 bytes
ASM Cache                  25165824 bytes
ASM diskgroups mounted

SQL> select name,state from v$asm_diskgroup;

NAME              STATE
----------------  -----------
DATA              RESTRICTED
FRA               RESTRICTED
```

When you try to start a database while the ASM instance is in restricted mode, you will receive the following error message:

```
SQL> startup
ORA-01078: failure in processing system parameters
ORA-01565: error in identifying file '+DATA/ICEMAN/spfileICEMAN.ora'
ORA-17503: ksfdopn:2 Failed to open file +DATA/ICEMAN/spfileICEMAN.ora
ORA-15056: additional error message
ORA-17503: ksfdopn:DGOpenFile05 Failed to open file +DATA/iceman/spfileiceman.ora
ORA-17503: ksfdopn:2 Failed to open file +DATA/iceman/spfileiceman.ora
ORA-15236: diskgroup DATA mounted in restricted mode
ORA-06512: at line 4
```

The restricted option can be specified at the diskgroup level to provide a granular level of restriction.

■**Note** In the world of RAC, the `restricted` start-up option at either the instance level or the diskgroup level will prohibit other ASM instances participating in the RAC cluster from having access to the diskgroups.

Let's look at how to enable restricted access at the diskgroup level:

```
SQL> alter diskgroup data mount restricted;

Diskgroup altered.

SQL> select name, state from v$asm_diskgroup;

NAME                STATE
------------------  --------------------
DATA                RESTRICTED
FRA                 MOUNTED
```

The restricted option can be used in RAC or non-RAC environments to perform a maintenance task such as a rebalance operation. In restricted mode, a rebalance mitigates ASM to ASM extent relocation messaging, making the rebalance operation much faster.

ASM Diskgroup Maintenance

Oracle Database 11*g* introduces the `force` option to the mount and drop diskgroup syntax. In Oracle Database 10*g*, to mount a diskgroup, DBAs would issue the following command:

```
SQL> alter diskgroup data mount;
```

In Oracle Database 11*g*, you can force the mount of the diskgroup even if not all the disks participating in the diskgroup are available:

```
SQL> alter diskgroup data mount force;
```

By default, the mount of the diskgroup is done with the `noforce` option. All disks must be available for the mount to succeed. With the `force` option, ASM simply offlines any disks that are missing and mounts the diskgroup with the available disks. This option can cause problems if used incorrectly. The issue could be something as simple as an incorrect `asm_diskstring` parameter. By using the `force` option to mount a diskgroup, you can cause more problems than not. The `force` option should be used cautiously. The `force` option can be leveraged with ASM redundancy diskgroups. ASM will force a mount of a diskgroup even with missing or damaged failure groups. In a RAC environment, only one RAC node may mount a diskgroup with the `force` option. Once a diskgroup is mounted, the remaining nodes will receive an alert when it tries to mount the diskgroup with the `force` option.

In the world of ASM, it is common practice to use the `dd` utility to clear out the header of disks. In Oracle Database 10*g*, in order to drop a diskgroup, it had to be mounted. If the diskgroup cannot be mounted, you can clear the disk(s) using the `dd` command.

■**Note** You can use the dd command to zero out the first 10MB of each of the raw partitions.

```
dd if=/dev/zero of=/dev/sdb1 bs=1M count=10
10+0 records in
10+0 records out
```

In Oracle Database 11g, ASM introduces the force option to the drop diskgroup command. The force option can be used if the target diskgroup cannot be mounted. The force option marks the headers of disks with a "FORMER" status.

In Oracle Database 11g, Oracle lifts the requirement that the diskgroup has to be mounted to drop the diskgroup. It is considered a best practice to mount the diskgroup to issue the drop diskgroup command. Only when the diskgroup cannot be mounted should you use the force option. You can use the following syntax to drop the diskgroup:

```
SQL> drop diskgroup data force;
```

When using the force option, you can include the including contents option:

```
SQL>  drop diskgroup data force including contents;
```

Similarly, you can perform a drop diskgroup operation using Enterprise Manager Database Console. From the Diskgroup main page, go to the ASM Instance Main page and then the Diskgroup tab, and you will see a Remove button. You can drop a particular diskgroup by selecting a diskgroup from the list and clicking the Remove button. On this screen, you have the option to drop with force or without force, as displayed in Figure 9-9.

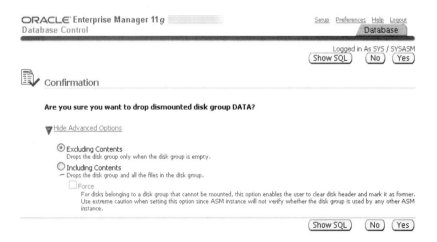

Figure 9-9. *ASM diskgroup drop*

You will also notice that there is a drop-down list for the rebalance operation. You can choose your power limit for the rebalance after the drop operation.

ASM performs some minor checks prior to dropping a diskgroup. First, ASM checks to see whether the diskgroup is being used by another ASM instance in the same SAN storage subsystem.

If so, ASM checks to see whether the ASM diskgroup is participating in the same cluster. If so, the command will return an error. Next, ASM will check to see whether the diskgroup is mounted by any other cluster. If so, the command will return an error. Please use extreme caution when dropping diskgroups with the `force` option. The effects are irreversible, and the damage can be severe. ASM does perform minor checks, but they are not definitive. After a successful drop force of a diskgroup, you can view the ASM alert logs for details:

```
SQL> alter diskgroup data dismount
NOTE: cache dismounting group 1/0x5E08702D (DATA)
NOTE: cache dismounted group 1/0x5E08702D (DATA)
NOTE: De-assigning number (1,0) from disk (ORCL:VOL1)
NOTE: De-assigning number (1,1) from disk (ORCL:VOL2)
SUCCESS: diskgroup DATA was dismounted
SQL> drop diskgroup data force including contents
NOTE: Assigning number (1,0) to disk (ORCL:VOL1)
NOTE: Assigning number (1,1) to disk (ORCL:VOL2)
Thu May 31 04:55:33 2007
NOTE: erasing header on grp 1 disk VOL1
NOTE: erasing header on grp 1 disk VOL2
NOTE: De-assigning number (1,0) from disk (ORCL:VOL1)
NOTE: De-assigning number (1,1) from disk (ORCL:VOL2)
SUCCESS: diskgroup DATA was force dropped
```

You can also perform ASM diskgroup `mount` and `dismount` operations using Enterprise Manager Database Console. The Diskgroup Mount/Dismount button is located on the Diskgroup main screen on the ASM Home ➤ Disk Groups tab. When you choose to mount a particular diskgroup by selecting a diskgroup from the list and clicking the Mount button, you will be directed to the Diskgroup Mount page, as shown in Figure 9-10.

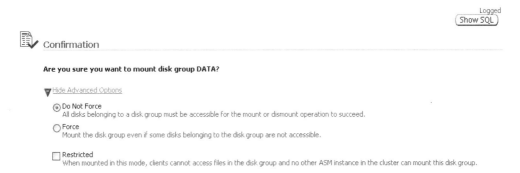

Figure 9-10. *ASM diskgroup mount*

You will also notice that you can check a box to mount the diskgroup in restricted mode. On the other hand, you may have to dismount a diskgroup. You can dismount a particular diskgroup by selecting a diskgroup from the list and clicking the Dismount button. On this screen, you have the option to dismount with force or without force, as displayed in Figure 9-11.

Figure 9-11. *ASM diskgroup dismount*

Diskgroup Checks

Starting in Oracle Database 11g, you can validate the internal consistency of ASM diskgroup metadata using the alter diskgroup ... check command. The check clause does the following:

- Checks the link between the alias metadata directory and the file directory

- Checks the alias directory tree links

- Checks the ASM metadata directories for unreachable allocated blocks

- Checks the consistency of the disk

- Checks the consistency of file extent maps and allocation tables

The alter diskgroup check command is applicable to a specific file in a diskgroup, one or more disks in a diskgroup, or specific failure groups in a diskgroup. This command also checks all the metadata directories. The following example checks the DATA diskgroup:

```
SQL> alter diskgroup data check;
```

A summary of errors is logged in the ASM alert log file. Here's an excerpt from the alert log file:

```
SQL> alter diskgroup data check
WARNING: Deprecated privilege SYSDBA for command 'ALTER DISKGROUP CHECK'
NOTE: starting check of diskgroup DATA
kfdp_checkDsk(): 9
kfdp_checkDsk(): 10
Tue Sep 11 03:17:59 2007
SUCCESS: check of diskgroup DATA found no errors
SUCCESS: alter diskgroup data check
```

The default behavior of the check clause is to repair the discovered errors. However, you can choose the norepair option if you do not want ASM to resolve the errors automatically. The good news is that you will still receive alerts about inconsistencies:

```
SQL> alter diskgroup data check norepair;
```

In the previous release, you had the following options to the check command: all, disk, disks in failgroup, and file. These options are now deprecated. If these options are specified, the commands will continue to work, but messages will be generated to the alert log.

You can also perform diskgroup checks using Enterprise Manager Database Console. The diskgroup Check button is located on the Diskgroup tab of the ASM Home page, as shown in Figure 9-12.

Automatic Storage Management: +ASM1_rac11.dbaexpert.com
Home
Performance
Disk Groups
Configuration
Users
Mount
Dismount
Rebalance
Check
Delete
Select All | Select None
Select
Name
State
Redundancy
Size (GB)
Used (GB)
Used (%)
DATA
MOUNTED
EXTERN
5.75
2.14
37.26
FRA
MOUNTED
EXTERN
1.92
0.52
26.98

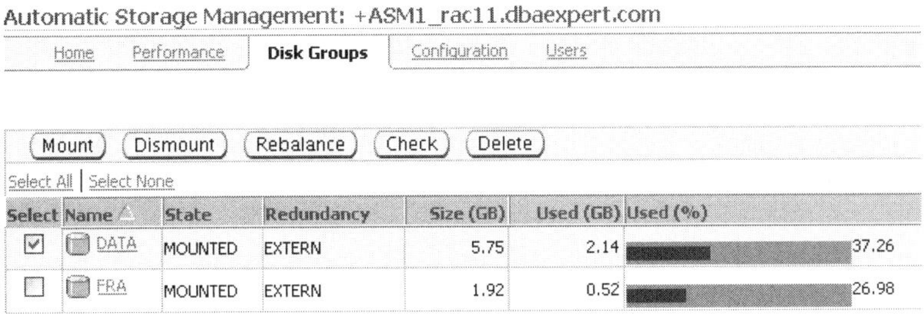

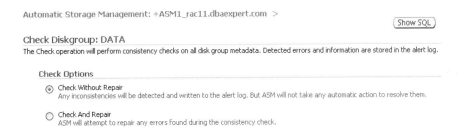

Figure 9-12. *ASM diskgroup Check button*

Clicking the Check button will direct you to the Check Diskgroup page. On this screen, you have the option to check the diskgroup with or without the repair option, as displayed in Figure 9-13.

Automatic Storage Management: +ASM1_rac11.dbaexpert.com >
Show SQL
Check Diskgroup: DATA
The Check operation will perform consistency checks on all disk group metadata. Detected errors and information are stored in the alert log.
Check Options
Check Without Repair
Any inconsistencies will be detected and written to the alert log. But ASM will not take any automatic action to resolve them.
Check And Repair
ASM will attempt to repair any errors found during the consistency check.

Figure 9-13. *ASM diskgroup check*

Diskgroup Attributes

Oracle Database 11*g* introduces a new concept called *ASM attributes.* Attributes provide a granular level of control for DBAs at the diskgroup level. Here are the attributes you can set:

- Allocation unit (AU) sizes. Starting in Oracle Database 11g, AU can be specified at diskgroup creation time. The AU can be 1, 2, 4, 8, 16, 32, or 64MB in size.
- The `compatible.rdbms` attribute.
- The `compatible.asm` attribute.
- `disk_repair_time` in units of minute (M) or hour (H).
- The `redundancy` attribute for a specific template.
- The `stripping` attribute for a specific template.

The attributes for the diskgroup can be established at `create diskgroup` time or can be modified using the `alter diskgroup` command later. All of the diskgroup attributes can be queried from the V$ASM_ATTRIBUTE view.

■**Note** For ASM to populate the contents of the V$ASM_ATTRIBUTE view, the diskgroup compatibility must be set to `11.1`.

Now we'll show how attributes can be set and modified for ASM diskgroups. First, we'll create a diskgroup with 10.1 diskgroup compatibility and then advance it to 11.1 using the `alter diskgroup` command. You can use the `compatible.asm` attribute to advance this attribute to 11.1:

```
create diskgroup data
disk  '/dev/raw/raw1',
      '/dev/raw/raw2',
      '/dev/raw/raw3'
attribute 'compatible.asm' = '10.1'
SQL> /
```

Alternatively, if you use ASMLIB, you can create the diskgroup using the ASMLIB disk names:

```
create diskgroup data
disk 'ORCL:VOL1',
     'ORCL:VOL2',
     'ORCL:VOL3'
attribute 'compatible.asm' = '10.1'
SQL> /
```

Now, we'll show the syntax to advance the diskgroup ASM attribute to 11.1. Please remember that once you advance an attribute to a higher version, you cannot reverse this action. Once you set any attributes to 11.1, you cannot go back to 10.x.

```
SQL>  alter diskgroup data set attribute 'compatible.asm' = '11.1.0.0.0';
```

You can also set ASM and RDBMS attributes for the diskgroup using Enterprise Manager Database Console. The Advanced Attributes section of the diskgroup is on the Diskgroup main screen on the ASM Home ➤ Disk Groups tab. Click the diskgroup, as shown in Figure 9-14.

Clicking the Edit button will direct you to the Advanced Attributes for Diskgroup page. On this screen, you have the option to set the diskgroup compatibility for ASM and RDBMS, as displayed in Figure 9-15.

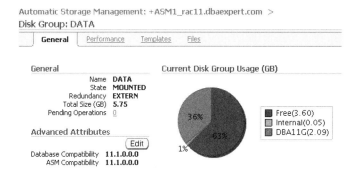

Figure 9-14. *ASM diskgroup attributes Edit button*

Automatic Storage Management: +ASM1_rac11.dbaexpert.com > Disk Group: DATA >
Edit Advanced Attributes for Disk Group: DATA

Disk Group Compatibility

Advancing the disk group compatibility enables the user to use new features available in the newer version. This operation can not be reversed.

Database Compatibility	`11.1.0.0.0`
	The minimum software version required for a database instance to use files in this disk group.
ASM Compatibility	`11.1.0.0.0`
	The minimum software version required for an ASM instance to mount this disk group.

⦿ **TIP** The database compatibility has to be less than or equal to the ASM compatibility.

Figure 9-15. *ASM diskgroup attributes*

On the successful advancement of the diskgroup to 11.1, the following message is listed in the ASM alert log file:

```
NOTE: Advancing ASM compatibility to 11.1.0.0.0 for grp 1
NOTE: initiating PST update: grp = 1
Wed May 30 19:48:02 2007
NOTE: Advancing compatible.asm on grp 1 disk VOL1
NOTE: Advancing compatible.asm on grp 1 disk VOL2
NOTE: PST update grp = 1 completed successfully
SUCCESS: Advanced compatible.asm to 11.1.0.0.0 for grp 1
```

Let's query the V$ASM_ATTRIBUTE view to confirm that the compatible is truly set:

```
  select name, value
  from v$asm_attribute
  where group_number=1
SQL> /
```

```
NAME                    VALUE
--------------------    --------------------
disk_repair_time        5H
au_size                 1048576
compatible.asm          11.1.0.0.0
compatible.rdbms        10.1.0.0.0
```

Using the DATA diskgroup we created earlier, let's change the compatible.rdbms attribute to 11.1:

```
SQL>  alter diskgroup data set attribute 'compatible.rdbms' = '11.1';
```

By querying V$ASM_ATTRIBUTE, you can see that the compatibility for the RDBMS is set:

```
select name, value
from v$asm_attribute
where group_number=1
SQL>  /
```

```
NAME                    VALUE
--------------------    --------------------
disk_repair_time        5H
au_size                 1048576
compatible.asm          11.1.0.0.0
compatible.rdbms        11.1.0.0.0
```

You can specify a combination of attributes at diskgroup creation time. We'll show another example where the au_size and compatible.asm attributes are specified in a single create diskgroup command:

```
create diskgroup fra disk '/dev/raw/raw11',
                          '/dev/raw/raw12',
                          '/dev/raw/raw13'
attribute 'au_size' = '16M', 'compatible.asm' = '11.1'
SQL>  /
```

Again, you can create this same FRA diskgroup with the ASMLIB syntax:

```
 create diskgroup fra disk 'ORCL:VOL3',
                           'ORCL:VOL4',
                           'ORCL:VOL5'
  attribute 'au_size' = '16M', 'compatible.asm' = '11.1'
SQL>  /
```

■**Note** ASM best practices recommend only two diskgroups. The general philosophy is that two diskgroups, DATA and FRA (for the flash recovery area), will suit the majority of the technical requirements of most companies. There are site-specific considerations that may need to be considered. For example, if your company utilizes a combination of RAID 1+0 and RAID 5 on the same server, you must create separate diskgroups since you do not want to mix multiple RAID levels in a single diskgroup. In this case, this particular company had terabytes of ASM storage on RAID 5 for BLOBs and RAID 1+0 for relational OLTP data.

Additionally, if you have differently sized disks, you have another candidate for additional diskgroups. Another good case for a separate diskgroup is when the disk attributes and speed are different from others.

Allocation Unit (AU) Sizes

Prior to Oracle Database 11*g*, the AU size could not be specified at diskgroup creation time. All AUs were 1MB. There is a workaround, but not very many DBAs are aware that you can have multiple au_sizes in Oracle Database 10*g*. Specifying au_size in Oracle Database 10*g* means setting an underscore initialization parameter and creating the diskgroup. If you want multiple AU sizes, you must set the initialization parameter and bounce the ASM instance with the new AU size. The following underscore initialization parameters allow a 16MB AU size and 1MB AU stripe size. This is recommended only for VLDB databases or may be suitable for databases that have large objects (BLOBs and CLOBs).

- _asm_ausize=16777216

- _asm_stripesize=1048576

In Oracle Database 11*g*, the au_size attribute can be specified only at diskgroup creation time. Because it involves storage characteristics, this attribute cannot be modified using the alter diskgroup command.

Starting in Oracle Database 11*g*, you can set the ASM allocation unit (AU) size from 1MB all the way to 64MB in powers of 2. As of Oracle Database 11*g*, the valid extent sizes are 1, 2, 4, 8, 16, 32, or 64MB. The larger AUs can be beneficial for large VLDB databases or data warehouses that perform large sequential reads. In addition, organizations that store BLOB or SecureFiles inside the database can benefit from larger AUs.

Variable-Size Extents

Variable-size extents provide support for larger ASM files. Moreover, this feature reduces the SGA requirements to manage the extent maps in the RDBMS instance. Setting the AU to a higher number also reduces the metadata space usage since it reduces the number of extent pointers associated with the metadata. Moreover, variable-size extents can significantly improve database open time and reduce memory utilization in the shared pool. Variable-size extents allow you to support databases that are hundreds of TB and even several PB in size.

Variable-size extents dynamically change extent size depending on how many AUs have been allocated. The management of variable-size extents is automatic and does not require manual intervention. The ASM variable extent feature will kick in and start allocating 8× AU extent sizes after 20,000 extents have been allocated. Variable-size extents are similar to the uniform extent allocation in the database and are allocated in 1, 8, and 64 AU chunks. This is automatically handled by ASM. Variable-size extents minimize the overhead associated with maintaining ASM metadata. After 40,000 extents, the extents are allocated at 64× AU size. The largest size extent supported in Oracle Database 11*g* will be 64MB.

ASM files larger than 20GB and up to 128TB are great candidates for variable-size extents.

■**Note** Even though the maximum database size file is 128TB, Oracle Database 11*g* ASM files can be up to 140PB for external redundancy. For normal and high redundancy, ASM supports up to 42PB and 15PB files, respectively. In Oracle Database 10*g*, the maximum file size for external redundancy was 35TB.

We'll now take the default 1MB allocation unit and provide an example of how this works. When the file hits 20GB (20,000 extents), the extent size will change from 1MB to 8MB since 8MB is 8 times the AU. At this point, AU will grab 8MB chunks until it reaches 40,000 extents; 20,000 additional extents at 8MB will be 160,000GB. When the file reaches the 180GB threshold (160GB + 20GB), the AU will change to 64MB.

There is a rare incident where large amounts of noncontiguous small data extents are allocated and freed and can cause situations when large contiguous space becomes unavailable. This causes fragmentation to occur in the diskgroup. The remedy is simple—rebalance the diskgroup to reclaim large contiguous space. If you do not perform a rebalance, it can cause a slight degradation in performance since ASM automatically performs defragmentation if extent allocation cannot sequester the storage.

Manually Allocate Larger Extents

Starting with Oracle Database 11*g*, you can allocate larger size extents when you create a diskgroup. Instead of the 1MB-sized extent, you can create diskgroups with larger AU. You can change the allocation unit size to 16MB for the DATA diskgroup using the create diskgroup command and setting the appropriate attributes for the diskgroup, as displayed here:

```
SQL> create diskgroup data
     disk 'ORCL:DISK1',
          'ORCL:DISK2'
     attribute 'au_size' = '16M',
               'compatible.asm' = '11.1'
               'compatible.rdbms' = '11.1';
```

RDBMS and ASM Compatibility

Two kinds of compatibility settings are relative to ASM and the database. When DBAs think about compatibility, they think about the initialization parameter in the init.ora file or spfile that dictates which version of functionality will be available to the ASM or database instance.

The `compatible` parameter is one of the two kinds of compatibility settings. The `compatible` parameter can be set for either ASM or the database instance. Here are the valid `compatible` values for both the ASM and database instance:

- `10.1`

- `10.2`

- `11.1`

Obviously, 10.1 is the lowest level of compatibility since ASM was introduced as a feature in 10.1. Setting the initialization parameter to a lesser value than the software release will exclude availability of the new features introduced in the new release. For example, if the `compatible` parameter is set to `10.2` for an 11.1 ASM instance, the new Oracle Database 11g features will not be available such as `drop diskgroup` with the `force` option as mentioned earlier. Similarly, the `compatible` parameter for the database plays a key role in negotiating what features are supported.

The other compatibility setting applies to ASM diskgroups and the functionality provided at the diskgroup level. There are attribute settings at the diskgroup level that control what features are available to the ASM diskgroup and which capabilities are available at the database level. These attributes are called *ASM compatibility* (`compatible.asm`) and *RDBMS compatibility* (`compatible.rdbms`). At each diskgroup level, you can adjust these two compatibility settings to meet the business or technology requirements. The diskgroup compatibility information is stored in the diskgroup metadata and provides the multiple-level support of different versions (10g, 10g Release 2, and 11g) of the databases.

RDBMS Compatibility

The terms *RDBMS compatibility* and *ASM compatibility* refer exclusively to diskgroup-level compatibility. RDBMS compatibility is classified by the `compatible.rdbms` attribute. Surprisingly, the `compatible.rdbms` attribute defaults to `10.1` in Oracle Database 11g. This attribute dictates the minimum `compatible` version setting of a database that is allowed to mount the diskgroup, and controls the format of the messages exchanged between the ASM and RDBMS instances.

■**Note** Similar to the `compatible` initialization parameter, if the `rdbms.compatible` diskgroup attribute is set to `11.1`, it cannot be reversed.

ASM Compatibility

ASM diskgroup compatibility is defined by the `compatible.asm` attribute and controls the persistent format of the disk ASM metadata structures. Similar to the `compatible.rdbms` attribute, ASM defaults the `compatible.asm` attribute to `10.1`. The general rule to remember is that the `compatible.asm` attribute must always be greater than or equal to the RDBMS compatibility level.

■**Note** Similar to the `compatible` initialization parameter, if the compatibility is set to `11.1`, it cannot be reversed to a lower version.

An ASM best practice informs the Oracle community to have two diskgroups: DATA and FRA. With multiple versions of ASM and RDBMS compatibility, it may make sense to create additional diskgroups during the upgrade process since the `compatible.rdbms` and `compatible.asm` attributes are set independently at the diskgroup level. This way, DBAs are able to support 10.1, 10.2, and 11.1 diskgroups. In addition, creating additional diskgroups for different `compatible.rdbms` levels can be useful if your server supports multiple versions of the database. In a RAC world, you will generally not see multiple versions of the database on a cluster; however, in a non-RAC ASM implementation, it will be common to see multiple versions of the database running on a single server.

The `compatible` attributes can be either in short form or in long form for the version number. The range of values for `compatible.rdbms` or `compatible.asm` can be from one version all the way to five versions: 11.1 to 11.1.0.0.0. For example, the `compatible` attribute can specified as `11.1` or `11.1.0.0`. Similarly, for Oracle Database 10*g* environments, it can be set to `10.1` or `10.1.0.0.0`. The combination of `compatible.asm` and `compatible.rdbms` attributes control the persistent format of the disk ASM metadata structures. These attributes influence whether a database instance can mount a diskgroup. Three things determine whether a database instance is allowed to mount a diskgroup:

- The `compatible` initialization setting of the database

- The `compatible.rdbms` attribute of the diskgroup

- The software version of the database

Even though you upgrade an ASM instance to Oracle Database 11*g*, the `compatible.asm` and `compatible.rdbms` attributes for the diskgroups still remain at 10.1, which is the default and the lowest attribute level for ASM. You can see here that the ASM compatibility and RDBMS compatibility are still at 10.1 for the FRA diskgroup:

```
select name, block_size,
allocation_unit_size au_size, state,
compatibility asm_comp,
database_compatibility db_comp
from v$asm_diskgroup
SQL> /
NAME    BLOCK_   AU        STATE       ASM_COMP     DB_COMP
        SIZE     SIZE

-----   -------  --------- ----------  -----------  ----------
DATA    4096     1048576   CONNECTED   11.1.0.0.0   11.1.0.0.0
FRA     4096     1048576   CONNECTED   10.1.0.0.0   10.1.0.0.0
```

ASM instances can support multiple databases on different versions. Each of the databases can have a different compatibility setting. The key point to remember is that the `compatible` initialization parameter must be greater than or equal to the RDBMS compatibility of all disk-groups used by the database.

As stated earlier, ASM compatibility of a diskgroup can be set to 11.0, while its RDBMS compatibility could be 10.1. This implies that the diskgroup can be managed only by ASM software version 11.0 or higher, while any database software version must be 10.1 or higher. To determine the software version and compatibility setting of the database, you can query the V$ASM_CLIENT view, as displayed here:

```
select db_name,
status,software_version,compatible_version
from v$asm_client
SQL> /
```

```
DB_NAME      STATUS         SOFTWARE_      COMPATIBLE_
                           VERSION        VERSION
----------   ------------   -------------  ------------
DBA11g1      CONNECTED      11.1.0.6.0     11.1.0.0.0
DBA11g1      CONNECTED      11.1.0.6.0     11.1.0.0.0
```

Fast Mirror Resync

In Oracle Database 10*g*, ASM offlines a disk when it is not able to write an extent or access the disk and is not needed anymore, shortly after the disk is dropped from the diskgroup. At this point, ASM will perform a rebalance on the extents of the surviving disk members in the diskgroup using the mirror extent copies. This rebalance operation is extremely costly and can take hours. Even for nondisk problems such as bad cables or problems with HBA or controllers, disks may get dropped from the diskgroup, and rebalance activity may occur. ASM is ignorant of what is causing the issue. ASM just knows that it is not able to complete a write operation.

In Oracle Database 11*g*, Oracle assumes the content of a dropped disk is not damaged or modified and preserves its membership in the diskgroup. Oracle introduces a new feature called *ASM fast disk resync* and does not automatically drop a disk from the diskgroup for a write failure. When a disk goes offline, Oracle now tracks all modified extents for a specified duration and keeps the disk membership in the diskgroup intact.

■**Note** The tracking mechanism is similar to a bitmap index. It allocates 1 bit for each modified allocation unit in the disk's metadata, thus providing an efficient and scalable architecture.

Once the disk is repaired or the temporary problem is resolved (that is, cable issue, controller, HBA, and so on), ASM can resynchronize the tracked extents that were modified during outage. In Oracle Database 11*g*, the time to recover from a perceived disk failure is directly relative to how many extents have changed during the outage. ASM can quickly resynchronize the changed extents on the failed disk with its surviving disks. The potential increase in performance for the fast disk resync feature is proportional to the number of changed allocation units. Resync activities that take hours in Oracle Database 10*g* can perceivably be down to minutes in Oracle Database 11*g*.

Disk Repair Time

We'll now talk about how the disk repair timer works. In Oracle Database 11g, the fast mirror resync feature is implemented using a grace period allotted to repair an offline disk. There is a new diskgroup attribute called `disk_repair_time` that allows you to specify the maximum amount of time before dropping a failed disk from the diskgroup. The purpose of `disk_repair_time` is to prevent dropping the disk from the diskgroup since a resynchronization operation is significantly less expensive than a rebalance operation. The default value of `disk_repair_time` is 3.6 hours, or 12,960 seconds.

■**Note** Note that 3.6 hours for `disk_repair_time` should be adequate for most companies.

The maximum allowable value for this attribute is 136 years. To take advantage of the fast disk resync feature, the compatibility attribute of the ASM diskgroup must be set to 11.1.0.0 or higher. The V$ASM_ATTRIBUTE view provides information about the compatibility level of the diskgroups:

```
SQL>  select name,compatibility
  2* from v$asm_diskgroup
SQL> /

NAME          COMPATIBILITY
----------    -----------------------
DATA          10.1.0.0.0
FRA           10.1.0.0.0
```

By default, the compatibility for diskgroup is set to 10.1. You need to advance this to 11.1 to take advantage of `disk_repair_time`. You cannot set the `disk_repair_time` attribute with the `create diskgroup` syntax. It can be set only with the `alter diskgroup` command. In this example, we'll show how to advance the `compatible.asm` and `compatible.rdbms` attributes for the DATA diskgroup to 11.1 to take advantage of the repair timer:

```
SQL> alter diskgroup data set attribute 'compatible.asm' = '11.1';

Diskgroup altered.
SQL> alter diskgroup data set attribute 'compatible.rdbms'='11.1';

Diskgroup altered.
```

Now you can query the V$ASM_ATTRIBUTE view to confirm the settings:

```
SQL> select name, value from v$asm_attribute;
```

```
NAME                        VALUE
-------------------         --------------------
disk_repair_time            3.6h
au_size                     1048576
compatible.asm              11.1.0.0.0
compatible.rdbms            11.1
```

If you need to increase the duration of the disk_repair_time to five hours, you can change it with the following command:

```
SQL> alter diskgroup data set  attribute 'disk_repair_time' = '5H';
```

You can specify this disk_repair_time unit in minutes (M or m) or hours (H or h). If not specified, the default is hours. As you can see here, you can also set the disk_repair_time at the minute granularity:

```
SQL> alter diskgroup data set  attribute 'disk_repair_time' = '40M';
```

You can query the REPAIR_TIMER column to see the remaining time left in seconds before ASM drops an offline disk in the V$ASM_DISK or V$ASM_DISK_IOSTAT view. In addition, the disk resynchronization operation appears as a "SYNC" value in the OPERATION column of the V$ASM_OPERATION view.

Oracle's background process, Diskgroup Monitor (GMON), wakes up every three minutes and checks all mounted diskgroups for offline disks. GMON will notify a slave process to increment their timer values (by three minutes) and initiate a drop for the offline disks with the timer values exceeding their deadlines if it detects an offline disk. This is shown in the REPAIR_TIMER column of V$ASM_DISK.

Online and Offline Disks

Associated with this grace period attribute of the diskgroup, Oracle Database 11g ASM also provides the online option to the alter diskgroup disk command to initiate a disk resynchronization operation. This statement will copy all the extents that are marked as stale using the redundant copies:

```
SQL> alter diskgroup disk data_0001 online;
```

Similar to onlining a disk, you can offline a disk with the alter disk group disk offline SQL command for preventive maintenance:

```
SQL> alter diskgroup data offline disk data_0000 drop after 20 m;
```

You can accomplish this same onlining and offlining of diskgroups using the Enterprise Manager Database Console. From the Diskgroup main page for the specific diskgroup, you will notice the Online and Offline buttons, as displayed in Figure 9-16.

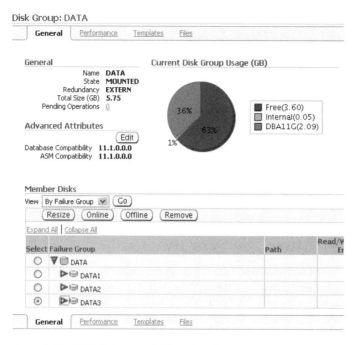

Figure 9-16. *ASM diskgroup Offline disk button*

You can pick the disk in question and click the Offline button. This will direct you to the Disk Offline Confirmation page. You can choose the appropriate disk repair time and offline-specified disk. Figure 9-17 shows this example.

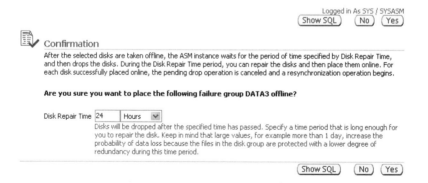

Figure 9-17. *ASM diskgroup offline disk*

ASM will update the MOUNT_STATUS and MODE_STATUS columns as MISSING and OFFLINE states. Also, the REPAIR_TIMER column will start counting down to drop the disk from the diskgroup. The following example will query the V$ASM_DISK view to check the status of the disk and to look at the REPAIR_TIMER column to see the remaining time:

```
select name, header_status,
mount_status, mode_status, state, repair_timer
from v$asm_disk
where group_number=1
SQL> /
NAME        HEADER_    MOUNT_     MODE_      STATE   REPAIR_
            STAUS      STATUS     STATUS             TIMER
---------   ---------  -------    --------   ------  -------
DATA_0003   MEMBER     CACHED     ONLINE     NORMAL        0
DATA_0002   MEMBER     CACHED     ONLINE     NORMAL        0
DATA_0001   MEMBER     CACHED     ONLINE     NORMAL        0
DATA_0000   UNKNOWN    MISSING    OFFLINE    NORMAL      840
```

Assuming the disk did not drop from the diskgroup, you can online the disk using `alter disk group disk online` once the maintenance is complete.

The following is an excerpt from the ASM `alert.log` file during the offline and online of the disk:

```
SUCCESS: Advanced compatible.asm to 11.1.0.0.0 for grp 1
SQL> ALTER DISKGROUP data OFFLINE DISK VOL1
NOTE: DRTimer CodCreate:  of disk group 1 disks
 0
WARNING: initiating offline of disk 0.3951611545 (VOL1) with mask 0x7e
NOTE: initiating PST update: grp = 1, dsk = 0, mode = 0x15
NOTE: group DATA: updated PST location: disk 0001 (PST copy 0)
NOTE: PST update grp = 1 completed successfully
NOTE: initiating PST update: grp = 1, dsk = 0, mode = 0x1
NOTE: group DATA: updated PST location: disk 0001 (PST copy 0)
NOTE: PST update grp = 1 completed successfully
Thu May 31 07:47:19 2007
NOTE: cache closing disk 0 of grp 1: VOL1
Thu May 31 07:47:31 2007
SQL>  ALTER DISKGROUP data ONLINE DISK VOL1
Thu May 31 07:47:31 2007
NOTE: initiating online of disk group 1 disks
 0
WARNING: initiating offline of disk 0.3951611545 (VOL1) with mask 0x7e
NOTE: initiating PST update: grp = 1, dsk = 0, mode = 0x1
NOTE: PST update grp = 1 completed successfully
NOTE: initiating PST update: grp = 1, dsk = 0, mode = 0x1
NOTE: PST update grp = 1 completed successfully
Thu May 31 07:47:31 2007
NOTE: cache closing disk 0 of grp 1: VOL1
NOTE: F1X0 copy 1 relocating from 0:2 to 0:4294967294
NOTE: F1X0 copy 2 relocating from 1:2 to 1:2
NOTE: F1X0 copy 3 relocating from 65534:4294967294 to 65534:4294967294
NOTE: initiating PST update: grp = 1, dsk = 0, mode = 0x19
Thu May 31 07:47:31 2007
```

```
NOTE: group DATA: updated PST location: disk 0001 (PST copy 0)
NOTE: PST update grp = 1 completed successfully
NOTE: requesting all-instance disk validation for group=1
Thu May 31 07:47:31 2007
NOTE: disk validation pending for group 1/0xeac83e65 (DATA)
WARNING: ignoring disk  in deep discovery
NOTE: cache opening disk 0 of grp 1: VOL1 label:VOL1
SUCCESS: validated disks for 1/0xeac83e65 (DATA)
NOTE: initiating PST update: grp = 1, dsk = 0, mode = 0x5d
NOTE: group DATA: updated PST location: disk 0001 (PST copy 0)
NOTE: group DATA: updated PST location: disk 0000 (PST copy 1)
NOTE: PST update grp = 1 completed successfully
NOTE: initiating PST update: grp = 1, dsk = 0, mode = 0x7d
NOTE: PST update grp = 1 completed successfully
NOTE: F1X0 copy 1 relocating from 0:4294967294 to 0:2
NOTE: F1X0 copy 2 relocating from 1:2 to 1:2
NOTE: F1X0 copy 3 relocating from 65534:4294967294 to 65534:4294967294
NOTE: initiating PST update: grp = 1, dsk = 0, mode = 0x7f
NOTE: PST update grp = 1 completed successfully
NOTE: completed online of disk group 1 disks
```

Once the disk issue is resolved, you can bring the disk back online using the online option to the alter diskgroup command:

```
SQL> alter diskgroup data online disk data_0000;
```

■**Note** You can also issue the alter diskgroup data online all command.

You should see now see that REPAIR_TIMER is set back to 0 and all the status of the disks are back to ONLINE. You can query the V$ASM_DISK view to confirm that the disk is ONLINE, as displayed here:

```
select name, header_status, mount_status,
mode_status, state, repair_timer
from v$asm_disk
where group_number=1
SQL> /
```

NAME	HEADER_ STAUS	MOUNT_ STATUS	MODE_ STATUS	STATE	REPAIR_ TIMER
---------	--------	-------	-------	--------	-------
DATA_0003	MEMBER	CACHED	ONLINE	NORMAL	0
DATA_0002	MEMBER	CACHED	ONLINE	NORMAL	0
DATA_0001	MEMBER	CACHED	ONLINE	NORMAL	0
DATA_0000	MEMBER	CACHED	ONLINE	NORMAL	0

SAN administrators and SAs may receive alerts from the SAN monitoring tools that a particular disk may go bad soon. For such situations, disks will have to be replaced and measures will need to take place so that it does not become an outage.

asmcmd Commands

Released as an ASM feature in Oracle Database 10*g* Release 2, asmcmd is a command-line utility to access and manage files associated with the ASM diskgroups. The asmcmd utility has a myriad of enhancements in Oracle Database 11*g*. asmcmd provides backward compatibility with Oracle Database 10*g* ASM instances. You can use the Oracle Database 11*g* asmcmd utility to manage your Oracle Database 10*g* ASM environments. Oracle will support copying of the asmcmd executable from the Oracle Database 11*g* software binary directory to an Oracle Database 10*g* Release 2 software binary directory. The asmcmd utility will allow various 11.1 functionality to be leveraged against a 10.*x* Oracle release.

There are numerous improvements and additional options to the existing commands to asmcmd. The key commands set that will be discussed are as follows:

- ls
- lsdg
- lsct
- lsdsk
- cp

ls

The ls command now incorporates the -c and the -g options. The -c option displays information from the V$ASM_DISKGROUP view or from the GV$ASM_DISKGROUP view if the -g flag is also provided. The -g option displays information from the GV$ASM_DISKGROUP_STAT or GV$ASM_DISKGROUP view if the -c flag is also provided. The -g flag queries the GV$ASM_DISKGROUP view and reports the instance ID (INST_ID) in the output. Here's a sample output from the -gc option:

```
ASMCMD> ls -gc
Inst_ID  Name
      1  DATA/
      1  FRA/
```

lsdg

The lsdg command lists all diskgroups and their attributes from V$ASM_DISKGROUP. The syntax for the lsdg command is as follows:

```
lsdg [-cgH] [group]
```

In Oracle Database 11*g*, two new options are provided—the -g and -c flags to the lsdg command. The -g flag queries the GV$ASM_DISKGROUP view and reports the instance ID

(INST_ID) in the output. If used with the -c flag, the GV$ASM_DISKGROUP_STAT view will be queried.

lsct

The lsct command lists all clients and their attributes from V$ASM_CLIENT:

```
ASMCMD [+] > lsct
DB_Name      Status      Software_   Compatible_   Instance_
                         Version     Version       Name
DBATOOLS     CONNECTED   11.1.0.4.0  11.1.0.0.0    DBATOOLS
DBATOOLS     CONNECTED   11.1.0.4.0  11.1.0.0.0    DBATOOLS
```

In Oracle Database 11g, the -g option is provided. This option queries the GV$ASM_CLIENT view and includes INST_ID in the report.

lsdsk

The lsdsk command is new to Oracle Database 11g. This command lists ASM-visible disks. Valid options for lsdsk are as follows:

```
lsdsk [-ksptcgHI] [-d <diskgroup_name>] [pattern]
```

The pattern keyword restricts the output to only disks that match the pattern. Wildcard characters and slashes (/ or \) can be part of the pattern. In connected mode, asmcmd uses the V$ and GV$ tables to retrieve disk information. In nonconnected mode, asmcmd scans disk headers to retrieve disk information using an ASM disk string to restrict the discovery set. The connected mode is always attempted first. Table 9-1 lists flags for lsdsk that are worth mentioning.

Table 9-1. *Important* lsdsk *Flags*

Flag	Description
-d	Displays disks that belong only to the specified diskgroup.
-K	Reads the following V$ and GV$ views to return relevant disk information: V$ASM_DISK.TOTAL_MB, V$ASM_DISK.FREE_MB, V$ASM_DISK.OS_MB, V$ASM_DISK.NAME, V$ASM_DISK.FAILGROUP, V$ASM_DISK.LIBRARY, V$ASM_DISK.LABEL, V$ASM_DISK.UDID, V$ASM_DISK.PRODUCT, V$ASM_DISK.REDUNDANCY, V$ASM_DISK.PATH
-S	Reads the following V$ and GV$ views to return relevant disk information: V$ASM_DISK.READS, V$ASM_DISK.WRITES, V$ASM_DISK.READ_ERRS, V$ASM_DISK.WRITE_ERRS, V$ASM_DISK.READ_TIME, V$ASM_DISK.WRITE_TIME, V$ASM_DISK.BYTES_READ, V$ASM_DISK.BYTES_WRITTEN, V$ASM_DISK.PATH
-T	Reads the following V$ and GV$ views to return relevant disk information about CREATION_DATE, MOUNT_DATE, REPAIR_TIMER, and PATH: V$ASM_DISK.CREATE_DATE, V$ASM_DISK.MOUNT_DATE, V$ASM_DISK.REPAIR_TIMER, V$ASM_DISK.PATH

Table 9-1. *Important* lsdsk *Flags*

Flag	Description
-g	Selects from GV$ASM_DISK or GV$ASM_DISK_STAT if the -c flag is also specified; GV$ASM_DISK.INST_ID will be included in the output.
-c	Selects from V$ASM_DISK_STAT, or GV$ASM_DISK_STAT if the -g flag is also specified.
-H	Suppresses the column header from the output.

Let's look at some examples of the lsdsk command with the new parameters. The -k option reports the total size and amount of free space information in megabytes at the disk level. It also provides failgroup, disk label, and redundancy information, as shown here:

```
ASMCMD> lsdsk -k -d DATA
Total_MB  Free_MB  OS_MB  Name  Failgroup  Library
          Label  UDID  Product  Redund  Path
   1961     1909   1961  VOL1  VOL1       ASM Library - Generic Linux, version
                                             2.0.2 (KABI_V2)
          VOL1                   UNKNOWN  ORCL:VOL1
   1961     1909   1961  VOL2  VOL2       ASM Library - Generic Linux, version
                                             2.0.2 (KABI_V2)
          VOL2                   UNKNOWN  ORCL:VOL2
```

Another parameter worth mentioning is the -s option. The -s option provides information about disk performance metrics including read and write times. This option also reports errors encountered at each disk level. You can use the -s option to gather performance characteristics of each disk. You can review the following read and write times and confirm IO distribution across all the disks in the diskgroup.

```
ASMCMD [+] > lsdsk -s -d DATA
Reads  Write  Read_Errs  Write_Errs  Read_time  Write_Time  Bytes_Read
Bytes_Written  Path
 1023   1306         0           0      2.491      1.166     4194304

          ORCL:VOL1
 1011   1306         0           0      2.809      3.387     4141056

          ORCL:VOL2
```

The -t option provides information about when the disks were created and mounted. It also provides the remaining duration for the disk repair time. You can leverage the -d option to specify just the DATA diskgroup in conjunction with the -t option to show creation and mount times, as displayed here:

```
ASMCMD> lsdsk -t -d DATA
Create_Date  Mount_Date  Repair_Timer  Path
30-MAY-07    30-MAY-07              0   ORCL:VOL1
30-MAY-07    30-MAY-07              0   ORCL:VOL2
```

cp

Anybody who has been supporting ASM on a day-to-day basis will admit that the copy command (cp) is the most anticipated ASM enhancement. Now, DBAs can copy ASM-supported files using the standard cp command from the asmcmd utility. The asmcmd cp command can be used to copy files in these situations:

- From local diskgroup to another local diskgroup

- From diskgroup to OS

- From OS to diskgroup

- From local diskgroup to a remote diskgroup

In addition, the asmcmd cp command can be used to copy all ASM-supported files such as Data Pump dump files, spfiles, block change tracking files, controlfiles, Data Guard Broker configuration files, and so on. The cp command has the following options:

```
cp [-ifr] <[\@connect_identifier:]src> <[\@connect_identifier:]tgt>
```

The three flags, -ifr, are similar to the flags from the Unix cp, rcp, and scp commands (interactive, force, and recursive copy). The interactive option prompts prior to a file overwrite. The force option will remove an existing file and perform a copy.

We'll now show some examples of using the copy command to copy files in and out of ASM. Let's start by copying a Data Pump dump file from the OS into the ASM DATA diskgroup:

```
ASMCMD [+] > cp /home/oracle/encrypted.dmp +data
source /home/oracle/encrypted.dmp
target +data/encrypted.dmp
copying file(s)...
file, +DATA/encrypted.dmp, copy committed.
ASMCMD [+] > cd +data
ASMCMD [+data] > ls -ltr
Type      Redund  Striped  Time            Sys  Name
                                           Y    ASMTESTING/
                                           Y    DBA10G/
                                           Y    DBA11G/
                                           N    encrypted.dmp =>
               +DATA/ASMTESTING/DUMPSET/TESTING.296.632600587
```

Only ASM-supported files are allowed to be copied into ASM. If you attempt to copy in a non-ASM file such as a text file, an error message will be generated.

Now let's copy an Oracle datafile from one ASM instance to another ASM instance. In Oracle Database 11g, an active database is no longer required to transfer files between one ASM instance diskgroup to another. We will copy one of the docs_d1 datafiles from the ASM instance on rac103 to another ASM instance on rac1. A database named DBA11g1 is running on the remote database server. In this example, we will rename the datafile from +DATA/DBA11g/DATAFILE/DOCS_D1.289.631914611 to xxx on the process:

```
ASMCMD [+DATA/DBA11g/DATAFILE] > cp
               +DATA/DBA11g/DATAFILE/DOCS_D1.289.631914611
```

```
                          sys@rac1.+ASM:+DATA/DBA11g1/datafile/xxx
Enter password: *********
source +DATA/DBA11g/DATAFILE/DOCS_D1.289.631914611
target +DATA/DBA11g1/datafile/xxx
copying file(s)...
file, +DATA/dba11g1/datafile/xxx, copy committed.
```

The syntax for the remote ASM diskgroup copy is as follows:

```
cp [srcfile] username@<hostname>.<SID>.<port>:<path>
```

The username can be any username in the ASM instance that has the sysasm privilege. Notice the dot (.) notation between the hostname and the ASM instance. The port assignment is optional if the LISTENER is not listening on port 1521. The last delimiter is a colon (:) followed by the fully qualified directory or file name. Note that the target ASM instance must be registered with the LISTENER for the remote copy between ASM diskgroups to work.

You can verify on the remote ASM instance that the copied file exists:

```
ASMCMD> pwd
+DATA/DBA11G1/DATAFILE
ASMCMD> ls -l xxx
Type      Redund  Striped  Time            Sys  Name
                  N     xxx => +DATA/ASMTESTING/DATAFILE/TESTING.278.632611175
```

You will also notice that the xxx file is created as an alias, and the actual file resides in the +DATA/ASMTESTING/DATAFILE directory. Because we specified the fully qualified file name, OMF will create an alias.

Another important point to note is that the -f option does not work with aliases. In the following example, we attempt to overwrite an existing alias, which results in an ORA-15005 error:

```
ASMCMD [+DATA/DBA11g/DATAFILE] >  cp -f
  +DATA/DBA11g/DATAFILE/DOCS_D1.289.631914611
  sys@rac1.+ASM:+DATA/DBA11g1/datafile/docs_d1.dbf

Enter password: *********
error
source +DATA/DBA11g/DATAFILE/DOCS_D1.289.631914611
target +DATA/DBA11g1/datafile/docs_d1.dbf
ASMCMD-08015: can not create file->'+DATA/DBA11g1/datafile/docs_d1.dbf'
ORA-15056: additional error message
ORA-17502: ksfdcre:4 Failed to create file +DATA/dba11g1/datafile/docs_d1.dbf
ORA-15005: name "dba11g1/datafile/docs_d1.dbf" is already used by an existing alias
ORA-06512: at "SYS.X$DBMS_DISKGROUP", line 142
ORA-06512: at line 3 (DBD ERROR: OCIStmtExecute)
ASMCMD-08016: copy source->'+DATA/DBA11g/DATAFILE/DOCS_D1.289.631914611'
              and target->'+DATA/DBA11g1/datafile/docs_d1.dbf' failed
```

Continuing with the cp examples, this is how to perform a datafile copy from one directory to another directory on the local ASM instance:

```
ASMCMD> cp  +data/DBA11g1/DATAFILE/ALERT_D1.267.631889077
             +FRA/DBA11G1/alert_d1.dbf
source +data/DBA11g1/DATAFILE/ALERT_D1.267.631889077
target +FRA/DBA11G1/alert_d1.dbf
copying file(s)...
file, +FRA/dba11g1/alert_d1.dbf, copy committed.
```

The syntax to copy files between one local diskgroup to another local diskgroup is straightforward. You can copy files between one diskgroup to another diskgroup or even to the same
diskgroup. You can also leverage the copy command to copy files from ASM to a local file system.
As the last example, we'll copy the docs_d4 datafile to the /oradata/DBATOOLS/ directory on the
file system:

```
ASMCMD> cp +DATA/DBA11G1/DATAFILE/DOCS_D4.276.631890065
                     /oradata/DBATOOLS/docs_d4.dbf
source +DATA/DBA11G1/DATAFILE/DOCS_D4.276.631890065
target /oradata/DBATOOLS/docs_d4.dbf
copying file(s)...
file, /oradata/DBATOOLS/docs_d4.dbf, copy committed.
```

Metadata Backup and Restore

As far as the ASM ecosystem is concerned, there isn't much to back up. The only files that can
be backed up are the initialization file or the spfile depending on the database standards for the
company. Possibly, the $ORACLE_BASE/diag directory may need to be backed up if you are inter-
ested in preserving the log files.

Oracle Database 11g provides the capability to back up the ASM diskgroup structure and
attributes including ASM aliases, directories, or templates. In Oracle Database 10g, objects
such as aliases, directories, or templates have to be manually re-created after the restore. Prior
to Oracle Database 11g, ASM metadata for the diskgroups could not be backed up because the
metadata resides on the disk headers. We recommend that DBAs utilize the ASM Metadata
Backup and Restore (AMBR) utility coupled with a solid RMAN backup strategy to provide the
complete database recovery solution. Using the AMBR tools, you can protect the diskgroup
structures since AMBR tools provide the facility to back up and restore the original ASM diskgroup with the same template and alias directory structures. Oracle Database 11g introduces
AMBR's md_backup and md_restore commands to provide a comprehensive level of protection
for the ASM environment. Extensions to the asmcmd utility provide this extra level of protection
for ASM:

- md_backup [-o <backup_file_path>] [-g diskgroup_name [-g diskgroup_name …]]

- md_restore [-t full|nodg|newdg]-fi <backup_file> -g dgname [-g dgname] [-o
  <override>] [-of <override_file>][-i] [-l< log_file>]

Backup Diskgroup Using md_backup

The md_backup command captures information about ASM disks, diskgroup and failure group
configurations, and template and alias directory structures, and it creates a user-designated

backup text file. The md_restore command uses this text file and converts it into SQL commands to restore the custom user-defined metadata for the diskgroups. You can view the ASM alert log file to see the SQL generated by the md_restore command. We'll provide an example of this in the next section when we demonstrate a complete ASM diskgroup backup and recovery.

With the md_backup command, users have the option to back up one or more diskgroups. The diskgroup names are delimited by commas. By default, the MDB file is created in the current working directory. This can be overwritten by providing a fully qualified file name. Not specifying the diskgroup(s) to the md_backup command will, by default, build metadata information for all diskgroups that are mounted.

Because the MDB file is a text file, users will be tempted to modify this file. You should be extremely cautious when modifying this file because ASM does not validate the syntax or accuracy of the flat file. The md_restore command simply converts this file into SQL statements and executes it. Please back up this file before making any modifications to it. Having said all this, modifying the MDB backup file can be very useful. You can manipulate this file so that only certain ASM objects are restored instead of restoring the entire diskgroup.

You will see in the "Metadata Backup and Restore Demonstration" section that the MDB file has four distinct sections: disk information, diskgroup information, alias information, and template information. This tag is used by the md_restore command to locate the section in the backup file.

■ **Caution** As mentioned, please exercise caution when modifying the MDB backup file. User errors can cause sections to be skipped.

In the disk section of the MDB file labeled as DISKSINFO, information about diskgroup name, disk label name, disk path, OS size/ASM size of the disk, and failgroup name will be captured. For the diskgroup section labeled as DGINFO, characteristics of the diskgroup name, redundancy type, ASM/RDBMS compatibility, and AU size will be captured. For the alias direction information section labeled as ALIASINFO, the MDB file has information about the diskgroup name, directory level, and alias name with the full path of the alias entry. Lastly, the template section labeled as TEMPLATEINFO houses relevant information for all system and nonsystem (user-defined) templates. For each template, the diskgroup name, template name, redundancy, stripe, and system designator is stored. All of this information is pertinent to the md_restore command.

Restore Diskgroup Using md_restore

The md_restore command of asmcmd performs an ASM metadata restore for a diskgroup. This utility reads the MDB backup file and essentially builds the required SQL statements to rebuild all the components of the diskgroup including templates, aliases, directories, and diskgroup names. This utility restores only the ASM diskgroup metadata information. Coupled with RMAN, you can achieve a higher level of data protection. You must still have a good RMAN backup. After a successful restore of the ASM diskgroup metadata, you can restore the database using RMAN.

This utility has several options. It can be used to restore the MDB backup file as is, or it can perform transformations of the diskgroup name. At the same time, you have the option to restore just one diskgroup or multiple diskgroups or all the diskgroups specified in the backup file.

Most important, the md_restore command will re-create all user-defined templates. It will also generate all the system templates and ASM alias directories including user-created directories.

```
md_restore -b <backup_file> [-li]
            [-t (full)|nodg|newdg] [-f <sql_script_file>]
            [-g '<diskgroup_name>,<diskgroup_name>,...']
            [-o '<old_diskgroup_name>:<new_diskgroup_name>,...']
```

Now we'll explain what some of these options mean. First, the -t option specifies the type of restore to be performed. The full tag specifies that all the diskgroups should be re-created using the same configuration from the MDB backup file. The nodg option can be used to skip the diskgroup creation and just restore the metadata in an existing diskgroup provided as an input parameter. The newdg option can be used to allow the user to change disk specification/ failure group specification/diskgroup name/AVD file specification, and so on.

Obviously, the -f option specifies the backup file created by the md_backup command. Another important option is the -o option for override. This option can be used only in conjunction with the newdg option. The override option allows the user to remap the diskgroup name, disk name, paths, and failure groups. An example of such an override option is in the form DGNAME=DATA:DATA_NEW, where the old diskgroup name is specified followed by a colon followed by the new designated diskgroup name. Another important option to note is the -i option to ignore errors. By default, the md_restore command aborts when it encounters an error. Lastly, the -l option can be used to log all messages to a log file.

Metadata Backup and Restore Demonstration

Now we'll show how to perform a complete backup of ASM metadata. To demonstrate AMBR's capability to back up and restore all the metadata pertaining to a diskgroup, we'll simulate all the potential elements of the diskgroup including custom directories, templates, and aliases. After the backup is complete, a diskgroup will be dropped to simulate a failure of some sort, and a restore of the metadata will be performed.

Prior to performing a backup using the md_backup command, we create additional diskgroup objects for demonstration purposes. The following code example will create additional directories, templates, and aliases. This is essential to the backup output that we'll present later.

```
  1* alter diskgroup data
     add alias '+DATA/dbatools/datafile/system.dbf'
     for '+DATA/dbatools/datafile/system.256.623974863'
SQL> /

Diskgroup altered.

SQL> alter diskgroup data add directory '+DATA/oradata';

Diskgroup altered.

SQL> alter diskgroup data add directory '+DATA/oradata/DBATOOLS';

Diskgroup altered.
```

```
SQL> alter diskgroup data add  template temp2 attributes (fine  unprotected);

Diskgroup altered.

SQL> alter diskgroup data add  template data2 attributes (fine mirror);

Diskgroup altered.

SQL> alter diskgroup data add directory '+DATA/oradata/WWJD';

Diskgroup altered.

SQL> alter diskgroup data
     add alias '+DATA/oradata/DBATOOLS/sysaux.dbf'
     for '+DATA/dbatools/datafile/sysaux.257.623974863';

Diskgroup altered.

SQL> alter diskgroup data
     add alias '+DATA/dbatools/datafile/users.dbf'
     for '+DATA/dbatools/datafile/users.259.623974865';

Diskgroup altered.

  1* alter diskgroup data
     add alias '+DATA/dbatools/tempfile/temp.dbf'
     for '+DATA/dbatools/tempfile/temp.264.623975155'
SQL> /

Diskgroup altered.

SQL> alter diskgroup data
     add alias '+DATA/dbatools/datafile/undotbs1.dbf'
     for '+DATA/dbatools/datafile/undotbs1.258.623974865';

Diskgroup altered.
```

The previous code example created the ASM templates TEMP2 and DATA2. To prove that the ASM templates are valid and exist within the ASM instance, you can query the V$ASM_TEMPLATE view, as shown here:

```
SELECT name, redundancy,stripe
from v$asm_template
where system='N'
SQL> /
```

NAME	REDUND	STRIPE
TEMP2	UNPROT	FINE
DATA2	MIRROR	FINE

Similarly, all the directories created using the alter diskgroup can be confirmed too:

```
select name,file_number,alias_directory
from v$asm_alias
where system_created='N'
and alias_directory='Y'
SQL> /
```

NAME	FILE_NUMBER	A
oradata	4294967295	Y
DBATOOLS	4294967295	Y
WWJD	4294967295	Y

The diskgroup backup can be invoked using the md_backup command similar to what is displayed here:

```
ASMCMD>  md_backup -o asm_backup.mdb -g data,fra

###User defined intermediate backup file is

         asm_backup.mdb

Disk group to be backed up: DATA#

Disk group to be backed up: FRA#
Current alias directory path: oradata/WWJD
Current alias directory path: oradata
Current alias directory path: oradata/DBATOOLS
```

Unfortunately, the md_backup command does not have the ability to override a backup metadata file if it already exists. You will get an error that looks similar to this when you specify the backup file of the same name:

```
ASMCMDAMBR-09357, A file with name 'asm_backup.mdb' already exists.
```

This command can be run in noninteractive mode, and the backup file path can be fully qualified:

```
asmcmd md_backup -o /tmp/asm_backup.mdb -g data,fra

###User defined intermediate backup file is

         /tmp/asm_backup.mdb
```

```
Disk group to be backed up: DATA#

Disk group to be backed up: FRA#
Current alias directory path: oradata/WWJD
Current alias directory path: oradata
Current alias directory path: oradata/DBATOOLS
```

The asm_backup.mdb file contents are shown next. You can clearly see that this file is a text file. The majority of the data from the TEMPLATEINFO section was deleted to make this output presentable. This section of the file contains the bulk of the information since there were 15 predefined system TEMPLATEINFO items to each diskgroup. You will notice the two custom templates that were created, DATA2 and TEMP2, in the MDB backup file.

```
+ASM1 > cat /tmp/asm_backup.mdb
@diskgroup_set = (
                  {
                    'DISKSINFO' => {
                                    'VOL1' => {
                                               'VOL1' => {
                                                          'TOTAL_MB' => '1961',
                                                          'FAILGROUP' => 'VOL1',
                                                          'NAME' => 'VOL1',
                                                          'DGNAME' => 'DATA',
                                                          'PATH' => 'ORCL:VOL1'
                                                         }
                                              },
                                .. 
                                ..
                               },
                    'DGINFO' => {
                                 'DGTORESTORE' => 0,
                                 'DGCOMPAT' => '11.1.0.0.0',
                                 'DGNAME' => 'DATA',
                                 'DGDBCOMPAT' => '11.1.0.0.0',
                                 'DGTYPE' => 'NORMAL',
                                 'DGAUSZ' => '1048576'
                                },
                    'ALIASINFO' => {
                                    '1' => {
                                            'DGNAME' => 'DATA',
                                            'LEVEL' => 1,
                                            'ALIASNAME' => 'oradata/WWJD',
                                            'REFERENCE_INDEX' => '16777799'
                                           },
                                    '0' => {
                                            'DGNAME' => 'DATA',
                                            'LEVEL' => 0,
                                            'ALIASNAME' => 'oradata',
```

```
                                            'REFERENCE_INDEX' => '16777693'
                                    },
                        '2' => {
                                    'DGNAME' => 'DATA',
                                    'LEVEL' => 1,
                                    'ALIASNAME' => 'oradata/DBATOOLS',
                                    'REFERENCE_INDEX' => '16777746'
                                }
                },
        'TEMPLATEINFO' => {
                        ..
                        ..
                        '2' => {
                                    'DGNAME' => 'DATA',
                                    'STRIPE' => 'FINE',
                                    'TEMPNAME' => 'DATA2',
                                    'REDUNDANCY' => 'MIRROR',
                                    'SYSTEM' => 'N'
                                },
                        ….
                        ….
                        '3' => {
                                    'DGNAME' => 'DATA',
                                    'STRIPE' => 'FINE',
                                    'TEMPNAME' => 'TEMP2',
                                    'REDUNDANCY' => 'UNPROT',
                                    'SYSTEM' => 'N'
                                },
                        ...
                        ...
                    }
        },
        {
          'DISKSINFO' => {
                        'VOL3' => {
                                    'VOL3' => {
                                                'TOTAL_MB' => '1952',
                                                'FAILGROUP' => 'VOL3',
                                                'NAME' => 'VOL3',
                                                'DGNAME' => 'FRA',
                                                'PATH' => 'ORCL:VOL3'
                                            }
                                },
                        ..
                        ..
```

```
                    'DGINFO' => {
                                'DGTORESTORE' => 0,
                                'DGCOMPAT' => '11.1.0.0.0',
                                'DGNAME' => 'FRA',
                                'DGDBCOMPAT' => '10.1.0.0.0',
                                'DGTYPE' => 'NORMAL',
                                'DGAUSZ' => '16777216'
                    },
              'ALIASINFO' => {},
              'TEMPLATEINFO' => {
                    ….
                    ….,
                        '11' => {
                                'DGNAME' => 'FRA',
                                'STRIPE' => 'FINE',
                                'TEMPNAME' => 'CONTROLFILE',
                                'REDUNDANCY' => 'HIGH',
                                'SYSTEM' => 'Y'
                        },
                    ...
                    ...
                }
          }
        );
```

Since the metadata backup is complete, you are ready to simulate a complete diskgroup failure. The following dismount and drop diskgroup commands will completely expunge everything in the DATA diskgroup:

```
SQL> alter diskgroup data dismount;
```

■**Note** The dismount command must be performed on all nodes of the cluster that have that ASM diskgroup mounted. Prior to this command, since this is a simulation, please make sure you have a solid RMAN backup including the spfile, the database, the archivelogs, and the controlfiles.

```
SQL> drop diskgroup data force including contents;
```

Now it's time to perform the restore from the previous md_backup command:

```
ASMCMD> md_restore -t full -g DATA -b /tmp/asm_backup.mdb
```

```
Disk group to be restored: DATA#
```

```
ASMCMDAMBR-09358, Option -t newdg specified without any override options.
```

```
Current Diskgroup being restored: DATA
Diskgroup DATA created!
Template DATA2 created/altered!
Template TEMP2 created/altered!
User Alias directory +DATA/oradata
                created!
User Alias directory +DATA/oradata/WWJD
                created!
User Alias directory +DATA/oradata/DBATOOLS
                created!
```

Note In the RAC node, each instance must manually mount the diskgroup after the restore is successfully executed.

At this point, if you examine the alert log of the ASM instance, you will see the SQL statements that were executed behind the scenes. Here's an excerpt from the alert log file located in the new diag directory, /apps/oracle/diag/rdbms/dbatools/DBATOOLS/trace/alert_+ASM1.log:

```
SUCCESS: diskgroup DATA was mounted
SQL> alter diskgroup DATA alter template AUTOBACKUP attributes (MIRROR COARSE)
SQL> alter diskgroup DATA alter template DATAGUARDCONFIG attributes (MIRROR COARSE)
SQL> alter diskgroup DATA alter template CONTROLFILE attributes (HIGH FINE)
SQL> alter diskgroup DATA add template DATA2 attributes (MIRROR FINE)
SQL> alter diskgroup DATA alter template DUMPSET attributes (MIRROR COARSE)
SQL> alter diskgroup DATA alter template PARAMETERFILE attributes (MIRROR COARSE)
SQL> alter diskgroup DATA alter template ARCHIVELOG attributes (MIRROR COARSE)
SQL> alter diskgroup DATA alter template TEMPFILE attributes (MIRROR COARSE)
SQL> alter diskgroup DATA alter template ASM_STALE attributes (HIGH COARSE)
SQL> alter diskgroup DATA add template TEMP2 attributes (UNPROTECTED FINE)
SQL> alter diskgroup DATA alter template CHANGETRACKING attributes (MIRROR COARSE)
SQL> alter diskgroup DATA alter template BACKUPSET attributes (MIRROR COARSE)
SQL> alter diskgroup DATA alter template DATAFILE attributes (MIRROR COARSE)
SQL> alter diskgroup DATA alter template ONLINELOG attributes (MIRROR FINE)
SQL> alter diskgroup DATA alter template FLASHBACK attributes (MIRROR FINE)
SQL> alter diskgroup DATA alter template ASMVDRL attributes (MIRROR COARSE)
SQL> alter diskgroup DATA alter template XTRANSPORT attributes (MIRROR COARSE)
SQL> alter diskgroup DATA alter template ASMVOL attributes (MIRROR COARSE)
SQL> alter diskgroup DATA add directory '+DATA/oradata'
SQL> alter diskgroup DATA add directory '+DATA/oradata/WWJD'
SQL> alter diskgroup DATA add directory '+DATA/oradata/DBATOOLS'
```

Since the DATA diskgroup is restored, you are ready to perform the RMAN restore of the database!

Additional md_restore Examples

Here we provide some additional examples of the `md_restore` command. To perform a restore of the DATA diskgroup from the MDB backup file, use this:

```
md_restore -t full -g DATA -f /tmp/backupfile
```

If you want the `md_restore` command to just re-create the metadata for the DATA diskgroup, you can use the following command. The assumption is that the DATA diskgroup already exists.

```
md_restore -t nodg -g DATA -i /tmp/backupfile
```

Now let's look at how to create a different diskgroup name. In this example, the diskgroup name DATA is remapped to DATA2:

```
md_restore -t newdg  -o "DGNAME=DATA:DATA2"  -i /tmp/backupfile
```

The `-of` option lets you specify override options in a text file. This example will apply the override options as specified in the `dg_over.txt` file and restore from the backup file:

```
md_restore -t newdg -of /tmp/dg_override.txt -i /tmp/backupfile
```

Bad Block Recovery with ASMCMD

Another new feature of the `asmcmd` utility is the bad block recovery, which runs automatically for normal and high redundancy disks. When bad spots occur on disks, ASM can detect these spots and recover them by restoring the data from its mirror extent from the other failure group(s). When ASM detects an IO error from an attempted read, it will automatically try to repair that block or blocks from the mirrored extents and write out a relocated copy to produce a successful read. This process occurs only for read blocks and happens automatically.

For the `remap` command to work, the diskgroups must be in a mounted state. The purpose of the `remap` command is to read mirrored extents to produce good IO for the primary extent. This is supposed to happen automatically, but you can use the `asmcmd` repair interface if there are reports of disk errors on the physical block. At this point, you can use the `remap` command to initiate a read on that block to trigger the repair. The syntax for the `remap` command is as follows:

```
remap <diskgroup name> <disk name> <block range>
```

You can use the `remap` command for a range of physical—not virtual—blocks on a disk. `<diskgroup name>` is the name of the diskgroup in which a disk needs to be repaired. `<disk name>` is the V$ASM_DISK.NAME of the disk that needs to be repaired. `<block range>` is a range of physical blocks to repair, in this format: `from-to`. Here are a couple of examples of this utility. The first command repairs blocks 25 to 100 for the VOL1 disk in the DATA diskgroup. The latter command repairs blocks 5230 to 5300 of the VOL4 disk in the FRA diskgroup.

```
ASMCMD> remap DATA VOL1 25-100
ASMCMD> remap FRA VOL4 5230-5300
```

ASM can repair only one extent at a time. If multiple block extents need to be repaired, `asmcmd` must make multiple passes to repair them one at a time. The `remap` command assumes that the physical block size is 512 bytes and the allocation unit size is 1MB.

Oracle Direct NFS

Oracle Database 10*g* introduced ASM by allowing direct IO to the database files. In Oracle Database 11*g*, Oracle provides a similar enhancement to NFS. Oracle Database 11*g* pioneers the database world with Direct Network File System (Direct NFS). Oracle Direct NFS is an NFS client built directly into the database kernel. With Oracle Direct NFS, the database kernel performs all the tuning processes automatically. DBAs and system administrators are no longer responsible for being intimate with all the tuning parameters associated with NFS.

Oracle RAC implementations on NFS are a common industry practice. Debates about implementing RAC on NFS vs. ASM have become a hot topic among database architects. The debate centers on cost, performance, and manageability. NFS on appliances such as Network Appliance has become a trend for RAC implementations. The introduction of Oracle Database 11*g* Direct NFS fuels the fire for NFS implementations.

For improved NFS performance, Oracle recommends the Direct NFS client that ships with Oracle Database 11*g*. Instead of using the operating system NFS client, you can access NFS version 3 servers directly using an Oracle internal Direct NFS client. If Oracle's Direct NFS is not able to open the NFS server, Oracle will utilize the operating system's NFS client as specified in /etc/fstab and post an error message in the alert log.

Set Up Direct NFS

Oracle Direct NFS setup involves manipulating the oranfstab file. The oranfstab file can reside in several locations. Oracle will always check the $ORACLE_HOME/dbs directory first. If the oranfstab file does not exist, it will search in the /etc directory. If an oranfstab file does not exist, Oracle will use the operating system /etc/mtab file. Oracle's Direct NFS client looks for mount point settings in the following order:

- $ORACLE_HOME/dbs/oranfstab

- /etc/oranfstab

- /etc/mtab

If there are duplicate entries in these files, Oracle Direct NFS client will use the first entry found.

To implement Oracle Direct NFS, an existing NFS mount point must already exist. The mount options for NFS are irrelevant since Oracle Direct NFS will override and configure settings optimally. The NFS mount options in the /etc/fstab file for this particular example are as follows:

```
nas103:/apps/oracle/share  /oradata nfs
rw,bg,hard,nointr,rsize=32768,wsize=32768,tcp,
actimeo=0,vers=3,timeo=600
```

It is important to note that in order to enable Direct NFS, you must disable reserved port settings on the NFS server.

Oracle uses the Oracle Disk Manager (ODM) to control NFS. To enable Direct NFS, you must replace the standard ODM driver with the ODM NFS library. For the client to work, you need to shut down the database and create a symbolic link from the standard ODM library to point to the NFS ODM library. Before you create the symbolic link, you will rename the original file `libodm11.so` to `libodm11.so.ORIG`. Next, you will create the symbolic link `libodm11.so` to point to `libnfsodm11.so`. Here are the steps to set up the NFS ODM library file:

1. `cd $ORACLE_HOME/lib`

2. `mv libodm11.so libodm11.so.ORIG`

3. `ln -s libnfsodm11.so libodm11.so`

Once the setup is complete, you will list the file to confirm that it is pointing to the right file:

```
DBA11g1 > ls -l libodm11.so
lrwxrwxrwx  1 oracle oinstall 14 Sep  5 09:02 libodm11.so -> libnfsodm11.so
```

Next, create the `oranfstab` file in the `$ORACLE_HOME/dbs` directory. Since Oracle first looks for the `oranfstab` file in the `$ORACLE_HOME/dbs` directory, DBAs can implement Direct NFS without the Unix system administrator's intervention.

The `oranfstab` file is not a requirement to implement Direct NFS. The `oranfstab` file is a special file to list additional options specific for Oracle Database to Direct NFS. The `oranfstab` file has the following attributes for each NFS server to be accessed using Direct NFS:

- `Server`: NFS server name

- `Path`: IP or hostname of up to four network paths to the NFS server

- `Export`: Exported path from the NFS server

- `Mount`: Local mount point for the NFS server

■**Note** For RAC implementations, you must use the `oranfstab` file from `/etc`. The `oranfstab` file must be synchronized across all the RAC servers.

For our simple demonstration, we will just have one entry in the `oranfstab` file. The contents of the `oranfstab` file look like this:

```
DBA11g1 > cat oranfstab
server: nas103
path:  192.168.1.103
export: /apps/oracle/share mount: /oradata
```

An example of an `oranfstab` with multiple paths looks like this:

```
server:  nas103
path:  nas1
path:  nas2
path:  nas3
path:  nas4
```

```
export: /oradata/share1 mount: /oradata1
export: /oradata/share2 mount: /oradata2
export: /oradata/share3 mount: /oradata3
export: /oradata/share4 mount: /oradata4
```

In this example, four paths are specified in the oranfstab file. The Direct NFS client will perform load balancing across nas1, nas2, nas3, and nas4. If an IO request to a specific path fails, Direct NFS will reissue the IO request over the remaining paths.

Validate Direct NFS

Once all the setup and configuration is complete, it's time to start the database. Starting the database shows the following entry in the alert log:

```
Oracle instance running with ODM: Oracle Direct NFS ODM Library Version 2.0
```

After the database is up and running, you can create a tablespace on the Direct NFS mount point. In this example, we will create a 10MB datafile for the nfs_data tablespace on the /oradata Direct NFS mount point:

```
SQL> create tablespace nfs_data datafile
     '/oradata/DBA11g1/nfs_data_01.dbf' size 10m;

Tablespace created.
```

In the alert log, you should see a message similar to this:

```
create tablespace nfs_data datafile '/oradata/DBA11g1/nfs_data_01.dbf' size 10m
Direct NFS: mount complete dir /apps/oracle/share on nas103
          path 192.168.1.103 mntport 923 nfsport 2049
```

You can now confirm from the database that Direct NFS is enabled. You can query the V$DNFS_SERVERS view to display the server name, directory names, and associated NFS ports, as shown here:

```
SQL>    select svrname, dirname, mntport, nfsport from  v$dnfs_servers;

SVRNAME    DIRNAME              MNTPORT    NFSPORT
---------  -------------------  --------   -------
nas103     /apps/oracle/share      923       2049
```

Other views that are relevant for Direct NFS client usage include the following:

- *V$DNFS_FILES*: Displays files currently open using Direct NFS

- *V$DNFS_CHANNELS*: Displays open network paths (or channels) to servers for which Direct NFS is providing files

- *V$DNFS_STATS*: Displays performance statistics for Direct NFS

Disable Direct NFS

You may need to disable Direct NFS for one reason or another. To disable Direct NFS, you can perform one of the following tasks:

- Put the standard ODM library file back in the `$ORACLE_HOME/lib` directory.

  ```
  cd $ORACLE_HOME/dbs
  cp libodm11.so.ORIG libodm11.so
  ```

- Remove the `oranfstab` file in either `$ORACLE_HOME/dbs` or `/etc`.

- Remove the NFS server or export path from `oranfstab`.

Network Interface Card Bonding

For network interface card (NIC) bonding, two common problems need to be addressed. First, expensive Ethernet switches are required to support advanced Ethernet switch support. Second, the network card bonding can be done only with homogeneous network cards.

With Oracle Direct NFS, you no longer need to deal with buying and configuring switches that can handle bonded network interfaces. And you don't even have to deal with configuring bonded network interfaces for performance and redundancy since Oracle Direct NFS utilizes the multipath IO internally.

Direct NFS Performance

The Oracle Direct NFS client provides support for direct and asynchronous IO out of the box. Using Direct NFS client functionality available in Oracle Database 11g, customers can realize better IO performance, more efficient system resource utilization, and lower operating costs in NAS environments. According to Hewlett-Packard, customers can see significant database throughput with improvements as high as 40 percent measured in internal testing. Most important, customers do not have to worry about optimizing NFS client configuration for database workloads, thus reducing administrative burden and costs.

What is better, ASM or Direct NFS? This is the million-dollar question debated by database, SA, and SAN architects. With the promise of the 10GB network cards and switches, this will make the debate even more exciting.

For continued discussions on Direct NFS vs. ASM, stay tuned at the `http://DBAExpert.com/blog` site.

CHAPTER 10

■■■

Data Guard

Oracle Hot Standby, introduced in Oracle version 7.3, was marketed to the database community as a disaster recovery (DR) solution. In Oracle version 7.3, many of today's automated processes had to be programmed to deliver successful implementations of disaster recovery using Oracle Hot Standby. Simple tasks such as transferring archivelogs had to be done manually by scripting the rcp/rsh or ftp process. In Oracle 8i, the Hot Standby product introduced new features such as the managed recovery process and read-only mode for standby databases.

In Oracle 9i Database, features such as logical standby database and Oracle Data Guard Broker made this product significantly more viable as a product for disaster recovery. Not only could it be used for high availability, but it could also be used for complex reporting systems. Unknown to a lot of the Oracle community, Oracle Data Guard was introduced as a product in Oracle 8i. It is in Oracle 9i Database that Hot Standby evolved into what we know today as the Data Guard technology. Oracle 9i Database introduced the marketing nomenclature known to all DBAs as Maximum Performance and Maximum Protection modes. In Oracle Database 10g, Data Guard is integrated with the flashback database and guaranteed savepoints. In this release, Oracle provides the capability to open the Data Guard database in read/write mode and flash back to a guaranteed restore point. In Oracle Database 11g, two major improvements have been added to the Data Guard product: the ability to open the database in read-only mode and still continue to apply redo known as *real-time query standby* and *snapshot standby*. The snapshot database provides the ability of the Data Guard database to open in read/write mode for operations such as stress/load testing, hotfix testing, code push validation, and so on, and be able to roll back the database to the precise point prior to opening the database in read/write mode and continue applying archivelogs.

■**Note** Oracle introduces another licensing option called Oracle Active Data Guard, which licenses the real-time query feature and the ability to use RMAN block change tracking on the standby database. This is an additional cost beyond the Enterprise Edition license.

Oracle packs significant new features in the Oracle Database 11g Data Guard technology stack. In this chapter, we will focus on all the latest and greatest Data Guard advancements:

- Real-time query standby database

- Snapshot standby database

- Logical standby database improvements

- Redo log compression

- Data Guard Broker enhancements

- Recovery Manager (RMAN) integration with Data Guard

- Rolling upgrades with the physical standby

- Fast-start failover improvements

Active Physical Standby Database Duplication

RMAN network-based duplication is one of the key new Oracle Database 11*g* features; with it, you can clone a database without a backup of the primary database server. This section will provide simple steps for creating a physical standby from an active database using RMAN.

Some preparation steps are required prior to initiating an active physical standby database duplication over the network. First, create a blank initialization file with just one parameter in the file, specifically, `DB_NAME=PRIMARY_DATABASE{DR}` in the `$ORACLE_HOME/dbs` directory.

Second, the password file for `sys` must be the same on both the primary and Data Guard servers. You must use `sftp/scp` to transfer the files from the primary `$ORACLE_HOME/dbs` directory to the disaster recovery database server. You also need to create the required Oracle Database 11*g* Optimal Flexible Architecture (OFA)–related directories:

- `$ORACLE_BASE/admin/$ORACLE_SID/adump`

- `$ORACLE_BASE/admin/$ORACLE_SID/pfile`

- `$ORACLE_BASE/admin/$ORACLE_SID/wallet`

Now, it's time to create the `listener.ora` and `tnsnames.ora` file entries on both the primary and disaster recovery nodes. You need to make sure the appropriate entries are on both of the `tnsnames.ora` files. If you are planning to use the broker, you need to pay particular attention to the `LISTENER` file's `global_dbname` parameter. The name of `global_dbname` must include the `_dgmgrl` parameter to it. For example, the following `listener.ora` entry is provided with the appropriate `global_dbname` parameter:

```
SID_LIST_LISTENER =
  (SID_LIST =
    (SID_DESC =
      (SID_NAME = PLSExtProc)
      (ORACLE_HOME = /apps/oracle/product/11.1.0/DB)
      (PROGRAM = extproc)
    )
                (SID_DESC =
                    (GLOBAL_DBNAME = DBA11gDR_DGMGRL.dbaexpert.com)
                    (ORACLE_HOME = /apps/oracle/product/11.1.0/DB)
                    (SID_NAME = DBA11gDR)
                )
  )
```

```
LISTENER =
  (DESCRIPTION_LIST =
    (DESCRIPTION =
      (ADDRESS = (PROTOCOL = IPC)(KEY = EXTPROC1521))
      (ADDRESS = (PROTOCOL = TCP)(HOST = bpo40.dbaexpert.com)(PORT = 1521))
    )
  )
```

After the appropriate changes are made, the database instance and the listeners need to be restarted on both the primary and physical standby database servers.

Lastly, the standby redo logs should be added on the primary standby database so that they will be duplicated as part of the active network–based physical standby duplication.

Mike Smith, a principal member of the technical staff in the High Availability group at Oracle, has provided a script to build a standby database. This RMAN script can single-handedly create a physical standby database over the network. This single integrated RMAN script will duplicate the source database over the network, copy the spfile, copy the controlfile, and duplicate the database. During the process, both the primary and standby initialization parameters will be updated to accommodate the Data Guard configuration.

You can use the following script to create a physical standby database from the remote node:

```
rman <EOF
connect target sys/oracle123@DBA11g;
connect auxiliary sys/oracle123@DBA11gDR;

run {
   allocate channel prmy1 type disk;
   allocate channel prmy2 type disk;
   allocate channel prmy3 type disk;
   allocate channel prmy4 type disk;
   allocate auxiliary channel stby type disk;

   duplicate target database for standby from active database
     spfile
         parameter_value_convert 'DBA11g','DBA11gDR'
         set 'db_unique_name'='DBA11gDR'
         set 'db_file_name_convert'='/DBA11g/','/DBA11gDR/'
         set log_file_name_convert='/DBA11g/','/DBA11gDR/'
         set control_files='/apps/oracle/oradata/DBA11gDR/control.ctl'
         set log_archive_max_processes='5'
         set fal_client='DBA11gDR'
         set fal_server='DBA11g'
         set standby_file_management='AUTO'
         set log_archive_config='dg_config=(DBA11g,DBA11gDR)'
         set log_archive_dest_1='service=DBA11g LGWR ASYNC
               valid_for=(ONLINE_LOGFILES,PRIMARY_ROLE)
             db_unique_name=DBA11g'
   ;
  sql channel prmy1 "alter system set log_archive_config=''dg_
config=(DBA11g,DBA11gDR)''";
```

```
  sql channel prmy1 "alter system set log_archive_dest_1=
              ''service=DBA11gDR LGWR ASYNC valid_for=(online_logfiles,primary_role)
 db_unique_name=DBA11gDR''";
  sql channel prmy1 "alter system set log_archive_max_processes=5";
  sql channel prmy1 "alter system set fal_client=DBA11g";
  sql channel prmy1 "alter system set fal_server=DBA11gDR";
  sql channel prmy1 "alter system set standby_file_management=auto";
  sql channel prmy1 "alter system set log_archive_dest_state_1=enable";
  sql channel prmy1 "alter system archive log current";
  allocate auxiliary channel stby type disk;
  sql channel stby "alter database recover managed standby database
              using current logfile disconnect";
 }
EOF
```

Once the script successfully creates a standby database, you will be able to configure the additional options discussed in this chapter. For a complete log of this script, you can consult a blog entry on the DBAExpert.com web site in the Data Guard blog category: http://dbaexpert.com/blog/.

■**Note** We recommend that the DR database db_unique_name parameter should be named $ORACLE_SID{DR}. The db_unique_name parameter of the primary database can be retrieved on the standby database by querying the PRIMARY_DB_UNIQUE_NAME column in the V$DATABASE view.

The db_unique_name parameter is treated differently in Oracle Database 11g. Databases with the same db_unique_name parameter will not be able to participate in a Data Guard configuration. If the primary and Data Guard standby database db_unique_name parameter is the same, these databases will not be able to communicate with each other after the upgrade.

Real-Time Query Standby

By far, the biggest enhancements to Oracle Database 11g Data Guard physical standby are the real-time query standby and snapshot standby features. The real-time query standby feature is marketing terminology for the physical standby database that is capable of applying redo while the database is open in read-only mode. Prior to Oracle Database 11g, when a database was open in read-only mode via alter database open or alter database open read only, subsequent archivelogs from the primary host could no longer be applied to the reporting database or disaster recovery site. This restriction is cleared and makes Data Guard truly a real-time reporting database in Oracle Database 11g Data Guard. The redo apply process continues to remain active while the database is open in read-only mode. The real-time query standby database continues to provide the protection modes (Maximum Protection, Maximum Availability, and Maximum Performance). The real-time query reporting database feature maximizes the return on investment of the budget allocated for the Data Guard database.

No one can argue that the real-time query standby database is by far one of the most innovative improvements to Oracle Database 11g. Not only does Oracle provide a disaster recovery solution, but at the same time, it also provides a complete return on investment. The real-time query feature is the same as the physical standby database that you are accustomed to, except now you can have the database open in read-only mode with almost real-time synchronization of your mission-critical data from your primary database.

There are two important restrictions to opening the physical standby database for read-only with redo apply. First, the `compatibility` initialization parameter must be set to 11.1.0 or higher. Second, the `alter database set transaction read only` command has to be issued prior to performing any kind of distributed queries over the database link.

Start the Real-Time Query Standby

To open the standby database in real-time read-only mode, you must stop the redo apply using the `alter database recover managed standby database cancel` command. Once the database is open, you can start or stop the redo apply at any time. The following steps are all that is required to change a standby database for real-time reporting:

```
SQL> alter database recover managed standby database cancel;
Database altered.

SQL> alter database open;
Database altered.

SQL> alter database recover managed standby database disconnect;
Database altered.
```

The managed recovery process, initiated after the database is open, is the key difference in implementing the real-time query standby database. In previous releases, the managed recovery process is started while the database is mounted.

Validate the Real-Time Query Standby Database

Now you have enabled the real-time query capability in the standby database. Let's perform a simple validation to prove that DDL (and even user creation in this example) can be propagated in the real-time query standby database. On the primary database, we will create a user called `rodba` to demonstrate how the real-time query standby database applies archivelogs while the database is in read-only mode. Once the archivelog is applied, you will be able to log in as `rodba`.

Immediately after the user account is created on the primary database, you can confirm that you cannot connect to the `rodba` user on the real-time query standby database, as shown here:

```
DBA11gDR $ sqlplus rodba/rodba

SQL*Plus: Release 11.1.0.6.0 - Production on Wed Aug 15 05:50:02 2007

Copyright (c) 1982, 2007, Oracle.  All rights reserved.

ERROR:
ORA-01017: invalid username/password; logon denied
```

To validate that the real-time query standby database can apply archivelogs while the database is open in read-only mode, manually issue a log switch command, and check the sequence number from the V$LOG view on the primary database. Immediately after, confirm that the sequence numbers on the primary and physical standby databases match to ensure that both databases are synchronized. First, force a log switch on the primary database, as displayed here:

```
SQL> alter system switch logfile;

System altered.

SQL> select max(sequence#) from v$log;

    MAX(SEQUENCE#)
    --------------
                13
```

Next, confirm on the real-time query standby database that the maximum sequence is at 13, as shown here:

```
SQL>  select max(sequence#) from v$log;

    MAX(SEQUENCE#)
    --------------
                13
```

Since the archivelog that housed the create user DDL is successfully applied, you should now be able to connect as the rodba user on the real-time query standby database. The following SQL*Plus connection proves that the real-time query feature is capable of applying DDL even while the database is open for read-only transactions:

```
DBA11gDR $ sqlplus rodba/rodba

Copyright (c) 1982, 2007, Oracle.  All rights reserved.


Connected to:
Oracle Database 11g Enterprise Edition Release 11.1.0.6.0 - Production
With the Partitioning, OLAP, Data Mining and Real Application Testing options

SQL>
```

You can offload all your reporting requirements to the real-time query standby database at the local data center or at the disaster recovery site. The primary database can be the recipient of all OLTP traffic while the real-time query standby database(s) can handle all your reporting needs.

Design the Real-Time Query Database

Just as you can have a farm of web servers to scale out your web applications, you can architect a farm of real-time standby reporting databases. This implementation technique is referred to as a *reader farm*. A reader farm allows you to integrate multiple real-time read-only physical standby databases as an alternative architecture to provide scaled-out read performance. In addition, a *reader farm* provides a higher level of availability by isolating faults to a specified read-only standby database and provides greater scalability by enabling more workload capacity on the primary database by offloading all reports.

By adopting RAC in conjunction with real-time query standby with flashback technologies, companies can achieve the maximum availability architecture.

■**Tip** You can implement invisible indexes on the primary database to create a customized indexing requirement for your reporting databases. The only caveat is that the application must be able to hard-code hints to be able to access the invisible indexes.

There are additional design considerations with real-time query standby databases. If your reporting application has the requirement to create temporary tables or perform aggregated inserts to staging tables, you can use database links to a non–Data Guard target database. This implies that the target database must be local and must have a high-speed, low-latency network.

Because real-time query standby can participate in Maximum Protection configuration (no data loss), you can effectively architect true real-time reporting configurations. Since data is synchronously replicated to the standby database, companies that invest in redundant networks with low latency and high throughput can take advantage of this benefit. Fortunately, the majority of the companies do not have real-time requirements for reports. Companies that can opt for near real-time reports can implement Maximum Availability or Maximum Performance configurations.

Snapshot Standby

Another great new Data Guard feature in Oracle Database11*g* is the snapshot standby database. Now in Oracle Database 11*g*, you can open a physical standby database in full read/write mode, allow modifications to the database, and, after a specified period, revert to a physical standby database. Simply stated, a snapshot standby database is an updatable standby database. To create a snapshot standby database, you simply convert a physical standby database using the following syntax:

```
alter database convert to snapshot standby;
```

While the standby database is in snapshot standby mode, you continue to receive archivelogs, but the archivelogs cannot be applied. Archivelogs from the primary database will be automatically applied when the snapshot standby database is converted to a physical standby database. If your protection mode is Maximum Protection, you cannot convert a physical standby database to a snapshot standby database if it is the only standby database participating in Maximum Protection mode.

■**Note** For RAC databases, you will need to shut down all the RAC instances except for the one you are planning to convert to a snapshot standby database. Once you convert the physical standby database on the single RAC instance, you can restart the other RAC instances.

With the snapshot standby database, companies can leverage their disaster recovery hardware for alternative solutions such as QA test validations and performance benchmarks, allowing the reallocation of money spent on purchasing Oracle licenses for QA database environments to go to additional Oracle licenses to support a Data Guard environment. By leveraging a production-sized database to support QA activities such as hotfix testing, load testing, functional testing, or even stress testing, hardware allocated for disaster recovery does not sit idle. The snapshot standby database facilitates maximum return on investment for both hardware and Oracle database licensing.

Convert to Snapshot Standby

Converting a physical standby database to a snapshot standby database is a, well, snap. To create a snapshot standby, the MRP process must be shut down, and you cannot be in read-only or real-time mode. The following example will result in an error since the database was still in real-time query mode (from the previous example):

```
SQL> alter database convert to snapshot standby;

ALTER DATABASE CONVERT TO SNAPSHOT STANDBY
*
ERROR at line 1:
ORA-38784: Cannot create restore point 'SNAPSHOT_STANDBY_REQUIRED_04/30/2007
16:30:23'.
ORA-01153: an incompatible media recovery is active
```

You must be in mount mode to convert the database to snapshot standby. Once you issue the command to convert to snapshot standby, Oracle dismounts your database. If you attempt to mount the database, you will receive an error, as shown here:

```
SQL> alter database mount;
alter database mount
*
ERROR at line 1:
ORA-00750: database has been previously mounted and dismounted
```

Behind the scenes, Oracle replaces the standby control file with the primary controlfile. Even though you are dismounted, you have to shut down the database and restart the database. In the following steps, we will shut down the database and open the database:

```
SQL> shutdown immediate;
ORA-01507: database not mounted
ORACLE instance shut down.

SQL> startup
ORACLE instance started.

Total System Global Area    1071333376 bytes
Fixed Size                  1302468 bytes
Variable Size               478150716 bytes
Database Buffers            587202560 bytes
Redo Buffers                4677632 bytes
Database mounted.
Database opened.
```

Next, we will query the open_mode column in the V$DATABASE view to confirm that the database is truly in read/write mode:

```
SQL> select open_mode from v$database;

OPEN_MODE
--------------------
READ WRITE
```

Additionally, we will query the database_role column in V$DATABASE to verify that the database is in snapshot standby mode:

```
SQL> select primary_db_unique_name,
            db_unique_name, database_role
from v$database;

PRIMARY_DB_UNIQUE    DB_UNIQUE_NAME   DATABASE_ROLE
-----------------    --------------   ----------------
DBA11G               DBA11GDR         SNAPSHOT STANDBY
```

■**Note** Oracle Database 11g introduces a new column in V$DATABASE called PRIMARY_DB_UNIQUE_NAME. Now, you are able to see the primary database unique name and the standby database unique name in a single view. Starting from Oracle Database11g, databases with the same db_unique_name parameter will not be able to participate in a Data Guard configuration.

Now you can perform DDL and DML on the snapshot standby database. In this example, we will create a table called docs_dr and insert rows:

```
SQL> create table docs_dr (doc_id number, name varchar2(4000), lob_content blob);

Table created.

SQL> insert into docs_dr (doc_id, name) values
            (1, 'Oracle Maximum Availability Architecture');
1 row created.

SQL> commit;
Commit complete.
```

Since you do not apply archivelogs while the database is in standby mode, over time the snapshot standby database deviates from the primary database. The duration a snapshot standby database can continue in this mode is dependent on the company's recovery point objectives (RPOs) and recovery time objectives (RTOs). The snapshot standby database can be ideal for short testing scenarios such as a load test to confirm that a schema or an application patch or a major upgrade will cause performance issues. The good news is that even though the database continues to be in snapshot standby mode, you can continue to ship archivelogs from the primary database to the disaster recovery site. The DBA should know how many archivelogs can be applied per hour, and based on the RPO/RTO, they will know how long they can continue in the snapshot standby mode without compromising the business's RPO/RTO. There are two factors to consider while the physical database is in the snapshot standby database mode:

- The number of archivelogs generated from the primary database source

- The amount of data updated while the standby database is in updatable mode

Businesses can reap the benefits from a temporary snapshot of the primary database and justify the return on investment from the amount of money spent on disaster recovery licenses.

Behind the scenes, Oracle creates an implicit guaranteed restore point on the physical standby database prior to converting the snapshot standby database. GAP detection and resolution continue as usual while the database is in snapshot standby mode. Once the database is ready to be flashed back to the point prior to opening the database in updatable mode, a guaranteed restore point is used to flash back a snapshot standby to the point in time prior to converting the physical standby database to the snapshot standby database. By default, the guaranteed restore point is named with the SNAPSHOT_STANDBY_REQUIRED_ prefix appended by the system date. You can query the V$RESTORE_POINT view to determine the name of the restore point, as revealed here:

```
SQL> select name, storage_size from v$restore_point;

NAME                                    STORAGE_SIZE
------------------------------------    -------------------------
SNAPSHOT_STANDBY_REQUIRED_05/01/2007    8192000
```

You can accomplish the equivalent of the snapshot standby database in Oracle Database 10g Release 2 Data Guard using the guaranteed restore points. The only caveat is that the DBA has to perform all the steps required to convert the physical standby database to the snapshot standby database manually. In addition, you must perform the steps required to convert the snapshot standby database to the physical standby database manually. These steps are significantly more complicated in Oracle Database 10*g* Release 2 than in Oracle Database 11*g*. Many DBAs are not aware that the snapshot standby database equivalent capability is available in Oracle Database 10*g* Release 2. For complete details, please refer to the case study on Oracle's Maximum Availability Architecture web site:

```
http://www.oracle.com/technology/deploy/availability/htdocs/FNF_CaseStudy.html
```

The syntax to convert the snapshot physical database to the standby physical database is as follows:

```
alter database convert to physical standby;
```

Convert Back to Physical Standby

Similarly, the database must also be in a mounted state to convert to physical standby mode. If you are not in a mounted state, you will receive this error if you attempt to convert back to a physical standby:

```
SQL> alter database convert to physical standby;

alter database convert to physical standby
*
ERROR at line 1:
ORA-01126: database must be mounted in this instance and not open in any Instance
```

Once you mount the database, you will be able to convert back to a physical standby, as shown here:

```
SQL> alter database convert to physical standby;

Database altered.
```

Now you need to shut down the database again, mount or open the database, and restart managed recovery. The conversion process back to physical standby will discard all the changes that were made while the database was in snapshot standby mode. As stated earlier, Oracle utilizes an implicit guaranteed restore point created earlier during the conversion from the physical standby to the snapshot standby. Oracle issues a flashback database to the specific guaranteed restore point. Before the snapshot standby is converted to the physical standby, the guaranteed restore point is dropped. As the Data Guard database is brought back into the physical standby mode, redo apply will apply all the redo data received while the database was in the snapshot standby mode.

Once the conversion back to physical standby is complete, the docs_dr table created in the earlier example disappears. In the following several queries, you will notice that the database is opened in read-only mode and the docs_dr table no longer exists:

```
SQL> alter database recover managed standby database cancel;

Database altered.

SQL> alter database open;
Database altered.

SQL> select open_mode from v$database;
OPEN_MODE
--------------------
READ ONLY

SQL> desc rodba.docs_dr
ERROR:
ORA-04043: object rodba.docs_dr does not exist
```

Using the Physical Standby for Rolling Upgrades

Oracle 10.1.0.3 introduced the feature to be able to perform rolling upgrades of the database software for the logical standby database. For a short interim, the databases can run different releases of Oracle software on the primary and logical standby databases. With careful planning, you can upgrade the disaster recovery site and then switch over the database. The amount of downtime can be as little as the amount of downtime to perform a switchover.

Once the applications are switched over, the original primary database can be upgraded. This approach of a rolling upgrade can be achieved with minimal downtime on the production database. The ability to perform this kind of rolling upgrade is now possible with the physical standby database. The physical standby database goes through a transient conversion to a logical standby and is converted to a physical standby.

Prepare the Primary Database

On the primary database, you need to confirm that flashback is enabled, you need to create a restore point, and you need to back up the standby controlfile, as shown here:

```
SQL> alter database flashback on;
Database altered.

SQL> create restore point pre_upgrade_11g guarantee flashback database;
Restore point created.

SQL> alter database create physical standby controlfile
     as '/tmp/control01.standby.ctl' reuse;
Database altered.
```

Pay particular attention that you don't delete this file. You will use this controlfile to switch over your primary to standby. The database must be in Maximum Availability or Maximum Performance mode to qualify for a rolling upgrade. You must downgrade databases that are in Maximum Protection mode to either one of the other modes.

Convert to Logical: Keep Your Identity

In Oracle Database 11g, you can temporarily convert the physical standby database to a logical standby to perform a rolling upgrade. The conversion from physical to logical standby is identical as in the previous release except for one step. Instead of using the command `alter database recover to logical standby database_name`, you will use the `keep identity` clause in lieu of `database_name`. You can temporarily convert a physical standby to a logical standby database using the new `keep identity` clause option:

```
SQL> alter database recover to logical standby keep identity;

Database altered.
```

The `keep identity` clause tells Oracle Data Guard to behave as a logical standby database even though it is really still a physical standby database. The `DBID` and `DB_NAME` of the standby database will remain the same. The `keep identity` clause should be used only in context of rolling upgrades of the physical standby database.

Please be aware that as you are converting into the logical database, you have to be concerned about the unsupported datatypes. You can query the DBA_LOGSTDBY_UNSUPPORTED view to find all the unsupported datatypes on the database, as shown here:

```
SQL>  select distinct owner, table_namefrom dba_logstdby_unsupported;
```

At this point, you need to be extra cautious to keep all your archivelogs. You will need the archivelogs later during the rolling upgrade process. You should make sure to disable the automatic archivelog deletion process while the database is engaged in keep-identity mode. In addition, you need to start the SQL Apply process. You can achieve both of these steps in the manner specified here:

```
SQL> execute dbms_logstdby.apply_set ('LOG_AUTO_DELETE', 'FALSE');

SQL> alter database start logical standby apply immediate;
```

Now, you can exercise the same steps you would usually apply to perform a rolling upgrade to a logical standby database. Once the logical standby upgrade process is complete on the transient logical standby database server, your disaster recovery site will be running the new Oracle software and become the primary database, and the primary database will be switched over to become the logical standby database.

Next, you will have to perform the following steps to turn the original database (at the primary data center) into a physical standby for the new primary database (at the disaster recovery site):

1. Shut down the database.

2. Start up in mount mode.

3. Flash back the database to the guaranteed restore point created earlier (`pre_upgrade_11g`).

4. Shut down again and start up in nomount mode.

5. Restore the controlfile from the backup taken earlier (`/tmp/control01.standby.ctl`).

6. Shut down again.

7. Switch the binary to the new Oracle software version. At this point, both sites will be running the new version of Oracle software.

8. Start up in mount mode.

9. Start MRP, and make sure that both databases are in sync.

Your database will be synchronized again running the new version of Oracle software. You can perform a switchover again to bring the primary database back to the original data center. At this point, both sites are running the new version of Oracle software with the original Data Guard configuration.

Improvements in Redo Transport

One of the changes made to the redo log transport mechanism in Oracle now defaults to asynchronous mode. In Oracle Database 11*g*, the default behavior of the log transport mechanism is set to asynchronous mode. One way to confirm the new default asynchronous redo transport mode is to invoke the Data Guard command-line interface (DGMGRL) and review the verbose output from the SHOW command. You will notice that the last line of the following output (logxptmode=async) reflects the asynchronous mode of redo transport:

```
DGMGRL> show database verbose dba11gdr

Database
  Name:                   dba11gdr
  Role:                   PHYSICAL STANDBY
  Enabled:                YES
  Intended State:         APPLY-ON
  Instance(s):
    DBA11gDR
  Properties:
    DGConnectIdentifier         = 'dba11gdr'
    ObserverConnectIdentifier   = ''
    LogXptMode                  = 'async'
```

The redo transport mechanism in Oracle Database 11*g* can also take advantage of authentication using SSL. The redo transport network transmission sessions can now use the remote login password file to perform encrypted SSL connections.

Block Change Tracking Support

Oracle Database 10*g* introduced the block change tracking feature to improve incremental backup performance. Block change tracking enables fast incremental RMAN backups by reading and backing up only the changed data blocks during incremental backups. Oracle Database 11*g* allows for block change tracking on the Data Guard configuration. To enable block change tracking, you can submit a SQL statement similar to the following example on the standby database:

```
SQL> alter database enable block change tracking using file '+DATA';
```

```
Database altered.
```

This example enables block change tracking and places the file in the DATA diskgroup.

■**Note** Use of real-time query or RMAN block-change tracking on a Data Guard standby database requires a license for Oracle Active Data Guard.

BCT enabled on the standby database provides greater ammunition to leverage backups at the disaster recovery site. Performing backups on the disaster recovery site can offload resources on the primary data center.

RMAN Understands Data Guard Configurations

Previously, DBAs had to create a standby controlfile from the primary database and push the controlfile using sftp/scp to the standby database server to create a physical standby database. Oracle Database 11g eliminates this step. Using the RMAN repository, you are able to register the physical standby database. Once you register the standby database with RMAN, RMAN has the ability to resynchronize file names and update the information back in the controlfile by performing a reverse resynchronization. This is an automatic process on physical standby databases.

Improved Integration with RMAN

There are numerous improvements made to RMAN integration with Data Guard. The majority of these improvements revolve around the db_unique_name parameter and the ability to maintain site persistence. Improvements relative to RMAN and Data Guard integration include the ability to do the following:

- Restore a standby controlfile from an existing controlfile backup.

- Set up persistent configuration at the site level instead of connecting to a database as a target using the new db_unique_name option.

- Back up, restore, and recover works transparently with any database configuration.

- Back up the spfile based on db_unique_name.

- Define a backup accessibility group.

    Please refer to Chapter 6 for additional details.

Compressed Redo Traffic

Oracle Database 11g introduces the capability to compress redo log data as it transports over the network to the standby databases. This is an important feature for Data Guard implementers who have high-latency and low-bandwidth WAN networks. This compressed redo feature can be turned on by enabling the `log_archive_dest_1` parameter with the `compression` parameter. Compression becomes enabled only when a GAP exists and the standby database needs to catch up to the primary database. When a GAP resolution is detected, the redo transport can be enabled to ship logs in compressed mode. This will reduce the network bandwidth. By default, the `compression` attribute is disabled and is optional. To enable compression of redo transport, you can use the `alter system` syntax:

```
SQL> alter system set log_archive_dest_1 = 'SERVICE=DBA11GDR COMPRESSION=ENABLE';

System altered.
```

Alternatively, you can enable compression using Data Guard Broker by setting the `RedoCompression` property to `enable`. In the following example, the `RedoCompression` property will be set on both the primary and physical standby databases:

```
DGMGRL> edit database 'dba11g' set property redocompression=enable;

Property "redocompression" updated
```

On the standby database, you can enable redo compression also:

```
DGMGRL> edit database 'dba11gdr' set property redocompression=enable;

Property "redocompression" updated
```

Once you set compression, either through Data Guard Broker or by modifying the `log_archive_dest_1` parameter, you can query the V$ARCHIVE_DEST view to confirm that redo log compression is enabled, as shown here:

```
SQL> select dest_name, compression from v$archive_dest;

DEST_NAME               COMPRESSION
--------------------    -----------
LOG_ARCHIVE_DEST_1      ENABLE
```

Redo log compression can also be disabled by using the `disable` option with Data Guard Broker or by setting the `log_archive_dest_1` initialization parameter. When adding a database to the Data Guard configuration, Data Guard Broker will detect the archive destination compression setting and adjust the `RedoCompression` property.

■Note Using network compression with Data Guard redo transport services requires a license for Oracle Advanced Compression.

Usage of Histograms for the NET_TIMEOUT Attributes

The optional `net_timeout` parameter to the `log_archive_dest_n` initialization parameter allows the DBAs to specify the number of seconds the log writer process (LGWR) waits for a response from the logwriter network server (LNS) process before terminating the connection. This parameter by default is set to 30 seconds.

■ **Note** Oracle recommends that you set the net_timeout parameter for the Maximum Protection and Maximum Availability databases.

The net_timeout parameter populates a histogram of response time values for the V$REDO_DEST_RESP_HISTOGRAM dynamic view. There is one entry for every synchronous redo transport destination. The maximum allowable value for the net_timeout parameter is 1,200 seconds.

You can query V$REDO_DEST_RESP_HISTOGRAM to determine the response time for each transport destination. The DEST_ID column correlates to the log_archive_dest_n parameter. The DURATION column can have the following values:

- 1–300 (shows actual seconds rounded up)

- 600 (301–600 seconds show the value of 600)

- 1,200 (601–1,200 seconds show the value of 1,200)

- 2,400 (1,201–2,400 seconds show the value of 2,400)

- 4,800 (2,401–4,800 seconds show the value of 4,800)

- 9,600 (anything greater than 4,801 seconds shows the value of 9,600)

For ease of management, the numbers in this column are reported in seconds only for the first 300 seconds. For all values less than 300 seconds, the DURATION column reports the time rounded to the nearest second. For values larger than 300 seconds, Oracle rounds up to the next increment of 600, 1,200, 2,400, 4,800, or 9,600 seconds. This is the makeup of the histogram view:

```
SQL> desc V$REDO_DEST_RESP_HISTOGRAM
 Name                            Null?     Type
 ------------------------        --------  ---------------
 DEST_ID                                   NUMBER
 TIME                                      VARCHAR2(20)
 DURATION                                  NUMBER
 FREQUENCY                                 NUMBER
```

You should carefully observe the FREQUENCY column to review the bucket counts to determine an appropriate value for net_timeout. A high bucket count suggests a good value for the net_timeout attribute.

Here's a sample query to display a response time histogram for the second archive destination:

```
SQL> select frequency, duration
       from v$redo_dest_resp_histogram
      where dest_id=2
        and frequency>1;
```

You can also determine the fastest response time by using the `max` function on the `DURATION` column. Likewise, to determine the slowest response time, you can use the `min` function on the `DURATION` column.

Fast-Start Failover for Maximum Performance Mode

In the previous release, fast-start failover was available only when the redo transport was set to synchronous mode. This meant that unless your Data Guard was set up for Maximum Availability, you could not take advantage of fast-start failover. Oracle Data Guard 11*g* now enables fast-start failover to function for databases that are in Maximum Performance mode using the asynchronous transport mode. Setting up the flashback recovery area is a requirement for Data Guard with Maximum Performance implementations. DBAs can configure the tolerable data loss for fast-start failover in Maximum Performance mode depending on the company's RPO/RTO.

Logical Standby: SQL Apply

While the physical standby applies redo and archivelog blocks to the disaster recovery database, the logical standby database mines the redo log entries and reexecutes the SQL against the target database. Logical standby databases provide these key benefits:

- Reports are near real time since SQL Apply can occur while the database is up and running.

- Reduces the workload on primary database because the logical standby database is updated in almost real time, and reports can be offloaded to the logical standby.

- Modification of the schema on the target to take advantage of reports. (For example, additional indexes and even bitmapped indexes can be utilized on the logical standby database.)

One restriction that prohibits a company's acceptance of the logical standby is its datatype limitation. Oracle Database 11*g* logical standby adds datatype support for XMLType stored as CLOBs. The compatibility parameter must be set to `11.1.0`. The logical standby still does not support the following:

- Bfile

- Collections (including varrays and nested tables)

- Multimedia datatypes (including Spatial, Image, and Context)

- `ROWID` and `UROWID`

- User-defined types

- LOBs stored as SecureFiles

- XML stored as binary XML

Support for Transparent Data Encryption (TDE)

TDE supported on the primary database allows encrypted data protection. For Data Guard logical standby TDE support, both the primary and logical standby databases must have compatibility set to 11.1.0. TDE in the context of user-held keys or hardware security modules are not available in Oracle version 11.1 logical standby databases. There are numerous rules to consider when you replicate tables using TDE. First, the wallet created on the primary database must be accessible by the logical standby database to decipher encrypted redo logs. We recommend you copy the wallet file from the primary database to the logical standby database server. If you change the master key on the primary database, you need to recopy the wallet to the logical standby. You should not attempt to rekey the wallet at the logical standby site while logical standby is performing SQL Apply. Rekeying the wallet can cause the SQL Apply process to shut down on the standby site.

Commands associated with opening and closing a wallet are not replicated to the logical standby database. Unless the auto-open wallet is used, the wallet must be manually opened and closed on the logical standby database.

▓**Note** The password for the wallet does not have to be the same. You can have different passwords to open the wallet on the primary site and on the logical standby database.

Encrypt Tables and Columns

If you do plan to rekey the table at the standby site, you should downgrade the guard setting to none and perform the rekey function. Encryption levels and the key at the table and column level on the standby database can be different from the primary database. For example, the Social Security column on the per_all_people_f HR table can be AES256 on the primary database, and the encryption algorithm on the logical standby can be set to AES192. Likewise, the encryption level can be set to none on the standby site also. To rekey the table on the logical standby database, you can use a rekey option command similar to this:

```
SQL> alter table docs rekey using '3DES168';

Table altered.
```

Encrypt Tablespaces

Oracle Database 11g Data Guard logical standby supports TDE with tablespace encryption. Similar to column-level TDE support, Oracle requires that you copy the wallet from the primary site to the disaster recovery host. Whenever the key from the primary site changes, you will need to manually copy the new key to the disaster recovery site.

Dynamically Set the Data Guard SQL Apply Parameters

Traditionally the DBMS_LOGSTDBY.APPLY_SET procedure was used to set Oracle database initialization parameters. The negative aspect of this procedure was that the SQL Apply engine had to be shut down. Oracle Database 11g lifts this restriction, and the apply_set procedure can set these parameters without stopping SQL Apply:

- apply_servers
- event_log_dest
- log_auto_del_retention_target
- log_auto_delete
- max_events_recorded
- max_servers
- max_sga
- prepare_servers
- record_applied_ddl
- record_skip_ddl
- record_skip_errors
- record_unsupported_operations

For example, you can now dynamically adjust the number of parallel servers used by SQL Apply to ten without bouncing the SQL Apply engine:

```
SQL> exec dbms_logstdby.apply_set ('MAX_SERVERS', 10);

PL/SQL procedure successfully completed.
```

In Oracle Database 11g, new columns, UNIT, SETTING, and DYNAMIC, are added to the DBA_LOGSTDBY_PARAMETERS view. This view provides the list of parameters used by the SQL Apply engine. The SETTING column shows parameters set as default or those modified by the DBAs. The value of system indicates that the parameter was not explicitly set by a DBA. The UNIT column displays the unit of value when applicable. The DYNAMIC column provides information on whether the SQL Apply parameter must be shut down to activate. By querying this view, you can see that the preserve_commit_order parameter is the only parameter that is not dynamically modifiable:

```
SQL>  select *
  2  from dba_logstdby_parameters
  3* order by name
SQL> /
```

NAME	VALUE	UNIT	SETTING	DYNAMIC
APPLY_SERVERS	5		SYSTEM	YES
EVENT_LOG_DEST	DEST_EVENTS_TABLE		SYSTEM	YES
LOG_AUTO_DELETE	TRUE		SYSTEM	YES
LOG_AUTO_DEL_RETENTION_TARGET	1440	MINUTE	SYSTEM	YES
MAX_EVENTS_RECORDED	10000		SYSTEM	YES
MAX_SERVERS	9		SYSTEM	YES
MAX_SGA	30	MEGABY	SYSTEM	YES
PREPARE_SERVERS	1		SYSTEM	YES
PRESERVE_COMMIT_ORDER	TRUE		SYSTEM	NO
RECORD_APPLIED_DDL	FALSE		SYSTEM	YES
RECORD_SKIP_DDL	TRUE		SYSTEM	YES
RECORD_SKIP_ERRORS	TRUE		SYSTEM	YES
RECORD_UNSUPPORTED_OPERATIONS	FALSE		SYSTEM	YES

13 rows selected.

Support for VPD and FGA

Oracle Database 11*g* logical standby provides support for row-level security (VPD) and fine-grained auditing (FGA) by replicating the DBMS_RLS and DBMS_FGA packages. Now security implementations from the primary database server replicate to the logical standby database. This will automatically enable by default if the logical standby database is created from an Oracle Database 11*g* database. Databases upgraded to Oracle version 11.1 will need to have this feature enabled manually. When the DBMS_RLS and DBMS_FGA procedures are executed on the primary database, additional information is captured in the redo logs, which allows the logical standby to rebuild the procedural call. Both the primary and logical standby must have the compatibility set to 11.1 to have security enabled with VPD and FGA.

DBMS_SCHEDULER Support

Oracle Database 11*g* Data Guard logical standby now provides support for DBMS_SCHEDULER. The scheduler is capable of running jobs on both the primary and logical standby databases. Using the DBMS_SCHEDULER.SET_ATTRIBUTE procedure, you can set the database_role attribute to be the primary database or logical standby. By setting this attribute, you specify that the jobs can run only when operating in that particular database role.

A job created on the primary database will, by default, run only in the primary database role. Let's take an example of a job that already exists in the database called EDBA_UPDATE and change the database role attribute to logical standby using the set_attribute procedure:

```
SQL> BEGIN
  2   DBMS_SCHEDULER.SET_ATTRIBUTE(name   => 'EDBA_UPDATE',
  3        attribute    => 'database_role',
  4        value        =>'LOGICAL STANDBY');
  5   END;
  6   /

PL/SQL procedure successfully completed.
```

Once you change the database role for the job, you can query the DBA_SCHEDULER_JOB view to confirm that the EDBA_UPDATE is targeted to run on the logical standby, as depicted here:

```
 SQL> select job_name, database_role from dba_scheduler_job_roles;

JOB_NAME                               DATABASE_ROLE
------------------------------         ----------------
XMLDB_NFS_CLEANUP_JOB                  PRIMARY
FGR$AUTOPURGE_JOB                      PRIMARY
BSLN_MAINTAIN_STATS_JOB                PRIMARY
DRA_REEVALUATE_OPEN_FAILURES           PRIMARY
HM_CREATE_OFFLINE_DICTIONARY           PRIMARY
ORA$AUTOTASK_CLEAN                     PRIMARY
PURGE_LOG                              PRIMARY
MGMT_STATS_CONFIG_JOB                  PRIMARY
MGMT_CONFIG_JOB                        PRIMARY
RLM$SCHDNEGACTION                      PRIMARY
RLM$EVTCLEANUP                         PRIMARY
EDBA_UPDATE                            LOGICAL STANDBY  <--
```

The DBMS_SCHEDULER package automatically establishes the switching of roles for switchover or failover conditions. Since the scheduler log replicates to the logical standby, log history is available after a failover or switchover condition.

Logical Standby Archivelog Storage

Oracle Database 11g logical standby allows the flash recovery area to be used as the archivelog destination for the log_archive_dest_n parameter. You can modify this parameter using the alter system command, as shown here:

```
SQL>  alter system set log_archive_dest_1='LOCATION=USE_DB_RECOVERY_FILE_DEST';

System altered.
```

By default, the logical standby architecture automatically deletes an archivelog once it is applied. Now in Oracle Database 11g, this is an option that can be controlled using the log_auto_delete initialization parameter. The log_auto_delete parameter must be coupled with the log_auto_del_retention_target parameter to specify the number of minutes an archivelog is maintained until it is purged. This parameter is set to 1,440 minutes, or 24 hours, by default. For archivelog retention to be effective, the log_auto_delete parameter must be set to true, and the flash recovery area must not be used to store the archivelogs. Here's an example of setting `log_auto_del_retention_target` to two days and `log_auto_delete` to true:

```
SQL> exec dbms_logstdby.apply_set('LOG_AUTO_DELETE', 'TRUE');

PL/SQL procedure successfully completed.

SQL> exec DBMS_LOGSTDBY.APPLY_SET('LOG_AUTO_DEL_RETENTION_TARGET', 2880);

PL/SQL procedure successfully completed.
```

SQL Apply Event Messages

Prior to Oracle Database 11*g*, SQL Apply events were written to the alert log and the SYSTEM. LOGSTDBY$EVENTS table. Oracle Database 11*g* introduces the new `event_log_dest` parameter that dictates whether the SQL Apply engine will write out specified events to the SYSTEM. LOGSTDBY$EVENTS table and/or to the alert log. You can modify this parameter using the DBMS_ LOGSTDBY.APPLY_SET procedure to set a specified value. This value can also be unset using the DBMS_LOGSTDBY.APPLY_UNSET procedure.

The `event_log_dest` parameter has two valid values: `dest_all` and `dest_events_table`. By default, this value is set to `dest_events_table`, which specifies that the events will be recorded only to the LOGSTDBY$EVENTS table. By setting this parameter to `dest_all`, as in the following example code, SQL Apply will record events to both the alert log and the LOGSTDBY$EVENTS table:

```
SQL> exec dbms_logstdby.apply_set('EVENT_LOG_DEST', 'DEST_ALL');

PL/SQL procedure successfully completed.
```

You can view the contents of the LOGSTDBY$EVENTS view as shown here to view error and informational messages posted by SQL Apply:

```
  1  select event_time, error
  2  from system.logstdby$events
  3* where error like 'APPLY_SET%'
SQL> /

EVENT_TIME                      ERROR
-----------------------------   --------------------------------------------
14-AUG-07 09.29.56.536531 PM    APPLY_SET: MAX_EVENTS_RECORDED changed to 200
14-AUG-07 09.32.09.984015 PM    APPLY_SET: MAX_SERVERS changed to 10
14-AUG-07 09.43.18.058327 PM    APPLY_SET: EVENT_LOG_DEST changed to DEST_ALL
```

This parameter influences the behavior of other parameters such as the `record_skip_errors`, `record_skip_ddl`, `record_applied_ddl`, and `record_unsupported_operations` parameters.

Data Guard Broker

Numerous enhancements have been made to Data Guard Broker. Data Guard Broker simplifies the management of the physical and logical standby databases by providing an easy-to-use command-line interface. The amount of learning curve associated with Data Guard Broker syntax is significantly less than learning the Data Guard initialization parameters and syntax required to maintain Data Guard.

■**Note**   We recommend that customers leverage Data Guard Broker to maintain the Data Guard configuration. Once you set up the environment to leverage the features of Data Guard, it is a committed relationship. It is an all-or-nothing model. You cannot maintain just the portions of the Data Guard infrastructure using Data Guard Broker and yet continue to modify the initialization parameters manually using SQL*Plus.

Unfortunately, Data Guard Broker setup features are not available in Database Console. You must implement the Enterprise Manager Grid Control that requires an Oracle Management Server and Grid Control repository. For high-availability considerations, Oracle recommends separating the management server from the database repository.

Data Guard Broker Command-Line Interface

As mentioned previously, one of the new features in Data Guard is the ability to convert a physical standby database to a snapshot standby database. The broker also has the ability to convert a physical standby database to a snapshot standby database with ease. Data Guard Broker can convert a physical standby database to a snapshot standby database with just one command. At this point, you can utilize the database to perform tests such as a QA load test or other activities that require read/write access to the database. Once such tasks are complete, the database can be reverted to physical standby managed recovery mode. Data Guard Broker again can bring the database back to a physical standby database with just one command.

Oracle cannot make the physical standby to snapshot standby conversion easier. The syntax to convert the physical database to a snapshot standby is as follows:

```
convert database db_unique_name to snapshot standby;
```

Here you will see a single convert statement that will convert a physical standby to a snapshot standby:

```
DBA11gDR $ dgmgrl sys/oracle@dba11g
Welcome to DGMGRL, type "help" for information.
Connected.

DGMGRL> convert database 'dba11gdr' to snapshot standby;

Converting database "dba11gdr" to a Snapshot Standby database, please wait...
Database "dba11gdr" converted successfully
```

Believe it or not, that was it! Now, let's put the snapshot standby back to a physical standby database. Again, it takes only a single convert statement to put it back. Here you will see a single convert statement that will convert a snapshot standby into a physical standby:

```
DGMGRL> convert database 'dba11gdr' to physical standby;

Converting database "dba11gdr" to a Physical Standby database, please wait...
Operation requires shutdown of instance "DBA11gDR" on database "dba11gdr"
Shutting down instance "DBA11gDR"...
Database closed.
Database dismounted.
ORACLE instance shut down.
Operation requires startup of instance "DBA11gDR" on database "dba11gdr"
Starting instance "DBA11gDR"...
ORACLE instance started.
Database mounted.
Continuing to convert database "dba11gdr" ...
Operation requires shutdown of instance "DBA11gDR" on database "dba11gdr"
Shutting down instance "DBA11gDR"...
ORA-01109: database not open

Database dismounted.
ORACLE instance shut down.
Operation requires startup of instance "DBA11gDR" on database "dba11gdr"
Starting instance "DBA11gDR"...
ORACLE instance started.
Database mounted.
Database "dba11gdr" converted successfully
```

We just demonstrated how executing the new convert database to physical/snapshot standby command transforms a physical standby database into a read/write database. Other commands that are new to the Data Guard command-line interface are disable fast_start failover, enable fast_start failover, and show fast_start failover. These new command-line options are discussed in further detail in the following sections.

Unfortunately, the Data Guard Manager does not have the ability to convert a physical standby database to a real-time query standby database. You must use SQL*Plus to convert the physical standby to a real-time query standby database. The feature to convert a physical standby database to a real-time query standby database will be available in Oracle Enterprise Manager Grid Control 11*g* when it is released.

Using Data Guard Broker simplifies the management of the redo transport and apply layer in Oracle Database 11*g*. The logic is that the primary database will be in transport-on or transport-off mode. This is an attribute of the LogShipping property and corresponds to the log_archive_dest_state_n initialization parameter. transport-off will indicate that this parameter is being set to defer, whereas transport-on will set this parameter to enable. The same logic applies to the physical standby database. The physical standby database will either be in apply-on or apply-off mode.

Customize Fast-Start Failover Events

Oracle Database 11g Data Guard Broker introduces numerous enhancements to the Data Guard Manager command-line interface. Enhancements include the ability to customize what initiates the fast-start failover conditions. Prior to Oracle Database 11g, the fast-start failover conditions were induced by database health checks provided by Oracle. Now, the fast-start failover can be induced by certain configurable conditions. For example, the fast-restart failover process can be initiated when the primary database archivelog destination runs out of space by setting the fast_start_failover condition to the value of Stuck Archiver:

```
DGMGRL> enable fast_start failover condition "Stuck Archiver"
Succeeded.
```

Alternatively, you can enable the fast_start failover condition for a specified ORA- error message. Although you would never want to fail over from just an ORA-600 error message, the following example is provided to demonstrate the ease of specifying a generic ORA-600 error condition:

```
DGMGRL> enable fast_start failover condition 600;
Succeeded.
```

If you issue the new show fast_start failover status command in Data Guard Broker, it reports that the ORA-600 error will initiate a failover:

```
DGMGRL> show fast_start failover;

Fast-Start Failover:        ENABLED
  Threshold:                45 seconds
  Target:                   dba11g
  Observer:                 bpo40.dbaexpert.com
  Lag Limit:                30 seconds
  Shutdown Primary:         FALSE
  Auto-reinstate:           TRUE

Configurable Failover Conditions
  Health Conditions:
    Corrupted Controlfile            YES
    Corrupted Dictionary             YES
    Inaccessible Logfile             NO
    Stuck Archiver                   YES
    Datafile Offline                 YES

  Oracle Error Conditions:
    ORA-00600: internal error code, arguments:
            [%s], [%s], [%s], [%s], [%s], [%s], [%s], [%s]
```

Now, the show configuration verbose command also displays fast-start failover–related information.

■**Tip** DBAs often get surprised when they realize that commands to DGMGRL can also be scripted. DBAs can issue commands in the command-line interface by invoking dgmgrl in Unix similar to what is shown here:

```
DBA11g $ dgmgrl sys/oracle "edit database 'dba11g'
        set property faststartfailovertarget='DBA11gDR';"
DGMGRL for Linux: Version 11.1.0.4.0 - Beta
Copyright (c) 2000, 2005, Oracle.  All rights reserved.
Welcome to DGMGRL, type "help" for information.
Connected.
Property "faststartfailovertarget" updated
dgmgrl sys/oracle "edit database 'dba11gdr'
                set property faststartfailovertarget='DBA11g';"
```

Initiate Fast-Start Failover from Applications

Oracle Database 11g also introduces the new DBMS_DG PL/SQL package, which can be customized by applications to initiate a request for fast-start failover of the primary database. Data Guard Broker will perform some preliminary validations such as checking the readiness of the failover state or checking that the lag limit is within the threshold on the primary database and communicates with the observer to initiate a failover. If no parameters are specified, the default string of "Application Failover Requested" will be logged in the broker log file and in the database alert log file. You can see from the function description here that the function expects a condition string for the fast-start failover:

```
SQL> desc dbms_dg

FUNCTION INITIATE_FS_FAILOVER RETURNS BINARY_INTEGER
 Argument Name        Type            In/Out Default?
 ------------------   -------------   ---------------
 CONDSTR              VARCHAR2        IN
```

This function can return any one of the following return codes:

- *ORA-00000*: Normal, successful completion.

- *ORA-16646*: Fast-start failover is disabled.

- *ORA-16666*: Unable to initiate fast-start failover on a standby database.

- *ORA-16817*: Unsynchronized fast-start failover configuration.

- *ORA-16819*: Fast-start failover observer not started.

- *ORA-16820*: Fast-start failover observer is no longer observing this database.

- *ORA-16829*: Fast-start failover configuration is lagging.

You can query the V$FS_FAILOVER_STATS dynamic view on the primary database to obtain the cause of failure information and when it occurred, as shown here:

```
select last_failover_time, last_failover_reason
from v$fs_failover_stats;
```

New Data Guard Manager Properties

In addition to the RedoCompression property, there are new Data Guard Manager properties worth mentioning, as shown in Table 10-1.

Table 10-1. *New Data Guard Manager Properties*

Property Name	Description
FastStartFailoverAutoReinstate	By default, this parameter is set to true by the broker. This parameter specifies that the observer should automatically reinstate the primary database after a fast-start failover when connectivity to the primary is reestablished. If diagnostic or troubleshooting efforts are required on the primary database server, you should set this to false. This can be done using the following command: DGMGRL> edit configuration set property FastStartFailoverAutoReinstate = false; Property "faststartfailoverautoreinstate" updated
FastStartFailoverLagLimit	The minimum value is 10. By default, this parameter is set to 30. This parameter is applicable for Maximum Performance fast-start failover configurations and specifies the acceptable lag-time limit time in seconds that the physical standby can fall behind the primary database; otherwise, fast-start failover is not permitted. This can be done with the following command: edit configuration set property faststartfailoverlaglimit = n; This attribute is ignored for SYNC destinations.
FastStartFailoverPmyShutdown	By default, this parameter is set to false. If this value is set to true, the primary database will be shut down with the abort option in the event of a fast-start failover. There are three possible triggering events for this: Redo generation stalls and the primary database loses connectivity with the observer and standby database for longer than FastStartFailoverThreshold seconds. By a user-configured fast-start failover condition. The application invokes the DBMS_DG.INITIATE_FS_FAILOVER function (a new Oracle Database 11*g* PL/SQL package). DGMGRL> edit configuration set property FastStartFailoverPmyShutdown = false; Property "faststartfailoverpmyshutdown" updated
ObserverConnectIdentifier	This parameter sets the connect string that the observer uses to connect to the target database.

There are new values for the `FS_FAILOVER_STATUS` column in the V$DATABASE dynamic view for fast-start-enabled databases. The valid values for this column are as follows:

- `tag under lag limit`

- `tag over lag limit`

The `tag under lag limit` value indicates that the database is valid for fast-start failover. The `tag over lag limit` value indicates that the database is behind and cannot perform a fast-start failover because the standby database apply is behind the `FastStartFailoverLagLimit` property.

Detect Lost-Write Conditions Using a Physical Standby

Most everyone will agree that the highest priority of a DBA is to protect the data. DBAs are constantly architecting and rearchitecting to find the best solution that will protect the enterprise from faults introduced by the inevitable such as block corruptions, lost writes, and failed disks. Previously, DBAs were only able to architect database resilience strategies to protect against lost-write failures using third-party hardware solutions. Oracle Database 11*g* Data Guard provides a mechanism to detect lost-write failures on the physical standby. With the proper architecture including the flashback recovery area, the database can recover from these lost-write faults.

First, let's discuss what lost-write failures are. A lost write can occur for several reasons. The most common reason is when the SAN disk array receives an acknowledgment for a successful disk block write to disk when it really did not. A subsequent read of an allegedly written block will return old content. The physical standby is now able to detect lost-write block corruptions by comparing SCNs of the redo blocks on the primary database and SCNs of the blocks on the physical standby database. Oracle Data Guard detects a lost-write corruption when the primary database block SCN is lower than the standby database block SCN.

There are steps for recovery when lost-write corruption is detected from the physical standby database. In addition, it is assumed that all the data contained on the corrupted lost-write block will be lost. When such errors are detected on the standby (ORA-00752) database, you must fail over to the physical standby:

```
SQL> alter database activate standby database;
```

DBAs must also realize that the old primary database must be completely rebuilt. The old primary database can no longer participate in a Data Guard configuration. The traditional options such as flashing back the database or reinstating the database are not an option when dealing with lost-write detection errors. For additional information on lost-write detection, please refer to Chapter 2.

Support of Heterogeneous OS Data Guard Configuration

Oracle Database 11*g* Data Guard now lifts the same OS requirements for a Data Guard configuration. The initial deployment of this heterogeneous Data Guard configuration is limited in scope. Effective with Oracle Database 11*g*, the Data Guard configuration can be composed of a hybrid of Linux and Windows primary and standby. Previously in Oracle Database10*g*, different combinations such as HP-UX PA-RISC and Itanium platforms were supported for the heterogeneous Data Guard configuration. For a table of different platform combinations supported

by Data Guard, please refer to MetaLink note 413484.1, "Data Guard Support for Heterogeneous Primary and Standby Systems in Same Data Guard Configuration."

Oracle Database 11*g* Data Guard Over Storage Vendor Solutions

A lot of customers build high-availability solutions using storage vendor technologies. Solutions are typically supplied by third-party companies that provide business continuity using
some sort of sync and split technologies. For example, as a file system is added to the primary
database, the Business Continuity Volumes (EMC solution) or Shadow Images (Hitachi solution) can be added on both the primary and disaster recovery site to continue this traditional
high-availability block for block data replication. EMC provides Data Guard–equivalent solutions using TimeFinder. Hitachi provides similar equivalency through TruCopy. Moreover,
Network Appliance has a similar technology called SnapMirror for Oracle that performs pointer-
based block replication to the disaster recovery site.

Oracle's Data Guard is comparable or even better than the storage vendor's snapshot
technologies. With the new real-time query and snapshot standby technologies, DBAs should
definitely consider Data Guard options over hardware-level HA technologies. Oracle's goal is
to provide these similar technologies as a native option to the Enterprise Edition. Oracle Database 11*g* provides real-time query and snapshot standby database features in addition to providing
disaster recovery while using a single copy of the storage.

■■■

Application Development

Ｏne of the focuses of this book is to expose major new Oracle Database 11*g* development features to the development community. This chapter dives deep into the new features of development in the areas of PL/SQL, Java, and XML support. Furthermore, this chapter briefly covers Application Express and PHP to describe what is available in Oracle Database 11*g*. The PL/SQL and Java portions of this chapter are dedicated to developers, with minor emphasis on DBAs. DBAs with previous development backgrounds can definitely enjoy this chapter, though. Also, DBAs who are aspiring developers can benefit from all the new Oracle Database 11*g* features offered to increase database productivity. Let's get started with a discussion on PL/SQL.

New PL/SQL Features

Oracle includes quite a cast of new features for PL/SQL in Oracle Database 11*g*. Although the new features don't offer new functionality that could not be achieved in Oracle Database 10*g*, albeit with some difficulty, they provide enhanced performance, simpler coding, and greater readability.

CONTINUE Statement

Finally, PL/SQL has a CONTINUE statement for its loops. Syntactically it is the same as the EXIT statement, and it allows for an optional WHEN clause and label. In the following example, an interface table is queried, and records that are flagged as comments are skipped:

```
LOOP
  FETCH cur BULK COLLECT INTO rows;
  EXIT WHEN rows.COUNT=0;
  FOR I IN 1..rows.COUNT LOOP
    CONTINUE WHEN NOT EVALUATORS.single_line_comment(rows(i));
    -- process responsive data
    ...
  END LOOP;
END LOOP;
```

For comment rows, control moves to the end of the loop, and the next I is processed.

Sequences Without Dual

It is no longer necessary to execute a SELECT statement in PL/SQL when you are retrieving either NEXTVAL or CURVAL from a sequence. The following shows how to access a sequence named my_sequence from within PL/SQL:

```
DECLARE
  new_Val NUMBER;
BEGIN
  new_Val := my_sequence.nextval;
 ...
END;
```

It couldn't be simpler.

Native Compilation

PL/SQL can now directly create native compiled PL/SQL code. Prior to this, you had to create C code translated from your PL/SQL and compile that manually using the platform's C compiler. An example of native compilation of a PL/SQL package is shown in the "SIMPLE_INTEGER" section. To utilize this feature, DBAs may need to set up a special directory to contain the share libraries. Specific requirements for each platform are given in the installation guide. You can find instructions on setting up the database in the PL/SQL language reference guide.

SQL-intensive PL/SQL programs will not see significant performance improvements since the SQL is interpreted by the database anyway, but computation-intensive tasks may see an order of magnitude improvement in speed (see the "SIMPLE_INTEGER" section for an example). Not only can you compile the individual PL/SQL modules you create, but you can also compile all the PL/SQL in the database. You're cautioned, of course, to perform a full backup before attempting this.

SIMPLE_INTEGER

A new datatype, which is a subtype of PLS_INTEGER, has been included. This datatype has the same range, –2,147,483,648 to 2,147,483,647, but PLS_INTEGER cannot be null. Also, instead of throwing some overflow or underflow exception when an expression results in values out of its range, variables of this datatype wrap from smallest to largest and from largest to smallest. Thus, incrementing a variable set to the maximum value results in the variable having the minimum value, and decrementing the minimum value results in the maximum value. The following example demonstrates this:

```
DECLARE
  cnt SIMPLE_INTEGER:=-2147483646;
BEGIN
  dbms_output.put_line('Decrementing');
  FOR I IN 1..4 LOOP
    cnt:=cnt-1;
    dbms_output.put_line(to_char(cnt,'999,999,999,999'));
  END LOOP;
  dbms_output.put_line('Incrementing');
```

```
  FOR I IN 1..4 LOOP
    cnt:=cnt+1;
    dbms_output.put_line(to_char(cnt,'999,999,999,999'));
  END LOOP;
END;
```

Executing the previous code yields the following results:

```
Decrementing
  -2,147,483,647
  -2,147,483,648
   2,147,483,647    -- Smallest minus one = Largest
   2,147,483,646
Incrementing
   2,147,483,647
  -2,147,483,648   -- Largest plus one = Smallest
  -2,147,483,647
  -2,147,483,646
```

Using this datatype in native compiled PL/SQL will result in a significant performance increase over the same code with PLS_INTEGER used instead. The following package compares SIMPLE_INTEGER with PLS_INTEGER and the NUMBER datatypes:

```
CREATE OR REPLACE
PACKAGE SI_DEMO AS
  PROCEDURE test_si;
  PROCEDURE test_pls;
  PROCEDURE test_num;
  PROCEDURE test;
END;
/
CREATE OR REPLACE
PACKAGE BODY SI_DEMO AS
  MAX_COUNT CONSTANT PLS_INTEGER:=10000000;


  PROCEDURE test_si IS
    numVal SIMPLE_INTEGER:=0;
    startTime PLS_INTEGER;
  BEGIN
    startTime:=dbms_utility.get_time;
    FOR i IN 1..MAX_COUNT LOOP
      numVal:=numVal*2-(numVal+8)*2;
    END LOOP;
    dbms_output.put_line('SIMPLE_INTEGER elapsed time(seconds):'||
    to_char((dbms_utility.get_time-startTime)/100,'990.90'));
  END;
```

```
  PROCEDURE test_pls IS
    numVal PLS_INTEGER:=0;
    startTime PLS_INTEGER;
  BEGIN
    startTime:=dbms_utility.get_time;
    FOR i IN 1..MAX_COUNT LOOP
      numVal:=numVal*2-(numVal+8)*2;
    END LOOP;
    dbms_output.put_line('PLS_INTEGER elapsed time(seconds):'||
    to_char((dbms_utility.get_time-startTime)/100,'990.90'));
  END;


  PROCEDURE test_num IS
    numVal NUMBER:=0;
    startTime PLS_INTEGER;
  BEGIN
    startTime:=dbms_utility.get_time;
    FOR i IN 1..MAX_COUNT LOOP
      numVal:=numVal*2-(numVal+8)*2;
    END LOOP;
    dbms_output.put_line('NUMBER elapsed time(seconds):'||
    to_char((dbms_utility.get_time-startTime)/100,'990.90'));
  END;


  PROCEDURE test IS
  BEGIN
    si_demo.test_si;
    si_demo.test_pls;
    si_demo.test_num;
  END;
END;
```

Compiling the SI_DEMO package as interpreted and executing the test() procedure yields the following:

```
SIMPLE_INTEGER elapsed time(seconds):   1.60
PLS_INTEGER elapsed time(seconds):      1.75
NUMBER elapsed time(seconds):           3.84
```

Repeated execution of the test() procedure, although not exactly matching the same timing, always resulted in PLS_INTEGER being a little slower than SIMPLE_INTEGER and resulted in NUMBER being more than twice as slow as SIMPLE_INTEGER.

The following compiles the SI_DEMO package into native code:

```
alter package si_demo compile plsql_code_type=native;
```

Executing yields the following results:

```
SIMPLE_INTEGER elapsed time(seconds):    0.10
PLS_INTEGER elapsed time(seconds):       0.80
NUMBER elapsed time(seconds):            3.22
```

The native code runs more than an order of magnitude faster for SIMPLE_INTEGER, twice as fast for PLS_INTEGER, and (not so surprisingly) just a little bit faster for Oracle NUMBER types. Clearly, if you are performing a great deal of integer arithmetic, SIMPLE_INTEGER is a must.

Regular Expression Enhancements

A new argument to REGEXP_INSTR() and REGEXP_SUBSTR() allows you to select the *n*th subexpression in the regular expression being evaluated. Subexpressions are identified in the regular expression by enclosing that bit of the pattern in parentheses. There is also a new function, REGEXP_COUNT(), which counts the number of matches. In the following expression, REGEXP_INSTR() is being used to determine the location of the repeated word *the* in the evaluated string:

```
SELECT REGEXP_INSTR('When in the the course of human events...' -- source
            ,'(the) (the)' -- regular expression with two subexpressions
            ,1 -- starting position to begin evaluation
            ,1 -- match occurrence
            ,0 -- 0 = return position of start, 1 = position after end
            ,'i' -- case insensitive search
            ,2 -- which subexpression to return position
            ) dup_loc
from dual;

DUP_LOC
---------------------
13
```

Subexpressions can be nested. The subexpressions are counted by the left parenthesis from one to a maximum of nine from left to right. The default is zero, which means the substring that matches the entire regular expression is used. In the example, 2 is given, which corresponds to the second *the* in the evaluated string. As you can see from the example, 13 is returned, which is the position of the *t* in the second *the*.

In the following example, REGEXP_SUBSTR() is used to retrieve either the timestamp, the severity code, or the message text from a hypothetical entry in a log file. Lines in the log file have the following form:

```
<timestamp>: [INFORMATION|WARNING|ERROR]: <text>
```

So, the regular expression assigned to the following parse_RE variable is constructed to return the relevant piece of the log line based on the subexpression number argument:

```
DECLARE
  log_Line VARCHAR2(256):='01-JAN-2007 13:56:03: ERROR: Network Unreachable';
  -- Constants to identify which piece of info is plucked from the line
  TS_IND CONSTANT SIMPLE_INTEGER:=1;
  SC_IND CONSTANT SIMPLE_INTEGER:=2;
  TB_IND CONSTANT SIMPLE_INTEGER:=3;
  -- The regular expression used. Three subexpressions.
  parse_RE VARCHAR2(4000):='(.*): (INFORMATION|WARNING|ERROR): (.*)';
  event_timestamp VARCHAR2(4000);
  event_severity VARCHAR2(4000);
  event_text VARCHAR2(4000);
  -- Function to improve readability.
  FUNCTION get_Match(pInd IN SIMPLE_INTEGER) RETURN VARCHAR2 IS
  BEGIN
    RETURN REGEXP_SUBSTR(log_Line,parse_RE,1,1,'i',pInd);
  END;
BEGIN
  pragma INLINE(get_Match,'YES'); -- request inlining
  event_timestamp:=get_Match(TS_IND);
  event_severity:=get_Match(SC_IND);
  event_text:=get_Match(TB_IND);
  dbms_output.put_line('Severity Level: '||event_severity);
  dbms_output.put_line('Timestamp: '||event_timestamp);
  dbms_output.put_line('Text: '||event_text);
END;
```

Executing yields the following:

```
Severity Level: ERROR
Timestamp: 01-JAN-2007 13:56:03
Text: Network Unreachable
```

A function, get_Match(), is declared to make the code easier to write and understand. The pragma INLINE(), which will be covered later in the "Subprogram Inlining" section, ensures that performance is not sacrificed for the sake of readability. REGEXP_SUBSTR() is called three times with different values for the subexp argument. In the first call, 1 is passed as the subexp number argument, and the text matching the first (.*) in the regular expression is returned. Likewise, for the second and third call, the matching text for (INFORMATION|WARNING|ERROR) and (.*) is returned accordingly.

REGEXP_COUNT() has been added to simply count the number of matches a regular expression has with the source text. The following counts the number of one-digit numbers found in a piece of text:

```
SELECT REGEXP_COUNT('In the sample only 1 person in 8 8 crackers', -- source text
       '[0-9]' -- regular expression
       ,1 -- starting position
       ,'i'  -- ignore case
       ) BAD_ONES
FROM dual
```

Executing yields the following:

```
BAD_ONES
--------------------
3
```

The starting position and case-insensitive arguments were included for completeness.

Named and Mixed Arguments in SQL Statement PL/SQL Function Calls

The use of NAME=>value is now supported in PL/SQL function calls that are contained in expressions in SQL statements. So for example, all of the following SELECT statements are now valid:

```
SELECT VENDORS_PKG.vendor_Id(vendor_name,organization_id)
FROM VENDORS;

SELECT VENDORS_PKG.vendor_Id(vendor_name,pOrgId=>organization_id)
FROM VENDORS;

SELECT VENDORS_PKG.vendor_Id(pVendorName=>vendor_name,pOrgId=>organization_id)
FROM VENDORS;
```

Subprogram Inlining

Inlining in PL/SQL is an optimization where the PL/SQL compiler replaces calls to subprograms (functions and procedures) with the code of the subprograms. A performance gain is almost always achieved because calling a subprogram requires the creation of a callstack entry, possible creation of copies of variables, and the handling of return values. With inlining, those steps are avoided. As an example, consider the following, where the PL/SQL optimization level is explicitly set to 2 for reasons explained later, and then an anonymous PL/SQL block is executed:

```
ALTER SESSION SET PLSQL_OPTIMIZE_LEVEL=2;

DECLARE
  PROCEDURE wr(pStr IN VARCHAR2) IS
  BEGIN
    dbms_output.put_line(rpad(lpad(pStr,15,'='),30,'='));
    dbms_output.put_line(dbms_utility.format_call_stack());
  END;
BEGIN
  wr('At Start');
  wr('Done');
END;
```

The procedure WR() in this block prints the passed-in string as well as the current call stack. Running this outputs the following:

```
=======At Start===============
----- PL/SQL Call Stack -----
    object      line   object
    handle     number  name
0x44b90390         5   anonymous block
0x44b90390         8   anonymous block


==========Done===============
----- PL/SQL Call Stack -----
    object      line   object
    handle     number  name
0x44b90390         5   anonymous block
0x44b90390         9   anonymous block
```

This is what you would expect—two calls to WR() on lines 8 and 9, with the call to dbms_utility.format_call_stack() on line 5 within the WR() procedure. Now, change PLSQL_OPTIMIZE_LEVEL to 3, which is the level that includes automatic inlining, and let's try that anonymous block again:

```
ALTER SESSION SET PLSQL_OPTIMIZE_LEVEL=3;

DECLARE
....
END;


=======At Start===============
----- PL/SQL Call Stack -----
    object      line   object
    handle     number  name
0x45d309a4         8   anonymous block


==========Done===============
----- PL/SQL Call Stack -----
    object      line   object
    handle     number  name
0x45d309a4         9   anonymous block
```

This is different. The PL/SQL optimizer has moved the code executed in WR() to the main body of the anonymous PL/SQL block. Although the performance increase in this example is negligible, the readability and maintainability of this code is superior to the case where WR() is not used and four DBMS_OUTPUT.PUT_LINE() are called instead. The example given for REGEXP_SUBSTR() would be an example where performance improvements could be realized.

The PLSQL_OPTIMIZE_LEVEL parameter has a default value of 2, which means inlining will occur only if the correct pragma INLINE directives are included in your code. Since it's possible your code will be maintained by someone who is unaware of inlining, it is a good practice to include this directive in your code for particularly critical sections where performance would suffer if inlining were not done. The following is the same anonymous block as before with two pragma directives added. The first requests inlining, and the second requests that inlining not be done.

```
ALTER SESSION SET PLSQL_OPTIMIZE_LEVEL=2;

DECLARE
  PROCEDURE wr(pStr IN VARCHAR2) IS
  BEGIN
    dbms_output.put_line(rpad(lpad(pStr,15,'='),30,'='));
    dbms_output.put_line(dbms_utility.format_call_stack());
  END;
BEGIN
  pragma inline(wr,'YES');
  wr('At Start');
  pragma inline(wr,'NO');
  wr('Done');
END;
```

Executing yields the following:

```
=======At Start===============
----- PL/SQL Call Stack -----
    object      line  object
    handle    number  name
0x44b0b99c         9  anonymous block

==========Done===============
----- PL/SQL Call Stack -----
    object      line  object
    handle    number  name
0x44b0b99c         5  anonymous block
0x44b0b99c        11  anonymous block
```

As you can see, the first pragma directive instructed the compiler to replace the call to WR() with the inline version, while the second pragma directive disabled inlining for the same subprogram. If the second pragma directive were not there, then the compiler would inline the second call, as you can test by removing the second pragma directive.

pragma INLINE(identifier, mode)

There are two arguments to the pragma INLINE compiler directive, as described in Table 11-1.

Table 11-1. *Pragma* INLINE *Compiler Directive*

Argument	Description
identifier	The name of the subprogram.
Mode	Either YES or NO. For NO, no inlining will occur for the subprogram. If YES and PLSQL_OPTIMIZE_LEVEL=2, the subprogram will be inlined. If YES and PLSQL_OPTIMIZE_LEVEL=3, the optimizer will place a high priority on inlining the subprogram. The optimizer may find a better optimization that does not need inlining.

PLSQL_OPTIMIZE_LEVEL Allowed Values

The PLSQL_OPTIMIZE_LEVEL initialization parameter specifies the level of optimization used to compile the PL/SQL library unit. Table 11-2 describes the PLSQL_OPTIMIZE_LEVEL allowed values.

Table 11-2. *PLSQL_OPTIMIZE_LEVEL Allowed Values*

Value	Description
1	No PL/SQL compilation optimizations are done. This is the debug level.
2	PL/SQL will rearrange code for performance but will not automatically inline subprograms. It will inline subprogram calls the developer has flagged with the pragma INLINE directive.
3	In addition to the level 2 optimizations, the PL/SQL compiler will automatically inline subprograms where performance gains are predicted, as well as place a high priority on inlining programmer flagged calls.

You can modify this parameter at the system level or at the session level. DBAs can use the ALTER SYSTEM command to set this level. In the following example, we will set PLSQL_OPTIMIZE_LEVEL to 3 for automatic inlining of subprograms:

```
SQL> alter system set PLSQL_OPTIMIZE_LEVEL = 3;

System altered.
```

Scope and Usage

Inlining may occur only with subprogram calls that reside in the same package, procedure, function, or anonymous PL/SQL block. The pragma INLINE directive, if present, must appear immediately before the subprogram call. When inlining subprograms in nonanonymous modules, the compiler can provide a number of useful warnings to help you verify that inlining did or did not occur. Table 11-3 shows several of the possible warning codes and descriptions associated with the warning codes.

Table 11-3. *Warning Codes Indicating That Inlining Did Not Occur*

Warning Code	Text and Description
PLW-05011	pragma INLINE for the procedure <subprogram name> does not apply to any calls. The pragma INLINE directive does not appear immediately before the call to the procedure identified as <subprogram name>. Note: this same message will be shown for functions as well.
PLW-06004	Inlining of call of procedure <subprogram name> requested. The compiler found the pragma INLINE and verified that it is before the identified procedure or function.
PLW-06005	Inlining of call of procedure <subprogram name> was done. The compiler inlined the identified procedure. If PLSQL_OPTIMIZE_LEVEL is 3, this warning will appear when automatic inlining is done regardless of whether the pragma INLINE directive is included.

Generalized Invocation

In prior versions of PL/SQL if you wanted to call an overridden method of a supertype from one of its subtypes, you would have to create a static method in the supertype and create an over-ridable wrapper member subprogram that called that static method. Within the subtypes, you would call the static member as needed. Here is an example of this idiom:

```
CREATE OR REPLACE TYPE SUP_T AS OBJECT(
      ...
      STATIC PROCEDURE super_init,
      MEMBER PROCEDURE init
)
NOT FINAL;

CREATE OR REPLACE TYPE BODY SUP_T AS
  STATIC PROCEDURE super_init IS
  BEGIN
  -- actual init code
  ...
  END;
  MEMBER PROCEDURE init IS
  BEGIN
  -- the wrapper procedure
  ...
  super_init;
  END;
END;

CREATE OR REPLACE TYPE SUB_T UNDER SUP_T(
  ...
  OVERRIDING MEMBER PROCEDURE init
)

CREATE OR REPLACE TYPE BODY SUB_T AS
  OVERRIDING MEMBER PROCDURE init IS
  BEGIN
  super_init;
  ...
  END;
END;
```

Although this works, the programmer would much rather cast SELF to the correct super-type and call the method directly. With Oracle Database 11g, this functionality has been added to PL/SQL. For the previous example, the syntax for calling init() in SUP_T from SUB_T is as follows:

```
(SELF AS SUP_T).init();
```

or,

```
init(SELF AS SUP_T);
```

The first essentially casts SELF to SUP_T and calls its init() procedure, while in the second, init(SELF AS SUP_T), the compiler selects the correct init() procedure based on the implicit first argument, SELF. We prefer the first style because it appears more like casting than overloading. This syntax is not limited to within method bodies of subtypes only. The pattern is as follows:

```
(<variable> AS <parent type>)
```

where <variable> is a variable instantiated to some type at or below the <parent type> in its type hierarchy.

The following example utilizes this new feature (highlighted in bold) in the simple hierarchy of PL/SQL subprograms and their implementations as either functions or procedures:

```
CREATE OR REPLACE type plsql_subprogram_t as OBJECT (
  name VARCHAR2(30),
  description VARCHAR2(256),
  MEMBER PROCEDURE print_doc)
  NOT FINAL NOT INSTANTIABLE;

CREATE OR REPLACE TYPE BODY plsql_subprogram_t AS
  MEMBER PROCEDURE print_doc IS
  BEGIN
    dbms_output.put_line('Name: '||name);
    dbms_output.put_line('Description: '||description);
  END;
END;

CREATE OR REPLACE TYPE plsql_procedure_t UNDER plsql_subprogram_t (
  overriding member PROCEDURE print_doc)
FINAL;

CREATE OR REPLACE TYPE BODY plsql_procedure_t AS
  OVERRIDING MEMBER PROCEDURE print_doc IS
  BEGIN
    dbms_output.put('PROCEDURE ');
    (self as plsql_subprogram_t).print_doc();
  END;
END;

CREATE OR REPLACE TYPE plsql_function_t UNDER plsql_subprogram_t (
  returning_type VARCHAR2(256),
  overriding member PROCEDURE print_doc)
FINAL;

CREATE OR REPLACE TYPE BODY plsql_function_t AS
  OVERRIDING MEMBER PROCEDURE print_doc IS
```

```
  BEGIN
    dbms_output.put('FUNCTION ');
    (self as plsql_subprogram_t).print_doc();
    dbms_output.put_line('Returning: '||returning_type);
  END;
END;
```

A noninstantiable type plsql_subprogram_t object is created with the single member procedure print_doc() that prints the subprogram name and description. Since the subprogram is an abstract concept implemented as either a function or a procedure, it is declared NOT INSTANTIABLE.

plsql_procedure_t is created as a subtype of plsql_subprogram_t and overrides the print_doc() member procedure to output the text "PROCEDURE" before calling the plsql_subprogram_t print_doc() member procedure to print the name and description.

plsql_function_t is created similarly as plsql_procedure_t except that it includes a returning_type attribute that identifies the datatype returned from the function. The print_doc() member procedure includes this as well as identifying itself as a function and calling the plsql_subprogram_t print_doc() member procedure.

The following example demonstrates these objects in use:

```
DECLARE
  TYPE subarr_t IS TABLE OF plsql_subprogram_t INDEX BY PLS_INTEGER;
  subs subarr_t;
BEGIN
  subs(1):=plsql_function_t('UPPER'
    ,'Folds lowercase characters in passed in string to uppercase.','VARCHAR2');
  subs(2):=plsql_procedure_t('DBMS_OUTPUT.PUT'
    ,'Writes characters to internal dbms_output buffer');

  FOR i IN 1..subs.COUNT LOOP
    subs(i).print_doc();
    dbms_output.new_line;
  END LOOP;
END;
```

Executing yields the following:

```
FUNCTION Name: UPPER
Description: Folds lowercase characters in passed in string to uppercase.
Returning: VARCHAR2

PROCEDURE Name: DBMS_OUTPUT.PUT
Description: Writes characters to internal dbms_output buffer
```

As you can see, plsql_subprogram_t print_doc() was called using this new language element and augmenting the subtype implementations of print_doc().

Cross-Session PL/SQL Function Result Cache

This new feature allows the developer to request that the result of a PL/SQL function call be cached in the SGA and returned from the cache if the same arguments are passed to the function in future calls. Functions that perform time-consuming queries on rarely modified tables are ideal candidates for this feature. As shown in the following example, the keyword RESULT_CACHE is added both to the function in the package specification as well as in the package body. Cached functions do not need to be declared in the package specification; they can be private functions. However, if they are public functions, they must include the RESULT_CACHE keyword.

```
CREATE PACKAGE FCACHE_DEMO IS
  FUNCTION GMOD(pNumb IN BINARY_INTEGER)
  RETURN BINARY_INTEGER
  RESULT_CACHE;
  PROCEDURE TEST;
END;
/
PACKAGE BODY FCACHE_DEMO IS
  FUNCTION GMOD(pNumb IN BINARY_INTEGER)
  RETURN BINARY_INTEGER
  RESULT_CACHE
  IS
   BEGIN
    dbms_output.put_line('GMOD: '||pNumb);
    RETURN pNumb*pNumb;
   END;
  PROCEDURE TEST IS
    ret BINARY_INTEGER:=0;
  BEGIN
    FOR i IN 1..1000 LOOP
      ret:=GMOD(MOD(ret+i,10));
    END LOOP;
  END;
END;
/
```

When executing FCACHE_DEMO.TEST(), the following ten lines are produced:

```
GMOD: 1
GMOD: 3
GMOD: 2
GMOD: 8
GMOD: 9
GMOD: 7
GMOD: 6
GMOD: 4
GMOD: 5
GMOD: 0
```

Usually, you would expect a very long list, but this list has only ten lines. From this you can see that the function body for GMOD() is executed a total of ten times (cache misses), while within the TEST() procedure GMOD() is called 1,000 times with a total of 990 cache hits.

This feature is handy when coupled with rarely changing tables. An additional clause, RELIES_ON(), can be inserted after the RESULT_CACHE keyword to identify tables and views that, if updated, will cause the function's cache entries to become invalid. Recompiling the function or the function's package will also invalidate the cache. The following code creates a table, VENDORS, and inserts a couple of rows into it. A cached function that relies on records in the VENDORS table is then created. This function looks up a vendor's VENDOR_ID when passed in the vendor's name. To identify function calls that are cached vs. those that are not, a DBMS_OUTPUT.PUT_LINE() is included in the function's body. Oracle recommends for cached functions that you do not include such "side effects" because the function's cache-hit behavior is not identical to the cache-miss behavior, but for proving that caching is working, as we are doing, inclusion is ideal.

```
CREATE TABLE vendors(vendor_id INTEGER NOT NULL primary key
            ,vendor_name VARCHAR2(80) NOT NULL UNIQUE);

insert into vendors values(1,'The Cookie Place');
insert into vendors values(2,'Tasty Pastries');

CREATE OR REPLACE FUNCTION find_Vendor_Id(pVendorName IN VARCHAR2)
RETURN vendors.vendor_id%TYPE
RESULT_CACHE RELIES_ON(vendors) IS
  CURSOR c_vendors(pName IN VARCHAR2) IS
    SELECT vendor_id
    FROM vendors
    WHERE vendor_name=pName;
  ret_Id vendors.vendor_id%TYPE;
  try_Name vendors.vendor_name%TYPE;
BEGIN
  dbms_output.put_line('cache miss: '||pVendorName);
  OPEN c_vendors(pVendorName);
  FETCH c_vendors INTO ret_Id;
  CLOSE c_vendors;
  RETURN ret_Id;
END;
```

The following anonymous block is then used to exercise this function and demonstrate when the caching is used:

```
DECLARE
  try_Number SIMPLE_INTEGER:=0;
  PROCEDURE TRY_IT(pNote IN VARCHAR2,pVendorName IN VARCHAR2) IS
  BEGIN
    try_Number:=try_Number+1;
    dbms_output.put_line(rpad(try_Number||'.',4)||pNote);
    dbms_output.put_line(rpad('=',40,'='));
    dbms_output.put_line('Calling find_Vendor_Id with: '||pVendorName);
```

```
      dbms_output.put_line('Returned Vendor_id : '||find_Vendor_Id(pVendorName));
      dbms_output.new_line;
   END;
BEGIN
   TRY_IT('First Call for "Tasty Pastries"','Tasty Pastries');
   TRY_IT('Second Call for "Tasty Pastries", no cache miss','Tasty Pastries');
   TRY_IT('First Call "The Cookie Place"','The Cookie Place');
   INSERT INTO vendors(vendor_id,vendor_name) VALUES(4,'Curiosity, A');
   TRY_IT('After INSERT INTO vendors, Call for "Tasty Pastries",
         notice cache miss','
   TRY_IT('After INSERT INTO vendors, Call for "Tasty Pastries",
         notice second cache      ,'The Cookie Place');
   TRY_IT('First Call for inserted "Curiosity, A", an uncommitted record'
     ,'Curiosity, A');
   TRY_IT('Second Call for inserted "Curiosity, A",
         an uncommitted record with a seco      ,'Curiosity, A');
    ROLLBACK;
   TRY_IT('After ROLLBACK, Call or "The Cookie Place", notice cache hit'
     ,'The Cookie Place');
  END;
```

Executing this anonymous block results in the following output:

```
1.  First Call for "Tasty Pastries"
=========================================
Calling find_Vendor_Id with: Tasty Pastries
cache miss: Tasty Pastries
Returned Vendor_id : 2


2.  Second Call for "Tasty Pastries", no cache miss
=========================================
Calling find_Vendor_Id with: Tasty Pastries
Returned Vendor_id : 2


3.  First Call "The Cookie Place"
=========================================
Calling find_Vendor_Id with: The Cookie Place
cache miss: The Cookie Place
Returned Vendor_id : 1


4.  After INSERT INTO vendors, Call for "Tasty Pastries", notice cache miss
=========================================
Calling find_Vendor_Id with: The Cookie Place
cache miss: The Cookie Place
Returned Vendor_id : 1
```

5. After INSERT INTO vendors, Call for "Tasty Pastries", notice second cache miss
=======================================
Calling find_Vendor_Id with: The Cookie Place
cache miss: The Cookie Place
Returned Vendor_id : 1

6. First Call for inserted "Curiosity, A", an uncommitted record
=======================================
Calling find_Vendor_Id with: Curiosity, A
cache miss: Curiosity, A
Returned Vendor_id : 4

7. Second Call for inserted "Curiosity, A", an uncommitted record with a second
cache miss
=======================================
Calling find_Vendor_Id with: Curiosity, A
cache miss: Curiosity, A
Returned Vendor_id : 4

8. After ROLLBACK, Call or "The Cookie Place", notice cache hit
=======================================
Calling find_Vendor_Id with: The Cookie Place
Returned Vendor_id : 1

Table 11-4 provides a running commentary on what happened in this anonymous block.

Table 11-4. *Code Execution Explanation*

Try Number	Explanation
1	Call to find_Vendor_Id() for "Tasty Pastries" requires the function body to be executed to retrieve the vendor_id.
2	Since try #1 already cached this entry, the value is retrieved from the cache without needing to execute the function body.
3	Call for "The Cookie Place" caches an entry for this vendor. INSERT INTO VENDORS invalidates the cache.
4	A call for "Tasty Pastries" indeed shows that the cache has been invalidated and the function body is executed to retrieve the value.
5	Another call to "Tasty Pastries" shows that while a session has outstanding changes to any of the RELIES_ON() tables, caching is not performed.
6 and 7	The same goes for the inserted or updated records: no caching. ROLLBACK executed.
8	The cache that was built in tries #1 and #3 is restored.

Tries #4 through #7 illustrate an important point about cached functions: to ensure that a session sees its uncommitted changes, caching is bypassed when the session has made changes to the tables identified in the RELIES_ON() clause. So as a general rule, do not rely on cached functions in subprograms that maintain the tables on which the cached functions rely.

What Does "Cross-Session" Mean?

The return values cached for function calls are available to all sessions that have EXECUTE privilege for this function. This means once a function call is cached, it remains cached for any future session that calls the function with a matching set of arguments.

Security Considerations

Since the cross-session caching mechanism will return cached values based solely on matching the passed-in arguments regardless of any special context processing, the existence of a virtual private database, or the security testing performed within the body of the function, functions that return sensitive data should probably not be created as public cached functions. If done, it is possible for someone without the appropriate privileges to view data they have no business seeing. Oracle's documentation shows a way of passing a user's context into a function to allow the caching of context-sensitive function calls. This method uses an argument with a default value being the value returned from a call to SYS_CONTEXT(). Although this works, there is nothing to prevent a malefactor from supplying a value for that default value and thus retrieving context-sensitive data that they might not be approved to view. Since cached functions do not need to be public functions, sensitive but time-intensive data can be cached by creating a private cached function (a function that appears only in the package body) and a noncached function that checks the caller's security context, called the *private cached function*, and returns the correct values as required by the security context.

Restrictions and Limitations

The following types of functions cannot be cached:

- No functions that have OUT or IN OUT arguments (which is bad form for functions anyway).

- No functions declared with invoker rights; the values returned from a function declared with AUTHID CURRENT_USER could vary according to the user.

- No functions defined in an anonymous block.

- No pipeline table functions.

- No functions with BLOB, CLOB, NCLOB, or ref cursor arguments.

- No functions with record, collection, or object arguments.

- The return type is not a BLOB, a CLOB, an NCLOB, a ref cursor, an object, or a record or collection that contains one or more of the preceding types.

Bulk In-Bind Table of Records in FORALL

Before Oracle Database 11*g*, attempts to use a table of records, as shown here, would result in the following error:

```
DECLARE
  CURSOR c1 IS SELECT rowid,bar FROM foo ;
  TYPE rows_t IS TABLE OF c1%ROWTYPE;
  rows rows_t;
BEGIN
  OPEN c1;
  FETCH c1 BULK COLLECT INTO rows;

  -- modify bar attribute of rows table

  FORALL I IN rows.COUNT
    UPDATE foo
    SET bar=rows(i).bar
    WHERE rowid=rows(i).rowid;
  ...
END;
/
```

The output of the previous PL/SQL block produces the following error:

```
PLS-00436: implementation restriction:
          cannot reference fields of BULK In-BIND table of records
```

PL/SQL did not support tables of records, which is why we used rows(i).bar and rows(i).rowid, while a more natural syntax was not allowed. The workaround was to create separate collections for each column, as shown here:

```
DECLARE
  CURSOR c1 IS SELECT rowid.bar from foo;
  TYPE rowID_t IS TABLE OF ROWID;
  TYPE bar_t IS TABLE of foo.bar%TYPE;
  rids rowId_t;
  bars bar_t;
  ...
BEGIN
  ...
  FETCH c1 BULK COLLECT INTO rids,bars;
  ....
  FORALL I IN rows.COUNT
    UPDATE foo
    SET bar=bars(i)
    WHERE rowid=rids(i);
```

Creating separate tables for each column returned from a SELECT statement made writing such code tedious and would encourage the programmer to not bother with bulk collects in cases where FORALL statements would be later used with that data, especially since with fewer lines of code the programmer could use a cursor FOR loop and achieve the desired brevity and clarity at the expense of performance.

With this release of PL/SQL, the restriction on tables of records in bulk operations has been lifted. This significant change means you can now use the more natural table of records within FORALL statements. In the following example, a small table is created and populated with ten rows. The anonymous PL/SQL block then immediately fetches all the rows and updates them using this new functionality (highlighted in bold):

```
create table nums(numb number,ita varchar2(256))
/
declare
  TYPE nums_t IS table of nums%ROWTYPE;
  ns nums_t:=nums_t();
begin
  -- create new records
  for i in 1..10 loop
    ns.extend;
    ns(ns.last).numb:=i;
    ns(ns.last).ita:='Insert='||i;
  end loop;
  -- insert into table using forall
  FORALL I in 1..ns.count
    INSERT INTO nums values ns(i);
  -- fetch them back
  SELECT * BULK COLLECT INTO ns FROM nums;
  -- update collection.
  FOR I IN 1..ns.count LOOP
    ns(i).ita:='Update='||i;
  END LOOP;
  -- update table.
  FORALL I IN 1..ns.count
    UPDATE nums
    SET ita=ns(i).ita
    WHERE numb=ns(i).numb;
end;
/
select * from nums
/
```

The following errors are emitted when the preceding code is run on Oracle Database 10*g*:

```
Error report:
ORA-06550: line 22, column 13:
PLS-00436: implementation restriction: cannot reference fields of BULK
           In-BIND tableORA-06550: line 22, column 13:
```

```
PLS-00382: expression is of wrong type
ORA-06550: line 23, column 16:
PLS-00436: implementation restriction: cannot reference fields of BULK
          In-BIND table...
<other peg-legging errors>
```

On Oracle Database 11*g*, this is the result:

```
NUMB                ITA
-------             --------------
1                   Update=1
2                   Update=2
3                   Update=3
4                   Update=4
5                   Update=5
6                   Update=6
7                   Update=7
8                   Update=8
9                   Update=9
10                  Update=10
```

The update was performed, and it was not necessary to declare separate variables for numb and ita. This is a fine improvement, especially with tables that have hundreds of columns.

Dynamic SQL Symmetry and New Functionality

The package DBMS_SQL and the native dynamic SQL in PL/SQL have been changed to support the mixing of the two in PL/SQL. For example, you can use DBMS_SQL to parse and execute a SQL statement with an arbitrary number of bind variables and convert that cursor into a ref cursor for use with native dynamic SQL statements such as FETCH-BULK COLLECT and the like. Likewise, the ref cursor created with an OPEN-FOR statement may be converted to a cursor for use in DBMS_SQL subprograms such as DBMS_SQL.FETCH_ROWS(); the only restriction on these conversions is that they are one-way. Once you convert away from its defining type, you cannot convert a cursor back. This means you will need to close the cursor using the target type's close mechanism (CLOSE or DBMS_SQL.CLOSE_CURSOR()) as required. The following example is a function that creates a ref cursor on the table POLY_ORDER_HEADERS, based on a variable number of passed-in conditionals. This function uses DBMS_SQL to create a cursor, parse it, bind variables with their correct datatypes, and execute the resultant cursor. The DBMS_SQL cursor ID is converted to the correct ref cursor and returned from the function.

```
CREATE OR REPLACE package poly_dyn_query AS
  TYPE order_cursor_t IS REF CURSOR RETURN poly_order_headers%ROWTYPE;
  TYPE conditional_rec_t IS RECORD
                            (column_name VARCHAR2(30),
                             operator VARCHAR2(10),
                             val varchar2(32000));
  TYPE conditionals_t IS TABLE OF conditional_rec_t;
  FUNCTION get_Matching_Orders(pConds conditionals_t) RETURN order_cursor_t;
end;
/
```

```
CREATE OR REPLACE package body poly_dyn_query AS
  FUNCTION get_Matching_Orders(pConds conditionals_t)
  RETURN order_cursor_t IS
    sqlStmt CLOB;
    cursorId NUMBER;
    idx PLS_INTEGER;
    ret PLS_INTEGER;
    whereOp VARCHAR2(30):=' WHERE ';
    retCur order_cursor_t;
    strval VARCHAR2(3200);
    numVal NUMBER;
    dateVal DATE;
    descTab DBMS_SQL.DESC_TAB;
    colCnt PLS_INTEGER;
    colType PLS_INTEGER;

    FUNCTION get_Column_Type(pColumnName IN VARCHAR2)
    RETURN INTEGER IS
    BEGIN
      FOR i IN 1..colCnt LOOP
        IF descTab(i).col_name=pColumnName THEN
          return descTab(i).col_type;
        END IF;
      END LOOP;
      RETURN NULL;
    END;

BEGIN
    sqlStmt:='SELECT * FROM poly_order_headers';
    cursorId:=DBMS_SQL.open_cursor;
    idx:=pConds.FIRST;
    WHILE idx IS NOT NULL LOOP
      sqlStmt:=sqlStmt||whereOp||pConds(idx).column_name||
                      pConds(idx).operator||':BIND'||idx;
      IF idx=pConds.FIRST THEN
        whereOp:=' AND ';
      END IF;
      idx:=pConds.NEXT(idx);
    END LOOP;
    DBMS_SQL.parse(cursorId,sqlStmt,DBMS_SQL.NATIVE);
    -- describe columns so right datatype can be bound
    -- to the bind variable
    DBMS_SQL.describe_columns(cursorId,colCnt,descTab);
    idx:=pConds.FIRST;
    WHILE idx IS NOT NULL LOOP
      colType:=get_Column_Type(pConds(idx).column_name);
```

```
      IF colType=2 THEN
        numVal:=to_number(pConds(idx).val);
        DBMS_SQL.BIND_VARIABLE(cursorId,'BIND'||idx,numVal);
      ELSIF colType=12 THEN
        dateVal:=to_date(pConds(idx).val,'YYYYMMDD hh24:MI:SS');
        DBMS_SQL.BIND_VARIABLE(cursorId,'BIND'||idx,dateVal);
      ELSE -- charaters and anything else
        DBMS_SQL.BIND_VARIABLE(cursorId,'BIND'||idx,pConds(idx).val);
      END IF;
      idx:=pConds.NEXT(idx);
    END LOOP;
    ret:=DBMS_SQL.execute(cursorId);
    retCur:=DBMS_SQL.TO_REFCURSOR(cursorId);
    return retCur;
  END;
END;
/
```

The following is a short anonymous PL/SQL block that exercises the get_Matching_Orders()
function:

```
declare
  rec poly_order_headers%ROWTYPE;
  cur POLY_DYN_QUERY.order_cursor_t;
  conds POLY_DYN_QUERY.conditionals_t:=POLY_DYN_QUERY.conditionals_t();
  idx SIMPLE_INTEGER:=0;
begin
  conds.extend;
  idx:=conds.last;
  conds(idx).column_name:='ORDER_TYPE';
  conds(idx).operator:='=';
  conds(idx).val:='CREDIT_CARD';
  conds.extend;
  idx:=conds.last;
  conds(idx).column_name:='ORDER_TOTAL_AMT';
  conds(idx).operator:='>';
  conds(idx).val:='100';
  conds.extend;
  idx:=conds.last;
  conds(idx).column_name:='ORDER_DATE';
  conds(idx).operator:='>=';
  conds(idx).val:='20070501 00:00:00';
  conds.extend;
  idx:=conds.last;
  conds(idx).column_name:='ORDER_DATE';
  conds(idx).operator:='<=';
  conds(idx).val:='20070601 00:00:00';
  cur:=POLY_DYN_QUERY.get_Matching_Orders(conds);
```

```
  LOOP
    FETCH cur into rec;
    EXIT WHEN cur%NOTFOUND;
    dbms_output.put_line(rec.header_id||' '||rec.order_total_amt);
  END LOOP;
  CLOSE cur;
end;
```

Note the following conditionals have been created:

- `ORDER_TYPE='CREDIT CARD'`

- `ORDER_TOTAL_AMT>100`

- `ORDER_DATE>= 1 May 2007`

- `ORDER_DATE <= 1 Jun 2007`

Executing yields the following:

```
15330 248
15333 288
15148 250
15149 192
15150 198
15151 208
15155 192
15426 132
15433 172
....
```

The results are, indeed, a subset of the orders actually residing in `poly_order_headers` for the month of May. Adding the following line:

```
idx:=dbms_sql.to_cursor_number(cur);
```

before the `CLOSE` cur call, as shown in this excerpt:

```
    EXIT WHEN cur%NOTFOUND;
    dbms_output.put_line(rec.header_id||' '||rec.order_total_amt);
  END LOOP;
  idx:=dbms_sql.to_cursor_number(cur);
  CLOSE cur;
end;
```

causes the following error to be thrown:

```
Error report:
ORA-01001: invalid cursor
ORA-06512: at "SYS.DBMS_SQL", line 2508
ORA-06512: at line 35
01001. 00000 -  "invalid cursor"
```

```
*Cause:
*Action:
```

This demonstrates that attempting to convert a cursor to its starting form will now work.
`OPEN-FOR, EXECUTE IMMEDIATE,` and `DBMS_SQL.parse()` all now accept CLOB arguments,
so the former 32KB limit has be lifted. The `get_Matching_Orders()` function described earlier
demonstrates this new functionality.

New Trigger Features

There are three major improvements to triggers in Oracle Database 11g. You now have some
control over the order of triggers firing; you can create triggers `ENABLED` or `DISABLED`; and there
is a new type of trigger, the compound trigger, that maintains a common state over the life of a
DML operation.

Trigger Ordering: The FOLLOWS Clause

When creating a trigger, a new clause may be included in the `CREATE TRIGGER` statement. Here
is a snippet showing the new `FOLLOWS` clause:

```
CREATE TRIGGER B4I_DONATIONS_JOU BEFORE INSERT ON DONATIONS
FOLLOWS B4I_DONATIONS_VAL,B4I_DONATIONS_SEC
WHEN ...
```

This new clause instructs Oracle to call `B4I_DONATIONS_JOU` after calling the two other triggers
listed in the `FOLLOWS` clause (`B4I_DONATIONS_VAL, B4I_DONATIONS_SEC`).

Creating Triggers As ENABLED or DISABLED

Two new keywords, `ENABLED` and `DISABLED`, have been added to the trigger creation statement.
These mutually exclusive keywords appear immediately before the optional `WHEN` clause and
after the optional `FOLLOWS` clause. Here's the `B4I_DONATIONS_JOU` trigger created initially disabled:

```
CREATE TRIGGER B4I_DONATIONS_JOU BEFORE INSERT ON DONATIONS
FOLLOWS B4I_DONATIONS_VAL,B4I_DONATIONS_SEC
DISABLED
WHEN ...
```

Compound Triggers Type

In prior versions of Oracle, to maintain and share data between different triggers on the same
table, a handler package was usually employed to contain global variables holding the "state"
for the particular DML operation underway. Although this did work, the fact that the state stored
in the package was not bound to the statement being executed meant that the developer had
to ensure that the state was initialized in a `BEFORE` statement trigger and that any resources
consumed, such as collections and cursors, were freed in an `AFTER` statement trigger. Exceptions, of
course, would cause the `AFTER` statement trigger to not be executed, and any significant resources
normally freed by the `AFTER` statement trigger could be hung up in the trigger's handler package
until the `BEFORE` statement trigger was called again or the session terminated. A new type of

trigger has been introduced in Oracle Database 11*g*, the compound trigger, to overcome these shortcomings of what are now known as *simple triggers*.

Compound triggers differ from simple triggers in that the compound trigger implements all of the timing-point logic (before statement, before each row, after each row, after statement) within its body, and all of those sections share the same set of variables declared in the trigger's common declaration section. The following example shows a compound trigger that collects donor names and amounts as part of a telethon system. At the end of the DML statement, a call to a package LIVE_FEED is called, presumably to update the totals board and maybe add the donor to a crawl on the bottom of the television screen.

```
create sequence donations_s
/
create table donations
(  donation_id INTEGER NOT NULL PRIMARY KEY
  ,donor_name VARCHAR2(256) NOT NULL
  ,donation_amount NUMBER NOT NULL
  ,address_1 VARCHAR2(256) NOT NULL
  ,address_2 VARCHAR2(256)
  ,address_3 VARCHAR2(256)
  ,city VARCHAR2(80) NOT NULL
  ,state VARCHAR2(2) NOT NULL
  ,postal_code VARCHAR2(80)
  ,country VARCHAR2(2)
  ,phone VARCHAR2(80)
  ,email VARCHAR2(256)
)
/


CREATE OR REPLACE TRIGGER donation_ins_trg
FOR INSERT ON donations
COMPOUND TRIGGER
  livePipe LIVE_FEED.pipe_t;
  messQueue LIVE_FEED.messTab_t:=LIVE_FEED.messTab_t();
BEFORE STATEMENT IS
BEGIN
  livePipe:=LIVE_FEED.getPipe();
EXCEPTION
  WHEN NO_DATA_FOUND THEN
    livePipe:=NULL;
END BEFORE STATEMENT;
BEFORE EACH ROW IS
BEGIN
  IF :new.donation_amount<=0 THEN
    RAISE_APPLICATION_ERROR(-20001,'Donations must be positive');
  END IF;
END BEFORE EACH ROW;
AFTER EACH ROW IS
```

```
BEGIN
  IF livePipe IS NOT NULL THEN
    messQueue.EXTEND;
    messQueue(messQueue.LAST).donor_name:=:new.donor_name;
    messQueue(messQueue.LAST).donation_amount:=:new.donation_amount;
  END IF;
END AFTER EACH ROW;
AFTER STATEMENT IS
BEGIN
  IF livePipe IS NOT NULL THEN
    LIVE_FEED.enqueue(livePipe,messQueue);
  END IF;
END AFTER STATEMENT;
END donation_ins_trg;
```

This code collects donor/amount pairs in the messQueue collection. When the after trigger is called, the LIVE_FEED.enqueue() procedure is called. If a negative donation amount, or some table constraint is violated, the after trigger is not called, except in certain cases with FORALL that will be covered later.

The following example shows a somewhat stubby implementation of LIVE_FEED:

```
CREATE OR REPLACE
package LIVE_FEED as
  SUBTYPE pipe_t IS PLS_INTEGER;
  TYPE messRec_t IS RECORD(donor_name VARCHAR2(256),donation_amount NUMBER);
  TYPE messTab_t IS TABLE OF messRec_t;
  FUNCTION getPipe RETURN pipe_t;
  PROCEDURE enqueue(pPipe pipe_t,messArr messTab_t);
end;
/
CREATE OR REPLACE
package body LIVE_FEED IS
  FUNCTION getPipe RETURN pipe_t IS
  BEGIN
    RETURN 14553;
  END;
  PROCEDURE enqueue(pPipe pipe_t,messArr messTab_t) IS
  BEGIN
    FOR i IN 1..messArr.COUNT LOOP
      dbms_output.put_line('Donor: '||messArr(i).donor_name
                ||' Amount: '||messArr(i).donation_amount);
    END LOOP;
  END;
END;
/
```

That's pretty simple—the example just uses DBMS_OUTPUT to list the enqueued records. The following is a test of the trigger using a simple insert statement:

```
insert into donations
select 1,'John Q Public',100,'101 Main St.'
  ,null,null,'Anytown','ST','0000000','US','111-555-3333','jqpublic@email.net'
from dual
  union all
select 2,'Percival Lowell',200,'100 Cactus Ln'
  ,null,null,'Flagstaff','AZ','86001','US','928-555-0000','plowell@email.net'
from dual
  union all
select 3,'Jane Doe',400,'101 Elm'
  ,null,null,'Peaceville',null,'0000000','US','333-555-2222','jdoe@email.net'
from dual;
```

Running yields the following:

```
Donor: John Q Public Amount: 100
Donor: Percival Lowell Amount: 200
Donor: Jane Doe Amount: 400
```

Changing Jane Doe's donation amount to –400 causes the following to be output:

```
SQL Error: ORA-20001: Donations must be positive
ORA-06512: at "DEMO.DONATION_INS_TRG", line 17
ORA-04088: error during execution of trigger 'DEMO.DONATION_INS_TRG'
```

The after trigger did not fire. Returning the donation amount to 400 and executing again yields the following:

```
Donor: John Q Public Amount: 100
Donor: Percival Lowell Amount: 200
Donor: Jane Doe Amount: 400
```

If this were written as a simple trigger, there would have been five lines listed since the declaration of messQueue also initialized the variable.

Compound triggers behave a little differently when used with FORALL statements. The following shows the prior example written as a PL/SQL anonymous block that creates the records in the PL/SQL table and uses FORALL to bulk insert them:

```
declare
  TYPE donTab_t IS TABLE OF donations%ROWTYPE;
  SUBTYPE donRec_t IS donations%ROWTYPE;
  donArr donTab_t:=donTab_t();
  FUNCTION newDonRec_t(donation_id IN PLS_INTEGER,doner_name IN VARCHAR2
                ,donation_amount IN NUMBER,address_1 IN VARCHAR2
                ,address_2 IN VARCHAR2,address_3 IN VARCHAR2
                ,city IN VARCHAR2,state IN VARCHAR2
                ,postal_code IN VARCHAR2,country IN VARCHAR2
                ,phone IN VARCHAR2,email IN VARCHAR2)
  RETURN donRec_t IS
    tmp donRec_t;
```

```
  BEGIN
    tmp.donation_id:=donation_id;
    tmp.donor_name:=doner_name;
    tmp.donation_amount:=donation_amount;
    tmp.address_1:=address_1;
    tmp.address_2:=address_2;
    tmp.address_3:=address_3;
    tmp.city:=city;
    tmp.state:=state;
    tmp.postal_code:=postal_code;
    tmp.country:=country;
    tmp.phone:=phone;
    tmp.email:=email;
    return tmp;
  END;

BEGIN
  donArr.EXTEND;
  donArr(donArr.LAST):=newDonRec_t(donations_s.nextval,'John Q Public',100,
  '101 Main St.',null,null,'Anytown','ST','0000000','US',
  '111-555-3333','jqpublic@email.net');
  donArr.EXTEND;
  donArr(donArr.LAST):=newDonRec_t(donations_s.nextval,'Percival Lowell',200,
  '100 Cactus Ln',null,null,'Flagstaff','AZ','86001','US',
  '928-555-0000','plowell@email.net');
  donArr.EXTEND;
  donArr(donArr.LAST):=newDonRec_t(donations_s.nextval,'Jane Doe',400,
  '101 Elm',null,null,'Peaceville','ST','0000000','US',
  '333-555-2222','jdoe@email.net');
  -- insert the records
  FORALL I IN 1..donArr.COUNT
    INSERT INTO donations VALUES donArr(i);
END;
/
```

The function newDonRec_t() initializes a record of type donations%RECTYPE. When this block is executed, the same result is seen. However, when you change Jan Doe's donation amount to –400 as before, the following is emitted:

```
ORA-20001: Donations must be positive
ORA-06512: at "DEMO.DONATION_INS_TRG", line 17
ORA-04088: error during execution of trigger 'DEMO.DONATION_INS_TRG'
ORA-06512: at line 36

Donor: John Q Public Amount: 100
Donor: Percival Lowell Amount: 200
```

The after trigger is called in this case. The after trigger will be called unless the first record in the collection has an exception. The following is the trigger with some work-around code added:

```
CREATE OR REPLACE TRIGGER donation_ins_trg
FOR INSERT ON donations
COMPOUND TRIGGER
  livePipe LIVE_FEED.pipe_t;
  messQueue LIVE_FEED.messTab_t;
  badCnt SIMPLE_INTEGER:=0;
BEFORE STATEMENT IS
BEGIN
  livePipe:=LIVE_FEED.getPipe();
  messQueue:=LIVE_FEED.messTab_t();
EXCEPTION
  WHEN NO_DATA_FOUND THEN
    livePipe:=NULL;
END BEFORE STATEMENT;
BEFORE EACH ROW IS
BEGIN
  badCnt:=badCnt+1;
  IF :new.donation_amount<=0 THEN
    RAISE_APPLICATION_ERROR(-20001,'Donations must be positive');
  END IF;
END BEFORE EACH ROW;
AFTER EACH ROW IS
BEGIN
  badCnt:=badCnt-1;
  IF livePipe IS NOT NULL THEN
    messQueue.EXTEND;
    messQueue(messQueue.LAST).donor_name:=:new.donor_name;
    messQueue(messQueue.LAST).donation_amount:=:new.donation_amount;
  END IF;
END AFTER EACH ROW;
AFTER STATEMENT IS
BEGIN
  IF livePipe IS NOT NULL AND badCnt=0 THEN
    LIVE_FEED.enqueue(livePipe,messQueue);
  END IF;
END AFTER STATEMENT;
END donation_ins_trg;
```

The badCnt variable is incremented in the BEFORE EACH ROW section and decremented in the AFTER EACH ROW section. If some error occurs, the AFTER EACH ROW section will not be called, and badCnt will retain a nonzero value. The AFTER STATEMENT trigger checks the value of badCnt and calls LIVE_FEED.enqueue() only if there's a pipe and badCnt is zero.

XML DB Improvements

XML DB makes major advancements since its inception in Oracle 9*i* Database Release 2. Oracle has long offered native XML support to allow storage of XML in object-relational or character large object (CLOB) formats. Since its introduction into the database engine, Oracle has made incredible progress toward a high-performance native storage XML engine inside the database. Oracle even provides easy-to-implement user interfaces in Enterprise Manager Database Console to set up XML DB in the database. This configuration includes the ability to set up HTTP and FTP access to the database. In Oracle Database 11*g*, XML DB adopts features such as Binary XML, XML index, repository events, XQuery compliance, and much more. These new features in Oracle Database 11*g* allow for simplified XML manageability and supportability for DBAs and application developers.

Repository Events

Repository operations on files and folders (resources) include check in, check out, create, delete, link, lock, open, render, submit for version control, uncheck out, unlink, unlock, and update. Business requirements may require certain action when particular repository operations occur. For example, you may want to make a copy of a file prior to a delete operation on a specific folder for auditing purposes. Events allow for the XML DB repository to be programmable like database triggers allow the database to be programmable.

Support Content Repository API for Java: JSR-170

Oracle Database 11*g* XML DB Content Connector provides support for the Content Repository API for Java Technology, also known as JSR-170. JSR-170 specifications developed under the Java Community Process (JCP) program promise a unified API for accessing any compliant repository in a vendor- or implementation-neutral fashion. JSR-170 is often called the JDBC of content repositories. Currently, customers write to proprietary APIs from each vendor to access their content repositories. The goal of the JSR-170 specification is to create a single content API that can be used to access data in any number of content repositories. You can plug in additional repositories as needed. Oracle Database 11*g* provides access of the XML DB repository using the JCR 1.0 Java API.

ACL Security

Oracle Database 11*g* enhances the ACL-based security model. XML DB ACL now complies with the industry-standard DAV ACL specifications and security standards in a WebDAV environment. Clients will notice improved interaction with the DAV ACL security model. In addition, the ACL security model can be extended for user-defined ACLs to secure other kinds of database objects. ACLs allow for a time-based security model with this release. You can set policies to enable access to resources during a certain time period or automatically publish and expire content based on the ACL.

New XMLType

Until now, there were three XMLType storage models supported by Oracle: structured, unstructured, and hybrid. The structured XMLType implies that the XML is well defined. Data in a structured XMLType is stored as a set of objects. This is also known as object-relational storage and object-based persistence. The unstructured XMLType is stored in character LOBs datatypes. This is also known as *text-based persistence*. Oracle Database 11g introduces a new XMLType datatype known in the XML industry as Binary XMLType, also recognized as post-parse persistence.

The Binary XMLType introduces advantages to the XML world in the database. Binary XML format generally reduces the verbosity of XML documents, and thus the cost of parsing is reduced. Even though the XML is stored in a parsed state, data is still accessible via XPath. No encoding checks are performed on loading. Thus, Binary XML brings forth no overhead (or at least reduced overhead) in parsing, validation, or conversions, which saves in time in IO and CPU cycles, which therefore translates into faster load times. Binary XML is capable of preserving infoset and DOM fidelity. If the XML data is going to be retrieved, Binary XML is the new solution for Oracle Database 11g.

Binary XML is the closest thing to a universal storage model for XML data by providing the storage benefits of both structured and unstructured data. Like structured storage, you can perform piecewise updates on Binary XML. Similar to unstructured storage, Binary XML data is kept in document order. Similarly, like structured XML, data and metadata can be separated at the database level. Another great benefit of Binary XML is that you can leverage binary storage for XML schema-based data even if the XML schema is not defined in completeness. Furthermore, with Binary XML, you can store XML schemas in the same table and query across common elements.

There are numerous advantages to Binary XML storage. First is high throughput including fast DOM loading. Though Binary XML storage takes up more space than object-relational storage, it does considerably better than CLOB storage. Binary XML storage provides the most schema flexibility of the three storage models. You have the option to store data and metadata together or separately. You can even use multiple schemas for the same XMLType table. Binary XML supports SQL scalar datatypes and SQL constraints. Binary XML supports indexing with XMLIndex, function-based indexes, and Oracle Text indexes. The performance of XPath-based queries produce good results. Streaming XPath evaluation circumvents DOM construction and evaluates multiple XPath expressions in a single pass. Using XMLIndex, you can improve the performance of XPath-based queries. XMLIndex will be discussed in detail in subsequent sections. Lastly, for XML schema–based data, inserted rows are fully validated during DML activity.

Let's look into how to create and manage this new XML datatype. First, let's create an XML table of Binary XML:

```
SQL> create table edba_xml
  2  of sys.xmltype xmltype
  3  store as securefile
  4  binary xml ( tablespace users
  5              retention auto keep_duplicates
  6*             compress high ) tablespace users
SQL> /
Table created.
```

You'll notice in this example that the XMLTYPE STORE AS SECUREFILE BINARY XML syntax distinguishes this XMLType as Binary XML. You will also notice that the SECUREFILE with KEEP_ DUPLICATES clause is utilized. For complete detailed information on the SECUREFILE option, please refer to Chapter 12.

Oracle Enterprise Manager Database Console provides full support for XML including the new Binary XMLType table. By utilizing the EM Database Console, you can easily implement Binary XML. One thing to note with Oracle Database 11g Enterprise Manager Database Console is that the location of the XML database management menus are located somewhere else. The XML database management options are located on the Schema tab on the middle left of the screen (see Figure 11-1).

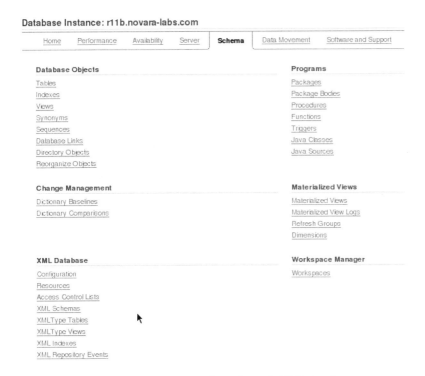

Figure 11-1. *Enterprise Manager Database Console XML database management menu options*

Now, let's create your first Binary XMLType table using Enterprise Manager Database Console by clicking the XMLType Tables link; just select Schema ➤ XML Database ➤ XML Type Tables.

The easiest way to create an XMLType table is to base it on another XMLType table, as depicted in Figure 11-2.

Figure 11-2. *XMLType table*

Please pay particular attention to the Go button in the middle of the screen next to the Create Like drop-down list. You can use this to create an XMLType table based on another predefined XML Type. The Create Like option will create the table as a copy of the source. So if the source table name is an object-relational storage type, then the target table must also be an object-relational storage type. In this particular example, the EDBA_SECURITY Binary XMLType table will be created based on the X$SECURITYCLASS table, as shown on the Binary XML Create Like screen (see Figure 11-3).

XML Type Tables

Search

Schema

Object Name

Go

By default, the search returns all uppercase matches beginning with the string you entered. To run an exact or case-sensitive match, double quote the search string. You can use the wildcard symbol (%) in a double quoted string.

Selection Mode Single

Create

Edit View Delete Actions Create Like   Go

Previous 25 26-37 of 37 Next

Select	Owner	Table Name	XML Schema	Element Name	Storage Type
⊙	XDB	X$SECURITYCLASS	http://xmlns.oracle.com/xs/securityclass.xsd	securityClass	BINARY
○	XDB	aggregatePrivilege174_TAB	http://xmlns.oracle.com/xs/securityclass.xsd	aggregatePrivilege	BINARY
○	XDB	fallback42_TAB	http://www.w3.org/2001/XInclude.xsd	fallback	OBJECT-RELATIONAL
○	XDB	fallback43_TAB	http://www.w3.org/2001/XInclude.xsd	fallback	OBJECT-RELATIONAL
○	XDB	fallback61_TAB	http://www.w3.org/2001/csx.XInclude.xsd	fallback	BINARY
○	XDB	fallback62_TAB	http://www.w3.org/2001/csx.XInclude.xsd	fallback	BINARY
○	XDB	ftp-log21_TAB	http://xmlns.oracle.com/xdb/log/ftplog.xsd	ftp-log	OBJECT-RELATIONAL
○	XDB	http-log20_TAB	http://xmlns.oracle.com/xdb/log/httplog.xsd	http-log	OBJECT-RELATIONAL
○	XDB	include47_TAB	http://www.w3.org/2001/XInclude.xsd	include	OBJECT-RELATIONAL
○	XDB	include66_TAB	http://www.w3.org/2001/csx.XInclude.xsd	include	BINARY
○	XDB	privilege173_TAB	http://xmlns.oracle.com/xs/securityclass.xsd	privilege	BINARY
○	XDB	xdb-log13_TAB	http://xmlns.oracle.com/xdb/log/xdblog.xsd	xdb-log	OBJECT-RELATIONAL

Edit View Delete Actions Create Like   Go

Previous 25 26-37 of 37 Next

Figure 11-3. *Binary XML Create Like screen*

After you click the Go button, you will be redirected to the Create Table screen. You can see that the binary storage is defined by the XDB.http://xmlns.oracle.com/xs/securityclass.xsd schema, as shown on the Binary XML Create Table screen (see Figure 11-4).

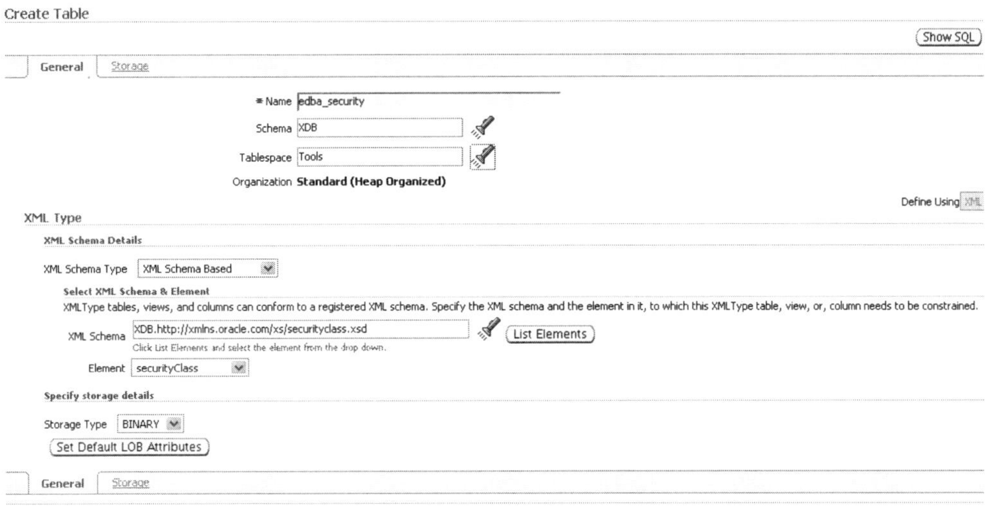

Figure 11-4. *Binary XML Create Table screen*

The following SQL statement is generated by Enterprise Manager Database Console:

```
CREATE TABLE "SH"."EDBA_SECURITY" OF SYS.XMLTYPE XMLTYPE
STORE AS BINARY XML ( TABLESPACE "TOOLS")
XMLSCHEMA "http://xmlns.oracle.com/xdb/schemas/XDB/
                xmlns.oracle.com/xs/securityclass.xsd"
ELEMENT "securityClass"
TABLESPACE "TOOLS" PCTFREE 10 INITRANS 1 MAXTRANS 255
STORAGE ( INITIAL 64K BUFFER_POOL DEFAULT)
LOGGING NOCOMPRESS
```

Once this table is created, you can describe the table and verify that an XMLType table has been created:

```
SQL> desc edba_security
 Name                                     Null?    Type
 ---------------------------------------- -------- -----------------
TABLE of XMLTYPE(XMLSchema
"http://xmlns.oracle.com/xs/securityclass.xsd" Element"securityClass")
STORAGE BINARY
```

Alternatively, you can create the Binary XMLType table without a schema definition. To create the Binary XMLType table, you can click the Create button. This will take you to the Create Table screen for XMLType tables. Oracle, by default, will create a Binary XMLType table (see Figure 11-5).

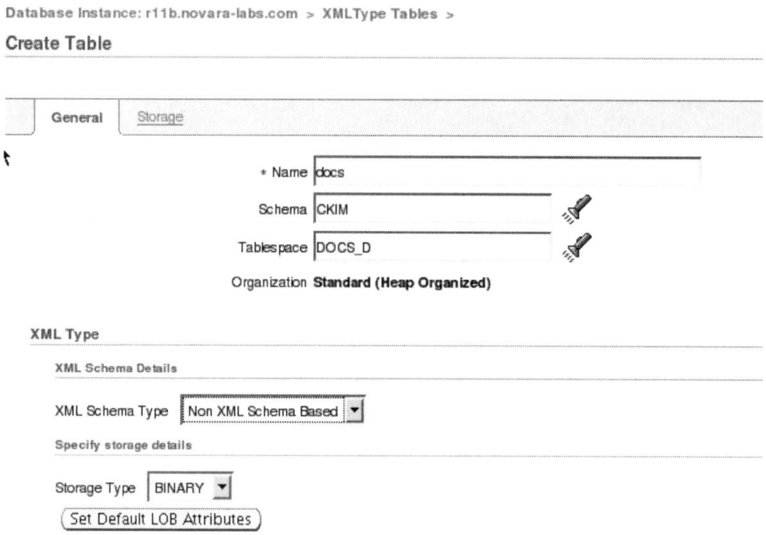

Database Instance: r11b.novara-labs.com > XMLType Tables >

Create Table

General	Storage

* Name `docs`

Schema `CKIM`

Tablespace `DOCS_D`

Organization **Standard (Heap Organized)**

XML Type

XML Schema Details

XML Schema Type   `Non XML Schema Based ▼`

Specify storage details

Storage Type   `BINARY ▼`

(Set Default LOB Attributes)

Figure 11-5. *Create Table screen for XMLType tables*

From a command-line perspective, creating an XMLType table is as simple as this:

```
SQL>  create table edba_po
      of sys.xmltype xmltype
      store as securefile
      binary xml (tablespace tools)
SQL> /

Table created.
```

Binary XMLType can be implemented as XMLType tables and columns. Here's another example of Binary XML on a column range-partitioned by the CREATION_DATE column:

```
create table edba_xml_tab
( edba_xml_tab_id number not null,
  creation_date date not null,
  xml_data sys.xmltype not null
)
tablespace xml_data
  xmltype column xml_data store as binary xml
  partition by range (creation_date)
(
  partition year_2006
  values less than (to_date('01-jan-2006','dd-mon-yyyy'))
  tablespace xml_data_2006,
  partition year_2007
  values less than (to_date('01-jan-2007','dd-mon-yyyy'))
```

```
  tablespace xml_data_2007,
  partition year_xxxx
values less than (maxvalue)
 tablespace xml_data
)
/
```

XMLIndex

Previously, you had the option of XPath function–based indexes (using extract or extractvalue) or Oracle Text. Both XPath and Oracle Text have limitations. Oracle Database 11g introduces the new XMLIndex geared to index the internal structure of the XML data. XMLIndex overcomes the indexing limitations of CLOB storage by indexing the XML tags of the document, and determines fragments based on the XPath expressions. XMLIndex also indexes scalar node values and tracks document hierarchy information for each node it indexes. It tracks the parent-child, ancestor-descendant, and sibling relationships.

Why Use XMLIndex?

SQL functions such as XMLQuery, XMLTable, XMLExists, XMLCast, extract, extractValue, and existsNode can take advantage of XMLIndex to improve the performance of XML retrieval. There are many advantages to using XMLIndex. Let's review the major advantages of XMLIndex. First, the XMLIndex can be used in any part of a query. XMLIndex is not bound to be used as part of a WHERE clause. XMLIndex can participate in range queries, aggregates, and arithmetic functions. If all the columns are used, XMLIndex can even fulfill fast full-index scans. Also, XMLIndex can be used to extract document fragments since it can be used as part of the SELECT clause and the FROM clause. Function-based and CTXXPath indexes are not capable of extracting fragments from documents. Second, XMLIndex can be used for both schema-based or non-schema-based XML documents. It is not restricted on the storage options for the XML: Binary XML, hybrid, or unstructured storage. XMLIndex can handle your XML as relational tables or as CLOBS. This can eliminate the need to shred your XML. (Of course, you may have specific reasons to continue XML extractions.) Third, XMLIndex can handle XPath expressions that target collections. Fourth, XMLIndex supports parallelism for index creation and maintenance. Updates to XMLIndex on Binary XML can be executed in a piecewise manner for enhanced performance.

■**Note** As of Oracle Database 11g, the CTXSYS.CTXXPath index is deprecated. XMLIndex renders all the functionality that CTXXPath provided and replaces the CTXXPath index. Oracle recommends replacing CTXXPath with XMLIndex.

XMLIndex Components

The XMLIndex is based on the XMLType datatype. The XMLIndex is a domain index relevant for the domain of the XML data. It is also a logical index with three components:

- Path index

- Order index

- Value index

The path index indexes the XML tags of the document and determines the document fragments. The order index indexes the hierarchical position of the nodes in the XML document. The value index obviously indexes the values of the XML document. This value index is what provides access for the WHERE clause predicate. Values can be retrieved on exact values or by range scans.

XMLIndex utilizes a shadow table for each XMLIndex referred to as the *path table*. The path table stores the row ID, locator (document fragment and datatype information), the order key (hierarchical position of the node represented in decimal key) for each indexed node, and the value (text of an attribute node).

XMLIndex Path Table

Let's look at how the XMLIndex path table looks. The path table information can be retrieved from the DBA_/ALL_/USER_XML_INDEXES view. The Oracle XDB schema ships with an XMLIndex for the XDB$ACL table. You can query the DBA_XML_INDEXES view to retrieve the index name and the path table name, as shown here:

```
SQL> select table_owner||'.'||table_name table_name,
  2         table_owner||'.'||path_table_name path_table_name,
  3         index_name
  4* from dba_xml_indexes
SQL> /


TABLE_NAME      PATH_TABLE_NAME      INDEX_NAME
------------    -----------------    --------------------
XDB.XDB$ACL     XDB.XDBACL_PATH_TAB  XDB$ACL_XIDX
```

Let's look at the path table associated with this XMLType table:

```
SQL> desc XDB.XDBACL_PATH_TAB
 Name                    Null?           Type
 ---------------         --------        --------------
 RID                                     ROWID
 PATHID                                  RAW(8)
 ORDER_KEY                               RAW(1000)
 LOCATOR                                 RAW(2000)
 VALUE                                   VARCHAR2(4000)
```

The path index is represented by the PATHID and the RID; likewise, the order index is represented by the ORDER_KEY and the RID. The PATHID and ORDER_KEY columns are automatically indexed by Oracle. The data in the ORDER_KEY column is in a decimal format. This is similar to the decimal format that you see in the Dewey Decimal system used in libraries. If the decimal number for the ORDER_KEY column resembles something like 1.11.12, this number would represent the node position of the 1st child of the 11th child of the 12th child of the document root node. The LOCATOR column is used for fragment extraction. If the locator is for Binary XML of schema-based data, the datatype information would also be stored in this column. The VALUE column stores the text value of the simple element node without children or attribute nodes. All comments are ignored during indexing. The VALUE column truncates any value larger than 4,000 bytes since it is a VARCHAR2(4000) datatype. For incidents where the VALUE column exceeds 4,000 bytes, the LOCATOR value is updated so that the complete value can be retrieved from the base table. In addition to the 4,000-byte limitation of the VALUE column, Oracle imposes another limit for the size of the key for the secondary index created on this column. This limit is determined by the DB_BLOCK_SIZE parameter of the database. This is not just for XMLIndex but also applies for B-tree and function-based indexes. It is important to note that neither the VALUE column limitation of 4,000 bytes nor the index key size affects the results of the query. The only perceivable impact is on performance.

Detailed conceptual information is provided for the path table. Unfortunately, you cannot access the path table. If you try to access the path table, you will get an error resembling this:

```
SQL> select order_key from XDB.XDBACL_PATH_TAB;
select order_key from XDB.XDBACL_PATH_TAB
                       *
ERROR at line 1:
ORA-30967: operation directly on the Path
Table is disallowed
```

The only thing you are allowed to do with the path table is create secondary indexes on the path table columns. Besides this, you really cannot do anything else. You do not even gather statistic on the path table. The only object(s) you would want to gather statistics is on the XMLIndex or the base table for the XMLIndex.

At index creation time, you have the option of specifying the path table name using the PATH TABLE option in the PARAMETERS clause. If you do not specify a path name, a system-generated path name will be created. Also, you can specify the tablespace location to the path table. By default, the storage properties for the XMLIndex path table and the secondary indexes automatically inherit the storage properties of the base table of the XMLIndex. You can customize the storage parameters in the PARAMETERS clause. Here's an example of the storage options:

```
('path table edba_po_path_table
(pctfree 5 pctused 90 initrans 5
storage (initial 1k next 2k minextents 3 buffer_pool keep)
nologging enable row movement parallel 3)
path id index edba_po_path_id_idx (logging pctfree 1 initrans 3)
order key index edba_po_order_key_idx (logging pctfree 1 initrans 3)
value index edba_po_value_idx (logging pctfree 1 initrans 3)');
```

The following CREATE INDEX syntax illustrates all the XMLIndex options that have been discussed so far:

```
SQL>  create index edba_security_xmlindex
   2   on edba_security v (value(v))
   3   indextype is xdb.xmlindex
   4   parameters('path table edba_security_path_table
   5*          (tablespace tools) async (sync manual)')
SQL> /

Index created.
```

This particular syntax was generated by Oracle Database 11g Enterprise Manager Database Console.

Another big feature of Oracle's XMLIndex indexes is that they can be created in parallel mode and can fully leverage Oracle's parallel query server processes. In this example, you take the same query and add the parallel option at the end of the CREATE INDEX syntax:

```
SQL>   create index edba_security_xmlindex
   2   on edba_security v (value(v))
   3   indextype is xdb.xmlindex
   4   parameters('path table edba_security_path_table
   5              (tablespace tools) async (sync manual)')
   6*  parallel 8
SQL> /

Index created.
```

Please note that indexes created with the parallel degree option do incur storage for each of the parallel processes as defined by the initial extent clause. If the initial extent of the index is 100MB and you specify a parallel degree of 8, Oracle will create 8×100MB extents during the index build.

EM Database Console to Create XMLIndex

Let's see how XMLIndexes are created using the Enterprise Manager Database Console. Oracle Database 11g Enterprise Manager Database Console produces another menu option for the XMLIndex. From the home screen, navigate to the XMLIndex screen by selecting Schema ➤ XML Database ➤ XMLIndex. On the XMLIndex screen, click the Create button. The General XMLIndex screen will look like Figure 11-6.

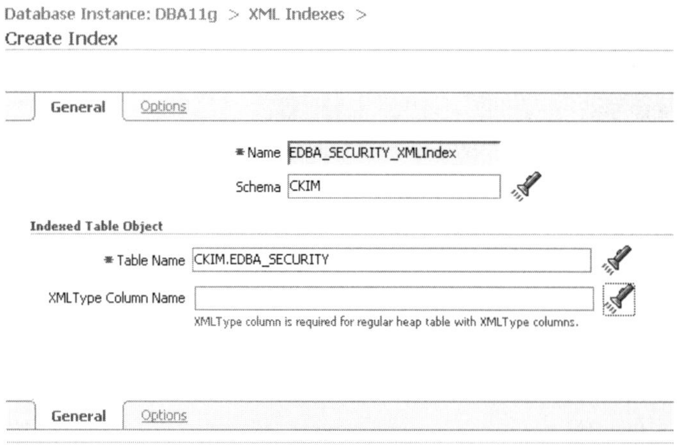

Figure 11-6. *General XMLIndex screen*

Once you enter the table name and the index name for the schema, click the Options tab to provide the path table name and tablespace information (see Figure 11-7).

Database Instance: DBA11g > XML Indexes >
Create Index

General | **Options**

XML Index Options
☑ Path Table Name `EDBA_SECURITY_PATH_TABL`
☑ Path Tablespace Name `TOOLS`
☐ Path Subsetting Options
    ⦿ Include All Paths
    ○ Include Below Path(s)
    ○ Exclude Below Path(s)

☑ Create Asynchronous Index
    ○ Manual
    ○ On-Commit
    ○ Frequency `1` `Seconds ⌄`

General | **Options**

Figure 11-7. *XMLIndex options*

There are additional options on this screen; the XML Subsetting and Asynchronous options will be explained in the upcoming sections.

Now, the XMLIndex is created, so let's see how you can retrieve this information from the data dictionary. You can query DBA_/ALL_/USER_INDEXES to retrieve high-level information about what table has XMLIndex indexes:

```
SQL>  select table_name, index_name , index_type
  2  from dba_indexes
  3  where owner='SH'
  4* and ityp_name=  'XMLINDEX'
SQL> /


TABLE_NAME        INDEX_NAME           INDEX_TYPE
------------      ------------------   --------------------
EDBA_SECURITY     EDBA_SECURITY        FUNCTION-BASED DOMAIN
                  XMLINDEX
EDBA_PO           EDBA_PO_XMLINDEX     FUNCTION-BASED DOMAIN
```

Earlier, the XMLIndex was referred to as a domain-level index, and querying the DBA_ INDEXES view indicates that the XMLIndex is a function-based domain index type. Also, note the ITYP_NAME column has the new value for XMLIndex.

You can also query the DBA_/ALL_/USER_XML_INDEXES view to get detailed information pertaining to an XMLIndex:

```
SQL>  select table_name table_name,
  2            path_table_name path_table_name,
  3            index_name, async
  4* from dba_xml_indexes
SQL> /


TABLE_NAME        PATH_           INDEX_            ASYNC
                  TABLE_NAME      NAME
-------------     --------------  ----------------  -----------
EDBA_SECURITY     EDBA_SECURITY_  EDBA_SECURITY_    MANUAL
                  PATH_TABLE      XMLINDEX
EDBA_PO           SYS71294_EDBA_PO EDBA_PO_XMLINDEX
                  XM_PATH_TABLE
XDB.XDB$ACL       XDBACL_PATH_TAB XDB$ACL_XIDX
```

You can see that SYS71294_EDBA_PO_XM_PATH_TABLE is the system-generated name for the path table for EDBA_PO_XMLINDEX.

Index Maintenance

You can perform index maintenance on XML index. You can rename an XMLIndex using the ALTER INDEX command. For example:

```
SQL> alter index EDBA_PO_XMLINDEX rename to EDBA_PO_XMLINDEX_idx;

Index altered.
```

Changing an XMLIndex index name does not change the name of the path table. The path table will need to be renamed independently. Just like regular indexes, you can perform index rebuild functions. You can rebuild an index but cannot change tablespaces during this process. If you try to change the tablespace for the XMLIndex during a rebuild operation, you will receive an error that looks like this:

```
SQL>  alter index EDBA_PO_XMLINDEX_idx rebuild tablespace docs_d;
 alter index EDBA_PO_XMLINDEX_idx rebuild tablespace docs_d
            *
ERROR at line 1:
ORA-29871: invalid alter option for a domain index
```

XMLIndex supports parallelism for index rebuilds:

```
SQL> alter index EDBA_PO_XMLINDEX_idx rebuild parallel 8;

Index altered.
```

■**Note** For smaller indexes, please be aware that the space consumption for indexes created with a parallel degree can be significantly higher since storage parameters are applied to each of the parallel query server processes.

XMLIndex Secondary Indexes

You can create one or more secondary indexes on the VALUE column of the path table. If you do not explicitly specify a secondary index on the VALUE column, a default secondary is created for you. The default secondary index is created based on the text data only. Optionally, you can index the VALUE column to be of another datatype. If you create a secondary index of NUMBER type, this index is used only when it is necessary. In addition to different datatype indexes, you can also create secondary indexes to be function-based or Oracle Text indexes. Let's look at examples of creating secondary indexes using function-based indexes on the path table:

```
SQL> create index edba_po_xmlindex_upper_idx
    on sys71294_edba_po_xm_path_table
    (upper(substr(value, 1,120))));

Index created.
```

If the values are compared for uppercase values for the first 120 bytes, the UPPER(SUBSTR()) function can become useful.

You can also create Oracle Text context-based indexes on the VALUE column for full-text queries that utilize ora:contains XPath functions:

```
SQL> create index edba_secxmlindex_ctx
    on edba_security_path_table(value)
    indextype is ctxsys.context
    parameters('TRANSACTIONAL');

Index created.
```

In the previous example, Oracle will utilize the VALUE column during predicate evaluation. The secondary index is by default a text-based index on the VALUE column of the path table. If all the data in the VALUE column happens to be numeric, you will want to change the datatype of the secondary index to NUMBER using the function-based index with the to_number(VALUE) clause. If there are any text values, you will receive an ORA-01722, "invalid number," error during index creation. If you get this error, you can still create an index but must use the DBMS_XMLINDEX stored package. Oracle provides a CreateNumberIndex procedure to allow the creation of a numeric index.

As you see here, the CreateNumberIndex procedure takes three parameters. The third parameter is the name of the numeric datatype index you want to name.

```
procedure createnumberindex
 argument name             type           in/out default?
 ---------------------- ----------- ---------------
 xml_index_schema        varchar2      in
 xml_index_name          varchar2      in
 num_index_name          varchar2      in
```

Let's see this in action:

```
SQL> begin
  2  dbms_xmlindex.createnumberindex
     ('SH', 'EDBA_PO_XMLINDEX_IDX',
      'EDBA_PO_XMLINDEX_IDX_N');
  3* end;
SQL> /

PL/SQL procedure successfully completed.
```

Likewise, you can use CreateDateIndex to create a DATE datatype secondary index on the VALUE column of the path table. The CreateDateIndex procedure accepts one additional parameter, XMLTYPENAME. This parameter can be DATE or DATETIME, as shown here:

```
SQL> begin
  2  dbms_xmlindex.createdateindex
     ('SH', 'EDBA_PO_XMLINDEX_IDX',
      'EDBA_PO_XMLINDEX_IDX_D', 'DATETIME');
  3* end;
SQL> /

PL/SQL procedure successfully completed.
```

Data Dictionary Views for XMLIndex Secondary Indexes

You created indexes on the VALUE column of the path table to improve the performance of your queries. Let's see how you can determine from the data dictionary what is indexed. The following example queries the data dictionary and identifies what the path table is, what the secondary index name is, and what columns of the path table are indexed:

```
SQL> select table_name, index_name, column_name, column_position
  2  from dba_ind_columns
  3  where table_name in (select path_table_name from dba_xml_indexes
  4  where index_name like '%DBA%')
  5* order by index_name, column_name
SQL> /
```

TABLE_NAME	INDEX_NAME	COLUMN_ NAME	COL_ POS
SYS71294_EDBA_PO_ XM_PATH_TABLE	EDBA_PO_ XMLINDEX_FIDX	SYS_NC00006$	1
SYS71294_EDBA_PO_ XM_PATH_TABLE	EDBA_PO_ XMLINDEX_IDX_D	SYS_NC00009$	1
SYS71294_EDBA_PO_ XM_PATH_TABLE	EDBA_PO_ XMLINDEX_IDX_D2	SYS_NC00010$	1
SYS71294_EDBA_PO_ XM_PATH_TABLE	EDBA_PO_ XMLINDEX_IDX_N	SYS_NC00008$	1
SYS71294_EDBA_PO_ XM_PATH_TABLE	EDBA_PO_ XMLINDEX_UPPER_IDX	SYS_NC00007$	1

EDBA_SECURITY_ PATH_TABLE	EDBA_ SECXMLINDEX_CTX	VALUE	1
SYS71294_EDBA_PO_ XM_PATH_TABLE	SYS71294_EDBA PO_XM_ORDKEY_IX	ORDER_KEY	2
SYS71294_EDBA_PO_ XM_PATH_TABLE	SYS71294_EDBA_ PO_XM_ORDKEY_IX	RID	1
SYS71294_EDBA_PO_ XM_PATH_TABLE	SYS71294_EDBA PO_XM_PATHID_IX	PATHID	1
SYS71294_EDBA_PO_ XM_PATH_TABLE	SYS71294_EDBA_ PO_XM_PATHID_IX	RID	2
SYS71294_EDBA_PO_ XM_PATH_TABLE	SYS71294_EDBA PO_XM_VALUE_IX	VALUE	1
EDBA_SECURITY PATH_TABLE	SYS71312_EDBA SECUR_ORDKEY_IX	ORDER_KEY	2
EDBA_SECURITY PATH_TABLE	SYS71312_EDBA SECUR_ORDKEY_IX	RID	1
EDBA_SECURITY PATH_TABLE	SYS71312_EDBA SECUR_PATHID_IX	PATHID	1
EDBA_SECURITY PATH_TABLE	SYS71312_EDBA SECUR_PATHID_IX	RID	2
EDBA_SECURITY PATH_TABLE	SYS71312_EDBA SECUR_VALUE_IX	VALUE	1

```
16 rows selected.
```

You can clearly see where the table name and/or index names are system generated.

Asynchronous Maintenance of XMLIndexes

Just like any other index, the XMLIndex index is updated with each insert, update, and delete of each row on the table. By default, the underlying base table and the XMLIndex are always synchronized. With XMLIndex, you can change this characteristic and defer the index updates as applicable to the business. In situations where you have a lot of data processing, you may want to defer the index maintenance until the job is complete. Similar to the way that simple materialized views are refreshed, XMLIndex can be synchronized on an interval basis or at a specified time. An XMLIndex index that is synchronized on an interval basis can be referred to as a *stale index*.

A stale index should be considered only if the business can tolerate data latency. An important fact to note is that a stale index can have an effect on query results. The query result is only as good as the last XMLIndex synchronization. You compromise data latency for the performance of database load. Basically, if the XMLIndex is not up-to-date, queries that hit the underlying base table will also reflect the data as of the last synchronization time.

If you are planning on using deferred XMLIndex synchronization, you need to be aware of operations that automatically update the XMLIndex. Any DDL commands against the XMLIndex will implicitly force the XMLIndex resynchronization. This includes the creation of secondary indexes against the path table. Also, any DDL commands issued on the base table will cause the XMLIndex to resync. This includes using ALTER TABLE commands, creating indexes, or dropping indexes on the base table.

Let's examine how asynchronous (ASYNC) maintenance can be implemented. The ASYNC option is part of the PARAMETERS clause of the CREATE INDEX or ALTER INDEX syntax. The ASYNC option has several possible values:

- (ALWAYS)

- (ON COMMIT)

- (EVERY "repeat_interval")

- (MANUAL)

- (STALE)

The default value for the ASYNC option is ALWAYS. The ON COMMIT option can be compared to the two-phased commit. The commit command will not return the "Commit Complete" status message until the synchronization is complete. You may encounter a small delay in response since the synchronization is performed as a separate transaction. The EVERY option with repeat_interval is the same as the repeat_interval specification for DBMS_SCHEDULER. You can have complete control over when to refresh the XMLIndex. One thing to note is that to use the EVERY option, you must have the CREATE JOB system-level privilege. MANUAL implies that the resynchronization will never occur automatically. A manual resync of the index will happen only with the DBMS_XMLINDEX.SYNCINDEX command.

The STALE value should not be changed. It is provided only for future use. The only thing you will have to know is that the staleness is set to TRUE when synchronization is set to ALWAYS; otherwise, this value is set to FALSE. Setting this value incorrectly will cause an error message to be generated.

Earlier, the XMLIndex was created with the ASYNC(SYNC MANUAL) clause. This implies that you have to manually synchronize the index with the DBMS_XMLINDEX package like you see here:

```
SQL> begin
  2  dbms_xmlindex.syncindex('JJONES', 'EDBA_SECURITY_XMLINDEX');
  3  end;
  4  /

PL/SQL procedure successfully completed.
```

You can re-create this index and have it refresh when commits occur with the ON COMMIT value:

```
SQL> create index edba_security_xmlindex
  2  on edba_security v (value(v))
  3  indextype is xdb.xmlindex
  4  parameters('path table edba_security_path_table
               ( tablespace tools) async (sync on commit)')
  5* parallel 8
SQL> /

Index created.
```

You can synchronize the XMLIndex using the repeat interval attribute. To create a refresh schedule of every 30 minutes, you can set the repeat interval with the FREQ=MINUTELY and INTERVAL=30 parameters:

```
SQL> create index edba_security_xmlindex
  2  on edba_security v (value(v))
  3  indextype is xdb.xmlindex
  4  parameters('path table edba_security_path_table
              ( tablespace tools)
        async (sync every "freq=minutely; interval=30")')
  5* parallel 8
  6  /

Index created.
```

When XMLIndex synchronization is set to DEFERRED, changes made to the underlying base table are recorded in a pending table. Oracle records the ROWID and the operation of the DML. This is similar to the way the snapshot logs work. A row is inserted into the pending table for every row that is inserted, updated, or deleted. The pending table is system generated. You have to query the DBA_/ALL_/USER_XML_INDEXES view and the PEND_TABLE_NAME column to determine the pending table name:

```
SQL> select index_name, stale, async, pend_table_name
  2  from dba_xml_indexes
  3* where index_name='EDBA_SECURITY_XMLINDEX'
SQL> /


INDEX_NAME        STALE  ASYNC   PEND_TABLE_NAME
--------------    -----  -----   ---------------
EDBA_SECURITY_           EVERY   SYS71484_EDBA_
XMLINDEX                         SECUR_PEND_TABLE
```

Once you determine the pending table, you can describe it to see the table attributes:

```
SQL> desc SYS71484_EDBA_SECUR_PEND_TABLE
 Name                               Null?    Type
 --------------------------------- -------- ----------------------------
 RID                                         ROWID
 OPERATION                                   VARCHAR2(2)
 ERRNUM                                      NUMBER
 ERRMSG                                      VARCHAR2(2000)
```

Similarly to the path table, you cannot perform any DML against the pending table:

```
SQL> select count(*) from sys71484_edba_secur_pend_table;

ERROR at line 1:
ORA-30958: operation directly on the Pending Table is disallowed
```

As synchronizations are complete, rows from the pending table are removed.

XMLIndex Path Subsetting

A great benefit of XMLIndex is that you do not have to know XPath expressions. By default, XMLIndex indexes all XPath locations of the XML data. Just like any other index, the smaller index size will yield the faster retrieval of data. With XPath expressions, you can narrow your search criteria and, in effect, reduce the data of the XMLIndex index. This ultimately will lead to highly tuned XML applications by limiting the nodes of the XML document to be indexed. The XMLIndex XPath subsetting is achieved in two possible methods:

- Exclusion

- Inclusion

Exclusion implies that you want to exclude fragments from the complete XPath expression. On the flip side, *inclusion* implies that you want to start from an empty set and add paths as you go. XML subsetting can be accomplished by including the PATHS option to the CREATE INDEX or ALTER INDEX command.

Let's review how this great feature works. First, let's create a new XMLIndex with certain nodes included:

```
SQL> create index edba_po_idx on edba_po
     (object_value) indextype is xdb.xmlindex
  2  parameters ('paths
  3  (include
  4  (
  5  /PurchaseOrder/LineItems//*
  6  /PurchaseOrder/Reference
  7  /PurchaseOrder/Actions
  8  )
  9  )'
 10* )
SQL> /

Index created.
```

In this particular example, the elements for LineItems, Reference, and Actions are included in the initial index build process. The LineItems elements and their descendants are included in this index. Let's assume that a new requirement came about to include the Requestor elements to the index. To add the Requested nodes, you can use the INCLUDE ADD parameters:

```
SQL> alter index edba_po_idx rebuild
  2  parameters ('paths (include add (/PurchaseOrder/Requestor
  3* ))')
SQL> /

Index altered.
```

If for some reason you need to add all the possible paths, you can use the ALL parameter. You can issue the options INCLUDE ADD (ALL) or EXCLUDE REMOVE (ALL). Both of these have equivalent results. Even though you can include all paths, you cannot exclude all paths.

```
SQL> alter index edba_po_idx rebuild
  2* parameters ('PATHS (include add (ALL))')
SQL> /

Index altered.
```

This would be equivalent to issuing the index REBUILD command that you are accustomed to using:

```
SQL>  alter index edba_po_idx rebuild;

Index altered.
```

Just like you can add nodes to an existing index, you can remove node entries from an XMLIndex using the EXCLUDE ADD option:

```
SQL> alter index edba_po_idx rebuild
  2* parameters ('PATHS (EXCLUDE ADD (/PurchaseOrder/Reference))')
SQL> /

Index altered.
```

Native Web Services for Oracle XML DB

For DBAs and developers who spend considerable time with web development, the new native web services for Oracle XML DB provide an easy technology stack to implement XML applications on the Web. You no longer need to have Oracle's Internet application server to serve XML services over the Web. This integration solution in the database provides another toolkit for the DBAs and developers.

Two services come natively with Oracle XML DB web services: the SQL and XQuery web service and the PL/SQL web service. The SQL and XQuery web service allows you to query and return data as XML data. The PL/SQL web service allows you to access stored procedures and functions over the Web. The native web services for Oracle XML DB rely on the following technology stack components:

- Simple Object Access Protocol (SOAP) V1.1

- HTTP post method

- The Accept-Charsets field of the HTTP input header

- Web Services Description Language (WSDL)

SOAP is a critical component for the XML DB web services. SOAP 1.1 is used by the HTTP POST method and for error handling.

All XML DB configuration files reside in the xdbconfig.xml file located in the root of the XML DB repository.

HTTP and FTP for XML DB

Oracle XML DB is part of the standard database creation process. By default, the XDB schema is locked out of the database. You must enable the XDB schema and also set up the appropriate HTTP and/or FTP ports. The FTP port is not a requirement for native web services for XML DB.

The ability to access the XML DB using HTTP or FTP is not a new Oracle Database 11g feature, but it is crucial to explain how to configure HTTP since it is the essence of enabling web services for XML DB. The good news is that you can set up HTTP and FTP access to XML DB using Enterprise Manager Database Console. Using Enterprise Manager Database Console, the setup process is as simple as clearing out the zeroed-out port numbers and resetting them to the desired port designations. The XML DB configuration URL is located in the XML Database section of the Schema tab. The XML DB Configuration screen even allows secure access to the XML DB repository using HTTPS.

■**Note** By default, the HTTP and FTP ports for WebDB are 8080 and 2100, respectively. For security concerns, you should change the port numbers for HTTP and FTP.

To confirm you have everything set up prior to HTTP or FTP access, you can use the lsnrctl status command. If everything is set up correctly, you should see line entries for HTTP and FTP similar to what is shown here as part of the lsnrctl status output:

```
(DESCRIPTION=(ADDRESS=(PROTOCOL=tcp)(HOST=rac1.dbaexpert.com)(PORT=8080))
    (Presentation=HTTP)(Session=RAW))
 (DESCRIPTION=(ADDRESS=(PROTOCOL=tcp)(HOST=rac1.dbaexpert.com)
    (PORT=2100))
      (Presentation=FTP)(Session=RAW))
```

Please remember that if FTP is enabled, files that are being transferred with FTP will be uploaded to the XML DB repository. You can control security for HTTP and FTP using access control lists (ACLs). Once you have successfully set up the HTTP port for XML DB, you can verify connectivity by pointing your URL to http://servername.domain.com:8080.

You should at this point be prompted for the XDB user ID and password.

Setup XML DB Servlet

For security reasons, native web services for Oracle XML DB are not set up in the database. You must manually enable XML DB web services. There are a couple of steps needed to set up the XML DB servlet. First, as the sys user, you need to grant the XDB WEBSERVICES role to the user:

```
SQL> grant XDB_WEBSERVICES to xdb;

Grant succeeded.
```

Alternatively, you can also grant the XDB_WEBSERVICES_OVER_HTTP role to the user. The XDB_WEBSERVICES role allows only for HTTPS communication with the database. This role is a requirement for XML DB web services. The XDB_WEBSERVICES_OVER_HTTP role allows for HTTP traffic.

```
SQL> grant XDB_WEBSERVICES_OVER_HTTP to xdb;
```

Grant succeeded.

You may choose to grant the XDB_WEBSERVICES_WITH_PUBLIC role to the user. This role enables access to all the objects that are granted to PUBLIC over the web services. With this role enabled for the user, the user would have access to the PUBLIC objects as if they were logged in the database; otherwise, the security permissions would be given access to database objects less the PUBLIC objects.

Second, you must add the web services configuration servlet using the DBMS_XDB package:

```
DECLARE
SERVLET_NAME VARCHAR2(32) := 'orawsv';
BEGIN
  DBMS_XDB.deleteServletMapping(SERVLET_NAME);
  DBMS_XDB.deleteServlet(SERVLET_NAME);
  DBMS_XDB.addServlet(NAME => SERVLET_NAME,
          LANGUAGE => 'C',
          DISPNAME => 'Oracle Query Web Service',
          DESCRIPT => 'Servlet for        SCHEMA => 'XDB');
  DBMS_XDB.addServletSecRole(SERVNAME => SERVLET_NAME,
                             ROLENAME => 'XDB_WEBSERVICES',
                             ROLELINK => 'XDB_WEBSERVICES');
  DBMS_XDB.addServletMapping(PATTERN => '/orawsv/*',
                             NAME => SERVLET_NAME);
END;
/
```

Once the orawsv servlet is added, you can review the xdbconfig.xml file to verify the setup. Another way to verify correct setup is to use XQuery to query the orawsv keywords from the xdbconfig.xml file.

Validate the XML DB Web Service

Now you can access the XML DB servlet using your web browser of choice. The web service has a WSDL associated with it. The WSDL document specifies the location of the service and the operations (or methods) the service exposes. The access path of the WSDL document is as follows:

```
http://host:port/orawsv?wsdl
```

In this particular example, for the host rac11, you can access the WSDL document using the following URL:

```
http://rac11:8080/orawsv?wsdl
```

This web page shows the following output:

```
<definitions name="orawsv" targetNamespace="http://xmlns.oracle.com/orawsv">
-
    <types>
-
```

```
    <xsd:schema targetNamespace=http://xmlns.oracle.com/orawsv
     xsi:schemaLocation="ht

    <xsd:element name="query">

    <xsd:complexType>

    <xsd:sequence>

    <xsd:element name="query_text">

    <xsd:complexType>

    <xsd:simpleContent>

    <xsd:extension base="xsd:string">

    <xsd:attribute name="type">

    <xsd:simpleType>

    <xsd:restriction base="xsd:NMTOKEN">
<xsd:enumeration value="SQL"/>
<xsd:enumeration value="XQUERY"/>
<xsd:enumeration value="XQUERYX"/>
<xsd:enumeration value="PLSQL"/>
<xsd:enumeration value="TABLE"/>
</xsd:restriction>
</xsd:simpleType>
</xsd:attribute>
</xsd:extension>
</xsd:simpleContent>
</xsd:complexType>
</xsd:element>
..
..
..
<service name="ORAWSVService">
<documentation>Oracle Web Service</documentation>

    <port name="ORAWSVPort" binding="tns:ORAWSVBinding">
<soap:address location="http://rac11:8080/orawsv"/>
</port>
</service>
</definitions>
```

Validate the PL/SQL Web Service

Once the servlet is defined and verified for successful access, you can proceed to access the stored packages or procedures inside the database for web service access. The PL/SQL web services are located here:

```
http://host:port/orawsv/SCHEMA_OWNER/PACKAGE_NAME/PROCEDURE_NAME
http://host:port/orawsv/SCHEMA_OWNER/PROCEDURE_NAME
```

■**Note** The schema owner, package name, and procedure name have to be accessed in uppercase. If the uppercase schema owner or package name is not specified, you will receive an "Incorrect Input Doc/URL" page, as shown here:

```
<soap:faultcode>
<soap:Value>soap:Sender</soap:Value>
</soap:faultcode>
<soap:faultstring>Error processing input</soap:faultstring>
    <soap:detail>
<OracleErrors>
        Incorrect Input Doc/URL
      </OracleErrors>
</soap:detail>
</soap:Fault>
```

Each stored function or procedure is associated with a dynamic web service that generates its own WSDL document. The WSDL for the stored functions can be accessed using the URL path specified earlier except you would simply replace the procedure with the function name. Let's create a simple package called DBA_SALARIES with a function called MAXSALARY:

```
CREATE OR REPLACE PACKAGE dba_salaries AUTHID CURRENT_USER AS
  FUNCTION maxsalary (p_org_name    IN OUT VARCHAR2,
                      p_high_salary OUT    NUMBER)
  RETURN NUMBER;
END dba_salaries;
/

CREATE OR REPLACE PACKAGE BODY dba_salaries
AS
FUNCTION maxsalary
   (p_org_name    IN OUT VARCHAR2,
    p_high_salary OUT    NUMBER) return number
IS
CURSOR c1 IS
SELECT MAX(salary)
FROM edba_master
WHERE org_name=p_org_name;
```

```
BEGIN
  OPEN c1; FETCH c1 INTO p_high_salary;  CLOSE c1;
  RETURN p_high_salary;
END;
END;
/
```

Once the package is created, you can validate the PL/SQL web service for the stored package. The DBA_SALARIES package that was created in the earlier example can be accessed using the following URL:

```
http://rac11:8080/orawsv/XDB/DBA_SALARIES?wsdl
```

Or you can ask for the WSDL document from the fully qualified PACKAGE.FUNCTION name instead. Notice that the package name is a separate virtual directory from the stored procedure or function. Continuing from the DBA_SALARIES package, we will access the MAXSALARY function:

```
http://rac11:8080/orawsv/XDB/DBA_SALARIES/MAXSALARY?wsdl
```

Here's the output:

```
- <definitions name="MAXSALARY" targetNamespace=
  "http://xmlns.oracle.com/orawsv/XDB/- <types>
- <xsd:schema targetNamespace=
  "http://xmlns.oracle.com/orawsv/XDB/DBA_SALARIES/MAXSA
- <xsd:element name="SNUMBER-MAXSALARYInput">
- <xsd:complexType>
- <xsd:sequence>
  <xsd:element name="P_ORG_NAME-VARCHAR2-INOUT" type="xsd:string" />
- <xsd:element name="P_HIGH_SALARY-NUMBER-OUT">
  <xsd:complexType />
  </xsd:element>
  </xsd:sequence>
  </xsd:complexType>
  </xsd:element>
- <xsd:element name="MAXSALARYOutput">
- <xsd:complexType>
- <xsd:sequence>
  <xsd:element name="RETURN" type="xsd:double" />
  <xsd:element name="P_ORG_NAME" type="xsd:string" />
  <xsd:element name="P_HIGH_SALARY" type="xsd:double" />
  </xsd:sequence>
  </xsd:complexType>
  </xsd:element>
  </xsd:schema>
  </types>
```

```
- <message name="MAXSALARYInputMessage">
  <part name="parameters" element="tns:SNUMBER-MAXSALARYInput" />
  </message>
- <message name="MAXSALARYOutputMessage">
  <part name="parameters" element="tns:MAXSALARYOutput" />
  </message>
- <portType name="MAXSALARYPortType">
- <operation name="MAXSALARY">
  <input message="tns:MAXSALARYInputMessage" />
  <output message="tns:MAXSALARYOutputMessage" />
  </operation>
  </portType>
- <binding name="MAXSALARYBinding" type="tns:MAXSALARYPortType">
  <soap:binding style="document" transport="http://schemas.xmlsoap.org/soap/http" />
- <operation name="MAXSALARY">
  <soap:operation soapAction="MAXSALARY" />
- <input>
  <soap:body parts="parameters" use="literal" />
  </input>
- <output>
  <soap:body parts="parameters" use="literal" />
  </output>
  </operation>
  </binding>
- <service name="MAXSALARYService">
  <documentation>Oracle Web Service</documentation>
- <port name="MAXSALARYPort" binding="tns:MAXSALARYBinding">
  <soap:address location="http://rac1:8080/orawsv/XDB/DBA_SALARIES/MAXSALARY" />
  </port>
  </service>
  </definitions>
```

In-Place XML Schema Evolution

Oracle Database 11g introduces new, in-place XML schema evolution capability. This particular feature enables certain kinds of changes to XML schemas with zero downtime. In-place schema evolution makes alterations to an existing XML schema without copying, deleting, or reinserting elements of the data.

Schema evolution capability is a much longed for feature for a lot of companies that are reluctant to use schema-based XMLTypes. Here are the general restrictions for in-place schema evolution:

- You cannot change the storage model.

- You cannot make transformations that invalidate existing documents.

To implement in-place schema evolution, you use the DBMS_XMLSCHEMA.INPLACEEVOLVE procedure. This procedure accepts three parameters:

```
procedure inPlaceEvolve(schemaURL IN VARCHAR2,
    diffXML IN XMLType,
    flags IN NUMBER := EVOLVE_PRESERVE_VALIDITY | EVOLVE_TRACE_ONLY);
```

The first parameter identifies the URL of the XML schema to be evolved. The `diffXML` parameter specifies the XML schema differences document that specifies the changes to apply. The `FLAG` parameter is an optional bit mask parameter that controls the behavior of the procedure. There are two possible flags for this parameter: `EVOLVE_SCAN_DATA` and `EVOLVE_PRESERVE_VALIDITY`. By default, `EVOLVE_PRESERVE_VALIDITY` is set, and `EVOLVE_SCAN_DATA` is not set. This implies that the validity of the document is ensured by inspecting the XML schema changes. You should accept the default parameter for the `FLAG` option only if the validity of the document can be guaranteed without scanning the instance documents. If the `EVOLVE_PRESERVE_VALIDITY` bit is not set, then the procedure will try to make changes to the XML schema even if it may introduce invalidity.

One of the options to the `inPlaceEvolve` procedure is `diffXML`. The `diffXML` document needs to be created before you can apply the in-place evolution of the schema. This document is the blueprint to delta changes that need to be applied to the XML schema. Changes are executed in order of operation as specified in the `diffXML` file. There are several ways to create the `diffXML` document: the XMLDiff JavaBean, the `xmldiff` command-line interface, or the `XMLDIFF` SQL function.

XQuery Enhancements

Oracle introduced XQuery to the database in Oracle Database 10*g* Release 2. Oracle continues to make improvements to enhance this feature set. Oracle Database 11*g* introduces two new functions: `XMLExists` and `XMLCast`.

XMLExists

The `XMLExists` function checks to see whether a specified XQuery returns a nonempty sequence. `XMLExists` is similar to the `existsNode` operator except it returns a `TRUE`/`FALSE` Boolean value and accepts an arbitrary XQuery expression.

■**Note** Oracle recommends you utilize `XMLExists` rather than use `existsNode`.

Let's see how the `XMLExists` function works:

```
SQL> select object_value
  2  from edba_po
  3  where XMLExists('/PurchaseOrder[Requestor="John Z. Chen"]'
  4* PASSING OBJECT_VALUE)
SQL> /
```

```
OBJECT_VALUE
--------------------------------------------------------------------------------
<PurchaseOrder xmlns:xsi="http://www.w3.org/2001/XMLSchema-instance" xsi:noNames
<PurchaseOrder xmlns:xsi="http://www.w3.org/2001/XMLSchema-instance" xsi:noNames
<PurchaseOrder xmlns:xsi="http://www.w3.org/2001/XMLSchema-instance" xsi:noNames
<PurchaseOrder xmlns:xsi="http://www.w3.org/2001/XMLSchema-instance" xsi:noNames
<PurchaseOrder xmlns:xsi="http://www.w3.org/2001/XMLSchema-instance" xsi:noNames
<PurchaseOrder xmlns:xsi="http://www.w3.org/2001/XMLSchema-instance" xsi:noNames
<PurchaseOrder xmlns:xsi="http://www.w3.org/2001/XMLSchema-instance" xsi:noNames
<PurchaseOrder xmlns:xsi="http://www.w3.org/2001/XMLSchema-instance" xsi:noNames
<PurchaseOrder xmlns:xsi="http://www.w3.org/2001/XMLSchema-instance" xsi:noNames

9 rows selected.
```

You can use the `XMLExists` function in SQL queries and in function-based indexes. To use `XMLExists` in a SQL statement, you must wrap it inside the `CASE` statement:

```
CASE WHEN XMLExists(...) THEN 'TRUE' ELSE 'FALSE' END.
```

XMLCast

Also with Oracle Database 11g XQuery, Oracle adds the `XMLCast` function. The `XMLCast` function takes the first argument and casts it to the second argument. The second argument must be of scalar SQL datatypes: NUMBER, VARCHAR2, DATE, and any derivate of date timestamps. Here is an example of how to use `XMLCast`:

```
SQL> select XMLCast(XMLQuery
                    ('/PurchaseOrder/Reference' PASSING OBJECT_VALUE
  2   RETURNING CONTENT)
  3   AS VARCHAR2(100)) "REFERENCE"
  4   from edba_po
  5   where XMLExists('/PurchaseOrder[Requestor="John Z. Chen"]'
  6*  PASSING OBJECT_VALUE)
SQL> /

REFERENCE
--------------------------------------------------------------------------------
JCHEN-20021009123337123PDT
JCHEN-20021009123337223PDT
JCHEN-20021009123338475PDT
JCHEN-20021009123335961PDT
JCHEN-20021009123336462PDT
JCHEN-20021009123337633PDT
JCHEN-20021009123337733PDT
JCHEN-20021009123337764PDT
JCHEN-20021009123337443PDT

9 rows selected
```

XMLCast supports casting of XML only to scalar SQL datatypes; it does not support casting of scalar SQL datatypes to XML or XML to XML.

XML Developer's Kit (XDK) Improvements

New to Oracle's XDK are the XMLDiff and XMLPatch SQL operators. With XMLDiff, you can compare two XML documents for anomalies. The output of this analysis is another XML document. With XMLPatch, you can take the output from XMLDiff and apply it to the source document. As you apply the delta output from XMLDiff, you can easily transform the source document to be compliant with another document.

XMLDiff

The XMLDiff function compares two XML documents and captures the differences. For the first parameter, specify the source XML document. For the second parameter, specify the XML document that you want to compare to the first document. Here's an example of using the XMLDiff operator:

```
SQL> SELECT XMLDiff(
  2     XMLTYPE('<?xml version="1.0"?>
  3     <bk:book xmlns:bk="http://dbaexpert.com">
  4        <bk:tr>
  5           <bk:td>
  6                    <bk:chapter>
  7                            Chapter 1. Upgrade New Features
  8                    </bk:chapter>
  9           </bk:td>
 10           <bk:td>
 11                    <bk:chapter>
 12                            Chapter 2. 11g New Features in Database Diagnostics
 13                    </bk:chapter>
 14           </bk:td>
 15        </bk:tr>
 16     </bk:book>'),
 17     XMLTYPE('<?xml version="1.0"?>
 18     <bk:book xmlns:bk="http://dbaexpert.com">
 19        <bk:tr>
 20           <bk:td>
 21                    <bk:chapter>
 22                            Chapter 1. Upgrade New Features
 23                    </bk:chapter>
 24           </bk:td>
 25           <bk:td>
 26                    <bk:chapter>
 27                            Chapter 2. 11g Data Guard New Features
 28                    </bk:chapter>
```

```
 29            </bk:td>
 30        </bk:tr>
 31    </bk:book>')
 32    )
 33* FROM DUAL
SQL> /


XMLDIFF(XMLTYPE('<?XMLVERSION="1.0"?>
<BK:BOOKXMLNS:BK="HTTP://DBAEXPERT.COM"><BK
--------------------------------------------------------------------------------
<xd:xdiff xsi:schemaLocation=
"http://xmlns.oracle.com/xdb/xdiff.xsd
    http://xmlns.oracle.com/xdb/xdiff.xsd" xmlns:xd=
    "http://xmlns.oracle.com/xdb/xdiff.xsd" xmlns:xsi=
    "http://www.w3.org/2001/XMLSchema-instance" xmlns:bk=
    "http://dbaexpert.com">
  <?oracle-xmldiff operations-in-docorder="true" output-model=
    "snapshot" diff-algorithm="global"?>
  <xd:update-node xd:node-type="text" xd:xpath=
    "/bk:book[1]/bk:tr[1]/bk:td[2]/bk:chapter[1]/text()[1]">
    <xd:content>
                     Chapter 2. 11g Data Guard New Features
    </xd:content>

  </xd:update-node>
</xd:xdiff>
```

The XMLDiff functionality comes in three flavors:

- The XMLDiff JavaBean (oracle.xml.differ.XMLDiff)

- The xmldiff command-line utility

- The XMLDiff SQL function

You can use any of the three options listed here to identify differences between two XML documents and create simple and repeatable processes that can replicate changes to XML documents.

XMLPatch

The XMLPatch function patches an XML document with the specified changes. A patched XMLType document is returned. You should specify the input XMLType document as the first argument. For the second argument, specify the XMLType document containing the changes to be applied to the first document. The changes should conform to the XDiff XML schema. Here's an example of the using the XMLPatch operator:

```
SQL> SELECT XMLPatch(
  2  XMLTYPE('<?xml version="1.0"?>
  3   <bk:book xmlns:bk="http://dbaexpert.com">
  4      <bk:tr>
  5          <bk:td>
  6                  <bk:chapter>
  7                          Chapter 1. Upgrade New Features
  8                  </bk:chapter>
  9          </bk:td>
 10          <bk:td>
 11                  <bk:chapter>
 12                          Chapter 2. 11g New Features in Database Diagnostics
 13                  </bk:chapter>
 14          </bk:td>
 15      </bk:tr>
 16   </bk:book>'),
 17  XMLTYPE('<?xml version="1.0"?>
 18  <xd:xdiff xsi:schemaLocation="http://xmlns.oracle.com/xdb/xdiff.xsd
 19    http://xmlns.oracle.com/xdb/xdiff.xsd"
 20    xmlns:xd="http://xmlns.oracle.com/xdb/xdiff.xsd"
 21    xmlns:xsi="http://www.w3.org/2001/XMLSchema-instance"
 22    xmlns:bk="http://dbaexpert.com">
 23    <?oracle-xmldiff operations-in-docorder="true" output-model="snapshot"
 24      diff-algorithm="global"?>
 25    <xd:delete-node xd:node-type="element"
 26      xd:xpath="/bk:book[1]/bk:tr[1]/bk:td[2]/bk:chapter[1]"/>
 27  </xd:xdiff>')
 28  )
 29* FROM DUAL
SQL> /

<?xml version="1.0"?>
<bk:book xmlns:bk="http://dbaexpert.com">
  <bk:tr>
    <bk:td>
      <bk:chapter>
                        Chapter 1. Upgrade New Features
                </bk:chapter>
    </bk:td>
    <bk:td/>
  </bk:tr>
</bk:book>
```

In this particular example, the second argument specified that the Chapter 2 element is the offset and should be excluded.

It is important to note that the documents specified in the XMLDiff and XMLPatch parameters must conform to the XDiff XML schema. If they do not conform, you will receive this error:

```
ERROR:
ORA-31011: XML parsing failed
ORA-19202: Error occurred in XML processing
LPX-00918: XmlPatch encountered an error in translating XPATH using XmlXVM


no rows selected
```

Beyond the 64KB Limit for XML Nodes

In previous releases of Oracle, there was a 64KB limit on text nodes and attribute values. In Oracle Database 11*g*, the limits imposed for XML text nodes and attribute values have been abandoned. Using new APIs available in PL/SQL, Java, and C abstract streams, XML nodes can scale as large as the datatype restrictions.

Oracle Data Pump Support for XMLType

Oracle recommends using Data Pump to import and export XMLType data. Oracle's conventional export utility (exp) does not support Binary XML tables or XMLType indexes. The following example clearly shows Oracle's deprecation of the export utility:

```
..
. . exporting table                    EDBA_SECURITY
EXP-00107: Feature (BINARY XML) of column SYS_NC_ROWINFO$ in
           table SH.EDBA_SECURITY
EXP-00112: Index EDBA_SECURITY_XMLINDEX is of XMLType and could not be exported
EXP-00078: Error exporting metadata for index EDBA_SECURITY_XMLINDEX. Index
           creation
Export terminated successfully with warnings.
```

Application Express (APEX) Enhancements

Starting in Oracle Database 11*g*, the Application Express stack is bundled with the Oracle RDBMS software. The Application Express 3.0 software stack is now part of ORACLE_HOME in the $ORACLE_HOME/apex directory.

APEX Configuration

There is a script called apxconf.sql located in the $ORACLE_HOME/apex directory that will allow you to configure the port assignment and the password for the Application Express admin user. APEX can be configured with the database-embedded PL/SQL gateway:

```
SQL> @?/apex/apxconf.sql

    PORT
----------
    8080
```

```
Enter values below for the XDB HTTP listener port and
the password for the ApplicatiDefault values are in brackets [ ].
Press Enter to accept the default value.


Enter a password for the ADMIN user            [] oracle123
Enter a port for the XDB HTTP listener [    8080] 8080
...changing HTTP Port

PL/SQL procedure successfully completed.


PL/SQL procedure successfully completed.


Session altered.

...changing password for ADMIN

PL/SQL procedure successfully completed.
```

Now you can unlock the anonymous user:

```
SQL> alter user anonymous account unlock;
```

```
User altered.
```

Once you have successfully set up the APEX environment, you can access the web site for rapid application development. The APEX database schema is now part of the standard database component of the Database Configuration Assistant. If you use the DBCA to create your database, it is part of the default database build process. Once you successfully set up APEX, you can access the admin page with the URL similar to what is shown here:

```
http://rac11:8080/apex/apex_admin
```

APEX Enhancements

Application Express packs enhancement after enhancement for Oracle Database 11g. Application Express provides added functionality to do the following:

- It provides the ability to print a PDF for report regions.

- It renders up to 18 different flash charts and converts scalable vector graphics to flash.

- It can migrate Access applications to Application Express using the Application Migration Workshop.

- You can use drag-and-drop layout pages for development productivity.

- It provides new item types such as date picker, pop-up list of values, shuttle, and new HTML text editor areas.

- It renders calendars by providing built-in wizards for daily, weekly, and monthly views.

- It supports loosely defined web services to support services created in JDeveloper and Oracle BPEL synchronous processes.

- It compares database objects in two separate schemas.

- It compares differences between two different applications.

- It facilitates bookmark pages within the application.

- It performs page and region caching for application performance.

- You can find items for CSS and images.

- It defines rules for password expiration, forces strong passwords, locks accounts, and forces password changes upon first login.

- You can manage workspace effectively by configuring sizes for new workspace and schema requests and additional space for existing workspace.

PHP Support Enhancements

With Zend Core for Oracle, you can easily develop PHP applications leveraging Oracle database technologies. Zend Core for Oracle is developed in partnership with Zend Technologies and can be downloaded from Oracle's OTN web site. This product is easy to install and fully integrated with Oracle. In Oracle Database 11g, Oracle provides enhanced support for PHP with the database. Oracle provides a feature called Database Resident Connection Pooling (DRCP) to provide considerable improvement in the scalability of PHP applications. In essence, DRCP provides a shared pool of connections similar to the way multithreaded sessions work. This allows for persistent connections without having to dedicate one for dedicated server processes for each of the PHP persistent connections.

From the application tier, you must append the following option to the connect string: (SERVER=POOLED). In the OCISessionPoolCreate() application call, you must specify this *connStr as an argument.

```
OCISessionPoolCreate ( OCIEnv          *envhp,
                       OCIError        *errhp,
                       OCISPool        *spoolhp,
                       OraText         **poolName,
                       ub4             *poolNameLen,
                       const OraText   *connStr,
                       ub4             connStrLen,
                       ub4             sessMin,
                       ub4             sessMax,
                       ub4             sessIncr,
                       OraText         *userid,
                       ub4             useridLen,
                       OraText         *password,
                       ub4             passwordLen,
                       ub4             mode );
```

The DBAs on the database tier can monitor the pooled connections using the DBA_ CPOOL_INFO view. For additional details, refer to Chapter 3.

Java Enhancements

The Oracle Database 11g JVM now supports J2SE 1.5. See http://java.sun.com/j2se/1.5.0/ docs/relnotes/features.html for a full list of all the features and enhancements. Quite possibly the biggest new feature is the introduction of generics in 1.5. Generics allow you to specify what classes are expected in generic collection classes. Generics are like a compiler hint.

Just-in-Time (JIT) Compiler and Native Compilation

Oracle has included a just-in-time compiler with Oracle Database 11g. This tool detects Java methods that would benefit from being compiled into native code and automatically performs the compilation. Behind the scenes, it runs as a slave process under the MMON background process. The DBMS_JAVA package has been enhanced with a collection of procedures to compile classes and methods. A helpful set of uncompile procedures will allow you to undo the compilation and allow you to mark the method or class as permanently uncompilable.

JIT compilation is automatically enabled by default and does not need any configuration. To turn off JIT compilation, you can use the ALTER SYSTEM command:

```
SQL> alter system set java_jit_enabled=FALSE;
System altered.
```

This initialization parameter is dynamically adjustable, so you can reenable JIT using the TRUE flag. There are advantages of using JIT with the database. First, JIT recompiles Java methods when they become invalid. Second, Oracle persists compiled Java methods across database sessions, calls, and instances.

JAR Support

Oracle supports the loading of JAR files into the database as database objects. What this means is although the loadjava program still needs to extract all the classes from the JAR file and create database objects for them, you can specify, via the -jarsasdbobjects option, that the JAR will be loaded as well and that the linkage between the classes and their JAR files will be retained. In cases where two JARs have the same class name, loadjava also provides the -prependjarnames option to prepend the JAR name to the Java class objects created. In the example, a simple Java program is created, loaded into the database as a JAR, and executed using the DBMS_ JAVA.runjava() function:

```
package hellooracle;

public class Main {
    public static void main(String[] args) {
        System.out.println("Hello, world");
    }
}
```

Hello, world, of course. This Java class was then compiled, and a JAR named HelloOracle.jar was created. To load it into Oracle, the following command was executed:

```
loadjava -u demo/demo -jarsasdbobjects HelloOracleB.jar
```

The following anonymous block was then executed in SQL*Plus:

```
set serverouput on
declare
  ret varchar2(32000);
begin
  dbms_java.set_output(20000);
  ret:=dbms_java.runjava(
      '-classpath JSERVER_CP/JAR/PRIVATE/SCHEMA/demo/HelloOracle.jar  \
        hellooracle.Main');
  DBMS_OUTPUT.PUT_LINE('return: '||ret);
end;
```

Executing this yields the following:

```
Hello world
return:
```

The backslash (\) character is not part of the program; it's just used to indicate that the argument to runjava() is on a single line.

In the first line of the code, a call to dbms_java.set_output() is called to direct that output from System.out.println() be sent to the dbms_output package. The second line is the actual call to the Java class. The classpath has a very specific format, which we'll cover in a bit, but apart from that, the call is just like you would make in a command-line call to java. As you can see from the resulting text, the class was executed as expected. The JSERVER_CP prefix to the classpath is replaced with the literal text jserver:/CP when the classpath entry is evaluated. The character immediately following the JSERVER_CP is used as the delimiter for the rest of the string. By convention, the / is typically used. There is another prefix string you should be aware of, JSERVER_SCHEMA. This one is replaced by jserver:/CP/SCHEMA. Table 11-5 explains what the arguments to these URLs are.

```
jserver:/CP/<type>/#2/#3/#4/#5
```

Table 11-5. *JServer URL Arguments*

Argument	JSERVER_SCHEMA	JSERVER_CP
Type	SCHEMA, a constant value.	JAR. RESOURCE. SHARED_DATA.
#2	A schema name. All classes in that schema are in this classpath.	The optional word PRIVATE. If not specified, the classes are loaded as shared classes. If PRIVATE is specified, the classes are loaded as private user class-loaded classes.
#3	N/A	The literal text SCHEMA.

Table 11-5. *JServer URL Arguments (Continued)*

Argument	JSERVER_SCHEMA	JSERVER_CP
#4	N/A	The schema this object is owned by.
#5	N/A	The actual object name for the object. This is case sensitive and should match the value found in USER/ALL/DBA_OBJECTS.

Improvements to the loadjava Tool

In addition to the ability to load JARs as database objects, the loadjava tool can now load JARs, classes, or resources from an HTTP URL. In the place of a file name, you specify a URL. Table 11-6 lists the new options to the loadjava program.

Table 11-6. *New loadjava Options*

Option	Description
-jarasresource	Loads JAR as resource in database. Does not extract classes from JARs.
-jarsasdbobjects	Loads JAR into database and also extracts classes.
-prependjarnames	Prepends the JAR name to the database object names that store the classes from the specified JAR (requires -jarsasodbobjects).
-nativecompile	Compiles loaded class to native code after loading and resolving them.

Improvements to the dropjava Tool

The dropjava tool has been enhanced to support dropping JARs that were previously loaded with the -jarasresource or -jarsasdbobject option, and you can now specify a list of objects to drop, with loadjava not failing if one or more of the listed objects do not exist. Table 11-7 lists the new options to dropjava.

Table 11-7. *New dropjava Options*

Option	Description
-jarasresource	Drops the entire JAR as resource from the database.
-jarsasdbobjects	Drops the JAR and the extracted classes from the JAR from the database.
-list	Drops the classes, sources, and resources listed from the database. Ignores missing objects.
-listfile <filename>	Same as -list except the specified file contains a list of objects, one per line, to be dropped.

Improvements to the ojvmjava Tool

A new option and command, -runjava, and a new command, connect, have been added to the ojvmjava tool. With the new connect command, you can connect to other database users. This is similar to SQL*Plus's connect command. runjava allows the user to specify whether the database's JVM or the ojvmjava tool should execute the Java, as the location of the classpath. This is how to use the command-line option -runjava:

```
ojvmjava ... -runjava [server_file_system]
```

Within the ojvmjava shell, the usage for the runjava command is as follows:

```
runjava [on|off|server_file_system]
```

Table 11-8 describes each of the possible settings for runjava.

Table 11-8. *runjava Options*

Command-Line Option	Shell Command	Description
-runjava	runjava on	Executable classes are run by ojvmjava. Classpath elements are on the local file system.
<no option>	runjava off	Executable classes are run with DBMS_JAVA by the database's JVM.
-runjava server_file_system	runjava server_file_system	Same as runjava on except the classpath elements are on the database server's file system.
N/A	runjava	Prints the current state of runjava.

In the following examples, the "Hello, world" program written earlier will be called from the ojvmjava shell. First, run ojvmjava without a -runjava option. This executes classes from the database.

```
r11b > ojvmjava -u demo/demo
--OJVMJAVA--
--type "help" at the command line for help message
$ java hellooracle.Main
Hello, world
```

In this case, the class hellooracle.Main was run from the database. Second, run with the -runjava option and Main.class present in the current directory:

```
r11b > ojvmjava -u demo/demo -runjava
--OJVMJAVA--
--type "help" at the command line for help message
$ java -classpath . hellooracle.Main
Hello, world

runjava call succeeded
```

The class was run from the file system, and `runjava` reported that it ran successfully. Third, run with the `server_file_system` option:

```
r11b > ojvmjava -u demo/demo -runjava server_file_system
--OJVMJAVA--
--type "help" at the command line for help message
$ java -classpath /home/oracle/Java hellooracle.Main
Hello, world

runjava call succeeded
```

The classes were loaded from the server file system and run locally.

The ojvmtc Tool

`ojvmtc` is a very nice tool that, given a list of classes and a classpath, will resolve all class references. If a class cannot be resolved, `ojvmtc` can either report the unresolved references or create a JAR containing stub versions of the unresolved classes. These stub versions throw a `java.lang.ClassNotfoundException` if they are called at runtime. In the following example, `ojvmtc` is called on a class as follows, where `packB.SwingThings` is not found in the classpath:

```
ojvmtc -list -server thin:demo/demo@localhost:1521:r11b Main.class
```

The program returns the following message:

```
The following classes could not be found:
packB/SwingThings
```

Execute `ojvmtc` again, but specify a JAR file to hold all classes in this closure set. The closure set is composed of all the classes specified on the command line and all classes generated as stubs by `ojvmtc`:

```
ojvmtc -jar rep.jar -server thin:demo/demo@localhost:1521:r11b Main.class
The set is not closed
1 classes are missing
generating stub classes
generating: packB/SwingThings
```

Checking out the contents of the newly created `rep.jar` shows the following:

```
r11b > jar tf rep.jar
packA/Main.class
packB/SwingThings.class
nov12.novara-labs.com:/home/oracle/Java/ojvmtc/run
```

The program added all referenced classes and JARs (`packA/Main.class`) as well as created a stub class (`packB/SwingThings.class`). `rep.jar` is loaded to the database using `loadjava`:

```
r11b > loadjava -u demo/demo -jarsasdbobjects rep.jar
nov12.novara-labs.com:/home/oracle/Java/ojvmtc/run
r11b > ojvmjava -u demo/demo
--OJVMJAVA--
--type "help" at the command line for help message
```

Invoking Main results in the following error:

```
$ java packA/Main
Hello
java.lang.NoClassDefFoundError: !!!ERROR!!! generated by genmissing
        at packB.SwingThings.<clinit>(Unknown Source)
         at packA.Main.main(Main.java:6)
```

The last three lines show the exception that's thrown when one of the stub classes is referenced. The generated stub classes are useful in cases where you are loading a class library that makes references to other libraries that are not needed and will not be loaded in the database. An example would be a statistics package that includes a graphics subsystem. In your usage of this library, you are interested only in time-series calculations, and you have no use for the graphics portion of the library. The generated stub routines allow you to load the statistics library and avoid having to write the stubs yourself.

CHAPTER 12

■■■

Data Warehousing

One of the primary focal points of Oracle Database 11g is to change the perception of how to utilize the database for content management. Typically, third-party applications are used to manage content within the database. Traditionally, the database served as a repository of metadata for content management. Oracle Database 11g provides tremendous improvements in the world of LOBs to fortify the native content management capabilities of Oracle Database.

To meet ever-demanding mission-critical business requirements, more and more Fortune 500 companies store their documents and images in the database. For example, corporate documents/images can be in the form of PDF, JPG/TIFF, or PNG. Even with Oracle Database 10g, large companies strategically architected solutions to store documents and images in the Oracle database. There are several critical reasons behind this decision to use Oracle Database as a repository for files. First, you can simplify backup solutions by moving documents in the database. Instead of backing up millions of files outside the database, companies can incorporate backup strategies to back up hundreds or thousands of Oracle datafiles depending on a company's database standards. In addition, backing up millions or hundreds of millions of documents on the file system can pose maintenance headaches, especially in the world of incremental backups. In addition, storing documents and images inside the database makes it easier to implement disaster recovery solutions. Oracle simplifies disaster recovery with Oracle Data Guard. A document stored in the database becomes just another transaction rolled forward to the disaster recovery database. You can implement physical or logical standby database technologies to provide up-to-the-second or even real-time data propagation to the disaster recovery site. Oracle also provides granular-level protection at the row level or, better yet, virtualized database record sets using virtual private databases.

Of course, on the flip side, some companies have not chosen to take advantage of documents inside the database. Slow performance used to be one of the largest concerns that led the decision away from documents and images in the database. With the performance improvements on LOB management in Oracle Database 11g, Oracle can meet or exceed the performance concerns of the past. Companies should reconsider their storage options to store the documents in the database.

This chapter will cover the multitude of new Oracle Database 11g features that surround information management. The objective of this chapter is to inform developers and DBAs of the new capabilities offered in Oracle Database 11g relative to data warehousing, Oracle partitioning, and SecureFiles. First, the discussion will center on the newly reengineered LOBs called SecureFiles. Next, the chapter will continue with the data warehousing enhancements followed by partitioning. Finally, the chapter will cover the high-level improvements made to Oracle

Multimedia. We cover an incredible amount of information in this chapter, so let's jump straight into Oracle LOBs.

Next-Generation LOBs

Oracle Database 11g breaks the barrier of large object (LOB) storage in the database. Though once perceived to be something handled only outside the database, Oracle Database 11g proves that files can easily be stored in the database with equal or better performance than in a traditional file system.

Although Oracle Database 10g provides file storage in the database using various utilities and applications, this technology was not well embraced by the Oracle community as a whole. Before Oracle Database 11g, LOBs were classified as either character LOBs (CLOBs) or binary LOBs (BLOBs). The only distinguishing factor between the two is that one is used to store large variable character data, and the other is used to store binary data. Oracle Database 11g completely reengineers LOB storage to what they call SecureFiles. The primary focus of the SecureFiles feature is to do the following:

- Improve performance

- Reduce space consumption

- Enhance security

SecureFiles vastly improves the management of large objects by introducing critical new functionality. First, LOB compression saves disk space for data at rest. Second, LOB encryption provides for data security at rest. Oracle offers the capability to deduplicate LOB segments and provides additional LOB APIs. For performance needs, LOB data path optimizations are included in Oracle Database 11g. We will be discussing all of these features in detail in the following sections.

SecureFiles Requirements

To take advantage of Oracle SecureFiles, you must satisfy a couple of requirements. First, the tablespace that houses the secure file must be in automatic segment space management (assm). Luckily, Oracle adopted the assm tablespace as a default feature when it was introduced in Oracle Database 10g and continues to be in Oracle Database 11g. Second, the compatibility for the database must be set to 11.0.0.0.0 or higher.

BasicFiles vs. SecureFiles

Oracle distinguishes the legacy large object storage from its next-generation large objects, referring to the legacy large objects now as BasicFiles. BasicFiles comprises all the CLOB and BLOB functionality as you know it up to Oracle Database 10g Release 2. Starting from Oracle Database 11g, the next-generation large objects are distinguished as SecureFiles. Let's drill down to the specific differences of SecureFiles.

What differentiates SecureFiles from BasicFiles is the storage parameter used when creating the table or adding the column. To leverage SecureFiles, you must specify the reserved store as securefile keyword of the LOB clause. Here's an example showing how to create a table leveraging the SecureFiles storage for the BLOB_CONTENT column in a table called SECURE_DOCS:

```
create table secure_docs
(       document_id number not null primary key,
        name varchar2(255) not null,
        edba_knowledgebase_category_id number not null,
        mime_type varchar2(128),
        doc_size number,
        dad_charset varchar2(128),
        last_updated date,
        content_type varchar2(128),
        blob_content blob
)
tablespace tools
lob (blob_content) store as securefile (
tablespace tools enable storage in row chunk 8192 pctversion 10
nocache logging)
/
```

By default, BasicFiles is created if the store as securefile clause is not specified. The following example creates a table named DOCS with a BasicFiles column named BLOB_CONTENT:

```
create table docs
(       document_id number not null primary key,
        name varchar2(255) not null,
        edba_knowledgebase_category_id number,
        mime_type varchar2(128),
        doc_size number,
        dad_charset varchar2(128),
        last_updated date,
        content_type varchar2(128),
        blob_content blob
)
tablespace tools
lob (blob_content) store as basicfile (
tablespace tools enable storage in row chunk 8192 pctversion 10
nocache logging)
/
```

■**Note** The term *FastFiles* is synonymous with SecureFiles.

LOB Performance

One of the promising features of SecureFiles is that the feature is highly performatory and capable of higher throughput than the file system. There are numerous performance optimizations for SecureFiles, including the following:

- SecureFiles allows for dynamic cache and nocache options. With Oracle Database 11*g* compatibility, you can provide a logging clause after the cache parameter. Oracle will determine when to cache or not cache the LOB into the buffer cache for performance. The logging setting is similar to the data journaling capabilities of file systems.

- The locking mechanism for SecureFiles uses the new distributed lock management semantics for LOB blocks to avoid cache fusion locks.

- The writing mechanism of LOBs is similar to the file system, in that LOB IOs are now capable of dirty cache writes on file servers. Similar to the file system, Oracle is capable of coalescing several IO requests into a single large IO call to the database, thus reducing the overhead from what it would take to manage several small IO requests. Moreover, Oracle Database 11*g* provides the option of prefetching LOBs at the OCI layer.

- The new SecureFiles storage option called filesystem_like_logging allows the logging of only the metadata changes. This is similar to the metadata journaling of file systems. filesystem_like_logging reduces the mean time to recovery.

Deduplication

Oracle Database 11*g* SecureFiles adds to the LOB paradigm the ability to detect duplicate LOB data and eliminate duplicates by using a secure hash SHA1 algorithm. Elimination of duplicate data is achieved by using the deduplicate LOB syntax. Deduplication allows companies to save storage without compromising performance.

By contrast, you can use the keep_duplicates option to continue to allow duplicate values in the same LOB segment to be stored in a table. The keep_duplicates option remains the default behavior for the deduplication feature in Oracle Database 11*g*. Continuing to utilize the documents table from the previous example, we'll show how you can implement this feature. First we'll create a table that allows for duplicate LOB segments. In the following example, we'll create a table called DEFAULT_DOCS with the keep_duplicates keyword:

```
 create table default_docs
(        document_id number not null primary key,
         name varchar2(255) not null,
         edba_knowledgebase_category_id number,
         mime_type varchar2(128),
         doc_size number,
         dad_charset varchar2(128),
         last_updated date,
         content_type varchar2(128),
         blob_content blob
)
tablespace tools
lob (blob_content) store as securefile (
keep_duplicates
tablespace tools enable storage in row chunk 8192 pctversion 10
nocache logging)
/
Table created.
```

Using a simple shell script to load a 189KB Microsoft Word document into the database, you can easily prove the usefulness of the deduplication functionality. The following scripts, the load.ksh shell script and a load.ctl SQL*Loader controlfile, are provided. The function of the load.ksh script is to simply increment the sequence number in the load.ctl file and invoke the SQL*Loader utility. Here's the content of the load.ksh shell script:

```
# load.ksh
export counter_file=load.seq
export controlfile=load.new
export filenum=$(cat $counter_file)
(( NUM = $filenum + 1 ))
echo $NUM > $counter_file
cat load.ctl | sed -e "s/NUMBER_TO_REPLACE###/$NUM/g" > $controlfile
sqlldr control=$controlfile userid=rodba/oracle123
```

The load.ctl file is the SQL*Loader controlfile to load a Microsoft Word document in the database. The size of the Word document is approximately 189KB.

```
#load.ctl
load data infile *
append
into table docs
fields terminated by '|'
(
 document_id,
 name,
 blob_content   lobfile(name) TERMINATED BY EOF
)
begindata
NUMBER_TO_REPLACE###|Chapter9-ASM.doc||
```

The load.ksh script was invoked 100 times to load 100 copies of the same document into the DEFAULT_DOCS table. By using the DBMS_SPACE.USED_SPACE procedure, the total bytes allocated for the LOB segment can be retrieved. The following simple PL/SQL script was created to retrieve the LOB segment size:

```
REM:  space.sql
define v_tab = '&1'
var a number;
var b number;
var c number;
var d number;

declare
v_used_blocks number;
v_total_bytes number;
v_segment_blocks number;
v_segment_bytes number;
v_segment_name varchar2(55);
```

```
cursor c1 is
select segment_name
from dba_lobs
where owner=user
and table_name=upper('&v_tab');

begin
open c1; fetch c1 into v_segment_name; close c1;

   dbms_space.space_usage (
      'sh', v_segment_name, 'lob'
      , v_segment_blocks, v_segment_bytes, v_used_blocks, v_total_bytes
      , :a, :b, :c, :d);

   dbms_output.put_line ('kb used: ' ||
                         to_char(round(v_total_bytes/1024,2)));
end;
/
```

This script takes an input parameter of the table name. Based on the table name, the PL/SQL logic queries the DBA_LOBS view and retrieves the LOB segment name associated with the table. This code example assumes that a table will have only one LOB segment. The LOB segment name is passed to the DBMS_SPACE.USED_SPACE procedure as one of the arguments. Using DBMS_OUTPUT, the total number of bytes used for the LOB segment is displayed.

We will save this script to a file named space.sql. We will use the space.sql script to determine the size of the SecureFiles LOB segments repeatedly throughout this chapter. In this particular example, the DEFAULT_DOCS LOB segment size is obtained using the space.sql script:

```
SQL> @space default_docs
old  12: and table_name=upper('&v_tab');
new  12: and table_name=upper('default_docs');
KB used: 19352

PL/SQL procedure successfully completed.
```

You can see from this output that the size of the LOB segment in the DEFAULT_DOCS table consumes about 19MB.

Next, let's create a table that is identical to the DEFAULT_DOCS table except with the deduplicate reserved syntax. Before we create the table, let's isolate this new table into a separate tablespace. Just to prove a point, we will create a tablespace called secure_docs_d with a single datafile 1MB in size:

```
SQL> create tablespace secure_docs_d datafile '+data' size 1m;

Tablespace created.
```

A table that is identical to DEFAULT_DOCS will be called SECURE_DOCS but will be created with the deduplication option, as shown here:

```
create table secure_docs
(       document_id number not null primary key,
        name varchar2(255) not null,
        edba_knowledgebase_category_id number,
        mime_type varchar2(128),
        doc_size number,
        dad_charset varchar2(128),
        last_updated date,
        content_type varchar2(128),
        blob_content blob
)
tablespace secure_docs_d
lob (blob_content) store as securefile (
deduplicate lob
tablespace secure_docs_d enable storage in row chunk 8192 pctversion 10
nocache logging)
/
```

Using SQL*Loader again, we are able to load the same 189KB document 100 times. The deduplication option is truly working since the 100 inserts of the document are resident in the 1MB tablespace. Let's see the actual size of the SecureFiles LOB segment using the same space.sql script created earlier:

```
SQL> @space secure_docs
old  12: and table_name=upper('&v_tab');
new  12: and table_name=upper('secure_docs');
KB used: 200

PL/SQL procedure successfully completed.
```

Amazingly, LOBs in the SECURE_DOCS table, using the deduplication option, consume only 200KB of space compared to the LOB column in the BASIC_DOCS table, which consumes about 19MB of storage.

By default, Oracle Database 11g allows duplicate LOB data to be loaded inside the database. When you query the DBA_LOBS view, you will see several distinct values for the DEDUPLICATION column, as shown here:

```
SQL>  select table_name, column_name, deduplication, securefile
  2  from dba_lobs
  3* where table_name in ('DEFAULT_DOCS', 'SECURE_DOCS', 'DOCS')
SQL> /
```

TABLE_NAME	COLUMN_NAME	DEDUPLICATION	SEC
DEFAULT_DOCS	BLOB_CONTENT	NO	YES
SECURE_DOCS	BLOB_CONTENT	LOB	YES
DOCS	BLOB_CONTENT	NONE	NO

SecureFiles LOB segments that do not allow for duplicate values will have a value of LOB in the DEDUPLICATION column. You can also see that the value of NONE is provided for BasicFiles LOB segments.

In addition to specifying deduplication when creating a LOB, you can also modify the deduplication attribute of a SecureFiles LOB column using the alter table command:

```
SQL> alter table default_docs modify lob(blob_content) (deduplicate lob);

Table altered.
```

When you issue such a command, Oracle Database will immediately read all values in the LOB column and remove duplicates.

DBMS_LOB.SETOPTIONS

Oracle also provides the capability to enable or disable deduplication/encryption/compression of LOBs at the per-LOB level using PL/SQL and using the LOB Locator API. The DBMS_LOB. SETOPTIONS stored procedure provides this granularity of control. Here's a description of the setoptions procedure:

```
procedure setoptions
  argument name              type                 in/out default?
  ----------------           ------------------   ---------------
  lob_loc                    blob                 in/out
  option_types               binary_integer       in
  options                    binary_integer       in
```

Encryption

LOB encryption is another superb enhancement to Oracle Database 11g SecureFiles. Now, you can encrypt LOB segments using Transparent Data Encryption (TDE). TDE requires an encryption key to be established and stored in Oracle's TDE wallet. For complete details on how to create a TDE wallet, please consult Chapter 5.

Continuing with our example from earlier with the SECURE_DOCS table, you can modify this table to be encrypted using the alter table encrypt clause. The following example shows how you can enable encryption for SecureFiles LOBs:

```
SQL> alter table secure_docs modify (blob_content encrypt using 'AES192');

Table altered.
```

Multiple levels of encryption are available in Oracle Database 11g for SecureFiles. The AES192-bit encryption algorithm happens to be the default encryption method. Other available encryption algorithms are as follows:

- 3DES168

- AES128

- AES256

Encryption for SecureFiles must use SALT. The option for NOSALT is not supported. SALT is a random value added to the data before it is encrypted. SALT in hashing algorithms strengthens the security of encrypted data by making it more difficult for hackers to crack using standard pattern-matching techniques. Encryption of the SecureFiles LOB segments occurs at the block level. You can encrypt LOBs on a per-column or on a per-partition basis.

You can query the USER_/DBA_ENCRYPTED_COLUMNS view to confirm that LOB columns are encrypted. You can also confirm that SALT is enabled by default with SecureFiles. Here's an example showing you that the default encryption is AES192-bit encryption and that it applies SALT:

```
SQL> select table_name, column_name, encryption_alg, salt
      from user_encrypted_columns
SQL> /


TABLE_NAME      COLUMN_NAME      ENCRYPTION_ALG      SAL
-----------     -------------    ----------------    ---
SECURE_DOCS     BLOB_CONTENT     AES 192 bits key    YES
```

Once a SecureFiles LOB column is encrypted, you can disable encryption using the decrypt keyword. The decrypt option will convert the encrypted column to clear text, as shown here:

```
SQL> alter table secure_docs modify (blob_content decrypt)
SQL> /

Table altered.
```

Compression

Customers with terabytes (or even petabytes) of storage allocated can greatly benefit from the compression option of Oracle Database 11*g* SecureFiles. Taking the document table from the previous examples, compression can be easily enabled by adding the keyword compress in the storage clause, as shown here:

```
 lob (blob_content) store as securefile (compress high)
```

There are two valid values for the compression option: medium and high. The default compression is set to medium. We'll demonstrate the medium and high compression options in this section to prove the enormous potential in space savings. SecureFiles with compression is the logical choice if your database has a large number of LOBs inside the database and is not updated frequently. To be able to demonstrate the compression capabilities, the keep_duplicate option is enabled so that Oracle will load the 100 LOB documents from the DEFAULT_DOCS table. Next, we will insert the same 100 documents into a table called SECURE_DUP_MEDIUM that has medium-level compression enabled:

```
SQL>  insert into secure_docs_medium select * from default_docs;
```

The same space.sql script, using the DBMS_SPACE.USED_SPACE procedure, can be used to determine how much space medium-level compression saves. With medium compression, the LOB segment consumes about 6.4MB of disk space, as shown here:

```
SQL> @space secure_docs_medium
old  12: and table_name=upper('&v_tab');
new  12: and table_name=upper('secure_docs_medium');
KB used: 6408
```

```
PL/SQL procedure successfully completed.
```

Another table with high compression is also created to show the compression capabilities of Oracle Database 11*g* SecureFiles. In this particular example, the LOB segment consumes about 5.6MB of disk space, as shown here:

```
SQL> @space secure_docs_high
old  12: and table_name=upper('&v_tab');
new  12: and table_name=upper('secure_docs_high');
KB used: 5608
```

```
PL/SQL procedure successfully completed.
```

You can change the compression algorithm by specifying the compress high syntax to the alter table command, as shown here:

```
SQL> alter table secure_dup_compressed_docs
        modify lob (blob_content) (compress high);
```

```
Table altered.
```

In this particular example, the difference between high and medium compression is not that noticeable since we are storing the same document 100 times. Obviously, the higher the degree of compression, the greater the CPU utilization will be to decompress the data. That higher CPU utilization will be reflected in the latency to retrieve and store the data. The gain of space saved in storage will be directly correlated with the penalty of retrieval and insertion times. For LOBs that are frequently updated, SecureFiles compression can save double, triple, quadruple or more the storage capacity for large corporations that have massive documents stored inside the database. Another factor that will determine the amount of compression will be the type of file. If the file is already compressed such as with JPEG or ZIP files, Oracle's SecureFile LOB compression will have little or no effect.

If you need to uncompress the LOB segment for one reason or another, you can use the nocompress keyword to achieve this. Here's an example of such a command:

```
SQL> alter table secure_docs_high modify lob (blob_content) (nocompress)
SQL> /
```

```
Table altered.
```

■**Note** Please exercise caution with the compress and nocompress options because compression/decompression occurs immediately and can be extremely time consuming for large LOB columns.

After the decompression of the LOB that was compressed with the high option, the size of the LOB is back up to 19MB, as shown here:

```
SQL> @space secure_docs_high
old  12: and table_name=upper('&v_tab');
new  12: and table_name=upper('secure_docs_high');
KB used: 19208

PL/SQL procedure successfully completed.
```

LOB compression can be enabled at the partition level. One partition can have LOB compression enabled while another partition does not. Likewise, a partition can have high compression for a partition and medium-level compression for another. See the following example that demonstrates the different compression options for partitions:

```
SQL> create table docs_compressed_mix2
  2  (document_id number,
  3   blob_content blob,
  4   document_category varchar2(55))
  5   partition by list (document_category)
  6  (
  7  partition p_dba1 values ('Data Guard') lob(blob_content)
  8          store as securefile(compress high),
  9  partition p_dba2 values ('ASM') lob(blob_content)
 10          store as securefile(compress medium),
 11  partition p_dba3 values ('Java') lob(blob_content)
 12          store as securefile(nocompress),
 13  partition p_dba4 values (default) lob(blob_content)
 14          store as securefile(compress high)
 15* )
SQL> /

Table created.
```

db_securefile Initialization Parameter

Oracle Database 11g implements a new parameter called db_securefile to provide you, the DBA, with control over the creation of LOB columns in a database. This parameter is dynamic and can be modified with the alter system command. There are five possible values for this parameter:

- always: This creates all LOBs as SecureFiles, but if the target tablespace is not ASSM, LOBs are created as BasicFiles. BasicFiles storage parameters are ignored. SecureFiles default parameters apply when storage options are not specified.

- force: Going forward, this forces all LOB objects to be created as SecureFiles. If the target tablespace is not ASSM, an exception will be reported to the user. BasicFiles storage parameters are ignored, and default SecureFiles storage parameters are used for parameters that are not specified.

- permitted: This is the default setting. SecureFiles LOBs are allowed to be created. By default, BasicFiles is created if the store as securefile clause is not specified.

- never: Going forward, this does not allow SecureFiles to be created. LOBs that are characterized as SecureFiles LOBs are created as BasicFiles LOBs. All storage parameters that are specific to SecureFiles will generate an exception error. If storage parameters do not exist, this defaults to the basic LOB defaults.

- ignore: This disallows SecureFiles storage parameters and forces BasicFiles. SecureFiles storage options are ignored.

Here's an example of modifying the db_securefile initialization parameter using the alter system command:

```
SQL> alter system set db_securefile='ALWAYS';

System altered.
```

Migrate from BasicFiles to SecureFiles

There are multiple approaches to migrate BasicFiles LOB segments to SecureFiles. Unfortunately, to take advantage of SecureFiles, the data must be completely rewritten into the new LOB. The most common approach is probably create table as (CTAS) or inserting all the rows from one table to another. Another option is to create a dummy column and update the data. Once you are done, drop the old BasicFiles LOB column and rename the SecureFiles LOB column to the original column name. The biggest advantage to this approach is that it requires the least amount of overhead in space consumption. You can use PL/SQL to perform batch inserts and commit every 10,000 rows or so to validate the progress along the way.

Another method would be to export and import the data. This still requires double the storage, one for the table and one for the dump file. Lots of companies would prefer to keep two copies of the data for a week or so before deleting the backup copies. By introducing export/import, you may be looking at triple storage to migrate to SecureFiles.

Online redefinition is another approach to migrate from BasicFiles to SecureFiles. The greatest benefit would be reduced or no downtime to perform the task. With online redefinition, the table can stay online during the entire duration of the migration, and the procedure can be performed in parallel. Again, double storage is required to perform an online redefinition. Here's a simple example of performing an online definition for the DOCS table to the SECURE_DOCS table:

```
declare
    error_count pls_integer
begin
dbms_redefinition.start_redef_table('sh','docs','secure_docs',
                'document_id, name, edba_knowledgebase_category_id,
                mime_type, doc_size, dad_charset,
                last_updated, content_type, blob_content');
dbms_redefinition.finish_redef_table('sh','docs','secure_docs');
end;
/
```

If the table being redefined is a partitioned table, then global indexes need to be rebuilt.

■**Note** As of Oracle Database 11*g* Release 1, Oracle Streams does not support SecureFiles, so this technology cannot be leveraged.

If the table being redefined happens to be a partitioned table, another great time-saving
technique will be to use the partition exchange option. During this process, Oracle recommends
using the `nologging` option of the SecureFiles LOB storage option. You can reenable logging
once the migration is complete. Using the documents table that is provided in the previous
example, you can perform a partition-by-partition exchange and migrate from BasicFiles to
SecureFiles LOB. First create a new table called DOCS2 with just one of the subsets of the range
partition key. In the following example, the table DOCS2 is created as a SecureFiles using the
CTAS approach:

```
SQL> create table docs2
  2  lob(blob_content) store as securefile (nocache nologging)
  3  tablespace tools
  4  as
  5  select * from documents_parted
  6* where edba_knowledgebase_category_id=2
SQL> /

Table created.
```

Now, once the partition data is converted into SecureFiles, you can perform the exchange.
You can use the following script to exchange the second partition (DOCUMENTS_P2) with the
temporary table (DOCS2) created earlier. The outage is incurred only for the single partition in
question.

```
SQL> alter table documents_parted exchange partition documents_p2
         with table docs2 without validation;

Table altered.
```

LOB Prefetch

Oracle Database 11*g* improves OCI access of smaller LOB and BFILES. LOB data can be prefetched
and cached while also fetching the locator. Now, you can customize the setting for the `oci_
attr_default_lobprefetch_size` variable in your OCI programs. This value determines the
prefetch data size for LOB locators. You can set this as an attribute of your OCI environment or
set it within your OCI program. The default value for this attribute is zero, which means there
is no prefetching of LOB data.

Data Warehousing New Features

Data warehousing features are rich with functionality to improve information management. The
functionality in Oracle Database 11*g* includes the ability to change reporting and aggregation

summary outputs with simple additions to the SQL language. In addition, Oracle captures and tracks change information and provides data staleness validation to businesses. These features are just a fraction of the functionality provided in the data warehouse environment. First we'll focus on the improvements introduced to materialized views. The next topic of discussion will center on the new ways to use pivot and unpivot operations to create executive reports using simple SQL statements.

Partition Change Tracking

Although partition change tracking (PCT) was introduced in Oracle 9*i* Database, Oracle did not expose this information in the data dictionary views. Oracle Database 11*g* exposes new views and adds columns to existing views to provide essential information to DBAs and developers to make well-informed decisions about materialized view refresh staleness. Materialized view refresh information is provided down to the partition level. Users can now query the data dictionary and see whether the materialized view partition is refreshed with updated data or is still stagnant with stale data.

■**Note** All the views that will be mentioned in this section apply to the DBA_, ALL_, and USER_ views. For simplicity, only the ALL_ view names will be used in the examples so that view names do not have to be repeated three times.

Four views are pertinent to materialized view freshness:

- ALL_MVIEWS

- ALL_MVIEW_DETAIL_RELATIONS

- ALL_MVIEW_DETAIL_PARTITION

- ALL_MVIEW_DETAIL_SUBPARTITION

The first two views, ALL_MVIEWS and ALL_DETAIL_RELATIONS, have additional columns. The ALL_MVIEW_DETAIL_PARTITION and ALL_MVIEW_DETAIL_SUBPARTITION views are new to Oracle Database 11*g*. Let's start with the ALL_MVIEWS view. When you describe ALL_MVIEWS, you will notice three new columns:

```
SQL> desc all_mviews
 Name                           Null?     Type
 ----------------------         --------  ---------
 ..
 ..
 NUM_PCT_TABLES                           NUMBER
 NUM_FRESH_PCT_REGIONS                    NUMBER
 NUM_STALE_PCT_REGIONS                    NUMBER
```

The NUM_PCT_TABLES, NUM_FRESH_PCT_REGIONS, and NUM_STALE_PCT_REGIONS columns are new additions to Oracle Database 11g to show how many detail partitions support PCT and the amount of stale and fresh PCT regions.

The ALL_MVIEW_DETAIL_RELATIONS view represents the named detail relations that either are in the from list of a materialized view or are indirectly referenced through views in the from list. Additionally, Oracle provides three new columns to the ALL_MVIEW_DETAIL_ RELATIONS view, as shown next, to inform whether PCT is supported and, if so, to show the number of fresh and stale partition regions:

```
SQL> desc all_mview_detail_relations
Name                            Null?         Type
-----------------------         -------       -------------
..
..
DETAILOBJ_PCT                                 VARCHAR2(1)
NUM_FRESH_PCT_PARTITIONS                      NUMBER
NUM_STALE_PCT_PARTITIONS                      NUMBER
```

The DETAILOBJ_PCT, NUM_FRESH_PCT_PARTITIONS, and NUM_STALE_PCT_PARTITIONS columns are new to Oracle Database 11g.

Oracle Database 11g introduces a new view called ALL_MVIEW_DETAIL_PARTITION to provide freshness information for each PCT partition, as shown here:

```
SQL> desc all_mview_detail_partition
Name                            Null?         Type
-----------------------         --------      -----------------
OWNER                           NOT NULL      VARCHAR2(30)
MVIEW_NAME                      NOT NULL      VARCHAR2(30)
DETAILOBJ_OWNER                 NOT NULL      VARCHAR2(30)
DETAILOBJ_NAME                  NOT NULL      VARCHAR2(30)
DETAIL_PARTITION_NAME                         VARCHAR2(30)
DETAIL_PARTITION_POSITION                     NUMBER
FRESHNESS                                     CHAR(5)
```

The ALL_ MVIEW_DETAIL_PARTITION view provides freshness information of each PCT detail partition in the materialized view. Also new to Oracle Database 11g is the ALL_MVIEW_ DETAIL_SUBPARTITION view. Similar to the ALL_ MVIEW_DETAIL_PARTITION view, this view provides freshness information for each PCT detail subpartition in the materialized view.

Materialized View Refresh Performance Improvements

Several enhancements to the materialized view refresh mechanism are introduced in Oracle Database 11g to reduce time and throughput. All of the enhancements are made automatically by Oracle. Prior to Oracle Database 11g, when a materialized view was created with a union all, an index was not created. To take advantage of the performance implications associated with a fast refresh, an index needed to be created manually. Oracle Database 11g creates this index for you automatically. Another improvement that is available is partition change tracking for materialized views with union all clauses. This materialized view improvement may be more noticeable of all the materialized view improvements. During the atomic materialized view refresh process, query rewrite against the materialized view will continue to work. Applications will see the data at the transactional state prior to the last materialized view refresh. For this to work, you must set the `query_rewrite_integrity` initialization parameter to `stale_tolerated`.

Materialized View QUERY REWRITE Enhancements

When a SQL query being executed equals the query that generated the materialized view, a rewrite occurs to use the materialized view instead of executing the query against the underlying base tables. The ultimate goal of the cost-based optimizer is to select an execution path with the least cost. The cost-based optimizer generates the plan using the materialized view and another plan against the base tables of the SQL statement and chooses the favorable plan based on cost. If there are situations of nested materialized views, the optimization process occurs again to see whether another rewrite operation can utilize another materialized view to reduce the amount of data. Query rewrite recursively occurs until all the possible materialized views are exhausted. This process of query rewrite can significantly improve performance by reducing the amount of data to be processed.

Oracle Database 11g increases the eligibility of query rewrites. In previous releases, the syntax of the inline views in the materialized view needed to exactly match the syntax of the submitted query. Oracle Database 10g treated the inline views as named views. In Oracle Database 11g, this functionality is enhanced by allowing equivalent inline views to be rewritten. An inline view is considered to be equivalent when it meets the conditions listed here:

- The select columns are the same.

- The `from` clause lists the same or equivalent objects.

- The `having` clause is the same.

- Join conditions, including `where` clauses, are equivalent.

Let's take a look at a materialized view that has `query rewrite` enabled. This particular materialized view joins data from two tables, `ORDER_HEADER` and `ORDER_DETAIL`, and contains an inline view:

```
SQL> create materialized view order_summary_mv
  2  enable query rewrite
  3  as
  4    select customer_id, order_date,
  5            sum(quoted_price) sum_quoted_price
  6    from (select customer_id, order_date, quoted_price
  7            from order_header oh, order_detail od
  8            where oh.order_id=od.order_id) iv
  9* group by order_date, customer_id
SQL> /

Materialized view created.
```

Let's look at the submitted query to see whether it qualifies for query rewrite. The following query does not match the inline view of the materialized view, but `query rewrite` will use the materialized view:

```
SQL> select iv.customer_id, iv.order_date,
  2          sum(iv.quoted_price) sum_quoted_price
  3  from (select customer_id, order_date, quoted_price
  4        from order_detail od, order_header oh
  5        where oh.order_id=od.order_id)  iv
  6* group by iv.order_date, iv.customer_id
SQL> /
```

If you observe carefully, the inline views do not match. Notice that the order of the table names in the from clause are listed in reverse order. In the previous release, this query would not be a candidate for a query rewrite. In Oracle Database 11g, Oracle is aware of the same table names in the inline views and matches the table names based on the object number. Query rewrite takes place and leverages the materialized view.

You can use an explain plan to identify the materialized view object usage or use the DBMS_ MVIEW.EXPLAIN_REWRITE procedure to validate whether a query rewrite truly occurred. Obviously, the best test-case scenario is if the query runs with the desired performance gain of using the materialized view. It never hurts to perform an explain plan to validate that query rewrite has truly occurred. Here, we will execute an explain plan for the submitted query and confirm that query rewrite has occurred:

```
SQL> explain plan for
  2  select iv.customer_id, iv.order_date,
  3          sum(iv.quoted_price) sum_quoted_price
  4  from (select customer_id, order_date, quoted_price
  5        from order_detail od, order_header oh
  6        where oh.order_id=od.order_id)  iv
  7* group by iv.order_date, iv.customer_id
SQL> /

Explained.

SQL> select operation, object_name from plan_table;

OPERATION                         OBJECT_NAME
--------------------------        -----------------------
SELECT STATEMENT
MAT_VIEW REWRITE ACCESS           ORDER_SUMMARY_MV
```

You can query the OPERATION and OBJECT_NAME columns from PLAN_TABLE to confirm that the query rewrite of the materialized view occurred. You should expect to see the operation mat_view rewrite access in the output, as illustrated earlier.

The following are elements that disqualify a query for rewrite:

- Grouping set clauses

- Set operators

- Nested subqueries

- Nested inline views

Query rewrite for remote tables is not supported, but query rewrite can be used on materialized views that reference remote tables. The gains achieved from query rewrite can be astronomical considering the elimination of a remote join and reducing (or even eliminating) network traffic. Because Oracle is not aware of the integrity constraints of the remote database, query rewrite will not use any constraint information. As usual, there are some caveats associated with this rule:

- The materialized view can reference only a single remote database.

- The materialized view must reside on the local database.

- The query_rewrite_integrity initialization parameter must be set to stale_tolerated.

Let's see an example of how this works. The following query will create a materialized view that references remote tables using a database link:

```
SQL> create materialized view order_summary_remote_mv
  2  enable query rewrite
  3  as
  4  select oh.customer_id, oh.order_date,
  5         sum(od.quoted_price) sum_quoted_price
  6  from order_header@PROD oh, order_detail@PROD od
  7  where oh.order_id=od.order_id
  8* group by order_date, customer_id;

Materialized view created.
```

In this example, all the remote tables are from the single database, and thus, the materialized view qualifies for query rewrite. Now, let's look at the submitted query to see whether it will take advantage of the new materialized view:

```
SQL> select oh.customer_id, oh.order_date,
  2         sum(od.quoted_price) sum_quoted_price
  3  from order_header@PROD oh, order_detail@PROD od
  4  where oh.order_id=od.order_id
  5* group by order_date, customer_id
SQL> /
```

Since this query references all the remote tables from a single database, Oracle will rewrite the query to utilize the local materialized view and thus eliminate network traffic to access the remote tables.

Pivot Operators

Pivoting records is a common business intelligence practice that produces executive summary information and calculations. Oracle Database 11g provides the ability to easily produce cross-tabular reports as part of the SQL statement. Oracle introduces the new pivot operator to transform multiple rows into more columns and, in the process, aggregate data. A pivot operation typically produces additional columns by condensing large data volumes into smaller understandable summaries.

The classic examples of using the `pivot` operation are monthly sales reports, quarterly sales reports, summarized marketing analysis data, and so on. For example, you can take the monthly sales data and pivot the rows so that each month of data presented in a row will now show up as a column in a single inline row.

In the previous releases of Oracle, you could accomplish a `pivot` operation using `case` statements, as shown here:

```
SQL> select video_name,
            sum(case when month = '01' then quantity_rented else null end) jan,
            sum(case when month = '02' then quantity_rented else null end) feb,
            sum(case when month = '03' then quantity_rented  else null end) mar,
            sum(case when month = '04' then quantity_rented else null end) apr,
            sum(case when month = '05' then quantity_rented else null end) may,
            sum(case when month = '06' then quantity_rented else null end) jun,
            sum(case when month = '07' then quantity_rented else null end) jul,
            sum(case when month = '08' then quantity_rented else null end) aug,
            sum(case when month = '09' then quantity_rented else null end) sep,
            sum(case when month = '10' then quantity_rented else null end) oct,
            sum(case when month = '11' then quantity_rented else null end) nov,
            sum(case when month = '12' then quantity_rented else null end) dec
from (select video_name, month, quantity_rented
      from video_mstr_vw )
group by video_name
order by 1
/
```

This same query can be rewritten with the `pivot` syntax:

```
select *
from (select video_name, month, quantity_rented
      from video_mstr_vw)
pivot (sum(quantity_rented)
for month in
('01' as jan,
  '02' as feb,
  '03' as mar,
  '04' as apr,
  '05' as may,
  '06' as jun,
  '07' as jul,
  '08' as aug,
  '09' as sep,
  '10' as oct,
  '11' as nov,
  '12' as dec ))
order by video_name desc;
```

The `pivot` operator is a breeze compared to the old way of writing the same code. This example shows that the `pivot` operation is performed on the month with aggregation functions on the QUANTITY_RENTED column. The cost-based optimizer is optimized to handle pivot aggregations more efficiently in Oracle Database 11*g*.

The pivot clause can be specified with multiple pivot columns. Additional options include the capability to aggregate on multiple columns, use wildcards, and use aliases. You can pivot on multiple aggregations using the syntax pivot (expression) as Alias, (expression) as Alias2 for column. The pivot column must be a column of the table. If an expression needs to be pivoted, you should create an alias. Now we'll show an example of pivoting on multiple columns. This example will use the alias names for the pivoted columns to perform the sorting:

```
 1  select *
 2  from (select video_name, month, quantity_rented, rental_type
 3          from video_mstr_vw) pivot (sum(quantity_rented)
 4  for (rental_type, month) in (
 5                     (10000, '01') as SR_jan,
 6                     (10001, '01') as IR_jan,
 7                     (10000, '02') as SR_feb,
 8                     (10001, '02') as IR_feb
 9                              )
10       )
11* order by SR_jan, IR_jan, SR_feb, IR_feb
SQL> /
```

VIDEO_NAME	SR_JAN	IR_JAN	SR_FEB	IR_FEB
The Pacifier	7500			
Mission Impossible III	10000			
Ray		15500		
Madagascar		47500		
Open Season			4500	
Walk the Line			5500	
Lord of War			11500	
Superman Returns			20000	
Sin City				10500
Hostage				14500
Fantastic Four				65500
..				
..				

Note that the output results in four aliased columns (SR_JAN, IR_JAN, SR_FEB, and IR_FEB) from the in list. If the in list does not have an alias, the column heading will be same as the values specified in the in list. Notice that we are able to leverage the alias names in the order by clause. You can see from the next example that without aliases in the in list, the column headings have the values of the in_clause as the column headings:

```
SQL>  select *
  2    from (select video_name, month, quantity_rented, rental_type
  3           from video_mstr_vw) pivot (sum(quantity_rented)
  4    for (rental_type, month) in (
  5                        (10000, '01'),
  6                        (10001, '01'),
  7                        (10000, '02'),
  8                        (10001, '02')
  9                           )
 10        )
 11* order by "10000_'01'", "10001_'01'", "10000_'02'", "10001_'02'"
SQL> /

VIDEO_NAME                  10000_'01'    10001_'01'    10000_'02'    10001_'02'
----------------------      ----------    ----------    ----------    ----------
The Pacifier                7500
Mission Impossible III      10000
..
..
```

Notice the virtual headings can be used in the order by clause. Oracle offers the facility to provide a wildcard argument or subquery in the pivoting columns. You can use the any keyword for wildcard, and all values of the pivot columns will be used as pivot columns. You can use the subquery option to specify pivot column values based on a query. The pivot xml keywords are required to specify a subquery or to use the any keyword in pivot_in_clause. The any and subquery syntax can be used if you are not familiar with the data or do not know the specific values to pivot on. The output of the XML pivot operation will result in XML.

Now, let's look at what the any keyword does. The any keyword acts as a wildcard. By specifying the any keyword for pivot_in_clause, all the values found in the pivot column will be used for pivoting. There are a couple of things to consider when using the any clause:

- The any operation can be used only as part of the XML operation.

- The value for each row must match the input columns from the FOR argument.

Here's an example of using the any keyword with the pivot xml syntax:

```
SQL> select *
     from (select video_name, rental_type, quantity_rented
           from video_mstr_vw)
     pivot xml (sum(quantity_rented)
     for rental_type in ( any ) )
     order by video_name desc
     /
```

```
VIDEO_NAME              RENTAL_TYPE_XML
------------------      ---------------------------------------------
Walk the Line           <PivotSet><item><column name =
                        "RENTAL_TYPE">10000</column><column name =
                        "SUM(QUANTITY_RENTED)">5500</column></item>
                        </PivotSet>

The Pacifier            <PivotSet><item><column name =
                        "RENTAL_TYPE">10000</column><column name =
                        "SUM(QUANTITY_RENTED)">7500</column></item>
                        </PivotSet>

Superman Returns        <PivotSet><item><column name =
                        "RENTAL_TYPE">10000</column><column name =
                        "SUM(QUANTITY_RENTED)">20000</column></item>
                        </PivotSet>
..
..
```

In this particular example, the output will display data only where a valid rental type transaction exists. Sometimes, the preferable situation may be to use a subquery in pivot_in_clause to retrieve the data. In this case, instead of using the any keyword, you can replace pivot_in_clause with the query select distinct rental_type from rental_types, as shown here:

```
SQL>  select *
      from (select video_name, rental_type, quantity_rented
            from video_mstr_vw)
      pivot xml (sum(quantity_rented)
      for rental_type in (select distinct rental_type from rental_types) )
      order by video_name desc
      /
```

```
VIDEO_NAME              RENTAL_TYPE_XML
------------------      ---------------------------------------------
Walk the Line           <PivotSet><item><column name =
                        "RENTAL_TYPE">10000</column><column name =
                        "SUM(QUANTITY_RENTED)">5500</column></item>
                        <item><column name =
                        "RENTAL_TYPE">10001</column><column name =
                        "SUM(QUANTITY_RENTED)"></column></item>
                        <item><column name =
                        "RENTAL_TYPE">10002</column><column name =
                        "SUM(QUANTITY_RENTED)"></column></item>
                         <item><column name =
                        "RENTAL_TYPE">10003</column><column name =
                        "SUM(QUANTITY_RENTED)"></column></item>
```

```
                              <item><column name =
                              "RENTAL_TYPE">20000</column><column name =
                              "SUM(QUANTITY_RENTED)"></column></item>
                              </PivotSet>

The Pacifier              <PivotSet><item><column name =
                              "RENTAL_TYPE">10000</column><column name =
                              "SUM(QUANTITY_RENTED)">7500</column></item>
                              <item><column name =
                              "RENTAL_TYPE">10001</column><column name =
                              "SUM(QUANTITY_RENTED)"></column></item>
                              <item><column name =
                              "RENTAL_TYPE">10002</column><column name =
                              "SUM(QUANTITY_RENTED)"></column></item>
                              <item><column name =
                              "RENTAL_TYPE">10003</column><column name =
                              "SUM(QUANTITY_RENTED)"></column></item>
                              <item><column name =
                              "RENTAL_TYPE">20000</column><column name =
                              "SUM(QUANTITY_RENTED)"></column></item>
                              </PivotSet>
..
..
```

By using a subquery, the XMLType will show values for RENTAL_TYPE even if there are no values in SUM(QUANTITY_RENTED). The subquery will typically result in a larger output than using the any clause in pivot_in_clause.

Unpivot Operators

The unpivot operation rotates data from columns into rows. The unpivot operation does not reverse a pivot operation. The function of the unpivot operator is to take columns and convert them into rows. The unpivot operation does not undo any aggregations/summarizations/ calculations that were performed by the pivot operator. Think of unpivot as a mechanism to normalize data structures. unpivot will essentially reduce the number of columns and create more rows. Like the pivot operator, you can use the unpivot operation on multiple columns. Additional options include the ability to measure columns and aliasing.

By taking the previous pivot example, you can see how the unpivot works. A table named VIDEO_RENTAL_PIVOT_TABLE is created as a ctas from the previous multicolumn pivot example. In the following example, the data set is unpivoted on the month column:

```
SQL> select * from video_rental_pivot_table
  2  unpivot ( (quantity_rented) FOR month  IN (Jan, Feb))
  3* order by video_name, month
SQL> /
```

VIDEO_NAME	MAR	APR	MON	QTY_RENTED
Fantastic Four			FEB	65500
Hostage			FEB	14500
Lord of War			FEB	11500
Madagascar			JAN	47500
Mission Impossible III			JAN	10000
Open Season			FEB	4500
Ray			JAN	15500
Sin City			FEB	10500
Superman Returns			FEB	20000
The Pacifier			JAN	7500
Walk the Line			FEB	5500

11 rows selected.

Similarly to the `pivot` operation, the `unpivot` operation can also be applied on multiple columns and aggregations. The following example will unpivot the data based on store rentals and Internet rentals:

```
SQL> select * from video_rental_multipivot_table
  2  unpivot ((Store_Rent, Internet_Rent)
  3  for rent_type in ((SR_JAN,SR_FEB) as 10000,
  4                    (IR_JAN,IR_FEB) as 10001 ))
  5* order by video_name, rent_type
SQL> /
```

VIDEO_NAME	RENT_TYPE	STORE_RENT	INTERNET_RENT
Fantastic Four	10001		65500
Hostage	10001		14500
Lord of War	10000		11500
Madagascar	10001	47500	
Mission Impossible III	10000	10000	
Open Season	10000		4500
Ray	10001	15500	
Sin City	10001		10500
Superman Returns	10000		20000
The Pacifier	10000	7500	
Walk the Line	10000		5500

11 rows selected.

Partitioning

Oracle partitioning provides the ideal environment for implementing information lifecycle management (ILM) solutions. By maintaining and implementing partitions on separate tablespaces, DBAs can place older data on less expensive storage tiers. New data continues to be stored in tier 1 storage, while the older data can be migrated to less expensive tier 2, 3, and 4 storage. In addition, the older data can be compressed, thus further reducing storage costs.

Partitioning also provides to DBAs the flexibility to make tablespaces read-only. By implementing the `skip readonly` tablespace syntax to the RMAN backup architecture, significantly less space will be required for backups performed to disk and tape.

Many companies do not implement partitioning because of the additional licensing cost associated with it. If DBAs, backup administrators, developers, and senior management carefully analyze their application to look for ways to implement partitioning with read-only tablespaces, the Oracle partitioning option pays for itself. For large companies that have storage in the terabyte or even petabyte range, the Oracle partitioning option can save them money in storage and backups.

Oracle offers four main partitioning mechanisms:

- Composite partitioning

- Hash partitioning

- List partitioning

- Range partitioning

Based on the business requirement, each of the partitioning methods has its appropriate justified need in today's corporations. Oracle Database 11*g* improves partitioning options and provides new options to meet today's demanding requirements.

New to Oracle Database 11*g* are numerous techniques for partitioning table data to increase the performance and organization of your corporate data. These partitioning techniques include the following:

- Reference that allows tables with a parent-child relationship to be logically equipartitioned by inheriting the partition key from the parent table without duplicating the key columns

- Interval that automatically creates maintenance partitions for range partitions

- Extended composite that allows data to be partitioned along two dimensions

- Virtual columns that allow virtual columns to be defined as partition key columns

Partition Advisor

Partitioning advice is available within the SQL Access Advisor as part of Enterprise Manager or the command-line interface. In Oracle Database 11*g*, the SQL Access Advisor will also recommend partitions. In addition to the normal recommendations to create or drop indexes, materialized views, and materialized view logs, Oracle will recommend to partition existing tables and indexes to improve performance. The Partition Advisor provides the appropriate SQL syntax to create a temporary partitioned table, copy data, and rename the table to the original table name. Furthermore, the Partition Advisor will show the potential performance improvements from implementing the recommended partitions. The Partition Advisor is integrated with the SQL Access Advisor and is licensed under Oracle's Tuning Pack.

In the initial SQL Access Advisor screen, available as an option on the Advisor Central screen, you can click the option to recommend new access structures, as shown in Figure 12-1.

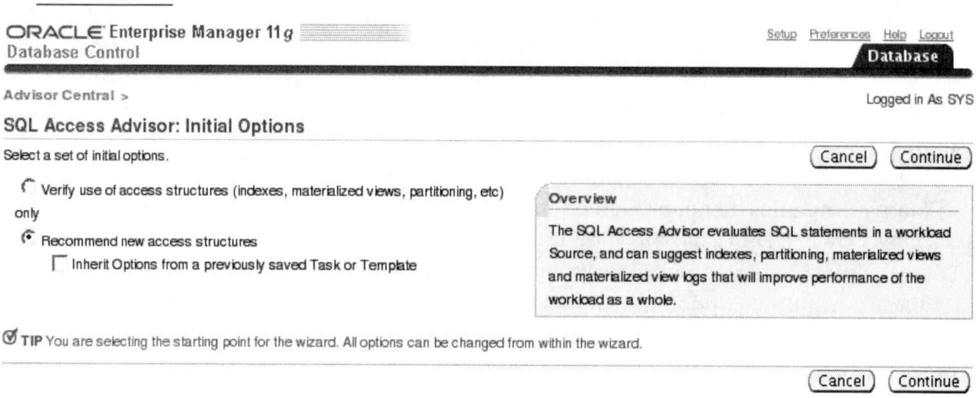

Figure 12-1. *SQL Access Advisor Initial Options screen*

Click the Next button, and you will be routed to the Workload Source screen. Here, you can select the source of the workload to analyze and select any filtering criteria. For demonstration purposes, keep the defaults on this screen. Click the Next button, and you will continue with the SQL Access Advisor to the Recommendation Options screen. On this screen, you can choose to select advice about indexes, materialized views, and partitions, as shown in Figure 12-2.

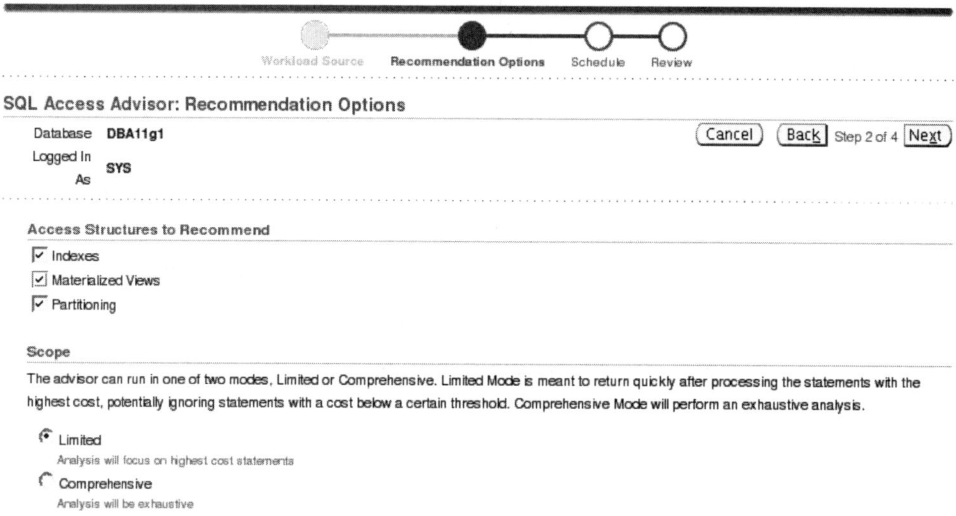

Figure 12-2. *SQL Access Advisor Recommendation Options screen*

Click the Next button, and you will be routed to the Scheduler screen. Click the Next button one more time to be routed to the Review Screen. Finally, click the Submit button to create a Scheduler job.

Once the job completes successfully, you can view the results of the SQL Access Advisor. Once again from the Advisor Central screen, locate the completed SQL Access Advisor result, as shown in Figure 12-3.

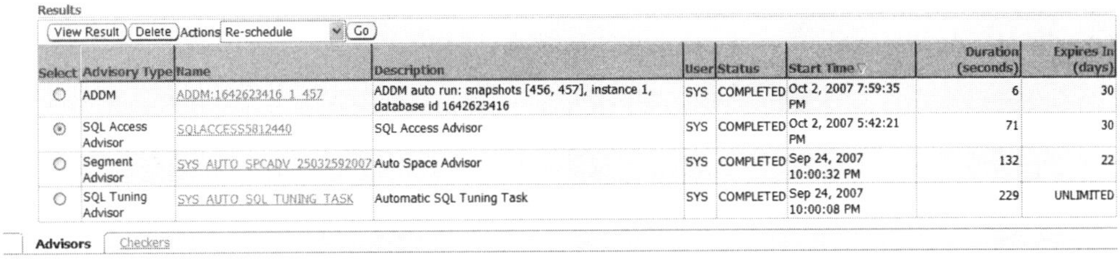

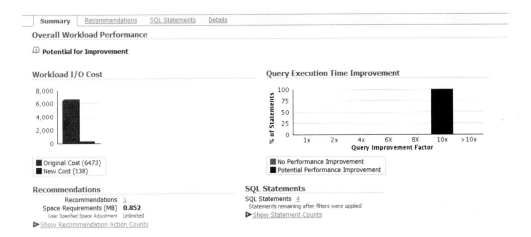

Figure 12-3. *SQL Access Advisor Results screen*

Click the respective row of the SQL Access Advisor, and click the View Result button. You will be redirected to the Advisor Central Summary page, as shown in Figure 12-4.

Figure 12-4. *SQL Access Advisor Summary screen*

The two graphs on this screen show incredible potential in performance improvements. The workload IO cost is reduced from 6473 to 138. The query improvement is expected to improve by a factor of ten times.

Click the Recommendations tab and notice the ID column on the bottom of the screen regarding recommendations for implementation. Please notice that there are four action items and action types with the color-coded squares shown in Figure 12-5.

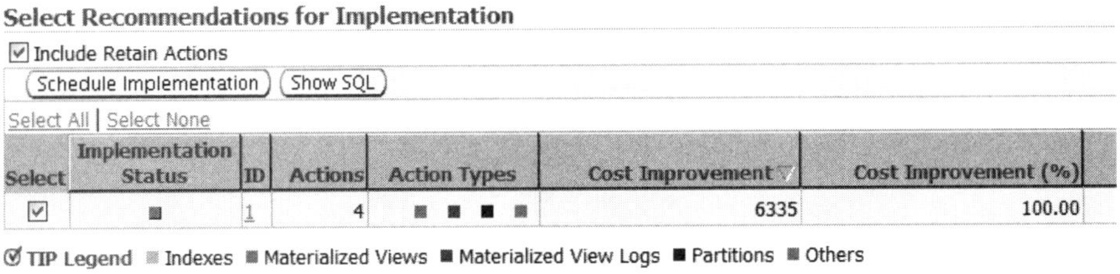

Figure 12-5. *Select Recommendations for Implementation screen*

Click the ID URL, and you will drill down to the detailed recommendation screen for the specific SQL Access Advisor result, as shown in Figure 12-6.

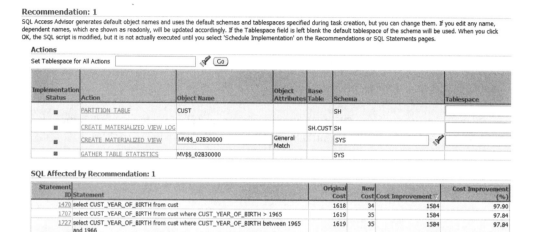

Recommendation: 1

SQL Access Advisor generates default object names and uses the default schemas and tablespaces specified during task creation, but you can change them. If you edit any name, dependent names, which are shown as readonly, will be updated accordingly. If the Tablespace field is left blank the default tablespace of the schema will be used. When you click OK, the SQL script is modified, but it is not actually executed until you select 'Schedule Implementation' on the Recommendations or SQL Statements pages.

Actions

Set Tablespace for All Actions [   ] [Go]

Implementation Status	Action	Object Name	Object Attributes	Base Table	Schema		Tablespace
■	PARTITION TABLE	CUST			SH		
■	CREATE MATERIALIZED VIEW LOG			SH.CUST	SH		
■	CREATE MATERIALIZED VIEW	MV$$_02B30000	General Match		SYS		
■	GATHER TABLE STATISTICS	MV$$_02B30000			SYS		

SQL Affected by Recommendation: 1

Statement ID	Statement	Original Cost	New Cost	Cost Improvement	Cost Improvement (%)
1470	select CUST_YEAR_OF_BIRTH from cust	1618	34	1584	97.90
1707	select CUST_YEAR_OF_BIRTH from cust where CUST_YEAR_OF_BIRTH > 1965	1619	35	1584	97.84
1727	select CUST_YEAR_OF_BIRTH from cust where CUST_YEAR_OF_BIRTH between 1965 and 1966	1619	35	1584	97.84
1793	select count(*) from cust	1617	34	1583	97.90

Figure 12-6. *SQL Access Advisor recommendation details*

Notice the PARTITION TABLE action for the CUST table. Click PARTITION TABLE to review the SQL script to convert the CUST table into a partitioned table. You will notice the following sections of the partitioning advice:

- Create new partitioned table

- Gather table statistics

- Copy constraints to the new partitioned table

- Copy referential constraints to the new partitioned table

- Populate new partitioned table with data from original table

- Rename tables to give new partitioned table the original table name

The Partition Advisor provides the following SQL syntax to convert the CUST table into an interval-partitioned table:

```
Rem
Rem Repartitioning table "SH"."CUST"
Rem

SET SERVEROUTPUT ON
SET ECHO ON

Rem
Rem Creating new partitioned table
Rem
```

```
CREATE TABLE "SH"."CUST1"
(    "CUST_ID" NUMBER,
    "CUST_FIRST_NAME" VARCHAR2(20),
    "CUST_LAST_NAME" VARCHAR2(40),
    "CUST_GENDER" CHAR(1),
    "CUST_YEAR_OF_BIRTH" NUMBER(4,0),
    "CUST_MARITAL_STATUS" VARCHAR2(20),
    "CUST_STREET_ADDRESS" VARCHAR2(40),
    "CUST_POSTAL_CODE" VARCHAR2(10),
    "CUST_CITY" VARCHAR2(30),
    "CUST_CITY_ID" NUMBER,
    "CUST_STATE_PROVINCE" VARCHAR2(40),
    "CUST_STATE_PROVINCE_ID" NUMBER,
    "COUNTRY_ID" NUMBER,
    "CUST_MAIN_PHONE_NUMBER" VARCHAR2(25),
    "CUST_INCOME_LEVEL" VARCHAR2(30),
    "CUST_CREDIT_LIMIT" NUMBER,
    "CUST_EMAIL" VARCHAR2(30),
    "CUST_TOTAL" VARCHAR2(14),
    "CUST_TOTAL_ID" NUMBER,
    "CUST_SRC_ID" NUMBER,
    "CUST_EFF_FROM" DATE,
    "CUST_EFF_TO" DATE,
    "CUST_VALID" VARCHAR2(1)
) PCTFREE 10 PCTUSED 40 INITRANS 1 MAXTRANS 255 NOCOMPRESS LOGGING
TABLESPACE "USERS"
PARTITION BY RANGE ("CUST_YEAR_OF_BIRTH") INTERVAL( 2) ( PARTITION VALUES LESS
THAN (1914) );

Rem
Rem Copying constraints to new partitioned table
Rem
ALTER TABLE "SH"."CUST1" MODIFY ("CUST_ID" NOT NULL ENABLE);

Rem
Rem Populating new partitioned table with data from original table
Rem
INSERT /*+ APPEND */ INTO "SH"."CUST1"
SELECT * FROM "SH"."CUST";
COMMIT;

begin
dbms_stats.gather_table_stats('"SH"', '"CUST1"', NULL, dbms_stats.auto_sample_size);
end;
/

Rem
```

```
Rem Renaming tables to give new partitioned table the original table name
Rem
ALTER TABLE "SH"."CUST" RENAME TO "CUST11";
ALTER TABLE "SH"."CUST1" RENAME TO "CUST";
```

You can execute this script manually in SQL*Plus or schedule this script to run as a job in Enterprise Manager.

Reference Partitions

Reference partitions are partitions based on the partitioning method of the parent table referenced by a foreign key. Reference partitioning relies on existing parent-child relationships and is enforced by an active primary key and foreign key constraint. The child table automatically inherits the partitioning key from the parent table without duplicating the key columns. The child table also inherits the maintenance operations from the parent table. This reduces the amount of human error introduced by manually duplicating efforts on the child table. Prior to Oracle Database 11g, you had to allocate redundant storage for the partitioned key for both the master and child tables. In addition, you had to perform double maintenance. Oracle Database 11g saves storage and maintenance by providing the reference partitions.

To create a reference partition, you can use the keywords partition by reference (foreign_key name) as part of your create table statement. Notice that you have to provide the foreign key name.

To show how reference partitions work, let's create the parent table called ORDER_HEADER partitioned by the ORDER_CATEGORY column. The syntax for the ORDER_HEADER table looks like this:

```
SQL> create table order_header
  2  (order_id number primary key,
  3  order_date date not null,
  4  customer_id number,
  5  order_category varchar2(55) not null)
  6  partition by list (order_category)
  7  (
  8     partition ord_cat_book values ('Book'),
  9     partition ord_cat_dvd values ('DVD'),
 10     partition ord_cat_music values ('Music'),
 11     partition ord_cat_camera values ('Camera'),
 12     partition ord_cat_cell values ('Cell')
 13* )
SQL> /
```

Now you can create a reference-partitioned table named ORDER_DETAIL based on the parent table, ORDER_HEADER, as shown here:

```
SQL> create table order_detail
  2  (order_detail_id number primary key,
  3   order_id not null,
  4   product_id number,
  5   quantity number,
  6   quoted_price number,
```

```
  7    constraint fk_order_detail foreign key (order_id)
  8               references order_header(order_id))
  9* partition by reference (fk_order_detail)
SQL> /
```

Table created.

In this example, the line with partition by reference (fk_order_detail) creates the reference partition against the ORDER_HEADER table. Now, the ORDER_DETAIL table has the same partitions as the ORDER_HEADER with the partitioning key on ORDER_CATEGORY. Notice that the ORDER_DETAIL table does not have the ORDER_CATEGORY column.

You have successfully created the reference partition. Now, you can query the USER_PART_TABLES view to validate that the ORDER_DETAIL table is a reference partition. The following example shows you that the partition type for the ORDER_DETAIL table is a reference partition:

```
SQL> select table_name, partitioning_type, ref_ptn_constraint_name
  2  from user_part_tables
  3* where table_name in ('ORDER_HEADER','ORDER_DETAIL')
SQL> /
```

TABLE_NAME	PARTITION	REF_PTN_CONSTRAINT_NAME
ORDER_DETAIL	REFERENCE	FK_ORDER_DETAIL
ORDER_HEADER	LIST	

You will notice that the REF_PTN_CONSTRAINT_NAME column lists the foreign key name used to create the reference partition. Furthermore, you can query the USER_TAB_PARITITIONS view to confirm that the partition name associated with the ORDER_DETAIL table is identical to the partition names associated with the ORDER_HEADER table, as shown here:

```
  1  select table_name, partition_name, high_value
  2  from user_tab_partitions
  3  where table_name in ('ORDER_HEADER','ORDER_DETAIL')
  4* order by partition_position
SQL> /
```

TABLE_NAME	PARTITION_NAME	HIGH_VALUE
ORDER_HEADER	ORD_CAT_BOOK	'Book'
ORDER_DETAIL	ORD_CAT_BOOK	
ORDER_HEADER	ORD_CAT_DVD	'DVD'
ORDER_DETAIL	ORD_CAT_DVD	
ORDER_HEADER	ORD_CAT_MUSIC	'Music'
ORDER_DETAIL	ORD_CAT_MUSIC	
ORDER_DETAIL	ORD_CAT_CAMERA	
ORDER_HEADER	ORD_CAT_CAMERA	'Camera'
ORDER_DETAIL	ORD_CAT_CELL	
ORDER_HEADER	ORD_CAT_CELL	'Cell'

10 rows selected.

Another thing to note is that the high_values of the reference partitions are set to null. The null value indicates that the values are derived from the parent tables.

Reference partitions will colocate the reference partition in the same tablespace of the parent table if the tablespace clause is not specified. The tablespace for the reference partition can be overridden by using the dependent tables clause. Here's an example of an alter table command using the dependent tables clause:

```
SQL> alter table order_header
  2  add partition ord_cat_pda values ('PDA')
  3  tablespace tools
  4  dependent tables
  5* (order_detail (partition ord_cat_pda_detail tablespace docs_d1))
SQL> /

Table altered.
```

The new partition for PDAs for the ORDER_HEADER table will reside in the tools tablespace, while the reference partition will reside in the DOCS_D1 tablespace. You can verify the different tablespace locations by querying the USER_TAB_PARTITIONS view again, as shown here:

```
SQL>  select table_name, partition_name, tablespace_name TS, high_value
  2  from user_tab_partitions
  3  where partition_name like 'ORD_CAT_PDA%'
  4* order by partition_name
SQL> /
```

TABLE_NAME	PARTITION_NAME	TS	HIGH_VAL
ORDER_HEADER	ORD_CAT_PDA	TOOLS	'PDA'
ORDER_DETAIL	ORD_CAT_PDA_DETAIL	DOCS_D1	

Reference partitioning works with range partitioning but does not support interval partitioning. Reference partitioning is supported with list, hash, and all combinations of composite partitioning.

By default, the partition name of a reference partition inherits the partition name of the referenced table if a name for the reference partition is not otherwise specified. Optionally, you can manually provide a partition name for the reference partition.

Interval Partitioning

Interval partitioning is an answered prayer for many DBAs who have to add new partitions to their data warehouse environment on a weekly, monthly, or quarterly basis manually. Having to create new partitions at the end of the week/month/quarter is a cumbersome task that can consume weekend time for DBAs. On the flip side, some DBAs preallocate partitions for the next year or several years to avoid partition maintenance tasks. This luxury is afforded to DBAs who have a lot of storage available to them. Oracle Database 11g introduces the new interval partitioning that fully automates the creation of range partitions based on an interval threshold. Interval partitioning is an extension of range partitions.

Let's create our first baseline interval partition and see how Oracle maintains partitions for us. Here's a table called EBDA_ALERT_NOTIFICATIONS that houses all the database alerts for the DBAs:

```
CREATE TABLE edba_alert_notifications
  (alert_notification_id number,
   subject varchar2(2000),
   hostname varchar2(55),
   database_name varchar2(55),
   severity varchar2(1),
   alert_log_id number,
   message varchar2(4000),
   creation_date date default sysdate,
   created_by varchar2(55),
   modification_date date default sysdate,
   modified_by varchar2(55))
partition by range (creation_date)
interval (numtoyminterval(1,'MONTH'))
( PARTITION p_jan2007 VALUES
 LESS THAN (TO_DATE('01-JAN-2007','DD-MON-RRRR')))
/

Table created.
```

You can see that CREATION_DATE is the partitioning key for this table using the numtoyminterval function based on the month. Let's query USER_TAB_PARTITIONS to verify that this table was created accordingly. The following query example shows that high_value for the partition is 2007-01-01 00:00:00:

```
SQL> col partition_name for a20
SQL> col high_value for a50 word_wrapped
SQL> select partition_name, high_value
  2  from user_tab_partitions
  3  where table_name='EDBA_ALERT_NOTIFICATIONS'
  4* order by partition_position
  5  /

PARTITION_NAME      HIGH_VALUE
----------------    -------------------------------------
P_JAN2007           TO_DATE(' 2007-01-01 00:00:00', 'SYYYY-MM-DD
                    HH24:MI:SS', 'NLS_CALENDAR=GREGORIAN')
```

Now, let's insert 12 rows to simulate 12 months of rolling partitions. These rows are fabricated, but the key point is that the CREATION_DATE column has the first day of each month for the year 2007.

```
insert into edba_alert_notifications values
(1, 'Critical Alert for DBATOOLS Database:  Tablepsace threshold exceeded',
'rac11.dbaexpert.com', 'DBATOOLS', 1, 1000,
'Resolve space issue on the alert_d tablespace: 98% utilized', '01-FEB-07', user,
sysdate, user);

insert into edba_alert_notifications values
(2, 'Critical Alert for ICEMAN Database:  Tablepsace threshold exceeded',
'rac15.dbaexpert.com', 'ICEMAN', 1, 1000,
'Resolve space issue on the tools tablespace: 91% utilized', '01-MAR-07', user,
sysdate, user);

insert into edba_alert_notifications values
(3, 'Critical Alert for JUMBO Database:  Tablepsace threshold exceeded',
'rac14.dbaexpert.com', 'JUMBO', 1, 1000,
'Resolve space issue on the users tablespace: 92% utilized', '01-APR-07', user,
sysdate, user);

insert into edba_alert_notifications values
(4, 'Critical Alert for NOBO Database:  Tablepsace threshold exceeded',
'rac18.dbaexpert.com', 'NOBO', 1, 1000,
'Resolve space issue on the system tablespace: 99% utilized', '01-MAY-07', user,
sysdate, user);

insert into edba_alert_notifications values
(5, 'Critical Alert for REDHAT Database:  Tablepsace threshold exceeded',
'rac01.dbaexpert.com', 'REDHAT', 1, 1000,
'Resolve space issue on the data tablespace: 95% utilized', '01-JUN-07', user,
sysdate, user);

insert into edba_alert_notifications values
(6, 'Critical Alert for ORAEL Database:  Tablepsace threshold exceeded',
'rac51.dbaexpert.com', 'ORAEL', 1, 1000,
'Resolve space issue on the docs_d tablespace: 93% utilized', '01-JUL-07', user,
sysdate, user);

insert into edba_alert_notifications values
(7, 'Critical Alert for SUSE Database:  Tablepsace threshold exceeded',
'rac61.dbaexpert.com', 'SUSE', 1, 1000,
'Resolve space issue on the docs_i tablespace: 97% utilized', '01-AUG-07', user,
sysdate, user);

insert into edba_alert_notifications values
(8, 'Critical Alert for ASMDB Database:  Tablepsace threshold exceeded',
'rac71.dbaexpert.com', 'ASMDB', 1, 1000,
'Resolve space issue on the sales_d tablespace: 91% utilized', '01-SEP-07', user,
sysdate, user);
```

```
insert into edba_alert_notifications values
(9, 'Critical Alert for RACDB1 Database:  Tablepsace threshold exceeded',
'rac81.dbaexpert.com', 'RACDB1', 1, 1000,
'Resolve space issue on the sales_i tablespace: 96% utilized', '01-OCT-07', user,
sysdate, user);

insert into edba_alert_notifications values
(10, 'Critical Alert for RACDB2 Database:  Tablepsace threshold exceeded',
'rac12.dbaexpert.com', 'RACDB2', 1, 1000,
'Resolve space issue on the oe_order_headers_d tablespace: 92% utilized', '01-NOV-
07', user, sysdate,user);

insert into edba_alert_notifications values
(11, 'Critical Alert for RACDB3 Database:  Tablepsace threshold exceeded',
'rac20.dbaexpert.com', 'RACDB3', 1, 1000,
'Resolve space issue on the mtl_inventories_d tablespace: 99% utilized', '01-DEC-
07', user, sysdate, user);

insert into edba_alert_notifications values
(12, 'Critical Alert for RACDB4 Database:  Tablepsace threshold exceeded',
'rac19.dbaexpert.com', 'RACDB4', 1, 1000,
'Resolve space issue on the hr_employees_d tablespace: 97% utilized', '01-JAN-08',
user, sysdate, user);
```

As you insert rows into an internal partition, Oracle will automatically create and maintain the range partitions that exceed the high_value of range partitions. You can query USER_TAB_PARTITIONS again and see Oracle's magic at work, as revealed here:

```
SQL> select partition_name, high_value
  2  from user_tab_partitions
  3  where table_name='EDBA_ALERT_NOTIFICATIONS'
  4* order by partition_position
SQL> /

PARTITION_NAME        HIGH_VALUE
---------------       --------------------------------------------
P_JAN2007             TO_DATE(' 2007-01-01 00:00:00', 'SYYYY-MM-DD
                      HH24:MI:SS', 'NLS_CALENDAR=GREGORIAN')

SYS_P41               TO_DATE(' 2007-03-01 00:00:00', 'SYYYY-MM-DD
                      HH24:MI:SS', 'NLS_CALENDAR=GREGORIAN')

SYS_P42               TO_DATE(' 2007-04-01 00:00:00', 'SYYYY-MM-DD
                      HH24:MI:SS', 'NLS_CALENDAR=GREGORIAN')

SYS_P43               TO_DATE(' 2007-05-01 00:00:00', 'SYYYY-MM-DD
                      HH24:MI:SS', 'NLS_CALENDAR=GREGORIAN')
```

SYS_P44	TO_DATE(' 2007-06-01 00:00:00', 'SYYYY-MM-DD HH24:MI:SS', 'NLS_CALENDAR=GREGORIAN')
SYS_P45	TO_DATE(' 2007-07-01 00:00:00', 'SYYYY-MM-DD HH24:MI:SS', 'NLS_CALENDAR=GREGORIAN')
SYS_P46	TO_DATE(' 2007-08-01 00:00:00', 'SYYYY-MM-DD HH24:MI:SS', 'NLS_CALENDAR=GREGORIAN')
SYS_P47	TO_DATE(' 2007-09-01 00:00:00', 'SYYYY-MM-DD HH24:MI:SS', 'NLS_CALENDAR=GREGORIAN')
SYS_P48	TO_DATE(' 2007-10-01 00:00:00', 'SYYYY-MM-DD HH24:MI:SS', 'NLS_CALENDAR=GREGORIAN')
SYS_P49	TO_DATE(' 2007-11-01 00:00:00', 'SYYYY-MM-DD HH24:MI:SS', 'NLS_CALENDAR=GREGORIAN')
SYS_P50	TO_DATE(' 2007-12-01 00:00:00', 'SYYYY-MM-DD HH24:MI:SS', 'NLS_CALENDAR=GREGORIAN')
SYS_P52	TO_DATE(' 2008-01-01 00:00:00', 'SYYYY-MM-DD HH24:MI:SS', 'NLS_CALENDAR=GREGORIAN')
SYS_P51	TO_DATE(' 2008-02-01 00:00:00', 'SYYYY-MM-DD HH24:MI:SS', 'NLS_CALENDAR=GREGORIAN')

13 rows selected.

Alternatively, you can convert a noninterval range partition table into an interval partition using the alter table command. If the EDBA_ALERT_NOTIFICATIONS table was not created as an interval partition table (it is a regular range partition), you can use the alter table command to convert it into an interval partition table. The following example creates the EDBA_ALERT_NOTIFICATIONS table as a noninterval range partition table and converts it to an interval partition table:

```
SQL> CREATE TABLE edba_alert_notifications
  2    (alert_notification_id number,
  3    subject varchar2(2000),
  4    hostname varchar2(55),
  5    database_name varchar2(55),
  6    severity varchar2(1),
  7    alert_log_id number,
  8    message varchar2(4000),
  9    creation_date date default sysdate,
 10    created_by varchar2(55),
 11    modification_date date default sysdate,
```

```
 12    modified_by varchar2(55)) partition by range (creation_date)
 13    ( PARTITION p_jan2007 VALUES
 14    LESS THAN (TO_DATE('01-JAN-2007','DD-MON-RRRR')));
```

Table created.

```
SQL> alter table edba_alert_notifications
  2  set interval (NUMTOYMINTERVAL(1, 'MONTH'))
  3  /
```

Table altered.

The only caveat that DBAs and developers may have is that they lose control over the partition name because it's system generated. The tablespace placement for each partition can be controlled using the store in clause. Even though you don't actually have complete control, Oracle provides the mechanism to place partitions in different tablespaces. The following sample script shows you how this can be accomplished:

```
CREATE TABLE edba_alert_notifications
  (alert_notification_id number,
  subject varchar2(2000),
  hostname varchar2(55),
  database_name varchar2(55),
  severity varchar2(1),
  alert_log_id number,
  message varchar2(4000),
  creation_date date default sysdate,
  created_by varchar2(55),
  modification_date date default sysdate,
  modified_by varchar2(55))
partition by range (creation_date)
interval (numtoyminterval(1,'MONTH'))
store in (alert_d1, alert_d2, alert_d3,
         alert_d4, alert_d5, alert_d6)
( partition p_jan2007 values
 less than (to_date('01-JAN-2007','DD-MON-RRRR')) tablespace alert_d1)
/
```

Notice that the store in clause lists six tablespaces, alert_d1 to alert_d6. Oracle will, in a round-robin fashion, create partitions in the tablespaces listed in the store in clause. You can see from the following query against USER_TAB_PARTITIONS that Oracle allocates the partitions in a round-robin fashion in the alert_d# tablespaces:

```
SQL>  select partition_name, tablespace_name
  2   from user_tab_partitions
  3* where table_name='EDBA_ALERT_NOTIFICATIONS'
SQL> /
```

PARTITION_NAME	TABLESPACE_NAME
P_JAN2007	ALERT_D1
SYS_P53	ALERT_D3
SYS_P54	ALERT_D4
SYS_P55	ALERT_D5
SYS_P56	ALERT_D6
SYS_P57	ALERT_D1
SYS_P58	ALERT_D2
SYS_P59	ALERT_D3
SYS_P60	ALERT_D4
SYS_P61	ALERT_D5
SYS_P62	ALERT_D6
SYS_P63	ALERT_D1
SYS_P64	ALERT_D2

```
13 rows selected.
```

At the same time, you have to ask yourself, "Is the price of a naming standard compromise worth the automation?" You can clearly see that interval partitioning is one of the best features in Oracle Database 11g for day-to-day manageability.

There are additional considerations that need to be reviewed for interval partitions. Interval partitioning has these restrictions:

- You can specify only one partitioning key column, and it must be of the NUMBER or DATE datatype.

- Interval partitioning does not supported index-organized tables.

- You cannot create a domain index on an interval-partitioned table.

Extended Composite Partitioning

Extended composite partitioning enhancement is a long-awaited feature for many DBAs and developers. Extended composite partitioning capabilities have been increased to address common business problems for companies in the 21st century. Prior to Oracle Database 11g, the only composite partitioning schemes were range-list and range-hash partitioning. Oracle Database 11g provides the complete composite partitioning options. In Oracle Database 11g, you now have the means to partition by two relevant date ranges. For example, you can partition a table by ORDER_DATE and SHIP_DATE or by HIRE_DATE and COMMISSION_DATE. You now have the flexibility to create a partition based on two relevant lists. For example, you can create a composite partition based on state and city or by region and product group. There are four new extensions to the composite partitioning paradigm, discussed next.

Composite List-Hash Partitioning

You can create a list partition subpartitioned by hash partitions. This enables the granularity for partition-wise joins. This new partition mechanism can increase performance and fulfills business requirements for partitioning.

Composite List-List Partitioning

Many multiterabyte partitioning implementations have the requirements to partition by list and subpartition by list. You can see that the composite list-list partitions will be one of the favorites for developers and DBAs who have relatively static data sets for partitioning keys.

For this example, let's take our documents table again. Let's assume that all the DBAs and developers groups across the entire organization share a common document repository, and the amount of documentation from each of the groups is enormous. We have a need to partition by the organization and then subpartition by DOCUMENT_CATEGORY. This can easily be accomplished in Oracle Database 11g using the new composite list-list partition, as shown here:

```
SQL> create table docs_list_list
  2  (document_id number,
  3   document_category varchar2(10),
  4   organization_id number,
  5   creation_date date,
  6   blob_content blob ) lob (blob_content) store as securefile
  7  partition by list (organization_id)
  8  subpartition by list (document_category)
  9  ( partition org1 values (1)
 10   ( subpartition p1_cat_dg values ('DG'),
 11     subpartition p1_cat_asm values ('ASM'),
 12     subpartition p1_cat_gen values ('GENERAL'),
 13     subpartition p1_cat_sql values ('SQL'),
 14     subpartition p1_cat_plsql values ('PLSQL'),
 15     subpartition p1_cat_rac values ('RAC'),
 16     subpartition p1_cat_def values (default) ),
 17    partition org2 values (2)
 18   ( subpartition p2_cat_dg values ('DG'),
 19     subpartition p2_cat_asm values ('ASM'),
 20     subpartition p2_cat_gen values ('GENERAL'),
 21     subpartition p2_cat_sql values ('SQL'),
 22     subpartition p2_cat_plsql values ('PLSQL'),
 23     subpartition p2_cat_rac values ('RAC'),
 24     subpartition p2_cat_def values (default) )
 25* )
SQL> /

Table created.
```

Composite List-Range Partitioning

Composite list-range partitioning will be another favorite partitioning scheme for developers and DBAs. Let's continue with the documents table again. In the following example, the document table can be partitioned by the organization and then subpartitioned by CREATION_DATE to create the list-range partition:

```
SQL> create table docs_list_list
  2  (document_id number,
  3   document_category varchar2(10),
  4   organization_id number,
  5   creation_date date,
  6   blob_content blob ) lob (blob_content) store as securefile
  7  partition by list (organization_id)
  8  subpartition by range (creation_date)
  9  ( partition org1 values (1)
 10  ( subpartition p1_cat_2007q1
                    values less than (to_date('01-APR-2007','dd-MON-yyyy')),
 11    subpartition p1_cat_2007q2
                    values less than (to_date('01-JUL-2007','dd-MON-yyyy')) ),
 12    partition org2 values (2)
 13  ( subpartition p2_cat_2007q1
                    values less than (to_date('01-APR-2007','dd-MON-yyyy')),
 14    subpartition p2_cat_2007q2
                    values less than (to_date('01-JUL-2007','dd-MON-yyyy')) )
 15* )
SQL> /

Table created.
```

Composite Range-Range Partitioning

One common implementation of composite range-range partitions is on two date columns.
Let's create a range-range partitioned table against the ALERT_NOTIFICATIONS table. In this particular instance, the data volume for this table is expected to be enormous because thousands of
systems and databases are monitored for thousands of companies. We will create a composite
range-range partition based on when the alert was generated and when the alert was actually
closed. The following create table syntax shows you how to create a composite range-range
partition partitioned by CREATION_DATE and subpartitioned by CLOSED_DATE:

```
SQL>  CREATE TABLE alerts_range_range
  2    (alert_notification_id number,
  3     subject varchar2(2000),
  4     hostname varchar2(55),
  5     database_name varchar2(55),
  6     severity varchar2(1),
  7     alert_log_id number,
  8     message varchar2(4000),
  9     creation_date date default sysdate,
 10     created_by varchar2(55),
 11     modification_date date default sysdate,
 12     modified_by varchar2(55),
 13     closed_date date)
```

```
14  partition by range (creation_date)
15  subpartition by range (closed_date)
16  ( partition p_Q1_2007 values
17    less than (to_date('01-APR-2007','dd-MON-yyyy'))
18    ( subpartition p_JAN2007 values
19      less than (to_date('01-FEB-2007','dd-MON-yyyy'))
20    , subpartition p_FEB2007 values
21      less than (to_date('01-MAR-2007','dd-MON-yyyy'))
22    , subpartition p_MAR2007 values
23      less than (to_date('01-APR-2007','dd-MON-yyyy'))
24    , subpartition p_PRE_Q1_2007 values less than (maxvalue)
25    )
26  , partition p_Q2_2007 values
27    less than (to_date('01-JUL-2007','dd-MON-yyyy'))
28    ( subpartition p_APR2007 values
29      less than (to_date('01-MAY-2007','dd-MON-yyyy'))
30    , subpartition p_MAY2007 values
31      less than (to_date('01-JUN-2007','dd-MON-yyyy'))
32    , subpartition p_JUN2007 values
33      less than (to_date('01-JUL-2007','dd-MON-yyyy'))
34    , subpartition p_PRE_Q2_2007 values less than (maxvalue)
35    )
36* )
SQL> /

Table created.
```

Once the range-range partition is created, let's insert two rows into the February subpartition:

```
insert into alerts_range_range
values (1,
'Critical Alert for DBATOOLS Database:  Tablepsace threshold exceeded',
'rac11.dbaexpert.com', 'DBATOOLS', 1, 1000,
'Resolve space issue on the alert_d tablespace: 98% utilized',
'01-FEB-07', user, sysdate, user, '10-FEB-2007');

insert into alerts_range_range
values (8,
'Critical Alert for ASMDB Database:  Tablepsace threshold exceeded',
'rac71.dbaexpert.com', 'ASMDB', 1, 1000,
'Resolve space issue on the sales_d tablespace: 91% utilized',
'01-FEB-07', user, sysdate, user, '10-FEB-2007')
;
```

By querying directly against the subpartition, you can verify that range-range composite partitioning is working as advertised:

```
SQL> select count(*) from alerts_range_range subpartition (p_FEB2007);

 COUNT(*)
---------------
        2
```

Virtual Column-Based Partitioning

As of Oracle Database 11*g*, the partition key can be based on the virtual column(s) of a table. Oracle Database 11*g* introduces what is known as *virtual columns*, which are derived by evaluation of a function or an expression. Values of virtual columns are not stored with the table; instead, virtual columns are evaluated on demand. Tables and indexes can be partitioned on virtual columns. For additional information regarding virtual columns, please refer to Chapter 3.

You can define a virtual column within a create table command or by using the alter table syntax. By allowing virtualization of the partitioning key, Oracle provides another level of enablement to meet ever-fluctuating business requirements.

By looking at the traditional HR_EMPLOYEES table, you will see the effectiveness of virtual column-based partitioning. Let's take the HR_EMPLOYEES table as an example and create a virtual column–based partition on the SALARY and the BONUS columns:

```
SQL> create table hr_employees
  2  ( employee_id number not null
  3  , first varchar2(55)
  4  , last varchar2(55)
  5  , middle varchar2(55)
  6  , email varchar2(55)
  7  , phone varchar2(55)
  8  , hiredate date
  9  , salary number
 10  , bonus number
 11  , position_id number
 12  , manager_id number
 13  , dept_id number
 14  ,total_package as (salary + bonus ) virtual
 15  )
 16  partition by range(total_package)
 17  ( partition p_10k values less than (10000)
 18  , partition p_10k_35k values less than (35000)
 19  , partition p_35k_50k values less than (50000)
 20  , partition p_50k_70k values less than (70000)
 21  , partition p_70k_100k values less than (100000)
 22  , partition p_100k_150k values less than (150000)
 23  , partition p_150k_200k values less than (200000)
 24  , partition p_200k_300k values less than (300000)
 25  , partition p_300k_500k values less than (500000)
```

```
26   , partition p_500k_1000k values less than (1000000)
27   , partition p_1000k_5000k values less than (5000000)
28   , partition p_other values less than (maxvalue)
29* )
SQL> /
```

Table created.

Now, let's create some dummy records to pinpoint where the rows are placed within the virtual partition keys:

```
SQL> insert into hr_employees
    (employee_id, first, last, email, salary, bonus)
     values
    (6, 'Allyson', 'Wu', 'allyson@dbaexpert.com', 300000, 250000);
```

1 row created.

```
SQL> insert into hr_employees
    (employee_id, first, last, email, salary, bonus)
     values
    (7, 'John', 'Lee', 'john@dbaexpert.com', 900000, 5000);
```

1 row created.

```
...
...
...

SQL> insert into hr_employees
    (employee_id, first, last, email, salary, bonus)
     values
    (10, 'Iceman', 'Kim', 'iceman@dbaexpert.com', 20000, 1000);
```

1 row created.

```
SQL> commit;
```

Commit complete.

With virtual columns, you have the same functionality as you would with any range or list partitioning key. Let's query the HR_EMPLOYEES table and look at the rows specific to employees who make $500,000 to $1 million as their total compensation package. You will see that both Allyson and John are the winners of the super-high salary award:

```
SQL> select first, last, salary, bonus, total_package
    from hr_employees partition (p_500k_1000k);
SQL> /


FIRST        LAST          SALARY       BONUS      TOTAL_PACKAGE
----------   ----------    ----------   ----------  -------------
Allyson      Wu            300000       250000     550000
John         Lee           900000       5000       905000
```

2 rows selected.

In the same regard, you can see that the partition pruning for virtual partitions works like any other range or list partitioning, as shown on this explain plan:

```
SQL> explain plan for
  2  select first, last, salary, bonus, total_package
    from hr_employees partition (p_500k_1000k);


Explained.


SQL> select * from table (dbms_xplan.display);
SQL> /


PLAN_TABLE_OUTPUT
-------------------------------------------------------------------------------
Plan hash value: 1171666257


-------------------------------------------------------------------------------
| Id  | Operation         | Name        |    Rows | Bytes | Cost (%CPU)| Time
| Pstart| Pstop |
-------------------------------------------------------------------------------
|   0 |    SELECT STATEMENT    |             |    2 |   194 |    3   (0)|
00:00:01 |      |       |
|   1 |             PARTITION RANGE SINGLE|    |    2 |   194 |    3   (0)|
00:00:01 |   10 |    10 |
|   2 |             TABLE ACCESS FULL   | HR_EMPLOYEES |2 |   194 |    3   (0)|
00:00:01 |   10 |    10 |
-------------------------------------------------------------------------------
Note


PLAN_TABLE_OUTPUT
-------------------------------------------------------------------------------
   - dynamic sampling used for this statement


13 rows selected.
```

System Partitioning

Oracle Database 11*g* complements Oracle's partitioning infrastructure with the concept of system partitioning. System partitioning enables you to create a single table that is composed of multiple physical partitions. The fascinating concept behind system partitioning is that it does not use partition keys. Because there are no partitioning keys, system partitions have no bounds for ranges or lists. At the same time, because there are no partitioning keys, you must explicitly specify the rows to the target table partition using partition-aware syntax. The mapping of a row must be specified to the partition level.

The benefit of system partitioning is that the application controls the partitioning for tables and indexes. The application controls the data placement and how it is retrieved. The database becomes the repository that provides the mechanism to break down an object into partitions without data-partitioning rules.

System partitions are created using the `partition by system` clause. Let's look at the syntax to create a system partition:

```
SQL> create table docs_system_parted
  2  (doc_id number,
  3   name varchar2(255),
     Description varchar2(1000),
  4   blob_content blob)
  5  partition by system
  6  (
  7   partition docs_p1 tablespace docs_d1,
  8   partition docs_p2 tablespace docs_d2,
  9   partition docs_p3 tablespace docs_d3,
 10   partition docs_p4 tablespace docs_d4
 11* )
SQL> /

Table created
```

System partitioning can continue to provide the benefits of partitioning as we know it (scalability, availability, and manageability), with the flexibility of data mapping in the control of the applications. To show the usefulness of system partitions, we'll show how data is added and deleted. When you add or delete records from system-partitioned tables, you have to provide the partition-aware syntax; otherwise, you will receive an ORA-14701 error, as shown here:

```
SQL> insert into docs_system_parted
  2  (doc_id, name)
  3  values
  4  (10001, 'Chapter 1: Installation and Upgrade');
insert into docs_system_parted
            *
ERROR at line 1:
ORA-14701: partition-extended name or bind variable must be used
for DMLs on tables partitioned by the System method
```

However, if you perform the inserts using partition-aware syntax, the rows get inserted successfully, as you can see here:

```
insert into docs_system_parted partition (docs_p1)
values
(1, 'Chapter 1 - Installation and Upgrade',
    'Complete documentation for Oracle Database 11g
     Installation and Upgrade by Sam and Charles', null)
/
1 row created.

insert into docs_system_parted partition (docs_p2)
values
(2, 'Chapter 2 - Diagnosibility',
    'Complete documentation for Oracle Database 11g
     Diagnosibility', null)
/

1 row created.
```

Like the insert command, the merge command must be performed with partition-aware syntax. Here's an example of alter table with the merge partition command:

```
SQL> alter table docs_system_parted
  2  merge partitions docs_p3,docs_p4
  3* into partition docs_p3
SQL> /

Table altered.
```

Update and delete operations can be performed with or without the partition-aware syntax. In the following script examples, you can see demonstrations of deletions using the partition-aware syntax:

```
  1  delete from docs_system_parted
  2  partition (docs_p2)
  3* where doc_id=10002
SQL> /

1 row deleted.

SQL> delete from docs_system_parted partition (docs_p2);

0 rows deleted.

SQL> delete from docs_system_parted partition (docs_p1);

1 row deleted.
```

```
SQL> rollback;

Rollback complete.
```

Partition pruning processes are not applicable to system partitions. Please be aware that when you perform updates and deletes without the partition-aware syntax, Oracle scans every partition on the table. For simplicity, you can perform updates and deletes without the partition-aware syntax, as shown here:

```
SQL> delete from docs_system_parted
  2* where doc_id=10001
SQL> /

1 row deleted.

SQL> delete from docs_system_parted;

1 row deleted.
```

Enhanced Partition Pruning Capabilities

Here's another feature that you get out of the box. Starting in Oracle Database 11g, partition pruning uses the bloom filtering and is automatically active for all joins with a partitioned object. In the previous release, the subquery pruning method was triggered on the cost-based decision model. The subquery pruning consumed internal recursive resources. The new bloom filtering is activated all the time without consuming additional resources.

Oracle Multimedia

Oracle interMedia is now called Oracle Multimedia. Oracle Database 11g continues to develop advancements to Oracle Multimedia. In today's increasing demand for higher-fidelity digitalization, Oracle bridges the technology with the database and supports the requirements in security, media, and entertainment, medical, and life sciences. With the lower cost in storage and higher technological advancement, customers are storing more and larger digital images, audio, and video in the database. Now, the information technology is entering an era where single media files can be tens of gigabytes in size. Oracle welcomes this challenge by providing rich features in Oracle Multimedia. Prior to the Oracle Database 11g release, the ORDIMAGE, ORDAUDIO, ORDVIDEO, and ORDDOC datatypes were bound to the 4GB size restriction. As of Oracle Multimedia, these datatypes can hold objects from 8TB to 128 TB depending on the database block size.

Enhanced DICOM Support

Oracle Multimedia continues to enhance functionality for Digital Imaging and Communications in Medicine (DICOM), which is a medical imaging standard initiated by the American College of Radiology (ACR) and the National Electrical Manufacturers Association (NEMA) to enhance the connectivity of radiological devices. In 1993, the ACR-NEMA standard was revised and renamed as DICOM (Version 3.0). Since then, the DICOM standard has become the dominant standard for radiology imaging and communication.

Oracle Multimedia recognizes stand-alone DICOM objects and extracts embedded attributes relating to patient, study, and series. Oracle Multimedia stores DICOM format data in database tables with columns of the ORDDICOM type.

ORDDICOM Object Type

Oracle Multimedia stores DICOM format data in database tables with columns of the ORDDICOM type. The ORDDICOM datatype is new to Oracle Database 11g and natively supports DICOM content produced by medical devices. Let's create a table that can house the ORDDICOM datatype:

```
SQL> create table medical_images
  2             (medical_image_id integer primary key,
  3              dicom        ordsys.orddicom,
  4              imageThumb   ordsys.ordimage,
  5              anonDicom    ordsys.orddicom)
  6* tablespace medical_images_d
SQL> /

Table created.
```

■**Note** Multimedia objects and procedures are defined in the ORDSYS schema.

The ORDDICOM object datatype stores the DICOM content and the extracted metadata. The setProperties method tells Oracle Multimedia to parse the DICOM data and extract DICOM metadata into ORDDICOM object attributes.

Image Processing

Using Oracle Multimedia, database users can perform image-processing functions that change image content. For example, you can scale and crop an image or convert it to a different file format. This level of processing requires interpreting pixel values of images. This can consume system performance and memory.

Another area of improvement is in the scale-down operations that provide the mechanism for fast generation of thumbnail images from very large source images (JPEG, TIFF, and DICOM with JPEG or RAW encoding).

Support for SecureFiles

Oracle Multimedia fully supports the next generation of LOBs, SecureFiles. SecureFiles complements the multimedia object types with the new performance improvements. Multimedia object types, methods, and packages are certified to work transparently with Oracle SecureFiles.

Note Oracle recommends using SecureFiles to store Oracle Multimedia object types. You can reap the performance benefits of Oracle's reengineered BLOB implementation.

Additional Multimedia Enhancements

Oracle Multimedia 11*g* adds the following medical imaging format support for DICOM:

- DICOM object creation capability

- DICOM object conformance validation enhancement

- DICOM metadata extraction enhancements

- The ability to make DICOM objects anonymous for security

Index

Find it faster at http://superindex.apress.com

Find it faster at http://superindex.apress.com

You Need the Companion eBook

Your purchase of this book entitles you to buy the companion PDF-version eBook for only $10. Take the weightless companion with you anywhere.

We believe this Apress title will prove so indispensable that you'll want to carry it with you everywhere, which is why we are offering the companion eBook (in PDF format) for $10 to customers who purchase this book now. Convenient and fully searchable, the PDF version of any content-rich, page-heavy Apress book makes a valuable addition to your programming library. You can easily find and copy code—or perform examples by quickly toggling between instructions and the application. Even simultaneously tackling a donut, diet soda, and complex code becomes simplified with hands-free eBooks!

Once you purchase your book, getting the $10 companion eBook is simple:

❶ Visit **www.apress.com/promo/tendollars/**.

❷ Complete a basic registration form to receive a randomly generated question about this title.

❸ Answer the question correctly in 60 seconds, and you will receive a promotional code to redeem for the $10.00 eBook.

THE EXPERT'S VOICE™

2855 TELEGRAPH AVENUE | SUITE 600 | BERKELEY, CA 94705

Offer valid through 5/08.